Hawaii

Hawaii

Kim Grant

with photographs by the author

SECOND EDITION

The Countryman Press ✳ Woodstock, Vermont

We welcome your comments and suggestions. Please contact Explorer's Guide Editor, The Countryman Press, P.O. Box 748, Woodstock, VT 05091, or e-mail countrymanpress@wwnorton.com.

Second edition

ISBN 978-0-88150-809-3
ISSN 1557-7961

Cover and text design by Bodenweber Design
Cover photograph and all interior photographs © Kim Grant
Maps by Mapping Specialists, © The Countryman Press
Text composition by PerfecType, Nashville, Tennessee

Published by The Countryman Press,
P.O. Box 748, Woodstock, Vermont 05091

Distributed by W. W. Norton & Company, Inc.,
500 Fifth Avenue, New York, NY 10110

Printed in Canada
10 9 8 7 6 5 4 3 2 1

DEDICATION

To my *ohana*
Beth Anderson, Catherine Direen, Lynette Molnar, and Julia Regan

EXPLORE WITH US!

Welcome to the second edition of this comprehensive guide to Hawai'i. In choosing what to include, I have tried to be highly selective but broadly inclusive, based on years of repeated visits, cumulative research, and ongoing conversations with locals. All entries—attractions, resorts, and restaurants—are chosen on the basis of personal experience, not paid advertising. As such, listings are generally ordered by preference unless otherwise indicated.

I hope you find the organization of this guide easy to read and use. The layout has been kept simple; the following pointers will help you get started.

INTRODUCTION

When is an introduction more than an introduction? When it helps answer the most important questions of all: Who is this person whose advice I am basing my dream vacation on? What does she know? How do I choose the right island? Or the right lodging? I'm a first-time visitor; what shouldn't I miss? I'm a repeat visitor; please give me some ideas for things to do that I haven't already explored.

WHAT'S WHERE

In the beginning of the book, you'll find an alphabetical listing of special highlights and important information that you can refer to quickly. Think of them as broad "best of" lists riddled with Web sites for ease of use. These headings and their contents will give you a good overview of the opportunities for exploration. They should also help you decide which island best suits your interests on any given visit. (If you're attracted to more things on the North Shore than the South Shore of Kaua'i, for instance, base yourself on the North Shore.) I tend to think of it as the book's collective wisdom—it summarizes everything from where to find the best beaches and botanical gardens to where to find the best spas, shopping towns, and scenic drives to where to go hiking and horseback riding.

BUILDING BLOCKS FOR PERFECT DAYS IN PARADISE

These regional, hour-by-hour planners will get you started on how best to dip into the islands. But a word of caution: If you try to do everything mentioned in the time allotted, you might not feel like you're on a vacation. Use them merely as a guide.

LODGING

Prices: Please don't hold us or the respective resorts responsible for the rates listed as of press time in late 2008. Changes are inevitable. At the time of this writing, the state and local room tax was about 14½ percent. Please also see *Lodging* in "What's Where in Hawai'i."

Price Codes for Double Occupancy:

$	=	$125 and under
$$	=	$125–$250
$$$	=	$250–$400
$$$$	=	$400 and over

RESTAURANTS

In most sections, note the distinction between *Dining Out* and *Eating Out*. Restaurants listed under *Eating Out* are generally inexpensive and more casual; reservations are often suggested for restaurants in *Dining Out*. A range of prices for main dishes is included with each entry.

Price Codes for Entrées:

$ = $1–10
$$ = $10–20
$$$ = $20–30
$$$$ = Over $30

KEY TO SYMBOLS

🏵   The "special-value" icon appears next to lodging entries, restaurants, and activities that combine exceptional quality with moderate prices.

✪   The "don't-miss-this" icon appears next to places, activities, and sights that you'll remember long after you return home.

✐   The "child and family interest" icon appears next to lodging entries, restaurants, activities, and shops of special appeal to youngsters and families.

☂   The "rainy-day" icon appears next to things to do and places of interest that are appropriate for foul-weather days (of which there are so few on the islands).

Y   The "martini-glass" icon appears next to restaurants and entertainment venues with good bars.

🏖   The "beach" icon appears next to worthy beaches that you'll pass along the way as you circle an island. Some are so worthy (for various reasons), they're reviewed under the bona fide *Beaches* section in each chapter.

I appreciate comments and corrections about places you discover or know well. You may e-mail me at hawaii@kimgrant.com or write to Explorer's Guide Editor, The Countryman Press, P.O. Box 748, Woodstock, VT 05091.

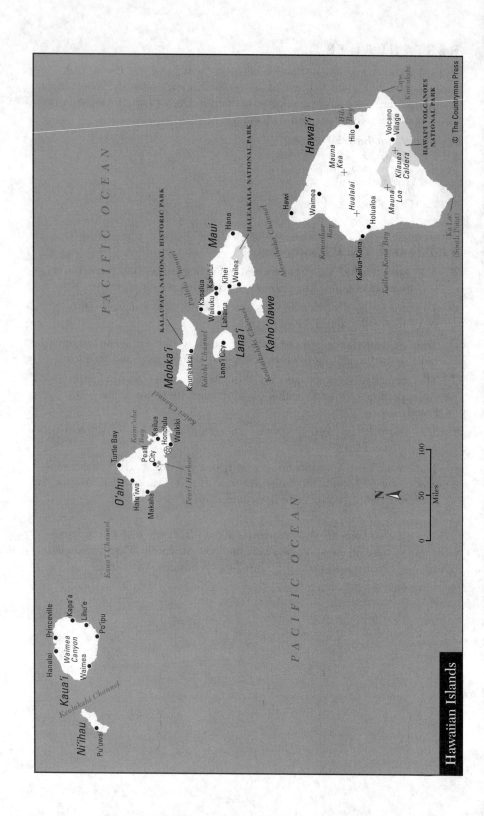

Hawaiian Islands

CONTENTS

LIST OF MAPS

INTRODUCTION

Sometimes I think the last thing the world needs is another travel guide to Hawai'i. Then the phone rings. And I get some e-mails. Friends are having a tough time wading through all the information available about Hawai'i. "Should we island-hop or stick to one island?" "Should we believe all this marketing hype about that resort?" "Should we take our one indulgent helicopter trip on Kaua'i or save it for the Big Island?" "We're going to be on Maui for seven nights; what are the seven best restaurants?" Or "We really don't want to spend a fortune on dining; is that even possible?" And then there's the big one: "I really need to rest, but I don't have time to research every option and I can't afford to make a bad decision. What should I do?"

And so I've written this guide from a conversational point of view for all those friends. Somewhere along the way, I've become a schizophrenic writer. I speak to a growing chorus of voices in my head as a project like this progresses. What does that mean? I hear my sister wondering where she can take her kids without having to raid their college savings plans, so I write with her in mind. My friend's well-off parents are celebrating a once-in-a-lifetime anniversary, and I include them in my perspective. My Dutch friends muse about how to divvy up their six-week holiday, and I talk about camping and hiking with them in mind. My San Francisco friends deliberate on long weekend getaways, so I write for them (with a secret jealousy). My gay friends want places where they won't be given a sideways glance, and I'm grateful to help make some lives a bit easier. If I wrote simply for myself, it would be a pretty skinny travel guide. But I write with a large circle in mind. Hopefully you'll think I write with you in mind. See *The Over-the-Top Life of a Travel Writer on O'ahu*; p. 84/O'ahu.

It's my fondest hope that you read this guide as if a friend has gone before you and she is simply telling it like it is. But who am I and why should you trust me? First things first: I'm not Hawaiian, and I don't live in Hawai'i. I bring an outsider's perspective to seeing and experiencing the islands. I've been writing travel guides since the first day after college graduation in 1984. I know how to play and rest. I value and guard my time and money with vigor. I have been smitten with Hawai'i since the mid-1990s, when I got my first assignment to author *Best Places to Stay in Hawai'i*. That's when I started spending two months a year in the state. And it's also when the spirit of the islands started seeping into my blood and spilling over into my mainland life.

Over the years, I have discovered the value of an $800-a-night hotel room, but I grew up appreciating what $50 a night would get you. There's still a time and a place for both. I'm just as happy to park at the beach and slurp a steaming bowl of saimin as I am to dine at ocean's edge by the light of tiki torches with waiters dressed in white hovering silently around as I indulge in a plate of panko-crusted mahimahi. I used to run around, seeing and doing five or six things a day on vacation. Then I scaled back to scheduling 10 perfect activities for 10 perfect days on vacation. Now I love to sit still and do nothing on vacation. But I still write for those three distinct personalities.

I try to convey the enchantment that arises in places like Hawai'i, those mystical qualities that separate Hawai'i from Dubuque. I try to summon the escapist allure that's such a potent aphrodisiac. I try to remind myself why I fell hard for the islands in the first place.

CHOOSING THE RIGHT ISLAND

How do I decide among the six major islands—which one is right for me? That's the most important question to ask. It's also the hardest to answer—and the one that most guidebooks don't address particularly well. What's the fundamental character of a place? What does each island have to offer, and for whom? The introduction to each of these islands addresses these questions.

Each year thousands of people return home from Hawai'i disappointed. They have tithed their annual income for an experience they enjoyed as much as their boss's birthday party. The beach in the travel brochure turned out to have so little sand they could count the grains, the neighborhood reminded them more of a New Jersey mall than their image of paradise, and their room looked out into a parking lot. The trip almost certainly had its moments of fun, but it wasn't what they expected.

If you don't have enough information to make an informed decision about where to go and what to do, travelers Bill and Cheryl Jamison's observation will ring true: "Most blind dates produce good stories at least. They just don't often lead to love." Take a little time up front to pick the right partner and your odds for happiness in Hawai'i will exponentially improve. This guide will help.

CHOOSING THE RIGHT LODGING

It's the second most critical decision, after picking the right island. It may seem like this guide has an exhaustive listing of places to stay, but trust me, it doesn't. If I wouldn't want to stay in a place for more than a couple of nights, I have not included it. It's my intention to describe a place objectively and evaluate the execution rather than the concept.

Cost, convenience, and comfort are important considerations. But perhaps the most important of all is the relationship of your room to the ocean or the beach, two variables that can make or break holidays. If wonderful beaches are among your reasons for going to Hawai'i, stay on one. If a good ocean view is even more important than a beachfront location, make sure you get one. Anyone who doesn't live directly on the sea at home is likely to be thrilled by the sight and sound of the Pacific surf. If cost is a consideration, get the least expensive room in the property of your choice. That way, you at least gain access to the two most stellar features of any given property: location and service.

To help you wade through the choices for each island, I've culled a list of the Best Romantic Hideaways, Best Intimate & Affordable Lodgings, Most Worldly Resorts, Best Condos, Best B&Bs, Best Family Resorts, and Best Resort Values. I've visited them all, stayed in most over the years, and spied them with a critical eye. I sit around a lot on the job: I settle into hundreds of lobby chairs and watch the check-in process. I eavesdrop on concierges as they problem-solve requests big and small. I ply bartenders with questions and talk to housekeepers. I talk to hundreds and hundreds of fellow travelers about their experiences and catalog these informal surveys for my reviews here.

ITINERARY HELPERS

To help in your voyage of discovery, each island has recommendations for **"Musts for First-Time Visitors"** and **"Ideas for Repeat Visitors."** And I've gone one step further with this edition: creating **"Building Blocks for Perfect Days in . . ."** for you to use as a quick glance of the best of the best. I trust you'll use it as a jumping off point of departure. A warning, though: If you try to do everything in the time allotted, your trip may feel like a forced march rather than a deserved holiday. I've also culled lists of the best beaches on each island for swimming and sunbathing, snorkeling and water sports, walking and watching sunsets, and family frolics.

Constructing an itinerary for Hawai'i is mainly a matter of deciding how many islands to visit. On any single island, select one spot and use it as a base for sightseeing. On Maui and the Big Island, you might want to move once or twice to get a better sense of their diversity, and some special-interest travelers—say, golfers—may want to sample more than one resort. But point-to-point travel is not necessary or generally desirable on an individual island.

I have two rules for Hawaiian itineraries: Visit at least two islands on any trip, and spend a minimum of five days on an island. The rules are clearly contradictory if you have less than 10 days, in which case I'd suggest extending your trip. You also need to anticipate a couple of days of low-energy jet lag on arrival. Depending on where you are starting and the time of year, Hawai'i is two to six time zones away.

When you can arrange only a week and it's your first trip to Hawai'i, forget the five-day rule and visit two islands. The islands are so different from one another and have so much to offer individually that it's important to experience some of the variety. A person who has been to one island and claims to have seen Hawai'i is like a New Yorker who has been to Los Angeles and claims to know the West.

If this is a return visit to the islands and you've gone beyond Waikiki and West Maui, a catalog of exceptions comes into play. Use Honolulu for a short stopover of less than five days on the way to another destination. Or pick a favorite spot on one island and sink into the sand for an extended stay. Or consider a two- or three-day jaunt to Moloka'i or Lana'i or a remote hamlet such as Hana for a change of pace. Once you have some acquaintance with at least O'ahu, Maui, Kaua'i, and the Big Island, these two itinerary rules become almost infinitely flexible.

Novices should be more cautious about breaking the two rules. They should design an itinerary with the two principles in mind and build it around their personal interests and the amount of time they have.

See *"Itinerary Suggestions"* (p. 17).

MANY MAHALOS

The new work paradigm does not include freelance researching and writing in a vacuum. To that end, a heartfelt *mahalo* goes out to a small cadre of folks who morphed from being friends to full-fledged colleagues and from being colleagues to full-fledged friends. Hawai'i brings people together. Bonnie Friedman is, first and foremost, a friend. She is also an extraordinarily sophisticated foodie who dines and wines with me whenever we get the chance (which is often), an inveterate Maui booster, and perhaps the most supportive *haole* that any native Hawaiian could want. I have learned a great deal about Hawai'i from her over the years.

Kim Bolger unraveled centuries of the Hawaiian monarchy, Captain Cook's conquering, and zealous missionary incursions. Michele Bigley provided an exceptional depth of knowledge about all things Kaua'i. Michael Clark, my alter ego (by way of Melbourne, O'ahu, and Berkeley), provided an eerily synchronistic voice-over in O'ahu. Julia Regan, a two-decade treasure, is just as comfortable outdoors as indoors and morphed into an activities expert. Bill and Cheryl Jamison and Bruce Shaw continue to get utmost kudos for introducing me to the islands in the first place.

Kermit Hummel practices the

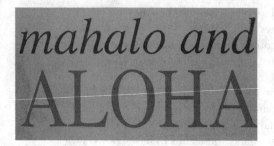
mahalo and ALOHA

patience of a sage; thank you for all your support. Jennifer Thompson, per usual, is the manifestation of efficiency. And to all the new authors that I hire in my role as Acquisitions Editor at Countryman, thank you for making me a compassionate colleague.

On the Big Island, *mahalo* to Aven Wright-McIntosh, Donna Kimura, Vicki Kometani, Leanne Pletcher, Cathey Tarleton, Michael Tuttle (a rain forest friend and rainbow coalition lifeline), Jeannette Vidgen, Laura Aquino, and Michele Gamble. On Oʻahu, *mahalo* forever to Joyce Matsumoto and to Caroline Witherspoon, Cynthia Rankin, and Sandi Yara. On Kauaʻi, a big *mahalo* to Rosemary Smith. . . . On Maui, *mahalo* to Bonnie Friedman (again), Keliʻi Brown, Janice and Tom Fairbanks, Bea Wolfe, Arabella Ark, Tanna Swanson, Mark Simon, Luana Paʻahana, and Cherie Attix. On Molokaʻi, Julie-Ann Bicoy, Michael Drew, and Dayna Harris get special thanks.

PLEASE WRITE FOR US AND TO US

In a departure from other Explorer's Guides, look for some first-person experiential anecdotes in this guide. And please consider sharing one of your own for possible inclusion in the next edition. (Send them to hawaii@kimgrant.com.) I think it is important that we collect and hear as many rich voices and inspirational stories as possible. I hope this alternative framework infuses the guide with a fresh perspective; I expect it to grow as a feature. I am only one person, albeit a professional traveler and trained observer, and although I try to maintain as fresh an eye as possible, I value other people's perspectives. In my travels, I constantly encounter a tapestry of understanding and wealth of humor that deserve to reach a wider audience.

I welcome readers' thoughtful comments, criticisms, and suggestions for the next edition of *Hawaiʻi: An Explorer's Guide*.

As with all editions, this one benefits from the accumulated knowledge that fellow explorers have shared with me, through letters and over breakfast at B&Bs.

ITINERARY SUGGESTIONS

I 've taken four prototypical personality types common among Hawai'i visitors and built an itinerary for each. Few of you are exclusively one of these types, but if you feel a particular kinship with one, the itinerary should work well for you.

FASHIONABLE FUN LOVER'S ITINERARY

Start in Waikiki and perhaps return here for your final two days. Waikiki remains America's most famous beach and offers more options for entertainment and nightlife than all the neighbor islands combined. The second stop is West Maui, at or near either the Ka'anapali or Wailea resorts. Ka'anapali is more active, while Wailea is more sensitively planned. The final destination is Kaua'i, which shows start-and-stop signs of displacing Maui as the choice of the chic. Split your days almost equally among the three islands, with some possible fluctuation between O'ahu and Kaua'i depending on whether you are a traditionalist or riding a new wave.

POLYNESIAN PURIST'S ITINERARY

Catch a flight to the Big Island. You may have to change planes in Honolulu, but don't leave the airport. Spend most of your two weeks on the Big Island. The best time to come is early April, during Hilo's Merrie Monarch Festival. If you can arrange this, use Hilo as a base for exploring the southern half of the island. In other periods, South Kona, Volcano, or Kailua-Kona may be a better headquarters. But concentrate your visit in the north, in the Kohala region. Don't miss the Pu'ukohola and Mo'okini *heiaus*, the Waipio Valley, the petroglyph fields and ancient fishponds of the Waikoloa and Mauna Lani resorts, and the Pu'uhonua O Honaunau National Historical Park. Near the end of your trip, fly to Moloka'i for a few days of native-style relaxation.

JADED ROMANTIC'S ITINERARY

If you're difficult to impress but can be stirred to passion by the authentically poetic, you should seek out some of Hawai'i's most idyllic hideaways. Hana is an imperative for one-third of your time. You might want to remain on Maui another four or five days in Makena, Kapalua, or Napili, or perhaps substitute a similar amount of time on the North Shore of Kaua'i. In winter, I would stick with Maui; in summer I'd elect Kaua'i. My third destination would include the South Kohala resorts of the Big Island. A well-off jaded romantic could not do better than dividing the days among these spots.

NATIONAL PARK NATURALIST'S ITINERARY

Your focus is Haleakala National Park on Maui, Hawai'i Volcanoes National Park on the Big Island, and the north coast of Kaua'i. On Maui, stay on the eastern half of the island, probably Upcountry, and make the drive to Hana one day. On the Big Island, choose lodging in Volcano Village. Kaua'i offers a range of accommodations moderately convenient to its natural splendors. I would opt for somewhere around Hanalei, probably Princeville, though the Kapa'a area is midway between the dramatic scenery of the North Shore and the South Shore's Waimea Canyon.

BUILDING BLOCKS FOR PERFECT DAYS IN PARADISE

These regional, hour-by-hour planners will get you started on how best to dip into the islands. But a word of caution: If you try to do everything mentioned in the time allotted, you might not feel like you're on a vacation. Use them merely as a guide.

HAWAIIAN CUISINE FROM PAST TO PRESENT

By Bonnie Friedman

There was a time—and it wasn't all that long ago—when Hawai'i was an epicurean wasteland. A "gourmet" meal consisted of a piece of frozen mahimahi—often from foreign waters—a baked potato, and some unidentifiable and completely overcooked vegetables. Sad, my friends . . . but oh, so true.

In the late 1980s, a group of "young Turk" chefs picked up the culinary challenge and ran with it. Led by the the Island of Hawai'i's Peter Merriman and Maui's Mark Ellman, a "gang of 12" kitchen warriors urged local growers to plant strawberries on the slopes of Mount Haleakala, purchased entire crops of luscious Waimea vine-ripened tomatoes, and prepared more varieties of local fish than you could shake a wok at. In Peter-the-Purist's case, he even dove for the sea urchins used in his signature soup. When you saw rancher Monte Richards having dinner at Merriman's, all you had to say was "I'll have what he's having," and you'd be overjoyed by a lamb dish that would make for a month of mouth-watering memories.

This diverse yet like-minded group of chefs (representing all the major islands) would become known as the founding fathers—and mothers—of Hawai'i regional cuisine. Basically, they did what was being done on the mainland and around the world. They realized that there's no place like home and that Hawai'i has access to a cornucopia of fantastic flavors and products, all awaiting inspired kitchen applications.

Let's step back a bit, though, shall we, because it's helpful to see where we've been in order to determine where we're going. First there were the Native Hawaiians, who in traditional times ate an exceptionally healthy diet of fish, *limu* (seaweed), bananas, sweet potato, and *kalo* (taro) in all its many forms (including the staple of the Hawaiian diet, *poi*). Contrary to popular myth, Hawaiians were not obese before we Westerners arrived. It was *Western cuisine*—food full of fat and sugar—that created problems for Hawaiians in the 1800s and beyond.

The diverse ethnic groups that now make up Hawai'i's population began to arrive in the mid-1800s, and they brought along their foods and their cooking styles. And so in a matter of a few decades, island cuisine comprised Chinese noodles, cabbage and other green vegetables (often cooked in a wok), Japanese rice, every form of soy imaginable, root vegetables, ginger, sushi, Portuguese bean soup, stews, sweet bread and sweet wine, Korean-style kalbi ribs, kimchi, and, yes, burgers, fries, corn on the cob, apple pie à la mode, and . . . Spam. It might surprise you to learn that more Spam is consumed in Hawai'i, per capita, than any place else in the world. Hawai'i even has Spam festivals. Now, before you go pooh-poohing this, consider: *Spam musubi*—a piece of grilled Spam sitting atop a bar of sushi rice all nicely wrapped in nori—is, if well made, one of the most delicious on-the-go lunches you will ever taste. Trust me.

One of the most lasting, popular, and beloved manifestations of the combination of these ethnic cuisines is the "plate lunch." Simply stated, a plate lunch is a meat or fish dish (chicken katsu, teriyaki beef, or salmon), two scoops of white rice (must be sticky!), and a scoop of macaroni or potato salad or the really authentic local-style combo—mac-potato salad! These hearty meals originally provided fuel for plantation laborers in the hot tropical sun. In an effort to keep up with more healthful dietary trends, tofu sometimes replaces meat, brown rice can be substituted for white, and green salad often supplants macaroni. But before you get all healthy on me, though, try the real thing once. There are myriad plate-lunch restaurants, stands, and carts throughout the islands.

Interestingly (perhaps ironically), the most difficult foods for visitors to find are traditional Hawaiian foods in all their modern manifestations. If you're lucky enough to be invited to a traditional lu'au, you'll likely encounter a vast array of strikingly unfamiliar foods—*kalua* pork, meat from a slow-roasted pig often cooked in an underground oven or *'imu*, served with or without cabbage; laulau ("packages" of fish and meat steamed and served in ti leaves); *lomi lomi* salmon, the Hawaiian version of ceviche or *poisson cru*; *poi*, black crab, breadfruit, and *'opihi* or limpets; squid *lu'au*, in which the leafy green tops of the *kalo* plant are

cooked with squid and coconut milk; chicken long rice (chicken with cellophane noodles); *pohole*, a native fern sometimes called Hawaiian asparagus; *haupia* or coconut pudding; and *kalolo*, which is *kalo* with coconut milk pudding. These foods are not for the faint of heart or the unadventurous. They are definitely acquired tastes for Western palates. With that caveat, these delicious dishes are certainly worth a try. A few restaurants, most notably 'Ono Hawaiian Foods in Honolulu, feature traditional Hawaiian fare.

BACK TO THE FUTURE

The original dozen chefs—Sam Choy, Roger Dikon, Mark Ellman, Beverly

Gannon, Jean-Marie Josselin, George Mavrothalassitis, Peter Merriman, Amy Ferguson-Ota, Philippe Padovani, Gary Strehl, Alan Wong, and Roy Yamaguchi—took the traditional and stirred in dashes of their own personal and creative styles. In turn, they crafted what came to be known as Hawai'i regional cuisine. Seared and blackened ahi, tropical fruit salsas, ethnic seasonings, fresh-from-the-farm produce, and fresh-from-the-ocean fish—these became the trademarks, the exciting culinary trend of the 1990s.

The 21st-century stars are pushing things farther. Chefs like D. K. Kodama of Sansei Seafood Restaurant & Sushi Bar (Maui and O'ahu), James McDonald of Pacific'O and I'o (Lahaina, Maui), Chai Chaowasaree of Singha Thai Cuisine and Chai's Island Bistro (Honolulu), Wayne Hirabayashi of Hoku's at the Kahala Hotel & Resort (O'ahu), Russell Siu of 3660 on the Rise (Honolulu), and Jackie Lau, corporate chef for Roy's in Hawai'i, have picked up the mantle. They're thrilling diners with daily innovations.

Even in more casual dining segments, the evolution continues. An influx of Latin American labor—most notably from Mexico and Guatemala—now influences island cuisine.

All indications are that the changes will continue. Thanks in large measure to the University of Hawai'i's fantastic community college culinary programs, local young people (and some from the mainland, too) are learning the ways of Hawai'i regional cuisine. Better, yet, they're making it their own.

And what of the original dozen? Sam Choy is going strong with restaurants on O'ahu, a line of food products, several cookbooks, and a local cooking show. Roger Dikon left Hawai'i to perform culinary magic in South Florida. Mark Ellman created Maui Tacos, a chain of Maui-Mex fast-food restaurants in Hawai'i and on the mainland and has opened two successful tapas-style restaurants on Maui. Beverly Gannon's Hali'imaile General Store and Joe's Bar & Grill, both on Maui, continue to earn rave reviews. Bev is also the corporate chef for Hawaiian Airlines and published her first cookbook in 2001. Jean-Marie Josselin is making his mark in Las Vegas like so many mainland celebrity chefs. George Mavrothalassitis's Chef Mavro restaurant (Honolulu) is a perennial award winner; Chef Mavro—as he's affectionately known—won a James Beard Award in 2003. He also now owns and operates a more casual Honolulu restaurant called Cassis. Peter Merriman's original restaurant, Merriman's (Island of Hawai'i), continues to be on the cutting edge, as does his Kohala Coast (Island of Hawai'i) eatery. He is slated to open another Merriman's in Kapalua, Maui in 2008. Amy Ferguson-Ota delights visitors at O's (Island of Hawai'i). Philippe Padovani is back in Honolulu and is a partner in a restaurant called 'Elua. Gary Strehl, last I heard, was cooking in Washington, DC. As for the two biggest names? Alan Wong's eponymous Honolulu restaurant is consistently named "Best in Hawai'i," and he has another in Japan. His Pineapple Room in Honolulu continues to thrive, and the newest in his empire is the Hualalai Grille in the Four Seasons Resort there (Island of Hawai'i). Roy Yamaguchi is the undisputed king of East-meets-West cuisine. His namesake restaurants blanket Hawai'i and stretch from coast to coast on the mainland.

We've come a long, long way from frozen mahimahi, no?

Bonnie Friedman, principal of Grapevine Productions, has been writing about Hawai'i's foodie scene for upwards of two decades. She is the co-author of *The Hali'imaile General Store Cookbook* and *D. K.'s Sushi Chronicles from Hawai'i*. In May 2007, Bonnie became a certified pastry cook.

HAWAIIAN HISTORY

The epic drama of Hawaiian history is an apt match for its breathtaking landscape. From the languid tropical rain forests to the barren and foreboding lava fields, this has forever been a place of contrast and tumult. Centuries of relentless assault on native people and culture by explorers, missionaries, and corporations have been followed by the modern renaissance of the Hawaiian Islands, culminating in today's quest for sovereignty. These, the remotest islands on earth, the "land of the raging fire," have been oasis, bounty, and burial ground for a stunning array of adventurers and marauders living out sagas of conquest and hope amid unbelievable beauty. And through it all, as unvanquished by time and change as Kilauea, the tolerance and welcome of *"aloha"* lives on.

INHABITATION AND EARLY CULTURE OF THE ISLANDS

The first inhabitants of Hawai'i arrived at Ka La'e (South Point) on the Big Island between A.D. 500 and 750 not by accident—unlike many who were to follow. The Polynesians paddled there to colonize, probably from the Marquesas Islands. They traveled more than 2,500 miles in double-hulled canoes up to 100 feet in length, with platforms and shelters containing their families, dogs, and small livestock. They also carried the future staples of the Hawaiian diet and economy: coconuts, bananas, *taro*, breadfruit, and sugarcane. Their masterful early navigation techniques included following stars, migrating birds, and wind and ocean currents.

There was no formal economy, but land was apportioned by mighty aristocratic chiefs or ali'i, according to the rules of a rigid caste system. It was divided into wedge-shaped pieces called *ahupua'a*, literally, "place where the hogs are stored." Each section was larger at the coast, where the natives lived, and narrowed as it went inland into pasture and wooded areas. The land was irrigated and farmed by ordinary citizens (*maka'ainana*), who were taxed to live on and cultivate it, in the feudal style. The ali'i won rank by physical power and force of personality, and individual dynasties waged constant battles of conquest within and between islands. With the arrival of the Tahitians around A.D. 1000, the first chapter in a long history of subjugation in the Hawaiian Islands was written. The original Polynesians were subdued by force and put to work building fishponds, temples, and further infrastructure.

There is no written history from the time humans arrived in the Hawaiian Islands until the first contact of the natives with the white man. Chants, talk stories, and petroglyphs carved in lava are the only record of the wars between tribes and islands, of building shelter to sustain life without metal or clay, or of humankind's relationship to the gods.

MANA, SACRIFICE, AND SURFING

Just beneath the *ali'i* in status, the authorities in religious and spiritual matters were the *kahunas* or high priests. Religion consisted of prayer and offerings from the harvests to gods, who would in turn ensure safety, health, and plenty. Around the 12th century Pa'ao, a mighty Tahitian *kahuna*, believing the existing rituals insufficient, further codified prayer and worship, and introduced human sacrifice in temples (*luakini heiau*) built for that purpose.

The *heiaus*, containing taboo, prayer, and drum towers, were commonly tributes to Lono, the god of the harvest, or Ku, the god of war. Often located in majestic settings, temple sites were chosen for their perceived *mana* or spiritual power. Most were built for specific times or purposes; if the *mana* of the location was perceived to diminish or the occasion passed, the temple was relocated or fell into disuse.

Pa'ao also instituted and entrenched *kapu*—a persistent coda of taboos that ruled all things social and most matters of daily life. *Kapus*, for instance, dictated

that women were not allowed to eat certain fish, coconuts, bananas, and pork, while men could not eat dog meat. Women and commoners were forbidden to eat or fraternize with royal males. A commoner (*maka'ainana*) or slave (*kauwa*) could be put to death for crossing paths with a chief or a king. Husbands maintained separate homes and pounded, cooked, and ate poi separately from their wives. Husband and wife—who were particularly celebrated if they were incestuous siblings of royal birth—could sleep together only in a structure built for that purpose, the *hale noa*. Polygamy was the norm, and the population grew to about a million people.

Where there was a difference in social standing, even between husband and wife, *kapu* ruled. It is claimed that one of Kamehameha the

Great's wives was so superior in status to him that he was reduced to approaching her only if he was unclothed and on his hands and knees. Breaking *kapu* could result in death, but penalties were variously enforced, and each island had a place of escape or *pu'uhonua* that sheltered offenders from death.

Even then, as ancient petroglyphs attest, surfing was the most popular hobby in the islands. But in sport, as in all else, caste was key—the *ali'i* used 16-foot-long boards while commoners were relegated to the 5- to 7-footers of inferior wood.

THE DEPARTURE OF LONO

Among the many legends the natives passed down from generation to generation was one about the enigmatic chief Lono. He arrived from heaven astride a rainbow, landing in Waipi'o Valley on the Big Island. There he met, fell in love with, and married the lovely Kaikilani and moved with her to the Kona Coast. Lono suspected another chief of coveting his bride and beat her savagely in a jealous rage. With her dying breath, Kaikilani declared her love for Lono alone. In abject grief, Lono traveled around the islands for months, challenging men to wrestling and other contests. Finally his guilt led him to quit the islands altogether in an enormous canoe laden with food and provisions. He vowed to return one day, sailing clockwise into the bay atop a floating island abundant with chickens and pigs. In Lono's honor, each year from October to February the natives held a cease-fire and harvest festival called *makahiki* complete with athletic contests, games, and festivities.

THE ARRIVAL OF CAPTAIN COOK AND THE FLOATING ISLAND

As the end of the 18th century neared, the Hawaiian Islands remained divided into feuding factions—the standout in battle, a 20-year-old warrior named Kamehameha. Not many on the island, warrior or otherwise, had seen Europeans until 1778, although the term for "white man"—*haole*, literally "one without breath," to describe their sickly paleness—was already in use, probably based on talk stories from sightings of Spanish explorers.

British captain James Cook, at 50, was the most celebrated explorer of the 18th century. Nevertheless, he missed both Maui and the Big Island before sailing to Kaua'i while in search of the nonexistent Northwest Passage to the Atlantic. On January 18, 1778—during the festival of *makahiki*—Cook's ships *Discovery* and *Resolution* sailed into Waimea Bay. He dubbed them the Sandwich Islands, in honor of the Earl of Sandwich.

Cook and his men were amazed by many things they saw. First, the natives looked so Tahitian in dress and features. Next, these "Tahitian" men and women were paddling and swimming out to his ships in great numbers to give gifts and bid him welcome. He was surprised to find them completely uninterested in the beads and cheap trinkets he had used successfully to barter with indigenous people elsewhere in his travels. Instead they wanted what they did not have: nails, bits of the ship, anything made of metal. In fact, a native man who attempted to take a piece of iron from one of the ships was shot to death, giving the natives the first of many experiences with firearms and supporting the growing suspicion that Cook was a god.

Mindful of infecting the natives with venereal disease, Cook had given an order against fraternization. But the willpower of his sea-weary crew was no match for the gaggles of native women who were warmly welcoming the men with dances and affection. The natives were certain by now that the huge clockwise-sailing ships—arriving, as they had, at *makahiki*—that had returned to their midst were none other than the god Lono and his attendants. Thus gonorrhea and syphilis were introduced to the islands. In the years to come, exposure to these diseases would kill or sterilize large portions of the native population. Cook and his men stayed in Kaua'i for several idyllic days, restocking provisions, before continuing north to continue their search for a passage to the Atlantic.

On the return trip, a year later, they returned to their fondly remembered paradise. As they sailed into Kealakekua Bay on the Big Island, they were greeted by even greater and more enthusiastic crowds of *makahiki* celebrants, chanting "Lono" at Cook and falling to the ground, covering their heads and faces in a worshipful posture. Drawings made on this trip by the ship's artist, John Webber, offer one of the few surviving firsthand visual accounts of people and life in Hawai'i at that time.

This visit by Cook and his men was longer and ultimately far less successful. At first they enjoyed a cultural exchange. Cook was shown the thick mountain forests and a demonstration of canoe making, and the natives watched black-smiths and listened to flute and violin music for the first time. But weeks passed, and the greedy crew nearly exhausted local provisions and connubial hospitality. As they finally departed, they unceremoniously tore down a fence and took carved wooden icons of a seaside temple, ironically to Lono, to be used as firewood.

All might have been well if they had sailed off and disappeared on February 4, 1779, as planned. But storms damaged one of Cook's ships, and they returned less than a week later. For many reasons, including that the festival of *makahiki* was now over and that they sailed counterclockwise in a crippled ship, they did not receive a warm greeting. Cook was never aware that the festival had to do with his reception in Hawai'i; he believed this treatment was accorded all visitors and was surely confused by the markedly changed atmosphere that greeted his third arrival.

Rather than gifts, Cook and company were met with thievery. After several incidents, a cutter was stolen and Cook retaliated with a blockade of the bay and a plan to kidnap a chief as hostage until his equipment was returned. En route to find his intended hostage, High Chief Kalaniopu'u of the Big Island, the English fired on a canoe sailing out of the bay. A lower chief, Noekema, was killed. The attempted kidnapping of Kalaniopu'u was foiled by his wailing wife, but as Cook and his troops retreated, Cook fired at a native blocking his way. Just as the shot missed its mark, word of the death of Noekema reached the roiling mob. In an angry frenzy, the crowd of Hawaiians took turns striking and stabbing Cook and four of his sailors to death.

Cook's men retaliated by beheading two natives and setting fire to a village before rowing back to their ship. Days passed, and the natives, despite having un-masked him as a commoner, gave Cook an *ali'i* funeral rite by removing his bones and stripping the skin from his skull. These remains were presented to his horrified crew, who buried him at sea, in turn causing the islanders to place a *kapu* on the bay. The British ships finally parted from Hawaiian waters in mid-March 1779, having unleashed more destruction in one year—with guns, disease, dissolution of native blood, and tales of bounty, along with accurate maps that soon established Hawai'i as a port of call for a steady stream of traders and plunderers—than had been seen in the entire 700 years prior.

KAMEHAMEHA THE GREAT

Kamehameha was born at Kohala on the Big Island in 1758 to parents of royal blood. He was a fierce and driven soldier, said to be over 6 feet 6 inches tall, thus a valuable asset to his uncle, Chief Kalaniopu'u. The young warrior was present at the scene of James Cook's death. Even today Kamehameha is deified as the most enduring hero in Hawaiian history. The sad irony is that his acquisitive conquest of Hawai'i and his courting of trade just at the time when the isolation of the islands was coming to an end provided a singular platform for exploitation by the outside world and the beginning of the end of native culture and self-determination.

Kamehameha's unification of the islands was ultimately made possible by firearms bought or raided from trading ships. His series of battle campaigns for unification lasted more than 10 years. His ultimate victories over rival chiefs Keoua and Kahekili required the services of paid *haole* patrons, including John Young and Isaac Davis, upon whom Kamehameha conferred chieftain status.

Young and Isaac helped equip Hawaiian fleets with cannons and mercenary soldiers; when the wars were successfully concluded, they married Hawaiian women and settled permanently in the islands. This was the story of hundreds of British, French, Welsh, Chinese, and Spanish by then. More than the human population boomed; Kamehameha was forced to import cowboys (*paniolo*) from Mexico and Spain to cope with the burgeoning herds of wild cattle and horses on the islands.

A lover as well as a fighter, Kamehameha had 21 wives, including the noblewoman Keopuolani, whom he married in 1795. Her lineage assured him children of the *ali'i* rank, although only three of 11 offspring lived to adulthood. Although his social aspirations lay with Keopuolani, the king's heart belonged to Ka'ahumanu, a tall, audacious, 200-pound beauty who, though childless, would utterly alter Hawaiian history in her own inimitable way.

SANDALWOOD—A CAUTIONARY TALE

The story of sandalwood is a fitting metaphor for the forces that subsumed Hawai'i as dealings with trade grew. In the early years, native Hawaiians practiced an innate ecology and primitive but highly effective conservation. There was a *kapu*, for instance, against harvesting certain kinds of trees without planting two more in their place. As Yankee traders found their way to Hawai'i, these ancient practices fell prey to more modern mercantile interests, particularly the newfound native demand for firearms.

In the 1790s, American sea captains identified that Hawai'i had vast groves of sandalwood trees—a fragrant wood much in demand in Asia. A trade route, which became disproportionately profitable to the sea merchants, was opened. Shiploads of sandalwood were delivered from the islands to Canton and traded for china and silks, which were in turn delivered to New England. In New England, the Asian bounty was unloaded and the boats were reloaded with items coveted in Hawai'i—from weapons to furniture, depending on trends and tastes.

Kamehameha had been an old-style conservationist, but his successor son Liholiho allowed chiefs to import luxury items with promissory notes of future deliveries of sandalwood. These debts mounted, and the frenzied harvests that followed crippled and maimed indentured commoners who carried the wood miles and miles on their backs from the interior to the waiting ships. The logs were amassed in piculs or log pits carved into the mountains in the exact dimension of a ship's hull. One picul sold in China for 34 cents. Written records exist of chains of laborers, thousands long, in painful lockstep toward the sea. Within a few short years of Kamehameha's death, the sandalwood forests were utterly bare, the agricultural system had collapsed from lack of focus on other crops, and the credit-happy chiefs were deeply in debt with no way to pay.

KAMEHAMEHA II (LIHOLIHO)

On Kamehameha's deathbed in 1819, Ka'ahumanu, the wife who would not be denied her place in history, claimed he asked her to guide the fate—as the *kuhina nui*—of the kingdom and his heir, Kamehameha's 20-year-old son Liholiho, crowned Kamehameha II.

Her first official act was to enhance her own power by supplanting the ancient hold of *kapu*. Less than six months after her husband's death and secret burial at Kailua-Kona, she convinced the weak-willed Liholiho—whether by intoxicants or sheer persuasion—to throw a lavish feast attended by royals. At the dinner she pressed Liholiho to sit by her, flaunting the ancient *kapu* against men and women dining together. Social engineer Ka'ahumanu had personally placed forbidden foods and then encouraged the consumption of them by the male and female guests—including dog meat, which Liholiho was reported to have tasted.

The world did not end, the heavens did not weep, and the gods did not exact revenge. In one libertine evening, centuries of taboos and traditions succumbed. The response across the land was gleeful and destructive as Hawaiians splintered and torched temples and idols in fits of wanton disobedience. They were blissfully unaware in those episodes of carefree wilding that a religion with equally divisive and far-reaching consequences was, even then, scant months from their shores.

Liloliho was at loose ends as Ka'ahumanu ran the islands and the first whaling ships landed, fast-forwarding Westernization with new diseases and liquor. He decided in 1823 at the age of 28 to visit England and pay an uninvited call to ask for kingly advice from George IV. Despite his bounty of $25,000 in gold coins and a shipload of sperm oil, he was not only not received by King George but also broadly caricatured by British newspapers, which called him a "cannibal" among other racial epithets. As Liholiho sought intervention and grooming to become worthy of the king's audience, he and Kamamalu, his sister and his favorite of five wives, contracted measles, died, and were buried with Christian rites in 1824.

When word of his death reached the islands, Liholiho was succeeded on the throne by the second of Kamehameha I's sons, Kauikeaouli, crowned Kamehameha III. Ka'ahumanu, however, was very much the power behind the throne and would remain so for roughly another decade. A less likely development was her role as a fervent promoter of Christianity.

CHRISTIANITY COMES ASHORE

The end of the old religion and *kapu* left a sense of moral anarchy, particularly felt by older, more traditional Hawaiians. In 1820, *Thaddeus*—the first missionary ship—landed within shouting distance of the site of the dinner party that sunk *kapu*. The sojourners were freshly tutored in the Hawaiian language and, after six months at sea, ripe to preach. This group of 23, led by Hiram Bingham and Asa Thurston, was the first of a dozen from New England's American Board of Commissioners of Foreign Missions. This troupe was moved to their mission in Hawai'i by an encounter with a Hawaiian expatriate named Henry Opukaha'ia, who had died in Boston with the wish on his lips that people in his homeland could hear and be comforted by the word of Christ, as he had been.

When she took gravely ill in 1824, the mighty trendsetter Ka'ahumanu was nursed back to health by Bingham's wife, Sybil. In her joyful recovery, Ka'ahumanu saw the hand of the Christian god of Sybil's prayers; she was converted, and she set about converting others. Even the most royal Keopuolani, the mother of the king, converted, and a massive movement of the population toward Christianity began in earnest.

The missionaries had their hands full. The existing offenses—the suggestive undulations of the hula, bare-breasted women, polygamy, incest, promiscuity, and the frayed remnants of pagan religion—had been augmented recently by the tastes of traders to include tobacco, liquor, and prostitution. The missionaries even took umbrage at innocent but indolent and "lewd" pastimes like kite flying, surfing, and wearing leis.

Clad in thick, dark, itchy wool, the missionaries forced the women into modest tentlike dresses called *mu'umu'us*. There went dancing, leis, boxing and wrestling, drinking and smoking, and lighting fires on the Sabbath. The normally spirited Hawaiians might have argued had they not been freshly parted from their centuries-old traditions, but they fell quickly into the new order, relinquishing

almost all that remained of their native ways.

They learned to read in droves, using the missionaries' oversimplified 12-letter Hawaiian alphabet, which permanently altered the character of their language. This seemed to the missionaries a small price to pay for Hawaiians becoming, by 1846, the most literate people in the world. They had printing presses and were dictating their oral histories into book form. The missionaries were far from universally generous about their new converts. Asa Thurston described Kailua as a "filthy village," and Bingham wrote that the Hawaiians were "stupid and polluted worshippers of demons."

The overarching religion of the missionaries, however, seemed to be capitalism. It is often repeated in Hawai'i that the preachers came to do good and stayed to do well. They formed the first tier of the emerging middle class by intermarrying and, when the laws changed to allow it, purchasing land and importing immigrant labor to work their fields.

KAMEHAMEHA III (KAUIKEAOULI)

Kamehameha III took the throne at nine and ruled for nearly 30 years, aided at the beginning of his reign, of course, by the omnipresent *kuhina nui*, Ka'ahumanu. He was educated as a Christian by Bingham himself, but he resisted internalizing Western values and fundamentally embraced Hawaiian culture and beliefs—rejecting Bingham's suggestion to make scripture the law of the islands.

In 1833 Ka'ahumanu died, just months after her baptism. She was succeeded as regent by Kauikeaouli's sister Kinau, a devout Christian. The two rulers disagreed, and in an argument over religion he stripped her of her title. For a time there was resurgence of old customs. Then the king reinstated Kinau to her throne and, in apology for his haste, declared her son Alexander Liholiho his successor. Bingham and the reinstated Queen Kinau established firmer religious order, including exile colonies where sinners and offenders were sent for punishment.

The true love affair of Kamehameha III's dynasty was his marriage to his sister Nahi'ena'ena, which produced one stillborn child. She died at 20, and the king moved the site of his monarchy from the Big Island to Maui to be near her grave site. Many Hawaiians were dying in the 1840s—reportedly of epic sadness. Oral histories refer to this time when imported racism was beginning to convince Hawaiians of their inferiority as the time when *Na kanaka okuu wale aku no i kau uhane*—"People dismissed their souls and died."

In addition to enhancing Hawai'i's political infrastructure with the first constitution and legislature, Kamehameha III bought land commission called the Great Mahale (divide) in 1848. This instituted, for the first time, private ownership of Hawaiian land and allowed land to be bought and sold. Title was transferred from the king to chiefs and, primarily, divided into 3-acre farm plots called *kuleana*. All who desired land were required to pay a tariff and register the plots. This was intended to turn the islands into a land of small farms, but the result was that only a few thousand wealthier Hawaiians carried through and registered. Commoners, who were required to pay the tax in cash, were largely unable to pay or simply did not grasp the idea of private landownership until it was too late. In 1850, foreigners were allowed to purchase land, and so many relished the opportunity that within 20 years, 80 percent of the property in Hawai'i was owned by foreigners and missionaries. Native Hawaiians were marginalized in their own land. The distribution of lands in the Great Mahale continues to cause contention today.

KAMEHAMEHA IV (ALEXANDER LIHOLIHO)

Further struggles of identity with the West marked the nine-year reign of the nephew Kamehameha IV. He married Emma Rooke, granddaughter of *haole* chieftain John Young, whose weapons and advice had helped Kamehameha I unify the islands. Their efforts in the monarchy were spent in health-care initiatives to try and stave off the decimating diseases brought to the islands by Chinese, Japanese, Filipino, Korean, Portuguese, and Puerto Rican immigrants imported to work the sugarcane fields. Queen Emma established the Queen's Hospital, which still exists today. But their efforts made scant inroads into the plagues of leprosy and other dread diseases.

After a series of tragedies, including the death of their only son—and the only possible continuation of the monarchy—as a toddler and the death of a close friend from a shooting during an argument, Kamehameha IV died from complications of emotional exhaustion, liquor, and asthma at 29.

KAMEHAMEHA V (LOT KAMEHAMEHA)

By the reign of Alexander's brother Lot, Kamehameha V, the wealth of the missionaries had led them into the sugar business—some of the many white men becoming entrenched in the political and mercantile life of the islands. This was the last king of a lineage that stretched back to the 12th century. His unrequited love for Princess Bernice Pauahi—who jilted him to marry an American—made him a lifelong bachelor and guaranteed no heirs. He was an advocate of bringing back the indigenous culture and again increased the power of the monarchy over constitutional government, but no real inroads into a renaissance were forthcoming. Lot died with no heir and no successor named.

WILLIAM C. LUNALILO

The outcome of a power struggle with David Kalakaua, William C. Lunalilo's reign as Hawai'i's first elected king lasted one year before his years of fast living, womanizing, and drinking caught up with him and he died of tuberculosis. His advisers and officials were overwhelmingly American, and their most lasting action was the groundwork to a treaty of trade reciprocity with the United States, born of the sugar plantation owners' distaste for the heavy tariff paid on sugar imported into the United States. The movement was afoot by the growers to annex Hawai'i to the States as a means of eliminating the tax and increasing their profit. The United States cared little about the sugar tax and annexation, but was quite keen on the concept of a naval outpost on O'ahu. General Schofield was sent to inspect the site that became Pearl Harbor and was well pleased, and soon—despite significant protest—there was a naval base in Pearl Harbor, in exchange for duty-free Hawaiian sugar.

DAVID KALAKAUA

After David Kalakaua successfully contested Queen Emma, wife of Kamehameha IV, for the throne, a riot by her followers had to be calmed by the military. Kalakaua, the Merrie Monarch and Hawai'i's last king, made a priority of returning life to more native influences. He reinstituted the hula, surfing, and a native-style state song. Among his wide travels, he visited the United States to convince President Ulysses Grant to honor the reciprocity agreement with the islands. Understanding that Hawai'i needed liaisons to survive in the increasingly complex world, he tried to broker a Polynesian-Pacific empire and proposed prudent marriages to solidify power bases. He built the lavish 'Iolani Palace, to the chagrin of sugar plantation owners who feared his lifestyle of spending. These owners introduced a new constitution severely limiting his power and granting the vote only to property holders, a very small minority of Hawaiians. King Kalakaua died in San Francisco in 1891.

LILIUOKALANI

Queen Liliuokalani, the final Hawaiian monarch, was the wife of the governor of O'ahu. In her two-year reign, she attempted to restore royal power. As she did so, *haole* businessmen, led by the grandson of missionary Asa Thurston, addressed this threat to their earnings by overthrowing the monarchy by force and charging treason in order to imprison Liliuokalani in 'Iolani Palace for eight months. They placed Sanford Dole at the head of a provisional government. An appeal to President Grover Cleveland brought the queen a brief reprieve, but in the end his support was rhetoric in the face of the potential political damage of supporting a Native Hawaiian government over white American business interests. The republic, with Dole as president, prevailed. Cleveland later wrote, "Hawai'i is ours. As I . . . contemplate the means used to complete the outrage, I am ashamed of the whole affair."

When Liliuokalani died in 1893, the people of Honolulu spilled into the streets to bid a tearful farewell to the embattled woman who remained queen in their hearts. In 1898, Hawai'i was officially annexed to the United States by Congress, and Stanford Dole was appointed governor. In 1901, the first tourist hotel, the Moana Surfrider (now a Sheraton), was built on Waikiki Beach.

On December 7, 1941, nearly 3,000 were killed as the Japanese bombed the U.S. naval station at Pearl Harbor, forcing America into World War II. Japanese on the islands were subject to the same suspicion as they were on the mainland; many were sent to internment camps, and *nisei* (second-generation Japanese) were dismissed from the army, employment, and civic life. Late in the war, a *nisei* unit of the National Guard was formed and deployed, which performed with distinction in battle and at war's end produced, in the true spirit of *aloha*, some of Hawai'i's most talented and influential professionals and statesmen, including U.S. Senator Daniel Inouye. In 1959, the United States passed legislation granting Hawai'i statehood.

SOVEREIGNTY FOR HAWAI'I

In 1993, Native Hawaiians marked the 100th anniversary of the overthrow of Queen Liliuokalani with a call for sovereignty. Since the 1980s, the movement for sovereignty—to right some of the wrongs done to Native Hawaiians—has grown more strident. These calls were answered and encouraged in 1993, when the U.S. Congress and President Bill Clinton issued a resolution of apology to the Native Hawaiians for the overthrow and promised to provide "a proper foundation for reconciliation." Bills were subsequently introduced in the Hawaiian legislature proposing a new Hawaiian nation of varying descriptions, and a commission was formed to gather input and options for the form it would take.

Amid a modern renaissance of native language, dress, dance, and customs, polls now show that the majority of Hawaiians, regardless of ethnicity, support a vision of sovereignty as a nation-within-a-nation. The consensus and legislative process continue today, stewarded largely by descendants of Native Hawaiians.

SOME HISTORICAL DATES

A.D. 500–700: The first settlers, thought to be from the Marquesas Islands in Polynesia, arrive in Hawai'i. They navigate across the Pacific by the stars, sun, clouds, ocean swells, and currents.

A.D. 1000: The first Tahitians arrive in the islands and probably conquer the Marquesans.

1778: Captain Cook lands his ships, *Resolution* and *Discovery*, in Waimea, Kaua'i. He names the archipelago the Sandwich Islands, in honor of the Earl of Sandwich.

1810: Believing in his destiny, King Kamehameha I wages war on the rulers of other islands using Western weapons. In doing so, he unifies the islands for the first time under one leader.

1819: Whaling ships arrive in Kealakekua Bay on the Big Island and bring opportunity for industry and commerce.

1820: The first American missionaries arrive to spread Christianity.

1850: Foreigners (*haole*) are permitted to purchase land. The legislature approves hiring of foreign laborers, which encourages an influx of Chinese, Japanese, and Portuguese workers. The number of immigrants increases as the sugar and pineapple industries prosper.

1893: Tired of taxation and decreased sugar sales, sugar planters plot to end the monarchy with a United States takeover. The Annexationists overthrow Queen Liliuokalani. A provisional government is established and later replaced by the Republic of Hawai'i.

1898: The United States annexes Hawai'i and creates the Territory of Hawai'i. Later that year the U.S. acquires the Philippines and Guam.

1900: Duke Paoa Kahanamoku (1890–1968) puts the spotlight on Hawai'i by winning several Olympic gold medals and setting the world record in the 100-meter freestyle. He continues to set records at the 1924 and the 1928 Olympics.

1927: Matson places the deluxe passenger ship SS *Malolo* (flying fish) into service between San Francisco and Honolulu and times the inaugural voyage with the opening of the new Royal Hawaiian hotel in Waikiki.

1941: On December 7, the Japanese attack Pearl Harbor on O'ahu, and the United States enters World War II.

1958: Pan Am's Boeing 707 opens international travel to the islands.

1959: Hawai'i becomes the 50th state of the United States.

1970s: Native Hawaiians and local activists gain recognition through protests against the military's bombing practices on Kaho'olawe.

1993: The U.S. Congress apologizes for overthrowing the Hawaiian monarchy, and the state of Hawai'i creates a formal process to recognize Hawaiian sovereignty.

LANGUAGE

Hawaiian is a relatively new written language, first recorded in the mid-19th century when New England missionaries began assigning letters to the sounds they heard. With only 12 letters and two punctuation marks, it's the most minimal language in the world. It's also argued to be an oversimplification of the original spoken language. Still, the small number of letters and only 162 feasible syllables makes it much easier than other languages to learn.

Although English is—without question—the first language in Hawai'i, there has nonetheless been an effort to rejuvenate interest in the Hawaiian language for fear it will be lost. As such, you will hear a few consistently used Hawaiian words. You'll probably also feel more culturally involved if you sprinkle in a few choice words where appropriate. Besides, it's a beautifully lyrical, lilting language, and we all benefit from a little more lyricism in our lives.

Hawaiian locals have a language all their own—a form of pidgin English, which is a combination of Hawaiian, English, and slang. It's hard to tune your ear to or get a taste of *da kine* (true Hawaiian pidgin) unless you leave the tourist areas and engage with locals. If you want to be *akamai* (someone who's very smart), go to extreme-hawaii.com/pidgin, where you can see how pidgin words are spelled and listen to how they're pronounced.

When you're traveling around the islands, these basic pronunciation rules will come in handy:

CONSONANTS

h, **l**, **n**, and **m**	pronounced as they are in English
k and **p**	pronounced with less aspiration (breath)
w	usually pronounced like a soft *v*, but at the beginning of words or after an *a*, may be pronounced like a *v* or a *w*

VOWELS (UNSTRESSED)

a	*a* as in *above*
e	*e* as in *bet*
i	*y* as in *pity*
o	*o* as in *hole*
u	*u* as in *full*

When two vowels appear side by side (aka a diphthong), stress the first vowel but perhaps not quite as much as you would in English.

VOWELS (STRESSED)

a   *a* as in *bar*
e   *ay* as in *play*
i   *ee* as in *see*
o   *o* as in *mole* (but slightly longer)
u   *oo* as in *soon*

PUNCTUATION

The glottal stop ('), or *okina*, does not often appear on street signs or in writing, but it's very helpful in pronunciation. (A good example of this in English is *oh-oh*. If that was a Hawaiian word, it would appear as *oh'oh*.) It has the effect of creating a discernible pause. I have used the glottal stop in this book to help with pronunciation.

COMMON WORDS

For the best Hawaiian electronic dictionary, and a great reference for Hawaiian place-names, head to wehewehe.org/cgi-bin/hdict.

I also rely heavily on the *New Pocket Hawaiian Dictionary* by Mary Kawena Pukui and Samuel Elbert, published by the University of Hawai'i Press.

'*a*'*a*	the rough kind of lava
'*ae*	to say yes or offer consent
ahupua'*a*	a division of land encompassing terrain reaching from the mountains to the ocean—a "slice of cake," if you will, with the large piece being oceanfront
'*aina*	land or earth
akua	god, goddess, or spirit
ali'*i*	Hawaiian chief, royal, or person of high rank
aloha	welcome, hello, good-bye, love, or friendship
a'*ole*	no, never, not
brah	pidgin for friend
da kine	pidgin for thingamajig, whatchamacallit
halaua	hula group or school
hale	house or building
haole	Caucasian, mainlander, or foreigner
hapu'*u*	tree fern
heiau	ancient temple or place of worship
hui	group or club
hula	a form of dance and music
kahuna	priest or priestess; a person well versed in any field
kai	sea
kama'*aina*	resident of Hawai'i
kane	man

kappa	cloth made from bark (also known as *tapa* in other parts of the world)
kapu	sacred or forbidden
keiki	young child
kiawe	mesquite
koa	rare hardwood tree
kona	leeward
kukui	candlenut tree
lanai	balcony or patio
lau	leaf
lei	wreath of flowers or shells worn around the neck
mahalo	thank you
makai	toward the sea (used as a directional signifier)
malihini	stranger or newcomer
mana	a kind of spiritual power
mauka	toward the mountain (used as a directional signifier)
mele	ancient chant
Menehune	legendary, dwarflike ancient Hawaiian people
mu'umu'u	loose fitting gown or dress
nui	significant or important
'ohana	family
pahoehoe	the smooth kind of lava
pali	clifflike mountain
paniolo	cowboy
pau	finished or done
pili	a kind of grass
puka	hole or door
tutu	grandparent
wahine	woman
wai	water
wikiwiki	fast

FOOD TERMS

imu	pit-style oven
liliko'i	passion fruit
limu	seaweed
lomi lomi	type of raw salmon preparation
lu'au	traditional Hawaiian meal
mahimahi	white fish
'ono	delicious
'opae	shrimp
poi	a basic Hawaiian food made from *taro* root
poke	raw fish preparation
pua'	a pig
pupu	snack or appetizer
taro	Hawaiian food plant

WHAT'S WHERE IN HAWAI'I

ACTIVITIES DESKS

Where Hawaiian activities are concerned, it's a jungle out there. The best of these "desks" (kiosks) will make reservations for whatever you want to do. The worst will persuade you to endure time-share presentations in exchange for free tickets. Only you can decide what your time is worth. **Activity Warehouse** (travel hawaii.com), with outlets on Maui and Kaua'i, is quite reputable. Booking on your own through the Internet will usually save you 10 to 25 percent, but I for one can never predict what I'll want to do ahead of time. If you have your heart set on something in particular, though, book ahead to save disappointment.

AIRPORTS AND AIRLINES

Practically all major U.S. airlines fly into Honolulu (**O'ahu**), and many fly to **Maui** (Kahalui), **Kaua'i** (Lihu'e), and the **Big Island** (Kailua-Kona and Hilo). United offers the most flights; Continental offers direct service from Newark, New Jersey. No carriers fly to **Lana'i** or **Moloka'i** from the mainland.

For interisland air, contact Hawaiian Airlines (808-838-1555 or 1-800-367-5320; hawaiianair.com) and Go!

(1-888-435-9462; iflygo.com). Hawaiian also offers an increasing number of flights from the West Coast.

AQUARIUMS

The Waikiki Aquarium (808-923-9741; waquarium.org) on **O'ahu** and Ocean Center on **Maui** (808-270-7000; mauioceancenter.com) are both well worth your time.

AREA CODE

It's the same for all the islands: 808. Calling one neighbor island from another is akin to calling the mainland, so you'll have to dial 808 first. Calling from one place on an island to another place on that same island is considered a local call.

ART MUSEUMS

For statewide information, consult hawaiimuseums.org. In Greater Honolulu on **O'ahu**, don't miss the Contemporary Museum (808-526-0232; tcmhi.org) and Honolulu Academy of Arts (808-532-8700; honoluluacademy .org).

ATTIRE

The islands are delightfully casual. Aloha shirts for men are considered dressy, and a jacket and tie are required only at one or two places (and even there, they're provided). At the other end of the spectrum, you'll always need shoes and shirts at beachfront restaurants.

BANYAN TREES

I can't get enough of these magnificent trees that put down roots with abandon. On **O'ahu**, you can sip cocktails under two noteworthy specimens: at the Banyan Court (808-921-4600; Moana Surfrider hotel), made famous by the *Hawai'i Calls* radio program, and the Hau Tree Lana'i (808-921-7066; New Otani Kaimana Beach Hotel), where Robert Louis Stevenson lauded Hawai'i. On **Maui**, the Banyan Tree in Lahaina takes up an entire city block. On the **Big Island**, Banyan Drive in Hilo is impressive.

♈ BARS

Look for this symbol adjacent to restaurants and entertainment venues where it's romantic or fun to sip a tropical drink.

⚓ BEACHES

Look for this symbol wherever there are gorgeous strands of sand. In each chapter, if beaches are particularly great for swimming and other water activities, they are described under *Beaches,* usually in order of my preference. If they're more suited to gawking from scenic overlooks, they are listed under *To See & Do*. Dr. Stephen Leatherman, a self-appointed beach specialist, consistently includes Hawaiian sands on his Best Beaches lists (drbeach.org).

Are you planning on building your vacation around beach bumming? Go out of your way for these: On **O'ahu**, Waikiki is the granddaddy for tourists, but Lanikai Beach ("The Windward Coast") is downright incredible for quietude. On **Maui**, Makena Beach ("South Maui") and Hamoa Beach ("To Hana & Beyond") are well worth the effort. On **Lana'i**, head to tranquil Hulopo'e Beach. On **Moloka'i**, Papohaku Beach is the second longest in the state. Because the **Big Island** is the youngest island in the chain and erosion hasn't had as much time to work its magic, you'll find mostly small patches. Two exceptions are truly exceptional: the Kohala Coast's Hapuna Beach and Mauna Kea Beach (aka Kaunaoa Beach). The adventurous will want to check out Green Sands Beach (aka Papakolea Beach) in the South Point Area. On **Kaua'i**, the South Shore's Po'ipu Beach Park is without equal; Western Kaua'i's Polihale State Park is remote and desolate; and on the North Shore, Hanalei, Ke'e, Tunnels, and Anini beaches are impossible to beat as a foursome.

See also *Beach Safety Tips* (p. 466/The Big Island).

BICYCLING
Visit bikehawaii.com for complete information. On **Maui**, visitors enjoy saying they bicycled down a volcano, and Maui Downhill (808-871-2155; mauidownhill.com) is happy to oblige. On **Kaua'i**, off-road mountain bicycling is pretty decent, and options are varied. On the **Big Island**, there are a few options, but remember: It's a big island. Bike rentals are listed, whenever they are available, throughout this book.

BIRD-WATCHING
Hawai'i is home to birds that exist nowhere else on the planet, and the best birding is found on **Moloka'i** and Kaua'i. Serious birders will want to pick up the *Field Guide to the Birds of Hawai'i* (Princeton University Press, 1987). The University of Hawai'i (uhpress.hawaii.edu) also publishes a great selection of birding guides. On **O'ahu**, the Windward Coast is rife with bird-watching places, while the North Shore offers the Waimea Valley Center (808-638-

7766). On **Kaua'i**, the Hule'ia National Wildlife Refuge in the Lihu'e Area, accessible only via kayak, is thick with endangered birds. Terran Tours (808-335-0398) takes birders deep into West Kaua'i's Koke'e State Park in search of rare birds. On the North Shore, Kilauea Point National Wildlife Refuge and Hanalei National Wildlife Refuge are both rich with our fine feathered friends, but the latter is closed to visitors. Guides and tours are listed throughout this book.

BOAT EXCURSIONS
From hard-rubber rafts to outrigger canoes and kayaks, from schooners to catamarans, if it floats it probably takes paying passengers. Keep in mind that many excursions serve double duty by offering snorkeling, perhaps, along with some kind of other special-interest ride. On Windward **O'ahu**, Captain Bob's Adventure Cruises (808-942-5077) takes happy visitors out onto placid Kane'ohe Bay. In West **Maui**, Ocean Riders (808-661-3586; mauioceanriders.com) depart from Lahaina. On **Kaua'i**, the most dramatic trips head along the North Shore's Na Pali coastline, but they depart out of Western Kaua'i: Holoholo Charters (808-335-0815; holoholocharters.com) and Captain Andy's (808-335-6833; napali.com) depart out of Port Allen, Ele'ele. On the **Big Island**, myriad boats depart from Kailua-Kona (Kona Coast).

See also *Ferries*, *Paddling*, *Water Sports*, and *Whale-Watching*.

BOTANICAL GARDENS
On **O'ahu**, check out Foster Botanical Garden (808-522-7066) in Greater Honolulu. On **Maui**, the signature protea are impressive at Upcountry's

prepared. Carry bottled water or be prepared to decontaminate it. Also, your equipment needs may vary considerably. You'll need a down sleeping bag atop the volcanoes and a simple sleeping sheet at the beach. Break-ins are always a concern. Don't leave anything valuable in your tent or your car. What's a camper to do? Leave at home the laptops, iPods, cameras, PDAs, cell phones, and anything else that you don't want stolen. Or cross your fingers and hope for the best.

CANOEING
See *Water Sports*.

CAR RENTAL
I like Budget (1-800-527-0700) partly because they publish fabulous, four-color drive-guides to the islands. These guides are the single best investment (besides this guidebook) that you can make in your trip. Dollar (808-565-7227 or 1-800-533-7808) is the only car company conducting business on Lana'i.

Kula Botanical Garden (808-878-1715). On **Kaua'i**, make time for the South Shore's National Tropical Botanical Garden (aka Allerton and McBryde; 808-742-2623; ntbg.org). Kaua'i's North Shore boasts Na Aina Kai Botanical Gardens (808-828-0525; naainakai.com) and Limahuli Garden (808-826-1053; ntbg.org). All three are well worth a visit. On the **Big Island**, there are a couple of gardens on the Hamakua Coast, as well as the Japanese-style Liliuokalani Gardens in Hilo. For more about indigenous flora, read *Island Flora* (p. 532/Kaua'i).

CAMPING
Permits (and sometimes small fees) are required to camp at any state parks and dozens of county beach parks. In order to prevent squatters from residing at beaches permanently, and, ostensibly, in order to clean the facilities, camping areas are closed certain days of the week. For state parks, contact the Department of Lands and Natural Resources (808-587-0300; hawaii.gov/dlnr/dsp/). For county-run beach parks, each island has different contact numbers listed in the appropriate chapters.

Rain, mosquitoes, and contaminated water will conspire to make your camping life miserable unless you're

✐ CHILDREN, ESPECIALLY FOR
Look for this symbol throughout the guide, which will let you know quickly about activities, lodging, and restaurants particularly suited to families and children. Big resorts offer *keiki* programs, all-day and half-day programs designed for kids of a certain age. Some are akin to babysitting, but most offer culturally aware activities that enrich the wee ones. For babysitter referrals, contact People Attentive to Children (patch-hi.org). If you've forgotten anything (like strollers), or don't want to lug it from the mainland (like high chairs), contact Baby's Away (babysaway.com) on O'ahu (1-800-496-6386) and on Maui and the Big Island (1-800-942-9030). They deliver.

On **O'ahu**, Sea Life Park (808-259-7933; sealifeparkhawaii.com), the Aquarium (808-923-9741; waquarium.org), and the Honolulu Zoo (808-971-7171; honoluluzoo.org) keep kids happy. In West **Maui**, hop aboard the sweet Sugar Cane Train (808-667-6851; sugarcanetrain.com). On the **Big Island**, head to the Pana'ewa Rainforest Zoo (808-959-7224; hilozoo.com) in Hilo.

COCKTAILS
See *Bars*.

COFFEE
To test the strength of your coffee connection, check out *Coffee . . . Did You Know?* coffee-tasting terminology (p. 371/Big Island). For a history of coffee in the islands, consult kalaheo.com and coffeetimes.com. On **O'ahu**, the gigantic Hawai'i Coffee Company (808-843-4202; hicoffeeco.com) in Greater Honolulu offers tastings and tours of its production facility. On **Moloka'i**, Moloka'i Coffee Co. (808-567-9023; molokaicoffee.com) offers tours of coffee fields. On **Maui**, sip some java at Maui Coffee Roasters (808-877-2877; hawaiiancoffee.com). On **Kaua'i**, coffee trees have begun supplanting sugarcane, and the Kaua'i Coffee Company (808-335-3237) sells

the harvest in West Kaua'i. On the **Big Island**, dozens of little cafés serve local Kona coffee. The hills of Holualoa (on the Kona Coast) enjoy a preponderance of them.

COMMITMENT CEREMONIES
Getting married, committing, recommitting? You're not alone. According to recent statistics, half of the heterosexual couples getting married in Hawai'i are from the mainland or another country. Although gays and lesbians were denied the right to marry in Hawai'i in 1999 after a long battle, Hawai'i is *otherwise* a very accepting place (see *Gay & Lesbian*). If you fall into the former camp, you'll need a license from the Marriage License Office in Honolulu (808-586-4545; state.hi.us/doh/records). The rest gets trickier, but there are plenty of people willing to help you fulfill your fantasies: Use an in-house wedding specialist at a resort or find an independent wedding consultant. Many Web sites listed under *Packagers* have honeymoon specialists.

CRAFTS
On **O'ahu**, the Bishop Museum (808-848-4158; bishopmuseum.org), Contemporary Museum (808-526-0232; tcmhi.org), and Honolulu Academy (808-532-8700; honoluluacademy.org) all have good gift shops with high-quality crafts. On **Maui**, Upcountry's Maui Crafts Guild (808-579-9697; mauicraftsguild.com) and Central Maui's Historical Society Museum Gift Shop (808-244-3326; mauimuseum.org) are great places for crafts and local gifts. On the **Big Island**, Volcano Art Center (808-967-7565; volcanoartcenter.org) has a Pele-powerful collection.

CULTURE

Where to begin? Entire libraries have been written about Hawaiian culture. I've recommended a few books later in this chapter to get you started. As this guide evolves over the years, more and more introductory essays will be included to pique your interest in this rich culture. To get you started, you'll find snippets on *Hawaiian Quilts* (p. 111/Oʻahu), *Kapa* (p. 113/Oʻahu), the *ʻUkelele & Innocent Merriment* (p. 346/Molokaʻi), slack key guitars in *Loosen Up* (p. 451/Big Island), *Leis* (p. 524/Kauaʻi), *Hunting Wild Pigs* (p. 527/Kauaʻi), and the islands of *Kahoʻolawe* (p. 247/Maui) and *Niʻihau* (p. 511/Kauaʻi).

On **Oʻahu**, your first stop should be the outstanding Bishop Museum (808-847-3511; bishopmuseum.org) in Greater Honolulu. It will undoubtedly ignite a spark and enrich the rest of your visit. On the **Big Island**'s Kona Coast, visit Puʻuhonua O Honaunau National Historical Park (808-328-2288), a reconstructed place of refuge that was used in the 16th century. On the Web, consult alternative-hawaii .com and www.uhpress.hawaii.edu.

DINING

You will see that *Dining Out* and *Eating Out* are separated in this guide. Entries in the former category tend to be more formal and expensive than the latter. They also usually require reservations.

In general, islanders dine earlier than mainlanders. If you're dining around sunset, remember that it's light for only about 10 minutes after the sun actually sets. So get there on time.

To help you appease your hearty appetite, I've culled lists of the best places to eat on each island—from pricey and moderate places to cheap eats, classic seats, and best places for solo fine dining. The *Just So You Know* passing references throughout this guide alert you to choices that aren't worth a write-up but are still worth a mention for one reason or another. In **Waikiki**, there is also a convenient delivery service; see *Dining In* (p. 81/Oʻahu).

See also "Hawaiian Cuisine from Past to Present" (p. 19).

DISCOUNTS

Consider purchasing the Activities and Attractions Association Gold Card (808-871-7947 or 1-800-398-9698; hawaiifun.org) for $30. With it, you'll receive decent discounts at upward of 200 islandwide outfitters, restaurants, golf courses, car rentals, activities, and more. The card allows you to purchase up to four tickets to any one attraction, and it's valid for one year.

Big hotel chains like ResortQuest (1-800-922-7866; resortquesthawaii .com), Outrigger (1-800-688-7444; outrigger.com), Ohana Hotels (1-800-462-6262; ohanahotels.com), Castle Resorts & Hotels (1-800-367-5004; castleresorts.com), and Marc Resorts (1-800-535-0085; marcresorts.com) offer deals when you island-hop with them, and often throw in a rental car.

See also *Activities Desks*, *Packagers*, and *Web Sites*.

✪ DON'T MISS THIS

The "✪" icon appears next to places, activities, and sights that you'll remember long after you return home.

ECOSYSTEM

It's incredibly fragile here. Literally hundreds and hundreds of endangered plant and animal species exist here and nowhere else on the planet. Please tread lightly and heed warnings and signage pertaining to various ecological issues. Thanks. Cruise alternative-hawaii.com.

See also *Nene* (p. 396/Big Island).

EMERGENCIES

Call 911 from anywhere. Major hospitals are located in Greater Honolulu on **Oʻahu**; in Wailuku on **Maui**; in Lihuʻe on **Kauaʻi**; and in Hilo and Kealakakua (the Kona Coast) on the **Big Island**.

ENTERTAINMENT

Near the end of each section, you'll find this selection, in order of my preference unless otherwise noted.

ETIQUETTE

At the front doors of homes and B&Bs (as well as many vacation rentals and condos), you'll usually see a sign: MAHALO FOR REMOVING YOUR SHOES. This helps keep places clean; the local red soil is virtually impossible to remove from carpets and tiles.

FAMILIES

See *Children, Especially For*.

FERRIES

The SuperFerry (1-877-443-3779; hawaiisuperferry.com), a four-story catamaran, finally began Oʻahu to Maui service in late 2007, transporting cars and passengers daily. Details

for more interisland service was sketchy at press time. The *Molokaʻi Princess* (1-877-500-6284; maui princess.com) is a passenger ferry between Molokaʻi and Maui. Expeditions (1-800-695-2624; go-lanai.com) operates one between Lanaʻi and Maui.

FISHING

Sportfish Hawaiʻi (808-396-2607; sportfishhawaii.com) has statewide charter information. On the **Big Island**, charters go in search of "big game" like trophy-worthy marlin. Charter boats are listed throughout this book.

FLEA MARKETS

In Central & Leeward **Oʻahu**, the Aloha Stadium Swap Meet (808-486-6704; alohastadiumswapmeet.net) is huge. In Central **Maui**, the smaller Swap Meet (808-877-3100) is a more local affair.

FOOD

For your first course, the essay by noted food writer Bonnie Friedman, "Hawaiian Cuisine from Past to Present" (p. 19), will whet your appetite. If you want to get really creative with Spam, the statewide iconic food prod-

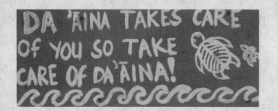

uct, pick up *Hawai'i's Second Spam Cookbook* by Ann Koudo Corum. Throughout this guide, look for essays on *Plate Lunches* (p. 129/O'ahu), *Malaadas Wars* (p. 132/O'ahu), *Shave Ice* (p. 164/O'ahu), mochi ice cream at Bubbies (p. 130/O'ahu), and Maui-made Roselani's (p. 299/Maui). On the **Big Island**, try *malasadas* at Tex Drive-In on the Hamakua Coast and macadamia nuts from the Mauna Loa Macadamia Nut Factory (808-966-8618; maunaloa.com) in Hilo.

GAY & LESBIAN

Waikiki has the only real "out" scene, but in general, same-sex couples will not have a problem in touristed Hawai'i. For everything you want to know about the confluence of the words *gay* and *Hawai'i*, consult gayhawaii.com and rainbowhandbook.com. Also cruise outinhawaii.com. *Odyssey* (odysseyhawaii.com) is a free (mostly men's) monthly magazine.

GOLF

To help beat the astronomical cost of greens fees, contact Stand-by-Golf (1-888-645-2665; hawaiistandbygolf.com) for same- or next-day tee times. **Lana'i** has two amazing courses that induce well-off patrons to fly over for

the day and play a round. On **Maui**, Kapalua (West Maui) and Wailea (South Maui) draw avid aficionados. On **Kaua'i**, the North Shore's Princeville Resort boasts world-class golf, but Po'ipu Bay is also quite worthy. On the **Big Island**, courses at Hapuna, Mauna Kea, and Mauna Lani (all on the Kohala Coast) are prime for serious players. Throughout the islands, expect to be distracted by rainbows, headwinds, and water hazards. On the Big Island, volcano views and lava are the norm. Plan on losing more balls in Hawai'i than you do elsewhere.

HAWAI'I REGIONAL CUISINE

See *Dining* and the essay "Hawaiian Cuisine from Past to Present" (p. 19). With the help of a few great cookbooks, you can bring the taste of Hawai'i home and try replicating it yourself. Beverly Gannon, one of Hawai'i's signature chefs and the owner of the Hali'imaile General Store on Maui, shares her recipes in *The Hali'imaile General Store Cookbook*. O'ahu native Dave "D. K." Kodama (owner of Sansei Seafood Restaurant on Maui) offers a primer on sushi and includes beginner and intermediate recipes in *D. K.'s Sushi Chronicles from Hawai'i*. Pick up 50

Thrifty Maui Restaurants, which reviews local restaurants, and the entertaining *Potluck: Stories That Taste Like Hawai'i*, both written by colleagues.

HAWAI'I TIME
See *A Note About Timing* (p. 65/ O'ahu).

HEIAUS
Please respect these utterly revered Hawaiian altars by not stepping on them or removing any stones. On **O'ahu**, the largest of these sacred temples is Pu'u O Mahuka Heiau (on the North Shore). **Maui**'s largest is Pi'ilanihale He'iau (in "To Hana & Beyond"). On **Kaua'i**, the Coconut Coast's well-preserved Poli'ahu Heiau is easily accessible. On the **Big Island**, the Pu'ukohola Heiau National Historic Site and Mo'okini Luakini Heiau (both in the North Kohala & Waimea area) are both quite sacred. The latter dates to about A.D. 500 but is difficult to reach.

HELICOPTER TOURS
Chopper tours are offered everywhere except O'ahu and Lana'i. Since most of **Maui**, the **Big Island**, and **Kaua'i** are virtually inaccessible, these whirlybirds offer the best chance to see near-vertical waterfalls, deeply carved valleys, and magical volcanic cones. **O'ahu**, by the way, offers unusual tours with Island Seaplane (808-836-6273; islandsea plane.com).

HIGH SEASON
Summertime, when families descend on Hawai'i, constitutes high season. So does wintertime (from mid-December through March), when a blanket of *brrrr* covers most of the mainland. Holiday periods like Thanksgiving and Easter also draw throngs. Be careful about coming in late April: There are three simultaneous holidays in Japan at that time, which means the Japanese are traveling in greater numbers than usual.

HIKING
Myriad resources will take you deep into the rain forests. The University of Hawai'i (www.uhpress.hawaii.edu) publishes a great selection of hiking guides, while the Department of Land and Natural Resources (808-587-0300; hawaii.gov/dlnr) in Honolulu has details on dozens of state park trails. Tours and trails are listed throughout this book.

On **O'ahu**, the biggest hiking bang-for-your-buck is Diamond Head (Southeast O'ahu). Without a doubt, the most dramatic and unusual hiking, though, is on **Maui** at Haleakala National Park (808-572-4400; www .nps/gov/hale) and on the **Big Island** at Hawai'i Volcanoes National Park (808-985-6000; www.nps.gov/havo). Don't miss the Waipi'o Valley (Hamakua Coast) on the Big Island, either. On **Kaua'i**, the most challenging hike is the Kalalau Trail in the Na Pali Coast State Park, but Waimea Canyon and Koke'e State Park also offer truly exceptional opportunities.

See also *Take the One Less Traveled By* (p. 546/Kaua'i).

HISTORIC HOUSES & MUSEUMS
For statewide information, consult hawaiimuseums.org. On **Maui**, Wailuku's Bailey House Museum (808-244-3326; mauimuseum.org) and Lahaina's Baldwin House (808-661-3262; hawaiimuseums.org) tell the missionaries' stories. The story of **Kaua'i** is told at Lihu'e's Kaua'i

Museum (808-245-6931; kauaimuseum.org) on the Coconut Coast. On the **Big Island**, drop in at the Parker Ranch Visitor Center & Museum (808-885-7655; parkerranch.com) for insight into the island's rich *paniolo* history and the Huliheʻe Palace (808-329-1877; daughtersofhawaii.org) for insight into Hawaiian royalty.

HISTORIC MUST-SEES
On **Oʻahu**, over 1 million visitors a year pay their respects at Pearl Harbor and the USS *Arizona* (808-422-2771; nps.gov/usar). Don't miss the ʻIolani Palace (808-522-0832; iolanipalace.org) in Greater Honolulu), Queen Emma Summer Palace (Windward Coast), and Kawaiahao Church and Mission Houses Museum (Greater Honolulu). On Lanaʻi, the leper colony of Kalaupapa National Historic Park (nps.gov/kala) is utterly haunting and disturbing, but the work of Father Damien was downright inspirational and uplifting.

HISTORY
It's a long, colorful, and often painful one. But it is also a joyous and rich one. For a briefing, please see this guide's history primer (p. 23) and time line (p. 34) for a few important dates to whet your appetite. Then head online to hawaiihistory.com, hawaiianhistory.org (published by the Historical Society), and hawaii-nation.org (a voice for independence and sovereignty).

HORSEBACK RIDING
On **Oʻahu**, ride at the North Shore's Turtle Bay Resort (808-293-8811; turtlebayresort.com). On **Maui**, ride at Mendes Ranch & Trail Rides (808-871-5222; mendesranch.com), outside Wailuku in Central Maui, and from the Hotel Hana-Maui (808-248-8211; hotelhanamaui.com) in Hana. Pony Express Tours (808-667-2200; ponyexpresstours.com) go into the volcanic Haleakala National Park. On **Kauaʻi**, the South Shore's CJM Country Stables (808-742-6096; cjmstables.com) takes riders along Mahaʻulepu Beach, while the North Shore's Princeville Ranch Stables (808-826-6777; princevilleranch.com) offers another distinct choice. The **Big Island** boasts Parker Ranch, one of the largest ranches in the country, where you'll find a few places to ride in the North Kohala & Waimea area. There are also riding opportunities in the Kona Coast and Hamakua Coast.

HULA
On **Oʻahu**, the Bishop Museum (808-847-3511; bishopmuseum.org) offers free weekday performances. **Molokaʻi** is considered the birthplace of hula, and the Ka Hula Piko festival celebrates it. On the **Big Island**, though, the Merrie Monarch Hula Festival (merriemonarchfestival.org) goes all out. See also *Halau, A Personal Story* (p. 194/Maui) and *Hula as We Know It* (p. 444/Big Island).

INFORMATION (GUIDANCE)
Prior to your visit, contact the Hawaiʻi Visitors & Convention Bureau (808-923-1811; gohawaii.com) and other official visitors bureau offices at the neighbor islands: **Oʻahu** (1-877-525-6248; visit-oahu.com); **Maui** (808-244-3530; visitmaui.com); **Molokaʻi** (1-800-800-6367; molokai-hawaii.com and visitmolokai.com); **Lanaʻi** (1-800-947-4774; visitlanai.net); **Kauaʻi** (1-800-262-1400; kauaidiscovery.com and kauai-hawaii.com); and the **Big Island** (1-800-648-2441; bigisland.org).

INTERNET
See *Web Sites*.

ITINERARY SUGGESTIONS
See the essay on p. 17 and *A Note About Timing* (p. 65/O'ahu). For each of the main islands (O'ahu, Kaua'i, the Big Island, and Maui), I have also created a week's worth of "A Perfect Day in . . ." Throw them out or use them as starting points with abandon.

KAYAKING
See *Water Sports*.

LANGUAGE
See the primer on p. 35 to get you started on pronunciation and common words that you may hear or read. To check the spelling and meaning of Hawaiian words, there's no better site than wehewehe.org/cgi-bin/hdict.

LODGING
Types of accommodations reviewed in this guide include everything from big resorts and hotels to small B&Bs and inns, motels and hostels to vacation rentals and cottages. All are listed in order of my preference and accept credit cards, unless otherwise noted. Rates quoted are for two people sharing one room and are "rack rates," published rates that often don't resemble what you will actually pay (except during high season). They serve as a useful comparison of what places cost relative to their competitors. If you want to stay at a bigger property, see if it's offered for less money by going to their Web site rather than by calling the hotel directly. Don't forget to add another 14½ percent in taxes to the bill. For the best bed & breakfasts, book through island-by-island agencies listed at the beginning of each island chapter. Remember that most inns and bed & breakfasts don't accept children under 10 or 12 years of age. Also consult expedia.com, travelocity.com, orbitz.com, and hotels.com along with hotline.com, priceline.com, and cheaptickets.com.

LU'AUS
On **O'ahu**, see *Local Lu'aus* (p. 171/O'ahu) for an islandwide rundown of these feasts that feature local food and Polynesian entertainment. If you're island-hopping and your time and money are limited (whose aren't?), save them for **Maui**'s Old Lahaina Lu'au (808-667-1998; old lahainaluau.com), described under *The Only Lu'au You'll Ever Need or Want* (p. 232/Maui). On the **Big Island**, see *Lovely Lu'au* (p. 413/Big Island) about Kona Village Resort.

MAPS
Everyday users will rejoice in the free maps produced in *This Week Magazine*, available on islands everywhere. The best choice for divers and snorkelers are Franko's Maps (frankosmaps.com).

MOVIES & TV
On **Kaua'i**, Hawai'i Movie Tours (808-822-1192; hawaiimovietour.com) highlights many of the silver screen's finest locations.

MUSEUMS
See *Art Museums*, *Culture*, and *Historic Houses & Museums*.

MUSIC
Hawaiian-music.com boasts old and new Hawaiian music. You name it, I bet they stock it. And if you can't name it, tell them what you're inter-

ested in and they'll steer you in the right direction. Also check buy hawaiianmusic.com. Tune in to hula records.com/radio for more information on the famed *Hawai'i Calls* radio program, which broadcast out of Waikiki from 1935 to 1975. See also *A Twenty from Mr. Tiny Bubbles* (p. 102/O'ahu), about aging icon Don Ho, and *Loosen Up* (p. 451/Big Island) about slack key guitars.

MYTHS & LEGENDS
Legends and Myths of Hawai'i (by David Kalakaua and Glen Grant) and *Hawaiian Mythology* (by Martha Beckwith) offer thorough tale tellings of charming stories passed down from generation to generation. In the ensuing editions of this guide, more myths and legends will be added, but to whet your appetite, see also M*aui Captures the Sun* (p. 270/Maui); *Maui Raises the Island* (p. 291/Maui); *Do You Believe?* (p. 483/Kaua'i), about the Menehune; and *A Sister and a Chief* (p. 544/Kaua'i).

NEWSPAPERS
The daily *Honolulu Advertiser* (honoluluadvertiser.com) and *Honolulu Star Bulletin* (starbulletin.com) keep folks up to speed. Neighbor islands publish regional papers, which are a great source of local news and island flavor.

NIGHTLIFE
O'ahu's Waikiki is the granddaddy of all. Period. It's got bars and clubs, movies galore, dinner shows, The spirit of Don Ho, and plenty of romantic places to drink cocktails and gaze into someone's eyes. Just a heads-up: **Kaua'i**, **Lana'i**, and **Moloka'i** are all pretty darn quiet in terms of nightlife. Little nightlife exists on the **Big Island** outside the resorts.

PACKAGERS
Discounts are out there, but as an individual traveler you may not have access to them. Read this guidebook, decide where you want to go and stay, and then call a packager to see if they have something that overlaps. Pleasant Holidays (1-800-742-9244; pleasantholidays.com) specializes in Hawai'i. Airlines also package trips to Hawai'i, and United is the biggest of the bunch (unitedvacations.com). Consult hawaii-aloha.com, bestof hawaii.com, and travel-hawaii.com.

PADDLING (OUTRIGGER CANOES)
On **O'ahu**, try paddling these ancient seafaring vessels off the shores of Waikiki Beach. Or watch 'em paddle the Ala Wai Canal (on the edge of Waikiki) in the late afternoon. **Moloka'i** has a fair number of formal and informal outrigger canoe clubs and races.

PARKING
Parking is getting pricier at resorts every day. It's always cost an arm and a leg in Honolulu (upwards of $25 a day at the big resorts), but now it's spread to neighbor island resorts, where it used to be free. See *Free Parking in Waikiki?* (p. 72/O'ahu).

PERFECT DAYS IN . . .
For each of the main islands (O'ahu, Kaua'i, the Big Island, and Maui),

I have created a week's worth of "A Perfect Day in . . ." that correspond to all the different regions of each island. Throw them out or use them as starting points with abandon.

PETROGLYPHS

On the **Big Island**, a huge district of ancient rock carvings can be found near the Mauna Lani Resort (Puako Petroglyphs), while the smaller Kaupulehu Petroglyphs are found near the Hualalai Resort; both are on the Kohala Coast.

PINEAPPLES

Central **Oʻahu** is covered in pineapple fields; stop at the little roadside Del Monte Pineapple Garden (near the Dole Pineapple Plantation store) to discern the differences among varieties. **Lanaʻi** once supplied a huge percentage of the world's pineapples. In West **Maui**, take the Pineapple Plantation Tour (808-665-5491; maui pineapple.com). Read *Slicing & Dicing a Pineapple* (p. 209/Maui).

PLANE TICKETS

They'll constitute a big chunk of your budget. Frequent-flier mileage is well spent to Hawaiʻi, but also try travel ocity.com, expedia.com, and ww.orbitz.com.

See also *Discounts* and *Packagers*.

POPULATION

According to U.S. census projections for 2004, there are 1.26 million residents statewide. Island by island, this breaks down to 891,000 on Oʻahu, 142,000 on Maui (including Molokaʻi and Lanaʻi), 58,000 on Kauaʻi, and 164,000 on the Big Island.

⬆ RAINY DAY ACTIVITIES

Chances are, if it were sunny every day we would take sunshine for granted. So when clouds move in and rain starts falling, be appreciative of the sun and look for this icon, which tells you where to head indoors.

RECOMMENDED READING—FICTION

The Folding Cliffs, by W. S. Merwin. A dramatic book-length poem that captures the history of Hawaiʻi.

Hawaiʻi, by James Michener. This blockbuster historical novel is thick with vivid writing.

Hotel Honolulu, by Paul Theroux. This is a hilarious tale of an ex-literati who marries a Hawaiian woman and works in a hotel to escape his life on the mainland.

Shark Dialogues, by Kiana Davenport. This first novel covers a 100-year sweep of Hawaiʻi history through fictional characters; it's the tale of victors and victims, at once provocative, magical, and meaningful.

Talking to the Dead, by Sylvia Watanabe. This collection of interwoven short stories introduces Hawaiian life.

The Warrior King, by Richard Tregaskis. This fictitious depiction of Hawai'i's legendary leader King Kamehameha makes a good read.

RECOMMENDED READING—NONFICTION

A Call for Hawaiian Sovereignty, by Michael Kioni Dudley and Keoni Kealoha Agard. This definitive book on Hawaiian sovereignty is one of the first to tell the history from the Hawaiian perspective. It creates a strong argument for the Native Hawaiians needing their own land and government for their culture to survive.

A Hawaiian Reader and *The Spell of Hawai'i*, by A. Grove Day and Carl Stroven. These two paperback anthologies are filled with various writings about the islands.

A World Between Waves, by Frank Stewart. A selection of essays on the natural history of Hawai'i by some of America's most renowned writers.

Hawai'i's Story by Hawai'i's Queen Lili'uokalani. This autobiographical account covers six decades of island history and is told in an elegant voice.

Hula: Historical Perspectives, by Dorothy B. Barrere, Mary K. Pukui, and Marion Kelly. This is a must-read for hula students or anyone interested in the history of hula.

Kaua'i, the Separate Kingdom, by Edward Joesting. The book jumps around a bit, but it's a readable account of the island's early history.

Letters from Hawai'i, by Mark Twain. A humorous compilation of letters Mark Twain was hired to write for the California paper the *Sacramento Union*.

Shoals of Time, by Gavan Daws. One of the best one-volume history books on the islands. It follows Hawaiian history from the arrival of Captain Cook to statehood.

Vagabond's House, by Don Blanding. For more about the poet, see also *The Double Life of a Vagabond Poet* (p. 141/O'ahu).

Voices of Wisdom, by M. J. Harden. This beautiful collection of black-and-white photographs paired with essays and interviews by Hawaiian elders is eloquent, sensitive, and timeless. Through chanters and activists to historians and healers, wisdom about Hawaiian culture is not lost.

Volcano, by Garrett Hongo. Japanese-American poet Garrett Hongo sets out to research his family heritage in this gripping tale.

RESORT FEES

What are they? Besides a personal pet peeve? They constitute a $15–25 daily surcharge for items that used to be rolled invisibly into the cost of your room—or, if you prefer, that used to be seen as an added-value bonus. What's irksome, though, is that the so-called complimentary items (like the morning newspaper, coffee, parking, unlimited local phone calls, and use of the gym) aren't complimentary at all. You pay a daily fee for them. And if you don't use the gym, read the paper, or drink coffee, you don't get your money back. Not all resorts tack on this obnoxious fee, but plenty do. If they're already charging you $450 for a room, why engender so much ill will with this tacked-on fee?

SAILING
See *Boat Excursions*.

SCENIC DRIVES
There's a basic assumption that you'll take the most scenic drives of all by simply circling the islands. On **O'ahu**, though, specifically don't miss the Tantalus Drive & Round Top Drive (Greater Honolulu), Nu'uanu Pali Highway & Lookout (Windward Coast), and the coastal route around Southeast O'ahu. On **Moloka'i**, the twisty road to the East End is breathtaking. On **Maui**, the road to Hana is the biggie, but the lesser-known Kahekili Highway is by far a personal favorite. On **Kaua'i**, follow the road beyond Princeville all the way to the end at Ke'e Beach for that real end-of-the-road feeling. The beach and jagged mountain views are stunning, while one-lane bridges hark back a century. On the **Big Island**, I love the desolation of Saddle Road, but car rental contracts technically forbid it. The quiet is deafening up there.

SCUBA
According to those in the know (to whom I defer), Hawai'i holds the top 10 dive sites in the world. Yes—in the world. For a first-person view of diving, see *Confessions of a Diver* (p. 216/Maui). On **Maui**, the most popular dive site is Molokini, but Extended Horizons Scuba (808-667-0611; extendedhorizons.com) offers many other trips as well. On **Kaua'i**, diving is more weather dependent than on other islands; contact Dive Kaua'i (808-822-0452; divekauai .com), Sea Sport Divers (808-742-9303; seasportdivers.com), Blue Dolphin Charters (808-335-5553; kauaiboats.com), and Bubbles Below Scuba Charters (808-332-7333;

bubblesbelowkauai.com). On the **Big Island**, Nautilus Dive Center (808-935-6939; nautilusdive hilo.com) is the go-to outfit, but you might also look into the snorkel-scuba hybrid snuba with Big Island Water Sports (808-324-1650; snubabig island.com).

SHOPPING
Each section concludes with "Selective Shopping," with entries listed in order of my preference unless otherwise noted. Without question, **Waikiki** offers the biggest selection in the state. Elsewhere on **O'ahu**, little Haleiwa on the North Shore is fun; in Greater Honolulu, pop into tiny lei shops in Chinatown and stop by Hilo Hattie (hilohattie.com) for everyday aloha wear. (Also see *The Thrill of the Hunt*; p. 104/O'ahu.) On **Maui**, make time to wander around Makawao and Pa'ia (both Upcountry). In West Maui, Lahaina is crammed with more T-shirts than treasures, but it's still fun. In South Maui, Wailea shops are decidedly upscale. On **Kaua'i**, funky Kapa'a (on the Coconut Coast) and tiny Hanalei and Kilauea (both on the North Shore) have interesting one-of-a-kind shops. On the **Big Island**, head to Hilo.

SMOKING

In late 2006, Hawai'i enacted some of the most stringent anti-smoking laws in the U.S. Smoking is not permitted in bars, restaurants, or most hotel rooms. It is also against the law to smoke within 20 feet of the doorways of these establishments.

SNORKELING

Even if you've never snorkeled, you can learn quickly and painlessly on a trip. Many offshore boat excursions include snorkeling as part of a half- or full-day trip. For independent snorkelers, Snorkel Bob's (snorkelbob .com) has a lock on rentals of masks, fins, and snorkels. Remember that it's unwise to snorkel alone. On **O'ahu**, Hanauma Bay (Southeast O'ahu) is the most popular area for a reason. On **Maui**, the same is true for Molokini (although it's accessible only by boat), but don't overlook the Black Rock and Kapalua Bay, both in West Maui. On **Kaua'i**, the North Shore's Ke'e Beach has the best reef fish. On the **Big Island**, the best area is accessible only by boat; head to the Kona Coast's Kealakekua Bay, but don't overlook Kahalu'u Beach.

SPAS

In Waikiki (on **O'ahu**), check out Mandara Spa (808-947-9750; man daraspa.com) at the Hilton, Spa-Halekulani (808-923-2311; haleku lani.com) at the Halekulani, and Abhasa Waikiki Spa (808-922-8200; www2.abhasa.com) at the Royal Hawaiian. In Central & Leeward O'ahu, the Ihilani Spa (1-800-626-4446; ihilani.com) at the Marriott is fantastic. In South **Maui**, the Spa Grande at Grand Wailea Resort Hotel & Spa (808-875-1234; grandwailea .com) has no peers, although the Spa

Kea Lani at Fairmont Kea Lani Maui (808-875-4100; fairmont.com/kealani) and The Spa at Four Seasons (808-874-8000; fourseasons.com/maui) are very, very good. West Maui also has many fine choices in Ka'anapali, including Spa Moana at the Hyatt Regency (808-661-1234; maui.hyatt .com) and the Heavenly Spa at the Westin Maui (808-667-2525; westin maui.com). Just up the road in Kapalua, relax into the Ritz-Carlton Spa, Kapalua (808-669-6200; ritz carlton.com). Or head to the independent training school, Spa Luna (808-575-2440; spaluna.com), in Upcountry. Quite simply, I could live out my days at Honua Spa at Hotel Hana-Maui (808-248-8211; hotel hanamaui.com) in Hana. On **Kaua'i**, ANARA Spa (808-742-1234; kauai .hyatt.com) at the Hyatt Regency is without equal. One dear friend flies over from her neighbor island for weekend indulges here. On the **Big Island**, the Kohala Coast resorts are very competitive, so you'll have many world-class spas to choose from, including the Four Seasons Resort Hualalai (808-325-8000; fourseasons .com/hualalai), Hilton Waikoloa Village (808-886-1234; hiltonwaikoloa village.com), Fairmont Orchid (808-885-2000; fairmont.com/orchid), Mauna Lani Bay Hotel (808-885-6622; maunalani.com), and Hapuna Beach Prince Hotel (808-880-1111; hapunabeachhotel.com).

SPECIAL EVENTS

For a complete and official list of events, consult calendar.gohawaii .com.

SPELUNKING

Lava tubes make for great exploring, and Maui Cave Adventures (808-248-

7308; mauicave.com), off the Hana Highway, offers really fun trips.

STARGAZING

Hawai'i's distinct absence of lights and other atmospheric pollution create some of the world's best stargazing conditions. In West **Maui**, take a nightly Tour of the Stars (808-661-1234) at the Hyatt Regency. But save your real focus for the **Big Island**'s Keck Telescope (see *Mauna Kea & Saddle Road*, p. 392/Big Island) and the Keck Observatory (808-885-7887; keckobservatory.org). And save time for the Ellison S. Onizuka Space Center (808-329-3441; hawaiimuseums .org/mc/ishawaii_astronaut.htm) on the Kona Coast.

SUBMARINE TRIPS

Atlantis Submarines (1-800-548-6262; atlantisadventures.com) has underwater reef viewing on **O'ahu** (at the Hilton Hawaiian Village), **Maui** (in Lahaina), and the **Big Island** (on the Kona Coast).

SUGAR

In Central **Maui**, learn the important story of sugar at the Alexander & Baldwin Sugar Museum (808-871-8058; sugarmuseum.com). On the Coconut Coast of **Kaua'i**, the story is told at the Sugar Mill and Grove Farm Homestead Museum (808-245-3202), as well as the little South Shore town of Koloa. See also *The Sweet Smell of Sugar Success?* (p. 484/Kaua'i).

SURF SCHOOLS

For Hawai'i surfing news, browse holoholo.org/surfnews. On **O'ahu**, stroll Waikiki Beach when in search of a quick lesson. On **Maui**, the Nancy Emerson School of Surfing (808-205-

0335; surfclinics.com) will get you on a board in no time. On **Kaua'i**, the South Shore's Margo Oberg's Surfing School (808-332-6100; surfonkauai .com) will do the same.

TAXES

The general excise tax (sales tax by another name) is 4 percent, and lodging tax is about 14½ percent.

TENNIS

Free municipal courts are scattered throughout the islands; contact numbers are provided in each chapter. Please limit your play to 45 minutes if someone is waiting. Additionally, excellent tennis is available at many resorts, including **Oahu**'s Turtle Bay Resort (808-293-8811; turtlebayresort .com) on the North Shore. On **Maui**, the Ka'anapali resort area in West Maui offers many choices, as do Wailea and Makena in South Maui. On the **Big Island**, the Kohala Coast resorts offer great tennis facilities.

THEATER

On **Maui**, the highest quality and best selection is offered through the Maui Arts & Cultural Center (808-242-7469; mauiarts.org).

TIME ZONE

Hawai'i is two hours earlier than Pacific Standard Time. (When it's 5 PM in San Francisco, it's 3 PM in Honolulu.) But since Hawai'i doesn't observe daylight saving time, when it's in effect on the mainland, Hawai'i is three hours earlier than the West Coast.

TO SEE & DO

In each chapter, this section generally unfolds in the manner you will probably explore that island. In the rare exceptions to this rule, sights are organized geographically.

TRAFFIC

Honolulu (**O'ahu**), the state's capital, is a major metropolitan area and subject to sobering traffic jams that resemble those on the mainland. You will encounter congestion at worktime rush hours around Wailuku on **Maui**, around Kailua-Kona on the **Big Island**, and around Kapa'a on **Kaua'i**.

✸ VALUE

This symbol appears next to entries that represent an exceptional value.

VOLCANOES

The entire archipelago was born from volcanic eruptions. On **O'ahu**, Diamond Head's presence is unavoidable and alluring. **Maui**'s Haleakala National Park (808-572-4400; nps.gov/hale) and the **Big Island**'s Hawai'i Volcanoes National Park (808-985-6000; nps.gov/havo) over-

whelm the senses. Contact the latter for up-to-the-minute information about Big Island lava flows.

See also *Vog* (p. 458/Big Island).

WATERFALLS

On **Maui**, Oheo Gulch ("To Hana & Beyond") is arguably the most dramatic. On **Kaua'i**, you can drive right up to 'Opaeka'a Falls on the Coconut Coast. On the **Big Island**, Rainbow Falls (Hilo) and Akaka Falls (Hamakua Coast) are worth seeking out.

WATER SPORTS

It's no exaggeration to say that you can do almost any water sport almost anywhere in Hawai'i, though some places are obviously better than others at various times of the year. For marine and ocean sports news, consult holoholo.org. On **O'ahu**, windsurfing (offshore) and ocean kayaking (out to the islands) are really big in Kailua Bay on the Windward Coast. Mesmerizing surfing competitions are held at the North Shore's Banzai Pipeline (at Ekuhai Beach Park). **Maui** is the island king of windsurfing; world-class events are held on

Ho'okipa Beach, and surfers hang out in P'aia (both found in "Upcountry"). On **Kaua'i**, the Coconut Coast's Wailua River State Park is perfect for kayaking, as is the North Shore's Hanalei River. You have to be fairly experienced to paddle along the Na Pali Coast. Novices will feel steady at the North Shore's Anini Beach. Outfitters and guides are listed throughout this book.

See also *Paddling* (*Outrigger Canoes*).

WEATHER

Temperatures in Hawai'i don't fluctuate much from season to season, but locals certainly feel the difference and refer to their version of winter. (Try explaining that to someone from the Upper Midwest!) Average summer temps hover around 85 degrees, winter around 78 degrees. Check with the National Weather Service (808-973-4381; nws.noaa.gov) when it matters most. And consult weather.hawaii .edu, hawaiiweathertoday.com, and weather.com. It's generally drier in the summer and wetter in the winter (November through March). Leeward sides (west and south) are mostly drier and hotter; windward sides (east and north) are mostly wetter and cooler. The islands are filled with microclimates; this is especially true in the town of Hana, Maui, and on the Big Island, where cacti thrive and where the summit of Mauna Kea can be capped with snow. Hilo is the wettest city in the United States, and yet 25 miles south it's dry as a bone. Tsunamis and hurricanes are rare occurrences, but they can be utterly devastating. Visit the Pacific Tsunami Museum on the Big Island in Hilo (808-935-0926; tsunami.org) for a fascinating look at the power of nature, and try to watch someone's video of Kaua'i's ferocious hurricane (see *Looking Iniki in the Eye*, p. 522/Kaua'i). There are always unexpected consequences of Mother Nature; see *Don't They Ever Sleep?* (p. 516/Kaua'i).

WEB SITES

For great, all-around information, consult these three related sites: search-hawaii.com, aloha-hawaii.com, and postcards-hawaii.com (with great photography). Also check hawaii.com. And see hawaiivisitor.com for packages, airfares, and activities, and hawaiiweb.com (a reliable statewide site).

WEDDINGS

See *Commitment Ceremonies*.

WHALE-WATCHING

Migrating humpbacks return to these waters from mid-December to mid-April. On **O'ahu**, boats for whale-watching (and dolphin sightings,

depending on the season) depart from Central & Leeward Oʻahu. On **Maui**, the nonprofit Pacific Whale Foundation (808-249-8811; pacificwhale.org) offers trips and insights from its research. On **Kauaʻi**, Holoholo Charters (808-335-0815; holoholocharters .com) in Western Kauaʻi offers trips. On the **Big Island**, Captain Dan McSweeney (808-322-0028; ilove whales.com) departs from the Kona Coast.

See also *Humpback Whales* (p. 244/Maui).

WINERIES
On **Maui**, Tedeschi Vineyards & Winery (808-878-6058; mauiwine.com) makes island-themed vintages.

O'ahu 1

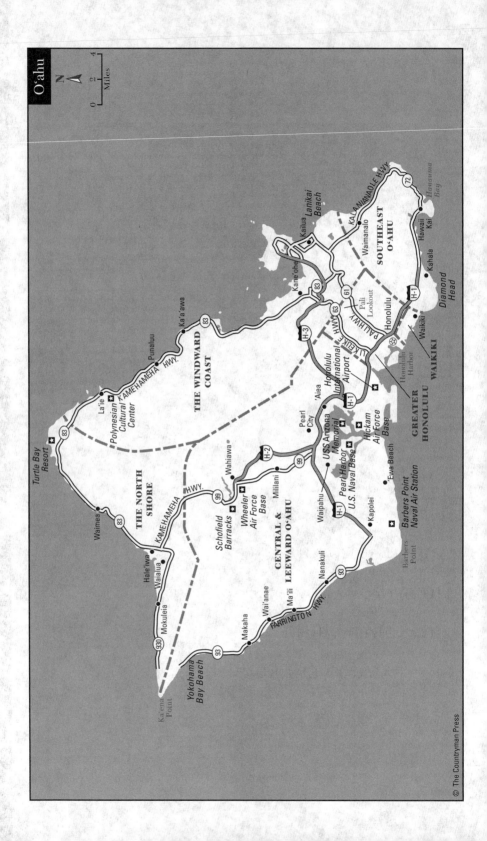

Oʻahu

N

0 2 4 Miles

THE NORTH SHORE

THE WINDWARD COAST

CENTRAL & LEEWARD OʻAHU

GREATER HONOLULU

SOUTHEAST OʻAHU

WAIKIKI

Turtle Bay Resort

Waimea

Haleʻiwa

Waialua

Mokuleia

Laʻie

Polynesian Cultural Center

Punaluu

Kaʻaʻawa

KAMEHAMEHA HWY.

Kaʻena Point

Yokohama Bay Beach

Makaha

Waiʻanae

Maʻili

Nanakuli

FARRINGTON HWY.

KAMEHAMEHA HWY.

Schofield Barracks

Wheeler Air Force Base

Wahiawa

Mililani

Waipahu

Pearl City

ʻAiea

USS Arizona Memorial

Pearl Harbor U.S. Naval Base

Hickam Air Force Base

Kapolei

Ewa Beach

Barbers Point

Barbers Point Naval Air Station

Kaneʻohe

Kailua

Lanikai Beach

Waimanalo

Kahala

Hawaii Kai

Hanauma Bay

Diamond Head

Waikiki

Honolulu

Honolulu Harbor

Honolulu International Airport

Pali Lookout

PALI HWY

LIKELIKE HWY.

KALANIANAOLE HWY.

930

83

83

83

93

93

99

99

H-2

H-1

H-1

H-1

H-3

61

63

72

© The Countryman Press

O'AHU IN BRIEF

Millions visit O'ahu each year, but few really get to know it. That's a shame. When travelers go to the neighbor islands, they generally rent a car and spend time exploring. On O'ahu they are likely to take a taxi or bus to Waikiki and disappear for the rest of their vacation under the shadows of skyscrapers. Few visitors get more adventuresome than taking an organized tour around the island, during which they experience a lot more of life on the bus than on O'ahu. Waikiki certainly has its attractions, but Greater Honolulu and the rest of the island have more.

Let's get a discussion of Waikiki out of the way first. Waikiki remains the center of Hawaiian tourism (and rampant consumerism) because it offers so much to do in such a compact setting. It's a 24/7 city, thanks to the jet-setters and jet-lagged. It's said that on any given day, half the visitors to Hawai'i (that's all the islands combined) are in Waikiki. Yes, the beach is a bit crowded, but it makes for great people-watching, and you can swim year-round in the usually gentle surf. Hop an outrigger canoe or take a surf lesson. In the early morning it's a beachcomber's delight. The view of crunchy white sand and gentle waves set against the backdrop of Diamond Head Crater is hard to match. By midmorning, however, this sunny mecca is alive with tourists from around the world exploring hundreds of designer stores and lesser knowns; discovering restaurants for every taste and budget; and claiming their own patch of sparkling beach. Just before sunset, Kuhio Beach Park at the Diamond Head side of Waikiki hosts free hula and Hawaiian music performances every day except Monday. In the evening, Waikiki kicks into nightlife mode. Open-air beach bars come alive with music and mai tais, but you can always find a mellow corner to kick back and enjoy things from a distance, if you prefer. By late evening you might be sweating on a crowded dance floor or just curling your toes into the cool sand under the stars. That's why I always end up liking Waikiki much more than I ever expect to. The city wears well over time, and I always leave with a greater affinity for it than when I arrived.

A full 70 percent of Hawai'i's 1.3 million residents live on O'ahu (the gathering place), and of those about half live in Greater Honolulu. The major metropolitan area is particularly attractive because it's squeezed between the extinct Diamond Head, the dramatic Ko'olau Mountains, and the boundless Pacific

Ocean. Pearl Harbor sits 'Ewa (at the easterly end). Yes, even today ancient Hawaiian terms are used to express directions in the city. Going inland toward the mountains is mauka (MOW-kah); reversing course toward the sea is makai (mahk-EYE). When you arrive at the airport and head to Waikiki, you are going "Diamond Head," and when you visit Pearl Harbor your direction is 'Ewa (AY-vah).

Almost a century ago Somerset Maugham expressed surprise at what a typical Western city Honolulu is, a reaction shared by today's visitors. The unofficial capital of the Pacific Rim has plenty of high-rises and traffic, but it also has accessible waterfalls, mountains, a rain forest, and beaches within its boundaries. Visitors are always surprised at this as well as the rural character of the rest of O'ahu.

But Maugham's impression can be partially dispelled with a little probing off the freeways. There is nothing conventional about the collection of Pacific anthropology and natural history at the Bishop Museum, an excellent spot for an introduction to the natural and human forces that have shaped modern Hawai'i. Chinatown and its vibrant markets are a historic potpourri of the Asian cultures blended so extensively into Hawaiian life. The 'Iolani Palace, the only royal residence in the United States, flaunts a 19th-century, European-inspired grandeur. Even downtown Honolulu is fascinating in many ways. While the buildings may resemble those in any other American city, the atmosphere is tropical, and business dress can be remarkably casual. You'll know you're not in Kansas anymore, Dorothy, when you see Spam on the breakfast menu at McDonald's. Give yourself at least a couple of days to explore Greater Honolulu.

As for the rest of O'ahu, two mountain ranges dominate her geography. Remnants of volcanoes that exploded into bedrock, the Ko'olau and Waianae Ranges run parallel to each other (north–south) for the length of the island. The shoreline around the Ko'olaus is sometimes dramatically beautiful and always intriguing for its profound variations. To give you an impression of O'ahu's size, it's convenient to know that the island is about 110 miles around (not including a detour up to Makaha). Without stopping (which would be silly), it would take you about three hours to drive around it. Although most visitors assume it's the largest island because of Honolulu's presence, O'ahu is actually the third largest, after the Big Island and Maui (in that order).

High above the city, just 15 minutes from downtown, at the Nu'uanu Pali Lookout, you can survey the other side of the Ko'olaus. Few vantage points take my breath away as regularly. Keep going to reach Windward O'ahu and Kailua, a pleasant commuter community. Beyond the adjacent town of Kane'ohe, the countryside becomes increasingly rural. The Valley of the Temples, with its striking Buddhist shrine, definitely deserves a visit. The Polynesian Cultural Center is more questionable (to me), though this Mormon re-creation of South Pacific villages and native crafts is Hawai'i's most popular paid-admission attraction.

Let me backtrack for a minute, though. While the panorama from the Nu'uanu Pali Lookout may be terrifically spectacular, the best way to reach the Windward Coast is to drive along the promontory of Southeast O'ahu. From Waikiki, hug the shoreline beneath Diamond Head and through the exclusive Kahala neighborhood. Koko Head, another extinct crater, is the next landmark, rising weatherworn above Hanauma Bay, where the contours of the Pacific and the beach will match anyone's image of paradise. From here the scenic coastal highway continues past beaches that are beautiful but dangerous for swimming, and into Kailua.

At the Turtle Bay Resort, the highway turns west off the Windward Coast to the North Shore, famous among surfers for its mighty waves. The beaches called Sunset, Banzai Pipeline, and Waimea attract the world's best board enthusiasts every winter for daredevil play and international championships. Admiring the waves years ago, Jack London marveled: "Why, they are a mile long, these bull-mouthed monsters, and they weigh a thousand tons." The sight and sound of one crashing ashore is, as London said, an ego-shrinking experience.

Beyond these death-defying beaches and the quaint town of Hale'iwa, the highway heads inland, back to Honolulu. It crosses the valley between Central O'ahu's two mountain ranges through sugarcane and pineapple fields. On the right is Schofield Barracks, site of James Jones's novel *From Here to Eternity* and the setting for the memorable movie version of the book. As you reenter the city, you get a good view of a more significant reminder of World War II, the intricate waterways of Pearl Harbor.

O'ahu's grand tour acquaints visitors with aspects of the authentic Hawai'i that cannot even be glimpsed in Waikiki. It is a must-do, and is best in a rental car so that you can follow your own pace and interests. However you manage it, get out of Waikiki for at least one, preferably two, day trips. To roost in Waikiki and pretend to have been to Hawai'i should be illegal.

GUIDANCE

Hawaiian Visitor's and Convention Bureau (808-923-1811 or 1-800-464-2924; gohawaii.com), 2270 Kalakaua Ave., Suite 801. Open 8–4 weekdays. Contact them before your trip for a visitor's packet, or stop in for tons of brochures, maps, and guides once you're there.

O'ahu Visitor's Bureau (808-524-0722 or 1-877-525-6248; visit-oahu .com), 733 Bishop St. Open 8–4:30 weekdays. Their *Island of O'ahu Travel Planner*, pocket map, and honeymooner's brochure are helpful.

MORE WEB SITES

state.hi.us/dlnr (Hawai'i's Department of Land and Natural Resources)

honolulumagazine.com (*Honolulu Magazine*)

NEWSPAPERS & RADIO

For news, pick up the daily *Honolulu Advertiser* (honoluluadvertiser.com) and *Honolulu Star Bulletin* (starbulletin.com), or the weekly *Pacific Business News* (bizjournals.com/pacific). The *Honolulu Weekly* (honoluluweekly.com) is a fine complimentary guide available at many restaurants and clubs. The free *101 Things to Do on O'ahu* and *This Week O'ahu* are also very helpful, and are loaded with coupons and maps.

For aloha tunes, dial the FM radio to 98.5 KDNN, 100.0 KCCN, 99.5 KHUI, 90.3 KTUH, and 105.1 KINE. For news, tune your AM dial to 590 KSSK. You'll find NPR programming on 88.1 KHPR.

INTERNET & POST OFFICE

ShakaNet is in the process of completing free WiFi throughout Waikiki.

WEATHER

Check with the **National Weather Service** (808-973-4381) when it matters most.

MEDICAL EMERGENCY

Queens Medical Center (808-538-9011), 1301 Punchbowl St., Honolulu. Open 24/7; includes a trauma center.

Straub Clinic and Hospital (808-522-4000), 888 S. King St., Honolulu. Open 24/7.

Ku'akini Medical Center (808-536-2236), 347 N. Ku'akini St., Nu'uanu. Open 24/7.

Holistica Hawai'i Health Center (808-951-6546; holistica.com), Hilton Hawaiian Village Beach Resort & Spa, 2005 Kalia Rd. This outstanding wellness center offers state-of-the-art scans with an EBT scanner.

GETTING THERE

By air from the mainland: Practically all major U.S. airlines fly into Honolulu.

By Interisland air: **Hawaiian Airlines** (808-838-1555 or 1-800-367-5320; hawaiianair.com), **Aloha Airlines** (808-484-1111 or 1-800-367-5250; alohaairlines.com), and Go! Airlines (1-888-435-9462; iflygo.com) fly to neighbor islands.

A NOTE ABOUT TIMING

Even though you'd be better off on "Hawai'i time," taking it easy and not planning too much, a few tips will take you a long way toward maximizing your time in Hawai'i. Don't try to cram too much into any one day. You can circle the island in a day, but only if you don't linger at any of the more significant sights. Visit the USS *Arizona* and Pearl Harbor early in the morning, before bigger crowds assemble. Plan on half a day at the Bishop Museum. Spend an afternoon (preferably not on the weekend) barefoot on the North Shore and in Hale'iwa. Hanauma Bay is closed on Tuesday; the Polynesian Cultural Center is closed on Sunday; Saturday mornings are the most colorful in Chinatown.

GETTING AROUND

From the airport: The quickest and easiest way from the airport to Waikiki is by taxi. **Star Taxi** (808-942-7827 or 1-800-671-2999; startaxihawaii.com) takes up to five passengers from the airport for a flat fee of $30, but you must book in advance. The ride takes 20–45 minutes, depending on the time of day. Shuttles to hotels are available through **Roberts Hawaii** (808-271-4765). Be sure you know the exact name of your hotel; many sound similar, and you don't want to get dropped off at the wrong one. Because of luggage restrictions, taking **TheBus** (see next page) is impractical unless you are traveling very light. Unless you're staying outside Honolulu, don't bother with a rental car at the airport. They are readily available and often less expensive in Waikiki, and you won't want to deal with driving and parking problems (including pricey overnight rates) upon your arrival.

By car in general: You'll regret it if you don't explore the wealth of O'ahu for a couple of days (at the very least). Besides, isn't that why you bought this book—to explore?

Directions are easy once you know four critical words: Diamond Head versus 'Ewa, and *mauka* versus *makai*. Locals don't generally use directionals like north, south, east, and west. Instead, you'll hear "head Diamond Head at the next corner," which means "head in the direction of Diamond Head." Or "turn 'Ewa when you reach the banyan tree," which means "head in the westerly direction toward the town of 'Ewa." *Mauka* means "head toward the mountains," and *makai* means "head toward the sea" (as in, "head *makai* for three blocks").

By bus: **TheBus** (808-848-5555; thebus.org). With over 70 routes and 4,000 stops, this incredibly well-developed bus system goes everywhere you'll want to go. Buses run from about 5 AM until midnight; they run every 15 minutes during the daylight hours and about every 30 minutes after dark. Tickets cost only $2; free transfers are available. Consider purchasing a four-day Visitor Pass from any ABC store for unlimited rides ($20).

Utilizing this system in Honolulu is quite easy. One of the more popular routes, with service every 10 minutes, is the No. 8 between Waikiki and Ala Moana Center (which takes 15 minutes). Hotel concierges usually have a bus route map for all the popular attractions, as does TheBus Web site. You can do a Circle Island tour in about four hours. The No. 55 runs counterclockwise along the South Shore, through Kane'ohe up to the North Shore. The No. 52 runs clockwise through Central O'ahu to the North Shore. To make it all the way around the island you have to transfer at Turtle Bay Resort.

ISLANDWIDE

Tours by foot: **Hawaiian Trail and Mountain Club** (htmclub.org), Honolulu. This group leads regularly scheduled hikes from 'Iolani Palace. For a schedule of upcoming hikes, visit their Web site.

Tours by bike: **Bike Hawai'i** (808-734-4214 or 1-877-682-7433; bikehawaii .com), Honolulu. This group offers mountain biking tours, all-day bike-hikes, and sailing and snorkeling options. Try their Downhill Biking Adventure through a lush rain forest combined with either a hike or a sail and snorkel. **Honolulu City & County Bicycle Coordinator** (808-527-5044; state.hi.us/dot/highways/ bike/oahu) has more information than you can shake a wheel at, including great regional maps.

Tour by air: **Island Seaplane** (808-836-6273; islandseaplane.com), 85 Lagoon Dr., Honolulu. Looking for a different vantage point? Something a little out of the ordinary? Try these 30- and 60-minute flights ($125 and $230 per person, respectively). Skimming into Honolulu Harbor harks back to an earlier time, and it's a heck of a lot of fun. The shorter tour takes in Diamond Head, Kahala, Hanauma Bay, and Kane'ohe Bay. The longer tour heads up the Windward Coast to the North Shore and returns via Central O'ahu and over Pearl Harbor. Take the latter if you can swing it.

DRIVING TIMES & DISTANCES

Waikiki to Kailua (via Southeast O'ahu) = 25 miles, about 50 minutes

Waikiki to Kailua (via Pali Hwy.) = 10 miles, about 30 minutes

Waikiki to Pearl Harbor = 11 miles, about 30 minutes

Kailua to Hale'iwa = 50 miles, about 2 hours

Waikiki to Hale'iwa (via H-2) = 30 miles, about 60 minutes

Waikiki to Yokohama Beach (Leeward O'ahu) = 44 miles, about 75 minutes

Hiking: **Mauka Makai Excursions** (808-255-2206; hawaiianecotours.net). This deservedly award-winning outfit specializes in full- and half-day eco trips that highlight places of cultural significance, like sacred archaeological sites. They're highly sensitive and knowledgeable, and they talk story with the best of them. Book any of their trips and be the richer for it.

O'ahu Nature Tours (808-924-2473; oahunaturetours.com) offers myriad excellent tours for all abilities.

Department of Lands and Natural Resources (808-587-0300; hawaii .gov/dlnr/dsp), 1151 Punchbowl St., Room 131, Honolulu. Check the Web site for details about 33 state park trails. It's an invaluable resource.

Na Ala Ele (808-973-9782; hawaiitrails.org) is an excellent resource for hiking, as is the Sierra Club (hi.sierraclub.org) and the Nature Conservancy (808-537-4508; nature.org).

Underwater: **Aaron's Dive Shop** (808-262-2333 or 1-888-847-2822; hawaii -scuba.com), 307 Hahani St., Kailua (see "The Windward Coast"). This full-service shop and tour company offers summertime beach dives off the North Shore and wintertime beach dives off the Leeward Coast (weather permitting, of course). Daily, two-tank boat dives, as well as wreck dives to places like Mahi, are more popular. Boat and beach dives begin at $125 per person, pickup and gear included. Make reservations a couple of weeks in advance during high season (a few days ahead in off season).

Art: **Arts with Aloha** (808-532-8713), 900 S. Beretania St., Honolulu 96814. This thick brochure covers the music, theater, and visual arts scene on O'ahu. Ask for one in advance of your arrival.

Camping: Permits (and sometimes small fees) are required for camping at the four **state parks** and a dozen **county beach parks** (not all of which are reviewed in this chapter). With the exception of Malaekahana Bay State Recreation Area, all are closed on Wednesday and Thursday in an effort to keep folks from living at the beach and, ostensibly, to give authorities time to clean the facilities. For state parks, contact the Department of Lands and Natural Resources, State Parks Division (808-587-0300), P.O. Box 621, Honolulu 96809. For county-run beach parks, contact the Honolulu Department of Parks and Recreation (808-523-4525), 650 S. King St., Honolulu 96813. Keep in mind that there's no place to rent camping gear on O'ahu.

Golf: To beat astronomical costs of greens fees, contact **Stand-by Golf** (1-888-645-2665; stand-bygolf.com; taking calls 7 AM–11 PM) for same- or next-day tee times.

✳ Special Events

For a complete list of islandwide events, consult calendar.gohawaii .com.

Late January: **Ala Wai Challenge**, Ala Wai Park, Waikiki. This all-day Hawaiian sporting event includes ancient games, tug-of-war, and a quarter-mile outrigger canoe race.

Late January–February: **Narcissus Festival** (808-533-3181), Honolulu. Part of the Chinese New Year celebration, this four-week festival includes food stalls, arts and crafts, and a beauty pageant.

February: **NFL Pro Bowl** (808-486-9300; nfl.com), Honolulu. The best professional football players get to come to Hawai'i for this prestigious postseason game.

Sand Castle Building Contest (808-956-7225), Kailua Beach Park, Kailua. Watch the students from the University of Hawai'i School of Architecture put their design skills to work building intricate sculptures.

Late March: **Prince Kuhio Celebrations**, statewide. On March 26 Hawai'i celebrates the birth of Jonah Kuhio Kalanianaole, who served as a congressional delegate from 1903 to 1921.

March or April: **Annual Easter Sunrise Service** (808-532-3720), National Cemetery of the Pacific, Punchbowl Crater, Honolulu.

May 1: **Lei Day**, statewide. The phrase "May Day is Lei Day" was coined by Grace Tower Warren in 1928 when Lei Day was conceived.

Late May: **Memorial Day** (808-532-3720), celebrated at the National Memorial Cemetery of the Pacific in Honolulu, includes a solemn 9 AM ceremony recognizing the soldiers who died defending their country.

May–August: **Outrigger Canoe Season** (808-261-6615; y2kanu.com), statewide. Canoe races are held most weekends across the state.

June: **King Kamehameha Celebration** (808-383-7798; hawaii.gov/dags/ king_kamehameha_commission), statewide. Hawai'i's longest-running festival honors King Kamehameha, unifier of the Hawaiian Kingdom.

July 4: **Fourth of July Fireworks** (808-656-0110), Desiderio and Sills Field, Honolulu. This all-day celebration includes games, entertainment, and, of course, fireworks.

Third Sunday in July: **Prince Lot Hula Festival** (808-839-5334), Moanalua Gardens, Honolulu.

July: **Queen Liliuokalani Keiki Hula Competition** (808-521-6905), Neal Blaisdell Center, Honolulu. Five hundred *keikis* (children), representing 22 schools, take part in this competition.

Mid- to late August: **Admissions Day**, statewide. On the third Friday

---

TOP 10 "MUSTS" FOR FIRST-TIME VISITORS

Stop at the Nu'uanu Pali Lookout
Get quiet at Pearl Harbor
Have a drink at House Without a Key
Visit the wonderful Waikiki Aquarium
Watch North Shore waves roll in
Tour the 'Iolani Palace
Hike Diamond Head
Take a walking tour of Chinatown
Stroll Waikiki Beach at sunset
Visit the Bishop Museum

in August, all islands celebrate the day Hawai'i became the 50th state.

September: **Aloha Festivals** (808-589-1771; alohafestivals.com), statewide.

November 11: **Veteran's Day** (808-532-3720), National Cemetery of the Pacific, Greater Honolulu. A solemn ceremony is held here. Call for time.

Mid-November: **Triple Crown of Surfing** (808-638-7266; triplecrown ofsurfing.com), North Shore. The world's best pro surfers demonstrate their versatility, strength, skill, and fearlessness. Prize money tops $1 million.

December: **Festival of Trees** (808-547-4371), Amfac Plaza, Honolulu. Year-round volunteers (self-proclaimed "glue sniffers") glue and sew stuffed animals, pillows, festive wreaths, and ornaments to sell at this charity benefit.

Festival of Lights (808-547-4397), Honolulu. Holiday festivities begin with the mayor lighting the trees in front of Honolulu Hale.

TOP 10 IDEAS FOR REPEAT VISITORS

Cruise the Honolulu Academy of Arts

Hang out at Lanikai Beach

Snorkel at Hanauma Bay

Play a round at Ko Olina Golf Course

Ride outrigger canoes on Waikiki Beach

Buy a lei from a tiny Chinatown shop

Drive Round Top and Tantalus Drives

Take an early-morning swim at Sans Souci Beach

Tour with Mauka Makai Excursions

Hike Manoa Falls Trail

Honolulu Marathon (808-734-7200; honolulumarathon.org). More than 30,000 runners take to the streets between Ala Moana Beach Park and the Kapi'olani Park Bandstand.

Rainbow Classic (808-956-6501), University of Hawai'i, Manoa Valley. Eight of the best NCAA basketball teams compete at the end of the month.

WAIKIKI

Waikiki is America's original romantic resort. In the 1920s and '30s, Hollywood and social registry celebrities made it their favorite hideaway. They cruised into Honolulu Harbor, where they were welcomed by lithe hula dancers in grass skirts handing out leis and kisses. A few elegant beachfront hotels, spread handsomely across the expansive sands, lodged, dined, and entertained their wealthy guests in sumptuous style. All-purpose beach boys were everywhere arranging picnics, demonstrating surfing, and playing the ukulele. In the evening lovers strolled in the moonlight in places where skyscrapers now loom.

In the early years the closest most Americans could get to the Pacific paradise was in postcard pictures and the *Hawai'i Calls* radio show, immensely popular broadcasts that became a siren song for Waikiki. World War II abruptly changed all that. When soldiers and sailors first took over the elite sands hoteliers thought it was a temporary turn, but the fighters' fond memories, coupled with growing opportunities for air travel, permanently transformed Waikiki into a middle-class vacation destination. The beach began to get crowded with people and buildings by the 1950s, a trend that escalated rapidly in the next two decades.

As Waikiki became the most wholesalable spot in the sun for the tourism industry, standards plummeted to undignified depths. Hotel lobbies were transformed into tacky shopping arcades. Entertainment degenerated into a crass spectacle. Restaurants served frozen fish. The 1980s, fortunately, heralded a remarkable renaissance in the old resort. Waikiki wasn't trying to regain the exclusivity of the early years, but it did want to reclaim its world stature that was rapidly disintegrating.

If any single event marked the reversal, it was the opening of the new Halekulani in 1983. One of the first hotels in Waikiki, and a playground for the rich during the Great Depression, the Halekulani was rebuilt to serve more people and do it with style and grace. Other hotels followed the lead, culminating in 1989 with the restoration of the Moana Surfrider, the oldest of them all. Then there was a lull until the early 2000s. If you haven't stopped in Waikiki since then (and especially since 2006 or 2007), you're in for a big surprise. The Beach is hopping, the streets are jumping, the cash registers are ringing, and the mood is lively. This is not your grandfather's Waikiki. Some lament the passing of Old Waikiki, but others are thrilled that the renaissance has created an upscale vacation destination.

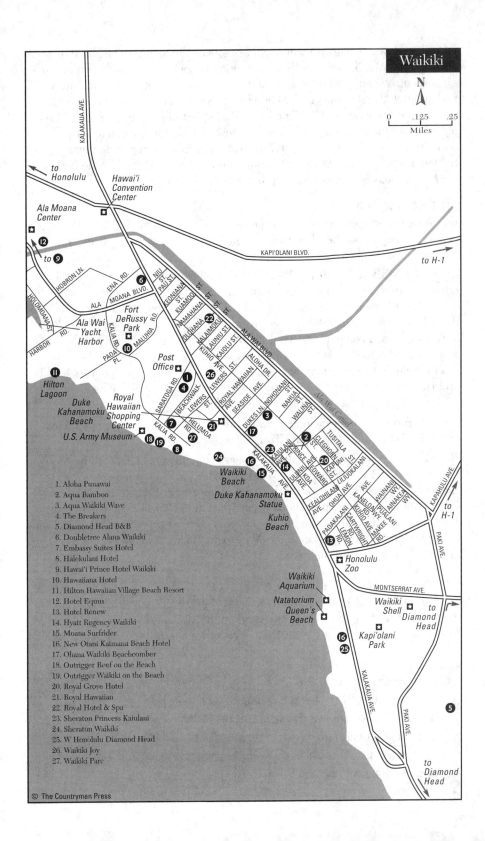

Waikiki

N

0   .125   .25
Miles

to Honolulu

Hawai'i Convention Center

Ala Moana Center

KALAKAUA AVE.

KAPI'OLANI BLVD.

to H-1

HOBRON LN.

ENA RD.

ALA

MOANA BLVD.

to 9

NIU ST.
PAU ST.

KEONIANA ST.

KUAMOO ST.

MAMAHANA ST.

OLOHANA ST.

KALAIMOKU ST.

KAIOLU ST.

KUHIO AVE.

KALAUNU ST.

ROYAL HAWAIIAN AVE.

SEASIDE AVE.

ALOHA DR.

ALA WAI BLVD.

Ala Wai Canal

Fort DeRussy Park

KALIA RD.

MALUHIA RD.

PADA PL.

Ala Wai Yacht Harbor

HARBOR

HOLOMOANA ST.

Post Office

SARATOGA RD.

BEACHWALK

LEWERS ST.

HELUMOA

KALIA RD.

Royal Hawaiian Shopping Center

Hilton Lagoon

Duke Kahanamoku Beach

U.S. Army Museum

INOHONANI ST.

NAHUA ST.

WALINA ST.

DUKES LN.

KAIULANI AVE.

PRINCE EDWARD ST.

KANEKAPOLEI ST.

CLEGHORN ST.

TUSITALA ST.

KAPUNI ST.

LILIUOKALANI AVE.

WANANI WY.

PUALANI WY.

AINAKEA WY.

KAPAHULU AVE.

to H-1

Waikiki Beach

Duke Kahanamoku Statue

Kuhio Beach

KALAKAUA AVE.

KEALOHILANI AVE.

OHUA AVE.

PADAKALANI RD.

KANEKOA

LEMON RD.

CARTWRIGHT RD.

KUHIO AVE.

MAKEE AVE.

PAKI AVE.

Honolulu Zoo

MONTSERRAT AVE.

Waikiki Aquarium

Natatorium

Queen's Beach

Waikiki Shell

to Diamond Head

Waikiki

Kapi'olani Park

KALAKAUA AVE.

PAKI AVE.

to Diamond Head

1. Aloha Punawai
2. Aqua Bamboo
3. Aqua Waikiki Wave
4. The Breakers
5. Diamond Head B&B
6. Doubletree Alana Waikiki
7. Embassy Suites Hotel
8. Halekulani Hotel
9. Hawai'i Prince Hotel Waikiki
10. Hawaiiana Hotel
11. Hilton Hawaiian Village Beach Resort
12. Hotel Equus
13. Hotel Renew
14. Hyatt Regency Waikiki
15. Moana Surfrider
16. New Otani Kaimana Beach Hotel
17. Ohana Waikiki Beachcomber
18. Outrigger Reef on the Beach
19. Outrigger Waikiki on the Beach
20. Royal Grove Hotel
21. Royal Hawaiian
22. Royal Hotel & Spa
23. Sheraton Princess Kaiulani
24. Sheraton Waikiki
25. W Honolulu Diamond Head
26. Waikiki Joy
27. Waikiki Parc

© The Countryman Press

Still, no level of transformation will bring back the idyllic atmosphere of a half century ago. Waikiki is primarily a destination for people who thrive on urban excitement. Within a 1.5-mile-long and 0.5-mile-wide stretch of high-rises, you'll find about 400 restaurants and 29,000 hotel rooms that run at an average year-round occupancy rate of 80–85 percent. That's a lot of people. This is a place for nightlife, for loud crowded beaches, for inexhaustible shopping, and for package tours from Japan and the mainland. It's Hawai'i's only metropolitan tourist center, and it's proud of it. If high-rise congestion and high-pitched hustle bother you, go to the neighbor islands or other areas of Honolulu or O'ahu.

GETTING AROUND

By car: A car is more trouble and expense than it's worth in Waikiki. But when you want one to tour the island (which I highly recommend), there are convenient outlets in Waikiki.

By trolley: **Waikiki Trolley** (808-593-2822; waikikitrolley.com). More like an open-air cable car than a bus, this narrated trolley runs between major sights in Waikiki and Honolulu from 8:30 AM to 11:30 PM daily. You can hop on and off all day. (Pick it up, among other places, in front of the DFS Galleria.) It may be relatively expensive compared to TheBus, but most folks think it's pretty convenient. A one-day trolley pass costs $25 for adults, $12 for ages 4–11. They also offer a roughly three-hour trolley tour to Southeast O'ahu, which covers Kahala and Hanauma Bay, but if you're traveling with someone you'll have far greater flexibility by renting a car (for about the same price).

By taxi: Taxi companies include **Aloha State Cab** (808-847-3566), **City Taxi** (808-524-2121), and **Royal Taxi Tour** (808-944-5513).

By foot: This compact area is easy to navigate, bound *mauka* (inland) by Ala Wai Canal and Ala Wai Blvd., and by Waikiki Beach. Diamond Head dominates to the east; downtown lies 'Ewa (to the west). Kalakaua Ave. is the main thoroughfare, running somewhat parallel to Waikiki Beach. Kuhio Ave. runs between Kalakaua and Ala Wai. Kapahulu Ave. borders the eastern edge of town and separates Waikiki from Kapi'olani Park. Ala Moana Blvd. spurs off Kalakaua Ave. and heads 'Ewa toward the harbor.

TOURS

By foot: ✪ **Waikiki Historic Trail** (808-441-1404; waikikihistorictrail.com). These great walking tours connect visitors to the Waikiki of yesteryear, the vestiges of which are quite different from what you see today. Call for reservations.

FREE PARKING IN WAIKIKI?

No, that's not a misprint. But it *is* subject to change. In the meantime, if you have a car in Waikiki, you might get lucky with free spots. Most side streets and Ala Wai Boulevard have free parking. For the time being, Kuhio Avenue at Lewers has free spots, and you can always park at the Zoo, although it might be a trek to your hotel. Good luck.

✳ To See & Do

WAIKIKI BEACH

Kapiʻolani Park is just beyond the east end of Waikiki, bordered by Kalakaua and Montserrat Avenues. This beautiful 500-acre park was Hawaiʻi's first, established by King Kalakaua in the 1870s and dedicated to his wife, Queen Kapiʻolani. Locals come here to jog, practice early-morning T'ai Chi Chih, play tennis and soccer, run their dogs, throw Frisbees, or simply enjoy a family picnic under the shade of a 100-year-old banyan tree. The park is also home to the graceful **Waikiki Shell** amphitheater, the site of frequent evening and weekend music and dance concerts. If you just feel like a walk in the park, this is the place.

Natatorium is on Kalakaua Ave. opposite Kapiʻolani Park. Officially the Waikiki War Memorial Natatorium, this classic 100-meter saltwater pool was carved out of the Pacific in 1927 to honor Hawaiʻi's World War I veterans and to serve as a competitive swimming arena. Johnny Weismuller, later of *Tarzan* fame, trained here before winning two gold medals at the 1928 Olympic Games in Amsterdam. Since the 1980s, the Natatorium has fallen into disuse because of structural problems. Today it's the center of a vocal debate on whether to restore it to its historic glory or tear it down and restore the beach to its own glory. For the time being, it's an elegant landmark.

✒ **Honolulu Zoo** (808-971-7171; honoluluzoo.org), 151 Kapahulu Ave. Open 9–4:30 daily. You'll know you're near the zoo when you see local artists displaying their paintings against the zoo fence on Kalakaua Blvd., a tradition that has endured for years. Inside, the zoo resembles a mini tropical oasis interspersed with lush gardens and well-managed displays of flamingos, alligators, elephants, zebras, and nene, the state bird of Hawaiʻi. On Wednesday evening in the summer months, the zoo is host to an early-evening music concert featuring local Hawaiian bands. Check the Web site for a whole host of terrific educational programs, including twilight tours and "Snooze in the Zoo." $8 adults, $1 ages 6–12.

✒ ✪ **Waikiki Aquarium** (808-923-9741; waquarium.org), 2777 Kalakaua Ave. Open 9–4:30 daily. This aquarium (the third oldest in the United States) is just big enough to have several terrific displays but not so large as to overwhelm. It's managed by the University of Hawaiʻi and dedicated primarily to coral reef aquatic life—that means reef sharks, living coral, and sea jellies. If you can't tell a parrotfish from a puffer and want to learn about biodiversity and coral reefs, then this is your place. You can go eye to eye with a black tip reef shark and find out which types of coral can survive large waves. A rare pair of Hawaiian monk seals that make their home in a large outdoor environment are an uncommon treat. The aquarium is a hit with grown-ups and kids alike, and it's a perfect place to go following a snorkeling adventure to identify what you saw or missed. $9 adults, $6 seniors, $4 ages 13–17, $2 under age 12.

Waikiki Beach Walk (waikikibeachwalk.com) is the area bound by Kalakaua Ave., Saratoga Rd., Lewers St., and Kalia Rd., one block from the beach. If you

BUILDING BLOCKS FOR PERFECT DAYS IN PARADISE

These regional planners will get you started on how best to dip into the island. Use them as building blocks to create perfect days. But a word of caution: If you try to do everything mentioned, you might not feel like you're on a vacation. Use them merely as a guide.

Building Blocks for a Perfect Day in Waikiki

Take a morning dip at San Souci Beach (1 hour)
Investigate sea creatures at the Waikiki Aquarium (90 minutes)
Watch outrigger canoes paddle through the Ala Wai Canal (15 minutes)
Learn to paddle an outrigger canoe or learn to surf (90 minutes)
Walk the Waikiki Historic Trail (2 hours)
Stroll through the Moana Surfrider & Royal Hawaiian hotels (30 minutes)
Have sunset drinks at a House Without a Key or Mai Tai Bar (1 hour)
Stroll Waikiki Beach (1 hour)
Photograph Diamond Head at dusk (30 minutes)

haven't been to Waikiki in a few years, are you in for a shock. During 2006 and 2007, a whopping 10 hotels were torn down; streets were broadened and planted with lush trees; and dozens of upscale shops and restaurants were added. Trump International Hotel is expected to come on line in mid-2009 as part of Phase Two. (Its 460 units sold out within hours of being on the market.) In case you're wondering, Outrigger Hotels financed the $460 million development of this prime 8-acre parcel in the heart of Waikiki.

Fort DeRussy Park, Kalakaua Ave., Waikiki. The U.S. Army appropriated this large piece of Waikiki a few years after the annexation of Hawai'i in 1898. Even then they were thinking location, location, location. Once a swampy marshland where Hawaiian kings went duck hunting, Fort DeRussy is now an army recreation center; its Hale Koa Hotel is restricted to the military. The beach and museum are open to civilians, however, free of charge.

U.S. Army Museum (808-955-9552; hiarmymuseumsoc.org), Fort DeRussy, at Saratoga and Kalia Rd., Waikiki. Open 10–4 Tues.–Sun. Erected in 1911 of reinforced concrete and known as Battery Randolph, this converted artillery bunker once held two 14-inch recoiling guns. When they were first tested in 1914, they rattled dishes and cracked windows in the neighborhood. Tourism eventually silenced them for good. The museum's eclectic collection is an interesting mix of modern and ancient weaponry, from woven shields to armored tanks. Donations accepted.

Ala Wai Yacht Harbor, Ala Moana Blvd. From dawn till dusk you'll see sailboats pull in and out of the picturesque harbor, along with joggers and walkers circling the perimeter of adjacent Magic Island. Late afternoon usually means outrigger canoe teams are gliding out of the canal and into the harbor. Did I

WAIKIKI BEACH WALK

mention the sunset? This is a great place to drink it in. (The Hawai'i Prince Hotel Waikiki has a stunning vantage point overlooking the harbor.)

Ala Wai Canal runs along Ala Wai Blvd. and scoots underneath the Ala Moana Blvd. Bridge. Stand along its banks to catch the uniquely Hawaiian sport of outrigger canoe races. The canal was built in 1922 to divert streams that flowed in the wetlands of Waikiki, altering forever what had once been hunting and farm land.

❋ Spas

Abhasa Spa (808-922-8200; abhasa.com), Royal Hawaiian, 2259 Kalakaua Ave. Open 9–9 daily. From ayurvedic specialty treatments to "body cocoons" (like seaweed or mud wraps) to hot stone massages, this hotel spa offers all the treatments you'd expect at an upscale resort. (It's one of the best in Honolulu.)

Mandara Spa (808-945-7721; mandaraspa.com), Hilton Hawaiian Village Beach Resort & Spa, Kalia Tower, 2005 Kalia Rd. Few spas on the mainland, much less in Hawai'i, deliver like Mandara, whose name comes from an ancient Sanskrit legend about "the gods' quest to find the elixir of immortality and eternal youth." With 25 treatment rooms offering a full complement of wet and body therapies, Mandara excels because of the staff. They're sensitive and skilled practitioners, trained in Hawaiian and Balinese ways of healing. You may not find eternal youth, but if you're anything like me, you'll feel 10 years younger for weeks after visiting here. And that's almost priceless.

Spa Halekulani (808-931-5322; halekulani.com), Halekulani Hotel, 2199 Kalia Rd.. Open 9–8 daily. Peaceful and pampering, graceful and timeless: These are the words that come to mind after indulging the mind and body at Spa Halekulani. From signature massages to a signature scent to scrubs designed to detoxify, this oh-so-evocative oasis reigns supreme. I'd expect nothing less.

❋ Outdoor Activities

BICYCLING

Big Kahuna Rentals (808-924-2736; bigkahunarentals.com), 407 Seaside Ave. Big Kahuna rents mountain bikes for $10 per half day, $20 for a 24-hour period, and $100 per week.

GOLF

Ala Wai Municipal Golf Course (808-733-7387; reservations 808-296-2000; co.honolulu.hi.us), 404 Kapahulu Ave. Supposedly the busiest course in the world, this flat course is within walking distance of Waikiki hostelries. Greens fees run $42, plus $16 for the cart. Reservations can only be made three days in advance.

SUBMARINE TRIP

Atlantis Submarines (800-548-6262; go-atlantis.com), the Pier at Hilton Hawaiian Village Beach Resort & Spa. Tours depart hourly every day. These subs descend 100 feet below the surface to see marine life in all its glory. Since the artificial reefs and sunken ships are a mile offshore, it requires a 20-minute boat ride to get there. The below-water tour inside the submarine, where cabin pressure is the same below surface as it is on land, lasts 45 minutes. (The whole trip lasts two hours.) If you're new to underwater exploration, try the 64-passenger sub with larger portholes and roomier seating. It's the world's largest passenger submarine, but regardless, if you're claustrophobic, you might want to skip this activity. It's a popular tour, so make reservations in advance. $79–99 adults, $42–45 ages 12 and under. Children must be at least 36 inches tall, and everyone must be able to climb a vertical ladder.

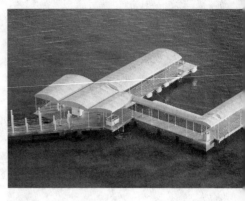

ATLANTIS SUBMARINE

TENNIS

Diamond Head Municipal Courts (808-971-7150), 3908 Paki Ave. Of the almost 200 free municipal courts on O'ahu, these are the most convenient—across from the beach in Kapi'olani Park. The four lighted courts (open 24/7) are available on a first-come, first-served basis.

WALKING

✪ **Waikiki Beach Walk** is a paved path that runs parallel to the shore for about 2 miles. In the early morning the beach belongs to walkers and joggers. Get there as close to sunrise as you can manage—the stroll down the nearly silent strip toward Diamond Head is a precious moment.

WATER SPORTS

Aloha Beach Services (808-922-3111), 2365 Kalakaua Ave., next to the Moana Surfrider and the Duke Kahanamoku statue. Open 7–4 daily. These conveniently located folks rent every kind of beach gear imaginable, as well as surfboards and surf gear—from body boards to windsurfers. Surfing lessons are $30.

Paddling. It could be the best $10 you ever spent. Hop aboard an outrigger canoe, parked on Waikiki Beach, and head out at sunset to catch a wave. If you miss it, try again. And don't worry about ending up in Tahiti; a surf boy goes out with you.

✳ Beaches

From northwest to southeast.

⊗ ⨍ **Waikiki Beach**, all along Kalakaua Ave. This world-renowned beach starts at the Hilton Hawaiian Village Beach Resort & Spa and runs about 2 miles to a small pier known as The Wall, at the bottom of Kapahulu Ave. First things first: Waikiki's glistening white sand was shipped in

WAIKIKI WATERFRONT BEACH WALK

from Moloka'i. Let's all say a collective "thank you." And because of natural erosion, it's been widened by the city recently. In fact, it's about 50 percent wider, to the tune of about $400,000. The strip is squeezed between a line of fancy resort hotels and the blue horizon, with Diamond Head always in view. An assortment of surfers, catamarans, outrigger canoes, swimmers, and snorkelers claim it for their own starting at 10 AM or so, when boogie board and surfboard vendors set up shop and catamarans offer sailing jaunts. By noon it's hard to walk the packed beach without stepping on oiled sunbathers and small children digging trenches with yellow plastic shovels. In fact, if you achieve this feat, consider it your good deed for the day. But at night, when visitors head to restaurants and clubs, a moonlit stroll along this beach is still romantic. It's hard to beat the skyline views, Diamond Head towering in the distance, the surf lapping at the shore, a fragrant breeze cooling the air, and stars lighting up the huge sky. Swimming is good, of course, but watch out for inflatable beach mattresses floating by. *Facilities*: Lifeguards, showers, restrooms, telephones, vendors.

Waikiki Beach might be termed Greater Waikiki Beach. Several sections have their own names, which usually reflect an adjacent park or hotel. But it's all basically one long, beautiful stretch of sand and sea. Of these sections, the best known are **Duke Kahanamoku Beach**, fronting the Hilton Hawaiian Village Beach Resort & Spa; **Gray's Beach**, fronting the Halekulani Hotel, the Royal Hawaiian, and the Sheraton Waikiki; and **Kuhio Beach Park**, toward the east end of Waikiki. Kuhio is my second favorite section because

AN OUTRIGGER CANOE RIDE

there are no hotels; it's just a thin stretch of grass and trees. It's also the scene of free hula performances every evening before sunset.

🏖 **Queen's Beach**, Kalakaua Ave., opposite the Honolulu Zoo. Just a few minutes' walk from bustling Waikiki Beach, Queen's is best known as Waikiki's gay beach. The peaceful and grassy park setting here is also ideal for family picnics under the shade of a monkeypod tree. The sandy beach itself is narrow, but there's a decent swimming area. *Facilities*: Lifeguards, showers, restrooms, telephones.

🏖 **Kapi'olani Beach**, Kalakaua and Montserrat Aves., opposite Kapi'olani Park. This beach simply continues the tree-lined theme between Queen's and Sans Souci.

🏖 ✪ **Sans Souci Beach** (aka **Kaimana Beach**), Kalakaua Ave., opposite Kapi'olani Park. Next to the New Otani Hotel, with its calm protected waters shielded by a coral reef close to shore, Sans Souci is my favorite stretch of beach. It attracts those who want to avoid crowded Waikiki. The calm waters make for good snorkeling, and it's a prized location for serious swimmers making daily laps out to the windsock marker. You can follow the Kapua Channel as it cuts through the reef, although be careful of currents that can pick up here. Check conditions with the lifeguard before venturing out. *Facilities*: Lifeguard, showers, on-street parking only.

✳ Lodging

This enclave is O'ahu's only developed destination area for lodging. Almost 90 percent of all visitors to O'ahu stay in Waikiki, which has upward of 29,000 rooms in 55 hotels and 27 "condo-tels" (a new entity that combines the services of a hotel with the feel of a condo). Occupancy rates are high year-round, but the best time to catch a deal is from mid-April to mid-June and September to mid-December. Fierce competition does two things to the market here: It keeps room quality relatively high and package deals front and center (except at the poshest places). Don't forget to factor in 11.96 percent for room tax; it adds up, as do daily parking fees if you're letting the car sit in the garage. And ask about hospitality suites if you arrive at some ungodly hour or if your flight departs long after checkout. Many hotels have a place for you to shower, freshen up, set up a laptop, that sort of thing.

DUKE KAHANAMOKU

Right on the Beach

RESORTS & HOTELS

🐚 𝆑 **Halekulani Hotel** (808-923-2311 or 1-800-367-2343; halekulani.com), 2199 Kalia Rd. The Halekulani, which radiates a serene spirit, sets the bar. You won't find a trace of flash or swagger at the "house befitting heaven," just genuine sophistication in all that matters. Staff address you by name, your folded laundry is returned to you in a wicker basket, and sunset cocktails are a gracious must. As for the guest rooms, they're a compelling blend of contemporary convenience and opulent comfort, from plush bathrooms and separate sitting areas to flat-screen TVs and WiFi. The main difference among guest rooms is their views. The Diamond Head rooms have the best views, as they are close to the sea and scan a long stretch of Waikiki Beach. As you might conjecture, the Halekulani's restaurants match the accommodations in magnificence. Neoclassical **La Mer** (see *Dining Out*) is easily among the top restaurants in Hawai'i. Even the so-called number-two restaurant, Orchids (see *Dining Out*), is superior. Light meals are also served at **House Without a Key** (see *Entertainment*), which was named after the 1925 Charlie Chan novel. Always setting the trend but remaining thoroughly dignified in doing so, the Halekulani has a romantic Vera Wang suite and boutique, as well as a small but wholly serene spa. Ask about complimentary passes to half a dozen top-notch cultural attractions, which could save you $100! *Rates*: $$$$; one child free in parent's room. *Facilities and amenities*: 454 rooms and suites, waterfront pool, three restaurants, **Spa Halekulani** (see

TOP 15 PLACES TO STAY IN WAIKIKI

Best Romantic Hideaways
Halekulani Hotel
Royal Hawaiian
W Honolulu Diamond Head

Most Worldly Hotels
Halekulani Hotel
Moana Surfrider
Hawai'i Prince Hotel Waikiki

Best Family Hotels
Embassy Suites Hotel
Hilton Hawaiian Village Beach Resort
Outrigger Waikiki on the Beach

Best Value Hotels
Hotel Renew
Waikiki Parc
New Otani Kaimana Beach Hotel
Doubletree Alana Waikiki
Royal Grove Hotel
The Breakers

HALEKULANI HOTEL

Spas), fitness center, shops, concierge, children's programs, parking (fee).

ʄ ♪ **Hilton Hawaiian Village Beach Resort & Spa** (808-949-4321 or 1-800-445-8667; hiltonhawaiian village.com), 2005 Kalia Rd. This 22-acre Hilton stands on the fairest section of Waikiki Beach, separated from the action by a park, which allows you to sun and swim without getting trampled. Hawaiʻi's largest hotel has more than 3,300 rooms in high-rise towers, a colossal convention center, and plenty of waterways filled with penguins, tropical birds, turtles, and fish. The urban atmosphere is quite popular with tour groups. The elegantly refurbished Aliʻi rooms are definitely the most desirable of all in the mammoth complex; you can count on personable, attentive service here. Rooms in other buildings are standard

HILTON HAWAIIAN VILLAGE

Hilton quality. While views get better and closer to the Pacific as the prices go up, all have the usual range of conveniences and comforts. The Hilton caters particularly well to families in all regards, including dining and recreation. On Friday evening enjoy the fireworks display. *Rates*: $$$–$$$$; children free in parent's room. *Facilities and amenities*: 3,386 rooms and suites, five pools, 20 restaurants (see **Golden Dragon** under *Dining Out*), fitness center (fee), **Mandara Spa** (see *Spas*), water sport rentals, concierge, more than 90 shops, children's programs, parking (fee).

ʄ ♛ ♪ **Outrigger Waikiki on the Beach** (808-923-0711 or 1-800-688-7444; outrigger.com), 2335 Kalakaua Ave. The shining star of the Outrigger chain on Oʻahu, this hotel is a gem when you consider price, value, and location. Right in the middle of town, with half the rooms overlooking Waikiki Beach, The Outrigger's guest rooms received a $20 million renovation in 2004 and feature lanais and Polynesian décor. *Rates*: $$$–$$$$; children free in parent's room. *Facilities and amenities*: 524 rooms and suites, pool, three restaurants (see **Duke's Canoe Club** under *Eating Out*), fitness center, Waikiki Plantation Spa, water sport rentals, concierge, children shuttled to Outrigger Reef for the "Cowabunga Kids Club," parking (fee).

ʄ ♛ **New Otani Kaimana Beach Hotel** (808-923-1555 or 1-800-356-8264; kaimana.com), 2863 Kalakaua Ave., on Sans Souci Beach. The New Otani, one of the most delightful small hotels in Hawaiʻi, balances a classy sophistication and casual naturalness that most places don't have the sense to seek. It's not surprising, then, that her **Hau Tree Lanai** (see *Dining Out* and *Entertainment*) is also the essence of Hawai'i—which is probably why it was used in Tom Selleck's *Magnum, P. I.* Many of the smartly stylish accommodations in the nine-story main building are oceanfront or junior suites. Though they are smaller than most Waikiki quarters with those labels, the rooms have been recently renovated and are also more affordable. In fact, these oceanfronts are among the best values in Honolulu. The moderate and ocean-view rooms are barely large enough to hold their queen-sized beds, though I have stayed in them without discomfort. To cut costs without sacrificing space, stay in the park-view studios and suites in the separate three-story Diamond Head wing. *Rates*: $$–$$$; Internet specials; children under 12 free in parent's room. *Facilities and amenities*: 125 rooms and suites, two restaurants, small fitness room, water sport rentals, concierge, parking (fee).

ℱ **Moana Surfrider** (808-922-3111 or 1-800-325-3535; moana-surfrider .com), 2365 Kalakaua Ave. In 2007 this venerable lady received a hefty nip and tuck and was rebranded as a Westin Resort. Prior to that, though, in 1989, she went under the knife for an extensive and authentic rehabilitation. As a result, the historic Surfrider became a symbol of Waikiki's renaissance as a distinguished destination. Architects scoured basements and archives for old plans, photos, renderings, menus, even china. And they executed the unearthed history with aplomb. Fire-eaters were sent packing, and the **Banyan Court** and **The Veranda** (see *Entertainment* for both) again became spots to dream, read, and dance. Accommodations in

NEW OTANI

the newer structures—the Diamond and Tower Wings—are mostly contemporary in tone but suggest the elegance of the original Moana, now known as the Banyan Wing. Banyan Wing rooms are a bit smaller but more enchanting; newer rooms have more frontal beach views. (Rates vary with the view, not the building.) In

DINING IN
Room service might sound absurd when you've just flown over the Pacific to reach Waikiki, but sometimes you're just in the mood to stay in. No longer are you limited to the room service of your resort or hotel; or perhaps your lodging doesn't offer room service. **Room Service in Paradise** (808-941-3463; 941-dine.com) makes house calls from dozens of area restaurants. For the price of the food, plus a small delivery charge and a tip, the world of Waikiki take-out is your oyster.

MOANA SURFRIDER

Hawaiian, by the way, *moana* means "broad expanse of ocean," an apt name for the Surfrider's location, as the beach here is wide and alluring. Although it does get crowded and clamorous, it's positively glorious here early and late in the day. Even if you're not staying here, come see how the "First Lady of Waikiki" graces the beach anew. Claim a front-porch rocker and newspaper and check out the scene. *Rates*: $$$$; children free in parent's room. *Facilities and amenities*: 795 rooms and suites, pool, two restaurants, Waikiki's only beachfront spa (opening in 2008), use of fitness room at Sheraton Waikiki, concierge, shops, children's programs, parking (fee).

✦ **Royal Hawaiian** (808-923-7311 or 1-888-488-3535; starwoodhotels.com), 2259 Kalakaua Ave. The Royal Hawaiian (closed at press time for an $8 million renovation) is the most romantic hotel on Waikiki Beach. Opened in 1927 and deemed the Pink Palace of the Pacific, in its heyday it was frequented by Gable, Fairbanks, Pickford, and assorted tycoons. While it's still an infatuating port of call, it no longer eclipses other luxury hotels in terms of service, cuisine, and accommodations. The main attraction today is the architecture and atmosphere in the original five-story building. Nostalgia buffs and other romantics love the Old World feel. Rooms in the hotel vary substantially. I steer clear of contemporary chambers in the adjacent 17-story Royal Tower. (Why come to the Pink Palace and spend more to stay nearby?) Within the original Palace, you can enjoy city, garden, or ocean views from a wonderful period room that's likely to feature a handsome carved door, high ceilings, floral wallpaper, and Queen Anne–style furnishings. While the Royal Hawaiian has dwindled in éclat since its glory years, you can still find much of the original élan. *Rates*: $$$$; one child free in parent's room. *Facilities and amenities*: 528 rooms and suites, pool, one restaurant, fitness center, **Abhasa Spa** (see *Spas*), concierge, shops, children's programs, parking (fee).

✦ **W Honolulu Diamond Head** (808-922-1700 or 1-877-946-8357;

ROYAL HAWAIIAN

starwoodhotels.com/hawaii), 2885 Kalakaua Ave. Nestled near the base of the Diamond Head crater, just beyond the bustle of Waikiki, the 12-story W opened its doors to great fanfare in late 1999. Intimate and ultratrendy—with attentive around-the-clock service—this sophisticated niche hotel marries substance with style. High-tech amenities cater to business needs, but comfort and style reign in the form of great beds and artsy detailing. W is doing with this signature line of hotels what Pottery Barn did for the home furnishings market. Earthy tones, natural light, and minimalist components prevail. Guest rooms have a distinctive Balinese motif, with contemporary teak furniture. They also include an oversized desk, lanai, Bliss bath products, terry-lined cotton piqué bathrobes, and luxe bedding. Rich fabrics and textures are used liberally throughout. If you imagine yourself with a lifestyle rather than simply a life, you'll feel right at home here. The only drawback is that it's one building (or one minute's walk) removed from the beach. *Rates*: $$$$; children free in parent's room. *Facilities and amenities*: 50 rooms and suites, Diamond Head Grill (see *Dining Out*), stylin' lounge (see *Entertainment*), fitness center, concierge, parking (fee).

 Sheraton Waikiki (808-922-4422 or 1-800-325-3535; starwood hotels.com), 2255 Kalakaua Ave. This 30-story Sheraton, the second-largest hotel in the state, puts you in the center of Hawai'i's most famous beach. Although it's primarily a convention center, many independent travelers like the location, the high-rise sunsets, and the beehive of activity. In fact, there is probably more free entertainment here than at any other hotel in Hawai'i; kids, in particular, are kept quite engaged. In a nutshell, the guest rooms (deftly renovated in 2007) are more standard than deluxe but compensate with fewer pretensions. All regular quarters are moderate in size and meet expectations for Sheraton-style comfort and convenience. (But I don't recommend the least-expensive rooms in the eight-story Manor Wing.) At the other end of the spectrum, this Sheraton has some of Waikiki's choicest views—in the oceanfront quarters facing Diamond Head. For similarly stunning views, don't leave without having a drink at the lofty Hanohano Room (see *Entertainment*). *Rates*: $$$–$$$$; children free in parent's room. *Facilities and amenities*: 1,695 rooms and suites, two pools, two restaurants, fitness center, water sport rentals, concierge, shops, children's programs, parking (fee).

 Outrigger Reef on the Beach (808-923-3111 or 1-800-688-7444; out rigger.com), 2169 Kalia Rd. Although this Outrigger was under construction through 2008, it promises to finally live up to its prime oceanfront location—

W HONOLULU DIAMOND HEAD

THE OVER-THE-TOP LIFE OF A TRAVEL WRITER ON O'AHU

All my friends would concur in a heartbeat: A travel writer works longer hours than almost any other white-collar worker. But they would also readily agree to one other truth: It sure does sound like a great life. So, at their request, I share with you the following:

- After a very long plane ride, a 21st-floor corner room yields a million-dollar twinkling view of Waikiki Beach and Diamond Head in the distance. The 11-hour flight was worth it for this view alone. I could go home a happy person tomorrow.

- My daily ocean forays revolve around one big question: Should I float or swim today? The contact with water becomes as necessary as breathing.

- Dave, a masseuse at a high-end spa, untangles knots and answers questions I never posed.

- I ditch the puritanical one-piece bathing suit and buy a bikini. "You mean a tankini?" questions my friend Julia. No, a bi-kini.

- I enjoy oceanfront cocktails with an old PR pal, followed by dinner with the GM of an oh-so-stylish boutique hotel. Apparently I sound cool enough to be put on the tightly controlled guest list for the hottest club in Honolulu.

- After a morning hike, I'm up for another four-hour, six-course dinner, this time with Chef "X," who joins me for dinner halfway through. The staff is simultaneously quaking in their boots (at having to serve him) and amused at their wacky, crazed chef eating with an actual patron. The next day, when I return to photograph him preparing a lamb dish, they ask with abandon, "Who the heck are you that the chef sat with you all night? We've been here since opening and have never seen him do that." Did someone tell him by mistake that I was writing for the *New York Times*?

- At an artful sushi bar, the chef prepares eight elegant plates that do not appear on the regular menu. Thankfully, I am never offered soy or wasabi. The chef and I talk for three hours about creativity and following one's heart.

although I can't conjecture whether rooms will be well priced for what they offer. For sure, guest rooms should be larger and more contemporary. *Rates*: $$–$$$$; children under 12 free in parent's room. *Facilities and amenities*: 639 rooms and suites, pool, two restaurants, fitness center, concierge, shops, spa, water sport rentals, Internet in rooms (free), WiFi in public areas (free), parking (fee).

Across from the Beach

RESORTS & HOTELS

⌀ Embassy Suites Hotel—Waikiki Beach Walk (808-921-2345 or 1-800-

- I enjoy dinner with Joyce Matsumoto, formerly of the world-renowned, ultra-famed Halekulani Hotel. In the mid-1990s Joyce was the first person I met on my first trip to Hawai'i, when she offered this unsolicited comment: "This is just the beginning of a long love affair with Hawai'i for you." We have so much fun that she cancels an appointment and invites me to breakfast the next morning.
- I encounter a strangely intriguing eight-course Kaiseki Japanese dinner that includes deep-fried fish bones. They call them "fish crackers." I call them "not particularly to my liking." But of course I eat them graciously. And then I drink a lot of very old, very rare sake.
- I'm offered a wonderful tour of the largest Kona coffee distributor in the state. I do in-house-only tasting and get buzzed on the caffeine.
- I bump into Chef "X" at a Chinatown hole-in-the-wall and slurp down the best noodles I've ever had while watching him do the same with pig's feet and knuckles. Small world.
- My bartender friend at the Wonderlounge (at the W Honolulu Diamond Head) plies me with apple martinis all night. I'm amazed at how badly many folks dance. No wonder *Queer Eye for the Straight Guy* is so popular.
- In 2005, I watch, listen to, photograph, and chat with Don Ho. But I can't make out a single word of what he's saying for the first hour. "Tiny Bubbles" is certainly recognizable because of the tune. Everyone in the audience is enamored.
- My friend Bonnie flies over from Maui for 48 hours to share my 1,500-square-foot suite overlooking the harbor.
- It takes me 14 days to notice my first rainbow. Rainbows in Hawai'i are everywhere, even on the state license plate. Have I not been paying attention?
- I'm driving for 30 minutes straight (a rarity on O'ahu), listening to a great CD that I brought from the mainland, when I notice that my cheeks hurt. Suddenly I realize that I've been smiling for 30 minutes. And that, of course, makes me smile even more.

362-2779; embassysuiteswaikiki.com), 201 Beachwalk St. In side-by-side 21-story towers, across the street from Waikiki Beach, this all-suite hotel packs a pretty punch. New in 2007, all of the one- and two-bedroom suites have two balconies; some feature sweeping ocean views; décor deftly blends Hawaiiana with contemporary amenities like flat-screen LCD TVs. From the lei greeting and manager's cocktail reception to the seated check-in process and all-you-can-eat breakfast, this hotel makes it easy to settle in for a week. It all feels quite opulent, especially the mattresses and linens. *Rates*: $$$–$$$$; children free in parent's room. *Facilities and amenities*: 421 suites, one pool, free breakfast, wet bar, children's programs during school vacations, 24-hour fitness center, 24-hour business center, shops, concierge, water sport rentals, WiFi (free), parking (fee).

☙ **Waikiki Parc** (808-921-7272 or 1-800-422-0450; waikikiparchotel.com), 2233 Helumoa Rd. The Parc deftly delivers on its promise of "affordable luxury" (a phrase that's more than marketing malarkey) and also positions itself as an "executive boutique." Rooms in the 22-story building, renovated in 2006, are all similar in size and appointments. Beautifully decorated with understated Zen-like elegance, they're smallish but have comfortable sitting areas, a tranquil color scheme, and a small lanai (sometimes just big enough for standing). The highest rate, for a deluxe ocean view, will place you on one of the top floors with a spacious lanai.

THE ROOFTOP WAIKIKI PARC POOL

You won't mistake the hotel for its big sister, the Halekulani, across the street, but the siblings share many basic attributes, including great service. The Waikiki Parc affords a level of classy comfort remarkable for its price range. *Rates*: $$–$$$$; one child free in parent's room. *Facilities and amenities*: 297 rooms, pool, **Nobu** restaurant (see *Dining Out*), fitness center, water sport rentals (at Halekulani Hotel), concierge, parking (fee).

☙ **Hotel Renew** (808-687-7700 or 1-866-406-2782; aquaresorts.com), 129 Paoakalani Ave. The elite diamond in the crown of Aqua boutique properties, Hotel Renew practically forces guests to relax and renew. The artfully designed interior is quite impressive—sleek yet warm and inviting. Zen-like in their simplicity (but not austere), the primarily black-and-white guest rooms include Shoji screens, 500-thread-count sheets, iPod docking stations, a dimmable light system, 80-inch projection TVs or LCD HDTVs, and an "Everything on Demand" entertainment system. Service is attentive, and the hotel boasts "green consciousness" as well as a no-smoking policy. Book it! *Rates*: $$$; children free in parent's room. *Facilities and amenities*: 72 rooms, one lounge, organic treats and small specialty plates, nearby fitness center (fee), concierge, WiFi (free), offsite parking (fee).

☙ **Ohana Waikiki Beachcomber** (808-922-4646 or 1-800-462-6262; waikikibeachcomber.com), 2300 Kalakaua Ave. Across from the beach, this value-oriented hotel operated by Ohana Hotels is right in the thick of things. Its guest rooms, which underwent a "soft" renovation in 2007, are quite pleasant in both size and appointments, made more so by a plethora of packages. I wouldn't hesitate to book a week's stay here. *Rates*: $$; children free in parent's room. *Facilities and amenities*: 494 rooms and suites, terrace pool, fitness center nearby, restaurant, activity desk, children's programs July–Aug., parking (fee).

Hyatt Regency Waikiki (808-923-1234 or 1-800-514-9288; hyattwaikiki .com), 2424 Kalakaua Ave. For the excitement and glitter of Waikiki, no hotel matches the huge Hyatt. Epitomizing the energy that attracts many visitors to this famous shore, here the tempo can approach casino level. Complete with an upscale shopping arcade, the hotel also boasts octagonal 40-story towers and a waterfall that recycles 30,000 gallons of water a day. In the hotel proper, though, the rooms are quiet and spacious. (They underwent a $14 million renovation in 2006.) Tasteful but not ostentatious, the chambers come with pleasant tropical furnishings, a lanai, and a writing desk. Regency Club rooms are available on the top floors, where a concierge will attend to your every need. Kids enjoy Camp Hyatt, where they can eat, play games, read Hawaiian children's books, and do arts and crafts. Adult activity at the Hyatt focuses on dancing, drinking, dining, and shopping. For urban bounty with contemporary flash, the Hyatt's your choice. *Rates*: $$$–$$$$. *Facilities and amenities*: 1,230 rooms and suites, pool, four restaurants, spa, fitness center, concierge, more than 60 shops, Camp Hyatt children's program June–Sept. (daily) and Oct.–May (Fri. and Sat.), parking (fee).

✦ **Sheraton Princess Kaiulani** (808-922-5811 or 1-800-782-9488;

princesskaiulani.com), 120 Kaiulani Ave. Perhaps the best bargain among the big Waikiki hotels, this Sheraton appeals to people who want to be near the center of Waikiki and don't mind a short walk to the beach. The face-lifted countenance and plethora of packages please families and anyone else looking for contemporary style at a good price. The Princess's towers burgeon with over 1,000 rooms, crowded into one city block. Most guest quarters have been spiffed up with new, albeit standard, Sheraton furnishings; some have Hawaiian quilts. (Avoid the least-expensive city rooms, which lack balconies and look onto a mundane back street and shopping area.) A couple of other pluses: The Sheraton's daytime activities and crafts demonstrations attract guests of all ages, and you're within walking distance of Kapi'olani Park, the zoo, and the aquarium. Absent the grandeur this site surely possessed when it was Princess Kaiulani's 10-acre estate, it still treats you royally for the price. *Rates*: $$$–$$$$; children free in parent's room. *Facilities and amenities*: 1,152 rooms and 14 suites, pool, two restaurants, fitness center ($8 daily), concierge, activity desk, children's programs, parking (fee).

✦ ❀ **Hawaiiana Hotel** (808-923-3811 or 1-800-367-5122; hawaiiana hotelatwaikiki.com), 260 Beachwalk St. They don't make 'em like this low-slung hotel anymore. You'll notice the difference right away (with the carved tiki totem and pineapple upon arrival), and the distinctions will continue throughout your stay (for example, Kona coffee is served poolside every morning and there is entertainment every week). Families are particularly well suited to the Hawaiiana because of kitchenettes and a staff readily dispensing aloha. Guest rooms are basic, but they're only a block from the beach. *Rates*: $–$$, children under five free in parent's room. *Facilities and amenities*: 93 rooms, two pools, WiFi in public areas (fee), barbecue, washer-dryer, fresh pineapple upon arrival, parking (fee).

❦ **The Breakers** (808-923-3181 or 1-800-426-0494; breakers-hawaii.com), 250 Beach Walk. The Breakers is one of my favorite Waikiki places; a cozy low-rise that dwarfs the skyscrapers in charm. You have to walk a short block to the beach, but no matter. This is distinctly old Waikiki, and they don't make 'em like this anymore. The accommodations are located in two-story ranch-style wooden buildings. Half look out into the tree-lined central courtyard, where a garden-party mood prevails around the swimming pool. The poolside rooms are slightly more expensive than the other standard rooms, and they can be a little noisier, but they are still my first choice. The second-floor rooms have a small lanai. When tropical laziness prevents you from walking the few steps to the restaurants and bars of Kalakaua Avenue, you'll be glad that all rooms have equipped kitchenettes. For a friendly atmosphere, casual comfort, and genuine value, the inn has few rivals in Honolulu. *Rates*: $–$$; children free in parent's room. *Facilities and amenities*: 64 rooms and suites, pool, activity desk, restaurant.

❦ **Royal Grove Hotel** (808-923-7691; royalgrovehotel.com), 161 Ulunlu Ave. When it's okay for function to trump form, you won't find a better bargain that this six-story, family-owned hotel. Aloha oozes from every pore of the Fongs' home away

from home, located just two blocks from Waikiki Beach. What do you get for your money? An occasional potluck dinner and a pool that's always the social center of the hotel. Inevitably you'll hear a member of the Fong family playing the ukulele, dancing hula, or singing old Hawaiian songs. Rooms come with kitchenettes and with and without air-conditioning; splurge on A/C, if for no other reason than to drown out some street noise. If you need daily maid service (rather than twice weekly), consider spending your hard-earned cash somewhere else. *Rates*: $; children under five free in parent's room as long as a crib is not required; weekly discounts. *Facilities and amenities*: 85 rooms and suites, pool, free water sports equipment, parking (fee).

❦ **Aloha Punawai** (808-923-5211 or 1-866-713-9694; alohapunawai.com), 305 Saratoga Rd. This is one of the best values in Waikiki. Family run since the late 1950s, it's a whopping two blocks from the beach and across the street from Fort DeRussy Park. What this throwback to another era lets you do is throw money back into your wallet. The rooms won't win any interior decorating awards, and the furniture is more mix-and-match than Crate and Barrel, but they sure are neat and tidy. And you can't beat the aloha. With all the recent construction around the Beach Walk, I sure hope they can hold out. *Rates*: $–$$; children free in parent's room. *Facilities and amenities*: 18 rooms, all with kitchenettes and private balconies; parking (fee).

❦ **Kai Aloha Apartment Hotel** (808-923-6723; kaialoha.magicktravel.com), 235 Saratoga Rd. A mere one block from the beach, this old-fashioned, apartment-style hotel rents studios and one-bedroom apartments (that can sleep up to five) to those savvy enough to save big bucks on their sleeping options. Okay, so Kai Aloha isn't going to win any design contests, but it wins for value. In addition to daily maid service, the hotel offers a nice deck on the second floor for escaping the bustle of Waikiki. *Rates*: $; children free in parent's room. *Facilities and amenities*: 18 units, three-night minimum; parking (fee) across the street.

Elsewhere

Hawai'i Prince Hotel Waikiki (808-956-1111 or 1-888-977-4623; prince resortshawaii.com), 100 Holomoana St. The Prince, opened in 1990, is an urban high-rise with class. Overlooking the marina, its location is unusual for Honolulu—directly on the ocean but a walk or quick shuttle ride to the beach. Waikiki is 10 minutes by foot, and Ala Moana Beach Park is a shorter distance the other way. The hotel substitutes service for sand, and it features attentive and professional staff. The polish is distinctly Prince, a Japanese chain known for its finesse. The rooms and suites start on the same level as the pool, giving everyone an elevated view of the Pacific across the yacht harbor. As for the rooms, they're similar (and quite large) but ascend in price as they go up in altitude. (A soft renovation in 2006 brought flat-screen TVs—among other plush necessities—de riguer these days for prime properties.) When you're feeling sleek and chic and deserving of personal attention, the Prince could well be the best address in town. *Rates*: $$$$; children free in parent's room. *Facilities and amenities*: 521 rooms and 57 suites;

pool; five-minute walk to beach; four restaurants, including **Prince Court** (see *Dining Out*); golf courses; fitness center; two tennis courts; day spa; concierge; parking (fee).

☙ **Doubletree Alana Waikiki** (808-941-7275 or 1-800-222-8733; double tree.hilton.com), 1956 Ala Moana Blvd. Affiliated with the Hilton Hawaiian Village, the Doubletree is one of the most artful hotels in Waikiki. At the top of the stairs, where you check in, you'll be greeted by *Hawai'i Wall*, a magnificent ceramic mural by Jun Kaneko. When you reach your room, you'll find more original artwork that adds to the already refined accommodations. The only thing minimal is the size of the bathroom, but even there you get Italian marble and a well-designed space. The regular

HAWAI'I PRINCE HOTEL WAIKIKI

rooms differ mainly in views, which at their optimum encompass parts of Waikiki, the ocean, and the yacht harbor. The closest section of Waikiki Beach is a 10-minute walk. Opened in 1992 and most recently renovated in 2005, the Alana has professional staff that pays great attention to detail. *Rates*: $$–$$$; children free in parent's room. *Facilities and amenities*: 317 rooms and suites, restaurant, pool, fitness center, activity desk, parking (fee).

🌸 **Aqua Bamboo & Spa** (808-922-7777 or 1-866-406-2782; aquaresorts.com), 2425 Kuhio Ave. Completely renovated in 2008, the 12-story Bamboo "condo-tel" is just a few minutes' walk from the beach and in the heart of Waikiki. As per usual with Aqua hotels, service is friendly and attentive, and lots of amenities are complimentary: There's no nickel and diming customers here. The stylish guest rooms have a decidedly Southeast Asian–inspired quality to them. For the money, this is another Aqua winner. *Rates*: $$–$$$; children free in parent's room. *Facilities and amenities*: 93 rooms and suites, saltwater pool, spa, Internet access in rooms (free), WiFi in lobby (free), continental breakfast (free), parking (fee).

🌸 **ResortQuest Waikiki Joy** (808-923-2300 or 1-877-997-6667; aston hotels.com), 320 Lewers St. Waikiki Joy may sound like a peculiar name for a hotel, but it's apt. Opened in 1988, this small boutique property fills a void in an area bursting with expensive behemoths. A couple of blocks from the beach, the Joy provides affordable contemporary luxury and personal service. The hotel's sleek design incorporates art deco accents throughout the open-air, barrel-vault-ed lobby. A tile deck a few steps above the reception desk holds a small pool and lounging area. As for guest quarters, superior rooms are in an 11-story tower, and the suites are in a separate eight-floor wing. Even the least-expensive quarters have a marble entry, handsome contemporary décor, and a lanai. Additionally, the Waikiki Joy may be the only Hawai'i hotel with whirlpool tubs in every room. And if you find that Waikiki moves you to song, the Joy has turned an entire floor of the hotel into private karaoke studios, rented hourly. *Rates*: $$–$$$; children free in parent's room; affordable Internet rates. *Facilities and amenities*: 94 rooms and suites, pool, restaurant, continental breakfast, fitness center, concierge, valet parking (fee).

🌸 **Royal Hotel & Spa** (808-943-0202 or 1-800-367-5666; royalgardens .com), 440 Olohana St. I've always appreciated this little boutique hotel (formerly called the Royal Gardens), set about three calm blocks from the beach. And after its 2007 renovation, I'm even more enamored with its quiet elegance. *Rates*: $–$$; children free in parent's room. *Facilities and amenities*: 210 rooms and suites, two pools, restaurant, lounge, small fitness room, parking (fee or free).

🌸 **Aqua Waikiki Wave** (808-922-1262 or 1-866-406-2782; aquaresorts.com), 2299 Kuhio Ave. A gem of an $8 million renovation turned the old 15-story Coral Reef hotel into a hot little boutique property. As is customary with Aqua properties, they tend toward hip and mod. Think white walls with bright splashes of color, flat-screen TVs, free WiFi in the rooms, live plants, free morning newspaper, and more. *Rates*: $$–$$$;

children free in parent's room. *Facilities and amenities*: 247 rooms and suites, small pool, two restaurants, fitness room, concierge, activity desk, WiFi in rooms (free), parking (fee).

🏇 **Hotel Equus** (808-949-0061 or 1-800-535-0085; hawaiipolo.com), 1696 Ala Moana Blvd. This boutique hotel, formerly called the Hawai'i Polo Inn and renovated in 2006, features friendly Aqua Resort service and comfortable rooms with lots of extras (for the price). All suites have microwaves; some rooms have lanais (and bamboo furniture); some have partial ocean views. Light sleepers should request a rear room, as Ala Moana Boulevard gets a constant din of traffic. If it's polo season (May–Oct.), ask the staff for free tickets and directions to the fields out in Mokuleia and Waimanalo. *Rates*: $–$$$; children free in parent's room. *Facilities and amenities*: 70 rooms and suites, pool, continental breakfast (free), Internet access in rooms (free), parking (fee).

🏇 **Diamond Head B&B** (808-923-3360 or 1-800-262-9912; diamondheadbnb.com), Noela Dr. Visitors to Waikiki needn't be confined to concrete towers—not when this homey Hawaiian house is available. *Kama'aina* (local residents) traveling to the city have long known of hosts Joanne and Brooke Trotter's bed & breakfast hidden in a quiet residential area near Kapi'olani Park. It features a comfortable living room filled with modern art, spacious rooms, and lots of koa furniture. Guest rooms in the main house, generally furnished with Hawaiian-style or Chinese furniture, are far enough from each other to offer privacy. The *Makai* Suite boasts a separate sitting area, 1940s vintage furnishings, and a screened lanai hidden by lush foliage. The Princess Ruth Suite features a larger-than-life-sized bed that was made especially for the 300-pound princess. Inquire about the availability of Grampa's apartment, which offers more privacy and is well suited to longer stays. Breakfast is served family style in the dining room, but the real gathering area is a large brick patio (where the host often has projects going on all around). A large backyard insulates you from neighbors. Sans Souci Beach is within walking distance, and all guests have access to beach towels, coolers, beach mats, and a refrigerator stocked with beverages. *Rates*: $$; children free in parent's room; two-night minimum. *Facilities and amenities*: three rooms, full breakfast, TV, no A/C, no smoking, credit cards not accepted.

Hostelling International–Waikiki (808-926-8313; hostelsaloha.com), 2417 Prince Edward St. This official Hawai'i hostel in an older, four-story building is a short walk from the beach and has typical hostel amenities. *Rates*: $. Office open 7 AM–3 AM; no curfew. *Facilities and amenities*: 63 dorm beds, a few private rooms, free water sport equipment, pay phone.

Polynesian Hostel Beach Club (808-922-1340 or 1-877-504-2924; hawaiihostels.com), 2584 Lemon Rd. Ensconced in a former motel at the Diamond Head end of Waikiki, these two- and four-bedded rooms boast in-room baths. *Rates*: $. Office open 24 hours; no curfew. *Facilities and amenities*: 48 dorm beds, nine semi-private rooms, three studios, beach, continental breakfast, free water sport equipment, Internet access, no A/C, no smoking, no phones.

✳ Where to Eat

Bask in Asian, Hawaiian, and other Pacific Rim fusion cuisine; there's quite a confluence in Waikiki. In addition to historic, romantic, and pricey beachfront eateries, you'll find a couple of way-above-average places serving very accessible dishes. Although almost every hotel and resort offers fine and casual dining, I have included only those worth seeking out. It's said that something like 100,000 visitors a day eat out at least once in Waikiki; good thing there are hundreds of eateries. To that end,

you'll also notice plenty of fast-food emporiums, nondescript plate-lunch places, and all-you-can-eat buffets. Most are unworthy of mention here.

DINING OUT
(Reservations are recommended, and usually essential, at all of the establishments listed.)

Right on the Beach
ƒ **La Mer** (808-923-2311; halekulani .com), Halekulani Hotel, 2199 Kalia Rd. Open for dinner nightly. The watchwords here are understated elegance—just like the hotel itself. While

CHAINS

🐟 **Aqua Resorts** (1-866-406-2782; aquaresorts.com). These folks burst on the scene in the mid-2000s with panache. Their better properties include **Aqua Waikiki Wave**, **Hotel Renew**, **Aqua Bamboo & Spa**, and **Hotel Equus** (see *Lodging*), but you might also want to check out **Aqua Aloha Surf** and **Aqua Palms & Spa**, both of which represent a great value.

Outrigger Hotels (1-800-688-7444; outrigger.com) and **Ohana Hotels** (1-800-462-6262; ohanahotels.com), various locations. Under the same parent company, these two chains offer an incomparable selection of values and packages. Think along the lines of a free rental car, six nights with the seventh free, island-hopper rates, and discounts for seniors and AAA members. They have dozens of Honolulu properties between them. Ohana hotels tend to be more blue collar in amenities and prices, while Outrigger hotels jump up a few notches on the economic scale. All room rates are pegged to their in-town location, room size, and views (or, more accurately, the lack thereof). Call for rates and information about facilities and amenities. Among the better properties, I like **Ohana Waikiki Beachcomber** (see *Across from the Beach*), **Ohana East**, and **Outrigger Luana**.

ResortQuest (1-866-774-2924; resortquesthawaii.com) also has a number of really decent, moderately priced condos and hotels in Waikiki. The best among them are **ResortQuest Waikiki Beach Tower**, **ResortQuest Waikiki Beachside Hotel**, and **ResortQuest Waikiki Beach Hotel**. One of the best amenities of them is "Breakfast on the Beach," where the hotel will pack a hot (free) breakfast that you can take across the street to eat on Waikiki Beach. Couldn't be sweeter.

WAIKIKI BEACH

it's arguably the "fanciest" in Hawai'i, nothing else in the Pacific really compares to this consistently award-winning restaurant. Without a doubt, your hard-earned money is worth this splurge. The room overlooks the ocean (*la mer* does, of course, mean "the sea" in French), and the menu interprets the cuisine of the south of France using local ingredients. The service is nothing short of superb, and the wine list, *c'est magnifique!* Jacket or long-sleeved dress shirt required for men. Prix fixe $$$$.

✦ **Orchids** (808-923-2311; halekulani .com), Halekulani Hotel, 2199 Kalia Rd. Open for breakfast and lunch Mon.–Sat., dinner nightly, and Sun. brunch. When you crave the same service and stunning oceanfront setting as La Mer, but without the formality, Orchids is a highly favored sibling. I particularly love this place for its leisurely breakfasts. It makes me feel rich in spirit. Popovers are sublime, as are eggs Benedict with crab cakes. And for me, one of the true hallmarks of great service is that when you ask for a quarter inch of milk in your espresso, they give it to you. Not a millimeter more or less. Sunday brunch is perhaps the best in the state. Children's menu. Breakfast $–$$$, lunch $$–$$$, dinner entrées $$$–$$$$.

✦ **Michel's at the Colony Surf** (808-923-6552; michelshawaii.com), 2895 Kalakaua Ave., Colony Surf Hotel. Open for dinner nightly. Steak and seafood dominate the menu. Tiki torches, San Souci Beach, ocean breezes filtering in through big open windows, live music, the Waikiki Beach and Diamond Head silhouettes clearly visible . . . it doesn't get more atmospheric than this. And thankfully, it's not as formal as it used to be when it opened in the mid-1980s. Signature dishes include French onion soup, escargot, and bouillabaisse, as you'd expect from a classy French restaurant. But vegetarians and seafood fanatics (try the onaga) will not be disappointed either. Dinner entrées $$$$.

TOP 10 PLACES TO EAT IN WAIKIKI

Pricey
La Mer
Orchids
Caffelatte Italian Restaurant
Michel's at the Colony Surf
Diamond Head Grill
Nobu

Moderate
Hula Grill Waikiki
Keo's
Sansei Seafood Restaurant

Inexpensive
Eggs 'n Things

🌶 **Bali by the Sea** (808-941-2254, hiltonhawaiianvillage.com), 2005 Kalia Rd., Hilton Hawaiian Village Beach Resort & Spa. Open for dinner Mon.–Sat. Another night, another impressive oceanfront dining room. It's hard to get enough of them. Request a window table for a view you'll never forget. Featuring Pacific Rim and Continental cuisine, Bali by the Sea's signature dishes include orange miso-glazed Kona kampachi, mac-crusted opakapaka with a kafir lime sauce, scallion-crusted ahi tempura, or oven roasted Colorado rack of lamb. Can't decide? Order the trio of opakapaka, prawns, and filet. Dinner entrées $$$$.

🌶 ♈ **Hau Tree Lanai** (808-921-7066; kaimana.com), New Otani Kaimana Beach Hotel, 2863 Kalakaua Ave. Open for all three meals daily. This institution, a charming open-air restaurant, is so close to glorious San Souci Beach that you risk, literally, getting sand between your toes. There's nothing quite like dining beneath the outstretched limbs of this stunning hau tree. (The Hau Tree Lanai is one of the few remaining outdoor beachfront restaurants in the state and is shaded by the ancient tree that used to shelter Robert Louis Stevenson.) I always come for breakfast—it's most highly recommended. The *poi* pancakes and *poi* waffles are without parallel. Or begin your evening in paradise with a sunset cocktail. Breakfast $$, lunch $$–$$$, dinner entrées $$$–$$$$.

🌶 🦞 ◐ **Hula Grill Waikiki** (808-923-4852; hulagrillwaikiki.com), 2335 Kalakaua Ave., Outrigger Waikiki on the Beach. Open for breakfast and dinner daily. One of the best values in town, with views that are worth a pretty premium, the Hula Grill is perhaps the best choice in town for a substantial morning meal. I'm particularly fond of the pineapple pancakes and crab cake eggs Benedict. The dinnertime atmosphere feels romantic when a 1930s Hawaiiana theme takes center stage. You won't be disappointed with regional seafood and steaks; I always go for the nightly special and have never been disappointed. Children's menu. Breakfast $–$$, dinner entrées $$$.

🌶 **Golden Dragon** (808-946-5336; hiltonhawaii.com), Hilton Hawaiian Village Beach Resort & Spa, 2005 Kalia Rd. Open for dinner Wed.–Sun. This is definitely not your father's (or mother's) neighborhood Chinese restaurant with Formica, paper napkins, and disposable chopsticks. This is serious gourmet Chinese dining in serene and gorgeous surroundings. The menu reflects the cooking of both the Canton and Szechuan regions, and every dish I've ever tasted has been truly delicious. The house specialties, Imperial Peking Duck and Imperial Beggar's Chicken, must be ordered 24 hours in advance. Don't be put off, though; they are totally worth the effort! Entrées $$–$$$$.

HAU TREE LANAI

Elsewhere

Nobu (808-237-6999; noburestaurants .com), 2233 Helumoa Rd., Waikiki Parc Hotel. Open for lunch weekdays and dinner daily. If you frequent Beverly Hills or Manhattan, you know Nobu. But from the moment Nobu burst onto the culinary scene in 2007, it's been met with high praise. Yes, it's expensive, but when your spirit and palate want to be pampered with fine service and sushi, owner and chef Nobu Matsuhisa won't disappoint. From ceviche and "new style" sashimi to tartar with caviar, every gastronomical whim is calculated and delicious. In a lighter mood? Enjoy drinks, dishes, and sushi from the stylin' lounge. Lunch $$–$$$, dinner entrées $$$$.

Caffelatte Italian Restaurant (808-924-1414), 339 Saratoga Rd. Open for dinner Wed.–Sun. This gem of a tiny trattoria, where Chef Laura makes everything from scratch, packs a big punch. It's everything a neighborhood eatery should be, even if the "neighborhood" is Waikiki, and worth every penny. All the traditional dishes like gnocchi, ravioli, bruschetta, and tiramisu are outstanding—arguably the best in Waikiki. Prix fixe only $$$$.

🍸 **Sansei Seafood Restaurant & Sushi Bar and D.K. Steakhouse** (808-931-6286; sanseihawaii.com), 2552 Kalakaua Ave., Waikiki Beach Marriott Resort. Open for dinner nightly. Located on the third floor, Chef D. K. Kodama's Sansei restaurant offers award-winning seafood and sushi menus. It's truly some of the most imaginative sushi I've ever tried. Don't miss the mango and crab salad hand roll, Japanese calamari salad, panko-crusted ahi sashimi, and Rock Shrimp Dynamite. The adjacent steak house is romantic and specializes in house-aged, bone-in rib eye steaks—paired with master sommelier Chuck Furuya's perfect wine list. As if that weren't enough, a million-dollar ocean view (across the street) completes the experience. Entrées $$–$$$$.

Diamond Head Grill (808-922-3734; w-dhg.com), W Honolulu Diamond Head, 2885 Kalakaua Ave. Open for all three meals daily. Although I didn't get a chance to eat here for this edition, relatively new Executive Chef Mariano Lalica is beginning to make his mark. Ask around to see what's up. The dining room is as stylish as ever—one of the most visually hip places in town, even without the bed as centerpiece. Entrées $$$$.

Prince Court (808-944-4494; princeresortshawaii.com), Hawai'i Prince Hotel Waikiki, 100 Holomoana. Open for all three meals daily. The main, and quite worthy, attractions here are the daily breakfast buffet and the extravagant weekend brunch. Because the hotel (and the entire chain to which it belongs) is Japanese owned,

SANSEI SEAFOOD RESTAURANT

many patrons are Japanese visitors. So if you've always wanted to taste a full Japanese breakfast (with miso soup, fish, and noodles), this is the place to do it. It's an interesting concept for Westerners to experience. Dinner focuses on Eurasian cuisine. Children's menu. Breakfast $$, lunch $$, dinner entrées $$$$.

Keo's (808-951-9355; keosthaicuisine .com), 2028 Kuhio Ave. Open for all three meals daily (closed midafternoon). Keo Sananikone, who also owns and operates the less-flashy but just as delicious Mekong I and Mekong II, is one of Hawai'i's best-known and most respected restaurateurs. He's known for two things: consistently good, unfussy Thai food and an extraordinary photographic collection of celebrity diners. If you want to try re-creating Keo's food at home, pick up his beautiful cookbook, *Keo's Thai Cuisine*. I also particularly like the open-air atmosphere here. Breakfast $–$$, lunch and dinner entrées $$.

Singha Thai Cuisine (808-941-2898; singhathai.com), 1910 Ala Moana Blvd. Open 4–11 nightly. Chai Chaowasaree's beloved (and first) restaurant deserves top billing for food, ambience, and entertainment. Chai uses French techniques and local ingredients to finesse his native Thai cuisine. Signature dishes include fresh ahi tempura with amazing Thai chili ginger and Thai light black bean sauces, both of which are available with tofu, lobster tail, or all of the fresh local fish you can shake a hook at. The exceptional cuisine here is complemented by a stunning interior and gorgeous Royal Thai dancers who perform nightly 7–9. (Chai is also the chef-owner of Chai's Island Bistro at

the Aloha Tower & Marketplace.) Entrées $$–$$$.

🦐 🍴 **Todai Restaurant** (808-947-1000; todaiwaikiki.com), 1910 Ala Moana Blvd. Open for lunch and dinner daily. Everything about Todai is b-i-g. Come to think of it, though, it's not big, it's h-u-g-e. Everything except the bill, that is. More than two dozen Todai restaurants across the United States and Hong Kong use the same successful formula. These all-you-can-eat Japanese seafood buffets seat up to 500 people, embrace familial special occasions, offer a gigantic selection of dishes (they have 40 different kinds of sushi, for example), and charge incredibly reasonable prices. Lunch buffet $$, dinner buffet $$$.

EATING OUT

Right on the Beach

🏄 🦐 🍴 ♗ **Duke's Canoe Club** (808-922-2268; dukeswaikiki.com), Outrigger Waikiki on the Beach, 2335 Kalakaua Ave. Open for all three meals daily. This homage to the world's most famous surfer, Duke Kahanamoku, is almost as much a surfing museum as it is a restaurant. Part of the wildly successful chain of TS restaurants, the restaurant's food is straightforward and utterly dependable—local fish, shrimp, steaks, salads, fries, and the company's signature Hula Pie (macadamia nut ice cream with an Oreo crust and topped with whipped cream). And with a spectacular setting right on the beach, it's a winning combination. Since lots of entertainers perform at Duke's, it's always a good idea to check the local papers or ask your hotel concierge about the schedule. Reservations recommended. Children's menu. Breakfast buffet $$, lunch $–$$, dinner entrées $$–$$$.

Elsewhere

🦞 🐚 **Cha Cha Cha** (808-923-7797), 342 Seaside Ave. Open daily for lunch and dinner. Across from the movie theater and in the mood for Mexican or Caribbean? You have a great option amid all the Waikiki glitz. Cha Cha Cha has a refreshingly neighborhood feel with an emphasis on fresh. The chef creates almost everything from scratch, from Caesar salad dressing to the mighty flavorful salsa on fish tacos or burritos. Try the jerk chicken, Jamaican chicken, or the blackened anything. It's also the perfect place for late afternoon *pupus* (appetizers) and fabu margaritas, too. Children's menu. Lunch and dinner $–$$.

Wolfgang Puck Express (808-931-6226; wolfgangpuck.com), 2570 Kalakaua Ave. Open 8 AM–10 PM daily. When I want a quick meal but I'm still in the mood for healthful, well-priced food, I remember this chic little place and become happy. Order in line and wait for your number to be called. Then chow down on gourmet pizzas, Puck's famous Chinois chicken salad, sandwiches, and Asian-inspired salads. Dishes $–$$.

🐚 ⅋ **Tiki's Grill & Bar** (808-923-8454; tikisgrill.com), ResortQuest Beach Hotel, 2570 Kalakaua Ave. Open 10:30 AM–midnight daily. Tiki's is packed with Hawaiian kitsch, big blue cocktails with little umbrellas, and the young, fit, and tan. It's the kind of retro place that screams Hawai'i, Hollywood style. As for the food, the upscale local menu features specialties like signature salmon, pan-seared ahi, and macadamia-nut crusted mahimahi. Live nightly

entertainment makes the place even livelier. Reservations recommended. Children's menu. Lunch $–$$, dinner entrées $$–$$$.

🦞 **Teddy's Bigger Burgers** (808-926-3444), 134 Kapahulu Ave. Open 10:30–9 daily. When too much fancy seafood overwhelms your senses and you long for a good old-fashioned burger (with, perhaps, fries and a milkshake), Teddy's seems like an oasis of normalcy. Lunch and dinner $.

Wailana Coffee House (808-955-1764), 1860 Ala Moana Blvd. Open 24/7/365. The coffeehouse draws an entertaining mix of folks—from late night post-karaoke participants and the budget-minded to those nursing hangovers and those with a hefty appetite. The coffeehouse dishes up strictly traditional diner fare; breakfast is served all day. I like the French toast made from Portuguese sweetbread. Dishes $–$$.

🦞 🐚 **Eggs 'n Things** (808-949-0820; eggsnthings.com), 1911-B Kalakaua Ave. Open 11 PM–2 PM daily. Yes, those

DUKE'S CANOE CLUB

hours are correct: Eggs 'n Things opens late, stays open throughout the night, and closes right after lunch. No matter when you patronize this landmark, a line will inevitably be snaking out the door—the food is that good. In addition to serving outrageously delicious omelets and pancakes, they're renowned for having some of Hawai'i's most efficient servers, all decked out in signature full-length aprons. Children's menu. Dishes $. No credit cards.

JUST SO YOU KNOW
Sunday Brunch on the Beach (808-923-1094; waikikiimprovement.com). Open (so to speak) 9–1:30 Sun. Heard of rolling out the red carpet? On Kalakaua Avenue, on the third Sunday of each month, the mayor's office rolls out the green carpet. Traffic is cordoned off, and buffets and tables are set up for brunch. Stroll along Kalakaua Avenue between the Moana

SUNDAY BRUNCH ON THE BEACH

Surfrider and the Hawaiian Regency, enjoy free entertainment, and sample (not free) food from upward of 14 hotel restaurant stations.

The easiest fast food is found at **International Marketplace Food Court** (808-971-02080; international markeplacewaikiki.com) at 2330 Kalakaua Ave. Open 10 AM–10:30 PM with live music in the early evenings.

✳ Entertainment
Strolling Waikiki Beach counts as big-time entertainment here. No wonder; it's magical. On Friday and Saturday evenings around dusk (say, 6:30) you'll find hula dancing and torch lighting in front of **Kuhio Beach Park** (Diamond Head end of Waikiki). Thanks to a program called **Sunset on the Beach** (808-923-1094), you can also watch free, first-run movies on a big screen set up on Queen's Beach. At the **Waikiki Shell amphitheater** (in Kapi'olani Park, bordered by Kalakaua and Montserrat Aves.), there are frequent evening and weekend music and dance concerts; check the newspapers. From boisterous dinner revues to mellow dinnertime sunset cruises, and high-energy dance clubs to quiet steel-guitar trios, this town has it all. In fact, every night could be a late night in Waikiki. Bar-hopping or clubbing (*holo-holo*) could very well be a sport here. Much of the entertainment takes place in hotel lounges (check with your hotel concierge), where you'll find solo ukelele strumming and big bands humming. On Friday night the **Hilton Hawaiian Village Beach Resort & Spa** (see *Lodging*) puts on fireworks for all to enjoy. Although packaged for visitors, many events produced at hotels evoke a bygone era surprisingly well.

AFTERNOON TEA

℣ **The Veranda** (808-921-4600; moana-surfrider.com), Moana Surfrider, 2365 Kalakaua Ave. Open for afternoon tea, 1–4 daily, with or without champagne. If you've always longed to experience Hawai'i at the turn of the 20th century (monarchal overthrow notwithstanding), head here for a refined tea—it's as close as it gets. Elegant servers bear china tea service, tiered plates of tiny sandwiches with the crusts cut off, and delectable sweets. Reservations recommended. Tea $$$–$$$.

ROMANTIC PLACES FOR COCKTAILS & HAWAIIAN MUSIC

All around Waikiki the lilting strains of Hawaiian music sail on sound waves as swiftly and surely as outrigger canoes glide across the azure seas.

℣ ☉ **House Without a Key** (808-923-2311; Halekulani Hotel) is utterly romantic, enchanting, and serene. Named for a Charlie Chan mystery in a time when houses were not locked, this almost open-air bar feels like Hawai'i of yesteryear. I never pass

HOUSE WITHOUT A KEY

through Honolulu without stopping here for one very strong mai tai. If you'd rather be outside, Halekulani Hotel offers classy beachfront entertainment (in the form of a steel-guitar combo) at sunset for the price of a drink. With the Pacific just steps away, Diamond Head in the distance, and a spot under the cover of a kiawe tree, you'll never want to leave.

℣ ☉ **Mai Tai Bar** (808-923-7311; Royal Hawaiian hotel), an outdoor beachfront bar that all visitors seem to experience at least once, is particularly pink at sunset. Even the beer is pink. There's often live entertainment.

BANYAN COURT AND THE VERANDA

Ψ **Banyan Court** (808-921-4600; Moana Surfrider) harks back to turn-of-the-20th-century Hawai'i, complete with live steel-slide guitar music (or the like). The evocative, nationally syndicated *Hawai'i Calls* radio program originated here and aired 1935–1975. In an effort to revive the flagging tourism industry during the Depression, it brought the aloha spirit of Hawai'i into the living rooms of mainlanders. Thus, the dreaming began. If you close your eyes and listen hard enough, you can almost still hear *Hawai'i Calls*. No wonder Robert Louis Stevenson loved to hang out here, under the protective arms of the sagelike banyan tree.

Ψ **Hau Tree Lanai** (aka **Sunset Lanai Lounge**) (808-921-7066; New Otani Kaimana Beach Hotel) is beachfront, quiet, and demure. It's a nice, slightly out-of-the-way place.

Ψ **Duke's Canoe Club** (808-922-2268; Outrigger Waikiki on the Beach) hosts popular contemporary Hawaiian concerts on the beach on weekends (4–6). Sunday always seems

DIAMOND HEAD GRILL

more crowded; there's no cover, and you don't have to buy anything on the lower lanai. At their **Barefoot Bar**, where it's always three deep at the bar, there's Hawaiian music nightly. It's a fun place, appealing to a middle-of-the-road crowd ranging in age from 20- to 50-somethings.

Ψ **Hanohano Room** (808-922-4422; Sheraton Waikiki). For stunning views of Waikiki's glittering skyline at dusk, head up to the 30th floor; romantic dancing heats up later in the evening. (Men need to wear collared shirts and long pants, women the equivalent.)

BARS & CLUBS

Ψ **Tiki's Grill & Bar** (808-923-8454; ResortQuest Beach Hotel), reviewed under *Eating Out,* appeals to groups (or singles) looking for outdoor fun with a capital *F.* It's almost like Duke's, just not on the beach.

Ψ **Wonderlounge at the W** (808-922-3734; w-dhg.com), W Honolulu Diamond Head, 2885 Kalakaua Ave. Hot and hip, this second-floor bar has the most "scenery" in Honolulu. Full of oh-so-beautiful young Honolulu professionals, the W has a tightly controlled guest list, but call and get your name on it to avoid the line and $15 cover charge. Then get ready to play the game of meeting, greeting, dancing, and drinking. I highly recommend the apple martinis. On Friday night it's six deep at the bar; no exaggeration. Although it's not very hip, you can get there before 9 PM to avoid the cover.

GAY HONOLULU

Ψ **Hula's Bar & Lei Stand** (808-923-0669; hulas.com), Waikiki Grand Hotel, 134 Kapahulu Ave. Open 10 AM–2 AM daily. Hawai'i's oldest gay bar is still a longtime favorite with the local and visiting gay community. It's a relaxed place with open-air seating overlooking Kapi'olani Park, Diamond Head, and the Pacific. By night the comfortable club (frequented by more men than women but welcoming to women nonetheless) also offers a terrific bar scene, where patrons mostly just hang out, enjoying the ambience and company. If you need more reasons to visit, consider the good drink specials, dancing, a pool table, go-go dancers, and myriad special events.

Fusion Waikiki (808-924-2422; gay hawaii.com/fusion), 2260 Kuhio Ave. Open 10 PM–4 AM daily. Look for female impersonators at this mixed club.

Angles Waikiki (808-926-9766; gay hawaii.com/angles), 2256 Kuhio Ave. Open 10 AM–2 AM daily. This mixed club is a relaxed bar by day (the open-air lanai overlooking the street is a nice feature) and a dance club by night.

In-Between (808-926-7060), 2155 Lau'ula St., behind Moose's. Open four PM–2 AM daily. In-Between is a small and intimate club with gay karaoke. It's mostly men, but women are welcome, too.

DINNER SHOWS & REVUES
If you want showroom diversions, Waikiki has them in abundance.

There are a number of other shows aimed at visitors (call for exact times and days) that you can attend with or without dinner. Prices below are for shows with one cocktail. Among them are: **Society of Seven** (1-800-404-3391; Outrigger Waikiki on the Beach; $38 adults, $24 ages 5–20), a dancing, singing, instrument-playing,

impersonating band of musicians that has been entertaining a revolving door of visitors since the early 1980s; **Creation: A Polynesian Journey** (808-931-4660; princess-kaiulani.com; Sheraton Princess Kaiulani; $45 adults and children), a kind of loose history of the settlement of the islands—complete with firedancing; **Magic of Polynesia** (808-971-4321; honuhawaii activities.com; Ohana Waikiki Beachcomber; $47 adults, $31 ages 4–11), full of sleights of hands and other illusions.

✳ Selective Shopping
Shopping in Waikiki is decidedly upscale and concentrated in malls and along Kalakaua Ave. All the designer boutiques in the world are represented here, and Japanese tourists, in particular, love to patronize them. At the other end of the spectrum, the ubiquitous **ABC** stores (of which there are upward of 40 in Waikiki alone) sell basic grocery items, suntan lotion, beach mats, and other sundries. I bet you'll enter one daily. **Long's**, rather than ABC, generally has better prices on Kona coffee and macadamia nuts.

CLOTHES
Bailey's Antiques and Aloha Shirts (808-734-7628; alohashirts.com), 517 Kapahulu Ave. For vintage aloha shirts (that can set you back as much as $600) and tasteful contemporary ones, too (more like $50). Open daily.

FARMER'S MARKET
Kapi'olani Community College Farmer's Market (hfbf.org/Farmers MarketKCC.html; park off Diamond Head Rd.). This lively place, Honolulu's only true farmer's market, boasts both the farmers and their goods.

A TWENTY FROM MR. TINY BUBBLES

Although icon Don Ho died in 2007, his spirit is so entwined with Waikiki that this essay remains timeless. If you long for the good old days, you can always pay your respects at Don Ho's Island Grill (808-528-0807; donho.com), 1 Aloha Tower Dr., Aloha Tower Marketplace. Open 10–10 daily. Serving contemporary Hawaiian cuisine amid a temple of nostalgic memorabilia. Dishes $$$–$$$.

My father and I went to Hawai'i to scatter, in a legal place, my mother's ashes and to enjoy, in a mostly legal fashion, the Don Ho concert.

My mother had died earlier that year, and my father and I took an opportunity to travel together to acclimate and remember Lu. We hiked Diamond Head, where we spread some of her ashes, and then, as if casting for an antidote, went to see the Don Ho show. Since my mother's passing, my quiet rebellions included ignoring signs like VIDEOTAPING OF DON HO CONCERT STRICTLY PROHIBITED. I was determined to videotape the show so my dad would have a memento of our *hegira*. After all, Don Ho is one of my father's favorite performers, and this would not only be a keepsake for us, but also a reminder of a trip some 12 years earlier in which he and my mother saw Don Ho together.

I was impressed by how accessible Hawai'i's musical ambassador was. When you walk into the celebrity photo-lined hall at the Ohana Waikiki Beachcomber, you're given a meet-'n'-greet photo opportunity that reveals an affable man who wears his 70-plus years well. His signature style and legendary stature conjure images of an Asian Elvis. An authentic performer, he has sincere appreciation for his fans.

My mother was the sort who got to know restaurant owners by name and would convince them her daughter should play their slightly out-of-tune Wurlitzer. My father, conversely, has always been a behind-the-scenes fellow, cheerfully and quietly waiting for the right moment for a witty one-liner so as not to take up much of your time. Suddenly, in Don Ho's presence, my mother was alive and well in the body of my father. "This is my daughter May-Lily; she plays the piano; she plays the guitar; she writes her own music; she blah blah blah . . ." I can't tell you what else could possibly have possessed my father, other than the spirit of my mother and the excitement of meeting Don Ho. "What kind of music?" Mr. Ho inquired.

"Folk rock," I coyly replied.

The concert was thoroughly enjoyable, like a musical sweeps week of my parents' generation. Think: hip Lawrence Welk in a Sino-Vegas lounge with the master of ceremonies working from a rattan-chaired podium alongside his loyal musical family. There were eclectic as well as treasured songs like "Ain't No Big Thing," "I'll Remember You," and "Tiny Bubbles." There was the Japanese country singer, Joe, playing mind-blowing banjo; there was Don Ho's engaging sidekick, Haumea, hula dancing gracefully; there was a cadre of other gifted island soloists. My father was entranced by the show, as was I. And all of this was captured on video. About midway through the concert, Don Ho announced: "May-Lily Lee, please come up to the stage." *Caught in the act! How embarrassing! Their technology is remarkable*, I thought. For a millisecond I was in a blind, maniacal panic wondering if I might have to turn in the camera. It wasn't until I saw my dad smiling like a knowing Buddha that I knew. As veteran audience members seem to know as well, Don Ho was making the casting call—inviting certain members of his audience to participate onstage. For his numerous shows, he calls on people to sing, share jokes, and more. He acknowledges anniversaries, birthdays, and honeymoons, and many concertgoers seem to know that this spirit of invitation is part of the experience. What a clever showman. *What a clever way to get me to stop recording.*

Shocked and elated, I nervously went onstage and sang, sounding like a slightly anemic Alison Krauss but belting out a song nonetheless, to my father's delight. In that rare moment I was one of the "stars." How *American Idol* to be onstage with Hawai'i's entertainment legend. I was even asked to tell a joke—which I did, poorly. I recall hearing only my father laugh.

The next night as my dad and I wandered around Honolulu, he asked, "Do you want to see Don Ho?" So we went again, and Don Ho's assistant immediately recognized us. I was startled that he called my father by name. I thought perhaps he called every Asian male *Mr. Lee* and got it right half the time. This time Don Ho asked me what else I could sing, and I offered up some Paul Simon. This time I was a *veteran*, meaning I sang with a bit more confidence than the night before. After the show Don Ho signed autographs and asked if I was a professional singer. I'm not. "You are now," he said, signaling for his assistant to get a $20 bill. He autographed it and gave me the signed $20. The solicitous, royal treatment we received from Don Ho and his staff, along with the cash, was unlike anything I'd experienced there or on any vacation. For my father and me, it was the highlight of our Hawai'i adventure. The experience made me feel only a little guilty for making the tape that my father has enjoyed on countless post-Hawaiian evenings. If Don Ho found out, I wonder if he would ask for his $20 back.

—May-Lily Lee

THE THRILL OF THE HUNT

For as consummate shopper as I am, the outdoor International Marketplace (see *Shopping Centers*) is a feast. It's probably a good idea to remember a landmark when entering because I wandered around in circles several times before I found my way out.

With the assistance of a young local who took me under his wing after watching me retrace my steps, I selected just the right T-shirts, an orchid cutting, and coral earrings as gifts. He made certain the black pearl necklace I bought was just right—bargaining with the vendor on my behalf. I learned all about black pearls from a "knowledgeable" woman selling the most beautiful ones in *her* stall; of course, there were several stalls selling pretty much the same thing. And I learned how to propagate native Hawaiian plants from the cuttings they were selling. Was I to believe that the coffee plants I saw grew from the little beans they were selling there? Vendors engaged me in discussions about who I was buying for, their likes, their ages, and how long would I be in Waikiki. Whatever their economic motivations for this interest, I found that the sounds of hawkers, the smells of wafting pork and pineapple, the riot of colors so typical of the island, and the textures of so many varied people left me happy to have experienced that teaming catacomb.

At the end of our walk-around, my "guide" smiled broadly, and it was obvious that he wished a "little something" for his efforts. We'd become quite friendly and by the end he pretty well knew me, my friends, and my family. What a good ambassador. However, caveat emptor to all.

—Martha Grant

Come for a variety of products, a hot breakfast, or scones and local coffee. Held 7:30 AM–11:00 AM on Saturday.

SHOPPING CENTERS

DFS Galleria (808-931-2700; dfs galleria.com), 330 Royal Hawaiian Ave. at Kalakaua Ave. As if shopping weren't enough of a distraction, this touristy emporium offers music and dance performances and houses a three-story replica of an old cruise ship—the kind that used to call in Honolulu port in the 1920s. As for shops, look for designer-happy boutiques and the largest cosmetics outlet in the state. Open until 11 PM daily.

Royal Hawaiian Shopping Center (808-922-2299; royalhawaiianshopping center.com), 2201 Kalakaua Ave. Not to be outdone by the Beach Walk shops and the general high-flying upgrade on Kalakaua Ave., that pantheon to commerce, the Royal Hawaiian has undergone a complete makeover. Stretching over three city blocks, this four-story center has more than 150 seriously upscale shops and offers cultural classes like lei making and ukulele lessons, free entertainment, and a nightclub/Polynesian review (Waikiki Nei) on the top floor. Open 10–10 daily (holiday and restaurant hours may vary).

International Marketplace (808-971-2080; internationalmarketplace waikiki.com), 2330 Kalakaua Ave. With over 130 little wooden stalls tucked under the protective outreach of an old banyan tree, this outdoor bazaar has lots of souvenirs (many imported from Southeast Asia). Open 10 AM–10:30 PM daily.

2100 Kalakaua (808-541-5136; 2100kalakaua.com), 2100 Kalakaua Ave. Modeled after a three-story town house, this newer complex contains world-renowned designer boutiques. Open 10–10 daily.

The Hilton Hawaiian Village Beach Resort & Spa and **Hyatt Regency** Waikiki have hundreds of shops on premises. Among the best is **Na Mea Hawaii** (808-949-3989; nativebookshawaii.com), which carries

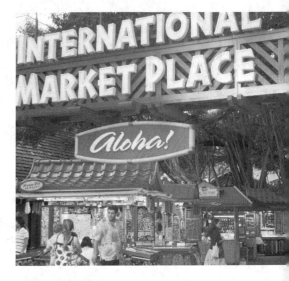

A WARREN OF OUTDOOR SHOPS

native Hawaiian books and crafts. It'll be well worth your time, I promise. Open 9–9 daily.

See also **Waikiki Beach Walk**, under *To See & Do*.

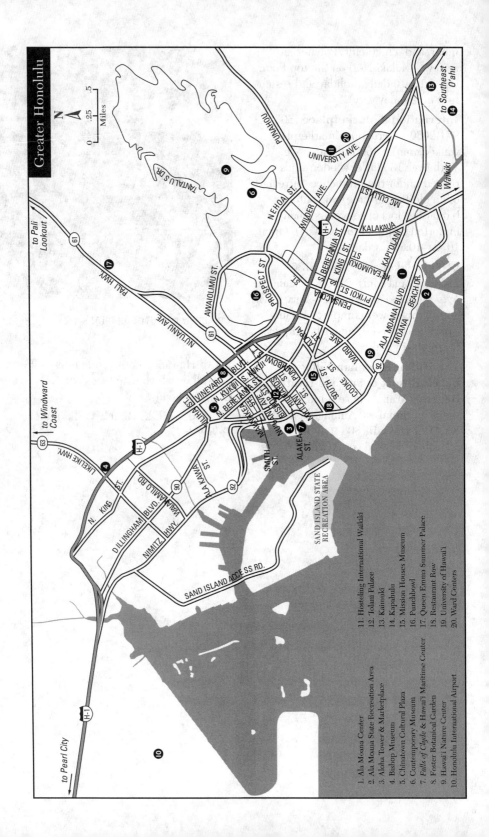

Greater Honolulu

N

0 .25 .5
Miles

to Pearl City

to Windward Coast

to Pali Lookout

H-1

LIKELIKE HWY.

PALI HWY.

NU'UANU AVE.

61

63

90

92

N. KING ST.

DILLINGHAM BLVD.

NIMITZ HWY.

WAIAKAMILO RD.

ALAKAWA ST.

SAND ISLAND ACCESS RD.

SAND ISLAND STATE RECREATION AREA

SMITH ST.

ALAKEA ST.

VINEYARD BLVD.

N. KUKUI ST.

N. BERETANIA ST.

ILIA ST.

NU'UANU AVE.

N. HOTEL ST.

PAUAHI ST.

MAUNAKEA ST.

PUNCHBOWL ST.

S. KING ST.

QUEEN ST.

HALEKAUWILA ST.

PENSACOLA ST.

WARD AVE.

COOKE ST.

SOUTH ST.

PIIKOI ST.

KEEAUMOKU ST.

PROSPECT ST.

AWAIOLIMU ST.

NEHOA ST.

TANTALUS DR.

PUNAHOU ST.

WILDER AVE.

MC CULLY ST.

KALAKAUA AVE.

KAPIOLANI BLVD.

S. BERETANIA ST.

ALA MOANA BLVD.

MOANA

BEACH DR.

UNIVERSITY AVE.

to Waikīkī

to Southeast O'ahu

92

17

61

4

5

6

7

8

9

11

12

13

14

15

16

18

19

20

1

2

3

10

1. Ala Moana Center
2. Ala Moana State Recreation Area
3. Aloha Tower & Marketplace
4. Bishop Museum
5. Chinatown Cultural Plaza
6. Contemporary Museum
7. Falls of Clyde & Hawai'i Maritime Center
8. Foster Botanical Garden
9. Hawai'i Nature Center
10. Honolulu International Airport
11. Hosteling International Waikīkī
12. Iolani Palace
13. Kaimukī
14. Kapahulu
15. Mission Houses Museum
16. Punchbowl
17. Queen Emma Summer Palace
18. Restaurant Row
19. University of Hawaii
20. Ward Centers

GREATER HONOLULU

Greater Honolulu keeps me busy for days with a wealth of first-rate cultural diversions, and it comes as a welcome relief from the packaged experiences in Waikiki. Downtown, the governmental and financial nexus, is chock-full of high-rises and business tycoons closing complex deals in aloha shirts. For mainlanders, it's a big-time disconnect. The compact and relatively quiet district is also home to missionary buildings and the only palace on American soil.

As for the waterfront, it's all too easy to turn your back on it since it's separated from downtown by the Nimitz Highway, but that would be a shame since so much of Honolulu's development was predicated on shipments arriving by sea. In the 1820s, dozens of ships fat from whaling anchored in the harbor. By the 1920s, cruise ships dispensed hundreds and hundreds of tourists who were greeted with leis and serenaded by the Royal Hawaiian Band.

Ala Moana Boulevard, which stretches along the harbor, offers prime shopping areas and a very good beach park. The farther west you go, the more industrial it becomes.

The 16-block Chinatown, perhaps more accurately called "Southeast Asiatown," is lively and bustling, especially on Saturday mornings. All your senses will come alive at the oldest Chinatown district in the United States. Shop for aromatic leis, enjoy inexpensive cuisine, or just drink in the sights. Visit an acupuncturist, herbal Chinese medicinal shop, or hole-in-the-wall bakery, or just watch the older men gather in the streets. But, do visit. It's always a highlight of my trip.

Manoa Valley, light years away in spirit from other neighborhoods in Honolulu, offers hiking trails, a great botanical garden, and rich university life. You'll probably be surprised at how green and verdant the area is, so close to downtown. The Punchbowl (and beyond) is similarly shocking in its views—it offers stunning vistas of Honolulu and Diamond Head. Make your way up.

Lastly, if I lived in Honolulu, I'd live in the very neighborhoody Kapahulu and Kaimuki, which offer nothing more to tourists than a wonderfully real glimpse of life in Honolulu. Have dinner or a coffee here at least once.

GETTING AROUND

By car: I prefer the autonomy and convenience of driving in Honolulu to The-Bus, but I'm probably in the minority. Whatever your preference, there are serious traffic problems on the H-1 before 9 AM and between 3 and 6 PM and on the Pali Hwy., which is crowded with commuters heading to and from Kailua. Honolulu, about 12 miles wide and 25 miles long, mostly stretches 'Ewa toward Leeward O'ahu since it's hemmed in by the sea, Ko'olau Mountain valleys, and Diamond Head. If you're exploring the neighborhoods of Kapahulu and Kaimuki (my favorites precisely because of their "neighborhoodness"), continue along Waialae Ave. to reach the Kahala Mall (see "Southeast O'ahu"), which seems like another world but isn't.

See also "O'ahu in Brief."

TOURS

By foot: ✪ Take a delightful two-hour walking tour of Chinatown with the **Chinese Chamber of Commerce** (808-533-3181; 76 N. King St.) on Mon. at 9:30 for $10, or with the **Hawai'i Heritage Center** (808-521-2749; 1168 Smith St.) on Wed. and Fri. at 9:30 for $5. Call for reservations. The **Hawai'i Geographic Society** (808-538-3952) offers expert two-hour treks of temples, archaeology, and more.

✳ To See & Do

✪ ✧ **Bishop Museum** (808-847-3511; bishopmuseum.org), 1525 Bernice St. Open 9–5 daily. Don't judge this extraordinary museum by its unassuming entrance. Only after you've found your way to the main gallery building, known as Hawaiian Hall, does this fine anthropological institute begin to reveal itself. Modernized by a major renovation in 2008 (that has enlivened Hawaiian history through diverse voices and an indigenous perspective), the Hawaiian Hall is still housed in a glorious 19th-century Victorian building with koa wood beams. The

THE HONOLULU SKYLINE, WITH DIAMOND HEAD IN THE BACKGROUND

museum's three distinctive tiers wrap around an open colonnaded interior, each one centered on one of the three real or mythical realms of Hawai'i: sea, land, and mountains. As you ascend the koa staircase you come closer and closer to modern-day Hawai'i.

The first level, Kai Akea, represents the watery regions of Hawai'i. It is the world of pre-Western contact; an isolated but tightly organized island society familiar with the land and the sea and used to battle. This is where visitors learn about the legends of Native Hawaiians and the pervasive and powerful presence of religion in ancient culture. The second floor, Wao Kanaka, displays artifacts from daily life and cultural traditions of Native Hawaiians. When taken as a whole, they reveal the hallowed place held by nature and the land. The journey ends in the realm of Wao Lani, where the visitor experiences the dynamism of contemporary Hawaiian culture and the resilience of the indigenous people and their traditions in the face of rapid change. Throughout, exhibits pulse with the chants and storytelling of Native Hawaiians, emphasizing the rich oral tradition of the native culture.

Despite the immense collection on display at the Bishop Museum, there is something personal about it. Charles Reed Bishop founded the museum in 1889 and dedicated it to his wife, Princess Bernice Pauahi Bishop, the last descendant of the royal Kamehameha family. Princess Pauahi loved hats, and her favorites are on display. She also intended that the museum augment the education of Native Hawaiian children and help develop their sense of heritage, and there are daily presentations of traditional Hawaiian culture that range from storytelling and quilting to lei making and hula dancing.

Try to visit the **planetarium** while you're there. Daily shows are at 11:30 AM, 1:30 PM, and 3:30 PM. The planetarium is noted for its portrayal of the skies according to ancient Polynesian star positions that guided the earliest Hawaiians across the Pacific. $16 adults, $13 ages 4–12.

Downtown

✪ **'Iolani Palace** (808-522-0832; iolanipalace.org), at S. King and Richard Sts. Open 8:30–4 Tues.–Sat.; guided, self-guided, and audio tours available. The only royal palace in the United States, 'Iolani was the focal point of events during Hawai'i's tumultuous 19th century. It was the residence of King Kalakaua and Queen Kapi'olani from 1882 to 1891 and of Queen Lili'uokalani for two years after that. It was in the ornate red and gold throne room that King Kalakaua indulged in one of his favorite pastimes—dancing the waltz and the polka. The palace was also the

BUILDING BLOCKS FOR A PERFECT DAY GREATER HONOLULU

Visit the Bishop Museum (4 hours)

Drive Tantalus Drive and Round Top Drive (90 minutes)

Tour the 'Iolani Palace (90 minutes)

Take a walking tour of Chinatown and buy a lei (90 minutes)

Take a walking tour of downtown (90 minutes)

Hike the Manoa Falls Trail (1 hour)

Sample Malasadas (15 minutes)

'IOLANI PALACE

sad scene, following the overthrow of the Hawaiian monarchy, of Queen Lili'uokalani's nine-month confinement to her own home after she was convicted of treason for opposing the takeover.

The palace later housed the capital of the republic, territory, and state of Hawai'i until 1969. In 1978, restored to its royal splendor, the palace reopened as the museum of today. The ticket window and gift shop are located in the former barracks of the Royal Household Guard. Also on the premises, the domed pavilion was built for the coronation of King Kalakaua (1853) and is the pleasant setting for Friday afternoon concerts by the Royal Hawaiian Band. A grassy mound surrounded by a wrought-iron fence marks the former graves of King Kamehameha II and Queen Kamamalu. It seems only fitting that the banyan tree between the palace and capitol was planted by Queen Kapi'olani. The grounds, by the way, are free and open to the public. Prices vary by tour; children under age 5 not permitted on the docent-guided Grand Tour.

Hawai'i State Art Museum (808-586-0900), 250 S. Hotel St. Open 10–4 Tues.–Sat. This museum (nicknamed HISAM) opened in 2002, a splendid addition to the city's several outstanding museums. Built in 1928 on the site of the original Royal Hawaiian hotel (O'ahu's first hotel), this Spanish mission–style gem sits just opposite 'Iolani Palace. The downtown museum is dedicated solely to Hawai'i's diverse artistic and cultural heritage and features a wide variety of artistic styles, from fine art and sculpture to photography and mixed media. Western and Asian art forms, along with traditional folk art of Hawai'i, are represented here. Free.

State Capitol (808-586-0178), 415 Beretania St. Open 7:45–4:30 weekdays. Built shortly after Hawai'i became the 50th state in 1959, the capitol's design is intended to mirror island themes, with legislative chambers shaped like volcanoes, palm-tree columns, a rotunda open to trade winds, and a large reflecting pool surrounding the building. It doesn't work for everybody, but visitors are free to walk through the rotunda and peer into the legislative chambers. In front of the capitol stands a statue of Father Damien, who worked selflessly with the lepers of Moloka'i and died

PLAQUE DETAIL AT 'IOLANI PALACE

HAWAIIAN QUILTS

Quilting, first taught to the Hawaiian royals by missionaries in the early 1800s, has played an integral part in preserving the history of the Hawaiian people. When first introduced to the art form, the Hawaiians thought it seemed silly to cut up pieces of cloth and resew them. (They were taught from a very early age not to waste anything.) So they created quilts out of one cut piece of cloth and sewed it to a background usually made of white muslin.

Bearing the names of flowers, famous Hawaiians, dead relatives, and gods, the quilts took their themes from everyday life. No quilt was made simply to pass the time; quilts were made for a purpose. The breadfruit 'ulu pattern, for instance, is said to bring prosperity to its maker. Quilt making often carried mystical meaning. Many quilts have a center opening, or puka, which may have been integrated into the design so Spirit would not become trapped. Quilts were often buried with their maker to reunite Spirit.

The Hawaiian Quilt Research Project spearheaded a formidable movement to preserve historical patterns and exhibit old quilts for educational purposes.

of the disease 16 years later at the age of 49. The sculpture, created by Venezuelan Marisol Escobar, stands across the street from the **eternal torch** dedicated to veterans of World War II.

Honolulu Hale (City Hall), 530 S. King St. Designed to resemble a Spanish mission, the 1927 building is set around an open courtyard with a red-tiled roof, ornate balconies, decorative frescoes, and arches and pillars completing the theme. The open-air courtyard is ideal for the frequent concerts and art exhibits hosted by the city. An eternal flame on the front lawn memorializes the victims of the September 11, 2001, attack on the World Trade Towers in New York City.

Washington Place (aka **Governor's Mansion**), 320 S. Beretania St., opposite the State Capitol. This colonial Greek Revival mansion was named for the first president of the United States and built for a clipper-ship captain, John Dominis, in 1846. Today, it serves as the governor's residence. Its best-known resident, however, was Queen Lili'uokalani, who lived here from the overthrow of the monarchy until her death in 1917. A plaque with the words to "Aloha O'e," the Hawaiian anthem she composed, stands near the house.

King Kamehameha statue, 957 Punchbowl St. The statue of the "great King" stands in front of Ali'iolani Hale (see below). Kamehameha's statue was cast of Florentine bronze in 1883, and every year it is draped with enormous (12-foot) leis on June 11, King Kamehameha Day, a designated statewide holiday.

Ali'iolani Hale (808-539-4994; jchhawaii.topcities.com), 417 S. King St. Open 9–4 weekdays. The name means "the house of the heavenly chiefs," and this Renaissance Revival building was originally designed as a grand palace but was later altered to house governmental offices. It remains the oldest government building in Honolulu, currently home to the Hawai'i Supreme Court. Built by the Hawaiian monarchy in 1874, ironically it was the very place where the monarchy's end was announced in 1893 by Sanford Dole. Free.

Kawaiaha'o Church (808-522-1333), 957 Punchbowl St. Open 8–4 weekdays. O'ahu's oldest church, first built of grass and thatch, was replaced in 1842 by the present New England Gothic church and was originally used only by Hawaiian royalty. The building consists of 14,000 coral blocks cut from Hawai'i's precious reef. Each slab, weighing in at 1,000 pounds, was ferried to shore by canoe. The tomb of King Lunalilo is at the main entrance, while in the rear early

KING KAMEHAMEHA & ALI'IOLANI HALE

KAWAIAHA'O CHURCH

missionaries are buried along with business tycoons like Sanford Dole, who overthrew the monarchy and became the first governor of the state. Donations accepted.

Mission Houses Museum (808-531-0481; missionhouses.org), 553 S. King St. Open 10–4 Tues.–Sat. The three original buildings of the Sandwich Islands Mission headquarters (Frame House, Chamberlain House, and Printing House) together make up this museum. The timbers for the Frame House, the oldest wooden building in Hawai'i (1821), were cut and fitted in Boston, then hauled around Cape Horn by the first missionaries. Its narrow windows, which had resisted the cold wind of New England's winters so well, blocked out Hawai'i's cooling trade winds, making for many a hot and airless night. Chamberlain House is made from blocks of offshore coral, considered expendable in the mission days. In the third building, early missionaries printed Hawaiian-language Bibles used in converting Hawaiians to Christianity. $10 adults, $8 seniors, $6 ages 6–18.

Foster Botanical Garden (808-522-7066; honolulu.gov), 50 N. Vineyard Blvd. Open 9–4 daily; guided tours Mon.–Sat. at 1 PM (reservations strongly recommended). Starting with a five-acre purchase from Queen Kalama in 1850, German botanist William Hillebrand began planting native trees near downtown Honolulu. Later Captain Thomas Foster bought the land and continued the planting. His widow, Mary Foster, left the garden to the people of Hawai'i, and in 1931 the garden as we know it today opened to the public. Some plants here could be star candidates in a science-fiction fantasy. Look for such exotics as the cannonball and sausage trees, Amazon cigar box tree, New Zealand kauri

MISSION HOUSES MUSEUM

KAPA

The making of *kapa*, or cloth from bark, is a cherished Hawaiian legacy and one kept alive by Na Hoa Hoala Kapa (friends of the reawakening of *kapa*). Primarily used for sleeping coverings and clothing, *kapa* was made from various plants, including *'akala* (endemic raspberry), *'ulu* (breadfruit), and *wauke* (paper mulberry). Specifically cultivated for *kapa*, *wauke*'s inner bark was soaked until it softened into a pliable pulp, then beaten several times, hung to dry, and stored until needed, at which point it was soaked again, beaten, and felted into rectangular pieces. Traditional colors for *kapa*—red, yellow, black, and various shades of blue-green—came from dyes made from charcoal, ochers, and other plant parts.

Kapa of the 18th century is relatively thick and sometimes displays a ribbed design, which was achieved by forcing the dampened cloth into grooves with a carved wooden instrument. These grooves provided an elastic quality, good for loincloths (*malo*) or other tight garments. The designs were based on combinations of linear elements, which made for bold patterns filled with triangles, squares, and short wavy lines. Kapa from the 19th century was thinner and finer in texture, decorated with "watermarks" pressed into the material during the second beating. The motifs were often achieved by stamps carved on the inside end of bamboo strips (*'ohe kapala*).

The Bishop Museum has an extraordinary and extensive collection of *kapa*.

tree, and Egyptian doum palm. Nutmeg, allspice, cinnamon, a huge black pepper plant, and other herbs all thrive in this botanical masterpiece. The beautiful 13-acre tropical garden is a short walk from Chinatown. $5 adults, $1 ages 6–12.

Along Ala Moana Blvd.

Ala Moana Center, Ala Moana Blvd., opposite Ala Moana Beach Park. Hawai'i's biggest shopping center (see *Selective Shopping*) is also home to airline offices, a small post office, two banks and several ATMs, a mini supermarket, and a huge food court with plate-lunch specials. Almost daily the Centerstage courtyard hosts free events of all kinds—from hula dancers and gospel singers to garage bands and ballet performances. Ala Moana Center is also Honolulu's main bus transfer point; you can catch a bus here to almost anywhere on O'ahu. Schedules are available near the main bus stop.

ʄ **Ala Moana Beach Park**. See *Beaches*.

Ala Moana State Recreation Area, Ala Moana Blvd., on the Waikiki side of Ala Moana Beach Park. Known locally as Magic Island, this is one of the nicest parts of the mile-long Ala Moana Beach Park. It's not an island at all, just a shaded grassy peninsula with everything you need for a day at the beach. High school outrigger canoe teams often practice in the late afternoon during the school year. You can walk around the perimeter of Magic Island and watch the boats sail in and out of the adjoining Ala Wai Yacht Harbor.

Ward Entertainment Center, Ward Warehouse, and Ward Center, 1200 Ala Moana Blvd. (between Ward Ave. and Pi'ikoi St.). Opposite the western end of Ala Moana Beach Park, you'll find a series of shops and restaurants and a movie theater. They are all part the Ward complex, beginning with the original Ward Warehouse shopping center (at Ward Ave. and A'uahi St.). Continuing east, Ward Center is the newest section of shops and restaurants and features valet parking for $4. You can park once, walk to any number of nearby shops and restaurants, then hop across the street to catch a movie at Ward Entertainment Center.

Hawai'i Coffee Company (808-843-4202; hicoffeeco.com), 1555 Kalani St. Open for tours 9–11 and 1:30–3:30 Tues.–Fri. Reservations required; six-person minimum; no children under 12. Speaking from personal experience, I can say that coffee junkies will enjoy this fun diversion: Tour the processing plant of the world's largest buyer and roaster of Kona coffee. Once a week the makers of Royal Kona and Lion coffee fling their doors open to share how they roast millions of pounds of coffee daily. Among other things, you'll see colorful historical paraphernalia dating to the 1880s, quality-control labs, and blending

HAWAI'I COFFEE COMPANY

machines. The best part, of course, is sampling half a dozen different types of coffee.

Restaurant Row, 500 Ala Moana Blvd. This complex of shops, restaurants, theaters, and nightclubs is a popular place to eat, especially for the downtown lunch crowd. But at night it livens up as moviegoers catch a film at the nine-theater multiplex.

Aloha Tower & Marketplace, Pier 9, at Bishop St. Built in 1926 at the edge of downtown, the 10-story Aloha Tower is a Honolulu landmark and symbol of old Hawai'i—check out the world depicted by the murals in the terminal. It was built in 1926, an icon of territorial Hawai'i and the first Honolulu building visible when approaching Honolulu by sea. The city's tallest building for years, it still offers a 360-degree view of Honolulu and the harbor from the observation deck. In the days when everyone arrived on ships, the four-sided clock tower's inscription ALOHA greeted every visitor. Today's cruise ships still disembark beneath it. Beneath the tower is the marketplace, with boutique shopping and several excellent restaurants, most of them with outdoor tables overlooking Honolulu Harbor.

Hawai'i Maritime Center (808-536-6373; bishopmuseum.org), Pier 7, Honolulu Harbor. Open 9–5 daily. Near the Aloha Tower, the museum covers everything from the arrival of Captain Cook to modern-day windsurfing. Displays on early tourism include a reproduction of a Matson liner stateroom and photos of Waikiki when only the Royal Hawaiian and the Moana hotels broke the skyline. The center is home to the 266-foot ***Falls of Clyde***, the world's last four-masted, four-rigger sailing ship. Built in 1878 in Glasgow, the *Falls* began carrying sugar, passengers, and then oil between Hilo and San Francisco in the 19th century, before she became a barge. Finally, just as she was to become a sunken breakwater off Vancouver, B.C., a Hawaiian group came to the rescue. Admission to the center includes a tour of the *Falls*. $7.50 adults, $4.50 ages 4–12.

Hokulea, nearby, is a replica of the outrigger sailing canoes used by the earliest seagoing Polynesian explorers who navigated their way to the Hawaiian Islands. If you're lucky enough to find it in port, you'll understand why it's such a source of pride to modern Hawai'i.

Honolulu Harbor, opposite downtown. The history of Honolulu Harbor is essentially the history of modern Hawai'i, at least since 1850, when Kamehameha III designated it the chief port of call for the Kingdom of Hawai'i. Trans-Pacific trade followed, and the whaling industry thrived—at least temporarily. Christian missionaries found Hawai'i at roughly the same time as the whalers and made life so unpleasant for the brothel and bar owners of Honolulu that the whaling captains soon discovered a port more welcoming to their thirsty crews— Lahaina on Maui.

THE *FALLS OF CLYDE* AT PORT 9

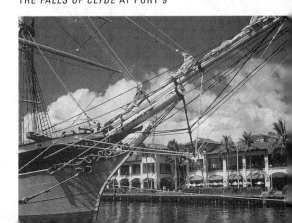

Sand Island State Recreation Area, Sand Island Access Rd. off Nimitz Hwy. (Hwy. 92), at the western end of Honolulu Harbor. Sand Island State Recreation Area is a popular local coastal park with camping and picnicking facilities, restrooms, and showers. With a boat ramp nearby, it has almost everything. Speaking of which, Sand Island also lies in the flight path of Honolulu International Airport, so it's great for plane-spotting, as well as watching big freighters and tankers come and go.

Chinatown

Hotel Street, between Nu'uanu Ave. and River St. Strolling along Chinatown's Hotel Street amounts to a walking historical tour of the last 120 years. This is where seamen and missionaries once competed for bodies and souls, and where today flower lei shops, noodle factories, and a variety of ethnic restaurants serve the entire community of Honolulu.

Yat Tung Chow Noodle Factory, 150 N. King St. The most famous of several working Chinatown noodle factories, each with its own character, Yat Tung Chow is a fast-paced operation marked by clouds of white flour that hang in the air and by the sweat on the workers' brows! There are no tours as such, but you can walk in and have a peek at the variety of noodle shapes that emerge from mechanical rollers.

O'ahu Market, corner of N. King St. and Keka'ulike St. Honolulu chefs head to this landmark each morning for fresh fish displayed in small buckets or boxes of ice. You can tell how fresh most fish is by the clearness of the eyes. (I always feel like I'm being watched here.) The fresh produce is less threatening (there are no potatoes with eyes), and the entire market bustles with energy.

River Street Pedestrian Mall, between N. Beretania St. and Kukui St. This low-key extension of River Street borders Nu'uanu Stream and marks the northwest edge of Chinatown. At the corner of North Beretania Street, a bronze statue of Dr. Sun Yat-sen honors the Chinese revolutionary leader. Farther along, several stone benches near the open-front Royal Kitchen are filled with local seniors gazing intently at mah-jongg and checkerboards. Between moves the old-timers may also be munching on a baked *mana-pua*—originally a northern Chinese pork bun, but these days it could be filled with anything from *kalua* pig to cinnamon apples.

MAUNAKEA STREET

Chinatown Cultural Plaza, between the Pedestrian Mall and Maunakea St., and N. Beretania St. and Kukui St. A little off the beaten path, this plaza has a relaxed ambience, perhaps because it's far less crowded than other Chinatown centers. There are a few excellent restaurants here, mostly frequented by knowing locals. Besides the popular Royal Kitchen (808-524-4461, Legend Seafood Restaurant (808-532-1868) and Legend Vegetarian (808-532-8218) are both worth a hunger detour.) On weekends you'll often find cultural performances on the plaza's small central stage.

Izumo Taisha Mission, corner of Kukui St. and College Walk. Just opposite the Cultural Plaza, this traditional Japanese shrine makes for a peaceful detour. Visitors are welcome, and you might begin at the small fountain near the entrance, where a delicate bamboo ladle is used for washing hands before proceeding. A

CHINATOWN

100-pound sack of rice inside the open shrine symbolizes good health. Outside, look for the peace bell, which Japanese schoolchildren from the sister city of Hiroshima visit each year to decorate with origami in a gesture to promote world peace.

Kuan Yin Temple (808-533-6361), Vineyard Blvd., at the entrance to Foster Botanical Garden (see under *Downtown*). You can't miss this bright red-and-green Buddhist temple, but the inside is far different. Walk up the interior stairs to the first landing, where you'll find a peaceful worship area awash in burning incense. Dedicated to the Kuan Yin Bodhisattva, goddess of mercy, the altar is usually adorned with fresh flowers and mounds of fruit. The large coils of incense are said to be a sort of calendar, each one taking exactly one week to completely burn.

Maunakea Street. This street, especially the two blocks between North King and Pauahi Streets, is the heart of Chinatown, anchored by the templelike Wo Fat Restaurant (which claims to be the oldest restaurant in Honolulu and dates to 1882). The lively thoroughfare is packed with small shops, Chinese bakeries, and Honolulu's most popular lei shops, where you're welcome to watch the lei makers weave and thread blossom after blossom. You can peek inside a Chinese herbal medicine shop or admire the red-glazed ducks hanging in the window at the butcher shop next door. The **Maunakea Marketplace** (808-524-3409; 1120 Maunakea St.) rivals the O'ahu Market for lively shopping, with everything from fresh fish and poultry to produce and imported dry goods. There's even a food court featuring every ethnic group in town—including Korean, Japanese, Filipino, Portuguese, Vietnamese, Thai, and even Chinese.

Nu'uanu Avenue, between N. King St. and Pauahi St. Nu'uanu Avenue is where Chinatown and downtown Honolulu merge, and it's a bit of both. On the downtown side is Indigo (see *Dining Out* and *Entertainment*), an upscale bar and restaurant that spills outside to a rambling street-side courtyard. On the Chinatown side is Hank's (808-526-1410; hankscafehonolulu.com; 1038 Nu'uanu Ave.), a sweet and cozy neighborhood bar with live music and open-mic nights. Nu'uanu Avenue is home to a growing gallery scene, which peaks on First Fridays (of each month), when locals arrive after work to take in the art and munch on free *pupus* and appetizers.

Hawai'i Theatre (808-528-0506 for changing tour times), 1130 Bethel St. All the elegance of territorial Hawai'i is on display at this neoclassical landmark between Chinatown and downtown. The city recently restored it to its former glory when it was hailed "the pride of the Pacific." Set in a beautifully restored historic building, it now serves as a center for the performing arts and cultural activities in Honolulu. Weekly tours are conducted.

Manoa Valley

Manoa Valley is Honolulu's hidden gem, home to the University of Hawai'i and only minutes from Waikiki by car or bus. The university area is full of small restaurants, a movie theater, and bookstores. But as you head toward the back of the valley, a small residential rain forest gives way to hiking trails that lead to waterfalls and panoramic views of the nearby city below.

University of Hawai'i (808-956-8111; uhm.hawaii.edu), University Ave. and Dole St. The central campus of the state's university system is home to over 20,000 students from both Hawai'i and the U.S. mainland, as well as around the Pacific Rim. In particular, students are drawn to strong academic programs in the marine sciences, astronomy, and language studies, among others. The school supports a healthy music and arts program, with frequent concerts and stage performances. As a bonus, frequent rainbows pop up with passing showers at the back of Manoa Valley.

Lyon Arboretum (808-988-0456; hawaii.edu/lyonarboretum), 3860 Manoa Rd. Open 9–4 weekdays; self-guided tours available. Lyon Arboretum maintains a place of honor among the Pacific's horticultural gardens. Along with rare species of palms, it is home to an herb and ethnobotanical garden. But the real pleasure here is in wandering along the paths of flowering ginger, exotic bromeliads, and hibiscus. For the most part, plants are in their natural settings and landscaping is minimal so you get a real sense of this tropical rain forest. The arboretum is also near the trailhead to Manoa Falls (see under *Hiking*). Donations requested.

Punchbowl & Beyond

Honolulu is spread out along a winding ribbon of land between the airport and Diamond Head. Within that official boundary, you'll find Pearl Harbor, the University of Hawai'i, the Bishop Museum, Makiki Heights, and Punchbowl, the popular name for the shallow crater that is home to the National Cemetery of the Pacific.

National Cemetery of the Pacific (aka **Punchbowl Crater**) (808-532-3720), Punchbowl Crater, 2177 Pu'owaina Dr. Open 8–6:30 daily. This extinct volcanic crater, once known as Pu'owaina (hill of sacrifice), was the place where King Kamehameha first battled O'ahu's warriors when he began his quest to unite the

Hawaiian Islands. Today the peaceful crater is the final resting place of over 30,000 servicemen and servicewomen from four wars, along with Ellison Onizuka, the Hawaiian-born astronaut who perished in the 1986 space shuttle disaster, and Ernie Pyle, the most famous war reporter of his day, who was killed while covering the last days of World War II. Free.

NATIONAL CEMETERY

✪ **Tantalus Drive** and **Round Top Drive**. Tantalus Drive is accessible from the west via Puʻowaina Drive, near Punchbowl. Round Top Drive is accessible from the east via Keʻeaumoku Street and Makiki Street. Toward the top of Mount Tantalus (2,013 feet), a looping 8-mile road offers some of the finest views in all of Hawaiʻi. Tantalus Drive is the name for the western side of the loop, and Round Top Drive is the loop's eastern side. Enticing you to stop now and then to soak up the views (or passing showers), the drive generally takes about two hours. The road is narrow but in excellent condition, and there is little traffic aside from a few local residents and backpackers on their way to one of several area trailheads. Along the way you'll pass dense forests of bamboo and eucalyptus fringed with elephant-ear taro and colorful ginger, often in misty clouds resembling a delicate Japanese or Chinese ink painting. Guides from the **Hawaiʻi Nature Center** (808-955-0100) lead walking tours into the forest on weekends.

Contemporary Museum (808-526-0232; tcmhi.org), 2411 Makiki Heights Dr. Open 10–4 Tues.–Sat., noon–4 Sun.; tours at 1:30. There are several reasons to visit this outstanding museum in the hills high above Honolulu. Start with the international collection of modern painting and sculpture, including an installation by David Hockney. While wandering around the galleries and grounds, stop for lunch at the excellent courtyard **Contemporary Café** (808-523-3362). On my last visit, lunch was accompanied by a classical guitarist. Finally, stroll through the terraced gardens; a narrow path leads to a lookout with panoramic views of Honolulu below. You may have to slap a few mosquitoes, though, if you linger too long! $5 adults, $3 seniors, free for ages 12 and under; free on the third Thurs. of each month.

✪ **Honolulu Academy of Arts** (808-532-8700; honoluluacademy.org), 900 S. Beretania St. Open 10–4:30 Tues.–Sat., 1–5 Sun.; tours of the different wings given most days at 10:15 AM, 11:30 AM, and 1 PM. Honolulu is rich with museums, but the academy is my personal favorite. As soon as you enter the building you find yourself outside again! The architecture of this 1927 masterpiece is elegant and inviting, with over 30 small galleries that seem to weave in and out of six garden courtyards, shaded corridors, and delicate lily ponds. There are excellent Asian, European, Hawaiian, and Oceania collections. You'll find peaceful Buddhas and modernist sculptures, classical Chinese paintings, Chagalls and Monets, and a superb collection of Japanese ukiyo-e prints in the small James Michener gallery. A recent addition to the museum, Shangri La is located about 15 minutes away and requires advance reservations. Beginning in the 1930s, **Shangri La** was the Diamond Head home of Doris Duke, a wealthy philanthropist who assembled one of the finest collections of Islamic art in the world today. The central garden is patterned after the Shalimar Garden of 17th-century Pakistan, a study in symmetry and grace. It's well worth a visit, although at the museum you can catch a video glimpse of the collection. The Academy also has a fine lunchtime restaurant, the **Pavilion Café** (808-532-8734), with lovely lanai seating. Try the signature flatbread Piadina sandwich. $10 adults, $5 seniors, free for ages 12 and under; free on the first Wed. of every month.

Pu'u Ualaka'a State Park. See *Hiking*.

Kapahulu & Kaimuki

Kapahulu Avenue (just "Diamond Head" or east of Waikiki) and nearby Kaimuki's **Waialae Avenue** form two of the most appealing commercial neighborhoods in all of Honolulu. The Kapahulu area in particular is a midrange restaurant row, with choices ranging from Egyptian to Hawaiian. A few blocks away, Waialae Avenue is more of a mixed commercial district, but as you approach 12th Avenue the hardware stores and barbershops give way to several popular Japanese, Italian, Korean, and Vietnamese eateries, along with a couple of good diners, Internet cafés, and bakeries. If I lived in Honolulu, this neighborhood would be my home.

See also **Nu'uanu Pali Highway & Lookout**, **Nu'uanu Valley Rain Forest**, and **Queen Emma Summer Palace** in "The Windward Coast." **Diamond Head** and **Kahala** are covered in "Southeast O'ahu"; for **Pearl Harbor**, see "Central & Leeward O'ahu."

✳ Outdoor Activities

BOATING

Navatek I (808-973-1311; atlantisadventures.com/oahu.cfm), Pier 6, Aloha Tower Marketplace. Why is it that people who are normally not water people always end up taking boat trips when they come to places like Waikiki? Because experiencing Waikiki and Diamond Head from the water is a remarkably fresh perspective on the destination. You won't regret it. And there's no need for seasickness pills on this vessel—Navatek guarantees it. Take a sunset dinner cruise or a lunchtime cruise (the best value). Dinner cruises from $72 adults, $48 children ages 2–12 (for a few dollars more get a window seat upgrade); lunch cruises $55 adults, $28 children.

HIKING

✪ **Manoa Falls Trail** (808-587-0300; hawaiitrails.org). This trail, at the end of Manoa Road, is one of the most accessible and popular on O'ahu. Less than 1 mile each way, it's so popular that tourists think nothing of making a quick detour here on a hot day—perhaps outfitted in their Waikiki finery, perhaps with flip-flops on their tender feet. This would be a big mistake. Although the trail is relatively short and extremely scenic, it's also part of a rain forest. Therefore, it's extremely damp and slippery. At the least you'll need good walking sandals that won't fly off or break the first time you catch your foot on a tree root. The trail is usually classified as easy, but that can be misleading. Along the way you'll encounter moss-covered boulders, Tarzan-worthy hanging vines, and the sweet melodies of songbirds, creaking eucalyptus trees, and gurgling streams. When you reach the 100-foot falls, think twice before jumping into the tempting pool to cool off. People do it, but if you read the warning signs nearby you'll learn that leptospirosis, an infectious disease that affects the liver and kidneys, lurks in many mountain streams and pools.

Pu'u Ualaka'a State Park (808-587-0300). The entrance to this state park is about 2.5 miles up Round Top Drive from Makiki Street. It's another 0.5 mile to a lookout that provides stunning views of Diamond Head, Waikiki, downtown Honolulu, Pearl Harbor, and even the Waianae Range on O'ahu's Leeward Coast. Closer in, you'll see Punchbowl Crater and the University of Hawai'i. My favorite time here is just before sunset, when the breeze and the birds put the flickering city lights below in proper perspective. It's arguably the best place to catch a Honolulu sunset.

See also **Tantalus Drive** and **Round Top Drive** under *To See & Do* for weekend tours by the Hawai'i Nature Center.

SAILING
Honolulu Sailing Co. (808-239-3900 or 1-800-829-0114; honsail.com), Honolulu Harbor. Trips daily. This well-established company takes folks on snorkeling,

---

TOP SIX PLACES TO STAY BEYOND WAIKIKI

Best Romantic Hideaways
Kahala Hotel & Resort (Southeast O'ahu)
'Ihilani Resort & Spa (Central & Leeward O'ahu)
Turtle Bay Resort (The North Shore)

Most Worldly Resorts
Kahala Hotel & Resort (Southeast O'ahu)
'Ihilani Resort & Spa (Central & Leeward O'ahu)

Best B&Bs and Cottages
Santa's (The North Shore)
Ke Iki Beach Bungalows (The North Shore)

Best Family Resorts
'Ihilani Resort & Spa (Central & Leeward O'ahu)
Kahala Hotel & Resort (Southeast O'ahu)
Marriott Ko Olina Beach Vacation Club (Central & Leeward O'ahu)

picnicking, and whale-watching trips. Full-day cruises are $150 for adults, $75 ages 12 and under; half-day cruises are half price.

☀ Beaches

✂ ⨍ **Ala Moana Beach Park**, Ala Moana Blvd., opposite Ala Moana Center. This very family-friendly, 76-acre beach park is safe, beautiful, and easy to get to. Its combination of sand, grass, shade, and showers is also hard to match. The mile-long beach park borders busy Ala Moana Boulevard, but it still has somewhat of a rural feel to it—it's spread out, dotted with shade trees and picnic tables. The beach itself is protected by a coral reef, so swimming is usually gentle and the water good for wading. The park is also a favorite late-afternoon stop-off for joggers and long-distance swimmers, who usually begin at the eastern end of the park's little peninsula, known locally as Magic Island. It's just opposite the Ala Wai Yacht Harbor, where outrigger canoe clubs come to practice. *Facilities*: Free parking, lifeguards, restrooms, showers, picnic tables.

☀ Lodging

Ala Moana Hotel (808-955-4811 or 1-800-367-6025; alamoanahotel.com), 410 Atkinson Dr. This 36-floor behemoth attached to the even bigger Ala Moana Center got a little cozier (if I can say that) when it was converted into a "condo-tel" in 2006. Because it's so close to the convention center, too, it's often used by groups, but individual travelers might find it appealing because of great Internet rates. Many of the rooms feel more like small apartments, and rooms on upper floors have great views of the city and Waikiki. There's a nice "recreation deck" with a pool, studios for yoga classes, and a fitness center. *Rates*: $$–$$$$; children free in parent's room. *Facilities and amenities*: 1,100 rooms and suites, pool, four restaurants, fitness center, concierge, water sport rentals, Internet access in rooms (free), parking (fee).

Manoa Valley Inn (808-947-6019; manoavalleyinn.com), 2001 Vancouver Dr. At press time, this property was for sale, and I can only hope that the future owners have the cash needed to bring this fantastic place back up to snuff. Having said that, in its heyday, and on its better days, it's intimate and elegant with a Victorian country style. Just 2 miles from Waikiki and downtown, it feels centuries from either. On the National Register of Historic Places, this 1915 home was saved from the bulldozer in 1978 by Rick Ralston, owner of the ubiquitous Crazy Shirts, Inc. His careful and expensive renovation included the restoration (or duplication by local artisans) of 32 different types of molding, wainscoting, and other decorative elements. The guest rooms and cottage vary in size and furnishings, but you can count on antiques, four-poster or iron beds, and historically accurate fixtures. Guests tend to linger over a continental breakfast on the shady, wicker-furnished lanai that overlooks the Honolulu skyline across a tropical garden. *Rates*: $$. *Facilities and amenities*: Eight rooms (some with a shared bath), expanded continental breakfast.

Camping is permitted Fri.–Sun. at **Sand Island State Recreation Area** (808-587-0300). Permit required; $5 nightly; gates locked 6:45 PM–7 AM.

✳ Where to Eat

With the exception of San Francisco and New York, you are unlikely to find as dense a cluster of fine dining anywhere in the United States as in Honolulu. Get beyond Waikiki for a real taste of Hawai'i regional cuisine and food as art (on South King Street), traditional and healthy plate lunches, Chinatown holes-in-the-wall, sublime sushi, trendy wine bars, and neighborhood bistros in Kapahulu and Kaimuki. The waterfront area (see *Chinatown, Restaurant Row, Aloha Tower & Marketplace, and Nearby*) has outstanding choices. And don't miss the mochi ice cream at Bubbies (see p. 130 sidebar). Dining can be as expensive or inexpensive as you want. Venturing beyond Waikiki is well worth the modest effort required.

DINING OUT

(Reservations recommended, and usually essential, at all of the establishments listed.)

Kapahulu & Kaimuki Areas

One of the best neighborhoods in Honolulu has some of the best neighborhood restaurants. I dine around here as often as time allows.

3660 on the Rise (808-737-1177; 3660.com), 3660 Waialae Ave. Open for dinner Tues.–Sun. This award-winning (and, at times, overlooked) option features Hawai'i regional cuisine at its best by chef Russell Siu. Signature dishes, including ahi and New York steak alaea, vie for attention with delectable desserts and a *Wine Spectator* award–winning wine list. The lovely interior is quiet and understated—the perfect complement to Siu's sophisticated cuisine. The whole well-rounded experience rises to heights rarely matched.

Reservations strongly recommended; children's menu. Entrées $$$–$$$$, prix fixe $$$$.

✐ Sam Choy's Diamond Head (808-732-8645; samchoy.com), 449 Kapahulu Ave. Open for dinner daily; Sunday brunch. Like Emeril Lagasse and Rachael Ray, Sam Choy has become an institution. This big, earthy guy began cooking at his folk's lu'au and parlayed that into a multimedia food empire. Portions are as big as him and regional flavors as accessible as his spirit. Try favorites like *poke* (marinated raw fish), macadamia-nut-crusted mahimahi, steamed seafood *laulau*, the fresh catch of the day, and Choy's cut, a 9-oz filet mignon in an au poivre sauce. Children's menu. Dinner entrées $$$–$$$$.

✐ town (808-735-5900), 3435 Waialae Ave. Open daily. When a hip restaurant dares to use the motto "local first, organic whenever possible, and with aloha always," it'd better be good. town with a lowercase *t* definitely is. (There are always drawbacks though—a foodie friend of mine thinks hype can trump taste at town.) It's got style to match its substance: stainless tables, concrete floors, hand-typed menus, and eardrum-shattering acoustics (if you're over age 40, request a table on the lanai for a more peaceful meal). Chef-owner Ed Kenney imagined an eclectic Mediterranean menu that changes daily and might include polenta with eggs and asparagus. Breakfast is inexpensive, but no matter the meal, service can be a tad lacking. Children's menu. Breakfast $, lunch $–$$, dinner entrées $$–$$$. BYOB and house wine list.

12th Avenue Grill (808-732-9469; 12thavegrill.com), 1145C 12th Ave., at

Waialea Ave. Open for dinner Mon.–Sat. When Chef Hanney opened this trendy but tiny eatery in 2004, it was an instant success for folks looking for comfort food with a pinch of panache. Think mac and cheese with house-smoked Parmesan cheese and kimchi steak (this is Honolulu after all). Grab a seat at the bar while you wait for a (noisy) seat and save room for sweet somethings at the end, baked by Sam Choy's supplier. Go at 5:30 or wait until 8:30. Small plates $–$$, large plates $$$.

Hee Hing (808-735-5544), 449 Kapahulu Ave. Open 10:30–9:30 daily. This local favorite features a huge, nicely appointed dining room that's far less noisy than most Chinatown places. The Cantonese menu, with an outrageously good garlic black bean sauce that can be paired with any seafood, is a fabulous alternative for Chinatown. Hee Hing is also popular with big groups of friends who gather around big tables on Sunday morning to enjoy more than 75 kinds of dim sum. Dishes $$–$$$.

South King Street Area
Chef Mavro (808-944-4714; chef

CHEF MAVRO WORKS HIS MAGIC.

mavro.com), 1969 S. King St. Open for dinner nightly. James Beard Award–winning chef George Mavrothalassitis is without rival. Loyalists have followed him from La Mer at Halekulani to Seasons at Four Seasons Wailea to this eponymous, elegant restaurant. Catering to an "NPR crowd," the uncompromising Chef Mavro serves Hawai'i regional cuisine prepared with his signature Provençal flair. Committed to local farmers and fishermen, the impassioned chef from Marseilles creates and executes signature dishes to reflect those relationships. Be sure to try the glorious *liliko'i malasadas* (Portuguese-style passion fruit doughnuts). As you might expect, wine pairings are also without equal. Interchangeable three- and six-course meals $$$$.

Alan Wong's (808-949-2526; alanwongs.com), 1857 S. King St., Third Floor. Open for dinner nightly. Arguably the most celebrated of Hawai'i's celebrity chefs, Alan Wong's eatery is consistently rated the state's best restaurant. He probably makes more creative use of traditional Hawaiian ingredients—*taro, kalua* pork, and the like—than any chef in Hawai'i. The room is low-key; single travelers will have a grand time dining at the counter of the exhibition kitchen. Entrées $$$$.

Sushi Sasabune (808-947-3800), 1417 S. King St. Open for dinner Mon.–Sat. Aficionados agree: This is the best sushi in Hawai'i, so only staunch sushi lovers need bother coming here. If you sit at the sushi bar—frankly, the only way to really experience Sasabune—you get what you get. The neon sign reads TRUST ME, and that sums up the story. The chef will explain which fish got flown in from where that morning; he will explain about the nori picked and dried in his mother's small village in Japan; he will instruct you in proper sushi-eating technique. It's very expensive, but it's worth every penny. Prices depend on how much you eat; $$–$$$$.

Café Sistina (808-596-0061; cafe sistina.com), 1314 S. King St. Open for lunch weekdays, dinner nightly. Chef-owner Sergio Mitrotti is as artistic with a paintbrush as he is with a whisk. To wit: He's responsible for the evocative murals on the walls and the luscious northern Italian food on the menu. He's a pasta master by trade and favors the smoky, earthy flavors of mushrooms, olives, and other Mediterranean ingredients. One foodie friend, a loyal Sistina patron, recalls taking leftovers home on a neighbor-island flight and having fellow passengers insist on knowing where the wildly aromatic leftovers came from. Dishes $$–$$$.

The Willows (808-952-9200; willows hawaii.com), 901 Hausten St. Open 10–9 daily. Patrons come here for the lush and tropical ambience, not for the Hawaiian-American buffets (more on those in a minute). Pond-fed fountains murmur, pavilion-like dining rooms are open air, and tables are shaded by umbrellas. What more could you want? Open since 1944, Willows specializes in *laulau* (fish and taro steamed in ti leaves), *poke*, curry dishes, and barbecue ribs. Let the valet park your car for a nominal fee. Lunch buffet $–$$$, dinner and Sunday brunch buffet $$–$$$$.

Chinatown, Restaurant Row, Aloha Tower & Marketplace, and Nearby

Ÿ **Vino Italian Tapas and Wine**

Bar (808-524-8466), Restaurant Row (with free validated parking at night), 500 Ala Moana Blvd. Open for dinner Wed.–Sat. Hot on the heels of Maui's Vino, Sansei's D. K. Kodama and master sommelier Chuck Furuya opened what Honolulu desperately needed— an intimate yet happening wine bar serving delicious "small plates." In addition to 20 wines by the glass, Vino offers palate pleasers that run the gamut from asparagus Milanese to grilled "monster" Ligurian shrimp. The whole place, including the sky ceiling, has been painted to resemble a Tuscan village. Small plates $–$$.

Chai's Island Bistro (808-585-0011; chaisislandbistro.com), Aloha Tower & Marketplace, 1 Aloha Tower Dr. Open for lunch Tues.–Fri., dinner nightly. Chef Chai Chaowasaree opened this truly lovely space so his Singha Thai loyalists (and a whole cadre of newer fans) could enjoy his wonderful Hawai'i regional cuisine creations. Signature dishes include Alaskan king crab cake, crispy duck spring rolls, and kataifi-macadamia-encrusted jumbo black tiger prawns. Chai's is also the place to catch top names in contemporary Hawaiian music nightly. (In fact, the music oftentimes overwhelms the dining service for me.) Lunch $$–$$$, dinner entrées $$$–$$$$.

Ÿ **Indigo** (808-521-2900; indigo -hawaii.com), 1121 Nu'uanu Ave. Open for lunch Tues.–Fri., dinner Tues.–Sat. Chef Glen Chu has created an exotic atmosphere in which to enjoy his just-as-exotic Asian fusion cuisine. Try the steamed Good Fortune Shiitake Mushroom and Chicken Bao Buns, Thousand Loved Crab Cakes, kaffir-lime-scented and pan-seared Pacific fish, or Mongolian lamb chops. Starting to get the idea? Or simply come for appetizers at the bar. Lunch $$–$$$, dinner entrées $$$–$$$$.

Hiroshi Eurasian Tapas (808-533-4476; hiroshihawaii.com), 500 Ala Moana Blvd., Restaurant Row. Open for dinner nightly. Calling all foodies. Chef Hiroshi Fukui explores the fusion of "East meets West" with sushi-centric tapas like foie gras with a teriyaki glaze; a significant selection of wines by the glass (thanks to master sommelier Chuck Furuya); and large plates as well, like a signature cioppino, a delectable combo of Manila clams, shrimp, fresh fish, shiitake mushrooms, and sugar snap peas. About three small plates per person should do it so that you have room for great desserts. Tapas $–$$, large plates $$$.

Sam Choy's Breakfast, Lunch & Crab & Big Aloha Brewery (808-545-7979; samchoy.com), 580 Nimitz Hwy. Open for all three meals daily. This gargantuan place, with gargantuan servings, has tables surrounding a huge "cage" where all manner of crabs and other seafoods are held and prepared. It's no wonder that Sam Choy's BLC, as it's affectionately known, is favored by locals. You can sit in an old boat for fun, or wash your hands in fountains set right out in the middle of the action. Many folks swear by the big guy's big plates of fried rice for breakfast. You can't go wrong with the crab of the day. Or the Big Aloha beer, which perfectly complements crab. Children's menu. Breakfast $–$$, lunch $–$$$$, dinner entrées $$–$$$$.

Ala Moana & Ward Areas
❦ **The Pineapple Room** (808-945-6573; alanwongs.com), Macy's, Ala Moana Center. Open for lunch and dinner Mon.–Sat., breakfast on weekends. After you've shopped till you've dropped—or to get the energy to hit the racks—check out Macy's third-floor restaurant created by celebrity chef Alan Wong. Wong's inimitable touches grace the lunch menu, which features a great Thai Cobb salad, juicy burger, and *kalua* pork BLT. Dinner is also prepared with Wong's signature style; I'm partial to his fresh fish and shellfish dishes, as well as whatever he happens to be doing with beef and pork. Children's menu. Breakfast and lunch $$–$$$, dinner entrées $$$–$$$$.

Mariposa (808-951-3420), Neiman Marcus, Ala Moana Center. Open for lunch and dinner daily. The ultimate "ladies who lunch" spot also appeals to folks who simply appreciate delicious food in serene surroundings. It all starts with their renowned popovers (enhanced by flavored but-

---

TOP 10 PLACES TO EAT IN GREATER HONOLULU
Pricey
Alan Wong's (Greater Honolulu)
3660 on the Rise (Greater Honolulu)
Hoku's (Southeast O'ahu)
Chef Mavro (Greater Honolulu)
Moderate
Hiroshi Eurasian Tapas (Greater Honolulu)
Side Street Inn (Greater Honolulu)
Cheap Eats
Little Village Noodle House (Greater Honolulu)
Café Laufer (Greater Honolulu)
Nico's at Pier 38 (Greater Honolulu)
Kaka'ako Kitchen (Greater Honolulu)

ter) and a tiny cup of chicken con-
sommé, which arrive like little surprises as soon as you're seated. Start
with thick corn chowder, perhaps, and
then consider sharing a salad and
sandwich—especially if you're planning to try on dresses after lunch! But
if you don't give a darn, desserts like
their legendary butterscotch pie are
absolutely scrumptious. Children's
menu. Lunch $$–$$$, dinner entrées
$$$–$$$$.

See also **Hoku's** in "Southeast O'ahu."

EATING OUT

Kapahulu & Kaimuki Areas
✦ **'Ono Hawaiian Foods** (808-737-
2275), 726 Kapahulu Ave. Open for
lunch and dinner Mon.–Sat. It's inter-
esting—ironic, really—that only a
handful of places in Hawai'i serve tra-
ditional Hawaiian food. If you want to
feel like one of the locals (who pat-
ronize this place for weddings, small
lu'aus, and all important family occa-
sions), 'Ono could very well be the
best place to do it. Dishes like
pipikaula, haupia, poi, lomi lomi
salmon, *laulau,* and *'opihi* will sound
foreign. And the flavors may be an
acquired taste. But if you're adventur-
ous, 'Ono is the place to stretch your
palate with traditional Hawaiian food.
Dishes $–$$; no credit cards.

✦ **Café Laufer** (808-735-7717),
3565 Waialae Ave. Open daily at 10.
European-style pastries are the main
event here. Look for luscious, fresh-
from-the-oven scones and linzer
tortes that may require you to retool
your definition of heaven. Or simply
enjoy a slice of fancy, gooey cake coupled with a steaming-hot cup of coffee. If you've come with more of an
appetite, sit down to great soups, sal-

ads, and sandwiches, all of which are
prepared with a European touch that
raises the culinary level of even the
simplest dishes. Lunch $$, dinner
entrées $$–$$$. BYOB.

South King Street Area
Neo-Nabe (808-944-6622; neonabe
.com), 2065 S. King St. Open 5 PM–
2 AM daily, until 5 AM Fri. and Sat.
Catering to a nightclub crowd, this
hip place specializes in trendy Japan-
ese hot pot dishes prepared right at
your table. You choose the ingredients
and sauce, and they'll whip it up.
When you're in the mood for food
and fun, this place will entertain you.
Dinner entrées $$–$$$.

Spices (808-949-2679; spiceshawaii
.com), 2671 S. King St. Open for
lunch Tues.–Fri. and dinner Tues.–
Sat. Popular with university students
because of its location, Spices dishes
up concoctions (and an interior de-
sign palette) rich in Southeast Asian
flavors—from Thailand to Vietnam.
Think curries, stir fries, soups, and
rice and noodle dishes. Vegetarians
rejoice. Dishes $–$$.

Chinatown, Restaurant Row, Aloha Tower & Marketplace, and Nearby
Char Hung Sut (808-538-3335), 64
N. Pauahi St. Open Wed.–Mon. 5:30
AM–2 PM. Open for take-out only, and
if you arrive after 10 AM you may not
get everything you want. This much is
also true: Folks throughout the islands
agree that Char Hung Sut makes the
best dim sum not only in Hawai'i, but
the entire galaxy. Try the *manapua*
(sweet buns steamed or baked and
stuffed with tasty *char siu* pork) and
little pork hash dumplings (a shrimp
mixture wrapped in rice dough and
shaped into half-moons). No, it's not

French) served up plate-lunch style (in take-out Styrofoam containers). It's tough to find fresher fish at lower prices. And it's on the edge of the pier to boot! Line up at lunchtime with blue- and white-collar workers who come for to-die-for, catch-of-the-day, pan seared ahi, chicken katsu, and beef stew. Children's menu. Breakfast and lunch $–$$.

To Chau (808-533-4549), 1007 River St. Open 8:30–2:30 daily. When locals and Asians line up for pho, they line up here. Don't come for ambience, service, or any other dish on the menu. (I've never even noticed other dishes on the menu, but I'm sure there are some.) The broth is clear, dreamy, steamy, and flavored like there is no tomorrow. Dishes $; no credit cards.

Ala Moana & Ward Areas

Side Street Inn (808-591-0253), 1225 Hopaka St. Open 4 PM–2 AM nightly. This place might as well be nicknamed "the Chefs' Hangout." Later in the evening it's filled with big-name chefs who've finished working at their own fancy restaurants and have come here to "grind." Don't let the look of the place deter you; it belies the quality of the food. Look for blackened ahi, pesto-crusted ahi, fresh-steamed Manila clams, shrimp scampi, escargots, barbecued baby back ribs, and 16-ounce charbroiled steaks. One big-name chef and I shared pork chops, spicy chicken, ribs, and ahi belly here. (Yes, all in the same sitting.) It's not the place for serious dieters. Call for directions; it really is on a side street and can be tough to find. Reservations recommended. Entrées $$–$$$.

Kaka'ako Kitchen (808-596-7488), Ward Center, 1200 Ala Moana Blvd. Open for all three meals Mon.–

particularly healthy, but it's so good that it just doesn't matter. Besides, you can eat a cleansing salad and fruit tomorrow. Dishes $–$$; no credit cards.

Little Village Noodle House (808-545-3008; littlevillagehawaii .com), 1113 Smith St. Open for lunch and dinner daily. Looking for fresh, perfectly prepared food in a clean, well-lighted place? Look no further. I love this place, as do my foodie friends (and Chef Mavro, whom I've bumped into here on numerous occasions). As you might expect, all the noodle dishes are absolutely yummy, as are the long lists of vegetarian choices. (There's plenty of fish, shrimp, and chicken, too, of course.) I'm particularly partial, though, to green bean and eggplant dishes. The servers here are extremely knowledgeable about combining menu items, so give yours some guidance on basic likes and dislikes (and dietary restrictions) and leave the ordering up to him or her. Dishes $$.

Nico's at Pier 38 (808-540-1377; nicospier38.com), 1133 N. Nimitz Hwy. Open Mon.–Sat. Local contacts of mine are always surprised when they find out that I eat at this tiny out-of-the-way place. It's so Honolulu—in that it's gourmet cuisine (in this case

Sat., breakfast and lunch Sun. This is home to the original gourmet plate lunch. Owned and operated by Russell Siu of 3660 on the Rise (see *Dining Out*), Kaka'ako isn't fancy, but it sure is good. Choices include a seared ahi sandwich with tobiko aioli, five-spice shoyu chicken, meat loaf, and three-bean chili. It's all served in Styrofoam. But hey, that's local style. Children's menu. Dishes $–$$.

Akasaka (808-942-4466), 1646B Kona St. Open for lunch daily and dinner Mon.–Sat. First things first: Call for directions. Akasaka is worth finding. This is the real deal when it comes to authentic Japanese sushi, and to boot, the tiny place is informal and neighborhoody. Open since 1981, they offer various noodle dishes, along with spicy tuna rolls and scallops grilled in butter. Live big and let the sushi chef decide what to serve you. Lunch $–$$, dinner entrées $$$.

 Kua 'Aina (808-591-9133), 1116 Auahi St., near the Ward Center. Open daily. The original and wildly popular branch of this American restaurant is on the North Shore. But if you (tragically) can't get up there and want to know what the fuss is about, they've made a convenient outlet just for you. Their burgers are legendary for size and toppings, but their salads, sandwiches, and fries are almost as worthy. Dine outside if you get lucky, or take it away. Children's menu. Dishes $.

See also Olive Tree Café in "Southeast O'ahu."

COFFEE & MARKETS
Coffee Talk (808-737-7444), 3601 Waialae Ave. Open 5 AM–11 PM daily.

PLATE LUNCHES & OTHER FAST FOOD
You've heard of them, but what are they, besides beloved? The plate lunch traditionally consists of two scoops of rice and macaroni salad alongside a hot meat dish like roasted pork or teriyaki something-or-other. They are the Hawaiian version of (generally) greasy, inexpensive fast food. And they've probably evolved from a morphing of Japanese bento boxes, tins carried by immigrant sugar-plantation workers, and blue-plate specials geared toward a lunch-pail crowd. Pick them up at lunch wagons (or *kaukaus*, parked at popular beach parks and well-traveled intersections), at sit-down eateries, and at take-out joints. Although most are not particularly healthy, there is a trend toward more nutritious combinations. Look for grilled meat instead of meat drenched in gravy, or brown rice instead of white.

No matter where you are, don't overlook local chains like **Todai Seafood Buffet** (808-947-1000; 1910 Ala Moana Blvd.), an impressive Japanese buffet with a tame price tag; or **L&L Drive-Inn** (there are more than 30 on O'ahu and another 10 or so on neighbor islands), with classic plate lunches (see *Eating Out* "The Windward Coast"); or **Zippy's** (specializing in zip-fast seafood and saimin). You can't go wrong at any of these places. And don't forget about **Kaka'ako Kitchen** (see *Eating Out*, "Greater Honolulu").

At Honolulu's hippest coffee place, life-sized mannequins recline lazily, the art is bold and colorful, and an old bank vault doubles as meeting space. Grab a coffee drink and homemade pastry and linger with the Sunday paper.

Down to Earth (808-947-7678), 2525 S. King St. Open daily 7:30 AM–10 PM. This natural food store has lots of veggie dishes (sold by the pound) at the deli, as well as a salad bar.

Kokua Market (808-941-1922), 2643 S. King St. Open 8:30–8:30 daily. Kokua is a co-op featuring an excellent selection of organic goods as well as tasty salads and sandwiches for picnics.

Maunakea Marketplace (808-524-3409), 1120 Maunakea St. Open daily. This Chinatown food court is deservedly popular and worth every minute of your time. Eat your way around the world with samples of Vietnamese, Chinese, Japanese, and Thai cuisine. It's loads of fun.

JUST SO YOU KNOW

If you're hungry and in a hurry, don't overlook the food courts in Ala Moana Center and the fast food joints in Ward Center.

✳ Entertainment

I beg of you: Venture beyond the controlled confines of Waikiki for a real taste of what it's like to live and play in Hawai'i's biggest city.

MOVIES & THEATER

Even when they're enjoying an exotic vacation in Hawai'i, a surprising number of visitors end up at the movies.

Honolulu Academy of Arts (808-532-8768), 900 S. Beretania St., screens art and international films.

Ward Entertainment Center (808-593-3000), off Ala Moana Blvd. on A'uahi St., is home to Ward Theatre 16, a state-of-the-art multiplex cinema.

Restaurant Row (808-526-4171), Ala Moana Blvd., has nine screens and free validated parking (for three and a half hours).

International Film Festival (808-443-0512) is held annually at various venues around Honolulu.

Hawai'i Theatre (808-528-0506 for changing tour times and box office), 1130 Bethel St., a beautiful beaux-arts performing arts venue and cultural center, hosts a number of activities. Check the local paper for listings.

BARS & CLUBS

Formaggio (808-739-7719; formaggio808.com), 2919 Kapi'olani Blvd., in the Market City Shopping Area. Open 5 PM–midnight Mon.–Thurs., until

---

✪ **Bubbies** (808-487-7218; bubbiesicecream.com), 1010 University Ave. Open noon–midnight daily. Especially popular with movie patrons from the Varsity Theater across the street, Bubbies has mouthwatering homemade ice cream in a seemingly endless list of innovative flavors. For many, though, *the* raison d'être is mochi ice cream. Dozens of popular flavors are delicately enrobed in soft, sweet mochi (rice flour) dough and frozen. Be careful. They're oddly addictive, and you can easily lose track of how many you've popped into your mouth. Treats $.

two AM Fri.– Sat. After a satisfying night of noshing in the Kaimuki and Kapahulu neighborhoods, and before heading back to your Waikiki hotel, stop in to sample one of 50 wines by the glass at this little hideaway. Two-ounce tasting portions mean you can sample a fair number of vintages and refine your palette. You may want to pair a glass with some equally fine cheese; this is called Formaggio for a reason!

Ⓨ **Mai Tai Bar** (808-947-2900; mai tairumble.com), Ala Moana Center, fourth floor. Open daily. This open-air bar, an equally relaxing place by day or night, is a nice place for after-noon apps and a strong signature drink. In the evening they have live entertainment.

Ⓨ **Ryan's Bar** (808-591-9132; r-u-i .com), Ward Center, 1200 Ala Moana Blvd. Open daily. If you want to min-gle with a postwork Honolulu yuppie crowd, head to this trendy place. There's a wide selection of beer, too many kinds of tequila and single-malt Scotches to count, and plenty of friendly conversation. Good thing the *pupus* are worthy—you might be here a long time.

Ⓨ **Brew Moon** (808-593-0088), Ward Center, 1200 Ala Moana Blvd. Open daily. When I feel like cruising with a bunch of friends, the hip and cool Brew Moon offers a microbrewery and creative New Orleans–style noshing.

Ⓨ **Compadres Bar & Grill** (808-591-8307), Ward Center, 1200 Ala Moana Blvd. Open daily. For the best margaritas this side of Juarez, Mexico, this bar is living proof (that's 80-proof) that fun really can be meas-ured in ounces.

Ⓨ **La Mariana Restaurant & Bar** (808-848-2800), Sand Island, 50 Sand Island Access Rd. Open daily, sing-alongs likely Fri.–Sat. As long as you promise not to eat here (the food tends toward frozen mahimahi), I'll tell you about it. Okay: They just don't make 'em like this anymore. As the *Honolulu Advertiser* so wisely stated, it's "a throwback to the 1950s Hawai'i that never was." About as kitschy and nostalgic as it gets, complete with tiki-inspired décor, this fun institution hidden on the industrial docks is great when you feel like singing around the piano.

Ⓨ **Indigo** (808-521-2900; indigo -hawaii.com), 1121 Nu'uanu Ave. Open daily, bar open until 1 AM. Their Green Room lounge and Opium Den & Champagne Bar are definitely places people go to be seen. In addi-tion to dangerous bubbly stuff, they shake a mean sake martini. Quiet jazz moves into more groovin' dance music as the night wears on. Indigo has a DJ, dancing, and live bands Tuesday through Saturday. Thursday is happenin'.

Ⓨ **Anna Bananas** (808-946-5190), 2240 S. Beretania St. Open 11:30 AM–

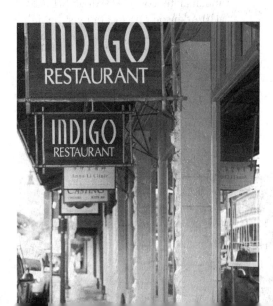

✪ THE MALASADAS WARS

Devotees of these sugary, deep-fried, doughnutlike pastries are obsessive in their pursuit of perfection. *Malasadas* are rather like a doughnut without a hole, or the hole *from* the doughnut. Asking two locals to agree on O'ahu's best *malasadas* is rather like asking New York Yankees and Boston Red Sox fans to reach consensus. Passions run deep. If your cholesterol levels can take it, conduct a taste test yourself. Head to **Champion Malasadas** (808-947-8778; 1926 S. Beretania St.; open at least 6 AM–9 PM daily except Mon.), whose pastries are light and airy, or **Leonard's** (808-737-5591; 933 Kapahulu Ave.; open 6 AM–9 PM daily), a longtime Portuguese bakery.

1:30 AM daily, live music Thurs.–Sat. This divey university haunt is a comfortable and incredibly beloved place to hang out and listen to live reggae, blues, world, alternative, and other music. It's the best (and oldest) blues venue on O'ahu; dancing gets pretty hot here.

Υ **Chai's Island Bistro** (see *Dining Out*), a fantastic restaurant within the increasingly popular Aloha Tower & Marketplace on the waterfront, has become one of the city's hottest venues for live Hawaiian music. Music often begins at 7 PM.

Υ **Rumours** (808-955-4811; ala moanahotel.com), Ala Moana Hotel, 410 Atkinson Dr., located just behind the shopping center. Open Fri. 5 PM–3:30 AM, Sat. 9 PM–3:30 AM. Loyal locals pack this place after work and dance beyond normal bedtimes. It appeals to a wide-ranging crowd, thanks to a lineup of Top 40, salsa, and oldies (I'm talkin' tunes from the 1960s to the 1990s). Call for the schedule. Come for Monday "afternoon" football in-season, starting at 3 PM.

See also **Hank's** under *To See & Do, Chinatown*.

DINNER CRUISES

A number of (I think kitschy) sunset cruises depart from the Aloha Tower & Marketplace and waterfront, including **Navatek/Atlantis Adventures** (808-548-6262; go-atlantis .com), which is designed to prevent seasickness, and **Ali'i Kai Catamaran** (808-954-8652 or 1-866-898-2519; robertshawaii.com).

❋ Selective Shopping

ART GALLERIES

Chinatown has a number of great galleries, including **Ramsay Museum** (808-537-2787; ramsaymuseum.org), 1128 Smith St. Open Mon.–Sat., it hosts group shows and has a lovely garden setting. The building itself is a National Historic Landmark.

CHINATOWN

Nohea Gallery (808-589-1174; noheagallery.com), Ward Warehouse, Ala Moana Blvd. Open daily. A superb collection of contemporary art in almost every medium imaginable.

BOOKSTORES

Borders (808-591-8995; borders stores.com), Ward Center, Ala Moana Blvd. Open daily.

Rainbow Books and Records (808-955-7994; rainbowbookshawaii.com), 1010 University Ave. Open daily. This university-area shop is odd, but it has tons of first- and secondhand Hawaiiana.

CLOTHES

Shanghai Tang (808-942-9800), Ala Moana Center. Open daily. For old-fashioned and Old World tailoring, the kind they used to do in China and Hong Kong, head here.

Hilo Hattie's (808-535-6500 or 1-888-526-0299; hilohattie.com), 700 N. Nimitz Hwy. Open daily. In recent years the quality of merchandise has improved here, and now it's worth taking the free daily shuttle from Waikiki to this retail outlet. Hilo Hattie's, by the way, is the "largest manufacturer of Hawaiian and tropical fashions." They also have a store at the Ala Moana Center.

FOODSTUFFS

Foodland (808-946-4654), 1460 S. Beretania St. Open daily. When it comes time to pull together a gourmet picnic to take to Leeward O'ahu, don't overlook this grocery store, which includes the **R. Field Wine Co.** (808-596-9463)—an outstanding wine shop.

Honolulu Chocolate Co. (808-591-2997; honoluluchocolate.com), Ward Center, 1200 Ala Moana Blvd. Open daily. So much smooth gourmet chocolate, so little time. I dare you to drink in the shop with your olfactory senses and not indulge your taste buds.

See also **Down to Earth** and **Kokua Market** under *Coffee & Markets*.

SHOPPING CENTERS

Ala Moana Center (808-955-9517; alamoana.com), Ala Moana Blvd. Open 9–9:30 daily, Sun. 10–6. Hawai'i's biggest shopping center is supposedly the world's largest open-air mall. Given the roughly 240 shops and 60 restaurants spread out over 50 acres, I believe it. Popular among visitors and residents (who fly over to shop here and then fly home), it has name-brand retailers like Sears, Macy's, and Neiman Marcus, as well as many small and unusual shops like the **Crack Seed Center**, which displays jars of pickled mangoes, candied ginger, and dried cuttlefish. Don't miss the great food hall on the second floor, especially the Japanese restaurant **Shirokiya** (808-973-9111). There is convenient bus service (aboard TheBus; $2; No. 8) from Waikiki, a 15-minute ride, or catch the Pink Line trolley ($2 each way, exact change only). Free parking.

Ward Center (808-591-8411; victoria ward.com), Ala Moana Blvd. Open

CARGO SHIPS IN

10–9 daily, Sun. until 6. Of the three Ward buildings, which harbor more than 100 shops and encompass four city blocks, the center is the most upscale. It also has lots of good bars and restaurants when you get tired.

Aloha Tower & Marketplace (808-528-5700; alohatower.com), Ala Moana Blvd., Pier 9, at Bishop St. Open 9–9 daily, Sun. until 6. This waterfront emporium has over 80 mostly one-of-a-kind shops and kiosks geared toward visitors. Parking is expensive and limited; try to take the trolley from Waikiki.

SPECIAL SHOPS
Antique Alley (808-941-8551), 1347 Kapiʻolani Blvd. Open Mon.–Sat. This jam-packed shop has tons of Hawaiiana; a bunch of sellers have banded together, so your chances of finding something to your liking are high.

Garakuta-Do (808-589-2262), 433 Koula St., *mauka* off Ala Moana Blvd. at Office Max. Open Tues.–Sat. This place has a luscious collection of antiques from Japan, from tansu chests and wood-block prints to screens and scrolls. It's fabulous.

✪ **Lita's Leis** (808-521-9065), 59 N. Beretania St., and **Sweetheart's Leis**

CHINATOWN LEI SHOPS

(808-537-3011), 69 N. Beretania St., both open daily, are two Chinatown institutions where you can get ultra-fresh leis ($3–25). Most lei shops are tiny stands—one-room storefronts really—where you can watch leis being strung with various flowers. To preserve the freshness and fragrance as long as possible, keep your lei in a plastic bag in the refrigerator when you're not wearing it. Although leis may seem touristy, residents consider giving and wearing them quite serious business. Remember, it's bad form to throw away a lei; instead return it to the land from where it came.

Honolulu Academy Gift Shop (808-532-8703; honoluluacademy.org; 900 S. Beretania St.), **Contemporary Museum Gift Shop** (808-523-3447; tcmhi.org; 2411 Makiki Heights Dr.), and **Pacifica Shop at the Bishop Museum** (808-848-4158; bishop museum.org; 1525 Bernice St.). All three shops carry an excellent selection of Hawaiian crafts and books. The only real equals they have are each other. The first two are open Tues.–Sun., the latter daily.

Macy's Kuʻu Home Island Gifts (808-941-2345), Ala Moana Center. Open daily. Up on the fourth floor of this national retailer you'll find a completely customized section with one of the best collections of Hawaiʻi-made gifts, products, and home accessories in the state.

✪ **Native Books/Na Mea Hawaii** (808-597-8967; nativebookshawaii.com), Ward Warehouse, 1050 Ala Moana Blvd. Open daily. Make sure to stop here at some point; from wooden bowls and books to baskets and Hawaiian crafts, this great shop will undoubtedly have something you want.

SOUTHEAST OʻAHU

One of Hawaiʻi's easiest drives yields a big bang, starting with the extinct volcanic crater Diamond Head—one of the most prominent and beloved landmarks in the Pacific. When you get beyond Koko Head you'll really feel as if you've left the big city behind. Along this breathtaking shoreline you'll encounter extinct volcanoes, daredevil surfers, accessible hikes, a snorkeling bay extraordinaire, a well-sited lighthouse, and the Hollywood of Oʻahu. Kahala, lined with gazillion-dollar manses and home to a fabulous resort, is the wealthiest community on the island.

GETTING AROUND

By car: This tour unfolds in geographic order, presuming you are beginning at the eastern edge of Waikiki and heading counterclockwise around the island. Hwy. 72 is also called the Kalanianaʻole Hwy. If you don't stop (which you will), it takes about one and a quarter hours to drive the 35 miles from Waikiki to Makapuʻu Point, up to Kailua, and back to Honolulu via the Pali Hwy.

✳ To See & Do

*In geographical order
from west to east.*

✪ **Diamond Head**, Diamond Head Rd. One of the most dramatic landmarks in the Pacific, Diamond Head owes its creation to a violent steam explosion that occurred late in Oʻahu's volcanic history. Ancient Hawaiians named it Leahi because it resembled the brow of the tuna. British whalers of the 19th century got so excited over the crater's sparkling surface, mistaking embedded calcite crystals for diamonds, that they dubbed it Diamond Head. In the early 1900s the U.S. Army turned the crater into a defense

---

**BUILDING BLOCKS FOR A
PERFECT DAY IN SOUTHEAST
OʻAHU**

Hike to the top of Diamond Head at
   sunrise (2 hours)
Drive around the posh neighbor-
   hood of Kahala (1 hour)
Have lunch at the Kahala Hotel &
   Resort (2 hours)
Snorkel at Hanauma Bay (3 hours)
Watch bodysurfers at Sandy
   Beach Park (1 hour)

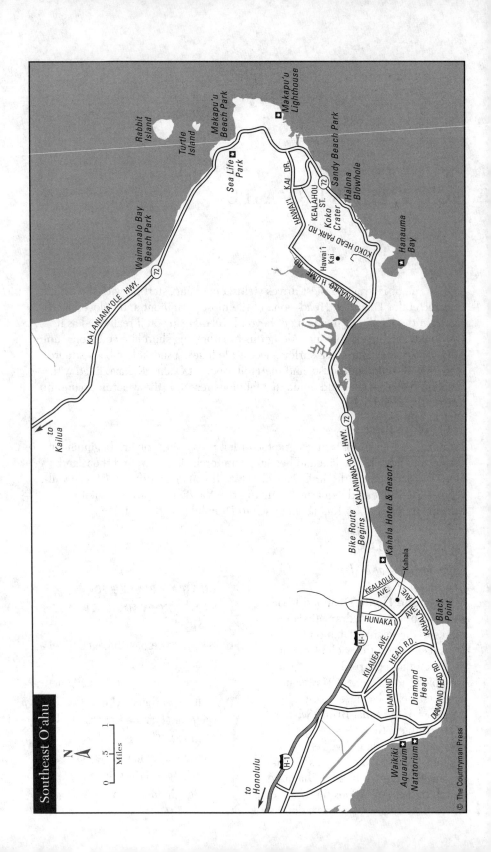

fortress, complete with a network of tunnels and rim-level cannons, bunkers, and lookouts. Today Diamond Head is a state monument with picnic tables, restrooms, and drinking water, but, alas, no shade. Bring a hat, especially if you want to hike to the crater rim for the best views in southern Oʻahu. Up here you take in Waikiki, Koko Head, and the Diamond Head Lighthouse.

SANDY BEACH PARK

Black Point, just off Kahala Ave., a quarter mile east of the Diamond Head Rd. junction, is a perfect spot to photograph Diamond Head and the southwest coast. It's also near the Doris Duke estate of **Shangri La** (see "Greater Honolulu").

✪ **Kahala**, between the H-1 Freeway and Kahala Ave. This very upscale neighborhood of mostly multimillion-dollar homes sits between Diamond Head and the Waialae Country Club. It's home to the exclusive Kahala Hotel & Resort, as well as the Kahala Mall, where Honokaʻa Street meets the H-1 Freeway.

Hawaiʻi Kai, Kalanianaʻole Hwy. About 20 minutes by car east of Diamond Head, this thoroughly suburban neighborhood is home to Kuapa Pond, a rambling waterway of homes and small-boat landings that spreads inland for miles. There are multiple shopping malls here, all good for last-chance shopping before reaching nearby Hanauma Bay.

Koko Head, Kalanianaʻole Hwy. A relic of Oʻahu's last volcanic activity, Koko Head, at an elevation of 645 feet, is a popular day-hike destination and home to Koko Crater Botanical Garden, a 60-acre dry-land exhibit (free). There are no facilities, but you can take a self-guided tour. From near the crater rim, you can look down to Hanauma Bay and west to Makapuʻu Point.

✦ ✪ **Hanauma Bay** (808-396-4229; friendsofhanaumabay.org or co.honolulu.hi .us/parks/facility/hanaumabay/welcome.htm), 100 Hanauma Bay Rd. Open 6–6 Wed.–Mon. (Apr.–Sep. until 7 PM), Hanauma Bay is a stunning, shallow coral cove of turquoise waters, colorful fish, and white-sand beach. It's also the most-visited snorkeling spot in the state, so it's best to arrive early (i.e., before 10 AM). Until a few years ago, Hanauma was overfished and the reef fish were overfed by tourists. Today the entire bay is a marine sanctuary, and visitors are required to view a short film at the impressive **Marine Education Center**, about its delicate ecology. It's a small price to pay for helping to preserve this coastal treasure. As a result, the entire cove is gradually returning to a healthier state. The reef is filled with life, from parrotfish and green sea turtles to shorebirds and sunburned tourists. Even if you don't intend to go in the water, it's worth a peek from the overlook near the parking lot.

Facilities: Snack bar, gift shop, lifeguards, showers, restrooms, snorkeling concession stand. $5 for adults and children ages 13 and up, $1 per vehicle, 50¢ to take the tram down to the bay.

✦ **Sandy Beach Park** (aka **Ka Iwi**). See *Beaches*.

Halona Blowhole, Kalaniana'ole Hwy. Less than 2 miles east of Hanauma Bay at scenic Halona Point, this blowhole is the unusual creation of a submerged lava tunnel with a spout in the rock ledge at the surface. First you hear a rushing sound, then a great *whoosh!* as the air is rapidly forced out by the surf crashing against the rocks and flowing into the compressed tunnel. As the pressure increases, a stream of water shoots up, often 30 feet into the air. Try to curb your curiosity; you really don't want to be looking into the blowhole when that happens.

ᛞ **Makapu'u Beach Park**. See *Beaches*.

ᛞ **Sea Life Park** (808-259-7933; sealifeparkhawaii.com), 41-202 Kalaniana'ole Hwy. Open 10:30–5 daily. Penguins in Hawai'i? This commercial marine park on a beautiful stretch of Waimanalo Bay features a sprawling 300,000-gallon aquarium of sea turtles, hammerhead sharks, and glittering reef fish. The park has an old-fashioned atmosphere with the usual crowd pleasers, including dancing dolphins. There are kid-friendly interactive displays, such as the chance to swim with graceful stingrays. There's also information on the park's continuing rescue efforts on behalf of seal and sea lion pups. It sure is expensive, though, for what they offer: $29 adults, $19 children ages 4–12.

Turtle Island and **Rabbit Island**, Kalaniana'ole Hwy. Just offshore between Sea Life Park and Makapu'u Point, Manana (Rabbit) and Kaohikaipu (Turtle) Islands are connected by a submerged coral reef. Rabbit Island is the larger of the pair, home to migratory shearwaters and a permanent population of rabbits. Occasionally they share the same burrows. Imagine.

ᛞ See *Beaches*.

✳ Outdoor Activities

GOLF

Hawai'i Kai Golf Course (808-395-2358; hawaiikaigolf.com), 8902 Kalaniana'ole Hwy., Honolulu. Greens fees at the Champion Course run $90–100 ($70 at twilight), while at the Executive Course they're $37–42. The latter course is

AROUND SOUTHEAST O'AHU

prime for novices. It's cheaper to book online than by phone, but either way make advance reservations.

Olomana Golf Links (808-259-7926; olomanagolflinks.com), 41-1801 Kalaniana'ole Hwy., Waimanalo. Greens fees are $80. This moderately difficult course, subject to frequent but short spurts of rain, has killer views of the Ko'olau Mountains.

HIKING

Diamond Head, Diamond Head Rd. The Diamond Head Trail is accessible only from inside the crater, a fairly steep climb best done early in the day before the heat hits this shade-free environment. Only 0.75 mile long, the trail is paved and features two sets of stairs, one with 99 steps, the other with 76. There's also a 200-foot tunnel to navigate; a flashlight is useful but not essential. When you reach the summit's observation deck, take in the unparalleled views and hold on to your hat; it's windy up there.

Koko Head Trail, Kalaniana'ole Hwy. Locals often take their daily walks here. The trail follows a rocky ledge, steep in places, and offers great views, especially of Diamond Head in the distance.

Makapu'u Head Lighthouse Trail, Kalaniana'ole Hwy. The mostly paved 1.5-mile trail to the lighthouse, marking the easternmost point of the island, is closed to vehicles. The lighthouse was built in 1909 and automated in 1974. In winter you can often catch a glimpse of humpback whales off the coast, with Moloka'i on the distant horizon.

SNORKELING

Snorkel Bob's (808-735-7944; snorkelbob.com), 700 Kapahulu Ave. Open daily. This statewide franchise rents boogie boards, surfboards, kayaks, and of course snorkeling gear for use at Hanauma Bay and elsewhere.

✳ Beaches

In order of preference.

⨍ **Hanauma Bay**. See *To See & Do*.

✪ ⨍ **Sandy Beach Park** (aka **Ka Iwi**), Kalaniana'ole Hwy. One of Hawai'i's premier bodysurfing beaches, and one of the few O'ahu beaches subject to high surf year-round, sits at the base of Koko Crater. Its pounding shorebreak challenges the very best bodysurfers and boogie boarders and is famous for sending people to the hospital. This is definitely not a swimming beach, but it's great for taking pictures because the surf breaks so close to shore. Sandy Beach is also popular with skim boarders, who run along the beach and drop their thin boards into the receding water, jump on, then shoot across the wet sand for a few brief moments. *Facilities:* Lifeguard, restrooms, showers, picnic and kite-flying area, weekend catering truck.

⨍ **Makapu'u Beach Park**, Kalaniana'ole Hwy. Located just below Makapu'u Point, Makapu'u Beach is a curved pocket of white sand with a pounding shorebreak that attracts only experienced bodysurfers and boogie boarders.

MAKAPU'U BEACH

When the surf is high, the waves break near the middle of the bay, yielding long rides for surfers and vicarious thrills for the spectators, who often fill the lookout above the beach. *Facilities*: Lifeguards, picnic areas with barbecues, showers, restrooms.

✄ ✦ **Waimanalo Bay Beach Park**, Kalaniana'ole Hwy. There are three beach parks along 3-mile-long Waimanalo Bay, each blessed with fine white sand, ironwood trees, and (usually) great swimming conditions. Close to Honolulu, this popular family beach provides a small, consistent shorebreak for novice wave riders. It's also famous for its stinging man-of-war jellyfish. Check with lifeguards or inspect the tide line, where seaweedlike debris accumulates. *Facilities*: Lifeguards, showers, restrooms, picnic areas, free parking. Camping is also available with a permit.

✳ Lodging

Although there's only one choice over here, a mere 4 miles from Waikiki, it's a doozy. I recall staying here once, majorly jet-lagged and exhausted, and finally realizing the value of a $700 room. If you had told me, after 48 hours at the Kahala Hotel & Resort, that I had to return to the mainland, I would have done so perfectly rested and completely sated.

✪ ✄ **Kahala Hotel & Resort** (808-739-8888 or 1-800-367-2525; kahalaresort.com), 5000 Kahala Ave. This

KAHALA HOTEL & RESORT

exclusive and secluded property would rise head and shoulders above her competitors, if she actually had any. In a class by herself, she's my favorite place to stay on O'ahu. This legendary refuge has attracted more international celebrities and royals than any other hotel in Hawai'i, and her style reflects this patronage: courtly and dignified, blissfully removed from the bustle. Since a mammoth renovation in the early 1990s, and a more modest one in 2008 when she and Mandarin Oriental management parted ways, the patrician refinement has been extended to all of the Kahala's rooms and suites. Décor includes parquet floors, four-poster beds, and rich fabrics. Even the smallest rooms are exceptionally spacious, with sitting areas and bathrooms boasting vintage fixtures. The best of the least-expensive rooms are lagoon-view quarters in the low-rise wing. These overlook fish, turtles, and dolphins that are trained several times

THE DOUBLE LIFE OF A VAGABOND POET: DON BLANDING (1894–1957)
To read Don Blanding's poetry is to see a complexity that is not all at once apparent. Masked within the perfect rhymes and jolly cadence is the story of a man who was deeply conflicted. The poet, who glorified traveling and seeing the world and was lauded for living "the vagabond life," was constantly searching for where he belonged.

Born in Oklahoma at the turn of the 20th century, Don Blanding spent the first years of his life in the sleepy Midwest, but directly after high school he began to wander. Always curious about what lay around the next corner, he traveled from town to town making his living in various ways. Because of this, Blanding is hard to define, and this is one of his most appealing traits. At different times in his life he was an actor, a director, a newspaper columnist and cartoonist, a designer, and a poet. He traveled to many places in the world and made his home in Hollywood, Carmel, Los Angeles, and Taos.

He loved the Hawaiian Islands and returned repeatedly, living for several years in Honolulu. He first began to publish his poems daily in the *Honolulu Star*, and with the encouragement of his editor, Blanding paid for the first printing of his book *Leaves from a Grass-House*. Many of the poems in this book were republished several years later in *The Vagabond House*, one of Blanding's most famous titles. *The Vagabond House* was greeted with immediate success; by 1948 it was in its 48th printing and had sold more than 150,000 copies.

Hawai'i so lauded the poet that he was made the state laureate. After he died of natural causes in his home in Los Angeles, Blanding's ashes were scattered at sea in Honolulu. Blanding's words continue to touch many people with their haunting ability to describe the possibilities for the future and the places yet to see, all the while mourning and treasuring the past.

a day before delighted guests. The beach offers rental kayaks, rafts, and sailboats, along with swimming and snorkeling. This is Hawai'i's finest metropolitan destination resort, and when you are feeling more regal than Polynesian, the hotel will pamper you graciously. *Rates*: $$$$; children free in parent's room. *Facilities and amenities*: 343 rooms and suites, large pool, great beach, 4 restaurants (see **Hoku's** and **Cabanas Seaside Grill** under *Dining Out*), nearby golf course, fitness center with steam

rooms and dry sauna, water sport rentals, concierge, shops, Kahala Keiki Club children's programs, parking (fee).

Camping is permitted at **Waimanalo Bay Beach Park** (808-768-3440; honoluluparks.com). No fee, but a permit is required; gates locked 6:45 PM–7 AM.

✴ Where to Eat

Home to one of O'ahu's best restaurants, this little region is proof that quality of choice reigns over quantity of choice.

DINING OUT

Hoku's (808-739-8780; kahalaresort.com), Kahala Hotel & Resort, 5000 Kahala Ave. Open for dinner nightly, Sunday brunch. Here's what elegant Hoku's has going for it: panoramic ocean view, a beautifully appointed dining room (which received a $750,000 overhaul in 2006), bamboo flooring, "A-plus" servers, and Executive Chef Wayne Hirabayashi's scrumptious Euro-island cuisine. Signature items include warm lobster and hearts of palm salad; anything from the kiawe grill; crisped whole island fish (for two); and wood-fired Australian rack of lamb. Don't even think about skipping dessert or Sunday brunch. Reservations recommended; children's menu; collared shirts with slacks or evening wear required. Entrées $$$$.

Roy's (808-396-7697; roysrestaurant.com), 6600 Kalaniana'ole Hwy., Hawai'i Kai. Open for dinner nightly. This is where the movement began. Whatever you call it—East meets West, Pacific Rim, Hawai'i regional cuisine—Roy Yamaguchi calls it Eurasian. Diners call it magnificent. And they've responded resoundingly. Roy now has over 30 restaurants in his empire. Along with beautiful views, you'll find Roy's signature ribs, ahi, a warm chocolate cake with liquid chocolate center, and a great wine list. This style of cuisine wraps everything you could possibly want on a dinner plate. Reservations recommended; children's menu. Entrées $$$$.

✪ **Cabanas Seaside Grill** (808-739-8770; kahalaresort.com), Kahala Hotel & Resort, 5000 Kahala Ave. Open for lunch daily. When you tire of formal service but still have a hankering for fine food served family style, Cabanas fits the bill beautifully. The relaxing beachfront location is alluring, romantic, and quiet. Lunch $$–$$$.

EATING OUT

Olive Tree Café (808-737-0303), 4614 Kilauea Ave., behind Kahala Mall. Open for dinner nightly. At this small, self-serve restaurant, the menu's building blocks include tomatoes, olives, feta cheese, pita bread, eggplant, sesame, lamb, lots of earthy herbs, and citrus. While it may sound strictly Mediterranean or Greek, it's not. You're in Hawai'i, after all, so you'll always find plenty of fish dishes. Service can be a bit slow, and it may take a while to snag a table, but the flavors and reasonable prices make up for any inconvenience. Entrées $–$$; no credit cards.

✳ Selective Shopping

Barnes & Noble (808-737-3323; barnesandnoble.com), Kahala Mall, 4211 Waialae Ave. Open 9 AM–10 PM daily.

Island Treasures (808-396-8827; kokomarinacenter.com), Koko Marina Center, 7192 Kalaniana'ole Hwy., just before Hanauma Bay. Open daily. For the perfect gifts for almost every budget, from art to home accessories, shop where the residents do.

Kahala Mall (808-732-7736; kahalamallcenter.com), 4211 Waialae Ave. This refined and quiet mall has many of the same stores as Ala Moana Center without the crowds. It also has the **Kahala eight-plex movie theater** (808-593-3000), open 10–9 daily, Sun. until 5.

THE WINDWARD COAST

Only 10 or so miles separates Honolulu from the Windward Coast, but it might as well be a world away. The transition is startling—going from one to the other side of the serrated Nu'uanu Pali—but it's my favorite transitional moment in Hawai'i. When I pass through, I feel like I'm home.

All three routes through the *pali* lead to the bedroom communities of Kailua and Kane'ohe, tucked into the base of the Ko'olau Mountains. Both are blessed with beautiful bays and filled with vacation rentals but no resorts. Trade winds blow steadily and strongly in Kailua Bay, and you can always count on seeing daredevil windsurfers in Kailua Beach Park. Its neighbor, Lanikai Beach, is one of the loveliest in the entire state, and because parking there is nonexistent, the best way to appreciate it is to walk from a nearby rental—preferably at the crack of dawn or after having a simple meal at a neighborhood restaurant.

Heading north, the coastal road hugs the shoreline, fringed with white sand. Sheer cliffs of the Ko'olaus provide a westerly backdrop. Deep valleys are generally inaccessible, but you will find some decent hikes along the way. Additionally, Windward Coast beaches are not great for swimming, but that doesn't mean they're not pretty to look at. As the two-lane road starts thinning out from traffic and development, you'll find a beautiful temple to explore, ancient fishponds, and the most-visited attraction in the state, the re-created Polynesian Cultural Center.

GUIDANCE

Kailua Chamber of Commerce & Information Center (808-261-2727; kailuachamber.com), Kailua Shopping Center, 600 Kailua Rd., Kailua. Open 8–4 weekdays, 10–2 Sat. Contact them before or during your trip to discover even more about this low-key destination. If you're going to be here more than an hour, it would behoove you to pick up a local map; it can be tough finding some of the restaurants listed here.

BUILDING BLOCKS FOR A PERFECT DAY ON THE LEEWARD COAST

Hold on to your hat (and breath) at the Nu'uanu Pali Lookout (30 minutes)

Drink in silence at the Byodo-In Temple (1 hour)

Visit the Polynesian Cultural Center (2 to 4 hours)

Enjoy a picnic, sunbathing, and windsurfing at Lanikai Beach (3 hours)

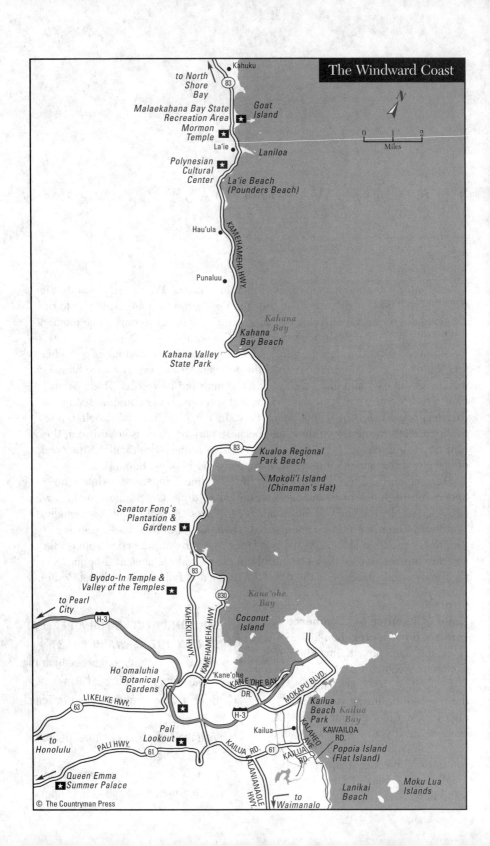

The Windward Coast

to North Shore Bay

83

Kahuku

Goat Island

Malaekahana Bay State Recreation Area

Mormon Temple

La'ie

Laniloa

Polynesian Cultural Center

La'ie Beach (Pounders Beach)

0   1   2
Miles

N

Hau'ula

KAMEHAMEHA HWY

Punaluu

Kahana Bay

Kahana Bay Beach

Kahana Valley State Park

83

Kualoa Regional Park Beach

Mokoli'i Island (Chinaman's Hat)

Senator Fong's Plantation & Gardens

83

Byodo-In Temple & Valley of the Temples

Kane'ohe Bay

830

to Pearl City

H-3

Coconut Island

KAHEKILI HWY.

KAMEHAMEHA HWY

Ho'omaluhia Botanical Gardens

'Kane'ohe

KANE'OHE BAY DR.

MOKAPU BLVD.

Kailua Beach Park

Kailua Bay

LIKELIKE HWY.

63

H-3

Kailua

KALAHEO AVE.

KAWAILOA RD.

to Honolulu

Pali Lookout

PALI HWY.

61

KAILUA RD.

61

KAILUA RD.

Popoia Island (Flat Island)

Queen Emma Summer Palace

KALANIANAOLE HWY.

to Waimanalo

Lanikai Beach

Moku Lua Islands

© The Countryman Press

By car: There are two ways to get to Kailua and the Windward Coast: by continuing counterclockwise around the island from Southeast Oʻahu, or by cutting through Pali Highway (Hwy. 61) tunnel from Greater Honolulu—the most dramatic and scenic of the two. You can also get here via the H-3 or via Likelike Highway (Hwy. 63); all roads seem to lead to Kailua. The coastal road is called Hwy. 83 and the Kamehameha Highway.

MEDICAL EMERGENCY
Castle Medical Center (808-263-5500), 640 Ulukahiki St., Kailua. Open 24/7.

✳ To See & Do

To Kailua
✪ **Nuʻuanu Pali Highway & Lookout**, Hwy. 61, halfway between Honolulu and Kailua. The Pali Highway cuts through the Koʻolau Range between Honolulu and Kailua, passing the Queen Emma Summer Palace, Hsu Yun Zen Temple, and the very picturesque Waikahulu Falls along the way. When the houses thin out and the greenery takes over, the mother of all 20-minute scenic drives unfolds. During the rainy season every hill and valley is veiled with little waterfalls and tropical ferns. Be sure to stop at the windy lookout (and hold on to your hat) to soak up the spectacular views. You'll be standing on the very spot where in 1795 King Kamehameha, in his bid to unite the Hawaiian Islands, drove the last of the Oʻahu defenders over the *pali* to their death.

Nuʻuanu Valley Rain Forest, 2 miles west of Nuʻuanu Pali Lookout. Coming from Honolulu, take the Nuʻuanu Pali Road turnoff to enjoy this 2-mile detour off the Pali Highway. You'll pass under a tropical canopy of wild ginger, hanging vines, and giant bamboo, the light of day barely flickering through.

Queen Emma Summer Palace (808-595-3167; daughtersofhawaii.org), 2913 Pali Hwy. Open 9–4 daily. This *pali* hideaway was once the residence of Queen Emma, consort of Kamehameha IV. Emma was three-quarters royal Hawaiian and a quarter English, a granddaughter of the captured British sailor John Young, who became a friend and adviser to Kamehameha I. The Youngs left the home to Queen Emma, who often slipped away from her formal downtown home to spend time at this retreat, with its columned porch, high ceilings, and beautiful grounds. The interior is decorated with period furniture from five of her homes, along with feather capes and robes, a cathedral-shaped koa cabinet displaying a gift of china from Queen Victoria, and a necklace of tiger claws given by the maharaja of India. $4 seniors, $6 adults, $1 ages 11–17.

NUʻUANU PALI LOOKOUT

Kailua & Nearby

⚔ **Kailua Beach Park**. See *Beaches*.

Ulupo Heiau State Monument, behind the Windward YMCA, on Manu-Oo Rd., off Kailua Rd. The stonework at this small *heiau* is well preserved and offers a glimpse into early Hawaiian life. In front of the temple an artist's rendition shows how it may have looked in the 1700s. Hawaiian legend holds that Menehune, credited for most ancient stonework, built the *heiau* quickly, according to their habit of finishing one project per night.

⚔ ✪ **Lanikai Beach**. See *Beaches*.

Flat Island (aka **Popoia Island**), just offshore from Kailua Beach. This tiny island is a bird sanctuary, as well as a popular and relatively easy kayaking destination.

Moku Nui Island and **Moku Iki Island**, just offshore from Lanikai Beach. Of the twin Moku Lua, you are only allowed to visit Moku Nui, usually by kayak, though local swimmers make it a daily habit. Both islands are bird sanctuaries. If you get the chance, don't miss a moonrise over the Mokus; it rivals a moonrise over Hernandez.

Kane'ohe & Hwy. 836

Kane'ohe Bay. This bay runs for 7 miles—from Chinaman's Hat (Mokoli'i Island) at the northern end to Kane'ohe Beach Park at the southern. Even though much of the bay is protected by an offshore reef, the water is generally silted and not good for swimming, especially compared to spectacular Kailua Beach. The nearly constant trade winds here are ideal for sailing, however, and you'll see sailboats and whitecaps most days.

Coconut Island (aka **Moku o Lo'e**), at the southeastern end of Kane'ohe Bay. Coconut Island, named for the coconut trees planted there by Princess Bernice Pauahi Bishop, was the location for the *Gilligan's Island* TV series in the 1960s. Today the University of Hawai'i's Institute of Marine Biology conducts research here.

Ho'omaluhia Botanical Gardens (808-233-7323), 45-680 Luluku Rd., Kane'ohe. Open 9–4 daily; guided hikes Sat. at 10 and Sun. at 1. *Ho'omaluhia* means "to make a place of peace," which Honolulu's largest botanical garden does. The garden was originally built by the Army Corps of Engineers to protect Kane'ohe from floods. Centered on a lovely 32-acre lake, it specializes in Polynesian plants, palms, and aroids (like philodendrons and anthuriums). You can drive through part of the complex, but walking is the only way to really appreciate these lush green gardens. Bring insect repellent and sensible shoes, as footing can be on the slippery side. Remind the kids not to eat the plants.

KO'OLAU MOUNTAINS

There are restrooms and a landscaped picnic area; parking and admission are free.

Along Hwy. 83 (the Kahekili & Kamehameha Hwys.) North from Kane'ohe

Haiku Gardens, 46-336 Haiku Rd. Surrounding a beautiful lily pond with a small pier that doubles as a wedding chapel, the lush, open setting is popular for sunset walks, which often coincide with happy hour at the adjacent restaurant, Haleiwa Joe's.

○ **Byodo-In Temple** (808-239-9844), 47-200 Kahekili Hwy. Open 9–5 daily. For most visitors the main attraction of the **Valley of the Temples** is Byodo-In, the "temple of equality." Constructed in 1968 to commemorate the 100th anniversary of Japanese immigration to Hawai'i, this red-and-gold replica of a 950-year-old temple in Kyoto features a 9-foot seated Buddha in the main hall, which catches the first rays of sunlight each day. Wild peacocks roam the grounds, and the 3-ton brass bell next to the large pond is said to bring tranquility and good fortune to those who ring it—and many do. (At least the line moves quickly!) Admission $2 adults, $1 ages 12 and under.

Senator Fong's Plantation & Gardens (808-239-6775; fonggarden.net), 47-285 Pulama Rd., Kane'ohe. Open 10–2 daily; walking tours at 10:30 AM and one PM. Although former U.S. senator Hiram Fong passed away in August 2004 at the age of 97, his inspired project from the 1950s continues to grow. It's both a nature preserve and a bird sanctuary; there are 700 acres of palms, ferns, and tropical flowers. $14.50 adults, $13 seniors, $9 ages 5–12.

Mokoli'i Island (aka **Chinaman's Hat**), off the Kamehameha Hwy., just beyond Kualoa Regional Park. Hawaiians called this cone-shaped islet Papale Pake, literally "hat Chinese," when Chinese laborers began arriving to work the fields of O'ahu. People sometimes explore the island by walking across to it at low tide, but you can reduce your chances of getting stranded by using a kayak when the tide is higher. The views of the coastline and Ko'olau Mountains are marvelous.

✦ **Kualoa Regional Park Beach**. See *Beaches*.

✦ **Pounders Beach** (aka **La'ie Beach Park**). See *Beaches*.

Polynesian Cultural Center (808-293-3333 or 1-800-367-7060; polynesia.com), 55-370 Kamehameha Hwy., La'ie. Open noon–9 Mon.–Sat. Better known locally as the PCC, this attraction is the work of the local Mormon church. The rambling grounds require most of a day to be enjoyed, so come prepared. For starters, there are seven theme villages representing the lifestyle and culture of Samoa, New Zealand, Fiji, Tahiti, Tonga, the Marquesas, and

BYODO-IN TEMPLE. THE VALLEY OF THE TEMPLES.

AT THE POLYNESIAN CULTURAL CENTER

Hawai'i. Authentic-looking huts and ceremonial houses, many built with twisted ropes and hand-carved posts, contribute to the theme. Polynesian descendants (often college students from nearby Brigham Young University) dress in traditional garb as they demonstrate *poi* pounding, coconut frond weaving, dancing, and handicrafts. There's also a replica of a 19th-century mission chapel, but the big attraction here is the evening lu'au and dance performance. The basic admission price also includes the Pageant of the Long Canoes; an optional 45-minute tram tour of the Mormon Temple grounds and BYU campus; and ocean-themed movies at the center's IMAX theater. Regular admission: $45 adults, $26 ages 3–11; admission with show package that includes preferred show seating: $65 adults, $50 children; lu'au package that includes evening meal and preferred show seating: $100 adults, $66 children.

Mormon Temple (808-293-2427), 55-600 Naniloa Loop, La'ie. The Church of Latter-Day Saints purchased the 6,000-acre plantation in La'ie that became the site of the Mormon Temple in 1919. It was the first built outside the U.S. mainland. The actual temple stands on an 11-acre section atop a gentle rise. There are free guided tours, although they do not include the temple interior.

✦ **La'ie Point**, at the end of Naupaka St. Located at the south end of La'ie Bay, the beach between La'ie Point and Malaekahana Bay State Recreation Area is great for surfing and bodysurfing. From the point there are magnificent views of the Ko'olau Range, the bay coast, and Mokuauia (Goat Island) just offshore.

✦ **Malaekahana Bay State Recreation Area**. See *Beaches*.

Goat Island (aka Mokuauia Beach), opposite Malaekahana Beach. Goat Island is a state bird sanctuary with a small sandy cove where swimming and snorkeling are permitted. When the tide is low and the water's calm you can walk there, especially if you have protective water shoes or sandals; you can also follow the locals there and use a kayak, boogie board, foam noodle, inner tube, or inflatable beach mattress. On the other hand, if you prefer to swim over at high tide, ask the lifeguard first about occasional riptides.

Kahuku, 2 miles north of La'ie. You could drive right through Kahuku and never know it, but that would be a loss. At the north end of the Windward Coast, this former sugar-mill town was once the province of the Kahuku Plantation, active from the late 1800s until 1971. The mill itself, once a proud landmark, has nearly disappeared, literally bit by bit. Today only the signature smokestack remains. Even so, there's a bit of spirit left here, perhaps best represented by the shrimp trucks (see *Eating Out* in The North Shore) that dot the highway and dispense heaping plates of fresh garlicky shrimp. Keep an eye out for the aquaculture ponds at the north end of town, which have become a local cottage industry.

BIRD-WATCHING
See **Flat Island** (Popoia Island), **Moku Nui Island**, **Moku Iki Island**, **Senator Fong's Plantation & Gardens**, and **Goat Island** under *To See & Do*.

BOAT EXCURSIONS
Captain Bob's Adventure Cruises (808-942-5077), Kane'ohe. Trips daily except Sun. Bob himself takes groups aboard his 42-foot catamaran. He sails around Kane'ohe Bay and stops alongside a sandbar 2 miles offshore, where you can practice your snorkeling techniques, enjoy a barbecue lunch, and take a coral-reef snorkel. It's a great trip. The boat leaves the pier at 10:15 and returns at 2:30. Shuttle bus service is available from Waikiki hotels. $83 adults, $65 ages 13–17, $63 children ages 12 and under.

GOLF
Kahuku Golf Course (808-293-5842), 56-501 Kamehameha Hwy., Kahuku. Greens fees at this nine-hole oceanside course are a mere $10, and playing time is first come, first served. Club rentals $12; cart rentals $4.

HIKING
Nu'uanu Pali Trail. Enter from Nu'uanu Pali Dr. or from Manoa Falls. This moderate-to-difficult trail is part of a larger circuit that takes in much of Nu'uanu and Manoa Valleys. Taken together, it's rigorous hiking and not just a walk in the rain forest. At the western end, **Jackass Ginger Pool** is the main attraction. At the eastern end, the **Manoa Falls Trail** (see *Hiking* under "Greater Honolulu") is one of several easier segments.

Maunawili Falls Trail, located near Waimanalo, off Kukuhau St. This popular 2.5-mile loop is a great introduction to hiking on O'ahu. The trail is moderate in difficulty, and its graceful contours take in a number of *pali* lookouts, with views of the Windward Coast, the Ko'olaupoko watershed, and several lush gulches.

Ka'iwa Ridge Trail, off A'alapapa Dr., Lanikai. More a path than anything, this gentle, mile-long ridge offers splendid views and mountain greenery for the price of a short walk.

Kahana Valley, 1 mile north of Crouching Lion Inn. Kahana Valley is home to Ahupua'a o Kahana State Park, a deep rain forest with two poorly maintained hiking trails and an orientation center. Worth a visit, however, is the ancient **Huilua Fishpond** on Kahana Bay. This valley, by the way, is the only publicly owned *ahupua'a* remaining in Hawai'i. In ancient times, land in Hawai'i was divided like pie wedges so that each major landowner would get property that ran from the mountains (with abundant sources of water) to the sea (with abundant fishing).

Hau'ula Loop Trail. Trailhead at Hau'ula Homestead Rd., opposite the north end of Hau'ula Beach Park. This short but sweet trail (about 5 miles total walking distance) is well maintained and offers great views of the coast as you pass by ohi'a, ironwood, and guava trees.

I try to do everything I write about, but I am not a scuba diver. For the best information, head to the oldest outfitter in the state: **Aaron's Dive Shop** (808-262-2333; hawaii-scuba.com), 307 Hahani St., Kailua. O'ahu is a great place for wreck diving, but if you're a diver, you already knew that, didn't you?

WATER SPORTS

Windsurfing (offshore) and kayaking (out to the islands) are really big here.

Kailua Sailboards & Kayaks (808-262-2555; kailuasailboards.com), 130 Kailua Rd., Kailua. Open daily. This outfit rents kayaks ($49–59 daily) and beginner's sailboards ($59–69 daily). They also offer four-hour group guided kayak eco-tours ($119) and windsurfing lessons ($89–174). Don't need lessons? Rent boogie boards, surfboards, and bicycles and take off on your own. As if that's not enough, they also provide lunch and transportation to and from Waikiki hotels.

Naish Hawai'i/Windsurfing (808-262-6068 or 1-800-767-6068; naish.com), 155-A Hamakua Dr., Kailua. Open daily. Located in a sheltered bay, this highly regarded, longtime outfitter has packages for both beginners and experienced windsurfers. Beginning lessons include 90 minutes of instruction and 90 minutes of practice on your own ($75). They also rent and sell high-quality gear for all water sports. Always call ahead to check wind conditions and make reservations.

Twogood Kayaks (808-262-5656; twogoodkayaks.com), 345 Hahani St., Kailua. Open daily. In addition to kayak rentals ($24.50 per person for a tandem), Twogood offers guided kayak tours with naturalists that include snorkeling and swimming ($109 per person) and packages that include a kayak, lessons, lunch, and hotel pickup ($69). Head out with these folks and let them show you the natural pool around the back side of one of the islands.

KAILUA BEACH PARK

✳ Beaches

In order of preference.

✈ **Kailua Beach Park**, Kawailoa Rd., at the end of Hwy. 61. Kailua Beach Park, divided into two sections by Kaelepulu Canal, is a glistening white beach framed by ironwood trees. The turquoise-blue ocean on the bay's west side is popular year-round for swimming, sailboarding, and kite surfing; the east side has a small boat ramp and a lighthouse on the hill above. And a newish bike path cuts through the park. The long stretch of beach has grassy areas shaded by ironwood trees, while the bay is gentle most of the time, even when it's windy. The nearby bird sanctuary of Flat Island

(Popoia Island) is easily reached by kayak. *Facilities*: Lifeguards, restrooms, showers, shaded picnic areas, phones; kayak, windsurfer, and sailboard rentals.

🏄 ✪ **Lanikai Beach**, Kailua Rd., 300 yards east of Kailua Beach Park. Gentle, beautiful, pristine, and totally lacking in parking, Lanikai Beach is easily one of the prettiest beaches in all Hawai'i—and that's no exaggeration! The twin Moku Lua Islands sit directly offshore and round out the idyllic picture. Sun worshippers should bathe in the morning since the beach is shaded by the afternoon. The beach fronts a very upscale residential neighborhood, and it is accessible by public walkways only. The best advice is to park at Kailua Beach Park and walk to Lanikai. *Facilities*: None, other than nearby Kailua Beach Park.

🏄 **Kualoa Regional Park Beach**, Kamehameha Hwy., opposite Chinaman's Hat. Hawaiian kings sent their sons to be raised at peaceful Kualoa, and this once-sacred spot was where outcasts sought refuge. Even now the tranquil beach park feels like a sanctuary, seldom crowded and perfect for relaxing and swimming. Nearby Apua Pond, a salt marsh, is a nesting area for the endangered aeo (Hawaiian stilt). *Facilities*: Lifeguards on weekends and during summer, picnic tables and barbecues, restrooms, showers, camping, phones.

🏄 **Malaekahana Bay State Recreation Area**, at the north end of La'ie Bay. Malaekahana Beach follows a beautiful strand between Makohoa Point to the north and Kalanai Point to the south. Ironwood trees facing the long, sandy beach provide plenty of shade. Swimming is often good year-round, although there can be strong currents in winter. The beach is a favorite for everything from bodysurfing to Frisbee. Kalanai Point, the main section of the state park, is less than a mile north of La'ie and has picnic tables, barbecue grills, fabulous camping, restrooms, and showers.

🏄 **Pounders Beach** (aka La'ie Beach Park), half a mile south of the Polynesian Cultural Center in La'ie. What's in a name? Well, this is a great bodysurfing beach, but the shorebreak can be punishing, especially in winter. Swimming in summer is mellow, and the ironwood trees near the beach offer shade. The area around the old landing is usually the calmest. *Facilities*: Showers, restrooms.

✳ Lodging

The bedroom community of Kailua is surprisingly close to Honolulu (about 30 minutes by car) and could make a great base for exploring most of the island. Other than a few vacation rentals, a passable motel-like value, and camping, there's mostly just exploring. (Incidentally, only a tiny percentage of the available lodging rentals are officially licensed.)

VACATION RENTALS & COTTAGES
Pat's Kailua Beach Properties (808-261-1653 or 808-262-4128; pats kailua.com), 204 S. Kalaheo Ave., Kailua. These folks represent about 30 area properties, with kitchens or kitchenettes, with or without ocean views, within walking distance of the beach.

Lanikai Beach Rentals (808-261-7895 or 1-800-258-7895; lanikaibeach rentals.com), 1277 Mokulua Dr. This agency offers several properties in the Lanikai and Kailua area. The majority of them accommodate two to four people; a few are even larger. All have kitchens or kitchenettes, TVs, and private phones; some come with washer-dryer and Internet access. *Rates*: $$–$$$$; five to seven night minimum stay; $45–100 cleaning fee.

MOTEL

La'ie Inn (808-293-9282 or 1-800-526-4562), 55-109 Laniloa St. (just off the Kamehameha Hwy.), La'ie. Adjacent to the PCC, this two-story motel has very basic rooms that barely fit the bill for area exploration. Every year there are promises that it will be demolished and rebuilt, so perhaps one day it will actually happen. Why include it here? The staff is extraordinarily friendly, it's really inexpensive, and there aren't many places to stay in this area. *Rates*: $; children free in parent's room. *Facilities and amenities*: 49 rooms, pool, A/C, activity desk.

CAMPING

FYI: There's no place to rent camping gear on O'ahu.

Kualoa Regional Park Beach (808-768-3440), Kamehameha Hwy., opposite Chinaman's Hat. Free (and excellent camping), but permit required; no camping Wed.–Thurs.; gates locked 8 PM–7 AM.

Malaekahana Bay State Recreation Area (808-293-1736), at the north end of La'ie Bay. Permit required; $5 nightly; gates locked 7 PM–7 AM; no camping Wed.–Thurs. This park offers the best camping on Windward O'ahu. Aside from campgrounds, several cabins and yurts can be rented.

Kahana Bay Beach Park (808-587-0300), Kamehameha Hwy. Permit required; $5 nightly; gates locked 8 PM–7 AM; no camping Wed.–Thurs. This stunningly situated campground offers great views of Mokoli'i Island.

Ho'omaluhia Botanical Gardens (808-233-7323), 45-680 Luluku Rd., off Kamehameha Hwy., Kane'ohe. Free permit required; camping only Fri.–Sun. nights; check for gate lockout times. This is one great place to camp.

✷ Where to Eat

Value-laden neighborhood eateries rule the roost. If you want to feel like a local, dine here. As you head north, stop at a lunch wagon for locally cultivated shrimp.

DINING OUT

♈ **Lucy's Grill 'n Bar** (808-230-8188; lucysgrillnbar.com), 33 Aulike St., Kailua. Open nightly for dinner. This deservedly popular neighborhood bistro specializes in Hawai'i regional cuisine. I prefer dining at the outdoor bar and lanai, but no matter where it's served, the fish offerings are always fabulous. I always try to save room for crème brûlée, although it's hard because the portions are so big. Reservations recommended; children's menu. Entrées $$–$$$.

♨ **Assaggio** (808-261-2772; assaggio kailua.com), 354 Uluniu St., Kailua. Open for lunch and dinner daily. A popular place with decent prices and a casual neighborhood atmosphere, Assaggio is the original in a family-owned chain of southern Italian restaurants. Hidden on a quiet side street, it's beloved by locals. As for specific dishes, I always stick with the most popular: chicken Assaggio and Sicilian chicken. Then again, there are myriad pastas that can be matched with myriad sauces for a blast of flavor. And to boot, dishes are available in two sizes! Unless you live in a city with a serious Italian neighborhood, save room for a cannoli. Reservations recommended. Lunch $$, dinner entrées $$–$$$.

Buzz's Original Steak House (808-261-4661), 413 Kawailoa Rd., Kailua. Open daily 11–3 and 4:30–10. For serious surf-and-turf eats, regardless of whether you've come from the beach or are heading into Honolulu après dinner, this steak house is a dependable option. In addition to a salad bar, look for teriyaki dishes. Reservations recommended. Lunch $–$$, dinner entrées $$–$$$; no credit cards.

EATING OUT

🦐 **L&L Drive-In** (808-262-1113; hawaiianbarbecue.com), 26 Hoʻolai St., Kailua. Open 10–9 daily. Franchises of Hawaiʻi's most successful plate-lunch chain are now found as far afield as Las Vegas. But right here in your backyard you'll find standard local fare like chicken katsu, chili and rice, fried fish, and stew. And, of course, they're all served with two scoops of rice and macaroni salad. It's not for the fainthearted, but everyone needs to try it once. Dishes $–$$.

🦐 **Kalapawai Market** (808-262-4359; kalapawaimarket.com), 306 S. Kalaheo Ave., Kailua. Open 6 AM–9 PM daily. One block from Kailua Beach Park, this neighborhood deli is a real local gathering place. And why not? It offers short-order breakfast dishes, lots of drip coffees, simple sandwiches (and specialty ones like feta veggie or turkey cranberry), and a great selection of wine.

🦐 **Down to Earth Natural Foods** (808-262-3838; downtoearth.org), 201 Hamakua Dr., Kailua. Open 8 AM–10 PM daily. Look for organic fruits and veggies, many of which are grown in Hawaiʻi. Why shop at Safeway (across the street) when you can shop locally? The deli has baked goods, waffles at breakfast, wraps at lunchtime, and smoothies.

🦐 **Cinnamons** (808-261-8724; cinnamonsrestaurant.com), 315 Uluniu St., Kailua. Open 7 AM–2 PM daily, dinner Thurs.–Sat. Do like the locals do: Come for breakfast-in-a-skillet or carrot crème pancakes, and leave very happy.

COFFEE

Morning Brew (808-262-7770), Kailua Shopping Center, 572 Kailua Rd., Kailua. Open daily. This independent coffeehouse is a good alternative to Starbucks (which happens to be across the way).

✳ Selective Shopping

Kim Taylor Reece Gallery (808-293-2000 or 1-800-657-7966; kimtaylorreece.com), 53-866 Kamehameha Hwy., Sacred Falls. Open noon–5 Thurs.–Sat. You've seen the sepia-tinged photographs of hula dancers on the beach; now you can see the gallery of their maker.

BookEnds (808-261-1996), Kailua Shopping Center, 600 Kailua Rd., Kailua. Open daily. This is a great independent neighborhood bookstore.

Agnes Portuguese Bake Shop (808-262-5367), 46 Hoʻolai St., Kailua. Open Tues.–Sun. To truly weigh in on the *malasadas* wars (see *Entertainment* under "Greater Honolulu"), you've got to try them here.

SHRIMP TRUCKS

THE NORTH SHORE

The North Shore epitomizes *laid-back*. It's best to slow down and enjoy the pace—unless, that is, you're a surfer dude competing in a world-class event. Then you'd better be on your toes, since mammoth winter waves routinely reach 30 feet and the beaches are filled with spectators watching you strut your stuff. You might wonder what the fuss is all about in summer, however, when the gentle swells are far from intimidating.

No matter the month, the North Shore is a step back in time, and Hale'iwa is the epicenter of the action. Deemed a Historic and Scenic District in the mid-1980s, Hale'iwa is a funky little town lined with old wooden buildings that house surf shops, low-key eateries (of surprisingly high quality), and one-of-a-kind retailers. Despite the presence of these little commercial operations, the North Shore is otherwise undeveloped for tourism. There are very few overnight accommodations (save for one big resort) along the shoreline. And therein lies a great part of the North Shore's appeal. It feels real. Slip off your sandals, hang around for an afternoon, slurp some shaved ice, ogle buff bodes at the competitions, and admire the athleticism and artistry of the master surfers. It's about an hour's drive from Honolulu. Relax, stay as long as you want, and discover the cadence of Hawai'i time.

To really get away from the crowds, take the Farrington Highway to its desolate, western conclusion just shy of Ka'ena Point, which is accessible only by foot. There is no circular road around O'ahu's shoreline.

GETTING AROUND

By car: You'll approach the North Shore in one of two directions: by continuing a counterclockwise tour of the

---

BUILDING BLOCKS FOR A PERFECT DAY ON THE NORTH SHORE

Shop, hang out, and have lunch in Hale'iwa (4 hours)

Eat Shave Ice from Matsumoto's (30 minutes)

Watch surfers at Sunset Beach & Banzai Pipeline (Ehukai Beach Park) (2 hours)

Visit the sacred Pu'u o Mahuka Heiau (1 hour)

Catch a snack at the shrimp trucks (45 minutes)

Linger over dinner at Turtle Bay Resort (2 hours)

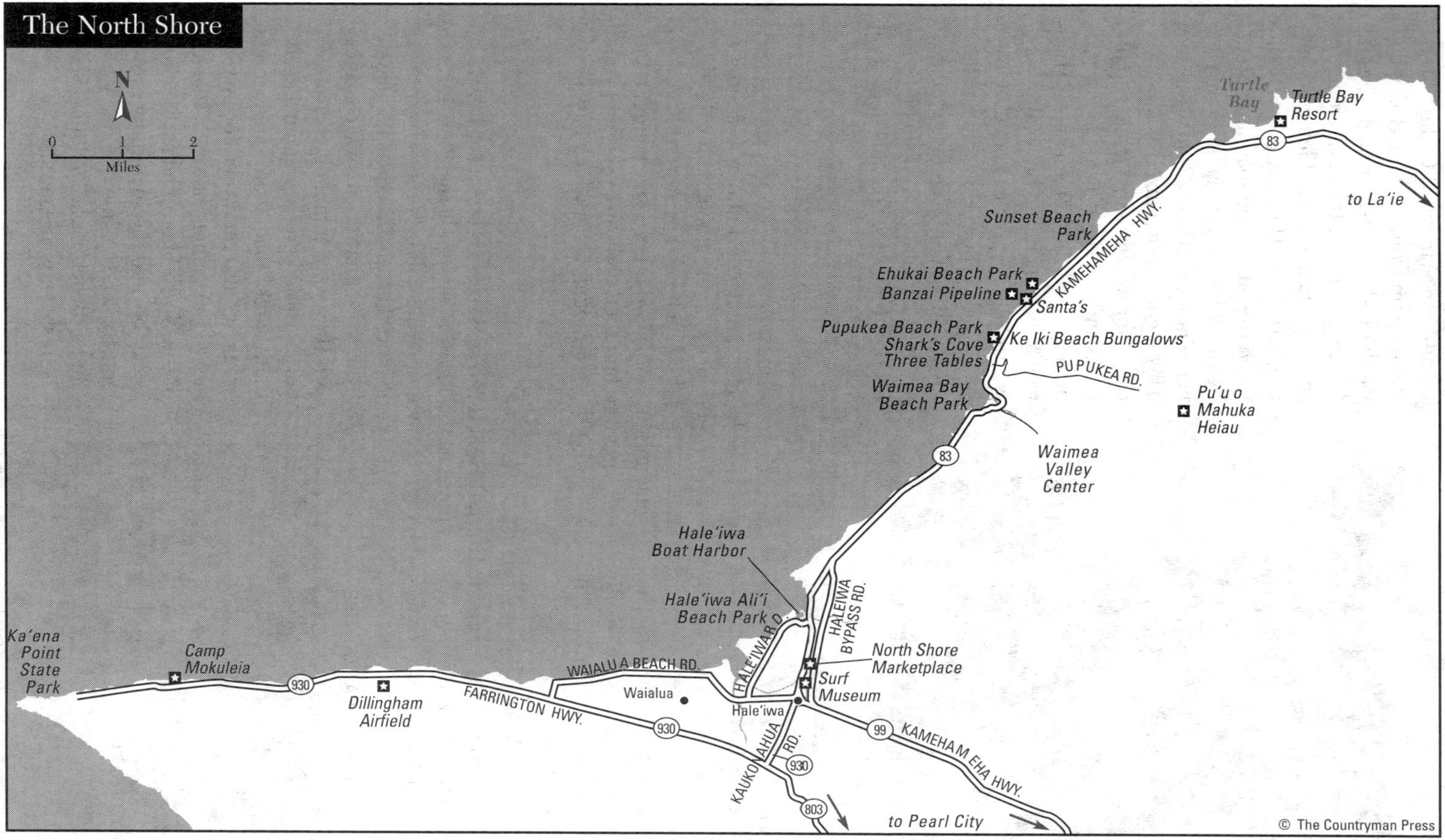

The North Shore

N

0 1 2
Miles

to La'ie

Turtle Bay Resort

Turtle Bay

KAMEHAMEHA HWY.

Sunset Beach Park

Ehukai Beach Park
Banzai Pipeline

Santa's

Pupukea Beach Park
Shark's Cove
Three Tables

Ke Iki Beach Bungalows

PUPUKEA RD.

Pu'u o Mahuka Heiau

Waimea Valley Center

Waimea Bay Beach Park

83

North Shore Marketplace

Surf Museum

HALE'IWA BYPASS RD.

HALE'IWA RD.

KAMEHAM EHA HWY.

99

KAUKONAHUA RD.

930

803

to Pearl City

Hale'iwa Boat Harbor

Hale'iwa Ali'i Beach Park

Hale'iwa

WAIALUA BEACH RD.

930

Waialua

FARRINGTON HWY.

Dillingham Airfield

930

Camp Mokuleia

Ka'ena Point State Park

© The Countryman Press

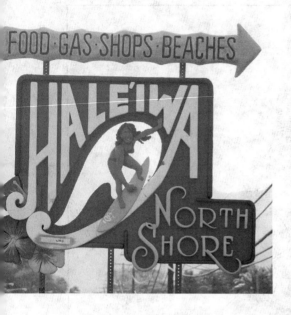

island from Windward Oʻahu or by shooting up from Greater Honolulu via the H-1 and H-2 through Central Oʻahu. For the latter, at the rotary just south of Haleʻiwa, head leftward on the Farrington Highway (Hwy. 930) to reach the end of the road near Kaʻena Point, or head right via the Kamehameha Hwy. (Hwy. 83) for Haleʻiwa. This section is organized as if you've opted for the former, a circle trip of the island. All sights listed below are on or just off the Kamehameha Highway. When there are big winter swells, North Shore traffic can crawl at a snail's pace. There is simply nowhere for cars to pull over and watch the action. The same is true, albeit to a lesser extent, on weekends in general.

✳ To See & Do

Turtle Bay to Haleʻiwa

Turtle Bay Resort, 57-091 Kamehameha Hwy., between Kahuku and Sunset Beach. Even if you're not staying here, pop in and make a beeline for the dramatic shoreline. The walking trails skirting the beach heading toward Kahuku are great for early-morning beachcombing, and there is good snorkeling in the protected, adjacent Kuilima Cove. If you're famished and can't wait until you reach Haleʻiwa, my preferred eatery is **Ola** (see *Dining Out*), which is right on the beach.

⨍ **Sunset Beach**. See *Beaches*.

✪ ⨍ **Banzai Pipeline** (at **Ehukai Beach Park**), across from Sunset Beach School. Banzai Pipeline, also known as the Pipeline or simply the Pipe, is one of Oʻahu's premier surfing spots when the winter swells roll in from the North Pacific. The pipeline gets its name from the extraordinary wave shapes, as if they were tumbling over huge but invisible barrels. Famous for its shallow reef that creates an awesome break, it's also renowned for breaking heads. In summer, however, like most of the North Shore, the surf is gentle as can be, and the swimming is excellent. Banzai Pipeline is actually part of Ehukai Beach Park. *Facilities*: Showers, restrooms, lifeguards.

SURFING THE BANZAI PIPELINE

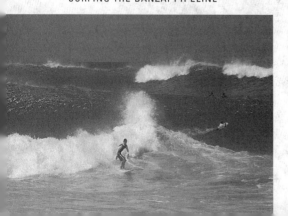

Shark's Cove, across from the old Shell gas station. Shark's Cove is a busy North Shore spot, well known around Oʻahu for excellent spring and summer snorkeling. You can rent snorkel sets nearby at Planet Surf (next to Foodland Supermarket). Ask locals how Shark's Cove got its name, and you'll hear a variety of amusing stories. More dangerous are the fantastic underwater caves just offshore, an area designated as **Pupukea Marine Life Conservation District**. Although these caves are popular with experienced divers, newcomers should enjoy them only in the company of a local expert.

 Three Tables Beach. See *Beaches*.

 Puʻu o Mahuka Heiau, 0.5 mile up Pupukea Rd., off Kamehameha Hwy. (turn at Foodland Supermarket); a sign points to the *heiau*, another 0.75 mile in. Well worth a side trip, this ancient *heiau* is the largest on Oʻahu. Portions of Puʻu o Mahuka are overgrown, but you can sense its spirit in the low stone walls, especially when you take in the panoramic view of the bay and beyond.

Waimea Valley Center (808-638-7766), 59-864 Kamehameha Hwy. Open 9–5:30 daily. This center opened in 2003 with the hope of reclaiming a once-pristine nature preserve that is home to over 5,000 species of flora and fauna. It encompasses several hundred lush acres of rare greenery and bird life. There are paths good for strolling and rich archaeological excavations, including several sacred *heiau* sites. Gardens are well labeled and there are birds galore, from common moor-hens and peafowl to red-crested cardinals and Caspian terns. The 40-foot **Waimea Falls** is one of the main attractions; you can even take a dip in the pool. $10 adults, $5 ages 4–12.

 Waimea Bay Beach Park. See *Beaches*.

Haleʻiwa

 North Shore Surf and Cultural Museum (808-637-8888), North Shore Marketplace, 66-250 Kamehameha Hwy., Haleʻiwa. Open 11–6 Wed.–Mon. This low-key house of surf memorabilia is a delightful collection of odds and ends, a lot like the North Shore itself! You'll find old wooden surfboards, surf movie posters, a photo gallery, and classic aloha shirts on display. If the surf's up, don't count on predictable open hours. We all have our priorities. Donations accepted.

West of Haleʻiwa

Waialua. Located between Haleʻiwa and Mokuleia, off Crozier Dr. via Haleʻiwa Rd. Waialua is an old sugar plantation town, although its sugar mill (Oʻahu's last) closed for good in 1996. There are a few shops serving the community around the old mill. Although the town itself has seen better days, coffee trees were planted after the mill closed in the hope of reviving the community. Several old

PUʻU O MAHUKA HEIAU

plantation buildings are worthy of a look-see, including a bank-turned-bar.

Farrington Highway (Hwy. 930) branches west past Dillingham Airfield toward the state park at Ka'ena. The main thoroughfare along the remote western section of the North Shore branches off just south of Waialua. Turn left on Farrington Highway to reach Waialua, Mokuleia Beach Park, and Dillingham Airfield. Beyond Dillingham, you'll eventually come to the North Shore entrance for **Ka'ena Point State Park**, a rugged coastal terrain accessible only by foot.

KAMEHAMEHA HIGHWAY, HALE'IWA

✷ Outdoor Activities

BICYCLING
Raging Isle (808-637-7707; ragingisle.com), 66-250 Kamehameha Hwy., Hale'iwa, rents mountain bikes for about $40 per 24-hour period.

BIRD-WATCHING
See **Waimea Valley Center** under *To See & Do*.

GOLF
Turtle Bay Resort (808-293-8574; turtlebayresort.com), 57-049 Kuilima Dr., Kahuku. Greens fees at the windy and challenging Palmer Course are $185 daily ($110 after 2 PM); at the more "forgiving" Fazio Course, they run $160 daily ($90 after 2 PM). Make reservations two weeks in advance.

HIKING
Turtle Bay Resort (808-293-8811; turtlebayresort.com), Kamehameha Hwy., Kahuku. This 800-plus-acre resort has a dozen miles of walking trails, including five that run along the shoreline. Ask for a free map from the concierge.

Kaunala Loop Trail, off Pupukea Rd. High above Waimea Valley, and overlooking all of Waimea Bay, this O'ahu hike is one of my favorites, although it's open only on weekends. The 4-mile trail takes about two and a half hours, and along the way there are swamp mahogany trees, streambeds to cross, and exotic tree ferns.

HORSEBACK RIDING
Turtle Bay Resort (808-293-8811; turtlebayresort.com), Kamehameha Hwy., Kahuku. Rides daily. These stables offer two slow-paced, follow-the-leader-type trail rides that go across beaches, cut through a magnificent ironwood forest, and conclude in a meadow. The 45-minute ride ($50) leaves at four specified times throughout the day. The one-and-a-half-hour trip starts at 4 PM ($80). Call ahead

for reservations and age and weight restrictions.

TENNIS

Turtle Bay Resort (808-293-8811; turtlebayresort.com), 57-091 Kamehameha Hwy., Kahuku. Open daily. Along with clinics and rentals, this popular facility has eight Plexipave courts. Court time costs $10 hourly; reserve in advance to avoid disappointment.

WATER SPORTS

Surf-n-Sea (808-637-9887; surfnsea.com), 62-595 Kamehameha

WAITING TO CATCH A WAVE

Hwy., next to the Rainbow Bridge, Haleʻiwa. Open 9 AM–7 PM daily. Look to the knowledgeable and enthusiastic staff here for one-stop shopping for water adventure tours and lessons. They also sell and rent equipment for snorkeling, diving (for certified divers and beginners), sea kayaking, and surfing. Lessons and excursions venture along the western and northern coasts, depending on the season and conditions. Dive in Shark's Cove ($75–135) or sign up for an all-inclusive surfing lesson ($85). These folks have whatever suits your pleasure, as long as you're getting in the water.

TOP BEACHES ON OʻAHU

For Swimming & Sunbathing
Lanikai Beach (Windward Oʻahu)
Ala Moana Beach Park (Greater Honolulu)
Sans Souci Beach (aka Kaimana Beach) (Waikiki)
Sunset Beach (North Shore)
Pokai Bay Beach Park (Central & Leeward Oʻahu)

For Walking
Kapiʻolani Beach (Waikiki)
Malaekahana Bay State Recreation Area (Windward Oʻahu)
Waikiki Beach (Waikiki)
Waimanalo Bay Beach Park (Southeast Oʻahu)
Lanikai Beach (Windward Oʻahu)

For Snorkeling & Water Sports
Hanauma Bay (Southeast Oʻahu)
Kailua Beach Park (Windward Oʻahu)
Three Tables Beach (North Shore)
Waimea Bay Beach Park (North Shore)

Hans Hedemann Surf School (808-924-7778; hhsurf.com), at the Turtle Bay Resort (and the Kahala Hotel & Resort and the Park Shore Waikiki Hotel . . . while we're at it). This championship surfer dude has been winning contests since, like, the mid-1970s. He can help anyone get their sea legs.

✳ Beaches

In order of preference.

✪ ✦ **Sunset Beach**, unmarked on the Kamehameha Hwy.; look for Mile Marker 9. Perhaps the most famous of several world-class North Shore surf spots, Sunset Beach is a 2-mile-long strip of white sand that borders crystal-clear seas. In spring and summer it's generally placid and perfect for swimming and sun-bathing. In winter months, though, it often sports 15- to 20-foot waves, attracting top surfers from Hawai'i and beyond. *Facilities*: Lifeguard, picnic tables, highway parking.

✦ **Banzai Pipeline** (at **Ehukai Beach Park**). See *To See & Do*.

✦ **Waimea Bay Beach Park**, just south of Pupukea Beach Park, Waimea. A gorgeous beach set in a tight cove, Waimea also has excellent swimming during summer months before it turns fierce come winter. Then it becomes another favorite of world-class surfers who challenge its monster waves and steep shore-break. When Waimea calms down, it's great for bodysurfing. When the surf's up in winter, come early to watch the pros and also to get one of the prized parking spots. *Facilities*: Lifeguard, showers, restrooms, picnic tables, free parking.

✦ **Three Tables Beach**, Kamehameha Hwy., 0.5 mile east of Waimea Bay. Adjacent to Shark's Cove, this beach gets its name from the three flat ledges rising just above the water. It has great snorkeling and diving in summer, when you can often spot (or swim with) giant sea turtles. Farther out, coral caves and lava arches await serious divers. This is a summer-only spot; in winter, dangerous riptides flow between the beach and the tables. The beach has several tide pools worth exploring, but beware of sharp rocks and coral. *Facilities*: None, except at nearby Shark's Cove.

✦ **Hale'iwa Ali'i Beach Park**, adjacent to the small Hale'iwa boat harbor. This well-protected beach park offers the North Shore's safest year-round swimming, especially at the south end. On winter weekends the county offers free surf lessons. If you get the fever, you can rent your own board from the shop that's closest: Surf-n-Sea (see *Water Sports*). The beach on the other side of the harbor is also good for swimming and features volleyball and basketball courts, plus a grassy softball field. *Facilities*: Both beaches have lifeguards year-round, picnic tables, showers, restrooms.

SUNSET BEACH

✱ Lodging

The pickings are slim up here, which is a shame because it's a downright dramatic place to stay. But perhaps that's part of the allure: It hasn't sold its soul to tourism. **Team Real Estate** (808-637-3507 or 1-800-982-8602; teamrealestate.com) has plenty of listings for North Shore vacation rentals.

✤ **Turtle Bay Resort** (808-293-8811 or 1-800-203-3650; turtlebayresort .com), 57-091 Kamehameha Hwy., Kahuku. The world's most celebrated surfing waves, where titanic peaks of water hammer the shoreline each winter, are just down the road from here. And although the waves are less menacing around the hotel, they still have an explosive, spellbinding majesty. Luckily, the hotel also has a calm, reef-protected beach (Kuilima Cove) for sunning, snorkeling, surfing, kayaking, or scuba diving. In this remote outback, guests basically have all the sporting facilities to themselves; there's no jockeying for position in lines of tourists. With a recent $35 million renovation (in 2004), the resort again compares favorably to its setting. An open-air lobby sets the stage with floor-to-ceiling windows displaying expansive ocean views. Rooms are soothing and blend nicely with the outdoor elements. As for the 42 lovely beachfront cottages—complete with a separate check-in area—snag one if you can. They feature marble bathrooms with great soaking tubs, hardwood floors, and lanais where you'll linger far too long on teakwood chaises. As of early June 2008, the resort was under new management and there were controversial plans afoot to develop the 848-acre parcel with five new hotels. The state

SURFING COMPETITION

is also considering purchasing a huge tract of the land to preserve it. *Rates*: $$$–$$$$, children free in parent's room. *Facilities and amenities*: 443 rooms, suites, and beach cottages; two heated pools; swimmable beach; five restaurants (including **21 Degrees North** and **Ola** [see *Dining Out*]; two golf courses; 10 tennis courts; fitness center; **Spa Luana**; concierge; shops; children's programs; resort fee (includes tennis courts, fitness center, snorkeling gear, and parking).

✤ **Santa's** (808-962-0100 or 1-800-262-9912; bestbnb.com), North Shore. This is a rare find because of one magic word: oceanfront. Occupying the first floor of a private residence (with the most accommodating hosts in the world), the apartment is on a

WAIMEA BAY BEACH PARK

TURTLE BAY RESORT

quiet little lane just off the main highway. On weekends, though, the area is hopping with surfers, tourists, and locals out for a drive. As the name implies, the Santa Claus theme pervades every nook and cranny at Santa's. The unit is also outfitted with every conceivable convenience for his elves. A small living room has a great entertainment center, tons of movies, and a sleeper sofa for an additional guest. The fully equipped kitchen is generously stocked with coffee and fruit (and more) to get you started. A very pleasant gazebo rests at sand's edge, the perfect place for a postsunset drink. As for sunset drinks, walk up the side of the house and down the steps onto the beach. It doesn't get

BLISSFUL BEACH AT SUNSET

any better. Book very, very early! There's only one Santa. *Rates*: $$; three-night minimum. *Facilities and amenities*: TV, phone, A/C, no smoking.

Ke Iki Beach Bungalows (808-638-8829 or 1-866-638-8229; keikibeach.com), 59-579 Ke Iki Rd., Haleʻiwa. It's hard to beat the rarefied beachfront location of these units. And now it's hard to beat the actual bungalows themselves. In 2007, the new owners plunged $1 million into enlarging two units and remodeling interiors. Each bungalow comes with a full kitchen, telephones, and TV. Book four to six months in advance. No kidding! *Rates*: $$. *Facilities and amenities*: 11 units, some on the beach and worth every cent of their higher price tag; cleaning fee $50–100 (ask about water sport equipment and bicycles), TV, A/C in one unit only, no smoking.

Backpackers Vacation Inn & Plantation Village (808-638-7838; backpackers-hawaii.com), 59-788 Kamehameha Hwy. For the surfer dude in all of us, this hostel, across from Three Tables Beach (between Shark's Cove and Waimea) offers Spartan and rustic dorms, studios, private rooms, and private cabins. *Rates*: $–$$. *Facilities and amenities*: dorms with shared bath and kitchen, cabins and studios with private bath and a full kitchen or kitchenette, TV, linens, bike rentals, (inexpensive) all-you-can-eat meals, water sports equipment rental.

Camp Mokuleia (808-637-6241; campmokuleia.com), 68-729 Farrington Hwy., west of Haleʻiwa and 4 miles east of Kaʻena Point. Way up on the northwestern tip of the North Shore, you'll find a 9-acre Episcopal camp and conference center that offers camping (on the beach and on grassy areas), cabins that sleep 14–22 people, a studio cottage, lodge rooms (with and without a private bath), and a three-bedroom beach house. This place is a gem of a getaway. Don't be put off by other groups staying here; it's just a fact, and there's plenty of privacy for all. Call for rates and reservations.

✳ Where to Eat

There are plenty of funky, vegetarian eateries up here that offer excellent value. A couple are O'ahu institutions. Hang out for a while, pretend you have time on your hands, and get into the spirit of the place. Unless otherwise noted, all eateries are in Hale'iwa. It's too bad there aren't more places to stay up here, because you could eat cheaply (and well) for days.

DINING OUT

✍ ⵉ **Hale'iwa Joe's** (808-637-8005; haleiwajoes.com), 66-011 Kamehameha Hwy. Open for lunch and dinner daily. This place has a great surfer-tropical atmosphere; it's situated at the Anahulu Bridge overlooking the harbor and great sunsets; it has wonderful seafood and American menu selections (fish is always a great bet), good service, and moderate prices; bar drinks and pupus are available throughout the day; lunches revolve around sandwiches and salads. What more could you want? Hopefully you'll get lucky and score a table on the lanai. Children's menu. Lunch $–$$, dinner entrées $$–$$$$.

Jameson's by the Sea (808-637-6272; restauranteur.com/jamesons), 62-540 Kamehameha Hwy. Open for lunch and dinner daily, brunch on weekends. Sunsets are the big draw

here. If you come, try their famous salmon pâté, grilled fish sandwiches, and crab and shrimp sandwich. I tend to skip the more pricey and formal upstairs dining room. Reservations recommended; children's menu. Brunch $–$$, lunch $$–$$$, dinner entrées $$$$.

✪ **21 Degrees North** (808-293-881 or 1-800-203-3650; turtlebayresort .com), 57-091 Kamehameha Hwy., Turtle Bay Resort, Kahuku. Open Tues.–Sat. for dinner. Even if you're not overnighting at the resort, it's worth the drive up from Honolulu to dine here (or at **Ola**; see below). It takes about an hour, depending on traffic. Views of Turtle Bay through floor-to-ceiling windows are one thing; the contemporary island cuisine paired with refined Asian influences are another. Look for sumptuous dishes like lacquered salmon filet, braised Kona lobster, and rosemary crusted Colorado rack of lamb. The chef also strives to use all organic produce. Dinner entrées $$$$.

🦐 **Ola at Turtle Bay Resort** (808-293-0801; turtlebayresort.com), 57-091 Kamehameha Hwy., Turtle Bay

Resort, Kahuku. Open for all three meals daily. Few locations rival that of Ola, in a tasteful, wooden pavilion-style building right on the beach. With that calling card, Chef Fred DeAngelo could have skimped on the cuisine. But he saw that bet and raised us one. I've never been disappointed here—by the romantic tiki torches after dark or the execution of such a discriminating menu. Since *ola* means "living or healthy," it's no surprise that all the produce used is grown in the area and that the fresh catch-of-the-day comes from nearby waters. Vegetarians and vegans are not slighted in the least. Children's menu. Breakfast $, lunch $–$$, dinner entrées $$$.

EATING OUT

🍴 🌿 **Kua 'Aina Sandwiches** (808-637-6067), 66-610 Kamehameha Hwy. Open 11–8 daily. I'll go out on a limb here: Kua 'Aina makes Hawai'i's best burgers. (After almost 30 years in the same small space, it moved in the early 2000s and has never missed a beat.) As many folks order in as take out to the beach. Although the majority of patrons order juicy burgers (topped with a dozen choices), a minority thoroughly enjoy fish or turkey sandwiches. But what's a burg-

---

SHAVE ICE

In the olden days before refrigeration, when huge blocks of ice were carved up for home delivery, children would gather around, collect the ice shavings, and munch them down. Eventually Chinese immigrant workers from the sugar plantations started pouring sweet cane juices on top of the plain shavings. And then little shops started springing up to sell the stuff from paper cones, to be eaten with little wooden spoons. As with *malasadas* and lunch wagons, everyone has their beloved outlet for shave ice. When you're on the North Shore, head to ✪ **Matsumoto Shave Ice** (808-637-4827; matsu motoshaveice.com; 66-087 Kamehameha Hwy.; open 9–6 daily). Since the early 1960s this family has been scooping the Hawaiian version of snow cones, doused with your choice of syrupy tropical flavoring. *Liliko'i*, banana, and coconut are the most popular. To do like the locals, order it with sweet adzuki beans (a paste, really) and a scoop of ice cream.

er without a fry, a Butch without a Sundance, a Jack Bauer without a Chloe? To that end, rest assured: The shoestring fries are as celebrated as the half-pound patties. Dishes $; no credit cards.

Hale'iwa Eats (808-637-4247), 66-079 Kamehameha Hwy. Open for lunch and dinner daily. This new, hip, and authentic Thai restaurant serves delicious curries (from Panang to Massaman), soups (from Tom Ka Gai to Tom Yum Goong), noodle dishes (from pad Thai to yellow curry), and sautés (from basil chicken to Thai sweet and sour). Dishes $–$$.

Café Hale'iwa (808-637-5516), 66-460 Kamehameha Hwy. Open 7–1:45 daily. This famed, authentic hole-in-the-wall is excellent for breakfast. Join the sleepy-headed surfers or urbanites kicking back at Formica tables for a huge omelet and double espresso. And while the service is only decent, the food is great. Dishes $–$$.

Cholo's Homestyle Mexican (808-637-3059), North Shore Marketplace, 66-250 Kamehameha Hwy. Open 10:30 AM–9 PM daily. It's hard to beat a trifecta of good prices, good atmosphere, and good service—unless you add good cuisine. The Tex-Mex and homestyle Mexican dishes here are great, from grilled veggie burritos and spinach quesadillas to shrimp tacos and chicken fajitas. Order à la carte or full dinners. Dishes $–$$.

Kono's Big Wave Café (808-637-9211), North Shore Marketplace, 66-250 Kamehameha Hwy. Open for breakfast and lunch daily. Another hole-in-the-wall, this one has terrific and cheap breakfast burritos, salads, smoothies, and sandwiches like mac-

CHOLO'S HOMESTYLE MEXICAN

nut pesto and chicken. Mike, the owner, is a great guy. Dishes $.

Ted's Bakery (808-638-8207), 59-024 Kamehameha Hwy. Open daily. Yes, it serves simple meals throughout the day to surfer dudes, but Ted's is best known for its knockout pies—especially the chocolate *haupia* pie. Haven't tried it yet? It's a layered chocolate pudding and coconut custard topped with whipped cream. Dishes $.

Giovanni's Shrimp Truck (808-293-1839), 505 Kamehameha Hwy., south-

KONO'S BIG WAVE CAFÉ

WAIALUA BAKERY

east of Turtle Bay Resort. Open noon-
ish to sunsetish daily. These fresh little crustaceans, grown and harvested
on the North Shore, represent all that
is good about the North Shore. The
best way to enjoy them is from a
truck-turned-diner, outdoors at a picnic table, and slathered in butter, garlic, or a knock-your-socks-off secret
spice. Dishes $$; no credit cards.

BAKERIES & COFFEE

Coffee Gallery (808-637-5355; roast
master.com), 66-250 Kamehameha
Hwy. Open 6:30 AM–8 PM daily. For a
wicked strong cup of joe, Internet
access, and lots of room to hang out,
this funky café rules. Most dishes $.

NORTH SHORE SWIMWEAR

Waialua Bakery (808-637-9079), 66-
200 Kamehameha Hwy. Open 9–4
Mon.–Sat. One storefront off the
main drag, this little place has smooth-
ies, sandwiches, and aromatic loaves
of cheese herb bread.

✳ Entertainment

Jameson's by the Sea (808-637-
6272; restauranteur.com/jamesons),
62-540 Kamehameha Hwy. If you're a
mai tai fan, you'll consider the bar
here a place of preeminent entertain-
ment. Just make sure you have a des-
ignated driver.

✳ Selective Shopping

Hale'iwa is favored for shopping be-
cause of its intimate scale and low-key,
offbeat boutiques. There are more surf
shops than you can shake a board at.

Oogenesis (808-637-4422), 66-249
Kamehameha Hwy. Open daily.
Loose-fitting women's clothes made
of natural fibers.

Patagonia (808-637-1245; patagonia
.com), North Shore Marketplace, 66-
250 Kamehameha Hwy. Open daily.
Although it's a national retailer, I can't
help but include it. They also have a
shop in Honolulu's Ward Center.

North Shore Swimwear (808-637-
7000 or 1-800-247-8487; northshore
swimwear.com), North Shore Market-
place, 66-250 Kamehameha Hwy.
Open daily. For a great selection of
custom swimwear and mix-and-match
tops and bottoms, this low-pressure
place gets high marks.

Celestial Natural Foods (808-637-
6729), 66-443 Kamehameha Hwy.
Open daily. This funky little place has
sandwiches and salads, but also myri-
ad natural groceries and locally infused
products.

CENTRAL & LEEWARD OʻAHU

Once brimming with pineapple and sugarcane fields, the central ʻEwa Plain, or Leilehua Plateau, is still rich with fertile volcanic soil. These days, though, Oʻahu's agricultural heartland is best known for new housing, the U.S. Army's Schofield Barracks, and Pearl Harbor. Except for the latter, which is a must-visit, Central Oʻahu is a pass-through kind of place. Do stop for a minute to learn the difference between pineapple varieties at the tiny, roadside Del Monte Pineapple Garden.

Heading west toward Leeward Oʻahu, off the beaten path, you'll encounter far more locals than tourists. But perhaps that's a misstatement: You won't exactly "encounter" them, because most have nothing to do with visitors. The largest concentrations of Native Hawaiians live in the coastal towns of Makaha, Waiʻanae, and Nanakuli. Strung out along the undeveloped Farrington Highway, these towns simply offer a few barbecue and drive-in places to eat, and nothing else—but some military presence. The singular manicured oasis, Ko Olina Resort, boasts well-rounded diversions. It makes a delightful tropical stop, whether for a spa treatment or for strolling around perfect coves. As for the physical landscape, this spectacular and somewhat barren environment is cut off from the rest of the island by the Waiʻanae Mountains, its valleys inaccessible to the likes of everyone but the folks who've grown up around here.

GETTING AROUND
By car: The oft-clogged H-1 and Farrington Highway run parallel to each other ʻEwa out of Honolulu. But the road really empties out once you reach Leeward Oʻahu. No matter if you're approaching Kaʻena Point from the south or the east (via the North Shore), the road stops just shy of circling around to the North Shore because of erosion.

✳ To See & Do
✪ Pearl Harbor
USS *Bowfin* Submarine Museum & Park (808-423-1341; bowfin.org), 11 Arizona Memorial Dr., Pearl Harbor. Open 8–5 daily. Just across the parking lot from the entrance to the USS *Arizona* Memorial, this museum is a good place to explore while waiting to visit the *Arizona*. The small park houses the USS

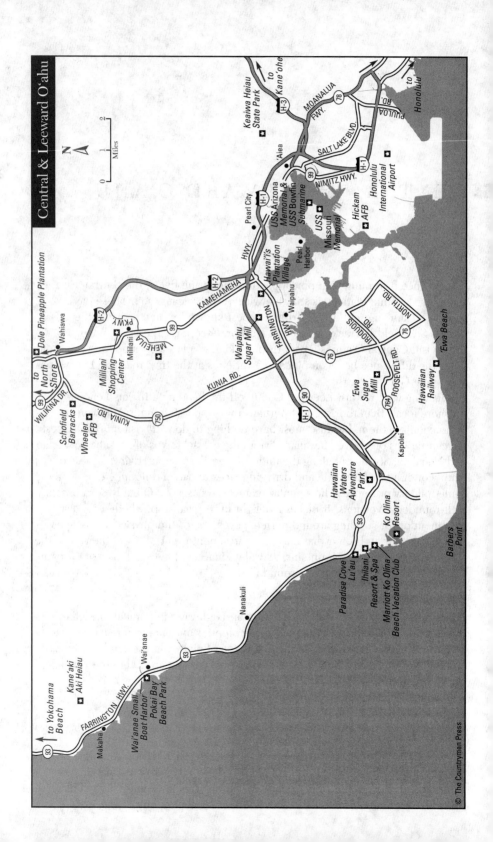

Central & Leeward Oʻahu

N

0 1 2 Miles

© The Countryman Press

Bowfin, a World War II submarine that sank 44 ships in the Pacific before the end of the war. Museum visitors take a self-guided tour, tracing submarine development from its beginnings. You'll find missiles and torpedoes (including a Japanese kaiten, a one-man suicide torpedo) spread around the grounds. $10 adults, $4 ages 4–12.

USS *Arizona* Memorial (808-422-2771; nps.gov/usar), Pearl Harbor. Open 7:30–5 daily. O'ahu's most popular destination receives over a million visitors annually and is reached via a small navy shuttle boat. Clearly visible 8 feet below the surface, the *Arizona* offers a haunting and humbling reminder of our vulnerability. Because the ship was so badly damaged (she took a direct hit, sinking in nine minutes with all hands on board), the *Arizona* was left in the 40 feet of water where she rests today, the tomb of her crew. Over 1,100 sailors, whose average age was just 19, were on board. As if breathing, she still leaks a few gallons of oil a day. It's a good idea to plan about four or five hours here and pick

USS *ARIZONA* MEMORIAL

up tickets in the morning: The quota of 4,500 is often filled by noon. The visitor's center has a snack bar and an interesting souvenir and gift shop, worth a look while you wait to board your shuttle boat. While you're waiting, rent the compelling **audio tour** for $5; it runs for 2½ hours and is worth five times the price. By the way, since 9/11, you are not allowed to carry any bags (including handbags and camera bags) onto the Memorial. But you can bring your camera without the bag. There are storage facilities on site for a fee; don't even think about leaving valuables in the trunk of your car. This is a high-theft area. Two last important notes: no baby strollers or sandals allowed. Free.

> **BUILDING BLOCKS FOR A PERFECT DAY IN CENTRAL & LEEWARD O'AHU**
> Visit Pearl Harbor in the morning (4 hours)
> Swim and sun on Ko Olina Resort beaches (2 hours)
> Drive Farrington Highway to the very end (2 hours)

USS *Missouri* Memorial (808-455-1600; ussmissouri.org), Battleship Row, Pearl Harbor. Open 9–5 daily. Nicknamed Mighty Mo, the USS *Missouri* is best known for her rendezvous with history on September 2, 1945, when the Japanese formally surrendered on her main deck, marking the end of World War II in the Pacific. Built in the New York Navy Yard, she was part of the invasion of Iwo Jima and was the only U.S. battleship on active duty in June 1950 when the Korean War began. More recently, she served in combat during the Persian Gulf War. Decommissioned for the last time, Mighty Mo was stricken from the Naval Register in 1995 and transferred to Pearl Harbor in June 1998, to rest near the Arizona. $16 adults, $8 ages 4–12; tours (including admission); $23 adults, $15 children.

Central O'ahu to the North Shore, Heading North

Keaiwa Heiau State Park, at the end of 'Aiea Heights Dr., 'Aiea. This popular local park is the site of an important stone medicinal temple that dates to the 1600s. The *kahunas*, or healers, grew and used medicinal herbs here to treat the sick. There are camping grounds, picnic facilities, and a scenic hiking trail.

PINEAPPLE FIELDS IN CENTRAL O'AHU

✐ **Dole Pineapple Plantation** (808-621-8408; dole-plantation.com), 64-1550 Kamehameha Hwy., Wahiawa. Open 9–5:30 daily. Dole's processing plant and gift shop seem to sit in the midst of endless pineapple fields; it's like a Beatles song with a twist. But you'll enjoy a beautiful bromeliad garden and large hibiscus hedge maze. The little steam train (Pineapple Express!) that encircles the entire

complex is a hit with kids. The gift shop sells everything from pineapple key chains to pineapples freshly packed for that last-minute carry-on gift. Train ride: $8 adults, $6 ages 4–12; tropical gardens: $4 adults, $3 ages 4–12; world's largest maze: $6 adults, $4 ages 4–12.

Kukaniloko Birthstones State Monument, 0.75 mile north of Wahiawa on Kamehameha Hwy. near Whitmore Ave. This complex of approximately 180 stones dates back to the 12th century, when ancient Hawaiian royalty came here to give birth. Free.

Schofield Barracks and the Tropic Lightning Museum (808-655-0438), Waianae Ave. Open 10–4 Tues.–Sat. Construction on the barracks began in 1908 and has continued adjusting to the demands of the military. It's the home base of the 25th Light Infantry, known as Tropic Lightning, and houses a museum with pictures and artifacts commemorating service in World War II, Korea, and Vietnam. This is the largest army base in Hawai'i, with over 14,000 military personnel and their families stationed here.

Leeward O'ahu, Heading West and North

Hawai'i's Plantation Village (808-677-0110; hawaiiplantationvillage.org), Waipahu Cultural Garden Park, 94-695 Waipahu St., Waipahu. Open for tours 10–2 Mon.–Sat. This low-key historic site consists of 30 homes, considered typical of Hawai'i's early immigrants. (Eight ethnic groups are represented.) A Japanese shrine and Chinese cookhouse are authentic remnants from the early 1900s. $13 adults, $10 seniors, $5 ages 4–11.

Hawaiian Railway (808-681-5461; hawaiianrailway.com), 'Ewa Station, 'Ewa Beach. Train departs only at 1 and 3 PM Sun. Experience some authentic Hawai-

LOCAL LU'AUS

If you're visiting a neighbor island, save your *lu'au* experience for later. Better yet, scan a local O'ahu newspaper for an organization hosting a *lu'au* fundraiser. It'll be one of the most authentic things you do in Hawai'i. If that fails, the **Royal Hawaiian** hotel (808-923-7311; $99 adults, $55 ages 5–12; 6 PM Mon. and Thurs.) hosts the most upscale *lu'au* on O'ahu. For a really kitschy and campy experience, try **Paradise Cove Lu'au** (808-842-5911 or 1-800-775-2683; paradisecovehawaii.com), which holds a nightly event at 7 PM. (The office is located at 1860 Ala Moana Blvd., Honolulu, but Paradise Cove is 30 miles away in Kapolei, in Leeward O'ahu.) Here's how it works: Buses (expect sing-alongs) truck up to 1,000 people from Waikiki hotels to a lovely 11-acre, westward-facing waterfront setting. After catching the sunset and craft demonstrations, participants turn their attention to the show and not-so-great buffet food. $75–125 adults, $65–112 ages 13–20, $55–100 ages 4–12.

The **Polynesian Cultural Center** (see "The Windward Coast" *To See & Do*), **Sea Life Park** (see "Southeast O'ahu" *To See & Do*), and **Turtle Bay Resort** (see "The North Shore" *Lodging*) also put on Polynesian revues.

ian heritage and hospitality aboard a 19th-century railway car as you follow the coastline from 'Ewa Beach up to Nanakuli. The restored narrow-gauge track covers 7 miles in each direction, and the narrated ride takes about 90 minutes. Parts of the original track were restored in the 1980s, and you can inspect several vintage engines and train cars at the open-air exhibit in 'Ewa. Before World War II, the railroad hauled sugarcane and molasses from the Leeward Coast to Pearl Harbor; another line carried passengers up to the North Shore for sightseeing on weekends. $10 adults, $7 seniors and ages 2–12; no credit cards.

Hawaiian Waters Adventure Park (808-674-9283; hawaiianwaters.com), 400 Farrington Hwy., Kapolei. Open daily in June and July; closed Tues. and Wed. in winter; hours vary daily. This wet and modern theme park has plenty of watery thrill rides, along with several places to chill out or recover your senses after dropping into a 65-foot free-fall slide or bodysurfing in a massive wave pool. If you don't want to waste all your adrenaline in a few seconds, however, try the more leisurely "downriver" inner-tube ride. There are also separate swimming areas for adults, teenagers, and *keikis*. $36 adults, $26 ages 3–11, $15 seniors.

✪ **Ko Olina Resort**, 92-1480 Ali'inui Dr. This plush resort boasts idyllic human-made lagoons, several walking paths, and great views up and down the sandy coastline. Built in the 1930s, the lagoons were immediately popular with local families. Today they attract both locals and tourists, who come to snorkel, swim, fish, and sail. It's one of the most relaxing places on O'ahu.

🏄 **Nanakuli**. The biggest town on the Wai'anae Coast (with a population of 11,000), Nanakuli is the site of a Hawaiian Homesteads settlement and, as such, has the largest group of Native Hawaiians on O'ahu. The sandy beach park has good swimming, snorkeling, and diving in summer; in winter the area is popular for whale-watching.

Wai'anae Coast. The Leeward Coast of O'ahu, compared to the lush tropical vegetation around the island, may seem a bit barren. To this day it remains separate from most of O'ahu; few tourists come this way following a tense past due to the high rate of theft in campsites and cars. Today things are much improved, and the boat harbor at Wai'anae town is the starting point for several dolphin-watching excursions in summer and whale-watching trips in winter. When I feel like getting away from the traffic and masses, I make a beeline for this coast.

KO OLINA RESORT

Kane'aki Heiau (808-695-8174), off Makaha Valley Rd., then off Maunaolu St. Open Tues.–Sun. 10–2, weather permitting. Using traditional materials, Honolulu's Bishop Museum undertook the restoration of this *heiau* site in 1970 and added elements that likely existed in King Kamehameha's time. The king used the temple until his death in 1819.

✦ **Makaha Beach Park**, midway between Waiʻanae and Kaʻena Point State Park. Makaha is best known for its winter surf and graceful crescent beach. Swimming and snorkeling are good during summer months, and divers can explore the arches and tunnels of the Makaha Caves to depths of 50 feet. Although visitors are welcome, technically this is a "local" beach, and you're advised to be respectful. *Facilities*: Lifeguards, showers, restrooms.

✦ **Yokohama Beach**, a mile-long park at the end of the road heading north. Named for Japanese immigrants who enjoyed fishing here, Yokohama Bay is a popular surfing and bodysurfing spot year-round. It's not for novices; the narrow shorebreak can be wicked, even on a seemingly calm day. *Facilities*: Restrooms, showers, lifeguard station at the south end of the beach near the guarded entrance to a satellite tracking station; plenty of parking, but break-ins are not uncommon.

✳ Spas

Ihilani Resort & Spa (808-679-3321; ihilani.com), 92-1001 ʻOlani St., Kapolei. Open 7–7 daily. Even if you don't stay at this resort, consider a half- or full-day program of massage, herbal wraps, body polishing, thalassic treatments, facials, and a spa lunch. It's one of the finest full-service facilities in the country, complete with Roman pools and Swiss showers. Really.

✳ Outdoor Activities

DOLPHIN- & WHALE-WATCHING CRUISES

Dream Cruises (808-592-5200 or 1-800-400-7300), Waiʻanae Small Boat Harbor. Two tours daily. These good five-hour dolphin tours aboard a 70-foot catamaran head along the Leeward Coast and into Yokohama Bay, the protected habitat of spinner and bottle-nosed dolphins, where you're guaranteed a sighting. Lunch is included. $70 adults, $42 children. Dream Cruises also offers snorkeling trips and wintertime whale-watching.

Dolphin Excursions (808-239-5579; dolphinexcursions.com), Waiʻanae Small Boat Harbor. This outfit also runs daily spinner dolphin tours at 7:30 and 10:30 AM and provides pickup at Waikiki hotels. These small trips (aboard large, hard-rubber rafts) include snorkeling, as well as possibile sea turtle sightings, albatross, and flying fish. From January through March, migrating humpback whales also make appearances. $105 adults, $55 ages 4–12.

See also **Nanakuli** under *To See & Do*.

Pearl Country Club (808-487-3802; pearlcc.com), 98-535 Kaonohi St., 'Aiea. Greens fees are $75–85; after 3:30 PM they drop to $25 for nine holes. This extremely popular course is packed with locals on weekends, but make no mistake about it: The folks who play here are not "weekend golfers." This course is too difficult to be fun for novices. Make reservations at least a week in advance.

✪ **Ko Olina Golf Course** (808-676-5300; koolinagolf.com), 92-1220 Ali'inui Dr., Kapolei. Greens fees are $170; after 2 PM they drop to $110. Collared shirts are requested; soft spikes are required. Make reservations in advance.

Makaha Golf Course (808-695-7111; makahavalleycc.com), 84-627 Makaha Valley Rd., Wai'anae. Greens fees run $65–85. Make reservations in advance and plan on playing midweek, when it's not so crowded. One of the best courses on O'ahu, it's situated beneath a dramatic volcanic mountain.

West Loch Municipal Golf Course (808-675-6076; 808-296-2000 for reservations), 91-1126 Okupe St., 'Ewa Beach. Greens fees are $50. The fairways are narrow, windy, and watery here, but for the price it's hard to beat. Reserve three days in advance.

HIKING

Ka'ena Point State Park. Ka'ena Point is accessible (by foot only) from both the Wai'anae Coast and the North Shore. The hiking trail that wraps around the northwest corner of O'ahu is the only way to see this unusual landscape. Bring plenty of water if you intend to hike even a portion of the trail. The area is usually hot and dry, with no shade unless you remember your hat. In winter the waves are often so big that they are considered unridable by the best surfers. During the other seasons, windsurfers can be spotted zipping back and forth just offshore.

✳ Beaches

Pokai Bay Beach Park, just north of Wai'anae. O'ahu's leeward side is mostly unprotected from ocean swells, which is why it's a prime surfing destination. However, the combination of long breakwater and Kaneilio Point at Pokai Bay makes for the only year-round safe swimming on the Wai'anae Coast. The calm waters also attract local outrigger canoe clubs, which come here to practice. The sandy-bottomed beach is popular with families, and you can do a bit of snorkeling near the breakwater. *Facilities*: Lifeguard, showers, restrooms, picnic tables.

See also Nanakuli, Makaha Beach Park, and Yokohama Beach under *To See & Do*.

KA'ENA POINT STATE PARK

✴ Lodging

It may feel remote over here, but that's part of the appeal. In actuality, it's only 35–45 minutes to downtown Waikiki, depending on traffic.

RESORTS

✧ **ʻIhilani Resort & Spa** (808-679-0079 or 1-800-626-4446; ihilani.com), 92-1001 ʻOlani St., Kapolei. I really like this place. The ʻIhilani offers all the conveniences that come with close proximity to Honolulu, as well as all the wonderful isolation that comes with being away from town. The 15-story property, which sits on four natural coves enhanced by developers, has perfect blue lagoons lined with sand and palms, ideal for swimming and water sports. There's also a glorious 3-mile coastal walking trail. Inland from the ocean, you'll find a stunning 18-hole golf course with a gem of a clubhouse that offers an air of grandeur. As for the guest rooms, they're quite spacious (almost 700 square feet) and well tailored to your needs, with a marble bathroom and teak furniture on an oversized lanai (which usually includes an ocean view). Upscale appointments abound. ʻIhilani, by the way, means "heavenly splendor," which is a completely apt description. The only full-fledged country-club resort on Oʻahu, it's an easy and elegant escape. *Rates*: $$$–$$$$; children free in parent's room. *Facilities and amenities*: 387 rooms and suites, two pools, beach, three restaurants, Ko Olina Golf Course, six tennis courts ($12 per person), fitness center, spa, water sport rentals, concierge, absolutely fantastic children's programs, parking (fee).

Marriott Ko Olina Beach Vacation Club (808-679-4700 or 1-877-229-4484; marriottvacationclub.com), 92-161 Waipahe Pl., Kapolei. It's another world out 45 minutes west of Waikiki: Quiet and spacious with lots of breathing room and crescent upon crescent of powdery white sands and swimming coves. Sure, this is first and foremost a vacation ownership property, but that doesn't mean that independent travelers are shunned. In fact, if you didn't know it, you'd never know. Set on 30 acres, choices range from hotel-style rooms to spacious two- and three-bedroom "villas" with gourmet kitchens, three TVs, private lanais, washer-dryers, and luxurious soaking tubs. *Rates*: $$$–$$$$; children free in parent's room. *Facilities and amenities*: 210 villas, two pools, golf, three restaurants, fitness room, concierge, access to Marriott's Spa at Ko Olina, children's programs, water sport rentals, high-speed Internet (fee), parking (fee).

Camping is permitted at **Keaiwa Heiau State Park** (808-587-0300).

ʻIHILANI RESORT & SPA

Permit required; $5 nightly; gates locked 6:45 PM–7 AM; no camping Wed.–Thurs.

✳ Where to Eat

Although Leeward O'ahu is almost a culinary wasteland, if you're passing through you won't starve. If you're heading here for any length of time, bring a picnic or assemble one from Mililani Restaurant.

Central O'ahu

✒ **Assaggio** (808-623-5115), 95-1249 Meheula Pkwy., Mililani. Open for lunch and dinner daily. Part of an excellent, family-owned chain of southern Italian restaurants, this eatery stands out among its peers. (Actually it has none, but it isn't resting on that fact.) It's low-key, always hopping, and highly worthwhile. Try the chicken Assaggio, a house specialty. Reservations highly recommended; children's menu. Lunch $$, dinner entrées $$–$$$. BYOB, with corkage fee.

✒ ∀ **Dixie Grill** (808-485-2722; dixie grill.com), 99-012 Kamehameha Hwy., 'Aiea. Open for lunch and dinner daily, breakfast on weekends. This great and popular barbecue joint (with indoor and outdoor seating) dishes up classic ribs, pulled pork, and pecan pie in a jacked-up atmosphere. It's a fun place; try their special Dixie BBQ ale. Children's menu. Dishes $$–$$$.

Mililani Restaurant (808-625-2000), 95-221 Kipapa Dr., Mililani. Open 10–8 daily. This really local place, hidden in a nondescript shopping mall, has classic plate lunches and picnic fixings (including "broasted chicken"). Eat in or take out. Dishes $.

Leeward O'ahu

✒ **Roy's at Ko Olina Restaurant** (808-676-7697), Ko Olina Golf Course, 92-1220 Ali'inui Dr., Kapolei. Open 11–9:30 daily. Dependably extraordinary—that's the perfect phrase for any new Roy's that opens. This one burst onto the Ko Olina scene in 2004 to typical success; the first one, in Hawai'i Kai (see "Southeast O'ahu"), opened in the late 1980s. You may know the formula by now: open kitchen, fabulous views, and signature Euro-Asian dishes like blackened ahi and Szechuan ribs. But this time the scenery and loud vibe has been supplanted by a romantic setting where you can actually whisper to your partner. Reservations recommended for dinner; children's menu. Lunch $$–$$$, dinner entrées $$$–$$$$.

✳ Selective Shopping

FLEA MARKET

Aloha Stadium Swap Meet (808-486-6704 or 808-486-9555), 99-500 Salt Lake Blvd., 'Aiea. Open 6 AM–3 PM Wed., Sat., and Sun. It's the same stuff they sell at the souvenir stands (plus lots of secondhand stuff), but here it's half price. Come to be entertained by hundreds of hucksters and vendors trying to lure you with bargains galore. Admission/parking 50¢, but if you take the **shuttle** (808-839-0911), which picks you up from Waikiki, it's $11 round-trip per person, not including admission.

Maui 2

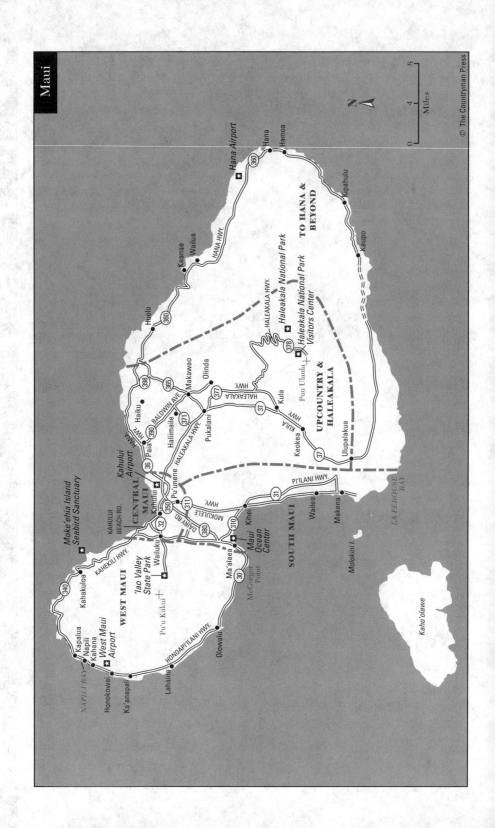

Maui

Moke'ehia Island
Seabird Sanctuary

NAPILI BAY

Kapalua
Napili
Kahana
Honokowai
Ka'anapali
Lahana

West Maui
Airport

WEST MAUI

340

Kahakuloa

KAHEKILI HWY.

Pu'u Kukui

'Iao Valley
State Park

Wailuku

KAHULUI
BEACH RD.

CENTRAL
MAUI

Kahului

Kahului
Airport

HONOAPI'ILANI HWY.

Olowalu

McGregor
Point

Ma'alaea

30

DAIRY RD.

32

350

380

311

Maui
Ocean
Center

310

MOKULELE HWY.

PI'ILANI HWY.

31

Kihei

Wailea

Makena

SOUTH MAUI

Molokini I.

LA PEROUSE
BAY

Kaho'olawe

36

Pu'unene

Paia

Haiku

HANA HWY.

HALEAKALA HWY.

390

BALDWIN AVE.

Haliimaile

371

Pukalani

377

Makawao

365

388

Olinda

Kula

37

Keokea

KULA HWY.

37

Ulupalakua

UPCOUNTRY &
HALEAKALA

Puu Ulaula

378

Haleakala National Park
Visitors Center

HALEAKALA HWY.

Haleakala National Park

TO HANA &
BEYOND

Kaupo

Kipahulu

Hana

Hamoa

360

Hana Airport

HANA HWY.

Keanae

Wailua

360

Huelo

N

0   4   8
        Miles

© The Countryman Press

MAUI IN BRIEF

Maui has been voted the world's best island destination by the haute arbiters of travel, *Condé Nast Traveler* and *Travel & Leisure*, for something like a zillion years in a row. As a result, over 2 million visitors flock to Maui annually. But when I talk to these visitors at the airport on arrival, they can't name one defining reason they decided to come. On the Big Island, it's always the volcano. On Kaua'i, it's always nature and ecotourism. And on O'ahu, it's the big-city allure of Honolulu and Waikiki. But Maui isn't so lucky. Or is it? In the end, these same visitors on departure have ended up doing seven great things in seven days. So perhaps it's the diversity of Maui that makes it so appealing. It has something—something very good—for everyone.

All this popularity comes at a price, though: Traffic can be a problem. The principal highways resemble a figure eight, and in order to get from one part of the island to the other, all traffic seems to end up crossing at the same place at the same time. No matter where you're staying, you'll be doing a lot of driving if you intend on exploring much. Development is also a problem—that is, if you're priced out as a local or if you remember Maui fondly B.C.C. (before condo construction), when open spaces were more plentiful and houses did not line every single inch of shoreline in West Maui and South Maui. It's not uncommon to see bumper stickers that read, NO MILLIONAIRE LEFT BEHIND, or posted signs that say, IF YOU DON'T LIVE HERE, YOU DON'T BELONG HERE.

To be sure, Maui got a major jump on the other neighbor islands in developing its tourism potential. The two factors that have made Hawai'i such a popular destination for Americans since the 1960s—statehood and jet air travel—were just aspirations when the Amfac Corporation decided

TOP 10 "MUSTS" FOR FIRST-TIME VISITORS

Drive to Hana

Watch sunrise atop Haleakala

Snorkel at Molokini

Experience the Old Lahaina Lu'au

Get lost Upcountry

Visit 'Iao Valley State Park

Take a helicopter tour

Ponder the passage of time under Lahaina's banyan tree

Pick up lunch from Pukalani Superette

Visit the Maui Ocean Center

to make Ka'anapali Beach in West Maui into Hawai'i's first master-planned resort development. The project seemed risky in many ways, but the company already owned the land, and the property was earning little profit as a sugarcane field. The resort opened in 1962, shortly after Congress granted statehood and the first big jets landed in Honolulu. In the 1970s, Maui began marketing itself separate from the other islands. It worked.

This act of vision gave Maui a dominant position in tourism among the neighbor islands. The half of Hawai'i's population employed in the travel trade attributes success to the old local saying "Maui no ka oi." When Hawai'i was a collection of warring kingdoms, the slogan meant "Maui over all." Currently it's interpreted as "Maui is the best." Maui's claim has been self-perpetuating, with popularity stimulating familiarity and familiarity maintaining popularity. The saying has equal parts truth and exaggeration. Promoters who use it today seem to forget that the historical boast eventually proved hollow. It was a king from the Big Island who won the conclusive battle on Maui, and even that wily warrior never conquered Kaua'i.

Maui is called the Valley Isle because of the flat isthmus in Central Maui that sits between two volcanoes, one dormant and one extinct. Pu'u Kukui dominates West Maui at 5,788 feet; at its core, it receives more than 400 inches of rain annually, making it one of the world's wettest areas. Don't worry about that rain impacting you; this area is inaccessible. It last erupted about 5,000 to 10,000 years ago. Mount Haleakala (10,023 feet) dominates eastern Maui. Because of these two striking mountains, visitors often think that Maui must consist of two distinct islands, separated by pineapple and sugarcane fields.

Maui's contemporary claim to superiority is bolstered by its beaches—more than 80 of them. None of the other islands comes close in total miles of sandy shore. Many of the beaches are wide, alluring crescents, ideal for seaside holidays, though Maui's advantage in this area is more quantitative than qualitative. Some of the most developed and heavily visited tourist destinations occupy rocky coasts or mediocre stretches of sand.

NEAR KEANAE, ALONG THE HANA HIGHWAY

The scenic sights are a more credible attraction. The summits of the two volcanoes that created Maui are usually covered in clouds, but their slopes roll grandly over much of the island toward the sea. The sweeping vista is interrupted near the ocean by an interminable line of automobile traffic and an almost seamless string of edifices along the water. But beyond these obstructions, the Pacific embraces the bewitching offshore islands of Moloka'i, Lana'i, Kaho'olawe, and Molokini. At almost any point along the western coast (whether you're in East Maui or West Maui), one or two of the islands capture the horizon, thrusting the craggy surfaces of timelessness between the blues of the sky and sea. As the sun sets over or between the islands, there is no better place in Hawai'i to catch the show. Even the easygoing locals consistently turn out for the evening extravaganza.

Few visitors miss the experience, but the vast majority overlook a more glorious asset: the largely unspoiled eastern half of Maui, which I've broken down into two chapters called "Upcountry & Haleakala" and "To Hana & Beyond." On the slopes of Mount Haleakala, the 10,023-foot crater dominates this region, where farmers grow exotic proteas, luscious sweet onions, guavas, avocados, and the potatoes that are made into famous chips. Rural villages dot the fields, ignoring the pandemonium almost visible at the resorts in the distance below. Higher up, the ashen Mount Haleakala Crater welcomes the sunrise as brilliantly as the surrounding islands bid farewell in the evening. After witnessing the spectacle, many visitors bike down the volcano, hike inside it, horseback ride through it, and camp in it.

Girdling the mountain along the eastern coast, a narrow road to Hana twists around sheer rock walls splashing with waterfalls and spans gorges overflowing with tropical vegetation. The spectacular drive brings you to the native settlement of Hana, one of the most remote, picturesque spots in the state. Period. Only a relatively small percentage of tourists get that far. Even though Upcountry and Hana are the only parts of Maui that rival Kaua'i's natural splendor and the Big Island's ancient harmony, most visitors hug the western shores (whether they're in West Maui or East Maui). They have come to Maui not to witness its beauty or Hawaiian personality but because it's famous. Most want to be a part of the action, mingle in the crowds, and relish the stimulation of popular resorts. If Maui is the best, it's because of its ability to encompass both worlds. The east and the west seldom meet on the island, but they both thrive in their separate, indomitable ways.

GUIDANCE

Maui Visitors Bureau (808-244-3530 or 1-800-525-6284; visitmaui.com), 1727 Wili Pa Loop, Wailuku. Open weekdays 8–4:30. The exceptional MVB dispenses free copies of the *Maui Travel Planner* and pocket maps. The out-of-the-way location seems to discourage casual drop-in visitors, but if you do drop in, folks are plenty friendly and you'll find a veritable mountain of information. There are also reams and racks of brochures at the Kahului Airport's Visitor Information Center. Look for *This Week Maui* for current events and happenings.

MORE WEB SITES

hawaiivisitor.com (packages, airfares, and activities)

kapaluamaui.com (Kapalua Resort)

kaanapaliresort.com (Ka'anapali Resort)

hanamaui.com (Hana)

nps.gov/hale (Haleakala National Park)

mauimapp.com (one-stop shopping)

state.hi.us/dlnr (Hawai'i's Department of Lands and Natural Resources)

NEWSPAPERS & RADIO

For local news, pick up the *Maui News* (mauinews.com) and the *Maui Times Weekly* (mauitime.com), which is free. Thursday's edition of the *Maui News* includes an entertainment roundup.

For aloha tunes, set your FM dial to 93.5 KPOA. For basic news on KAOI, tune to 1110 AM. If you're a dedicated NPR listener, tune the FM dial to 90.7 KKUA.

WEATHER

Call the **National Weather Service** (808-877-5111) to see just how much the weather is going to deviate from 80 degrees and sunny. For surfing conditions, call 808-877-3477 or 808-877-3611. For Haleakala National Park weather, call 808-572-4400.

MEDICAL EMERGENCY

Call 911. For hospitals, contact **Maui Memorial Medical Center** (808-244-9056), 221 Mahalani, Wailuku; **Hana Community Health Center** (808-248-8294), Hana Hwy.; and **Kula Hospital** (808-878-1221), 204 Kula Hwy., Kula.

GETTING THERE

By air from the mainland: Maui's major airport is **Kahului Airport**. The major carriers of American (1-800-433-7300; aa.com), United (1-800-241-6522; united .com), and Delta (1-800-221-1212; delta.com) all fly directly to Maui. Hawaiian Airlines (1-800-367-5320; hawaiianair.com) flies directly from Seattle and Portland (and San Diego in summer).

Interisland air: **Hawaiian Airlines** (1-800-367-5320; hawaiianair.com) provides direct interisland service to Kaua'i, the Big Island (Kona and Hilo), and Honolulu. Fares are commensurate with the distance traveled. **GO!** and **Go! Express** (1-888-IFLYGO2; iflygo.com) fly directly to Kona (Big Island), Moloka'i, Lana'i, and Honolulu.

Kapalua–West Maui Airport serves West Maui, and if you've based yourself in Ka'anapali or Kapalua, it might make sense to fly into here since it will save you an approximately 45-minute drive from Kahului. Island Air (1-800-323-3345; islandair.com) flies here from Honolulu, as does Hawaiian.

Hana also has a little airport reached by **Pacific Wings** (1-888-575-4546; pacific wings.com) from Honolulu and Kahului. As you'll read later, the drive to Hana from Central Maui takes about two and a half to three hours without stopping (which would be silly).

SAMPLE DRIVING DISTANCES

Kahului to Hana = 52 miles, about 3 hours without stopping much
Kahului to Lahaina = 21 miles, about 30 minutes
Lahaina to Ka'anapali = 5 miles, about 10 minutes
Ka'anapali to Kapalua = 5 miles, about 10 minutes
Kahului to Wailea = 20 miles, about 40 minutes
Lahaina to Wailea = 30 miles, about 45 minutes

Interisland ferry: **Moloka'i Princess** (808-667-6165 or 1-800-275-6969; mauiprincess.com), Lahaina Harbor. If you're traveling from Maui to Moloka'i, this 90-minute yacht ride provides an alternative to flying. $40 adults, $22 children one-way.

Lana'i Passenger Ferry/Expeditions Lahaina (808-661-3756; go-lanai.com), 658 Wharf St., Lahaina. The least expensive and most fun way to get to Lana'i is to take this ferry, which operates five boats daily. It takes approximately 45 minutes to cross the often-rough channel, so you might consider taking Dramamine. The boat docks at Lahaina Harbor and heads to Manele Bay Harbor on Lana'i. Round-trip: $50 adults, $40 ages 2–11 (under 2 free).

Hawaii Superferry (1-877-443-3779; hawaiisuperferry.com). The hotly contested passenger and car ferry now takes passengers between O'ahu and Kahului once daily. The trip takes three to four hours each way. $52–62 adults, $41–51 child/senior, $17 infants under two, $59–69 vehicles. Look for significant online discounts.

GETTING AROUND

By car: Getting around by car is really the only way. And it seems easy, because Maui's major roads cross the island like a figure eight. But because road names change in a few places, especially Upcountry, I bet you'll get lost once or twice—even if you study the map as you should. You can expect traffic to crawl between Lahaina and Ka'anapali, all through Kihei, and in and out of Kahului. There are major traffic jams in the Kahului area between 3 and 6 PM when locals are getting off work. Pay particular attention on Hwy. 311 (Mokulele Highway), between Kahului and Kihei, where there are far too many head-on crashes. And on Hwy. 30 (Honoapi'ilani Highway), which heads up to Lahaina, drivers are known to stop in the middle of the road during winter when they spot humpback whales just offshore. When there's an accident on this stretch, be prepared for considerable delays—this is the only road feeding West Maui.

TOP 10 IDEAS FOR REPEAT VISITORS

Drive around the back side of the West Maui Mountains

Take a wintertime whale-watch cruise

Really explore Lahaina

Visit the Sugar Mill Museum

Go horseback riding

Tour the Bailey House Museum

Swim at Oheo Gulch

Enjoy the Feast at Lele at sunset

Kayak around Makena Landing

Hang out at Hasegawa's General Store

TOP PLACES TO STAY ON MAUI

Best Romantic Hideaways
Napili Kai Beach Resort (West)
Aloha Cottage (Upcountry &
    Haleakala)
Hotel Hana-Maui (To Hana &
    Beyond)
Hamoa Bay House and Bungalow
    (To Hana & Beyond)
Cliff's Edge at Huelo Point (To Hana
    & Beyond)

Best Intimate & Affordable Lodgings
Plantation Inn (West)
Hana Oceanfront Cottages (To Hana
    & Beyond)
Huelo Point Lookout (To Hana &
    Beyond)
Punahoa Beach Apartments (South)
Aloha Pualani (South)

Most Worldly Resorts
Ritz-Carlton, Kapalua (West)
Four Seasons Resort Maui at
    Wailea (South)
Fairmont Kea Lani Maui (South)
Hotel Hana-Maui (To Hana &
    Beyond)
Heavenly Hana Inn (To Hana &
    Beyond)

Best Condos (or Almost-Condos)
Kahana Sunset (West)
Napili Surf Beach Resort (West)
Noelani Condominium Resort
    (West)
Makai Inn (West)

Best B&Bs
Old Wailuku Inn at Ulupono
    (Central)
The Guest House (West)
Two Mermaids B&B (South)
What a Wonderful World B&B
    (South)
Hale Ho'okipa Inn (Upcountry &
    Haleakala)

Best Family Resorts
Hyatt Regency Maui Resort & Spa
    (West)
Four Seasons Resort Maui at
    Wailea (South)
Grand Wailea Resort Hotel & Spa
    (South)
Sheraton Maui (West)
Ritz-Carlton, Kapalua (West)

Best Resort Values
The Whaler on Ka'anapali Beach
    (West)
Ka'anapali Beach Hotel (West)
Wailea Beach Marriott Resort
    (South)
Maui Coast Hotel (South)

Best Aloha Spirit
Ka'anapali Beach Hotel
Napili Kai Beach Resort
Old Wailuku Inn at Ulupono (Cen-
    tral)
House of Fountains (West)
Hale Ho'okipa Inn (Upcountry &
    Haleakala)

All major car rental companies are represented at the Kahului Airport. At Hana, you'll find Dollar, and at Kapalua–West Maui, you'll find Budget, Avis, and Alamo.

SpeediShuttle (1-877-242-5777; speedishuttle.com) takes folks from the Kahului Airport to all the major resorts in Kapalua ($74), Ka'anapali ($54), and Wailea ($39). All rates are one-way for one person. Call a day in advance. Unless you are going to simply vegetate and recuperate from life at your resort (something I've been known to do for days), this option might not be the smartest one.

By other methods: **Ali'i Taxi** (808-661-3688) offers 24-hour service around the island.

ISLANDWIDE TOURS

By land: **Maui Hiking Safaris** (808-573-0168 or 1-888-445-3963; mauihiking safaris.com). For guided hikes anywhere in Maui, Randy Warner is the go-to guy, especially since he's been doing it since the early 1980s. Half-day ($59–79) and full-day trips ($105–139), from easy to strenuous.

Hike Maui (808-879-5270; hikemaui.com). This is the oldest outfit in Hawai'i. It offers an array of hikes, from easy to strenuous, led by biologists and professors.

Maui Sierra Club (808-573-4147; hi.sierraclub.org). Contact this number for their monthly hike schedule.

See also **Maui Eco Adventures** under *Hiking* in "West Maui."

By sea: **Ann Fielding's Snorkel Maui** (808-572-8437; maui.net/~annf). Since Ann Fielding is a marine biologist, you'll find these small, shoreline guided tours quite educational. She goes out only two days a week (and she's often booked two months in advance), so call prior to your arrival on Maui. Depending on the time of year, she'll pick the best spot to meet. Half-day trips $95–140.

By air: ✪ **Blue Hawaiian** (808-871-8844 or 1-800-745-2583; bluehawaiian .com), at the Heliport at Kahului Airport, Kahului. Since most of the island is inaccessible and truly awe inspiring, I highly recommend seeing it from above. These high-tech whirlybirds take you around to the Garden of Eden (aka Hana) and over Haleakala. Professional pilots double as tour guides and jokesters, with the emphasis on making sure everyone has a good time. To that end, consider taking Dramamine before heading up, because once you're up there it's too late. Figure spending $165–192 for a 30-minute tour of the West Maui Mountains or $346–385 for a 90-minute one that includes West Maui, Hana, and Haleakala. Depending on whether or not you want to travel in an A-Star or Eco-Star, the rates are all over the map from $134 to $495. For the big bucks, you can fly over the Big Island as well.

✳ Special Events

Late January/Early February:
Chinese New Year (808-667-9175 or 1-888-310-1117). Lahaina hosts a traditional lion dance and fireworks.

Senior Skins Tournament (senior skinswailea.com), Gold Course, Wailea Golf Courses. Watch the best players in golf compete for thousands in prize money.

March: **Art Maui** (808-242-2787; art maui.com), Kahului. The island's biggest art show is held at the Maui Arts and Cultural Center.

Late March: **Prince Kuhio Celebrations**, statewide. Hawai'i celebrates the birth of Jonah Kuhio Kalanianaole, a congressional delegate from 1903 to 1921.

May 1: **Lei Day**, statewide. The phrase "May Day is Lei Day" was coined by Grace Tower Warren in 1928 when Lei Day was conceived.

May through August: **Outrigger Canoe Season** (808-879-5505; mauipaddlers.homestead.com/mchca.html). Canoe races are held most weekends across the state.

Early June: **King Kamehameha Celebration** (808-586-0333; hawaii .gov/dags/king_kamehamehacommis sion). Hawai'i's longest-running festival is celebrated statewide to honor King Kamehameha, unifier of the Hawaiian Kingdom.

Mid-June: **Maui Film Festival** (808-579-9244; mauifilmfestival.com), at three venues in Wailea and two in Kahului (at the MACC). Five days of movie premieres, movie-star sightings, hula, and contemporary music. Of the three venues under the stars, the Celestial Cinema is arguably the finest outdoor venue in the world for screening films. I'm not talking about stringing up a bedsheet between some palm trees. I'm talking Dolby surround sound and digital screens.

Early July: **Makawao Parade and Rodeo**, Makawao. With a parade on the fourth followed by a multiday festival, this serious event draws studs from the mainland thinking they can go head-to-head with the best Hawaiian *paniolo*. A fixture since 1965.

Kapalua Wine and Food Festival (1-800-527-2582; kapaluamaui.com), Kapalua. The Ritz-Carlton hosts fabulous tastings and enlightening panel discussions.

Mid- to Late August: **Admissions Day**, statewide. On the third Friday in August, all islands celebrate the day Hawai'i became the 50th state.

HALEAKALA NATIONAL PARK

September: **Aloha Festivals** (808-589-1771; alohafestivals.com), statewide.

September: **A Taste of Lahaina** and **Best of Island Music Festival** (1-888-310-1117; visitlahaina.com). Join 30,000 happy patrons in sampling signature dishes from some of Maui's best chefs.

Early October: **Maui County Fair** (808-242-2721; mauicountyfair.com), War Memorial Complex, Wailuku.

October 31: **Halloween in Lahaina** (808-667-9175), Front St., Lahaina. Almost 20,000 people come to this wacky costume party extraordinaire, which looks and feels like a micro Mardi Gras.

Early December: **Festival of Lights** (808-667-9175), Lahaina. A parade down Front Street features floats, marching bands, and Santa Claus. (I know it's hard to wrap your mind around a tropical Santa.) The banyan tree is also lit on the first weekend of December.

Late December: **First Light** (808-579-9996), Maui Arts and Cultural Center, Kahului. This spectacular movie festival should not be missed.

CENTRAL MAUI

Maui's industrial and commercial center, **Kahului**, was developed in the 1950s for sugarcane workers who dreamed of owning their own homes. But it proved bad timing: The sugar industry began its decline in the 1960s. It's not a particularly interesting place, and its waterfront is lined with warehouses, but since the airport is here you need to know about it.

Practically indistinguishable, the twin towns of Kahului and Wailuku are home to more than a third of the island's population. Where sugar and tourism were once the primary focus, the needs of residents hold the greatest sway today.

Wailuku, once the largest taro-growing region in the state and often referred to as "sleepy" Wailuku, feels like Maui's most real and genuine town. The spirit of the place is quite welcoming, quite relaxed. At its core, at Market and Main Streets, it's a walking town. Amid some junk stores and a few empty storefronts you'll also find some gems, some great-value ethnic eateries, and the renowned Bailey Museum. When exploring, be sure to wander over to Vineyard and High Streets just to get the full flavor of town. There's really no "there" there, but that's the point. Most people pass through on their way to the famed 'Iao Valley, but the country is worth more time than that.

GUIDANCE
The Kahului Airport has reams of information, and the islandwide Maui Visitors Bureau is also located in Wailuku. (See "Maui in Brief.")

GETTING AROUND
By car: Coming or going from Central Maui to West and South Maui, you'll pass by Ma'alaea Harbor many, many times (see "South Maui"). Its principal claims to fame are a small-boat harbor and the Maui Ocean Center. If you drive around the back side of the West Maui Mountains (and I highly recommend it), see Kahekili Hwy., *To See & Do*, "West Maui." Lastly, as you explore Central Maui, remember that Pa'ia (see "Upcountry & Haleakala") is only about 8 miles and 15 minutes east of the Kahului Airport.

TOURS
By air: See **Blue Hawaiian** under *Islandwide Tours* in "Maui in Brief."

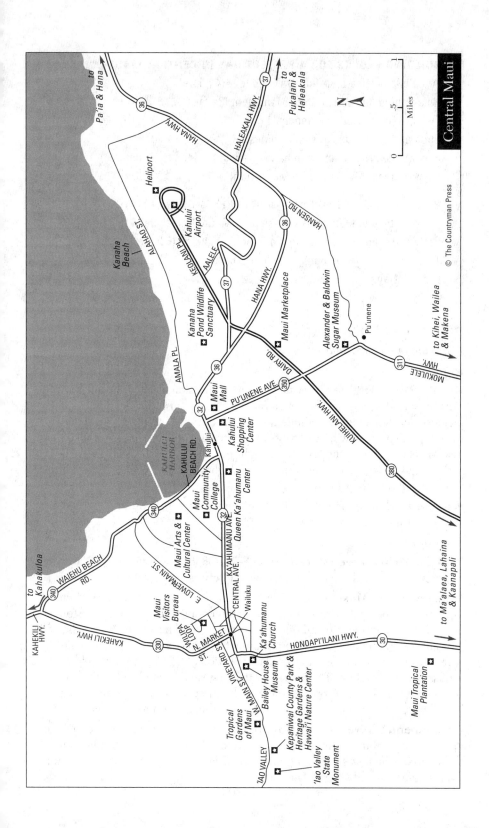

Central Maui

> **BUILDING BLOCKS FOR A PERFECT DAY IN CENTRAL MAUI**
> Try ethnic cuisine on a Tour Da Food tour (4 hours)
> Hike around 'Iao Valley State Monument (2 hours)
> Visit the Bailey House Museum (1 hour)
> Shop at Sig Zain Designs (45 minutes)
> Pop into Long's Drugstore to hang out with the locals (45 minutes)
> Enjoy a flight of wine at Café Marc Aurel (1 hour)
>
> **BUILDING BLOCKS FOR ANOTHER PERFECT DAY ON MAUI**
> Arrive in time to watch the sunrise over Mount Haleakala (4 to 6 hours)
> Go whale-watching (in season) or dolphin-sighting (6 hours)
> Take a day trip (if you don't have longer) to Moloka'i or Lana'i (all day)
> Drive to Hana and back (all day)

✳ To See & Do

Exploring in no particular order.

Kahului

Kanaha Pond Wildlife Sanctuary, near the junction of Hwy. 32 and Hwy. 36. This present-day saltwater lagoon, a rather ugly, greenish, murky place, is inauspiciously located about half a mile west of the airport. The former fishpond-turned-preserve is now home to lots of wading and endangered birds (like the black-necked stilt and the *'auju'u,* or night heron). Although you'll always be within sight of sugarcane smokestacks and highway traffic, you can take a little walkway out into the lagoon.

Kahului Harbor, on Hwy. 340, is Maui's only deepwater port and, as such, receives cruise and cargo ships.

Wailuku

Wailuku Main Street Association (808-244-3888; mauitowns.org), 2062 Main St., publishes a brochure about the town and offers walking tours on request.

🐾 **Bailey House Museum** (808-244-3326; mauimuseum.org), 2375A Main St. Open 10–4 Mon.–Sat. Visit this little museum operated by the Maui Historical Society to best appreciate and understand the general history of Maui. The 1833 lava-and-wood home belonged to prominent missionary Edward Bailey and his wife, Caroline. It contains an extensive collection of period furniture, clothing, artifacts, and tapa cloth. The house, by the way, sited at the head of the sacred 'Iao Valley, was formerly a royal compound until it was given over to become Wailuku's Female Seminary (1837–1849). $5 adults, $4 seniors, $1 ages 7–12.

Ka'ahumanu Church (808-244-5189), Main and High Sts. Sunday services at 8:30. When Queen Ka'ahumanu converted to Christianity in 1832, she founded this church, which was later built in a New England style (1876). Services and hymns are given and sung in Hawaiian.

✪ **ʻIao Valley State Monument** (& **ʻIao Needle**) (808-984-8100 or 808-984-8109), ʻIao Valley Rd. Open 7–7 daily; try to arrive before 9 AM to enjoy it in relative peace. Be sure to take the short drive into this very dramatic and very accessible valley, the result of wind and rain erosion. The mystical, oft-misty folded mountains are the stuff of dreams (and Japanese watercolor paintings). ʻIao, which means "supreme light," is often bathed in dramatic light and an occasional rainbow—that is, between deluges. The valley is 10 miles long, over 4,000 acres, and receives upward of 150 inches of rain a year, but the 6-acre park has a shelter from which

BAILEY HOUSE MUSEUM

you can view the ʻIao Needle, a 1,200-foot spire of lava tufted with a mossy green canopy. Prominent and spectacular, the velvety needle is viewed (when it's not shrouded) from a short but steep paved path that crosses a lovely little stream and waterfalls via a footbridge. In ancient times, Hawaiian royalty buried their families here, deep in hidden valley caves.

✎ **Kepaniwai County Park and Heritage Gardens**, ʻIao Valley Rd. Open dawn–dusk daily. Little structures commemorate the various groups that have made their homes here. Look for a New England saltbox, a Hawaiian *hale*, Chinese and Japanese pagodas, and the like. Adjacent to a stream, this makes a nice picnic spot. Wailuku, which roughly means "water of destruction" or "bloody water," is named for the 1790 battle between King Kamehameha the Great and Chief Kahekili. Fighting for nothing less than the control of Maui, the battle was so great and so many lives were lost that this riverside place, Kepaniwai, was called "damning of the waters." (King Kamehameha won the fight.)

A CENTRAL MAUI ROAD BY ANY OTHER NAME
Hwy. 30 = aka Honoapiʻilani Highway (south to West Maui)
Hwy. 32 = aka Kaʻahumanu Avenue (the main east–west thoroughfare through Wailuku)
Hwy. 36 = aka Hana Highway (east to Hana)
Hwy. 311= aka Mokulele Highway (south to Kihei)
Hwy. 340 = aka Kahului Beach Road in town, but aka Kahekili Highway as it heads northeast out of town
Hwy. 350 = aka Puʻunene Avenue
Hwy. 380 = aka Dairy Road in town, but aka Kuihelani Highway as it heads south out of town

☙ **Hawai'i Nature Center** (808-244-6500; hawaiinaturecenter.org), 'Iao Valley Rd. Open 10–4 daily. With over 30 hands-on natural history exhibits, this is an important place to get up to speed about Maui's environmental ecosystem. During my last visit, I learned about carnivorous caterpillars and dragonflies. Even local adults, who've lived on Maui all their lives, walk away with fascinating new-found knowledge. $6 adults, $4 ages 4–12.

On the Outskirts

☙ **Maui Tropical Plantation** (808-244-7643 or 1-800-451-6805; mauitropical plantation.com), Hwy. 30. Open 9–5 daily. Just south of Wailuku, this 60-acre working plantation is mainly a stop for tour buses. But they do offer an informative (if pricey) 35-minute tram ride alongside 20 different varieties of fruits and flowers, including sugar and pineapple fields. A store (surprise, surprise) sells Made in Maui goods. Free admission; tram tours: $11 adults, $4 children.

Pu'unene

✪ **Alexander & Baldwin Sugar Museum** (808-871-8058; sugarmuseum.com), 3957 Hansen Rd., off Hwy. 311. Open 9:30–4:30 Mon.–Sat. year-round, plus Sun. July–Aug. The rusting hulk of the Pu'unene Sugar Mill, puffing away billowing water vapors, dominates the plains of Central Maui. One of Hawai'i's "Big Five" sugar producers and Maui's most extensive landholder, this mill (and one in Kaua'i) are the only remaining operational sugar facilities in the state. The largest mill in the world until 2002, it is no longer the primary economic engine driving Maui's (or Hawai'i's) economy.

'IAO NEEDLE

This little museum—filled with documents and historic photos and ensconced in a former plantation manager's home—tells the vital economic and cultural story of sugar in Hawai'i. From the importation of laborers to the daily life of laborers (who were identified by tags rather than names), to the laborers' uniforms to the process of how sugar is refined—it's all covered here.

By the way, it wasn't until the sugar plantations started digging irrigation ditches in 1878 to move water from the wet eastern slopes of Haleakala to their plantations in Central Maui that this formerly dry region became verdant and productive. $5 adults, $2 ages 6–17.

❋ Outdoor Activities

BIRD-WATCHING
See Kanaha Pond Wildlife Sanctuary under *To See & Do*.

FITNESS
Maui Family YMCA (808-242-9007; mauiymca.org), 250 Kanaloa Ave., Kahului. $10 daily pass.

GOLF
Waiehu Municipal Golf Course (808-244-5934), off Hwy. 340 a few miles northeast of Wailuku. Greens fees cost $50, carts are $18.50 extra. Make reservations two days in advance.

The Dunes at Maui Lani (808-873-0422; dunesatmauilani.com), 1333 Maui Lani Pkwy., Kahului. Greens fees cost $99 in the morning and drop to $75 after 2 PM. Make reservations a few weeks in advance.

HIKING
See **'Iao Valley State Monument** under *To See & Do*.

HORSEBACK RIDING
Mendes Ranch & Trail Rides (808-244-7320 office, 808-871-5222 reservations; mendesranch.com), Hwy. 340, 4 miles northeast of Wailuku. This family-operated outfit offers narrated trail rides through West Maui's rolling pastures and rain forests. Morning and afternoon rides are offered (two hours, $110). If you'd like a *paniolo*-style barbecue thrown in, it'll cost $130. Make reservations four to five days in advance.

WINDSURFING
Maui Windsurfing Company (808-877-4816 or 1-800-872-0999; maui-windsurf.com), 22 Hana Hwy., Kahului. Open 8:30–6 daily. Board rentals include roof racks. Windsurf rentals cost $45 daily.

❋ Lodging
If you can live without the benefit of beachside lodging, and if you plan on exploring more than not, this centrally located region is a great bet. Luckily, it's also home to one of Hawai'i's absolutely best B&Bs.

🍲 **Old Wailuku Inn at Ulupono** (808-244-5897 or 1-800-305-4899; mauiinn.com), 2199 Kahookele St.

PU'UNENE SUGAR MILL

HALAU, A PERSONAL STORY

Before I moved to Maui in 1982, my idea of "hula" was pretty much the same as Hollywood's. Nothing could have been further from reality. After I'd lived here a few years—and the seeds of appreciation of this amazing culture began germinating—I had the extreme good fortune to meet master *kumu hula* (teacher) Hakuani Holt-Padilla. At the time, her *halau* (school) was on hiatus while she completed her college education. I was one of several hopeful students-to-be who badgered her relentlessly until one day she said, "It's time."

And so in 1992, I, along with about 20 others, embarked on the journey of the *haumana* (student). After more than a decade, I've learned a few things.

Halau is about much, much more than dancing. It is about essential Hawaiian values, including *aloha 'aina* (love of the land), from which inspiration, along with materials for adornments and implements, come. It's about *lau lima* (many hands) and *lakahi* (unity) making the "work" easier and *aloha kekahi i kekahi* (love for one another) making for everlasting bonds among hula sisters and brothers.

Kumu always tells us that not all of us will become great dancers. But if we are good students, she will help us become the very best dancer each one of us can be. I will never be a performance-level hula dancer. I do not have the gift of "hula genetic memory" nor, frankly, the extraordinary commitment level required. What I have gained in these years of classes, practices, fund-raisers, and parties (and yes, a few thrilling performances) is just the tiniest bit of understanding of a beautiful and spiritual way of life. And thanks to *kumu*, I *am* on this journey for a lifetime.

—Bonnie Friedman

(off Hwy. 30), Wailuku. This delightful and historic 1924 plantation house draws loyal repeat guests (that'd be me) and first-timers-in-the-know (that'd be you) like few other places in Hawai'i. Genial hosts Janice and Tom Fairbanks, who've used mainland B&Bs as benchmarks for their enterprise, have left nothing to chance. The completely renovated house features fine architectural details like beautiful Hawaiian ohi'a and eucalyptus floors. Guest rooms blend conveniences and luxuries you'd expect from a resort hotel with intimate touches only smaller places can pull off—like the Hawaiian-design quilts. Of the three rooms in the adjacent Vagabond House, the Muilani's "rainmaker" shower tempts me to forgo all efforts at water conservation. In the main house, the three ground-floor rooms are smaller than those upstairs but feature their own lanais and private walled gardens. The elegant Ulu Room is worth the higher rate it commands. Janice grew up on Maui and Tom is originally from O'ahu, so you'll learn more about Hawaiian lore than you could possibly digest from a thick history tome. I can't say enough about this place . . . . Oh, the full breakfasts—zucchini and Moloka'i sweet potato pancakes, for instance—are the real reason you need to return. *Rates*: $$; additional person (fee); two-night minimum. *Facilities and amenities*: 10 rooms, full breakfast, A/C, Internet.

Banana Bungalow (808-244-5090 or 1-800-846-7835; mauihostel.com), 310 N. Market St., Wailuku. The best private hostel on Maui has free tours, free Internet, free beach shuttle, a communal kitchen, and well-maintained dorms. Reception hours 8 AM–11 PM; quiet hours 10 PM–8 AM; no curfew. *Rates*: $ (singles, doubles, triples, bunks).

Kanaha Beach Park (808-270-7389; office open weekdays 8–4; co.maui.hi .us). There are seven beachfront (and 10 nonbeachfront), county-run campsites near the airport. Three consecutive-night maximum. Contact 1580 Ka'ahumanu Ave., Wailuku 96793 for a permit ($3 adults, 50¢ children per night).

✳ Where to Eat

If you value your dining dollars, and if you want to dine with locals more than mainlanders, I highly suggest poking around Central Maui's excellent (primarily ethnic) eateries. They probably won't knock your socks off with atmosphere, but you'll get some great food at great prices. Unless otherwise noted, all eateries are located in Wailuku.

DINING OUT

Ⴤ **Manana Garage** (808-873-0220), 33 Lono Ave. (off Ka'ahumanu Ave.), Kahului. Open for lunch Mon.–Sat., dinner nightly. Take one part high concept (a cool and colorful industrial-chic interior driven by a garage and car theme); add one part Latin-inspired cuisine (with signature dishes like ceviche, adobo barbecue duck with sweet-potato quesadillas, and mac-crusted snapper on mashed potatoes—by chef Ed Santos); throw in great margaritas and live Latin rhythms on Friday and Saturday nights, and you've got a serious recipe for a memorable evening. *Olé!* If you can, save room for the sweet potato–praline ice cream sandwich. Reservations recommended; limited children's menu. Lunch $$, dinner entrées $$$.

EATING OUT

🍴 ✎ **AK's Café** (808-244-8774; akscafe.com), 1237 Lower Main St. Open 11–2 and 5–9 Tues.–Sat. I love supporting endeavors that try to do the right thing. The brother-sister team of Chefs Elaine and Scott have a simple motto: "Eat better for life." Sounds good—low fat, low carbs, low

OLD WAILUKU INN AT ULUPONO

AK'S CAFÉ

sugar. Luckily, what Chef Elaine prepares tastes good, too! Together they are single-handedly trying to improve the health of all who come their way. Stop at this casual eatery once and you'll probably stop again. I'm not just talking tofu here (although the cashew, broccoli, and tofu stir-fry is great). I'm also talking grilled chicken breast with black bean–mango salsa and baked mahimahi with orange fennel relish. Lunch about $, dinner entrées $$.

🍴 **Main Street Bistro** (808-244-6816; msbmaui.com), 2051 Main St. Open 7–7 weekdays, later on Friday night; live music on Friday night. Be sure to dine here. Well known on the Maui foodie scene, Chef Tom Selman (of Lahaina Grill and Sansei fame) offers dishes to suit every taste—from onion rings with homemade smoky ketchup to a dinner trio of duck. Lunch specials rotate, but look for crystallized bubba baby back ribs on Wednesday and grilled shrimp burgers on Friday. Breakfasts include omelets, pancakes, and loco-mocos. Breakfast dishes $–$$, lunch dishes $–$$$.

🍴 **Sam Santo's** (808-244-7124), 1750 Wili Pa Loop Rd. Open for breakfast and lunch Mon.–Sat. Tucked away, this low-key joint frequented by locals but also peppered by in-the-know-visitors serves the island's best dry *mein* (hands down), *manju* (a bean cake pastry), and pineapple turnovers (don't even think of trying another kind—you'll be sorry, and then you'll want to share your friend's pineapple one). Their beef sticks are pretty darn good, too. Sam Santo's has been in business for something like 12,000 years, so you know they're doing something right. Dishes under $; no credit cards.

🍴 **Tokyo Tei** (808-242-9630), 1063 E. Lower Main St., Suite C101. Open for lunch Mon.–Sat. (closed midafternoon), dinner nightly. If Formica and Naugahyde don't turn you off, this Japanese food will certainly turn you on. I can usually tell all I need to know about a Japanese restaurant by its miso soup. Tokyo Tei's tells me to stay for a complete dinner! Eunice's family-owned institution since 1937, Tokyo Tei serves the island's freshest, best sushi and sashimi for the price. The salmon teriyaki and shrimp tempura are outstanding, too. Dishes $–$$.

A Saigon Café (808-243-9560), 1792 Main St. Open 10–9:30 daily. Longtime owner Jennifer Nguyen doesn't hang a sign, by design. You'll just have to look for a strip of lit neon that says OPEN. The large, primarily Vietnamese menu features summer rolls, great soups and noodle dishes, stir-fry, vegetarian dishes, and "shrimp pops burritos." The space is simple and certainly pleasant enough. Dishes $–$$.

BAKERIES, COFFEE & MARKETS
🍴 **Café Marc Aurel** (808-244-0852; cafemarcaurel.com), 28 N. Market St. Open 7 AM–9 PM Mon.–Sat. With

> **TOUR DA FOOD**
>
> ✪ In mid-2008, longtime resident and foodie Bonnie Friedman (who contributed the introductory essay "Hawaiian Cuisine from Past to Present," started offering personalized tours (tourdafood.com) to Central Maui's hidden culinary treasures. Designed for two to four people, these morning-long, palate-pleasing adventures bring folks to places they'd never find on their own. Inevitably, happy clients also say, "I *never* would have tried this on my own." I'm obviously partial here since I've been friends with Bonnie since the early 1990s, but I encourage you to check out the Web site and trust your gut. You'll walk away thrilled to have met local purveyors and tried local delicacies.

sidewalk tables and a decidedly funky, Gen-Y interior, this café is a cool place to pass a warm afternoon. The café features what the owner, Marc, loves: coffee, cigars, and wine. Offerings for the latter are quite sophisticated. On my last visit I tried a flight of wine called "Wow" because they didn't fit into any categories (like viogniers or chardonnays), but they inevitably elicited a "wow" response from patrons. They certainly did from me! Also visit for loose teas, strong espresso (hot or "on the rocks"), and bagel sandwiches.

Maui Bake Shop (808-242-0064), 2092 Vineyard St. Open 6:30–2:30 Tues.–Sat. This institution, run by French-trained Jose and Maui-native Claire, whip up popular strawberry shortcake, brilliant brioche, and fabulous focaccia. Any bread that comes out of the 1935 brick oven is a winner. Although the hearty lunch dishes change daily, look for spinach and mushroom stuffed croissants, croque monsieur, and the crème de la crème: homemade soups (my favorite is the vegetable soup). The atmosphere is homey, too; there are only seven tables; many longtime patrons catch up with neighbors and take out.

Stillwell's Bakery and Café (808-243-2243), 1740 Ka'ahumanu Ave. Open 6 AM–4 PM Mon.–Sat. While Maui Bake Shop might get more press and foot traffic among visitors because of its Vineyard Street location, Stillwell's gets my vote for serving better food. Their cream horns and coconut macadamia bread are utterly sinful, while their great salads (and dressings) will help you feel saintly. No credit cards.

🍲 **Down to Earth Natural Foods** (808-877-2661; downtoearth.org), 305 Dairy Rd. (Hwy. 380). Open at least

7 AM–9 PM Mon.–Sat. and 8–8 Sun. This health-food grocery store features a bountiful salad bar, as well as hot and cold prepared deli items. Take out or grab a seat upstairs.

Maui Coffee Roasters (808-877-2877; hawaiiancoffee.com), corner of Hwy. 36 and Hwy. 380. Open 7 AM–6 PM weekdays, 8–4:30 Sat., 8–2:30 Sun. Why beat around the proverbial coffee bush? If you're the type who rails against the global invasion of Starbucks (which has an outpost around the corner on Dairy Road), you've found your true home. Come hang out, nosh on great scones, and be sustained by their veggie sandwiches. Coffee simply can't get any fresher since roasting is done on the premises. Buy a pound to take home, and they'll throw in a free cup. The shop is conveniently located near the airport, but be sure to get decaf if you plan on trying to sleep on the plane!

JUST SO YOU KNOW

Homemaid Deli (808-244-7015; 1005 Lower Main St., Wailuku) serves the island's best *malasadas*—get 'em piping hot 5 AM–10 PM; the **Queen Ka'ahumanu Center** (Hwy. 32) has a very popular **food court**; and **Maui Mall** (808-871-1307; 70 E. Ka'ahumanu Ave.; mauimall.com) houses the fun **Genki Sushi** (808-873-7666; genkisushiusa.com), which offers sushi on a conveyor belt. Pick what looks good as it rides by and pay at the end. Within the **Maui Marketplace** on Dairy Road, **Maui Ocean Grill** (808-893-0263) has arguably the best, fastest, and least expensive food on Maui. Try their ahi salads, plate lunches, burgers, and fried mahi. If anyone would argue this, though, it'd be their Marketplace neighbor **Ba Le**

(808-877-2400). Both are open daily for lunch and dinner.

✳ Entertainment

Maui Mall Megaplex (808-249-2222), Ka'ahumanu Ave., Kahului. During the rainy season, you'll appreciate this 12-screen venue.

Maui Arts & Cultural Center (MACC) (808-242-2787; 808-242-7469 events line; mauiarts.org), off Kahului Beach Rd., Kahului. If a big-name entertainer is performing anywhere in Hawai'i, chances are they're performing here. That's right; the $28 million MACC draws an A-list crowd arguably unmatched by any other venue in the state. The beloved center boasts great temporary exhibits in the spacious gallery, tons of art shows, large and small theaters, weekly film screenings, and a large open-air amphitheater. Since it opened in 1994, the MACC has quickly become the heart and soul of Maui's performing arts community.

Castle Theater, at the MACC (808-579-9244; mauifilmfestival.com), off Kahului Beach Rd., Kahului. The Maui Film Festival draws dependable indie and alternative films to this luxe locale. As an added value, on Wednesday night the movies are often followed by musical offerings and poetry readings at the MACC's **Candlelight Café**, which is often referred to as "the weekend in the middle of the week." Nice.

'Iao Theater (808-242-6969), 68 N. Market St., Wailuku. Built in 1927, this art deco gem now houses the Maui Community Theater, which takes up residence here six times a year.

♉ **Manana Garage** (see *Dining Out*) is really fun for when you're looking for margaritas and music.

♇ **Café Marc Aurel** (see *Bakeries, Coffee & Markets*) is perfect for a before- or after-dinner drink.

❈ Selective Shopping

Kahului services the island's consumer needs with a couple of mega-malls and many more strip malls. On a bad day, you'll mistake it for home. **Wailuku**, on the other hand, is a "real" town, and a quick trundle along its Main Street (and Market Street) will reveal a few surprises. You'll find the small-town merchants old-time friendly.

BOOKSTORES
Borders (808-877-6160; borders.com), Dairy Rd., Kahului.

FLEA MARKET
Swap meet (808-877-3100), S. Pu'unene Ave., Kahului. Every Sat. 7–noon (but go early); 50¢ per person. Next to the post office, this popular attraction is lots of fun and draws locals and visitors alike. In addition to bushels of Upcountry produce and homemade foods, keep one eye open for the food wagon serving garlic noodles with chicken. As for nonedible goods, you never know what vintage, kitschy something-or-other you'll unearth. Perhaps a dashboard hula dancer? (They sure beat bobble-head baseball players!) If cheap Balinese imports and shells are your thing, you'll be happy here, too. The swap meet is particularly jammed with vendors in December.

SHOPPING CENTERS
In Kahului, the **Ka'ahumanu Center** (808-877-3369), Ka'ahumanu Ave., is anchored by Macy's, Gap, Sears, Foodland, an atrium food court, and a movie theater (see *Entertainment*). It also houses more than 100 specialty shops, including Maui Hands (see *Special Shops*). Thanks to a magnificent makeover, the **Maui Mall** (808-871-1307; mauimall.com), 70 E. Ka'ahumanu Ave., once derided, is now respectable again. Don't miss the **Tasaka Guri Guri Shop** (808-871-4513), which has been selling scoops of their namesake sherbet-like product since the early 1900s.

SPECIAL SHOPS
Maui Hands (808-667-9898; mauihands.com), 612 Front St., Suite D, Kahului. Open daily. The vast majority of products here are indeed handmade by islanders. The consignment shop offers well-priced goods that friends and family would be happy to receive as gifts. It's worth your time (and money). Look for additional outlets in Lahaina (at the Hyatt), Makawao, and Pa'ia.

Sig Zane Designs (808-249-8997), 53 N. Market St., Wailuku. Open Mon.–Sat. With patterns and designs based on Hawaiian botany and

WAILUKU'S MAIN STREET

mythology, Sig has single-handedly modernized aloha wear. The original shop is located on the Big Island in Hilo. Put Sig on your short list of all shops on Maui.

Gottling Ltd. (808-244-7779; gott ling.com), 34 N. Market St., Wailuku. Open 10–5 weekdays, 10–4 Sat. (It never hurts to call ahead, since they do interior design work off site occasionally.) From tiny figurines to sizable furniture, the items in this Asian specialty shop are priced from two to six figures. For anyone with more than a passing interest in the Asian aesthetic, this is a must-stop shop. The Buddha collection will test your attachment to money and desire to acquire.

Bird of Paradise (808-242-7699), 56 N. Market St., Wailuku. Open Mon.– Sat. If you yearn for the vintage Hawaiiana of yesteryear (I'm talking the 1930s and 1940s), or at least for a leisurely islandlike lifestyle, this antiques shop probably has what you need. I always get nostalgic here, and I'm not a nostalgia buff.

✪ Maui **Historical Society Museum Gift Shop** (aka **Bailey House Museum**) (808-244-3326; mauimuseum .org), 2375-A Main St., Wailuku. Open 10–4 Mon.–Sat. Quite simply, there is no better place on Maui to find authentic Hawaiian gifts with integrity—at reasonable prices. It's small, but it's crammed with more Hawaiiana per square inch than almost anyplace I've been. They have a great selection of history books and prints.

WEST MAUI

West Maui's core is magnificently dominated by the sculpted, velvety, and lush West Maui Mountains. Its western shore harbors a historic port (Lahaina), a famous resort (Ka'anapali), and a coastline riddled with resorts and other places to stay (from Napili to Kapalua). Continuing along the backside of the West Maui Mountains, you'll encounter one of the most dramatic drives in Hawai'i.

Lahaina is a historic port masquerading as a tourist trap. But try to look beyond that because it boasts great places to stay, places to eat, and historical sights. In the early 19th century, when the bustling town was the first royal capital of Hawai'i, American and British whaling ships turned Lahaina into a sailor's version of an ideal liberty port. The lusty whalers loved the warm weather, the Maui potatoes, and most especially the bare-naked ladies who sometimes swam out to greet the ships. In 1825, when the population was around 2,000, there were 23 grog shops along the waterfront, many of them operated by Hawaiian chiefs. That made the notorious town a focal point for conservative New England missionaries in their crusade to transform the natives into respectable Congregationalists. (They had the help of Queen Ka'ahumanu, the wife of King Kamehameha I, who feared that the sailors would unduly influence the locals. She invited a band of missionaries from O'ahu to come and clean up the town.) The rambunctious whalers and the ministers waged an intense struggle for the soul of Lahaina for half a century, occasionally resorting to such maneuvers as the shelling of missionary homes and the kidnapping of ship captains. Thanks to the fine efforts of the Lahaina Restoration Foundation, which helped achieve National Historic Landmark status for Lahaina, the 19th century is readily accessible if you're willing to use a bit of imagination, dig beneath the surface, and look beyond all the shops.

Yes, Lahaina is still catering to visitors, but today the lures are resort wear, local art, souvenirs, and a great lu'au. The remaining grog shops are a little calmer, and the harbor is now a center for oceangoing recreation, particularly scuba diving, fishing, and snorkeling tours.

Ka'anapali, which means "rolling cliffs," is just a few miles north of Lahaina. It's Maui's original resort development, dating to 1962, and it still flourishes. The fine 3-mile-long beach bulges with deluxe hotels and condos, none as tall or tightly spaced as in Waikiki (thank goodness). The Sheraton, the first resort to

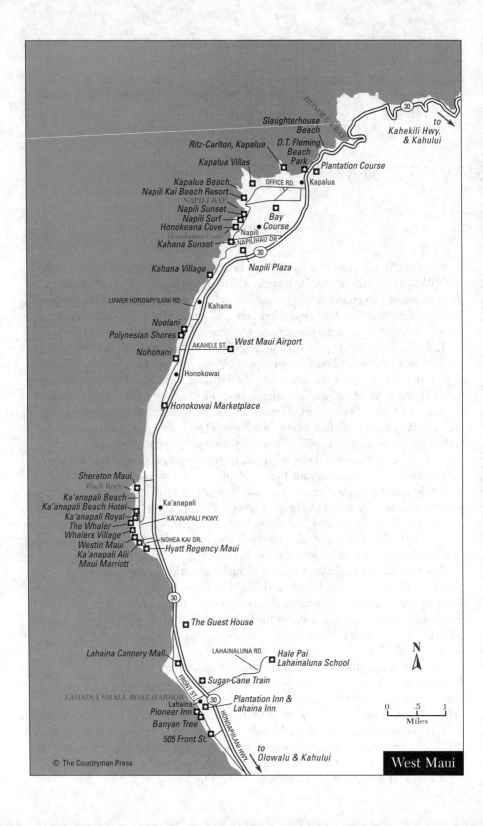

West Maui

open, in 1963, claimed the best spot and still feels the least crowded. (Back in 1963, they were charging a mere $15 nightly for their rooms.) The Ka'anapali Resort attracts an active crowd of families, conventioneers, and those interested in rubbing shoulders at all hours of the day with thousands of their peers. Many who come here never leave the confines of their coddling resorts, content to while away the day waterskiing, Jet Skiing, windsurfing, and cruising out their front doors directly onto the beach. Indeed, you can walk to a seaside mall, dine at a dozen restaurants, shop, and partake in every imaginable activity along this 3-mile stretch, which is connected by a wide walkway. Many consider it entertainment enough to simply wander through their neighbors' magnificent resorts! Ka'anapali also features three dozen tennis courts and two 18-hole golf courses. Its beach is only fair compared to other resorts, except in the area around the Sheraton. While a full mall occupies the center of the shore, most resorts also have their own (expensive) shops.

Kahana and **Honokowai** are coastal villages just up the road from Ka'anapali, with little more than tracts of condos. Most are low-slung, but there are a few high-rises, which tend to look rather like beached whales. (I have not included any of these as possible choices for you.) One beside another, developed in an unplanned and piecemeal manner, the towns have no golf courses or shared recreational facilities and few shops other than grocery stores. Occasional patches of sand dot the waterfront, but most of the condos overlook boulders or seawalls. Generally the condos provide very good values, and they're close enough to Ka'anapali and Kapalua to be convenient. They all draw their share of faithful repeat guests, but none more so than those in Napili.

Napili is a gem, a little beach hideaway on the fringes of Maui's action. With development restricted to low-rise buildings, the condos here gracefully border an enchanting bay and a broad half-moon beach. Resort facilities, shops, and restaurants are as limited as they are in Kahana, but Napili is a contained community with everything in walking distance, including the attractions of Kapalua. Unlike other parts of highly developed Maui, the shady and curving Lower Honoapi'ilani Road through Kahana and up to Napili is utterly pleasant and peaceful.

BUILDING BLOCKS FOR A PERFECT DAY IN WEST MAUI
Stroll the Ka'anapali Parkway at dawn before it gets too crowded (90 minutes)
Take a walking tour of historic Lahaina before it gets too warm (2 to 3 hours)
Ponder Lahaina's historic and magnificent banyan tree (30 minutes)
Drive the Kahekili Highway around the back side of the West Maui Mountains (4 hours)
Snorkel and swim off Black Rock in Ka'anapali (2 hours)
Participate in a cultural program at Ka'anapali Beach Hotel
Make reservations (as early as possible) for the Old Lahaina Lu'au (4 hours)
Dine on the waterfront (2 hours)
Sunset or evening drinks at the Hula Grill (1 hour)

Kapalua, which means "arms embracing the sea," is an exclusive enclave catering to affluent travelers who want to avoid the throngs. It thrives on a combination of natural beauty, splendid resort recreation, and elegant accommodations. All are spread artfully across hundreds of acres of scenic coastline and rolling hills bordered by a pineapple plantation and Norfolk pines. The resort boasts three exceptional golf courses, several ab-fab beaches (with a full range of water sports), a rain-forest preserve, and tennis facilities. Kapalua is serene compared with its Maui competitors, a resort area meant for pampered relaxation rather than playful exuberance. The mood matches the extraordinary setting, and together they guarantee guests a refined and serene retreat. Is there a downside (besides price)? It's often windy here, and it's certainly rainier (although not rainy) than its parched competition, Ka'anapali and Wailea.

The dramatic coastline beyond Kapalua is highlighted by lava-rock promontories that reach out into the Pacific between stretches of white sand (some accessible, some not). One of my favorite activities in West Maui is driving around the back side of the **West Maui Mountains**. The road gets less press than the drive to Hana, but I find it more exhilarating.

GUIDANCE
A visitor information center is located in the Lahaina Courthouse, but you should also check out the Lahaina Restoration Foundation ensconced in the Baldwin House for a free walking tour map of town (both are listed under *To See & Do*).

GETTING AROUND
By car: Honoapi'ilani Highway, the only road connecting all the West Maui resorts, is also referred to as Hwy. 30. Traffic around Lahaina, especially, can move at a glacial pace during high season and when there's an accident. North of Ka'anapali, Lower Honoapi'ilani Road runs parallel to Hwy. 30 through Honokowai and on up to Napili. Beyond Kapalua, Hwy. 30 is known as the Kahekili Highway as it descends into Wailuku.

WEST MAUI MOUNTAINS

TOURS
By air and boat to Moloka'i: **Paragon Air** (808-244-3356; paragon-air.com) offers a package from Maui to Moloka'i for $285 per person that includes airfare, lunch, and a tour of Moloka'i's famous Kalaupapa National Historic Park (more commonly known as the leper colony). Because of restrictions at the NHP, visitors must be at least 16 years old.

Moloka'i Princess (808-667-6165 or 1-800-275-6969; mauiprincess.com), Lahaina Harbor. Heading to Moloka'i for more than a day trip? Ask about their various tours: Drive-Cruise packages allow you to tour the island on your own; Ali'i Trips include a guided tour; Kalaupapa Tours include a hike and tour of the famous settlement (see "Moloka'i").

By air and boat to Lana'i: See **Trilogy** under *Boat Excursions.*

✳ To See & Do

Exploring clockwise from Ma'alaea Bay through Lahaina, Ka'anapali, and Kapalua, around the West Maui Mountains and back to Wailuku (see "Central Maui"). For activities and sights in Ma'alaea Harbor, see "South Maui."

McGregor Point, MM 9 on Hwy. 30. Folks stop at the scenic pullout in winter to watch whales frolicking around the reef that stretches from here to Olowalu. Many cars pull off a mile beyond McGregor Point at Papawai Point.

𝄞 **Olowalu Beach**. See *Beaches.*

Olowalu petroglyphs, off Hwy. 30. From the Olowalu General Store (at MM 15), turn *mauka* at the water tower (keep the water tower on your right) and take the dirt road through the sugarcane fields toward Olowalu Valley. After about 0.25 mile, you'll see an old set of stairs. The petroglyphs begin at ground level and continue about 50 feet upward.

Lahaina Outskirts

Lahainaluna School and **Hale Pa'i** (808-661-3262; lahainarestoration.org), *mauka*, Lahainaluna Rd., just south of town off Hwy. 30. Open 10–4 weekdays. Within a few years of this missionary school being founded in 1931 (it's the oldest secondary school west of the Rocky Mountains), the missionaries began printing the first Hawaiian-language newspaper. Next door at Hale Pa'i, where missionaries printed textbooks and Bibles, you'll find a little museum with a restored printing press. If you explore this far, you'll be rewarded with fine views of sugarcane and pineapple fields, as well as Lahaina Harbor. Head 2 miles up Mount Ball to reach the school. The school today, by the way, is a public high school. Classes in Hawaiian were given here until the 1970s.

𝄞 **Sugar Cane Train** (808-667-6851; sugarcanetrain.com), Hwy. 30, just north of Lahainaluna Rd. Open 10:15–4 daily. Officially called the Lahaina-Ka'anapali & Pacific Railroad by practically no one, this quaint little 1900s-era train travels through dense sugarcane fields for a 12-mile round-trip. Kids seem to like it. $21.50 adults, $15 children.

SUGAR CANE TRAIN

Lahaina Jodo Mission, Ala Moana St., off Front St. just north of town center. Built in 1968 to celebrate the centennial of the arrival of Japanese immigrants to Hawai'i, this reflective and peaceful parklike setting is perfect for contemplation. A giant Buddha turns his back on the West Maui Mountains, all the better for us to frame him at sunset. The small temple and three-tier pagoda (which memorializes the dead) are closed to the public.

Lahaina—Around Town

Baldwin House (808-661-3262; hawaiimuseums.org), 120 Dickenson St. Open 10–4 daily. At the corner of Front Street, this whitewashed coral-and-stone building dates to 1834 and claims to be Lahaina's oldest house. It was home to three generations of the Baldwin family from the mid-1830s to the late 1860s; the patriarch Baldwin was a noted doctor and missionary. The house, filled with period furnishings like a koa bedstead and heirloom piano (and Maui's first toilet), is much as he would have left it. It can be said that Baldwin gave much to the island, but he also gained much in return—specifically, 2,600 acres of land in Kapalua. Unsure of what to do with them, he experimented with growing pineapples on a small plot—and the rest is history. Next door to his homestead is the **Master's Reading Room**, built in 1833 and deemed the oldest building in town. The second floor served as a popular sailors' reading room during the period when grog shops were closed and prostitution forbidden. As soon as that ban was lifted, the reading room lost much of its popularity. Stop here to chat with the incredibly knowledgeable and dedicated **Lahaina Restoration Foundation** volunteers who are responsible for preserving much of the town's rich history. They also produce an excellent (and free) ✪ **walking tour map**. Baldwin descendants—of which there are quite a few, by the way—own the *Maui News*. $3 adults, $2 seniors, $5 families.

✪ **Banyan tree**, Front St., between Canal and Hotel Sts. The mother of all banyan trees, the largest in the state, this beloved specimen is a sight to behold. Take a few moments to savor the truly rare spectacle. Don't bother photographing it so that you can enjoy later; the width is impossible to take in, even with a 24mm lens. Planted in 1873 to mark the arrival in 1823 of the first Protestant missionaries (who came to do good and did quite well for themselves, as the saying goes), the tree was imported from India when it was a mere 8 feet tall. It now reaches some 50 feet, has 12 or so major trunks supporting its branches, and spreads for nearly an acre, easily one city block. Plenty of mynah birds enjoy perching in the canopy, so watch where you sit.

FRONT STREET, LAHAINA

Lahaina Courthouse (808-667-9175 or 808-667-9193), 649 Wharf St., in front of the banyan tree. Open 9–5 daily. In 1859, King Kamehameha III began building what would become a courthouse near here, but a storm destroyed the effort. Today the courthouse houses the **Lahaina Art Society** (808-661-3228) and a **visitor's center**. Free.

Brick Palace, Market St., on the waterfront in front of the Pioneer Inn. Formerly the site of a royal taro patch, only the cornerstones remain of what was King Kamehameha's palace built to welcome whaling captains. It's interesting to note that the king was in residence for only one year because his most revered wife didn't want to live here.

OLD LAHAINA COURTHOUSE

Pioneer Inn (see *Lodging*), 658 Wharf St. Built in 1901, this distinctive landmark was the rowdy center of Lahaina nightlife. The first-floor wraparound porch witnesses a constant parade of activity, while the second-floor balcony serves as a nice perch (if you're staying here) from which to take it in. It's a touristy but popular place to have a drink.

Seaman's Hospital, 1024 Front St. Originally built in the 1830s to house King Kamehameha III's court, it was later converted into a hospital to serve sailors. Note the circa-1900 sugar plantation residence next door.

Malu'ulu'olele Park, Front St. at Shaw St. This sacred spot, beneath the infield of a baseball field, was the compound of Prince Kauikeaolui and his sister Princess Nahienaena over 100 years ago. When the prince was a mere 10 years old he ascended to the throne as Kamehameha III and ruled for almost 30 years, including during the era when the kingdom became a constitutional monarchy.

Waiola Church and Cemetery (808-661-4349), 535 Waine'e St. near Shaw St. Hawai'i's first stone church was built in 1832 on this unlucky site. I say unlucky because two storms and two fires destroyed each subsequent structure. The present one dates to 1953. But the real reason to visit is the cemetery, where *ali'i,* commoners, and missionaries are all laid to rest side by side. Queen Keopuolani, one of King Kamehameha the Great's wives, was buried here in 1823. An early convert, she's "credited" (or not) with being quite influential in spreading Christianity to Hawaiians.

Hongwanji Temple, Waine'e St. This temple serves the island's largest Buddhist population.

WO HING SOCIETY

Hale Pa'ahao (aka **Old Prison**) (808-661-3262), Prison Rd. off Waine'e St. Open 10–3 weekdays. This "stuck-in-the-irons house" was built in 1852 by convicts. The most frequent transgressions, for which folks were confined to a ball and shackles, included public drunkenness and desertion. Free.

Wo Hing Society (808-661-5553), 858 Front St. Open 10–4 daily. This Chinese temple was built in 1912 to honor the contributions of Chinese immigrant laborers. It shows Thomas Edison's late-19th-century films taken in Hawai'i. Upstairs you'll also find Maui's only public Taoist altar. Admission $1 donation.

Ka'anapali to Kapalua, South to North

✦ **Ka'anapali Beach**. See *Beaches*.

○ **Ka'anapali Parkway**, a 3-mile paved walkway, links Ka'anapali to the resorts, restaurants, and shops from the Hyatt Regency Maui Resort & Spa in the south to the Sheraton Maui in the north. It's great for early-morning power walks and sunset meanderings. Wait too long, and you'll have to deal with strollers simply out to enjoy the incredible views! Imagine that!

Whalers Village Museum (808-661-5992; whalersvillage.com), on the second floor of Whalers Village mall, Ka'anapali Pkwy., Ka'anapali. Open 9 AM–10 PM daily. Also known as the **Whale Center of the Pacific**, this little museum tells the story of the region's whaling heyday (1825–1860). Check out the scrimshaw, a 30-foot sperm whale skeleton, historic photos, impressive little films, whaling paraphernalia, and a re-created "bedroom" for whalers. You'd have to travel to Nantucket or New Bedford, Massachusetts, to learn more about whaling. I'm always more impressed with each visit. Free, but donations gratefully accepted.

✦ **Napili Bay Beach**. See *Beaches*.

✦ **Kapalua Beach**. See *Beaches*.

Kumulani Chapel, Kapalua. Renovated in 1994, this wooden A-frame structure would look right at home in New England.

Burial Mounds near the Ritz-Carlton, Kapalua. There have long been issues between the wishes of developers and the preservation instincts of archaeologists. Add Native Hawaiians to the mix, and the issues can understandably become *really* incendiary. In 1986, as a Ritz-Carlton was breaking ground, archaeologists came in to study the site, as required by law. When they found an ancient burial site, all parties concerned agreed that the bones would be removed and interred elsewhere. But when it became clear just how extensive the burial ground was— upward of 900 sets of remains were found, along with other significant items— the project ground to a halt. Hawaiians all over the state rallied to the site, demanding that development stop. They drew a symbolic and literal line in the sand, so to speak, and said, in essence, "enough is enough." In 1989, the Ritz-Carlton agreed to push itself back from its preferred oceanfront perch. (It's still a very dramatic location, enhanced, I think, by the perspective.) The bones were then reinterred, and the site reverted to its former incarnation as a burial mound.

Also on the grounds of the Ritz-Carlton, you'll find a portion of the 16th-century King's Trail, a footpath that once circled the island.

Maui Pineapple Plantation Tour (808-665-5491; mauipineapple.com), Kapalua Villas Reception Center, 500 Office Rd., Kapalua. Tours at 9 and 11:45 weekdays. Maui's volcanic soil and growing conditions produce pineapples beyond compare. Take an informative tour with former plantation workers through the fields, and you'll learn everything you ever wanted to know about the history of this sweet thing. Like the fact that this plantation is Hawai'i's only remaining cannery; that pineapple will not ripen further once it is picked; that canned pineapple from Dole and Del Monte are no longer from Hawai'i. (Look for the 100% HAWAIIAN USA label once you're back home shopping.) And at the end of the tour, after a field tasting, you get to choose and harvest your own fruit. Sweet. $40 adults; no children under age five.

✂ **D. T. Fleming Beach State Park**. See *Beaches*.

✂ **Slaughterhouse Beach** (aka **Mokuleia Beach**). See *Beaches*.

✂ **Honolua Bay Beach** (see *Beaches*). In the mid-1970s, a 17-person, double-hulled canoe, a replica of an ancient sailing vessel, departed from here bound west for Tahiti. The modern-day voyageurs wanted to prove (and they did, with their successful round-trip) that early explorers could indeed navigate these waters without the aid of modern systems.

North Around the West Maui Mountains

○ **The Kahekili Highway** (Hwy. 340). I love this road more than almost any other in the state. Driving it is always the first thing I do on each return visit to Maui. It makes me feel like I'm home. In fact, I almost enjoy it more than the drive to Hana—perhaps because it's shorter, perhaps because it's less well known. I can't guarantee, though, that you will feel the same way. It's not for the faint of heart. Please do not attempt it if it's been raining. Calling this a "high-way" is perhaps the biggest understatement imaginable. (Okay, maybe that was!) The 20-mile stretch from Kapalua to Wailuku is paved, but a whopping 8 miles of that narrows to one lane—one lane with a sheer rock wall on one side and a sheer cliff on the other. They're not kidding when they say it follows an ancient footpath—with an emphasis on *foot!* Your odometer will rarely peg higher than 10 mph. All along, you'll enjoy pineapple fields that yield to high sea cliffs, fabulous sea views, neighborhood taro patches, cattle grazing on rolling pastures, locals selling banana bread from makeshift shelters, a couple of barely populated

SLICING & DICING A PINEAPPLE

Have you ever wondered how to properly slice a pineapple? Cut off the crown; then slice the pineapple in half lengthwise and then again, so you end up with four long quarters of fruit. Slice off the hard inner cores of each quarter, then cut the fruit from the shell with a sharp carving knife. Lastly, slice it into bite-sized chunks. When choosing pineapple at home, be aware that shell color is not necessarily an indication of ripeness. Ripe pineapple can vary from green to gold. If you're not going to eat a fresh pineapple immediately, cut it up and refrigerate it in an airtight container.

KAHEKILI HIGHWAY

deep valleys, Moke'ehia Island Seabird Sanctuary, and a perfectly positioned church or two.

Perhaps the loveliest spot of all is the tiny and remote village of **Kahakuloa**, easily identified by its red-roofed church. One of Maui's earliest settlements, Kahakuloa is the kind of place I never want to leave, although there is nothing to do here. Buy some banana bread or a cool beverage from the locals, talk story, and enjoy the simplicity of the adventure.

Hwy. 340 deposits you in Wailuku (see "Central Maui"), where you can take Hwy. 330 to Hwy. 30 to head back to Lahaina and Ka'anapali.

✳ Spas

Spa Moana at the Hyatt Regency Maui Resort & Spa (808-667-4725; maui.hyatt.com), Ka'anapali. This 15,000-square-foot oceanfront spa is the best in West Maui. The architecturally stunning place has wet and dry treatment areas, two-person treatment suites, a huge fitness center with aerobic studios, whirlpool, steam, sauna, and everything else you'd expect. Non–resort guests gain access with a $50 daily pass ($15 for in-house guests). Of course, the menu of spa treatments is additional. Fitness center open 24/7; treatment times keep shorter hours.

The spa at the Westin Maui (808-661-2588; westinmaui.com), Ka'anapali. Open 6:30 AM–8 PM daily.

Seaside Salon & Day Spa at the Sheraton Maui (808-661-0031; kaanapali beauty.com), Ka'anapali. Open 10–6 daily. This spa offers seaweed masks, peach body scrubs, volcano clay masks, and myriad massages.

Waihua at the Ritz-Carlton, Kapalua (808-669-6200), Kapalua. Open 5:30 AM–8 PM. Maui's swankiest resort fitness center offers traditional spa services. At press time, the spa was undergoing a $160 million renovation and was slated to be open full swing in late 2008. How could it promise anything less than greatness?

✳ Outdoor Activities

BOAT EXCURSIONS

Trilogy (808-661-4743 or 1-888-225-6284; sailtrilogy.com), Lahaina Harbor. This great outfit offers a couple of half-day and daylong catamaran trips to Lana'i, both of which include snorkeling. On Saturday, the trip includes a jeep tour of the island. Trips $39–199.

Ocean Riders (808-661-3586 or 1-800-510-3586; mauioceanriders.com), Lahaina Harbor. These small inflatable rafts clip the surface of the sea and travel to sea caves and other small places that big boats can't navigate into. I really like their snorkeling trip to the back side of Lana'i. Trips depart at 6:30 AM and return midafternoon. $115 adults, $99 children.

FARM TOURS
O'o Farm Tours (808-667-4341; pacificomaui.com). Tours Thurs. at 10:30; $50 per person, includes lunch. Maui soil produces fantastic edibles, and foodies will want to take this two-and-a-half-hour tour of a working Upcountry farm. The highlight is the seasonal luncheon featuring farm fresh ingredients, which are picked from the vines and plucked from the ground minutes before being cooked. The same holds true for desserts.

FISHING
Four- and eight-hour charters depart out of Ma'alaea and Lahaina Harbors. I recommend wandering around the harbor and talking to captains to get a feel for the person and boat. If you want to book ahead of time, contact **Sportfish Hawaii** (808-396-2607 or 1-877-388-1376; sportfishhawaii.com), which books captains and boats all across the state. Boats take six people max; count on spending $600–800 for half a day for the whole boat (private tour) or $200 per person for a shared boat. You can also count on regaling friends with stories about the ones that got away as well as the huge mahimahi, tuna, ono, and blue marlin that you'll reel in. I'm talking big-game fish.

GOLF
Ka'anapali
The North Course Royal (808-661-3691; kaanapali-golf.com), Ka'anapali Pkwy. Designed by Robert Trent Jones, this is more challenging than the South Course, but both afford pleasant Pacific and mountain views. Pay attention: North Royal has broad bunkers and really curvy greens. Bing Crosby played the opening round on the North Course in 1962. Greens fees cost $225 and drop to $110 after 2 PM. Ask about discounts if you are staying in the area. Make reservations up to 90 days in advance.

The South Course Kai (808-661-3691; kaanapali-golf.com), Ka'anapali Pkwy. Designed by Jack Snyder. Like its sister course, this one also has stunning ocean and mountain vistas. Fairways tend to be hillier and narrower than the North Course, perhaps to make up for the fact that it's shorter. Greens fees cost $185 and drop to $85 after 2 PM. Make reservations up to 90 days in advance. Ask about discounts if you are staying in the area.

Kapalua
Kapalua is the only Hawaiian resort with multiple golf courses that consistently rank in the state's top 10. You won't birdie or eagle many of the

ALONG THE KAHEKILI HIGHWAY

holes here, but keep your eyes peeled for these flying friends—all three Kapalua courses are certified Audubon Cooperative Sanctuaries. And the views are worth the price of admission even if you're not a golfer!

The Bay Course (808-669-8044; kapaluamaui.com), south of Office Rd. Designed by Arnold Palmer. A challenging dogleg on the fourth hole takes you to the top of a black lava peninsula, then you tee off across the surf to a green just above the biggest sand trap you've ever seen: the beach at Oneloa Bay. The greens are tough, but the fairways are wide here. Greens fees cost $215 and drop to $130 after 1:30. Make reservations 25 days in advance.

The Plantation Course (808-669-8044; kapaluamaui.com), near Fleming Beach. Designed by Ben Crenshaw and Bill Coore in 1991. The first hole can cream a golfer's ego: The scorecard gives you only four strokes to clear an elusive green that's both downhill and downwind. Greens fees cost $295 and drop to $150 after 1:30. Make reservations 25 days in advance.

Golf Academy (808-669-6500; kapaluamaui.com), Office Rd. off Hwy. 30. This state-of-the-art facility has clinics for all levels, video analysis, an 18-hole putting course, and a 23-acre practice facility.

HIKING

Maui Eco Adventures (808-661-7720 or 1-877-661-7720; ecomaui.com), 180 Dickenson St., Lahaina. The verdant West Maui Mountains are ripe for exploration, but they're also dense and seemingly impenetrable unless you have a knowledgeable local guide (four hours, $80 per person). Other hikes around the island allow you access to otherwise private lands, all ecologically diverse. Of all their offers, you'll particularly want to look into their six-hour waterfall and rainforest hike.

SCUBA DIVING

Extended Horizons Scuba (808-667-0611 or 1-888-348-3628; extendedhorizons .com and scubadivemaui.com), 94 Kupuohi St., Lahaina. With over 20 years in business, these folks know the area (including Molokini, of course; see "South

THE CATHEDRALS OF LANA'I

One of the most popular and majestic dives offered by Extended Horizons heads to this large lava tube, approximately 100 feet long and two stories tall. Looking toward the back wall, you'll see what looks like a stained-glass window, an effect produced by light reflecting off the crystal-clear blue water. Then note the large boulder just in front of the "window." During certain times of the year, light filters through the ceiling of the cathedral and illuminates the rock, giving it the feel of a traditional Catholic altar. After paying your respects, check out the nooks and crannies for sponge crabs, lobsters, big eye squirrelfish, and the occasional white tip reef shark and frogfish. This particular dive is generally done for 35 minutes at 55 feet.

Maui"). While guiding dive tours, their underwater naturalists point out sights you might otherwise miss. And after the dive, they elaborate on what was seen so you can benefit from their experience of reef ecology and fish behavior. Accommodating requests and taking weather into consideration, they'll choose from among 60 sites—ranging from lava tubes, caverns, and shipwrecks to green sea turtle cleaning stations and octopus dens. Site depths range from 25 to 95 feet. Each trip includes two dives, the first at about 60 to 70 feet and the second at about 50. They also offer deeper dives for more experienced divers and great night dives.

Maui Dive Shop (808-661-5388, Lahaina Cannery Mall on Front St. in Lahaina; and 808-661-5117, Whalers Village on Kaʻanapali Pkwy. in Kaʻanapali; mauidive shop.com) publishes a free 24-page *Maui Dive Guide.* Open 9 AM–10 PM daily.

SNORKELING

Snorkel Bob's (808-662-0104; snorkelbob.com), Dickenson Square, Lahaina; and 2 Kikei Rd., Napili. Open 8–5 daily. For freelance snorkeling at Honolua Bay, Kapalua Beach, Napili Bay Beach, and Olowalu Beach, Bob's has all the gear you'll need. Mask, snorkel, and fin rentals cost $2.50, $5.50, or $8 daily, depending on the quality of gear.

✪ **Black Rock** (Puʻu Kekaʻa), in front of the Sheraton Maui, Kaʻanapali, is one of the best and most accessible snorkeling spots on Maui. The extinct volcano crater is also considered one of the three great *uhane-lele* spots in the islands, where the souls of the dead followed the setting sun into the ocean and traveled with the outgoing tide to their final resting place in the sea of Kailalo. Kahekili, the last king of Maui, is reputed to have inspired his warriors to battle by leaping from this cliff into the ancestral spirit land and returning unharmed. The black rock cliff continues deep below the surface, harboring hundreds of crevices and ledges for eels, turtles, manta rays, and colorful fish to hide.

Lahaina Divers (808-667-7496), 143 Dickenson St., Lahaina, and the **Pacific Whale Foundation** (see *Whale-Watching*) both offer snorkeling trips out of Lahaina Harbor to the famed Molokini, the crème de la crème of offshore sights off the coast of South Maui. (See *Snorkeling* in "South Maui.")

SUBMARINE TRIP

✎ **Atlantis Submarine** (808-661-1210 or 1-800-548-6262; goatlantis.com), 658 Front St., Lahaina Harbor. Those who aren't licensed divers, or those who fear ocean swimming, can still explore the depths and wonders of Jacques Cousteau's world. Claustrophobics need not apply. Hop aboard this high-tech, 48-person vessel to head 100 feet below the ocean's surface. You'll be underwater for about 45 minutes; the entire trip takes about two hours. $80 adults, $41 children.

SURFING

The best area surfing is at **Honolua Bay** in winter.

Nancy Emerson School of Surfing (808-244-7873; mauisurfclinics.com), 505 Front St., Lahaina. The undisputed go-to gal for lessons, pro surfer Nancy trained these surfer-dude assistants who will get you standing on a board within an hour ($130–200). Group lessons, with a 5-to-1 student-instructor ratio, cost only $78 for a two-hour tutorial. Nancy uses three locations in and around Lahaina.

TENNIS

Hyatt Regency Maui Resort & Spa (808-661-1234, ext. 3174; maui.hyatt .com), 200 Nohea Kai Dr., Ka'anapali. This nice facility has six Plexipave courts and offers clinics, rentals, and lessons. But you'll pay a price for the convenience and plushness: $25 hourly for non–resort guests.

Lahaina Civic Center (808-661-4685), 1840 Honoapi'ilani Hwy., Lahaina. These five, lighted public courts are available on a first-come, first-served basis.

Kapalua Tennis Garden (808-665-9112; kapaluamaui.com), Kapalua. The most upscale facility in the area has a pro shop and 10 lighted courts that rent for $14–16 per person per day.

Royal Lahaina Tennis Ranch (808-661-3611, ext. 2296), Ka'anapali Beach Resort, 2780 Keka'a Dr., Ka'anapali. This outfit has a pro shop and 11 courts, half of which are available for nighttime play (at $10 per person per day).

WATER SPORTS

All manner of water sport rentals and charters, from sailing to paddling to kayaking, are offered from the hotels that line Ka'anapali Beach.

WHALE-WATCHING & DOLPHIN SIGHTINGS

✪ **Pacific Whale Foundation** (808-249-8811 or 1-800-942-5311; pacificwhale .org). Summertime snorkeling trips to Molokini and wintertime (late Nov.– mid-May) whale-watching trips are offered out of Lahaina Harbor and Ma'alaea Harbor. This nonprofit foundation, a pioneer in whale research, offers extremely informative trips. There are upward of 16 daily whale-watching trips; $23–80 adults, $17 ages 7–12, free 6 and under. Every dollar you spend at their stores and on their trips goes toward conservation and educational programs.

The foundation also offers ecofriendly **dolphin-sighting trips** out of Lahaina Harbor to Lana'i ($80 adult, $35 ages 7–12, free 6 and under). Practically no one knows more about the social interactions and behaviors of these intelligent and playful creatures than these folks. You can expect to see pods of 200 spinner dolphins. The six-hour trip departs at 8:00 AM.

WINDSURFING

In these parts, it's best at Honolua Bay.

✳ Beaches

In order of preference.

✦ **Ka'anapali Beach**, Ka'anapali Pkwy., Ka'anapali. This 3-mile stretch of powdery white stuff fronts the resorts. In winter, when parts of the beach become whisper-thin due to tides, the Sheraton Maui always has the most reliably wide section. Parking can be tough: Pay to park on the south end of the resorts or try your luck at the last northern turn off for Ka'anapali near the Maui Ka'anapali Villas.

✶ **Kapalua Beach**, off Hwy. 30, Kapalua. This deservedly popular crescent has a gentle slope. Its calm waters are protected by an offshore reef and rocky promontories. Engage in plenty of water sports, sunbathe, or simply snorkel: It's all very good here. Park on Lower Honoapi'ilani Road near the Bay Club restaurant or near Napili Kai Beach Club. *Facilities:* showers, restrooms, lifeguard, water sport rentals.

TOP FIVE BEACHES ON MAUI
For Swimming & Sunbathing
Kapalua Beach (West)
Makena/Big Beach (South)
With Walking Paths
Ka'anapali Beach (West)
Wailea Beaches (South)
For Snorkeling & Water Sports
Ka'anapali Beach (West)

✶ **Napili Bay Beach**, off Lower Honoapi'ilani Road, at the Napili Kai Beach Club, Napili. This perfect crescent offers good swimming and sunbathing and decent snorkeling. Even though it's backed by low-rise condos, its romantic appeal isn't diminished. *Facilities:* showers.

✶ **D. T. Fleming Beach State Park**, off Hwy. 30, below the Ritz-Carlton, Kapalua. The tides can be quite strong here, so think twice about swimming. Nonetheless, the lovely and sandy crescent is quite popular because of its length (1 mile). *Facilities:* parking, restrooms, showers, picnic tables (which are particularly popular on weekends).

✶ **Slaughterhouse Beach** (aka **Mokuleia Beach**), off Hwy. 30, just beyond Kapalua, part of the Marine Life Conservation District. You'll drive right by the beach unless you look for a green handrailing (*makai*) that leads down a steep set of stairs to the beach. The best beach for bodysurfing got its nickname not because killer waves take out daredevil bodysurfers; there's a more prosaic reason. A cattle slaughterhouse used to occupy the site. No facilities.

✶ **Honolua Bay Beach**, off Hwy. 30, north of Kapalua, part of the Marine Life Conservation District. Turn left down a dirt road near a pineapple field about 2 miles north of D. T. Fleming Beach and take the steep path down to the beach. As usual, don't leave valuables in the car. No facilities.

✶ **Olowalu Beach**, off Hwy. 30, south of Lahaina. Even though you're on the edge of the road here, there's great snorkeling at this sandy beach. In fact, the snorkeling is decent all along this stretch of Hwy. 30. No facilities.

NAPILI BAY BEACH

CONFESSIONS OF A DIVER

As a little girl, the aquarium in my room served as my night-light. Drifting off to sleep, I would stare at that tank, dreaming of being able to shrink down and swim through the rock formations with the colorful fish. I never would have imagined capturing that dream as an adult.

Upon arriving on the Hawaiian Islands in December 1986, I promptly picked up some snorkel gear and jumped into the water at Black Rock in Ka'anapali. There I was, back in that childhood aquarium! Swimming in the

✳ Lodging

An increasing number of folks aren't simply carousing Lahaina's busy Front Street only to sleep elsewhere. **Lahaina** has a surprisingly wide range of places to stay. As for the string of **Ka'anapali** hotels and resorts, which cater to the middle and upper middle class, they're oriented around their pools and grounds rather than to the sand beyond their hedges. Heading north, **Kahana** is less expensive than its southern neighbor, but real bargains are still rare. Some of the fancier places charge very high rates consider-

ing their surroundings, so I've included only a few of the smaller, attractive ones that provide value. Most of my lodging choices in **Napili** are located on a fabulous sandy cove. Moderately priced on the whole, these tend to be superb bargains. **Kapalua**, the most fashionable address on Maui, appeals to those with older, quieter money.

RESORTS

Ka'anapali

🌺 ✐ **Ka'anapali Beach Hotel**
(808-661-0011 or 1-800-262-8450;

warm, clear water, weightless and free, with so many amazing creatures around me. From that point on, I knew that I was *Home*.

When I try to explain to guests where I work that most of Maui's beauty is underwater, there's always an initial look of surprise. So many guests, though, change their perspective once they experience Maui's water for themselves. Truly weightless, using unfamiliar gear, and seeing things they've never seen, they exclaim, "We might as well be on Mars." The most common response is, "Once I put my face down into the water, this world as I know it ceases to exist."

How to explain emotions that you've never felt before? Like the euphoria that came when an 18-foot manta ray swam up to me inside Molokini and basically asked if I wanted a ride. I spent the next 15 minutes touring the glorious crater on the back of this gentle creature. How to explain the emotion during night dives, when, as I held a light to my own face, the squid, with their big curious eyes, would come right up to me and mimic my hand movements? They'd pulsate with color in an attempt to communicate. How to explain the emotion I felt when staring into the eyes of a green sea turtle while resting on the sandy sea bottom? I might well be looking into the eyes of God. For me, this is living, truly being one with nature. Moreover, it's right below the surface of the water, only hidden by the glare of our daily lives.

As fortunate as I have been to experience the underside of Maui, the real gift is sharing it. By being in the water, we grant ourselves the treat of becoming like little children again. So many guests return year after year, and I'm always tickled when I hear the familiar refrain, "Can Tanna come out and play?"

—Tanna Swanson

kbhmaui.com), 2525 Ka'anapali Pkwy. This oceanfront low-rise hovers near the top of my list of favorite Maui hotels solely because of its authentic Hawaiian spirit. That's especially true when compared to the larger resorts on Maui. The staff exude a genuine aloha spirit and extend their considerable knowledge about Hawaiian mythology, culture, values, and history to guests. As for the facilities, I prefer rooms in the original three-story Moloka'i Wing, which are furnished with an airy plantation style. All rooms have a balcony or lanai; guests can walk directly into the courtyard from many of the ground-floor rooms. The grassy courtyard, surrounded by four low-rise wings of the hotel, is delightfully simple, quiet, and relaxed by Ka'anapali standards. In addition to the pool being nicely set back from the beach, for a change there are palm trees under which you can set up a chaise lounge. *Rates*: rooms $$–$$$; children free in parent's room; plenty of packages. *Facilities and amenities*: 430 rooms and suites, pool, great beach, three restaurants, including the **Tiki Terrace** (which specializes in Hawaiian cuisine and has a popular Sunday brunch), access to golf courses, water sport rentals, concierge, children's programs (free), parking (fee).

☙ **Sheraton Maui** (808-661-0031 or 1-866-716-8109; sheraton-maui.com), 2605 Ka'anapali Pkwy. Ka'anapali's original hotel occupies the best stretch of beach, at the end of the strip just in front of Black Rock, which is perhaps Maui's most accessible and best snorkeling area. (See *Snorkeling*.) The family-friendly resort enjoys a sense of openness and tranquility not found in other resorts of this size because it's spread out on 23 acres. If you like being close to the action, avoid the premium oceanfront Hale Moana rooms, at the northernmost edge of the property on the other side of Black Rock. Thankfully, though, the majority of rooms in the other seven low-rise buildings also have some kind of ocean view, a refreshing change from most other area resorts. At some point during your stay, make your way to the Discovery Room atop Black Rock for surely the best views in Ka'anapali. Or watch the ceremonial sunset dive off Black Rock from the Lava Bar. *Rates*: rooms $$$$; children free in parent's room. *Facilities and amenities*: 510 rooms and suites, lagoonlike pool, the best stretch of beach among these resorts, three restaurants, nearby golf courses, three tennis courts (fee), fitness center, the small **Seaside Salon & Day Spa** (see *Spas*), water sport rentals, concierge, shops, children's programs, resort fee (includes self-parking, local phone calls and long-distance access, morning newspaper, in-room coffee, use of fitness center, and kids under 12 get to eat free).

☙ **Hyatt Regency Maui Resort & Spa** (808-661-1234 or 1-800-233-1234; maui.hyatt.com), 200 Nohea Kai Dr. A fantasy hotel that opened in 1980, the Hyatt spectacle begins in the lobby with cloisonné vases, Oriental opulence, and an impressive Asian and Pacific art collection. Outside, the developer tried to best Mother Nature with a 2-mile network of streams, a 40-acre Swan Lake, waterfalls, linked half-acre pools, and a swaying wooden bridge that crosses one end of the pool. In addition to a wildly and deservedly popular spa and excellent Camp Hyatt children's program, the resort also offers a rooftop **astronomy program** (see *Entertainment*). As for the guest rooms, they occupy three midrise buildings that form a half-moon around the water playground. Generally they're luxuriously appointed and large (although the lanai is smallish). Management is constantly renovating: In 2006 it was the golf course, in 2005 it was **Son'z**

KA'ANAPALI HOTEL GROUNDS

Maui, and in 2003 the **Spa Moana**. *Rates*: rooms $$$$; children free in parent's room. *Facilities and amenities*: 808 rooms and suites, enormous and fun pool, great beach, five restaurants (including Son'z Maui), nearby golf courses, six tennis courts (fee), excellent fitness center and Spa Moana (see *Spas*), water sport and bike rentals, concierge, shops, children's programs, self-parking (free), resort fee (includes local and toll-free phone calls, morning newspaper, one hour of tennis court time, in-room coffee, and use of fitness center).

✦ **Westin Maui** (808-667-2525 or 1-866-716-8112; westinmaui.com), 2365 Ka'anapali Pkwy. This splashy and spiffy water wonderland on the beach opened in 1987 to a great deal of fanfare, widely heralded as Ka'anapali's boldest tribute yet to glittery opulence and prodigal grandeur. And it's still true to this day. Beyond a profusion of Oriental and Hawaiian art in the lobby, you'll be drawn to Westin's "aquatic masterpiece," a dazzling water playground. Most guest rooms overlook this 55,000-square-foot pool area, which occupies the entire courtyard. (Oh, and most overlook the Pacific, too, but that almost seems secondary.) Most rooms are smallish, but they're seductively furnished with hand-crafted touches, custom lamps, and stone sculptures. The lanais, too, are better suited to standing than sitting. If you can afford them, I prefer the deluxe ocean-view rooms in the Beach Tower. In late 2007 these rooms were enlarged and received flat-screen TVs, practically de rigueur at these resorts now. *Rates*: rooms $$$$; children free in parent's room. *Facilities and amenities*: 758 rooms and suites, five pools, great beach, two restaurants, access to golf courses, access to tennis courts, fitness center and The **spa at the Westin** (see *Spas*), water sport and bike rentals, concierge, shops, children's programs, mandatory resort fee (includes parking, local phone calls, morning newspaper, in-room coffee, wireless, and use of fitness center).

Honokowai to Kapalua

✦ **Ritz-Carlton, Kapalua** (808-669-6200 or 1-800-262-8440; ritzcarlton.com), 1 Ritz Carlton Dr., Kapalua. After a full year of being "off-line" while undergoing a $160 million renovation, the Ritz reopened in early 2008. Wow. The one- and two-bedroom residential suites and guest rooms now enjoy renovated furnishings, dark wood floors, flat screen TVs, marble bath and tubs, spacious lanais, and wireless iPod docking stations. Also check out the environmental education center for kids and teens, lots of Hawaiian art, a new fitness center and spa, and the remodeled Terrace and Banyan restaurants. (Kai Sushi and the Onyx Bar are also brand new, but because of the timing of the opening, I didn't get a chance to sample these.) Overlooking a long white beach and set on 55 acres, this Ritz opened in 1992 amid the pineapple plantation influences of Cook pines and ironwood trees. The lobby frames the blue Pacific in the distance quite beautifully; I've spent many an hour just sitting there contentedly. Guest rooms are spread out in two long, six-story wings contoured gracefully to the sloping hilltop. And an immense three-level pool occupies much of the territory in between. *Rates*: rooms $$$$; children free in parent's room. *Facilities and amenities*: 463 suites, pool, beach, four restaurants, access to two golf courses, six tennis courts (free), fitness center, **Waihua at the Ritz-Carlton** (see *Spas*), water sport and bike rentals, concierge, shop, children's programs, self-parking (free), resort fee (includes fitness center, parking, resort shuttle, in-room coffee, tennis, and putting green).

🦅 🐚 **Napili Kai Beach Resort** (808-669-6271 or 1-800-367-5030; napilikai.com), 5900 Lower Honoapi'ilani Rd., Napili. The Napili Kai is the epitome of the casual Hawaiian hideaway, closer to more people's image of a relaxed, laid-back beach paradise than most other places on Maui. Adamantly unsophisticated compared with the upscale resorts, this 1962 classic nevertheless offers a comparable level of comfort, terrific ocean views, and one of the finest swimming beaches on the islands. Its devoted coterie of repeat guests comes looking for old Hawaiian character, pre-jet-set, and they find it at this charming place. A camaraderie develops between guests through morning coffee klatches and just enough organized activity to make you feel at home. Eleven two-story buildings sprawl over 10 acres, most of which have ocean views.

NAPILI KAI BEACH RESORT

Although there are more than a dozen floor plans, I like studios and suites in the renovated Lani I and Lani II. These have enormous terraces and even bigger vistas of the beach and bay. The bedroom is also oceanfront. With a pervasive *hookipa* (hospitality), the resort advertises its "unhurried way of life." It's a modest claim for one of Hawaii's classic beach hideaways. *Rates*: Rooms $$–$$$, studios $$$, one- to two-bedrooms $$$$; many packages. *Facilities and amenities*: 163 rooms and suites, great beach, Sea House restaurant, four pools, putting green, access to tennis courts (fee), fitness room, water sport equipment (free), concierge, complimentary children's programs, parking (free), wireless (free in lobby).

CONDOS, HOTELS & APARTMENTS
Lahaina

Lahaina Shores (808-661-4835 or 1-800-642-6284; classicresorts.com), 475 Front St. This seven-story hotel sits at the southern end of town, far from the crowds and adjacent to a few great restaurants. Rooms are nothing to write home about, but they're pleasant enough and come with every amenity you'll want (including a full kitchen and private lanai). The penthouse is a particularly great deal. The biggest deal, though, is that the property sits within yards of the ocean. It's hard to beat that. *Rates*: studios $$, one-bedrooms $$$, penthouse $$$; children free in parent's room. *Facilities and amenities*: 199 rooms and suites, pool, beach (not for swimming), activity desk, parking (fee), Internet (fee).

🦅 **Outrigger Aina Nalu Hotel Maui Resort** (808-667-9766 or 1-800-668-7494; ohanahotels.com), 660

Waine'e St. Outrigger converted this boutique resort, completely renovating and upgrading the property in 2005 into what they call a "deluxe condo." Basically what that means is that it features natural stone and tropical wood décor, contemporary gardens, new Hawaiian-style furnishings, and about half the number of units. Budget- and family-friendly, spread out on 9 acres, it's on a quiet side street close enough to town to make it convenient. It's quite a fine choice! *Rates*: $$$; children free in parent's room. *Facilities and amenities*: 135 units, two pools, activity desk, barbecue area, parking (fee), wireless (fee).

🐚 **Makai Inn** (808-662-3200; makai inn.net), 1415 Front St. At water's edge (although there is no beach) and a mere 20-minute walk to downtown, these small apartments are constantly being renovated with small tweaks here and there. And they're constantly booked; call well in advance and hope to get lucky. For the money, they're hard to beat. Orchid, Plumeria, Paradise Found, and Hibiscus offer the best ocean views, while families appreciate the two-bedroom Pineapple unit. *Rates*: $–$$. *Facilities and amenities*: 18 units, wireless (free), kitchens, house phone available (but no in-room phones), coin-op laundry facilities on site, parking (free), no TV.

Ka'anapali

The Whaler on Ka'anapali Beach (808-661-4861 or 1-877-997-6667; resortquest.com), 2481 Ka'anapali Pkwy. One of Hawai'i's earliest resort beach condos, The Whaler has earned its venerable reputation. In addition to an array of hotel-like services and rates that are moderate for the neighborhood, The Whaler also offers large guest accommodations in its twin 12-story towers. Of the four views from which to choose, I prefer the ones looking across the top of Whalers Village toward the Westin Maui. As for some specifics: The one-bedroom units are nearly twice as large as the studios; the two-bedrooms have an enormous wraparound lanai; the only difference between the deluxe hotel rooms and studios is the latter have kitchens. *Rates*: studios $$$, one- to two-bedrooms $$$–$$$$; children free in parent's room; two-night minimum. *Facilities and amenities*: 360 units, pool, great beach, access to golf courses, three tennis courts (free), Internet (free), children's program, parking (fee).

⚓ **Ka'anapali Ali'i** (808-661-3339 or 1-800-642-6284; classicresorts.com), 50 Nohea Kai Dr. Built in 1983, four high-rise buildings, 11 stories each, form a horseshoe around the landscaped central courtyard (and pool) that, in turn, opens onto the ocean. Since individual owners are required to upgrade their units frequently, you can count on high-quality furnishings. Additionally, all premier units were remodeled in 2006 and 2007. The one-bedroom units (with large lanais) are quite spacious, logging in at 1,500 square feet. With daily maid service and barbecue gas grills around the pool, the Ali'i offers the best of both worlds. *Rates*: one- to two-bedrooms $$$$; children free in parent's room; three-night minimum. *Facilities and amenities*: 264 units, pool, great beach, three tennis courts (free), fitness room, water sport rentals, concierge, parking (free).

Ka'anapali Royal (1-800-676-4112; whalersrealty.com), 2560 Keka'a Dr. In a secluded location above the 16th hole of a Robert Trent Jones golf course, this comely and quiet condo allows guests to sample the pleasures of the popular Ka'anapali Resort without getting lost in the crowds. The low-rise buildings are spread sparingly over 7 flowering acres, and most of the suites offer a view of Ka'anapali's most challenging links. The spacious condos, well designed for leisurely living, average 2,000 square feet, with two bedrooms, two baths, a handsome sunken living room, and daily maid service. Standards are high, and owners are required to renovate often. It's also a short walk to the beach and restaurants from here. *Rates*: $$$; children free in parent's room; five-night minimum (at Christmastime a 14-night minimum). *Facilities and amenities*: 18 of 105 units in rental pool, great beach nearby, pool, discounted rate at nearby golf courses, tennis courts (free), parking (free, but there is a vehicle registration fee).

Honokowai to Kapalua

These listings are ordered geographically, south to north, rather than by my usual preferential order.

Nohonani (808-669-8208 or 1-800-822-7368; nohonanicondos.com), 3723 Lower Honoapi'ilani Rd., Honokowai. The beach here extends right up to the pool's edge; that fact alone makes the rates a bargain for being so close to Ka'anapali. Although the facade of the two buildings (four stories each) is plain, the interior layout provides ocean views, and surf sounds are audible from the master bedroom. Décor is tasteful and comfortable, but mostly Nohonani provides a solid beach value and easy convenience when you want to save money for more of Maui's pleasures. In 2007, the two-bedroom units received a facelift. *Rates*: one- to two-bedrooms

$$; three-night minimum (at Christmastime a 14-night minimum). *Facilities and amenities*: 20 of 28 units in rental pool, pool, beach, activity desk, parking (free), on-site manager.

Polynesian Shores (808-669-6065 or 1-800-433-6284; polynesianshores .com), 3975 Lower Honoapi'ilani Rd., Kahana. This affordable, pleasantly planned seaside condo is easily mistaken for just another one of the many unexemplary condos strewn through Kahana. Upon closer inspection, though, you'll note that the two-story wooden buildings wrap around a manicured lawn that rolls down to the edge of the Pacific and envelops the oceanfront swimming pool. On the shore, a wooden deck extends over the rocks and water, luring sunbathers, sunset gazers, and snorkelers. Although individually owned, the units should please the fastidious. Each has a lanai and ocean view. Of the four layouts, I prefer the two-bedroom units (renovated in 2006 and 2007) with wraparound lanais. The Polynesian Shores may not fulfill all your leisure needs, but it addresses the most basic ones extremely well. *Rates*: one-bedrooms $$, two-bedrooms $$, three-bedrooms $$$; three-night minimum. *Facilities and amenities*: 52 units, pool, beach is 0.25 mile away, parking (free), wireless (fee).

Noelani Condominium Resort (808-669-8374 or 1-800-367-6030; noelani-condo-resort.com), 4095 Lower Honoapi'ilani Rd., Kahana. One of the few complexes along this road that offers oceanfront studios for couples, Noelani boasts the best rates on Maui, considering the proximity to the rocky, dramatic sea. For the price, it's hard to beat. Everything, including the refurbished quartzite stone pools and Jacuzzi, is only a lounge chair away from the Pacific surf. Though the neighborhood swarms with condos, from your lanai they don't intrude on the sunset views between Moloka'i and Lana'i at all. Although renovated in 2007, studio kitchens are still basic; the particularly bright two-bedroom apartments are situated on the corners with extra-large, wraparound lanais. There's nothing flashy here except for that single moment when the sun dips below the horizon each evening. *Rates*: studios $–$$, one-, two-, and three-bedrooms $$–$$$ (ask about packages); children free in parent's room; three-night minimum. *Facilities and amenities*: 50 units, two pools, beach (next door), fitness center, activity desk, Internet in lobby (free), parking (free), fitness center.

Kahana Village (808-669-5111 or 1-800-824-3065; kahanavillage.com), 4531 Lower Honoapi'ilani Rd., Kahana. These contemporary and stylish condos, in seven low-rise buildings, are some of the most luxurious on Maui's western coast. Additionally, the complex isn't as cloistered as others in the area. Each building stretches along the shore of a sand-fringed cove, providing Pacific vistas and quick access to a quiet beach. All units have spacious lanais and upgraded kitchen appliances and amenities. I prefer the second-floor units to the ground-floor ones because the former have vaulted ceilings and better ocean views. When you want the look of your lodging to be as smart as the choice, look no farther. *Rates*: two- to three-bedrooms $$$–$$$$; five-night minimum. *Facilities and amenities*: 42 units, large pool, beach, concierge, parking (free), Internet (free), local and long distance calls (free).

Kahana Sunset (808-669-8700 or 1-800-669-1488; kahanasunset.com), 4909 Lower Honoapi'ilani Rd., Kahana. This small low-rise complex, set in a garden on a beautifully protected cove, sits on an alluring beach, closer to Napili than the rest of the places in Kahana. These hideaway condos fall into three categories. The best are executive town houses located in the two oceanfront buildings (A and F). Regular two-bedrooms (in Buildings B, C, and D) are simply set a bit farther back from the beach and lack an extra half bath. Of these, it's definitely worth upgrading to Building B. The smaller, ground-level rooms take in much less of the Pacific Ocean. Even for a couple, I'd recommend a town house. Although the units aren't fancy or full of resort frills, this place is perfect for those who go to Hawai'i for marvelous beaches and value-filled retreats. And as an added bonus, you may see sea turtles frolicking in the bay and waves within a stone's throw of the beach. *Rates*: $$–$$$ for a one-bedroom, $$–$$$$ for a two-bedroom; children free in parent's room. *Facilities and amenities*: 49 of 79 units in rental pool, two pools, good beach, activity desk, parking (free), daily maid service, Internet (free).

Honokeana Cove (808-669-6441 or 1-800-237-4948; honokeana-cove .com), 5255 Lower Honoapi'ilani Rd., Napili. These condos are snugly gathered around a scenic inlet only five minutes by foot from Napili Bay and Napili Beach. The sea sweeps lazily into the rocky nook right up to the condo lanais and along the free-form swimming pool. You could almost say that the intimate complex appears to have grown organically out of the cove. The most abundant one-bedroom units come with or without a loft and with one or two bathrooms. Each unit is individually decorated, and all have some kind of ocean view. For a secluded oceanfront retreat, this place is hard to beat for the price. As the sun sets, perfectly framed by points of the cove, you may decide that your lanai alone is worth the cost. *Rates*: one-bedrooms $$, two-bedrooms $$–$$$, three-bedrooms $$$; weekly rates available; three- to five-night minimum. *Facilities and amenities*: 33 units, pool, parking (free), wireless (fee).

Napili Surf Beach Resort (808-669-8002 or 1-888-627-4547; napilisurf .com), 50 Napili Pl., Napili. This comely condo is smaller, quieter, and more affordable than most neighbor condos and only slightly less captivating. Since the beach tucks into the rocks in front of the Surf's main swimming pool, it's also the most sequestered and private spot on this gorgeous stretch of sand. There isn't much to do here except lounge in a chair. As for the accommodations, the concrete buildings are older than most in the area, but they're generally well cared for. Décor is contemporary and tropical. *Rates*: studios $$, one-bedrooms $$–$$$; each additional person $15; weekly rates. *Facilities and amenities*: 53 units, two pools, beach, parking (free), no credit cards, wireless (free).

⚘ ⚓ Napili Sunset (808-669-8083 or 1-800-447-9229; napilisunset.com), 46 Hui Dr., Napili. The prime attraction here is a great location, facing due west, right on the beach in the center of Napili Bay. Although the two-story condos are plain in appearance and the amenities minimal, the luxury hotels on Maui should envy this beachfront. Two of the complex's three buildings sit along the shore; the other sits across the street and overlooks a little pool and garden. Rooms in the latter are studios, fine for a family with one child. *Rates*: $$–$$$$; children under four free in parent's room. *Facilities and amenities*: 42 units, pool, beach, parking (free), daily maid service, Internet (free).

BED & BREAKFASTS AND INNS

⚘ The Guest House (808-661-8085 or 1-800-262-9912; mauiguesthouse .com), 1620 Ainakea Rd., off Fleming Rd. just north of Lahaina. One of the most welcoming yet hands-off B&Bs on Maui, The Guest House is only a mile from downtown Lahaina but seems worlds away. Guest rooms are spacious and breezy; two feature private backyard lanais. The large living room, communal kitchen, deep pool, private hot tubs, poolside grill, and extensive video library are some of its best aspects. Come for three days this year, and I bet you'll return for two weeks next year. Look for a big renovation in 2009, which promises to make this place better than ever. *Rates*: $$, including full breakfast. *Facilities and amenities*: four rooms, pool, use of full kitchen, hot tubs in every room, free water sports equipment, A/C.

⚘ Plantation Inn (808-667-9225 or 1-800-433-6815; theplantationinn .com), 174 Lahainaluna Rd., Lahaina. Designed to offer comfort and modern amenities, the inn demonstrates careful attention to detail in every respect, from the large verandas to exquisite decorating. Every room offers reason enough to lodge in Lahaina: Ground-floor rooms provide quick access to the pool from French doors, while lanais on the second floor provide a bit more privacy. (Standard rooms do not have a lanai.) Deluxe rooms distinguish themselves with a sitting area, while suites have a whole separate room that serves as a sitting and dining area. In 2008, the inn underwent a room-by-room renovation, which brought new furnishings, fixtures, and a switch from Victorian to island colors. You can also trust that poolside breakfasts are more elaborate than you'll find at almost any other inn in the state. I enjoy lingering here, since the enclosed courtyard is perfectly private. One more perk: Guests enjoy full privileges at the inn's sister property, the beachfront Ka'anapali Beach Hotel, just 3 miles up the road. *Rates*: $$–$$$, including full breakfast; children under five free in parent's room; seven-night minimum during Christmas. *Facilities and amenities*: 19 rooms, good pool, excellent restaurant (see **Gerard's** under *Dining Out*), A/C, parking (free).

House of Fountains (808-667-2121 or 1-800-789-6865; alohahouse.com), 1579 Lokia St., Lahaina. The tag line sounds about right: "Maui's most Hawaiian B&B." Situated in foothills of the West Maui Mountains in a quiet residential neighborhood, this B&B is filled with Hawaiian artifacts, arts and crafts (like quilts, warrior masks, and hula implements), and handmade Hawaiian-style furniture. In fact, the house is so richly appointed that hosts Daniela Clement and Don Kona Kamakani Atay offer house tours about Hawaiian culture and history. Completely renovated in 2006 and 2007, the contemporary and light B&B boasts a spacious patio and pool along with studios (*Makai*), rooms

(the cozy Ginger/Hibiscus room features a private garden *lanai*), and suites (Lokelani has ocean views and is good for families). Without a doubt, it's a great place to stay. *Rates*: $$. *Facilities and amenities*: six rooms, pool, Jacuzzi, TV, minifridge in each room, guest kitchen, Hawaiian-style full breakfast, phones, wireless (free), parking (free).

Lahaina Inn (808-661-0577 or 1-800-669-3444; lahainainn.com), 127 Lahainaluna Rd., Lahaina. This small, historic inn has been carefully restored to a period Victorian sensibility. Although the rooms and suites are smallish, they have the authenticity of a 1890s home. No detail was overlooked, from the leaded-glass lamps to the locksets. In a nod to modern trends during 2007, though, wallpaper was replaced with vintage Hawaiian patterns and large rain showers were added. Bedsteads are iron, brass, or wood. (I'd splurge for either the *Mauka* or *Makai* Suite because of their size.) Each has a lanai with a wooden rocker, but they're best enjoyed when your neighbor is out

THE GUEST HOUSE

since all lanais are attached. So-called mountain-view rooms overlook a parking lot, while harbor-view rooms look onto Lahainaluna Rd. and diagonally onto a slice of the harbor. *Rates*: $$; no children under 15. *Facilities and amenities*: 12 rooms, restaurant (see **Lahaina Grill** under *Dining Out*), A/C, phones, no TVs, adjacent parking (fee), wireless.

Pioneer Inn (808-661-3636 or 1-800-457-5457; pioneerinnmaui.com), 658 Wharf St., Lahaina. An inn in name only, this historic motel-like offering was constructed in 1901 as Maui's first hotel and set on the very same grounds that 50 years prior served as Hawai'i's capital. Now that Best Western is affiliated with it, it's rather subdued, except for the constant parade of tourists passing through the town's most memorable landmark (and bar). Before the renovation, crooked stairs led to creaky cubicles and shared baths aimed at adventurous pleasure seekers. (I knew two souls who lived here for a few dollars a week even as late as the 1950s.) Today, the historical character may be diluted, but the overall comfort level has been raised considerably. All rooms are on the

PIONEER INN

second floor and face the shaded courtyard, noisy Front Street, or barely less-noisy Hotel Street and the giant banyan tree. *Rates*: $$; children free in parent's room. *Facilities and amenities*: 34 rooms, courtyard pool, boisterous restaurant and boisterous bar, A/C, adjacent parking.

TOWN HOUSES

Pu'unoa (808-661-3339 or 1-800-642-6284; classicresorts.com), 45 Kai Pali Pl., Lahaina. An executive retreat extraordinaire, these 10 oceanfront town houses are the ultimate in luxe quarters. Truly beyond compare for rental properties, they come replete with every first-class amenity imaginable, including grocery delivery. Rare koa woods are used liberally, vaulted ceilings enhance a feeling of spaciousness, and, as you might expect, there's daily maid service. *Rates*: two-bedrooms $$$$; three-night minimum. *Facilities and amenities*: four units, pool, narrow beach, fitness room, concierge, parking (free).

✍ **Puamana** (808-667-2712 or 1-800-669-6284), Lahaina Cannery Mall, 1221 Honoapi'ilani Hwy. W., Lahaina. A quiet, self-contained seaside suburb, the family-friendly Puamana is essentially a community of private homes rather than a hotel or condo complex. The 60 low-rise buildings, most of which contain several town houses, are spaced over 28 oceanfront acres about a mile south of downtown. The beach here is narrow during summer, but it moves completely in winter to an adjacent beach park. Of the units in the rental pool, some are comfortably simple while others are more elaborate. (All are decorated by individual owners.) Because it's usually less expensive to book through an agency than directly through Puamana, I provide contact information for a rental agency located off property. You'll need to go here to pick up your keys. *Rates*: one-bedrooms $$, two-bedrooms $$–$$$, three-bedrooms $$$; children free in parent's room; three-night minimum. *Facilities and amenities*: about 15 units, three pools, complimentary tennis court, A/C (in some rooms), resort fee.

✎ **Kapalua Villas** (808-669-8088 or 1-800-545-0018; kapaluavillas.com), Kapalua. These 600 town houses and so-called villas are luxurious and a bargain (for what you get). Imagine that. It's especially true for families or groups. Ask about golf, tennis, and other packages. *Rates*: one- and two-bedroom condos $$$–$$$$, three-bedrooms $$$$; two- to seven-night minimum (depending on the season). *Facilities and amenities*: use of the pool, beach furniture, and fitness rooms (fee) at the Ritz-Carlton, Kapalua (see above), resort fee (includes Internet and long-distance phone calls).

✷ Where to Eat

You could enjoy fine, fine dinners in West Maui for a whole week and not exhaust the first-rate opportunities that'll expand your waistline. As for lunch, I keep it simple with a couple of beachfront and fast-ish food places. The choices I've included are excellent for what they offer. Once in town, you'll notice dozens of places that I've not reviewed. I am assuming that, at most, you'll be eating in Lahaina a few times. So I've narrowed your choices. It may sound maternalistic, but trust me.

If you're driving around the back side

of the West Maui Mountains, don't forget to check the *Where to Eat* listings in "Central Maui" since this great road deposits you in Wailuku.

Reservations are recommended for all *Dining Out* establishments.

DINING OUT

Lahaina

🏶 **Mala Ocean Tavern** (808-667-9394; malaoceantavern.com), 1307 Front St. Open for lunch weekdays, brunch on weekends, and dinner nightly. Owned by Mark and Judy Ellman, this small and wildly popular waterfront restaurant specializes in small plates and uses whole grains and organic ingredients most of the time. Favored entrées include Balinese fish stir-fry and prime flat iron steak. For lighter fare, try gado gado salad or calamari. Nab a lanai seat, or one of the few indoors. Or hang out at the bar with a mega martini and an ahi burger or sandwich. Weekend brunches are a simple way to say "French toast way worth the calories." Lunch and brunch $$–$$$, dinner entrées $$–$$$.

MALA OCEAN TAVERN

LAHAINA GRILL

℣ **I'O** (808-661-8422; iomaui.com), 505 Front St. Open for dinner nightly. Chef James McDonald's hip, hip, hip contemporary restaurant never, ever disappoints. Rarely will you find Pacific Rim, Asian, and Euro-American cuisine that consistently rises to this level. Because there are so many wonderful creations, I always order a bunch of appetizers in lieu of main dishes. Try the Thai curry asparagus soup, pinwheel carpaccio, or seafood martini. You'll inevitably utter to your dining companion something to the effect of "Honey, we're not in Kansas anymore." As for the open-air space,

I'O

nautical ship railings and an etched-glass aquarium merge with high-tech touches. Oh, and order anything chocolate for dessert. Children's menu. Entrées $$$–$$$$.

℣ **Pacific'O** (808-667-4341; pacifico maui.com), 505 Front St. Open for lunch and dinner daily. Per usual, this longtime place is absolutely great. For creative, contemporary Pacific Rim cuisine, no one rules like Chef James (of I'O fame). Try the coconut-mac-nut catch of the day or sesame-crusted lamb, shrimp and basil wontons, or Hapa Hapa tempura. Prime lunch choices include *kalua* quesadilla, Thai beef salad, and fish-and-chips. Not to be overlooked, pacifist vegetarians would revolt if Chef James's veggie specials were removed from the menu. The two-tiered setting couldn't be more romantic, with sunset views to Lana'i, tiki torches fluttering, palm trees swaying, and beachside tables. If you can't get the latter, consider dining at the bar. Children's menu. Lunch $$, dinner entrées $$$–$$$$.

℣ **Lahaina Grill** (808-667-5117; lahainagrill.com), Lahaina Inn, 127 Lahainaluna Rd. Open for dinner nightly. Although the namesake chef has departed, the reputation of this exceptional New American eatery survives completely intact. If you have limited fine-dining dollars, spend them here. This bustling hot spot, chic and cool, features trademark dishes like Maui-onion and sesame-crusted seared ahi, tequila shrimp and firecracker rice, grilled polenta stack, *kalua* duck, and rack of lamb. Because of sounds bouncing off the pressed-tin ceilings, this is not the place to come for an intimate conversation. Reservations are not accepted for the bar; children's menu. Entrées $$$–$$$$.

Gerard's (808-661-8939; gerards maui.com), Plantation Inn, 174 Lahainaluna Rd. Open for dinner nightly. This downright lovely (and dependably consistent) French bistro has been ensconced in the Plantation Inn and presided over by chef Gerard Reversade since the early 1980s. Chef Gerard has earned a loyal following with duck confit, rack of lamb, a fabulous wine list, and dessert classics like crème brûlée and profiteroles. Set with wicker chairs, Victorian accents, and lots of pink and green, the garden setting is utterly romantic: *C'est très bon*. Entrées $$$$.

Chez Paul (808-661-3843; chezpaul .com), Honoapi'ilani Hwy., Olowalu. Open for dinner nightly. Two fabulous French bistros within a few miles of each other in the middle of the Pacific Ocean? *Oui*. About 5 miles south of Lahaina in the blink-and-you'll-miss-it hamlet of Olowalu, this lovely bistro is pricey (especially since prices are in Euros) but worthy. Try the steak tartare—just one reason Chez Paul has been thriving since 1975. It tends to be a special-occasion place, with repeat patrons looking for the same cuisine they remember so well. Don't let the roadside exterior fool you; it belies an interior set with linen and china. Entrées $$$–$$$$.

✿ **Kimo's** (808-661-4811; kimosmaui .com), 845 Front St. Open for lunch and dinner daily; bar open until 12:30-ish. Although it may look like just a typical, casual, waterfront eatery on the strip, Kimo's offers a very good bang for the buck (especially for families)—as long as you're not expecting anything exotic. When you factor in oceanside tables and upstairs seating overlooking Front Street, it's easy to see why fans are devoted. Sig-

nature dishes include fish with a lemon-basil sauce, seared tuna, and prime rib (on and off the bone). The calorie cruncher Hula Pie was born here. Children's menu. Lunch $$, dinner entrées $$–$$$$.

✿ **Lahaina Fish Company** (808-661-3472; lahainafishcompany.com), 831 Front St. Open 11 AM–10 PM daily. It's the westward atmosphere that draws folks in here for dinner (especially), with tiki torches and tables cantilevered over the water. The affordable menu includes burgers, fish tacos, three or four daily fish specials (always my choice), and steaks. Children's menu. Lunch $–$$, dinner entrées $$–$$$.

Ka'anapali

✿ ⅋ **Hula Grill** (808-667-6636; hula grill.com), Whalers Village, 2435 Ka'anapali Pkwy. Open 11–11 daily. Long before there were high-rises on Ka'anapali Beach, there were low-rise beach houses like this. The outdoor tables alone, within a stone's throw of the beach, are worth the price of dinner. Chef Peter Merriman's always bustling, open-air eatery, which comes with a moderate or hefty price tag depending on what you order, blends Pacific, Euro, and Asian flavors into readily accessible cuisine. It's not going to knock your socks off, but it's very good. Seafood is the big draw. I tend to skip the enormous ice cream

---

TOP FIVE BEACHSIDE DINING
Pacific'O (West)
Mala Ocean Tavern (West)
Hula Grill (West)
Beachside Grill at Leilani's (West)
Mama's Fish House
(Upcountry & Haleakala)

sandwiches for dessert, but no one else seems to! Children's menu. Lunch $–$$, dinner entrées $$–$$$.

Son'z Maui at Swan Court (808-661-1234; sonzmaui.com), Hyatt Regency Maui Resort & Spa, 200 Nohea Kai Dr. When the owner of Nick's Fishmarket took over in 2006 and empowered Chef Geno Sarmiento, the former Swan Court morphed from very good to great. Although the atmosphere isn't my cup of tea, most diners love the setting: a grand staircase leads to a man-made lagoon with namesake swans. (It bears a resemblance to Hyatt's Tidepool restaurant on Kaua'i.) Try the traditional coq au vin, rack of lamb with pumpkin gnocchi, or scallops with bacon and tomatoes. Son'z also boasts the largest wine cellar in the state. Entrées $$$–$$$$.

Honokowai to Kapalua

✦ **Pineapple Grill** (808-669-9600; pineapplekapalua.com), 200 Kapalua Dr., Kapalua. Open 11 AM–10 PM daily. For superb Hawai'i regional cuisine by local chef Ryan Luckey, the Pineapple Grill has few rivals. Dine with a view of the West Maui Mountains or the ocean. I'd stake my reputation on their ahi steak with coconut-infused forbidden rice, catch of the day (relying on sustainable seafood), seafood paella, and pan-seared salmon. Save your budget and waistline to take full advantage of their wine pairings and deserts. At lunchtime, fare tends toward creative salads and sandwiches. Children's menu. Lunch $–$$, dinner entrées $$$–$$$$.

♀ ✦ **Roy's Kahana Bar & Grill/Roy's Nicolina Restaurant** (808-669-6999; roysrestaurant.com), Kahana Gateway Shopping Center, 4405 Honoapi'ilani Hwy., Kahana. Open for dinner nightly. These adjacent sibling eateries share similar characteristics: open kitchens, trademark Euro-Asian-Hawaiian fusion cuisine, and stunningly executed and creative dishes. Track lights, high ceilings, and modern artwork lend a mod feel. At Nicolina, which is quieter and a tad more romantic, keep it simple with a Thai chicken pizza or rack of lamb. Unless you're allergic, it'd be foolish not to order the chocolate soufflé for dessert. And just so you know, there are no views at this highway location; it's all about the food. Children's menu. Entrées $$$–$$$$.

Sansei Seafood Restaurant & Sushi Bar (808-669-6286; sansei hawaii.com), Kapalua Shops, 115 Bay Dr., Kapalua. Open for dinner nightly, with late-night dining Thurs. and Fri. With a cultlike following, Sansei garners accolades for its food the way Meryl Streep does for her acting. Why? Partly because Sansei defines the pinnacle of Euro–Hawaiian–Japanese–Pacific Rim fusion. The menu is so extensive, the flavors so exuberant, and the prices so (relatively) moderate that I could dine here nightly. Among the shining stars are

HULA GRILL

panko-crusted ahi sashimi, seared foie gras nigiri sushi, ravioli with lobster and crab, and mango crab hand roll. The miso soup is born of perfection. (By the way, I order apps two at a time and never get to the main dishes.) Appetizers $–$$, entrées $$–$$$.

☥ **Plantation House** (808-669-6299; theplantationhouse.com), Kapalua Plantation Golf Course, 2000 Plantation Club Dr., Kapalua. Open for all three meals daily. I can never decide whether it's chef Alex Stanislaw's food (eggs Benedict for breakfast and seafood later in the day) or the views (of the hills, ocean, fairways, and mountains) that's more impressive here. No matter. This spacious, clubby place with mahogany, teak, and wicker is the perfect setting for fish prepared a multitude of ways. The most popular is roasted with wild mushrooms. At lunchtime, sandwiches and salads are the order of the day. Children's menu. Breakfast $–$$, lunch $$, dinner entrées $$$–$$$$.

EATING OUT

Lahaina

🐚 🍴 ☥ **Aloha Mixed Plate** (808-661-3322; alohamixedplate.com), 1285 Front St. Open for lunch and dinner daily. My hands-down favorite in West Maui, this casual place has picnic tables on the water, a little bar, and great prices. Winning plates include shoyu chicken, coconut prawns, saimin, and burgers. There's a sweet, fun vibe upon entering, all throughout eating, and upon exiting. Adjacent to the Old Lahaina Lu'au (see *The Only Lu'au You'll Ever Need or Want*), you get the bonus of listening to and feeling the drumbeats from that exceptional production. To top it off, Aloha Mixed Plate even has free parking. See why I could come back

every night? Dishes $–$$.

🐚 🍴 **Cilantro** (808-667-5444; cilantrogrill.com), Old Lahaina Shopping Center, 170 Papalaua Ave. Open 10:30–9 daily. I love this place. From the first day it opened its doors, this kinda hip, pseudo-industrial alternative to Maui Taco has given the competition a run for its money. Frankly, I prefer it here for many reasons, not the least of which is the more relaxed atmosphere. The prices are perfect and the dishes are fresh. You know the offerings (they're just a bit more refined than the competition): tortas (classic Mexican sandwiches); combo plates (with margarita shrimp and adobo-roasted pork); tacos; burritos; and lemon herb chipotle rotisserie chicken. Children's menu. Dishes $–$$. BYOB.

🐚 🍴 **Penne Pasta** (808-661-6633; pennepastacafe.com), 180 Dickenson St. Open for lunch weekdays, dinner nightly. Are you tired of Pacific Rim cuisine and seared ahi? Is your wallet growing a bit thin? For a change of pace, this small eatery with sidewalk (and indoor) tables serves inexpensive pasta dishes. Unless you're a teenage boy, consider splitting the large servings. The flatbreads are tasty. Order at the counter and take a seat. Dishes $–$$.

ALOHA MIXED PLATE

THE ONLY LU'AU YOU'LL EVER NEED OR WANT

✪ **Old Lahaina Lu'au** (808-667-1998 or 1-800-248-5828; oldlahainaluau.com), across from the Lahaina Cannery Mall, 1251 Front St., Lahaina. The three-hour dinner show begins at 5:15 Oct.–Mar., 5:45 Apr.–Sept. Designed especially for this purpose, this *lu'au* venue couldn't be better: it's prime oceanfront real estate, it's relatively small, and it offers some traditional seating on the ground (on tatami mats). And in contrast to most *lu'aus*, the all-you-can-eat buffet is laden with very well-prepared food. Traditional offerings include *kalua* pig, *poi*, *lomi lomi* salmon, and coconut pudding (*haupia*), but there are also Pacific Rim preparations of seafood salads and mahimahi. As for "entertainment," the hula demonstrations range from ancient to modern; there's soulful chanting, drumming, and singing; and the Hawaiian and Tahitian performances are as authentic as it gets without heading farther west into the Pacific.

If you attend only one *lu'au* in your lifetime (and quite honestly, one is enough unless you get invited to a traditional one, for which you should drop everything and go), this is the state's best commercial offering.

If you can't afford the show, head to Aloha Mixed Plate (see *Eating Out*), an inexpensive outdoor restaurant adjacent to the *lu'au* grounds. You won't have a visual, but the evocative audio of drumming and chanting will burrow deep into your soul if you let it. Your imagination might be better than the "real" thing. Tickets $96 adults, $65 ages 12 and under. Serious advisory: Make reservations at least eight weeks prior to your visit, or you'll be sorry.

Ka'anapali

🦐 🏄 ⚲ **The Beachside Grill at Leilani's on the Beach** (808-661-4495; leilanis.com), Whalers Village, 2435 Ka'anapali Pkwy. Open for lunch and dinner daily. I prefer the downstairs beachside grill here, with torchlit tables and a lighter menu of burgers, *pupus,* and salads. Nothing beats casual cocktails on the sand. Dinner reservations recommended; children's menu. Lunch $$, dinner entrées $$–$$$$.

Honokowai to Kapalua

🏄 **The Gazebo Restaurant** (808-669-5621), Napili Shores Resort, 5315 Lower Honoapi'ilani Rd., Napili. Open for breakfast and lunch daily. Overlooking the beach, The Gazebo is popular with locals who happily line up for awesome breakfasts. You've never had mac nut pancakes until you've had them here. Children's menu. Dishes $–$$.

🏄 **Maui Tacos** (808-665-0222; mauitacos.com), Napili Plaza, 5095 Napili Hau St., Napili. Open 9–9 daily. For quick and cheap eats, these fish tacos, chicken enchiladas, and breakfast huevos rancheros are hard to beat. Thankfully, this inexpensive hole-in-the-wall has more comfortable seating than the one in Lahaina. At press time, there were five outlets on Maui. Dishes mostly under $.

🏄 **Pizza Paradiso** (808-667-2929; pizzaparadiso.com), Honokowai Marketplace, 3350 Lower Honoapi'ilani Rd., Honokowai. Open daily for lunch and dinner. This popular pizza joint dishes up traditional and create-your-own versions by the slice or by the pie. Try one with pineapple and roasted chicken. Take home, eat in, or have them deliver your pie for free. They aim to please, and they hit the mark. Dishes $–$$.

Honolua Store (808-669-6128), adjacent to the Ritz-Carlton, Kapalua. Open 6 AM–8 PM daily. The pickings are slim up here, but this godsend has a deli with sandwiches and affordable breakfast offerings.

Java Jazz (808-667-0787), Honokowai Marketplace, Lower Honoapi'ilani Rd., Honokowai. Open 5:30 AM–9 PM daily. You might prefer this place—for sandwiches, espresso, and music—simply because it is an independent alternative to Starbucks.

JUST SO YOU KNOW

The Whalers Village food court (808-661-4567) has decent take-away eats for the beach. It's certainly less expensive than whatever your resort is hawking.

The ubiquitous **Maui Taco** has a Lahaina franchise (808-661-8883; Lahaina Square, 840 Waine'e St.), but I prefer **Cilantro** (see *Eating Out*) for inexpensive and quick Mexican food. Also in **Lahaina**, Longhi's gets a lot of press because it's been around forever, but I've found it completely overpriced. The **Pioneer Inn**'s historic past draws in tourists to its nautical dining room, but if you're serious about food, go elsewhere.

All the big resorts offer lavish **Sunday brunches**, but only the **Ka'anapali Beach Hotel** (808-661-0011, ext. 124; reservations required) is worth it. Why? While the food is pretty good, what it really has to offer, hands down, is the most authentic Hawaiian experience. Adults $36, children $20.

MAUI

✳ Entertainment

A number of dinner and sunset cruises depart out of Lahaina Harbor, but to me none seem like a very good value in terms of how I want to spend my precious time and money. If you disagree and want to recommend one for me to check for the next edition, please let me know. Simply cruising down Front Street in Lahaina, people-watching, is entertainment enough for some.

DINNER & SHOWS

○ The Feast at Lele (808-667-1998 or 1-866-244-5353; feastatlele.com), 505 Front St., Lahaina. Show starts at 5:30 PM Oct.–Mar., 6 PM Apr.–Sept. This classy three-hour dinner show scores big-time with a trifecta: It has a stunning beachfront location; excellent food and wine; and Tahitian, Samoan, Tongan, and Hawaiian entertainment. No, it's not a luʻau; it's more about cultural island cuisine paired with a side order of not-exactly-authentic-but-still-spirited entertainment. (The chanting, singing, drumming, and dancing are representative of each island locale.) The Feast's success is a result of a partnership between chef James McDonald (see PacificʻO and IʻO under *Dining Out*) and the Old Lahaina Luʻau (see *The Only Luʻau You'll Ever Need or Want*). To boot, the sunsets are stupendous from here, the portions huge, and the individual tables set with candles and linen on the sand. It sounds just as romantic as it is. Tickets $110 adults, $80 ages 12 and under. Reservations are imperative, and it's best to book six weeks ahead.

Ulalena (808-661-9913 or 1-877-688-4800; ulalena.com), Maui Myth & Magic Theater, 878 Front St., Lahaina. Shows Mon.–Fri. at 6:30 PM, but call for show times because they sometimes add some. Although there's nothing "basic" about it, Ulalena basically tells the mythological and historical story of Hawaiʻi without the benefit of spoken word. It's all done through chanting, interpretive dance, performance art, and music. There's more than a touch of Cirque du Soleil to it, thanks to the high-energy acrobatics and high-tech lighting razzle-dazzle. Only the really hard-core culturalists are perturbed by the portrayal. Tickets $60–100 adults, $40–70 ages 3–15.

Napili Kai Beach Club Keiki Hula Show (808-669-6271; napilikai.com), 5900 Lower Honoapiʻilani Rd., Napili. Shows Tues. at 5 PM. Because this show isn't professional and perfect, it's thoroughly enchanting. Cynics can step aside so that the rest of us can smile through the *keiki*'s hour-long, heart-filled gift. Youngsters ages 6–18 perform Hawaiian and Polynesian dances draped in homemade ti-leaf skirts. It's all performed under the auspices of the Napili Kai Foundation, a nonprofit educational organization operated by the hotel staff to transmit the essentials of Hawaiian culture to the children of Maui. Tickets $10 adults, $5 *keiki*. Reservations. Your ticket price is tax refundable.

See also *The Only Luʻau You'll Ever Need or Want*.

DRINKS & MUSIC

⅄ Compadres Bar & Grill (808-661-7189), Lahaina Cannery Mall, 1221 Honoapiʻilani Hwy., Lahaina. Open nightly until 10 PM. If you're missing your basic urban creature comforts (like concrete floors and a shabby chic industrial look), Compadres delivers. Still, except for Taco Tuesday, when Compadres serves up $1 tacos with frisky $3 margaritas, I'd rather eat Mexican food at Cilantro (see *Eating Out*). The other plus to this industrial Tex-Mex place? From the back porch you're within earshot of the Old Lahaina Lu'au's primal drumbeats.

Y Cheeseburger in Paradise (808-661-4855; cheeseburgerland.com), 811 Front St., Lahaina. Music until 10 nightly. Although I am loath to mention this place because of its unabashed commercial appeal, they host raucous tropical bands starting in the late afternoon. (Don't come looking for a dance floor.) The open-air, second-floor balcony, always crowded, is a great place to people-watch.

Y Sly Mongoose (808-661-8097), 1036 Limahana Pl., Lahaina. If the words *Hard Rock Café* cause you to quiver in your sandals (yes, there is one in Lahaina), put on your scruffiest T-shirt and belly up to this divey but truly friendly bar. Watch out for the mai tais if you're driving.

Y Pacific'O (808-667-4341), 505 Front St., Lahaina. Open Thurs.–Sun. from 9 PM. With a bit of luck you'll catch some cool jazz on Saturdays in this stylin' waterfront restaurant.

See also **Mala Ocean Tavern**, with its stylin' little bar, under *Dining Out*.

MOVIES
Lahaina Center Movie Theater (808-249-2222), Lahaina Center, 900 Front St., Lahaina.

ROMANTIC PLACES FOR COCKTAILS
✪ Y Hula Grill (808-667-6636; hula grill.com), Whalers Village, Ka'anapali. This beach-style bungalow is right on the water (and beach) and features nightly Hawaiian music. It's the best place on the strip for a moonrise-over-the-water drink. Within feet of the sandy shores, it's also the closest you'll come to the beach.

See also **Pacific'O** under *Dining Out* and Leilani's on the Beach under *Eating Out*.

STARGAZING
✦ Tour of the Stars (808-661-1234, ext. 4727), Hyatt Regency Maui Resort & Spa (Lahaina Tower), Ka'anapali. Stargazing at 8, 9, 10, and 11 nightly. Tired of watered-down mai tais and overpriced mu'umu'us? If you're not heading to the Big Island, where stargazing is serious business, this activity provides a clear and present alternative. Overseen by an astronomer, the rooftop program includes peeping through a giant, reflecting deep-space telescope. It's a trippy journey through the planets. As if weekends are reserved for romance, the Friday and Saturday 11 PM shows include champagne and chocolate-covered strawberries. Tickets $25, $20 for Hyatt guests; $10 children; reservations required.

✷ Selective Shopping

ART GALLERIES
Lahaina galleries host **Art Night** every Friday (about 6–10 PM), flinging their air-conditioned spaces open to the warm night air. Strolling musicians provide an aural score to the festive atmosphere, and you may have a chance to talk story with artists whose work you admire.

Lahaina Arts Society Galleries (808-661-0111), 648 Wharf St., in the Old Courthouse, Lahaina. Open 9–5 daily. This highly regarded, members-only group produces a diverse body of work in various media—from ceramics and jewelry to fiber art and sculpture. The building houses the Banyan Tree Gallery and the Old Jail Gallery. The society also sponsors Art in the Park art fairs beneath the magnificent spread of the adjacent banyan tree (on the second and fourth Fridays and Saturdays of the month).

Village Galleries (808-661-5199; villagegalleriesmaui.com), Baldwin House, Masters Reading Room, Front and Dickenson, Lahaina. Open 9–9 daily. This long-standing gallery of quality art is one the finer showcases on Maui. Look for another shop at 180 Dickenson St. (with more contemporary gift fare) and at the Ritz-Carlton, Kapalua (808-669-1800).

BOOKSTORES

Old Lahaina Book Emporium (808-661-1399), 834 Front St., Lahaina. Open 10–7 daily. No offense to Amazon.com, but their used-book offerings have nothing on this remarkable bastion of recycled literature, history, and Hawaiiana. Its two stories will wow you with diversity and affordability.

OLD LAHAINA BOOK EMPORIUM

Barnes & Noble (808-662-1300), Gateway Mall, 325 Keawe St., Lahaina. Open daily. New in fall 2007, this great community center and bookstore is a welcome addition to West Maui.

MARKETS

Farmer's market, across from Honokowai Park and in the Hawaiian Moons parking lot on Lower Honoapi'ilani Rd., Honokowai. Mon., Wed., and Fri. 7–11 AM. Locally grown fruits and veggies, fresh breads and juices, assorted cheeses, onions, pineapples, and macadamia nuts.

SHOPPING AREAS

Lahaina's Front Street, like its mainland brethren of Provincetown and Key West, is packed like tin-can sardines with shops designed to reach deep into your wallets. Interspersed with dozens of T-shirt shops and purveyors of overpriced (and disarmingly similar) merchandise, though, are a few gems waiting to be unearthed. You'll have to expend a bit of shoe leather to find them.

Whalers Village (808-661-4567; whalersvillage.com), Ka'anapali Pkwy., Ka'anapali. An upscale but rather predictable pedestrian outdoor mall with more than 70 shops. It does have a little whaling museum (see *To See & Do*) and some outdoor exhibits (namely a 30-foot-long whale skeleton and a whaling boat with harpoons—never hurts to get a little culture in with the shopping). Lahaina Printsellers (see below) also has an outlet here.

SPECIAL SHOPS

Lahaina Printsellers (808-667-5815; printsellers.com), 505 Front St., Lahaina. Open 10–10 daily. If you're a heartfelt traveler struck with wanderlust, you don't have to be a cartographer to appreciate these original 18th- and 19th-century maps and engravings of Hawai'i and Polynesia. For the rest of the world, there are also high-quality reproduction prints. They also have a location in Whalers Village.

Lahaina Scrimshaw (808-667-9232; lahainascrimshaw.net), 845 Front St., Lahaina. Open 9 AM–10 PM daily. Although the connection to Maui's whaling industry may seem tenuous amid all the tourist-trap shops, it's real and dates to the 19th century. You might be surprised to learn that more scrimshaw is supposedly sold on this island than anywhere else. Pieces from $20 to 20,000.

Endangered Species (808-661-1139), Whalers Village, Ka'anapali. Open 9 AM–10 PM daily. A portion of the proceeds from shark and whale products help the respective causes.

WHALER'S VILLAGE

Hilo Hattie's (808-667-7911; hilohattie.com), 900 Front St., Lahaina. Open 9–9 daily. Head to this commercial institution for mass-produced aloha wear that you'll probably never don once you get home (but that you could very well wear every night of your vacation).

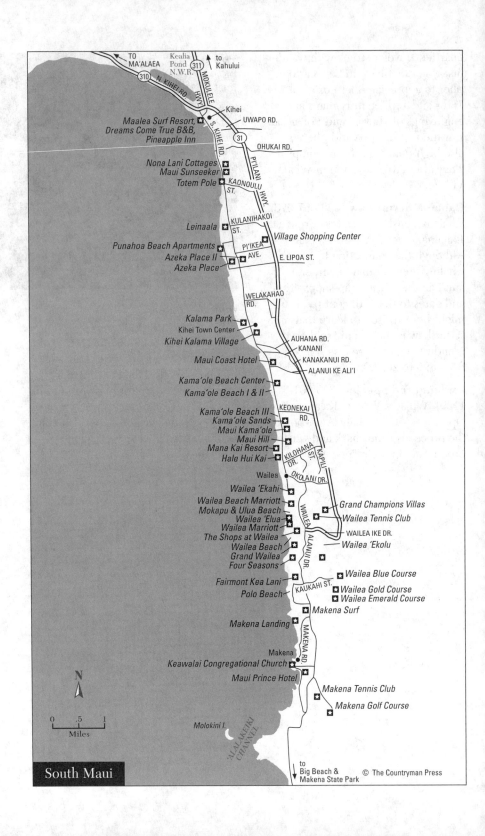

To MA'ALAEA

Kealia Pond N.W.R.

to Kahului

311 MOKULELE HWY.

310 N. KIHEI RD.

Kihei

S. KIHEI RD.

UWAPO RD.

Maalea Surf Resort,
Dreams Come True B&B,
Pineapple Inn

31

OHUKAI RD.

PI'ILANI HWY.

Nona Lani Cottages
Maui Sunseeker
Totem Pole

KAONOULU ST.

KULANIHAKOI ST.

Leinaala

Village Shopping Center

Punahoa Beach Apartments

PI'IKEA AVE.

E. LIPOA ST.

Azeka Place II
Azeka Place

WELAKAHAO RD.

Kalama Park

Kihei Town Center

AUHANA RD.

Kihei Kalama Village

KANANI

KANAKANUI RD.

Maui Coast Hotel

ALANUI KE ALI'I

Kama'ole Beach Center
Kama'ole Beach I & II

Kama'ole Beach III

KEONEKAI RD.

Kama'ole Sands
Maui Kama'ole
Maui Hill
Mana Kai Resort
Hale Hui Kai

KILOHANA DR.

KAPILI ST.

OKOLANI DR.

Wailea

Wailea 'Ekahi

WAILEA ALANUI DR.

Wailea Beach Marriott
Mokapu & Ulua Beach
Wailea 'Elua
Wailea Marriott
The Shops at Wailea
Wailea Beach
Grand Wailea
Four Seasons

Grand Champions Villas
Wailea Tennis Club

WAILEA IKE DR.

Wailea 'Ekolu

Wailea Blue Course

Fairmont Kea Lani
Polo Beach

KAUKAHI ST.

Wailea Gold Course
Wailea Emerald Course

Makena Surf

Makena Landing

MAKENA RD.

Makena

Keawalai Congregational Church

Maui Prince Hotel

Makena Tennis Club

Makena Golf Course

N

0   .5   1
Miles

Molokini I.

'ALALAKEIKI CHANNEL

to
Big Beach &
Makena State Park

© The Countryman Press

South Maui

SOUTH MAUI

From Kihei to Makena, the chances of clear skies are better for beach enthusiasts than anywhere else on Maui. But the scarcity of rain also produces a parched landscape that resembles Arizona as much as the tropics. Wailea and Makena compensate with irrigation. Kihei simply covers the arid plain with malls and condos.

But first there's **Ma'alaea Harbor**, which could just as easily be assigned to the Central or West Maui chapters as this one. A jumping-off point for boat trips, it's also home to the famed Maui Ocean Center.

In **Kihei**, from one end of South Kihei Road to the other, successions of inauspicious strip malls and developments choke both sides of the street, interrupted only intermittently along the ocean by a few patches of sand. (Along the northern stretch, in particular, there are fragile dunes between the road and ocean.) Often referred to as "condo hell," but also one of the fastest-growing communities in the United States, Kihei isn't much of a town. It stretches for 7 miles, 5 of which belong to highly trafficked South Kihei Road, along which you'll find almost every condo, restaurant, and beach you'll be interested in. Why stay here, then? Well, it offers a convenient location from which to explore the rest of the island, relatively pocketbook-friendly prices, and very dependable sun. Charming it's not, but you're also more likely to rub shoulders with friendly residents here than almost anywhere else on Maui. (One-third of Maui's population lives here.) When it's hot on Maui, it seems to be even hotter in Kihei.

Luxurious **Wailea**, not a bona fide town in the mainland sense of the word, came of age as a resort in the early 1990s with the opening of the oh-so-posh Four Seasons and oh-so-gauche Grand Wailea (an attraction in its own right). Although Ka'anapali and Wailea are similar in size, Wailea learned lessons in design from its older cousin. The density is much lower here, with buildings spread sparingly over the estate and limited to a moderate height. Wailea also stands in marked contrast to Kihei in that it's perfectly laid out, intensely green (thanks to world-class golfing), and oh-so-manicured. Once incorporated into Ulupalakua Ranch and completely barren save for stunted kiawe trees, this stretch of Maui was sold in the 1950s to Matson Cruise Lines, which expected to develop it. Instead they sold to sugar baron Alexander & Baldwin, which developed it in the 1970s.

As for beaches, a string of little bays doused with perfect white sand front the hotels along Wailea's coastline. Wailea's biggest draw is perhaps her three prime golf courses. Like the rest of the resort, they're sheltered by Mount Haleakala from the prevailing northern trade winds, providing the most predictably sunny playing weather on Maui. Another big plus is the Wailea Tennis Club, arguably unsurpassed in Hawai'i. The resort's five beaches, separated from each other by a rocky shoreline, are short, wide, and sandy. Almost all of Wailea's dining and entertainment options are located in the hotels and at The Shops at Wailea. But even with the scarcity of independent enterprises, the range of possibilities for everything should seem plentiful—unless perhaps you would really rather be in Ka'anapali.

> **BUILDING BLOCKS FOR A PERFECT DAY IN SOUTH MAUI**
> Walk the coastal walking trail in the morning before it gets too crowded (90 minutes)
> Visit the Maui Ocean Center (2 to 3 hours)
> Go snorkeling at Molokini in the morning when visibility is better (4 hours)
> Drive to the end of the road at Makena and go kayaking and sunbathing (4 to 6 hours)

Makena, a few miles south of Wailea, shares its neighbor's bright weather but is much smaller and less developed. Off the beaten path simply because it's at the end of the road, arid and wildish Makena is South Maui's last area to really be developed. The resort's two comely golf courses and other facilities are devoted primarily to hotel guests. This is the untamed side of South Maui, and it exudes a primal, end-of-the-road feel. When the road really does end, you'll be deposited where Haleakala last deposited her lava, back in 1790. Make the effort to get this far and you'll be rewarded with ubiquitous kiawe trees, a fabulous and empty beach, and dramatic lava fields.

Because of its proximity (as the crows fly and horses tread) to Ulupalakua Ranch, Makena was once Maui's second-largest port. Just days after assuming the throne, King Kalakaua and Queen Kapiolani arrived in Makena for a little holiday at Ulupalakua Ranch. Today, by the way, there is no direct road, and the trip is over 40 miles.

GETTING AROUND

By car: South Kihei Road is a necessary evil, lined with places to stay, eat, and swim. But there will come a tipping point when you've crawled along from traffic light to traffic light one too many times. To avoid reaching that point, learn the side roads and use Hwy. 31 (aka Pi'ilani Highway), a bypass road that runs parallel to South Kihei Road and leads to Wailea. Both roads eventually lead to South Makena Road, which takes you to the paved end of South Maui.

✳ To See & Do

Exploring from north to south.

Ma'alaea

Ma'alaea Small Boat Harbor, Hwy. 30 near the intersection of Hwy. 31. Plenty of fishing, snorkeling, and sightseeing boats depart from here.

⚓ ☉ **Maui Ocean Center** (808-270-7000; mauioceancenter.com), Hwy. 30, 192 Ma'alalea Rd., Ma'alaea. Open 9–5 daily, until 6 PM in July and August. Opened in 1998, this 5-acre tropical aquarium features a tunnel-like walkway that leads right through a large open-ocean tank. In essence, you'll be descending from sea level to the depths where reef fish, turtles, stingrays, and tiger sharks live. I haven't heard of anyone who's been disappointed by it. In addition to checking out the recently renovated marine mammal Discovery Center, you might also want to dive with the sharks. $24 adults, $21 seniors, $17 ages 3–12.

Kealia Pond National Wildlife Refuge (808-875-1582), off Hwy. 31 (N. Kihei Rd.), east of the Maui Ocean Center. This 700-acre preserve is home to endangered Hawaiian stilts, herons, ducks, and other waterfowl. Take a self-guided tour out onto the boardwalk (under construction at press time with no completion date set), along some dunes and ponds, where you'll find interpretive plaques and shelters. The boardwalk begins near MM 2 on the Pi'ilani Highway.

Kihei

Kihei Totem Pole, 575 S. Kihei Rd., across from the Aston Maui Lu Resort. A proverbial X marks the spot where Captain Vancouver (who named the western Canadian city for himself) landed in 1778 and officially "discovered" Kihei.

Kalama Park. Join the locals in watching a baseball or soccer game here.

⚓ See also Kama'ole III (aka Kam 3) under *Beaches*.

Wailea

⚓ See also **Ulua Beach**, **Wailea Beach**, and **Polo Beach** under *Beaches*.

☉ **Coastal Walking Trail**. This 1.5-mile paved walkway runs in front of all the resorts, between Wailea 'Elua Village and the Fairmont Kea Lani Maui. The path is pedestrian-friendly. If you want to do more than stroll, be sure to take it first thing in the morning (and I mean immediately after your first cup of wake-me-up coffee). Otherwise it's hot and crowded. Plenty of benches provide reason enough, though, to dally over native plants, perfect coves, black lava, and offshore island views. Pick up the path from any of the resorts or from one of the many shoreline access points.

Makena

⚓ **Makena Beach** (aka **Big Beach**) really consists of four beaches, including **Oneloa** and **Maluaka**. See *Beaches*.

Keawalai Congregational Church (808-879-5557), 5300 Makena Rd. Dating to 1855 with 3-foot-thick walls of lava rock, this church and graveyard are sited on prime oceanfront real estate. Hawaiian-language Sunday services are held at 7:30 AM and 10 AM.

La Perouse Monument, S. Makena Rd. A cairn and plaque mark the spot

MAKENA

SOUTH KIHEI ROAD ISN'T JUST CONDOS.

where the French explorer Admiral de la Perouse landed in 1786. Beyond Big Beach and 'Ahihi Bay, the road becomes gravelly and passes through *a'a* lava fields to La Perouse Bay. (I prefer tackling this bumpy, hardscrabble stretch with a four-wheel drive.) In case you're wondering, the last eruption ripped through here a mere two centuries ago, in 1790. (Perhaps it was Pele's reaction to the admiral's rather egotistical pronouncement of his so-called discovery.)

'Ahihi-Kina'u Marine Preserve, by the way, offers great morning snorkeling (and dolphin sightings), but it's harder to get into the water here than at La Perouse. More than usual, don't leave anything valuable in your car. You'll notice an abundance of broken window glass around here.

✳ Spas

🅰 **Spa Grand at Grand Wailea Resort Hotel & Spa** (808-875-1234, ext. 4949; grandwailea.com), Wailea. Open 8–7 daily. Weighing in at 50,000 square feet, the Spa Grand is the granddaddy of Hawai'i spas. It features a range of water treatments called the Terme Wailea Hydrotherapy Circuit. First you exfoliate and cleanse the skin with a loofah scrub, continue on to a cascading waterfall massage, then soak in a specialty bath (moor mud, seaweed, mineral salt, or tropical enzyme), and finish with a jet shower and a bit of lounging on the outdoor lanai. Stay all day, if you want, for the same price (a bargain at $85 for non–resort guests). The Romanesque spa is the Grand Wailea Resort's main attraction for many guests and nonguests. Specializing in individual attention, water therapy, and traditional Hawaiian treatments, the staff offer options such as seaweed baths, *lomi lomi* massages, volcanic ash wraps, and Maui mud masks. Since the Spa Grand's mission is to merge Hawaiian healing techniques with those native to Europe, India, and Asia, you'll find ayurvedic and Siddha treatments on the spa menu here.

Spa Kea Lani at Fairmont Kea Lani Maui (808-875-4100; fairmont.com), Wailea. Open 7:30 AM–8 PM daily. It may be small in comparison with other spas, but the state-of-the-art treatment rooms deliver the goods in style and substance.

The Spa at Four Seasons Resort Maui at Wailea (808-874-8000; fourseasons .com/maui), Wailea. Open 6 AM–9 PM daily. Try the signature Mango Salt Glow, an exfoliating procedure made exotic through the use of mango sorbet.

BIRD-WATCHING
See **Kealia Pond National Wildlife Refuge** under *To See & Do*.

FISHING
Four- and eight-hour charters depart out of Maʻalaea and Lahaina Harbors. I recommend wandering around the harbor and talking to captains to get a feel for the person and boat. If you want to book ahead of time, contact **Sportfish Hawaii** (808-396-2607 or 1-877-388-1376; sportfishhawaii.com), which books captains and boats all across the state. See *Outdoor Activities* in "West Maui." You can also count on regaling friends with fish stories about the ones that got away as well as the huge mahimahi, tuna, ono, and blue marlin that you'll reel in. I'm talking big-game fish. Shore fishing is great from sheltered spots along South Makena Road in Makena.

GOLF
Elleair Maui Golf Course (808-874-0777), 1345 Piʻilani Hwy., Kihei. This independent course, high above town with incredible views of Haleakala and the Pacific Ocean, is much less windy in the morning than afternoon. Greens fees cost $120 and drop to $65 after 3 PM. You can make reservations 30 days in advance.

Makena South & Makena North (808-891-4000; makenagolf.com), Makena Alanui Dr., Makena. Of these two fabulous Robert Trent Jones–designed courses, the North course is more difficult. The 14th hole challenges with a 200-foot elevation drop between the tee and green. Although the courses offer challenges and pleasures similar to those elsewhere on Maui, since they serve a smaller population of golfers there is a relative lack of competition for tee times. Sunset views of Molokini are unparalleled. Greens fees cost $170–190 in the morning and drop to $100–150 after 1 PM. (Fees are a bit lower for guests staying at area resorts.) Make reservations a couple of weeks in advance.

Wailea Blue, **Wailea Gold & Wailea Emerald** (808-875-7450; waileagolf.com), 100 Wailea Golf Club Dr., Wailea. Of these three magnificent sister courses, Blue is quite pop-

WAILEA BEACH

HUMPBACK WHALES

From late November to late April (more or less), humpbacks commune in the warm waters off the coast of the Hawaiian Islands to breed and, a year later when they return, to give birth. But according to the Hawai'i Whale Research Foundation, neither of these activities has ever been observed. The annual return of the humpbacks (from their summer home in Alaska) is always exciting and legendary. And since the whales come so close to shore, you'll want to be careful driving the coastal highways during this time. Folks are known to simply stop in the middle of the road, awestruck at the proximity and sheer number of these creatures!

Luckily for you, Maui is the best island for whale-watching. No specific time of day is best for sightings, but when the winds have died down and the water is calm, you'll have a better shot at spotting spouts of water when you scan the ocean. In West Maui, head to the scenic pullout at **McGregor Point** (MM 9 on Hwy. 30) and the stretch of highway between here and Olowalu overlooking **Olowalu Reef**. In South Maui, head to the **Wailea Coastal Walking Trail** or **Big Beach** in Makena, where you can climb high atop the Pu'u Olai cinder cone.

One of nature's most majestic spectacles is seeing these creatures heave their 30- to 40-ton bodies straight out the water and crash back down.

ular with its wide fairways, Gold is more challenging, and Emerald is perhaps more player-friendly—not to mention friendly on the eyes with stunning ocean views. (Emerald is also the hardest for booking tee times; weekdays are easier for all courses than weekends.) Blue was designed by Arthur Jack Snyder, but the other two are Robert Trent Jones Jr. courses. Greens fees cost $185–225 and drop in price later in the day only for the Blue course. Fees are a bit lower for guests staying at area resorts. Make reservations 30 days ahead of time.

KAYAKING

✪ **Makena Kayak Tours** (808-879-8426 or 1-877-879-8426), Makena Landing. After snorkeling and diving, the next best way to see reef fish and turtles is from sea level. This outfit is great for beginners as well as experienced paddlers. Because mornings see better weather conditions, the two-and-a-half-hour trips depart only at 7:30 and 8 ($55 per person). Groups are small, usually with only six guests per guide.

South Pacific Kayaks (808-875-4848 or 1-800-776-2326; southpacifickayaks .com), Kihei. Contact these folks for rentals ($40 single, $50 double per day), tours of secluded coastlines, and lessons. Remember that water conditions are usually best in the morning. All rentals must be arranged the day before.

To check out these behemoths up close, get in a kayak or raft or take a whale-watching cruise. Traveling next to a pod of whales is quite humbling.

Capt. Steve's Rafting and Excursions (808-667-5565; captainsteves.com) departs from Lahaina. Their two-hour rafting trips (Dec.–Apr.) cost $39–49 for adults, $29–35 for children under 12. (Some experts believe that afternoon trips offer the promise of more breaching, but they're also generally windier.) When thinking about which tour company to go with, consider what's most important to you. Would you rather have a biologist or a bartender on board? Would you rather be in a small boat where you can almost touch the surface of the water—but without facilities—or a bigger party boat with toilets? If you're really ecologically minded, consider simply watching the show from shore. Many experts believe that the profusion of tour boats is quite disruptive to the breeding animals.

To brush up on humpback factoids, head to the **Pacific Whale Foundation** (808-249-8811 or 1-800-942-3311; pacificwhale.org), Ma'alalea Harbor Village. You'll learn things about gestation period (11–12 months), birth weight (1–2 tons), and size (up to 50 feet long).

If you're not visiting Maui during humpback season, don't worry. At other times of the year you can spot different kinds of whales—pilot, sperm, false killer, melon-headed, pygmy killer, and beaked—traveling in pods (20–30 at a time).

SCUBA DIVING

❂ **Molokini**, just offshore from Wailea across the 'Alalakeiki Channel, is the most popular dive site by a long shot. See *Scuba Diving* and *Snorkeling* in "West Maui."

Maui Dive Shop (808-879-3388, 1455 S. Kihei Rd., and 808-879-1533, Kama'ole Shopping Center, both in Kihei; mauidiveshop.com) publishes a free 24-page *Maui Dive Guide*. See *Outdoor Activities*, in "West Maui.".

SNORKELING

Snorkel Bob's (808-879-7449; snorkelbob.com), Kama'ole Beach Center, 2411 S. Kihei Rd., Kihei. Open 8–5 daily. For freelance snorkeling, Bob's has all the gear you'll need. On your own, head to Kam III Beach in Kihei, *U'lua* Beach in Wailea, Makena Beach (weekdays are your best bet here), Pu'u Ola'i in Makena, and 'Ahihi-Kinau Marine Preserve past Makena. (See *Beaches* for location details.) Mask, snorkel, and fin rentals cost $8 daily, $32 weekly.

Trilogy (808-661-4743 or 1-888-628-4800; sailtrilogy.com), Ma'alaea Harbor. This fine outfit offers snorkeling trips, with breakfast and lunch, to Molokini. $110 adults, half price ages 3–15.

Four Winds II (808-879-8188 or 1-800-736-5740; mauicharters.com), Maʻalaea Harbor. This glass-bottomed catamaran takes folks out snorkeling at Molokini. If there are kids on board, or adults who are apprehensive of snorkeling in open water, they can still come along and have fun with their friends and family. Kids also like the on-board water slide. $89 adults, $59 ages 3–12, includes breakfast and a barbecue lunch. Afternoon trips are less expensive ($42 and $30, respectively) but conditions aren't as good and the barbecue lunch is $7 (optional). Book a week in advance to get 15 percent off.

✪ **Molokini**, a partially submerged volcano that looks like a crescent moon from above, offers the best snorkeling opportunities. Below the water's surface, at 10 to 80 feet deep, you'll find a bona fide marine sanctuary. Take a morning trip, when the waters will probably be clearer, with the **Pacific Whale Foundation** operating out of Maʻalaea Harbor (see *Whale-Watching*). With a bit of luck, you'll see porpoises playing and, if it's winter, humpback whales breaching.

TENNIS
Wailea Tennis Club (808-879-1958; waileatennis.com), 131 Wailea Iki Pl., Wailea. This full-service and upscale club, with 11 Plexipave courts, also offers lessons, rentals, ball machines, and clinics. It's an excellent facility. Courts rent for $15 per person.

Makena Tennis Club (808-879-8777), Makena Alanui, Makena. Six courts, two of which are lit, rent for $30 for up to four players.

WATER SPORTS
All manner of water sport rentals are available at the big resorts in Wailea.

Snorkel Bob's (see *Snorkeling*) rents boogie boards and such.

WHALE-WATCHING & DOLPHIN SIGHTINGS
Pacific Whale Foundation (808-879-8811 or 1-800-942-5311; pacificwhale .org). Summertime snorkeling trips to Molokini and wintertime (Dec.–mid-May) whale-watching trips are offered out of Lahaina and Maʻalaea Harbors. This nonprofit foundation, a pioneer in whale research, offers extremely informative trips. There are upwards of 13 daily whale-watching trips; $32 adults, $17 ages 7–12, free 6 and under. Every dollar you spend at their stores and on their trips goes toward conservational and educational programs.

The foundation also offers ecofriendly dolphin-sighting trips out of Lahaina Harbor to Lanaʻi ($80 adults, $35 ages 7–12, free 6 and under). Practically no one knows more about the social interaction and behavior of these intelligent and playful creatures than these folks. You can expect to see pods of 200 spinner dolphins. The six-hour trip departs at 8 AM.

WINDSURFING
It's best along the northern stretch of Kihei at **Ohukai Park**. There's plenty of parking and a good grassy strip for getting set up.

KAHO'OLAWE

Kaho'olawe's 45 square miles (it's 11 miles long and 7 miles wide) have long been barren and treeless, even as far back as the 1400s when a fire ravaged it. According to one legend, the desolation of Kaho'olawe resulted from a disagreement between two goddesses (one can only imagine the magnitude of the fight!).

The intervening years didn't get any better. In the 1840s, Kaho'olawe served as a penal colony. And when the island was later transformed into a sheep and cattle ranch, erosion continued unabated because of the grazing. Still, there were ancient religious sites on the island, and Native Hawaiians felt very protective of it. Enter the U.S. government. In 1953, President Eisenhower gave control of Kaho'olawe to the U.S. Navy for use as a target facility. It was taken with the postscript that when no longer needed, Kaho'olawe would be restored to its natural state and returned to theNative Hawaiians. For more than 40 years, gargantuan explosions could be seen and heard from Maui.

Primarily because of the tireless efforts of Protect Kaho'olawe 'Ohana, made up of young Hawaiian activists, the state of Hawai'i regained control of the island from the federal government in 1994. For the next 10 years, the navy "restored" it (or not, depending on whom you talk to) and officially pulled out on November 11, 2003. But the long process of restoring Kaho'olawe has barely begun. It will require strategies to control erosion, reestablish vegetation, recharge the water table, and gradually replace alien plants with native species. Plans include methods for damming gullies and reducing rainwater runoff.

Unauthorized entry onto Kaho'olawe and into the waters within 2 miles of Kaho'olawe are still prohibited. There are, however, opportunities for access. For more information call the **Kaho'olawe Island Reserve Commission (KIRC)** on Maui at 808-984-2400. You'll need to dial 60761 after the tone.

✳ Beaches

In order of preference.

Shoreline access signs indicate the entry points for beaches. Parking is always free, as is beach access along Wailea Alanui Drive.

✦ **Makena Beach** (aka **Big Beach** and **Oneloa**), Makena. Oneloa, which translates to "long sand," is definitely worth the trek. Easily the best in the region, at over 100 feet wide and 0.5 mile long, it's deservedly popular among visitors and residents. Because of its size, it rarely feels crowded. Be careful about incoming big waves and tread lightly in the water because the bottom can drop off rather

MAKENA BEACH

unexpectedly. There are three entrances; take the second dirt road past the Maui Prince Hotel and head past gnarly kiawe trees and cacti toward the water, where you'll find coarse, deep sand awaiting you. Snorkeling is best at the northern end. Use the first entrance if you're looking for **Little Beach**, just north of Oneloa on the other side of Pu'u Ola'i (a cinder cone hill). It's Maui's (un)official and illegal nudist beach. It also happens to be completely idyllic. *Facilities:* parking, portable toilets.

⚲ **Wailea Beach**, Wailea. Of the five little crescent bays along this pricey coastline, this probably comes as no surprise: The most perfect swimming beaches (complete with gentle bodysurfing waves) sit smack in front of the Four Seasons and Grand Wailea. And at sunset, with Kaho'olawe and Molokini in the foreground, there's no better place to be. Look for shoreline access signs with limited parking. *Facilities:* restrooms, showers.

⚲ **Kama'ole III** (aka **Kam 3**), Kihei. Of the three beach parks strung out along South Kihei Road, Kam 3 is most favored for swimming (and it has plenty of parking). But Kam I and Kam II also have grassy areas and places for kids to romp. Kam II has little shade. All are popular with locals and everyone at sunset. *Facilities:* restrooms, lifeguards, picnic areas, barbecue, showers, parking.

WAILEA BEACH

⚲ **Ulua Beach**, Wailea. Between the Wailea Beach Villas and Wailea Beach Marriott Resort, Ulua is good for families and snorkeling when the water is calm. Otherwise it's good for boogie boarding. It's particularly crowded in winter and summer. Look for shoreline access signs with limited parking. *Facilities:* showers, restrooms.

IT'S NOT SOUTH BEACH—IT'S KAM

⚓ **Polo Beach**, Wailea. Near the Fairmont Kea Lani Maui, Polo is smaller and less crowded than its neighbors, but it still has good swimming. Look for shoreline access signs with limited parking. *Facilities:* restrooms, showers.

⚓ **Maluaka Beach**, Makena. The strip closest to the Maui Prince Hotel is another short but wide crescent with exceptionally beautiful views of Molokini. You'll find the best snorkeling around Makena Landing. The shoreline access point is just off Makena Alanui Drive near the hotel. *Facilities:* restrooms, lifeguards, parking, showers.

✳ Lodging

Kihei is the budget center of South Maui, and my condo recommendations reflect that focus. While the town won't win any city beautification awards or give visitors much in the way of resort frills, it will lodge you for little more than the price of a mainland motel. Despite increasing crowds on the beach shared by the Four Seasons and Grand Wailea, **Wailea**'s resort-rich environment is more sedate and relaxed than that of Ka'anapali. When the trendy talk about going to Maui, they're probably talking about Wailea. In general, I tend to think of Wailea attracting the nouveau rich. **Makena**, at the end of

the road, is a remote place to base yourself if you expect to do any amount of exploring. If you want to stay put, though, it'll provide a perfect perch.

RESORTS

Wailea

Fairmont Kea Lani Maui (808-875-4100 or 1-866-540-4456; fairmont.com), 4100 Wailea Alanui Dr. This truly exceptional all-suites hotel can't avoid its eccentric facade. It's an attention-grabber, that's for sure. The Moorish-inspired architecture at the Kea Lani (which translates as "heavenly white") is studded with domes,

turrets, and arches. It's different in other ways, too. Even the smallest suites measure 850 square feet, boast an enormous lanai, and are genuinely luxurious. All guest rooms (and the pool) were renovated in 2006 and 2007 with new Bali-style furnishings in soothing green and tan. Marble bathrooms are also spacious. In fact, they'll make you want to move permanently to the Kea Lani. Oceanfront villas, if you can afford them, come with a private pool and a full kitchen. Whatever your first impression of the resort, you're likely to end up appreciating its uniqueness. *Rates*: $$$$; children free in parent's room; five-night minimum stay during Christmastime. *Facilities and amenities*: 450 rooms and suites, three large swimming pools, great beach, five restaurants (see Nick's Fishmarket Maui and Caffe Ciao under *Where to Eat*), access to the nearby golf courses, use of 11 courts at the Wailea Tennis Center (fee), great 24-hour fitness center, Spa Kea Lani (see *Spas*), water sport rentals, concierge, activity desk, shops, children's programs, parking (free), Internet (fee).

✿ **Four Seasons Resort Maui at Wailea** (808-874-8000 or 1-800-334-6284; fourseasons.com/maui), 3900 Wailea Alanui Dr. This elegant resort brims with élan. After years of operating exceptional urban hotels, Four Seasons decided to go on vacation. And did they ever! They came to Maui first, opening this hotel in 1990; it continues to be a prototype for translating cosmopolitan grandeur into absolutely top-rate leisure luxury. The midrise hotel is lofty in its formal poise but relaxed in its breezy island charm. Guest rooms achieve the same balance between tropical and traditional as public areas. Guest rooms, too, have all been renovated to "enter the 21st century" with new flat screen TVs and contemporary Hawaiian furnishings. Teak lanai furniture and evening turn-down service are equally

---

TOP PLACES TO EAT ON MAUI

Pricey
Lahaina Grill (West)
Plantation House (West)
Pineapple Grill (West)
Son'z Maui at Swan Court (West)
I'O (West)
Spago (South)
Duo (South)
Hali'imaile General Store
   (Upcountry & Haleakala)

Moderate
Mala Ocean Tavern (West)
Sansei (West, South)
Café O'Lei Kihei (South)

Colleen's (Upcountry & Haleakala)
Casanova Italian Restaurant
   (Upcountry & Haleakala)
Moana Bakery & Café
   (Upcountry & Haleakala)

Less Expensive
AK's Café (Central)
Main Street Bistro (Central)
Down to Earth Natural Foods (Central & Upcountry)
Cilantro (West)
Aloha Mixed Plate (West)
Pauwela Café
   (Upcountry & Haleakala)

appreciated. Bathrooms are exceptionally large and generously appointed. And if you can't really afford it but want to stay here anyway, rest assured that the least expensive rooms have great views that stretch up the slopes of Haleakala. At the cabana-lined pool, attendants spritz bikini-clad guests with cool Evian water. I could go on with a litany of exceptional services and offerings, many of which are included in the rates, but suffice it to say that even though this place is pricey, you'll get your money's worth. Without a doubt. *Rates*: $$$$; children free in parent's room. *Facilities and amenities*: 373 rooms and suites, three great pools, separate *keiki* pool, great beach, three restaurants (see Spago, Duo, and Ferraro's under *Dining Out*), access to the nearby golf courses, two tennis courts (lit at night), fitness center, exceptional spa (see *Spas*), water sport rentals, free bicycles, impressive concierge, shops, great "Kids for All Seasons" children's program, parking (fee), Internet (fee).

♪ Grand Wailea Resort Hotel & Spa

(808-875-1234 or 1-800-888-6100; grandwailea.com), 3850 Wailea Alanui Dr. This lavish, over-the-top resort was built at a cost of $600 million in 1991. It boasts a spa larger than all the others in Hawai'i combined, beautiful art collections (don't miss the Botero sculptures or the Picassos, Warhols, and Légers), and the most extensive children's camp in the tropics. The water features alone are worth a detour if you're not staying here, since the original owner sought to drown out the competition with them. He succeeded. The Grand Wailea also outflowers all the other resorts with colorful plantings spread

FOUR SEASONS RESORT

over 40 acres and six distinct gardens. Guest rooms are quite spacious and, as you might imagine, luxuriously appointed. Because of the terracing of the four- to eight-story wings, stretching out like legs of a spider, almost every room looks out onto the sea. Many views, though, from the Molokini, Haleakala, and Wailea Wings, are fairly distant. A significant 2008 renovation extended through to the Towers and onto a new slew of three-bedroom vacation rentals called Ho'olei. *Rates*: $$$$; children free in parent's room. *Facilities and amenities*: 780 rooms and suites, three pools, great beach, six restaurants, access to the nearby golf courses, use of 11 courts at the Wailea Tennis Center (fee), excellent fitness center, renowned Spa Grande (see *Spas*), water sport rentals, concierge, shops,

GRAND WAILEA RESORT

Camp Grande children's programs, resort fee (includes lei greeting, scuba clinic, sunrise power walk and yoga classes, entry into fitness center, art tours, local and toll-free phone calls, use of all water features, and water aerobics classes).

🦐 ✿ **Wailea Beach Marriott Resort** (808-879-1922 or 1-800-367-2960; marriott.com), 3700 Wailea Alanui Dr. The Marriott sits on 22 acres of prime real estate. Guest rooms are spread out in six low-rise wings and one seven-story tower. If you're fortunate enough to get one, there are also rooms in *hales* (buildings) 2, 3, 4, and 7 that are within 25 feet of the shore. (But more likely, the beaches will be a fair walk from your guest room.) The modern guest rooms were completely renovated in 2007 with new furnishings, and they bring the whole resort up to a "Marriott standard" with tile floors and a new adult pool. Its brand of casual copiousness has powerful allure for value-conscious travelers. *Rates*: $$$$; children free in parent's room. *Facilities and amenities*: 499 rooms and suites, four pools, four restaurants, access to the nearby golf courses, use of 11 courts at the Wailea Tennis Club (fee), fitness center, spa, water sport rentals, concierge, activity desk, shops, children's programs, resort fee (includes valet parking, Internet, dinnertime appetizers for two people, and local and long distance phone calls).

Makena

Maui Prince Hotel (808-874-1111 or 1-888-977-4623; mauiprincehotel .com), 5400 Makena Alanui Dr. From a distance, the Maui Prince looks like an oversized Concorde jet that's lost its tail and been plopped into a remote desert oasis. In actuality, the hotel is a serene hideaway that stands out for its scrubland surroundings. It's the "last resort" in a long line of resorts along this coastline, and that's one of the things I like most. Like some other Prince hotels, this won't hit you over the head with its boldness, but it will sneak up on you over time until you are a convert. Long after the glitz of other resorts fades, the old-fashioned graciousness of this one will remain. The lobby is an exquisite blend of traditional Japanese garden and a tropical jungle. Guest rooms emanate a restful composure through cream and pastel tones, understated décor, and requisite luxuries. As for the quarter-mile beach, it's separated from the grounds by a small rise, giving the white sands a sense of pristine seclusion. *Rates*: $$$–$$$$; children free in parent's room. *Facilities and amenities*: 310 rooms and suites, two pools, four restaurants (see Prince Court under *Where to Eat*), 36 holes of golf (fee), six Plexipave tennis courts (fee), fitness center, water sport rentals, concierge, activity desk, children's programs, parking (free), Internet (fee).

CONDOS, HOTELS & APARTMENTS

Kihei

These listings are ordered geographically, north to south, rather than by my usual preferential order.

🦐 **Aloha Pualani** (808-875-6990 or 1-866-870-6990; alohapualani.com), *makai*, 15 Wailana Pl., off S. Kihei Rd. New in 2003, this small two-story complex remains my favorite place to stay on the strip. It's romantic, elegant, chic, tidy, upscale, and it has a beautiful courtyard and pool. And to think: in Kihei. All units have ocean views, full kitchens, and a contemporary aesthetic. *Rates*: studios $$–$$$; no children under 16; two-night minimum. *Facilities and amenities*: six suites, beach across the street, pool, daily maid service, outdoor BBQ, A/C, TV/DVD, wireless (free).

Leinaala (808-879-2235 or 1-800-822-4409; mauicondo.com), *makai*, 998 S. Kihei Rd. Although this small condo is a low-rise cinder-block complex, it's oceanside, and that is a big deal. Set back from the water with a nice expanse of lawn, the units have a complete kitchen and private lanai. True to the layout at most other places, the living rooms, rather than the bedrooms, front the water. *Rates*: $$; children free in parent's room; four-night minimum. *Facilities and amenities*: 24 condos, pool, no credit cards.

Punahoa Beach Apartments (808-879-2720 or 1-800-564-4380; punahoabeach.com), 2142 Ili'ili Rd. These studios and one- and two-bedroom units tend to be booked faster than you can say "Do you have a vacancy on. . . ." Why? Because they're oceanfront with westward facing lanais and they're well priced. From here you can also walk to shops, walk down the lawn to a nice snorkeling spot, and walk next door to watch surfers. *Rates*: $–$$$; three-night minimum; $65 cleaning fee for stays less than five days. *Facilities and amenities*: 15 units, cable TV/DVD, phone, wireless (free), BBQ grill, laundry facilities, kitchenettes or full kitchens, parking (free).

Maui Coast Hotel (808-874-6284 or 1-800-895-6284; mauicoasthotel .com), *mauka*, 2259 S. Kihei Rd. Just a block from Kam I Beach and within walking distance of some restaurants, this hotel provides great value for the money. Each guest room comes equipped with a lanai, separate sitting area, and whirlpool jetted tub. *Rates*: $$–$$$; children free in parent's room. *Facilities and amenities*: 265 rooms and suites, pool, beach, two restaurants, two tennis courts (free), fitness center, activity desk, parking (free), A/C, Internet (fee).

Kama'ole Sands (808-874-8700 or 1-800-367-5004; castleresorts.com), *mauka*, 2695 S. Kihei Rd. Built in 1983, this lushly landscaped complex sits on 15 spacious acres. Although there are no views from the darkish bedrooms, the living rooms look onto the colorful gardens. All guest quarters come with private lanai, full kitchen, and daily maid service. *Rates*: one-bedrooms $$; two-bedrooms $$$–$$$$, two-night minimum; children free in parent's room. *Facilities and amenities*: 196 condos, pool, four tennis courts (free), water sport rentals, concierge, activity desk, parking (free), Internet (fee).

Maui Kama'ole Resort (808-874-8467; mauikamaole.com), *mauka*, 2777 S. Kihei Rd. Across the street

KIHEI CONDOS

from Kam III Beach, this newer low-rise complex has spacious one- and two-bedroom units, most with ocean views. *Rates*: one-bedrooms $$; two-bedrooms $$–$$$; four to six people maximum, depending on condo size; weekly rates; four-night minimum (or a cleaning fee). *Facilities and amenities*: 210 condos, two pools, sandy-bottomed Jacuzzi, four tennis courts (free), full kitchens in each unit, concierge, A/C, Internet (free).

Maui Hill Resort Quest (808-879-6321; mauilea.com), *mauka*, 2881 S. Kihei Rd. Because they're set high on a hill, most of these Moorish-style condos have ocean views (albeit distant ones) from the large lanais. In addition to full kitchens and all the other perks of upscale condos, the one-, two-, and three-bedroom units have access to many hotel-like amenities. As many as eight people can be accommodated in the three-bedroom units. *Rates*: one- to two-bedrooms $$–$$$; three-bedrooms $$$–$$$$; children free in parent's room. *Facilities and amenities*: About 57 of 140 units in rental pool, pool, putting green, tennis courts (free), concierge, Internet (free).

Mana Kai Maui Resort (808-879-2778 or 1-800-367-5242; crhmaui .com), *makai*, 2960 S. Kihei Rd. This eight-story property isn't much to look at (although it underwent a major renovation in 2007), but the location, on a nice sandy shore, is rare for Kihei. Guest rooms are smallish and have air-conditioning; the condos have lanais with ocean view, ceiling fans, and fully equipped kitchens. *Rates*: rooms $$; one-bedrooms $$–$$$; two-bedrooms $$$–$$$$; children free in parent's room; discounts for four- to six-night stays. *Facilities and*

amenities: 98 units, pool, beach, restaurant (see Five Palms under *Entertainment*), activity desk, wireless (fee).

Wailea

🏵 **Destination Resorts** (808-879-1595 or 1-800-367-5246; drhmaui .com). These folks manage a number of prime properties, all a tad different. **Makena Surf** offers the most sumptuous, secluded, and stylish seaside condos in the area. Most of the coastline on the gated property is rocky, better for snorkeling than swimming. The low-rise, Mediterranean-style buildings and their large, long lanais sprawl along the ocean in an isolated spot just before the Makena resort. **Wailea Grand Champions** Villas overlook the area's prodigious golf and tennis facilities. Built in 1990 and designed in a Newport Beach style, the wood-framed condos are the most attractive in Wailea. The grounds may be crowded, but the units are large and well designed. I prefer those with vaulted ceilings. **Wailea Villas** (ʻEkahi, ʻElua, and ʻEkolu) are 1970s-vintage low-rise units that vary in price but offer great value. Of the three villages, I find the gated ʻElua most enticing because the units are better positioned to maximize the views. ʻEkahi is only a small step down in luxury but a big step down in price. Less expensive upper-village ʻEkahi units are about an eight-minute walk to the beach; lower-village units are about three minutes. ʻEkolu condos feature sweeping golf-course views. And because these are farthest from the ocean, they are the least expensive. Then there are the new (in 2006) **Wailea Beach Villas**, where guests pretty much have the beautiful Ulua

Beach largely to themselves. *Rates*: condos $$–$$$$; children free in parent's room; minimum stays vary by property. *Facilities and amenities*: 320 condos, eight different properties, all with pools, use of 11 courts at the Wailea Tennis Center (fee), concierge, grocery pickup and delivery (expect to pay for delivery), parking (free), some properties have tennis courts on property (fee).

BED & BREAKFASTS

☙ **Two Mermaids B&B** (808-874-8687 or 1-800-598-9550; twomermaids.com), 2840 Umalu Pl., Kihei. Juddee and Miranda's place, on a quiet residential cul-de-sac, is easily one of the nicest and most professionally operated B&Bs on Maui. They've basically anticipated and fulfilled your every need, right down to delivering (outside your door so as not to bother you) a basket of exotic fruit and local bread each morning. With bright splashes of color everywhere, the units epitomize tropical island living. I particularly like the one-bedroom unit that has a large private deck, hot tub, and kitchenette. Because the studio unit (with a fun Murphy bed) is poolside, guests feel a greater sense of ownership of the pool area. Juddee, by the way, is a licensed minister and performs commitment ceremonies, vow renewals, and memorial ceremonies. *Rates*: front suite $$ (or a little more with an extra bedroom and bath), poolside suite $ (or $$ with an extra bedroom and bath); three-night minimum unless there are *pukas* (holes). *Facilities and amenities*: two units, pool, Kam III Beach a 10-minute walk, continental breakfast, beach equipment, A/C, wireless (free).

(1-800-943-5804; amauibedandbreakfast.com), 2828 Umalu Pl., Kihei. Hosts Eva and Jim Tantillo run one very fine B&B. If you're lucky enough to find an opening in their reservations, you're lucky indeed. They offer impeccable service, rates dripping with value, and an ideal location—a perfect trifecta. Views stretch from the ocean to Mount Haleakala to the West Maui Mountains. What a wonderful world, indeed. *Rates*: $$. *Facilities and amenities*: four rooms, full family-style breakfast, children under 11 free in parent's room, hot tub.

☙ **Eva Villa** (808-874-6407 or 1-800-884-1845; mauibnb.com), 815 Kumulani Dr., Kihei. Above Wailea in a quiet neihgborhood, hosts Dale and Rick Pounds offer a rooftop deck with 360-degreee views and a telescope, a waterfall, and guest room refrigerators stocked with breakfast items. The first-floor studio (weighing in at 600 square feet) overlooks the pool and Jacuzzi, while the separate cottage boasts a full kitchen and wraparound lanai. *Rates*: $$. *Facilities and ameni-*

TWO MERMAIDS B&B

ties: two rooms and one suite, pool, Jacuzzi, cable TV, BBQ, wireless (free), no credit cards.

❦ Dreams Come True on Maui (808-879-7099 or 1-877-782-9628; dreamscometrueonmaui.com), 3259 Akala Dr., Kihei. A mile from the ocean and tucked into a residential neighborhood, Denise McKinnon and Tom Croly's main house and separate cottage offer panoramic ocean views. The cottage is outfitted with a full kitchen, washer/dryer, TV, phone, Internet, and a nice lanai. The suites, located in the main house, have private entrances and lanais, and although each has a kitchenette, breakfast is also delivered to your room. It's a homey place where Tom shows movies nightly on an 8-foot screen and invites guests to join in. Ask about their two-bedroom condo across from the beach in Kihei. *Rates*: $–$$, four- to six-night minimum. *Facilities and amenities*: two suites, one cottage, Internet (free), beach towels, gear, coolers, snorkeling equipment, and outdoor kitchen and BBQ.

COTTAGES
Nona Lani Cottages (808-879-2497 or 1-800-733-2688; nonalanicottages .com), 455 S. Kihei Rd., Kihei. These old-fashioned cottages are an aberration for condo-happy Kihei. Dotted among palm trees on a couple of acres, complete with grassy expanses and hammocks, the cottages are a throwback to another era. If there was a possibility of rain keeping you indoors for days, I'd say stay elsewhere—although furnishings and carpets were renovated in 2007. But if you're going to be out and about more than not, it's hard to beat these

prices. *Rates*: $–$$ for cottages, discounts for longer stays; three- to four-night minimum. *Facilities and amenities*: eight cottages with full kitchen, no phones.

VACATION RENTALS
Kihei Maui Vacations (808-879-7581 or 1-888-568-6284; kmvmaui .com), one of many area agencies, represents dozens of vacation rentals and condos in South Maui.

✳ Where to Eat
There are dozens and dozens of large and small eateries lining the Kihei strip and ensconced in the Wailea resorts. But, assuming few readers will eat more than half a dozen meals here, I've culled the best in terms of price versus value, quickie stops versus places to linger, and casual hangouts versus romantic places to splurge. Reservations are recommended for all *Dining Out* establishments.

DINING OUT
Ma'alaea
𝒮 **Ma'alaea Grill** (808-243-2206; cafeoleirestaurants.com/thegrill), Ma'alaea Harbor Village, 300 Ma'alaea Rd. Open for lunch and dinner daily. With great views of the ocean, a casual and relaxed atmosphere, and lots of bamboo and teak, what's not to appreciate about this value-laden eatery? Owned by the same folks who run Café O'Lei Kihei, the grill espouses the same philosophy: healthy, good food at reasonable prices. As for the food, lunch options include creative salads (like quinoa or Asian-style) and grilled fish specials. Check out the grilled beef tenderloin, pastas, a good selection of shrimp dishes, and burg-

WEDDINGS, COMMITMENTS & BLENDING TRADITIONS

Locals and longtime residents say that if you're not meant to be on Maui, you'll know it. She will either embrace you or spit you out. When Maui embraced me, my dream became manifested soon after; it is truly a blessing to be part of this paradise. My vision has always been to be of service. For 20 years on the mainland I was the director of a community recovery center. Creating an environment to continue my life's dream on Maui has taken a few years, however. But now it's a reality. The process has been filled with guidance, a few mistakes, and lots of personal growth. As an on-site proprietor of our bed & breakfast, I am able to share the magic of Maui and talk story with guests, many of whom are honeymoon couples I have married.

I marvel at the spiritual gifts I receive as a minister on Maui. Having experienced the *mana* (spirit) of Maui for years, I now perform weddings, commitment ceremonies, and baptisms for couples and their children. I create ceremonies that integrate the cultural beliefs and values of each couple with gentle Hawaiian traditions. Among others, I have performed traditional lei exchanges, the Ceremony of Bitter and Sweet, the Lokelani Rose Ceremony, and the blending of sand or ocean water (an island metaphor for unions). I have even incorporated the Jumping the Broom ritual, an African American tradition, with a little *aloha* flavor. Performing these ceremonies in our island chapels, tropical gardens, and five-star resorts is like icing on the wedding cake. Couples appear in everything from casual aloha wear or shorts to bikinis, gowns, and tuxedos. As a certified diver, I've also performed underwater wedding ceremonies. After all, I am one of two mermaids. See, dreams really do come true. *Maui No Ka Oi.*

—Rev. Juddee A. Kawaiola
Ceremonies & Weddings by Two Mermaids

ers. You can't go wrong here. Children's menu. Lunch $–$$, dinner entrées $$–$$$.

The Waterfront Restaurant (808-244-9028; waterfrontrestaurant.net), Milowai Condo, 50 Hauoli St. Open for dinner nightly. Although it might look stuffy at first glance, what with a dark interior and an older waitstaff clad in bow ties, The Waterfront is a very friendly but conservative restaurant. Overlooking the boat-filled harbor, it's a picture-perfect setting for those who arrive early to catch the sunset. Try to reserve an outdoor table. In addition to almost a dozen fish preparations, look for good rack of lamb, lobster chowder, and onion soup. Ignore the fact that it's housed in an unappealing condo. It couldn't have this many loyal patrons for nothing. Entrées $$$–$$$$.

Kihei

🍴 **Café O'Lei Kihei** (808-891-1368; cafeoleirestaurants.com), Rainbow Mall, 2439 S. Kihei Rd. Open 10:30–

10 Tues.–Sun. Ignore the mall location and concentrate, instead, on how lucky you are to know about this tucked-away place that rises to the top of my best-dining-on-the-island list. From the open kitchen and big bar to hardwood floors and big picture windows, the café knows how to make patrons sit back and relax. Dine early or vie for tables with locals-in-the-know. For lunch I like the jumbo tiger shrimp salad and healthy plate lunch specials. For dinner you can't beat lobster tails, crab legs, and the mac-nut-crusted breast of chicken. I bet you'll return more than once. Lunch $–$$, dinner entrées $$–$$$$.

✐ ❦ ☖ **Roy's Kihei Bar and Grill** (808-891-1120; roysrestaurant.com), Pi'ilani Village Shopping Center, 303 Pi'ikea Ave. Open for dinner nightly. I marvel at how Roy's keeps living up to lofty expectations. Yes, it's formulaic—complete with an open kitchen, trendy food, a high-energy waitstaff (that can rush you if you let them), and a hip dining room buzz. But it works. And the Pacific Rim creations consistently wow diners from

SANSEI

execution to presentation. Since the menu changes daily, I usually opt for the fresh catch of the day or a lemongrass-crusted swordfish if they have it. Children's menu. Entrées $$$–$$$$.

✐ **Sansei** (808-879-0004; sanseihawaii .com), Kihei Town Center, 1881 Kihei Rd. Open for dinner nightly and for late-night dining (and karaoke Thurs.–Sat.) A South Maui outpost of the wildly popular phenomenon that catapulted out of nowhere in Kapalua (see *Dining Out* in "West Maui"), Sansei is simply a profound dining experience for those interested in Japanese–Euro–Pacific Rim seafood. (I confess to never having tried meat dishes here.) The more adventurous you are, the better, but it's not a requirement. It is not an exaggeration to report patrons lining up at 4:45 in anticipation of the doors opening at 5:30. Children's menu. Entrées $$–$$$$.

✐ ☖ **Stella Blues Café** (808-874-3779; stellablues.com), 1279 S. Kihei Rd. Open for all three meals daily. This stand-alone eatery in a suburban-style mall location doesn't appear to hold much promise. But it's a solid, consistent, all-around-decent eatery. When you tire of challenging your taste buds with pretentious food prepared with items you can't pronounce, Stella Blues will soothe the spirit and wallet. There's also probably something to satisfy everyone in your party—from burgers, interesting salads, and sandwiches at lunch to pasta, chicken, ribs, and steaks at dinner. The spacious interior is made more so by large picture windows; there are a few outdoor tables. Reservations recommended for larger parties only; children's menu. Breakfast $–$$, lunch $–$$, dinner entrées $$–$$$.

Wailea

♨ ♪ **Duo** (808-874-8000), Four Seasons Resort Maui at Wailea, 3900 Wailea Alanui Dr. Open for dinner nightly. This resort has the Midas touch when it comes to . . . well, everything. And this new (in 2007) steak and seafood restaurant is no exception. How many words do I have? Where to begin? With a Pacific pear martini or Downtown Duo aperitif, if you don't mind. On my last visit under the tutelage of chef Noel Badillo, the goat cheese fritter was light but so flavorful, and the tuna sashimi melted in my mouth. Carnivores take note: Duo is decidedly known for its excellent Kobe beef New York steak. And for seafood lovers, pick your fish (ahi "big eye" or the highly recommended island snapper or Keahole Maine lobster), and pair it with a dipping sauce of your choice—although the expertly trained waitstaff can offer suggestions as to what works best with what. Side dishes, offered separately, are portioned for two people. I love the matchstick curly hand-cut fries with truffle aioli and keet ketchup and the rich and cheesey Dauphinoise potatoes. As for dessert (as if anyone has room), s'mores are popular with families, but the chef and I prefer the subzero temptation of homemade ice creams, macaroons, and a tropical coulis. The Austrian pastry chef has dessert in her genes, I'm positive. Green cotton candy for all patrons tops off a delightful evening. Many patrons come back night, after night it's so relaxing. Entrées $$$$.

Υ ♪ **Spago** (808-879-2999; wolfgangpuck.com), Four Seasons Resort Maui at Wailea, 3900 Wailea Alanui Dr. Open for dinner nightly. When celebrity chef Wolfgang Puck opened this sophisticated dining room, it quickly became the place to drop a wad for a special evening. Surprise, surprise. The lovely setting, awash with fine art and lots of stone and wood for texture, sets the stage for the art of dining. It's open-air dining at its finest. Not content to merely trade on his reputation, Puck merges California, Hawai'i, and Pacific Rim flavors and sends them soaring. (The seasonal menu changes daily.) If you want to try the Spago experience without mortgaging your house, order *pupus* at the bar. Children's menu. Entrées $$$$.

♪ **Nick's Fishmarket Maui** (808-879-7224; tristarrestaurants.com), Fairmont Kea Lani Maui, 4100 Wailea Alanui Dr. Open for dinner nightly. Seafood reigns supreme at Nick's. Romantic and casually formal (only in Hawai'i), the Fishmarket traffics in lobster, tiger prawns, and local fish. And it's all fresh as can be. One of these days, they'll undoubtedly register a trademark for their blackened mahimahi. Join the crowd and order a Greek Maui Wowi salad, which really does wow me every time. Try to dine on the terrace. Children's menu. Entrées $$$$.

Ferraro's (808-874-8000), Four Seasons Resort Maui at Wailea, 3900 Wailea Alanui Dr. Open for lunch and dinner daily. With a primo location overlooking Wailea Beach, this open-air Italian restaurant is worth it for the cuisine, service, and atmosphere. Try a lobster salad or hearty sandwich at lunch; pair classical music and wine with any fish offering and locally grown pineapple cobbler for dinner; or grab a light bite between 4 and 6 PM. Lunch $$$–$$$, dinner entrées $$$–$$$$.

♈ ⌘ **Joe's Bar and Grill** (808-875-7767), Wailea Tennis Club, 131 Wailea Ike Pl. Open for dinner nightly. For homey and old-fashioned but upmarket cooking with flair served in a friendly and casual setting overlooking the Wailea Tennis Club with expansive views across to Lana'i, it's hard to beat Joe's. Joe and Bev Gannon (of Hali'imaile General Store fame) have created another winner. Mostly they serve Joe Gannon's favorite classics. Try the meat loaf with garlic mashed potatoes, any of the good salads, or the enormously thick pork chops. To call this place a "bar and grill" hardly does it justice. Children's menu. Entrées $$$–$$$$.

SeaWatch (808-875-8080; sea watchrestaurant.com), Wailea Golf Courses, 100 Wailea Golf Club Dr. Open 8 AM–9 PM daily. Hmmm. Is it the views or the food? You'll definitely enjoy a romantic candlelit sunset dinner in this lovely open-air setting, nestled among the golf links with distant ocean views. (Alfresco lunches,

ALEXANDER'S

away from the crowds, are also relaxing.) I always order the nightly specials, since the chef seems to be most excited about his nightly creations. You can expect fresh, clean flavors highlighting local fish and greens. As a bonus, SeaWatch is also one of the more affordable fine-dining experiences in Wailea. Children's menu. Breakfast and lunch $–$$, dinner entrées $$$–$$$$.

EATING OUT

Kihei

⌘ **Pita Paradise** (808-875-7679), Kihei Kalama Village, 1913 S. Kihei Rd. Open for lunch Mon.–Sat., dinner nightly. This informal place with a tropical courtyard provides a nice, healthy alternative to fast food. Order from the blackboard menu, grab a seat, and wait for the pitas, kebabs, and salads to be delivered in a basket. I'm talking chicken kebabs with sautéed veggies and herbed potatoes, Greek salads, lamb gyros, steak, and Kula onion pitas drizzled with their signature sauce. Lunch $$, dinner $$–$$$.

⌘ **Alexander's** (808-874-0788), Kihei Kalama Village, 1913 S. Kihei Rd. Open 11–9 daily. If you're like me, sometimes you just have a hankerin' for good old-fashioned fish-and-chips—lightly battered, of course, and fried in really fresh canola oil. Alexander's fits the bill perfectly. And you can always opt for broiled seafood. Order at the window and grab a chair outside. Dishes $–$$.

⌘ **Shaka Sandwich & Pizza** (808-874-0331), 1770 S. Kihei Rd. Open (more or less) 10:30–9 daily. For the best cheesesteaks this side of the City of Brotherly Love, and for the best thin-crust pizza east of the Hudson

River, Shaka rules. No exceptions. Dishes $–$$$.

Wailea
Caffe Ciao (808-875-4100), Fairmont Kea Lani Maui, 4100 Wailea Alanui Dr. Open for lunch and dinner daily (though they sometimes close in the middle of the afternoon). I'll recommend this place only if you promise to sit on the shady terrace and order a brick-oven pizza. Nothing else. My experience at the high-end deli? It's not like it used to be, but I do acknowledge slim take-out options in this neck of the woods. Lunch $$, dinner entrées $$$–$$$$.

COFFEE & MARKETS
The Coffee Store (808-875-4244; mauicoffee.com), Azeka *Mauka*, 1279 S. Kihei Rd., Kihei. Open 6–6 daily (until 5 PM on Sunday). As an alternative to two nearby Starbucks (down the street and around the corner), The Coffee Store delivers with strong espresso, simple breakfasts, and lunchtime turkey and veggie wraps. Get there early, though, since they often run out of dishes by early afternoon. Dishes $.

Hawaiian Moon's Natural Foods (808-875-4356), Kama'ole Beach Center, S. Kihei Rd., Kihei. Open 8 AM–9 PM daily. The combination of fresh Upcountry veggies, orgasmic organic offerings, and healthful groceries makes this a fertile feeding ground. (Or at least a great place to assemble a picnic, since there's no place to sit.) Forget outdated notions of what constitutes "health food." The selection of alternative cosmetics, soaps, shampoos, lotions, and potions—culled from producers around the state—is a veritable lesson in aromatherapy.

All the lavish Wailea resorts have equally lavish **Sunday brunches**, perhaps none more so than the **Prince Court** (at the Maui Prince Hotel in Makena; 808-874-1111), which is something of a retro throwback to the 1970s; views of Molokini, Kaho'olawe, and Makena Beach are unparalleled. A few **food trucks** park on the roadsides beyond the Maui Prince Hotel as you head to the end of the road in Makena. You'll find a **Maui Taco** branch, perfect for a quick burrito, at the Kama'ole Beach Center on South Kihei Road.

✳ Entertainment
Kukui Mall Movie Theater (808-875-4910), across from Kalama Park, 1819 S. Kihei Rd., Kihei. Four screens.

♉ **Five Palms** (808-879-2607), Mana Kai Maui Resort, 2960 S. Kihei Rd. Open daily. If you ignore the boxy hotel structure above you and remember that it's not about the food here, you'll quickly realize it's about long coastline views. The swaying palms and beachfront in the fore-

ON THE ROAD TO MAKENA

THE SHOPS AT WAILEA

ground help give the scene some depth. But really, only come here for a late-afternoon drink.

Sansei (808-879-0004; sanseihawaii .com), Kihei Town Center, 1881 Kihei Rd., has free karaoke 10 PM–1:30 AM Thurs.–Sat.

✳ Selective Shopping

If you like strip malls, you'll love Kihei. All but one are located on the main drag of South Kihei Road. The exception is Pi'ilani Village Shopping Center between North and South Kihei Roads off Pi'ikea Avenue.

MARKETS
Farmer's market, across from Suda's Store on S. Kihei Rd., Kihei. Mon., Wed., and Fri. 1:30–5:30. Locally grown fruits and veggies, fresh breads and juices, assorted cheeses, onions, pineapples, and macadamia nuts.

Hana Ka Lima, Wailea Beach Marriott Resort (808-879-1922), 3700 Wailea Alanui Dr., Wailea. This traditional crafts market is held 9–2 Tues. and Fri.

SHOPPING AREAS
The Shops at Wailea (808-891-6770), Wailea Alanui, are an ultra-upscale temple to consumerism. With them, the resort experience in South Maui is complete. In typical American fashion, Gucci and Tiffany coexist with Gap and Billabong. There is usually some kind of live entertainment or show on Wed. night.

SPECIAL SHOPS
Pacific Whale Foundation Gift Shop (808-879-8860; pacificwhale .org), adjacent to the Maui Ocean Center, 300 Ma'alaea Rd., Ma'alaea. Open 6–6 daily. Gifts with a whale theme to benefit the foundation.

See also Hawaiian Moon's Natural Foods under *Coffee & Markets*.

UPCOUNTRY & HALEAKALA

Upcountry—a term generally used to describe the small towns on the western slopes of Haleakala—will probably not conform to your conventional notions of Hawai'i. It's really another world. Some visitors even think of it as a separate island as they gaze across the central, flat isthmus from the West Maui Mountains and ask, "What island is *that*?" You'll find eucalyptus and redwood trees, *paniolos* and hitching posts, farmers and famed onions, and cool breezes and cooler nighttime temperatures. All of Maui's organic produce originates from these rich volcanic soils. With the exception of Haleakala Crater, Upcountry elevations fluctuate between 3,000 and 7,000 feet. Views are breathtaking. In trying to make sense of how you will explore, I have included here the coastal town of Pa'ia (and the almost coastal town of Ha'iku), which, depending on how much time you have, may or may not be better explored on your way to Hana.

Sitting at just over 10,000 feet, **Mount Haleakala**, "house of the sun," is one of the most ethereal and mystical places in Hawai'i. Throughout the day, the dormant volcano appears to hold up the clouds; it certainly looms over and dominates the landscape from practically every corner of the island.

For those who can adjust to Upcountry's slow pace, the region really merits the attention. The natural beauty is sublime, from jacaranda and hibiscus to cactus and rare silversword, and authentic communities are refreshing and friendly. Yes, there are good beaches and expert windsurfing conditions on its northern side, but

BUILDING BLOCKS FOR A PERFECT DAY UPCOUNTRY

Hang out in Pa'ia (2 hours)

Watch windsurfers at Ho'okipa Beach Park (30 minutes)

Gallery hop and shop in Makawao (2 hours)

Drive up Olinda Road (45 minutes)

Drive through the pineapple and sugarcane fields around Hali'imaile (30 minutes)

Stop at the Pukalani Superette (15 minutes)

Visit a protea or lavender farm in Kula (1 hour)

Stop in at the 'Ulupalakua Ranch Store or Tedeschi Vineyards (30 minutes)

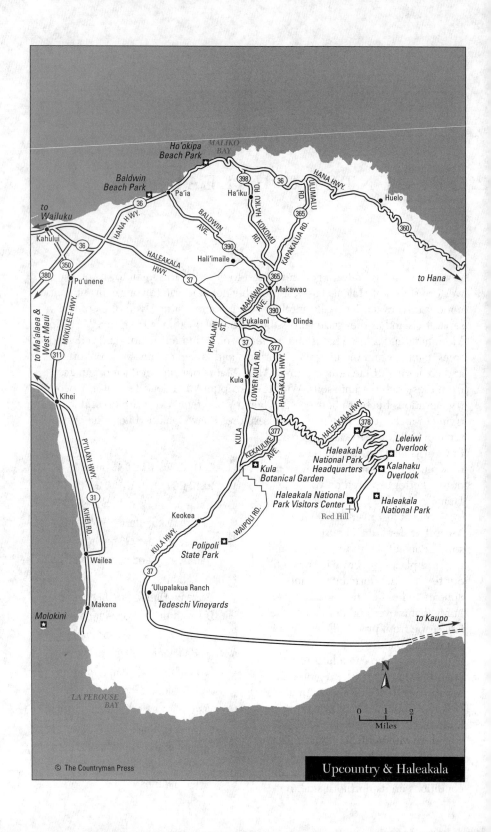

Upcountry & Haleakala

© The Countryman Press

beyond those pleasures, visitor activities are pretty well confined to exploring the volcano, a few little towns, and a few little attractions. Follow my motto: Slow down, see more. Generally, ideally, you'll want one day to explore Haleakala and another to get lost touring Upcountry.

Since most of you will have to pass by the Kahului Airport to reach Upcountry towns, for the purposes of organizing this tour I've oriented this section from there.

Although only 8 miles from the Kahului Airport in Central Maui, and technically not an Upcountry town, **Pa'ia** nonetheless feels more aligned with Upcountry than it does with the adventure I call "To Hana & Beyond." Because you could easily while away a morning shopping and eating, I suggest visiting on a separate trip from the one you take to Hana. So what's here? Well, these days it's a bunch of windsurfers, barefoot Rasta-braided hippies, granola-crunching kids strumming guitars, interesting shops and boutiques behind wooden storefront facades, and increasingly hip eateries. Back in the 1870s, though, Pa'ia camps and company stores sprang into existence to serve Alexander & Baldwin's sugar plantation community. A period of relative prosperity followed through World War II, when servicemen were stationed nearby. After the war, though, locals began moving to subdivisions in Kahului's "Dream City," also developed by Alexander & Baldwin. In the 1970s, beach bums and surfer dudes strolled in to fill the vacuum and never left. A strong counterculture atmosphere still prevails, at once tempered and fueled by good old-fashioned capitalism. It's a decidedly laid-back place, friendly and low-key.

Ha'iku, a short drive down the Hana Highway, seems off the beaten path but is surprisingly accessible. A former pineapple plantation town, Ha'iku's canneries have been converted to shops and restaurants. It's a pastoral place to explore, its ranches dotted with cattle, sheep, and horses. Head into town from the Hana Highway on Hwy. 398 (Ha'iku Rd.), meander along it until it merges back with the Hana Highway, and then cut back in again on Kapakalua Road (Hwy. 365).

From there, take a detour west into the speck of a village **Hali'imaile**, dominated by a pineapple plantation and one of Maui's best restaurants—worth a detour. Hwy. 371 runs alongside pineapple and sugarcane fields.

Or stay south on Hwy. 365 until it merges with Makawao Ave. in **Makawao**, which literally means "on the edge of the forest." Like Pa'ia (and just 7 miles from it if you come directly up from Baldwin Avenue), this little village grew to accommodate plantation workers in the 19th century. And then in the 1970s, artists and other West Coast exiles flocked here and began opening craft shops, art galleries, and New Age bookstores. Lush (and often wet) Makawao exists at the crossroads of Makawao and Baldwin Avenues. The old-fashioned wooden storefronts, complete with a hitching post or two, have the look of the Old West, but look closer and the tenants are more likely to be holistic entrepreneurs

CATTLE ENJOY THE COOL UPCOUNTRY.

carrying health food and advertising yoga therapy. Don't miss the Hui No'eau Visual Arts Center.

For an utterly lovely, rural, aromatic drive, head up, up, up the one-way Olinda Road. (which begins at the corner of Makawao and Baldwin Avenues) into **Olinda**.

From Makawao, take Hwy. 377 (Haleakala Highway) to **Pukalani**, which means "hole in the heavens," a quiet residential community with a

BALDWIN AVENUE, PA'IA

golf course, Starbucks coffee shop, and a very local grocery store, then through **Kula** (and possibly to Haleakala Crater), and merge with Hwy. 37 for the Tedeschi Winery. To be sure: I recommend exploring Haleakala separately from Upcountry, but if this is the only time for it, so be it.

Rural Kula is home to ubiquitous protea farms and small farms specializing in onions and orchids. As you continue south on Hwy. 37, the landscape becomes drier and drier, almost desolate with cacti and stunted trees. This is the cattle country of Ulupalakua Ranch, where Tedeschi Winery creates the only tiny excuse you need to come this far.

From here, you could continue around the back side of Haleakala to Hana (if the road has reopened because of a washed-out bridge, and if you're a real adventurer), but most people approach it from Ha'iku, from the clockwise direction. If you go this route, bring plenty of water and food, and fill up the gas tank in Pukalani. (See "To Hana & Beyond.")

GETTING AROUND

By car: Hwy. 37 (aka the Haleakala Highway out of Central Maui) comes from the Kahului Airport and heads toward Makawao and Kula. Just beyond the turnoff for Makawao, though, it can get confusing. Hwy. 37 then becomes known as the Kula Highway, while Hwy. 377 keeps the name Haleakala Highway and heads up to the Haleakala Crater (via the zig-zagging spur road of Hwy. 378). Lower Kula Road spurs off Hwy. 37.

Hwy. 36 (aka Hana Highway) comes from the Kahului Airport and heads east toward Pa'ia and Ha'iku.

On a map, it seems reasonable that you should be able to drive from Wailea to Kula. But no. You have to go all the way back toward the airport and then head Upcountry. It takes about 40 minutes to get from Wailea to Kula, about an hour to get from Lahaina to Kula. From Makawao, it takes about one and a half hours to reach either Haleakala or Hana.

✳ To See & Do

There aren't many traditional sights, and yet this is Maui's most diversified and interesting region. Expect to get lost on the quiet roads among the growing residential communities.

Pa'ia

⚲ 🎣 **Baldwin Beach Park**, about 6 miles east of the airport, 1 mile west of Pa'ia. See *Beaches*.

⚲ 🎣 **Ho'okipa Beach Park**, about 2 miles east of Pa'ia, on the Hana Highway. See *Beaches*.

Makawao

Hui No'eau Visual Arts Center (808-572-6560; huinoeau.com), 2841 Baldwin Ave., Makawao. Open 10–4 daily. This lovely, Mediterranean-style

HUI NO'EAU VISUAL ARTS CENTER

estate a mile south of town offers arts and crafts classes, lectures, workshops, a gallery, and a great gift shop. Don't miss the backyard pottery studio and reflecting pool. Begun by a group of women in 1934 and led by Ethel Baldwin (of sugar fame), the original collective (the so-called club of skills) painted, threw pots, and sketched here. Free.

Keokea

Dr. Sun Yat Sen Park, in this blink-of-an-eye nonvillage along Hwy. 37. This little park honors the first president of China, whose wife and family used to live on a nearby ranch when he was back in his homeland. Expansive views don't outweigh the unrelenting sun for me, but you might find it a nice place to picnic.

Kula

Holy Ghost Church, off Hwy. 37. This white octagonal Catholic church was built by Portuguese immigrants in the mid-1890s.

Kula Botanical Garden (808-878-1715), Hwy. 377 near Hwy. 37. Open 9–4 daily. The signature flower of the region, the colorful protea, is quite well represented here. In fact, almost three-quarters of Hawai'i's proteas are cultivated on this 200-acre plot. Some specimens grow over 12 inches wide. You can take a self-guided tour of 5 lovely acres, which also feature koi ponds, streams, little bridges, and over 700 varieties of plants—including birds-of-paradise, orchids, bamboo, koa, and kukui trees (the state tree). $7.50 adults, $2 ages 6–12.

Ali'i Kula Lavender (808-878-3004; aliikulalavender.com), 1100 Waipoli Rd., Kula. Open 9–4 daily. From lavender tea tours (complete with lavender-infused scones) to tours designed around how to cook with lavender, this one-note site is worth a stop because of its plantings and products.

Tedeschi Vineyards & Winery (808-878-6058; mauiwine.com), Hwy. 37. Open 9–5 daily; free tastings; free tours at 10:30, 1:30, and 3:00. Open to the public for tastings and 15-minute tours, the 22-acre winery sits in a former jail at the foot of Mount Haleakala. In addition to Hula O Maui sparkling wine and Upcountry Blush, the winery makes the requisite raspberry wine. The latter sounds more fun than it tastes, but this isn't Napa Valley, now, is it? The adjacent pictorial history of the ranch, polo, and *paniolo* is worthwhile.

'ULUPALAKUA RANCH STORE

'Ulupalakua Ranch Store (808-878-2561), Hwy. 37 across the street from Tedeschi Winery. Open 9:30–5 daily. Currently a cattle ranch, 'Ulupalakua encompasses 20,000 acres of the southwestern back slope of Haleakala. In the mid-1850s, it was developed as a sugar plantation by whaling captain James McKee, who, in his time, hosted such dignitaries as Robert Louis Stevenson and King David Kalakaua. King David really enjoyed his host's swimming pool, the first in the state. These days tourists pose at the ranch store to have their pictures taken with three wooden statues of *paniolo* and stop for a limited selection of snacks. Views of the West Maui Mountains, Molokini, and the Pacific are breathtaking from these parts.

Mount Haleakala

✪ **Haleakala National Park** (808-572-4400; nps.gov/hale), Hwy. 378. Established in 1916, this national park is a powerful and mystical place. Ascending the park road is an experience you won't soon forget, particularly the thrill of passing through clouds and then looking back down over them. It's also a place where people play: They bicycle down it (half way at least), ride horseback into it, drive up it at sunrise (and at sunset, though less so), camp in it, and hike through it. Upward of 1.3 million folks visit the park annually—that's an average of 3,500 per day. Since it sits at 10,023 feet, take altitude into consideration when you think about how best to approach your experience of the park.

Here are a few basic facts. It takes one and a half hours to drive to the summit from Kahului, longer from the resorts of Ka'anapali and Wailea. Almost no mat-

MOUNT HALEAKALA CRATER

ter where you're coming from, you'll take Hwy. 37 to Hwy. 377 (aka Haleakala Highway) to Hwy. 378 (aka Haleakala Crater Road). The road from sea level to summit traverses 37 miles and encompasses many switchbacks, and by the time you reach the top, you can expect the temperatures to be about 30 degrees colder than wherever you started. In wintertime, 40 mph winds and below-freezing temperatures are not uncommon. Wear as many layers of clothing as you can, bring your own food and water, and buy gas (last-chance) in Pukalani if you need to. To save your brakes, come down the volcano in low gear.

Dormant since 1790, the volcano's crater is 3,000 feet deep and measures 3 by 7 miles. It could swallow New York City in one gulp. So keep in mind, for perspective, that all those little cinder cones you'll see—which look like little blips on the crater floor—are actually hundreds of feet high. On a clear day, the view atop Haleakala extends for 100 miles.

It's a hearty but fragile ecosystem atop the volcano, and conditions for sustaining life are harsh. I'm thinking, in particular, of the endangered silversword plant, which looks like a yucca plant and grows only here on Hawai'i. It has a fragile root system that can be ruined if the topsoil is compacted by footsteps; takes 10 to 40 years to mature and blossom (between May and August); puts out a stalk that can reach 8 feet high and is rife with hundreds of purple flowers; and dies after blooming once.

After paying your park entrance fee ($10 per car, good for a week), **Hosmer Grove** (6,800 feet) offers a short loop trail that takes about 30 minutes and provides a nice introduction to this climatic zone with eucalyptus, cypress, fir, and juniper. The **park headquarters** (7,000 feet; open 8–4 daily) is just beyond it. Campers should stop here. The **Leleiwi Overlook**, at about MM 17 and 8,000 feet, offers a short trail that leads to fine panoramic crater views. If you're here in the late afternoon, you might get lucky and glimpse the "Brocken Specter," whereby you can see your own shadow on the clouds with a rainbow's arc overhead. Native Hawaiians referred to it as *aka ku anue nue* ("the seeing of one's soul").

Stopping at the **Kalahaku Overlook**, at about MM 19 and 9,300 feet, is permissible only on the way down. But keep it in mind because it has perhaps the best crater view of all and might, on a clear day, also take in Mauna Kea on the Big Island. If you haven't seen any yet, look for the rare silversword plants here.

At the **visitors center** (about 9,700 feet), you can learn about the when, where, and how of these volcanic eruptions through exhibits, photographs, and other displays. Rangers give morning talks on the hour about volcanology and ecology. Many visitors, preferring to enjoy otherworldly red-brown cinder slopes from the comfort of a glass enclosure, think this is the summit. But it is not. Before heading there, walk the short trail up to **Pa Ka'oao** (aka White Hill) for stunning 360-degree views. There's another parking lot just up the way that's closer to **Pu'u Ula'ula** (aka Red Hill), the highest point on Maui. Visitors gather here in the cold morning hours, behind the glass enclosure, to wait for sunrise. On a clear day you can squint and see O'ahu, 130 miles in the distance. The facility just beyond here, **Science City** (aka Haleakala Observatory), is operated by the University of Hawai'i and the Department of Defense to track satellites, conduct laser tests, and carry out solar and lunar research.

Haleakala National Park, by the way, consists of two distinct areas: the one mentioned above, and **Kipahulu** near Hana (see "To Hana & Beyond"). They aren't connected by road, and they couldn't be more different ecologically. Whereas the southwest slope of Haleakala is parched and lunar, the northeast slope is lush and tropical. The entire back side of southeast Maui is part of Haleakala National Park.

MAUI CAPTURES THE SUN

Hawaiians believe that during a legendary time long ago, when gods walked on earth as men and were known as "the People of Light," the father who held the heavens and the mother who guarded the path to the netherworld bore a son. This son was the demigod Maui.

Maui's mother, Hina, was well known for the fine bark cloth she made. One day while watching her, Maui said, "You spend all your time making *tapa,* mother." To which Hina replied, "The day is never long enough when I am making *tapa*. This piece is ready to dry, but Sun is already disappearing."

Maui, saddened by his mother's disappointment, decided to track down Sun and tell him he traveled too swiftly, that the days were too short.

Hina was not pleased with this idea. "No, Maui. Sun is much too strong. He is a powerful god. No one has ever gotten close to him, and I will be very afraid for you if you try."

"I will be the first to catch him; you will see, Mother. I will take my magic club and paddle, and I will catch the sun."

Maui traveled to Sun's home in a dead volcano and arrived while Sun was sleeping. In the secret darkness of the night, Maui set his snares. In the morning when Sun began to stretch his legs and arms in a big yawn, Maui quickly tied off four of his legs.

Sun was not pleased. With all of his fiery might he pulled and twisted, but the ropes held tight. "What do you want? Why are you doing this?" screamed Sun.

"My mother needs more hours in the day to dry her *tapa*."

"*Tapa!* Are you mad? I don't have time for this. Your people will die without my light. You need me!"

But Maui reeled and struck a mighty blow and broke off two of Sun's rays. "How about we make a deal. Half of the year you can travel at your normal speed, but the other half of the year, you will give us more sunlight." Sun, knowing he was trapped, agreed to these conditions.

From then on Sun moved slower for half the year, and every time he wanted to change his mind, he would look down at his broken limbs and remember the strength and courage of the half-god Maui.

✳ Spas

Spa Luna (808-575-2440; spaluna.com), Haʻiku Marketplace Cannery, 810 Haʻiku Rd., Haʻiku. Open weekdays; students work on Mon., Wed., and Fri. If resort prices leave you breathless, this holistic school for massage therapists might be just the thing to soothe your ragged wallet. The European-style day spa, a licensed training ground for aspiring professionals, offers massage, yoga, hydrotherapy, and more.

✳ Outdoor Activities

BICYCLING/RENTALS

Maui Downhill (808-871-2155 or 1-800-535-2453; mauidownhill.com). Once on Maui, you'll undoubtedly hear talk about biking down a volcano. Some visitors experience it as the most adventurous thing they've ever done; others find it expensive and a tad boring. If you want to try it, here's the story. A van will arrange to pick you up at your lodging at some ungodly hour, such as 3 AM. Bring as many jackets and layers of clothing as you can find. (Many people bring hotel blankets.) The van driver will transport your sleepy self to the top of Haleakala and serve you some pastries while you all wait for the sun to rise over the volcano. After it does, your van will drive you back down the mountain, to just outside the Park boundaries. By this time, you'll be donning Maui Downhill's requisite flaming yellow jacket, pants, and motorcycle helmet. With the aid of specially designed brakes, you'll then coast about 28 miles downhill in a few hours, always moderated by the pack leader with the slowest (usually lightest) person in mind. You need to appreciate the transitions along the way to really make it interesting. You'll go from a very cold clime to a warm and humid one (peeling off layers of clothing along the way); from a rocky and seemingly lifeless environment to one that becomes increasingly greener with grasses and is then dotted with cows and horses; from eucalyptus and plumeria forests to pineapple and sugar tracts; from 10,000 feet to sea level. The price is $140, but if you book online you'll save some serious cash.

Haleakala Bike Company (808-575-9575 or 1-888-922-2453; bike-maui.com), Haʻiku Marketplace, off the Hana Hwy. near MM 11, Haʻiku. If you have an aversion to group activities, this outfit will rent you a bike so you can ride down on your own. In October 2007, bike tours within park limits became off-limits. But individuals are still allowed to cruise downhill from the summit—if you can get yourself and the bike up there.

BIKING HALEAKALA

BOOGIE BOARDING

Head to **Baldwin Beach Park**; see *Beaches*.

Pukalani Country Club (808-572-1314; pukalanigolf.com), 360 Pukalani St., off Hwy. 37, Pukalani. When you tire of the sky-high fees at other courses, head to this fun and easier course. Greens fees cost $78 before 11 AM and drop to $63 after 1:30 PM. You can make reservations up to seven days in advance.

HIKING

Haleakala National Park (HNP) (808-572-4400). The extreme weather atop and inside the volcano can change in a nanosecond, so you've got to be prepared for anything. Even for short jaunts, bring a hat, water, layers of clothing, and sunscreen. Once you start hiking and get away from the crowds, the silence can be profoundly stunning when you stop crunching volcanic rock underfoot. Serious hikers will need to get much more detailed information from the NPS Web site (nps.gov/hale) before departing and from the visitors center on arrival.

Sliding Sands Trail, HNP, from the summit of Haleakala (just beyond the Pu'u Ula'ula building). A very strenuous trail that descends almost 4,000 feet in 4 miles to the crater floor. Consider taking it 1 mile into the crater and then hiking back up. Remember, though, it isn't called Sliding Sands for nothing.

Halemanu'u Trail, HNP, from the visitors center. Six miles to the crater floor and beyond. Not for the faint of heart.

Hosmer Grove, HNP. See Mount Haleakala, *To See & Do*.

Polipoli State Park (808-984-8109), Waipoli Rd. Chilly and misty, foggy and unspoiled, this magical area is quite rewarding for those who venture into its heart. Only accessible with a four-wheel drive, this enormous tract of land, part of the Kula and Kahikinui Forest Reserve, was reforested in the 1920s. It's now dense with redwoods, eucalyptus, cedar, ash, and cypress trees. You'll probably wonder if you're really in Hawai'i. The **Polipoli Loop Trail** affords exceptional panoramic island views. The 5-mile hike takes about three hours and sits at an elevation of 5,300 to 6,300 feet. Take Hwy. 37 south of Kula, turn left onto Hwy. 377, turn right onto Waipoli Road, and then head up and up for just over 10 miles to the end of the road. Along the way, you'll pass cattle grazing and open vistas stretching down to the ocean.

HORSEBACK RIDING

Pony Express Tours (808-667-2200; ponyexpresstours.com), Hwy. 378, on the road to Haleakala National Park. If you want to head deep into Haleakala Crater without exerting as much effort, these daylong jaunts are perfect ($182). Half-day ranch rides on the lower slopes of Haleakala cost $95–110. All levels of riders are accommodated. Reserve two weeks in advance in summer, one week in winter.

SURFING & WINDSURFING

Leave Ho'okipa to the pros, whether they're utilizing boards or sails. Windsurfers lay claim to morning waves, while surfers take their best shots in the

WEST MAUI MOUNTAINS FROM HOʻOKIPA BEACH

afternoon. (If you're visiting during March, April, or October, you can watch some serious big-board competitions.)

Hana Highway Surf (808-579-8999), 65 Hana Hwy., Paʻia. Board rentals cost $20 daily, but you need to leave a large deposit ($300–400) to take out their gear.

✳ Beaches

In order of preference.

✪ ⚐ **Hoʻokipa Beach Park**, about 2 miles east of Paʻia, on the Hana Hwy. Modern-day Maui surfing began at world-renowned Hoʻokipa. With plenty of invisible rocky ledges just beneath the water's surface, this beach is not for amateurs. Incessant winds make for great windsurfing in the morning, and by agreement, the professional surfers claim the liquid turf in the afternoon. There are great vantage points for watching the artful action, although it gets very crowded during weekend competitions. *Facilities:* parking, restrooms, showers, picnic tables.

⚐ **Baldwin Beach Park**, about 1 mile west of Paʻia, on the Hana Hwy. Good bodysurfing, and good swimming at either end of the curved beach.

✳ Lodging

💲 For the money, Upcountry lodging provides the most bang for the buck on Maui. But there are two conditions attached: Beach bums must drive for their sandy fixes, and visitors must want intimate lodging situations without resort coddling.

BED & BREAKFASTS AND VACATION RENTALS

💲 **Aloha Cottage** (808-573-8555 or 1-888-328-3330; alohacottage.com), 1879 Olinda Rd., Makawao. Four miles north of town, these elegantly comfortable and romantic cottages—the Thai Tree House and Bali Bungalow—

OLINDA ROAD

sit on the edge of an aromatic euca-lyptus gulch and a large tract of unde-veloped forest. A symphony of birds echoes from deep within the gulch; you can't be sure if you're in Thailand or Hawai'i. That feeling continues once you step inside. Top-of-the-line amenities and furnishings, from teak cabinets to granite countertops, from Ralph Lauren sheets to Oriental car-pets, indulge the senses. As befitting a property of this caliber, the getaways are perfectly private from the owner's house. Book today or hold your peace. *Rates*: $$$ (discounts for week-ly stays but more during holiday peri-ods); three-night minimum. *Facilities and amenities*: two cottages, dinner by advance arrangement, cleaning fee for stays of less than three nights, no A/C, phones.

🌿 **Banyan Tree House** (808-572-8482; hawaiimauirentals.com), 3265 Baldwin Ave., Makawao. This three-bedroom, plantation-style main house is great for families, especially since it has a pool and nicely landscaped grounds. Inside it's furnished in a breezy island style and features a

kitchen that might tempt you to cook. The four simple but cheery cottages also have access to the pool, ham-mocks, and distant ocean views. You can rent the house as suites or in its entirety; breakfast is included with the suites. *Rates*: two-person cottages $$; three-bedroom house (sleeps up to nine) $$$–$$$$; there-night mini-mum. *Facilities and amenities*: four cottages, one house, pool, kitchen or kitchenette, cleaning fee of $200, no A/C.

The Inn at Mama's Fish House (808-579-9764 or 1-800-860-4852; mamasfishhouse.com), 799 Poho Pl., Pa'ia. Adjacent to Ho'okipa Beach Park and on the grounds of a very popular restaurant where house guests receive a healthy discount (see *Dining Out*), these one- and two-bedroom cottages are the stuff of dreams. That's due in equal parts to the setting (within sandal shuffle of a coconut-tree-studded beach), the island-breezy furnishings, and the modern kitchens. The economy gar-den cottages, by the way, don't include maid service and are sur-rounded by a junglelike setting. The beachfront units boast a nice covered patio. *Rates*: $$–$$$$; three-night minimum. *Facilities and amenities*: nine cottages, beach, restaurant, full kitchens, cleaning fee, A/C, wireless.

🌿 **Hale Ho'okipa Inn** (808-572-6698; maui-bed-and-breakfast.com), 32 Pakani Pl., Makawao. One of the best values on Maui, this historic home was built in 1924 and converted to an inn in 1997 by longtime Mauian Cherie Attix. She's a passionate sup-porter of sustainable tourism and showing off Maui's best, the way Maui used to be. The inn's living room, lined with books and lovely woodwork, calls to you from the moment you set foot in the front door. Among the guest rooms, I like Rose with its bay window, claw foot tub, and extra day bed. Jasmine Room features an antique Hawaiian four-poster bed, while Hibiscus Room boasts an antique brass bed. Guests staying in the Kona suite have access to the kitchen. The breakfast spread, paired with good conversation at one round table, is generous: organic fixings, fruits from garden, local breads, jams and jellies. It's everything a B&B should be. *Rates*: $$. *Facilities and amenities*: three rooms and one suite, cable TV, continental breakfast, free wireless.

The Kula Lodge (808-878-1535 or 1-800-233-1535; kulalodge.com), 15200 Haleakala Hwy., Kula. These chalet-style accommodations in spacious A-frame chalets sit at 3,200 feet and project an atmosphere closer to Switzerland than Ka'anapali. Magnificent panoramas are the biggest selling point, but the other reason folks stay here is its proximity to Mount Haleakala. The closer you are, the longer you can sleep before waking at some ungodly hour to trek up the mountain for sunrise. But if you're trying to sleep in, be forewarned that hundreds of vans, buses, and cars will drive right by your door on their way up in the morning, too. Chalet 1 is the best of the lot, with the most expansive views, a gas fireplace, a brass bed, and a sleeping loft. *Rates*: $$. *Facilities and amenities*: five chalets, restaurant, no A/C, no TV, no phones.

Kula View B&B (808-878-6736; kulaview.com), 600 Holopuni Rd., west of Kula. Staying here, on the second floor of a private house, is like being up in a tree house with your

own private entrance and lanai. Guests come for the expansive views of Haleakala, but it doesn't hurt that the host has plenty of warm clothes for your sunrise trek up the volcano. The pleasant studio, which has rudimentary kitchen implements, is great for a few nights. *Rates*: $, including continental breakfast; two-night minimum. *Facilities and amenities*: one studio, phone, no TV (but will get you one by request), no credit cards.

CAMPING & CABINS

Polipoli State Park (808-984-8109; office open 8–4 weekdays). There's only one lone cabin (rented a year in advance) situated up at 6,300 feet on the slopes of Haleakala, but you can tent camp. The state allows up to 20 people at any given time ($5 per permit per night, but up to 20 people can go on one permit). Five-night maximum; free but permit required. Take Hwy. 37 to Kula, turn left onto Hwy. 377, right onto Waipoli Rd., and head up and up for just over 10 miles to the end. Contact the State Parks Division–Camping, 54 S. High St., Wailuku 96768.

HALE HO'OKIPA INN

Haleakala National Park (808-572-4400; visitors center open 8–4; nps .gov/hale). Be prepared for extreme conditions; there's a reason astronauts train here. Three cabins are well spaced for hiking, but there is no water or other facilities. And you have to be really lucky to get one. In fact, they're so popular that the NPS has created a lottery, which you can try for three months in advance ($40 nightly for one to six people; two nights maximum at any one cabin; three nights maximum in total). As for tenting, there are two wilderness areas inside the volcano and a more accessible one near Hosmer Grove. They're free, but a permit is required, and they're issued from the Haleakala Visitors Center on a first-come, first-served basis. Hosmer Grove, at 6,800 feet, is cold, but at least the sites are protected from the relentless winds. Three-night maximum. Contact Haleakala National Park, P.O. Box 369, Makawao 96768.

✳ Where to Eat

Upcountry doesn't boast the wealth of choices available in West and South Maui, but there's plenty of variety in terms of price, cuisine, and atmosphere. Fortunately, one of Maui's best foodie restaurants is here (at Hali'imaile). Reservations are recommended for all *Dining Out* establishments.

DINING OUT

🌸 ⑂ **Hali'imaile General Store** (808-572-2666; haliimailegeneralstore .com), 900 Hali'imaile Rd., Hali'i-maile. Open for lunch weekdays, dinner nightly. This 1920s company store, complete with wooden floors and high ceilings, is sitting pretty and squarely amid pineapple and sugar-cane fields. They're humble digs for high cuisine from one of the originators of the Hawai'i regional cuisine movement—the legendary Bev Gannon, who's been packin' 'em in since the late 1980s. My last dinner started with sashimi napoleon and moved on to rack of lamb Hunan style. Dynamite salmon is always a favorite, too. And please, please save room for desserts made by Celebrations Catering. To beat the high cost of dining here, consider simply having drinks and *pupus* at the bar. On my last visit, the bartender mixed a mind-blowing mai tai. And by the way, Bev's outstanding, eponymous cookbook makes a great gift. Children's menu. Lunch $$–$$$, dinner entrées $$$–$$$$.

🌸 ♪ **Colleen's** (808-575-9211), Ha'iku Cannery Marketplace, 810 Ha'iku Rd., Ha'iku. Open 6 AM–9 PM daily. Stylin' with high ceilings, a pseudo-industrial look, and an open kitchen, Colleen's is pleasantly unpretentious and beloved with locals. But that's not all. This is one of the best restaurants on the island, and, to boot, the prices are really reasonable

HALI'IMAILE GENERAL STORE

for the quality. If I lived around the corner, this would be my neighborhood eatery! Come for thicker-crust pizzas, seared ahi, and fish-and-chips. Come often. Early morning French toast and omelets are killers, as are burgers and creative salads at lunchtime. Breakfast and lunch $–$$, dinner entrées $$–$$$.

☙ ⅄ **Mama's Fish House** (808-579-8488; mamasfishhouse.com), Hana Hwy., Kuau Cove, 799 Poho Pl., Pa'ia. Open for lunch, *pupus,* and dinner daily. If you're hankering for the perfect fantasy island setting, complete with an intimate and curvaceous beachfront, striking palm trees, and lots of bamboo, lauhala, and lush plantings, then come to Mama's. Furthermore, consider dining at lunch on a fish sandwich to save some money and enjoy the view. There are always four or five catches of the day that you can pair with at least seven or eight different preparations. As if to emphasize the freshness, the menu highlights where and by whom the fish was caught. Careful; the good mai tais here pack a punch. Children's menu. Lunch $$$$, dinner entrées $$$$.

EATING OUT

Makawao

❧ ⅄ **Casanova Italian Restaurant** (808-572-0220; casanovamaui.com), 1188 Makawao Ave. Open for all three meals daily, except no lunch on Sun. In an old wooden building with a raised roadside porch (whose bar stools are frequented by locals and visitors reading the paper and talking story), Casanova offers plenty of options. From the informal deli side at breakfast, I never miss an opportunity to order a Brie and sun-dried

tomato omelet with buttermilk biscuits. At lunchtime, gourmet sandwiches supplant egg dishes and pastries. And for dinner, I head to the cozy, bona fide restaurant section and generally order a pizza from a wood-fired oven. You'll also be happy with large portions of great pasta dishes and Maui's best tiramisu. Reservations recommended. Breakfast $, lunch $–$$, dinner entrées $$–$$$$.

Keokea

Grandma's Coffee House (808-878-2140; grandmascoffee.com), Lower Kula Rd. Open 7–5 daily. This little roadside place makes an atmospheric stop for a cup of java and a slice of pineapple or banana cake (or other pastry). I wait to eat "real" food elsewhere. Family owned for generations, Grandma's also roasts their family-grown beans in the shop. Most dishes less than $.

Café 808 (808-878-6874), Lower Kula Rd. Open 6 AM–8 PM daily. Diagonally across from the Holy Ghost Church, and on a road that runs parallel to the beaten path, this really local place is off most visitors'

GRANDMA'S COFFEE HOUSE

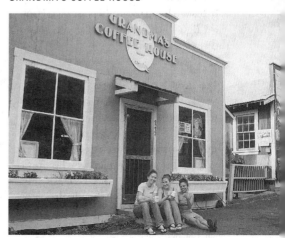

radar. The Spartan interior, complete with linoleum and a smattering of plastic chairs, always compels me toward a take-away burger. Most dishes less than $; no credit cards.

Ha'iku

Hana Hou Café (808-575-2661; hanahoucafe.com), Ha'iku Cannery Marketplace, 810 Ha'iku Rd. Open for dinner nightly (and from noon Thurs.–Sun.). This low-key place caters mostly to locals and windsurfers, but a few savvy tourists may also wander by. Order at the window and take away or grab an outdoor seat for "Sushi by Harry," plate lunches, fish, wild mushroom pasta, and steaks. The Hawaiian music begins most nights at about 7 PM. Dishes $–$$.

Pauwela Café (808-575-9242; pauwelacafe.com), 375 W. Kuiaha Rd. Open 6–2 daily. An easy detour off the Hana Highway about 5 miles east of Pa'ia, this café makes great breakfast burritos, bakes fabulous breads, and assembles a now famous *kalua* turkey sandwich. Casual and friendly, the café has only a few tables inside and out, but how many do you need? Don't let the corrugated-tin and cinder-block exterior put you off. It's located in a building that manufactures surfboards, and it's what passes for light industry around here. Most dishes less than $.

Pa'ia

Jacques North Shore (808-579-8844), 120 Hana Hwy., Pa'ia. Open for dinner nightly, sushi bar open Tues.–Sat. This eclectic place dishes up well-priced seafood to windsurfers and well-heeled, hip locals who appreciate great food. On my last visit, my companion and I practically drooled over the pumpkin fish and vegetable curry; French-Caribbean dishes are also popular. The other draws are outside dining under a giant awning and seats at the sushi bar. Ask about DJs and dancing on Friday nights. Sushi $, entrées $$–$$$.

Moana Bakery & Café (808-579-9999), 71 Baldwin Ave. Open for all three meals daily (except closes at 3 PM on Mon.). In all ways that are important, this is really the only decent place to eat in town. Breakfast omelets and pancakes dominate the early menu; soups, sandwiches, and salads take center stage midday. But at night, chef Don Ritchey, formerly of the Hali'imaile General Store, whips up more sophisticated Asian and Euro dishes, including excellent Thai curries. Usually there's live Hawaiian music in the evenings; call for a schedule. Children's menu. Breakfast and lunch $–$$, dinner entrées $$–$$$$.

MOANA BAKERY & CAFÉ

Café des Amis (808-579-6323), 42 Baldwin Ave. Open for all three meals daily. Appealing to 20- and 30-somethings, this crêperie offers a wide variety of the namesake options and also specializes in Indian-style curry wraps. Breakfast and lunch $, dinner entrées up to $$.

Ÿ **Milagros Food Co.** (808-579-8755), 3 Baldwin Ave. Open 8 AM–9:30 PM daily. Most people come here so they can sit at shady tables on a busy street corner to people-watch. In fact, happy-hour margaritas could almost be listed under *To See & Do*. If you get hungry, blackened ahi tostados and fish tacos should do the trick as long as you don't expect it to rival the real deal. It's rather like the Pacific Rim meets the American Southwest. Children's menu. Dishes $–$$$.

❧ **Pa'ia Fish Market** (808-579-8030), Baldwin Ave. Open for lunch and dinner daily. Windsurfer dudes outnumber visitors at this busy, small, and informal corner eatery. You can expect shellacked communal picnic tables, cold beers, good home fries, and mahi burgers. Don't bother with anything but the fish. Entrées $–$$.

BAKERIES, COFFEE & MARKETS
Makawao
Komoda's Store & Bakery (808-572-7261), 3674 Baldwin Ave. Open 7–5 Mon., Tues., Thurs., and Fri., 7–2 Sat. Long famous for cream puffs (but I really like the shortbread cookies), Komoda's also has hot dogs. Well, it's the buns, really. What? More than one local friend skips the dog and simply noshes on the bun. Arrive by 10 AM or risk the deflation that inevitably accompanies seeing empty shelves. Dishes $–$$; no credit cards.

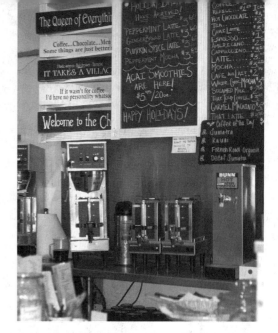

Down to Earth Natural Foods (808-572-1488; downtoearth.org), 1169 Makawao Ave. Open 8–8 daily. This health-food grocery store features a bountiful salad bar, as well as hot and cold prepared deli items. Head across the street to sit under the shady trees at the library.

Rodeo General Store (808-572-1868), 3661 Baldwin Ave., open 7 AM–10 PM daily. This old-fashioned general store underwent a marked makeover in 2008, but it still retains a rustic flavor and is true to its roots. The great wine selection and wine room is better than ever. By the way, it's pronounced *ROdeo,* as in bull riding, not *roDEo,* as in the drive in Beverly Hills.

Pukalani
❧ **Pukalani Superette** (808-572-7616), off Haleakala Hwy. Open 6:30 AM–9 PM weekdays, 7 AM–8 PM weekends. To feel oh-so-local, stop here at lunchtime with everyone else for hot deli items like chili chicken. My dear Upcountry friend Bonnie swears it contains a secret addictive ingredient.

Makawao Steak House (808-572-8711; Makawao) offers one of the only salad bars around; **Kula Lodge** (808-878-1535; Kula) is well known in travel guides for stunning sunset views of Upcountry and West Maui, but there are a dozen places I'd eat before here (except, maybe, in winter when the stone fireplace is warming).

✳ Entertainment
Ⴘ **Casanova** (808-572-0220), 1188 Makawao Ave., Makawao. The happenin' bar is open nightly, but locals really drive the distance (with good reason) to listen to live music and dance (9:45 PM–1:30 AM Wed.–Sat.). The lineup is a mixture of blues, reggae, rock, and country. When bands like Los Lobos travel through the islands, they'll often jam here, with or without local rock-and-roll exiles (like Willie Nelson and Kris Kristofferson). Wednesday night is ladies night, a DJ spins groovy tunes on Friday, and live bands play on Saturday. Although it doesn't get much better than this on Maui, it doesn't need to because this is pretty darn good. Cover.

MAUI CRAFTS GUILD

See also Jacques North Shore and Moana Bakery & Café under *Eating Out.*

✳ Selective Shopping
ART, ARTS & CRAFTS, ARTISANS
Maui Crafts Guild (808-579-9697; mauicraftsguild.com), 43 Hana Hwy., Pa'ia. Open daily. On the edge of town, in an old two-story wooden building, the crafts guild is a favorite Maui stop. Guild members work in a range of media, from raku to rare woods, from beads to banana bark, from sculpture to stained glass. Head upstairs for the furniture.

Hot Island Glass (808-572-4527; hotislandglass.com), the Courtyard, 3620 Baldwin Ave., Makawao. Open daily. If you can't stand the heat of this demonstration studio, you can cool off in their colorful gallery. The family-owned studio, which produces high-end pieces, is set back in the Courtyard. Call to make sure they're doing demonstrations the day you want to visit.

Viewpoints (808-572-5979; view pointsgallerymaui.com), the Courtyard, 3620 Baldwin Ave., Makawao. Open daily. So many Maui artists, so little time. Luckily, Makawao is a small town, and the galleries and cooperatives are close together. Viewpoints mostly represents painters and sculptors.

Maui Hands (808-572-5194; maui hands.com), the Courtyard, 3620 Baldwin Ave., Makawao. Open daily. Another fine gallery, with an additional location at the Ka'ahumanu Center in Kahului.

See also Hui No'eau Visual Arts Center under *To See & Do.*

HAWAIIANA

FARMER'S MARKETS

All around Upcountry, farmers cultivating the volcanic soil produce greener greens than you'll find almost anywhere in the United States. Check market listings under *Eating Out*.

FLOWERS

✪ **Sunrise Protea Farm** (808-876-0200; sunriseprotea.com), Hwy. 337 (a few miles past the Haleakala turn-off), Kula. Open 7–4 daily. Showy and dazzling, these flowers are easily shipped to the mainland. And while you're here, at 4,000 feet, you might as well take a self-guided walk through the colorful garden before buying.

✪ **Proteas of Hawai'i** (808-878-2533; proteasofhawaii.com), 417 Mauna Pl., Kula. Open 8–4:30 weekdays. The only appreciable difference between these folks and Sunrise is that Proteas of Hawai'i offer guided walking tours of the gardens. Call in advance to arrange a tour.

SHOPPING AREAS

✪ **Makawao**, Maui's coolest shopping town, caters to travelers with independent tastes. One-of-a-kind boutiques and a few down-home shops line Makawao's quiet crossroads.

✪ **Pa'ia**, also at a crossroads, boasts a dense thicket of laid-back, wooden-storefront shops that cater mostly to a surfer-dude kind of crowd.

SPECIAL SHOPS

Collections (808-572-0781), 3677 Baldwin Ave., Makawao. Open daily. This long-standing gift and clothing shop epitomizes everything breezy about island living.

Attitude (808-573-4733), 3660 Baldwin Ave., Makawao. Open daily. For women's clothes with a bit of attitude, brought to you by a delightful French proprietor with a great eye, few Maui shops match the low-key fashions collected under this roof.

Maui Girl (808-579-9266; mauigirl .com), 12 Baldwin Ave., Pa'ia. Open daily. Different size on top than the bottom? No worries here. These bathing suits and beachwear come in all manner of mix-and-match sizes.

BALDWIN AVE., MAKAWAO.

TO HANA & BEYOND

The Hana Highway began life as a footpath worn by ancient Hawaiians. It was paved in 1962 and improved in 1982 to handle the oncoming tidal wave of automobile traffic. Today, it's said that about 1,000 cars drive the route daily! Remember this and you'll enjoy the trip: It's the journey rather than the destination. There's good reason to believe you haven't experienced Maui until you've driven the Hana Highway and visited the tiny town of Hana. Not that there's much to *do* in town. In fact, visitors with high expectations are usually disappointed and wonder, "What's the fuss all about?" But Hana's appeal is its sedate and timeless quality, the old-Hawai'i character that's rapidly disappearing.

Although it's only 52 miles from Kahului to Hana, the last 29 miles are one blind curve after another (actually there are about 600 curves and 54 blind ones). Because the speed limit rarely exceeds 25 mph and often hovers around 10 mph, expect the trip to take almost three hours one-way (without stopping—which you will do).

For your effort, you'll be rewarded with a jagged coastline strewn with lava, one waterfall after another, pristine farmland dotted with grazing cattle, secluded swimming holes, pounding surf, stands of wild ginger and dense bamboo, monkeypod trees and thick ferns, rainbow eucalyptus, and lush rain forest. Try not to grow immune to the beauty as each curve exposes yet another magnificent vista. Oh, yes, and leave a few hours for the drive beyond Hana to Kipahulu (if the road is open), which is perhaps the most stunning section of the adventure.

Better yet, if that sounds like too much to do in one day, stay over for a few nights. For years, I "did" Hana as a day trip and knew its magical appeal only intellectually and theoretically. But Hana is not a drive-by kind of place. Now that I've stayed over many times, for many nights in a row, Hana's spirit has burrowed deep into my pores and soul. If I had only a month to live, I'd live in Hana (preferably at the Hotel Hana-Maui!). I'd watch a baseball game under the lights, eat Roselani Ice Cream on the harbor, ride horseback along the crashing shoreline, and watch sunrises speak to deafening silence.

Hana has always played a vital part in Hawaiian history, and it is still one of Hawai'i's most fiercely Hawaiian towns. Early Polynesians landed here and settled. In 1795, King Kamehameha left Hana to conquer the rest of the Hawaiian archipelago. (He needed only 15 years to do so.) Before the Europeans invaded

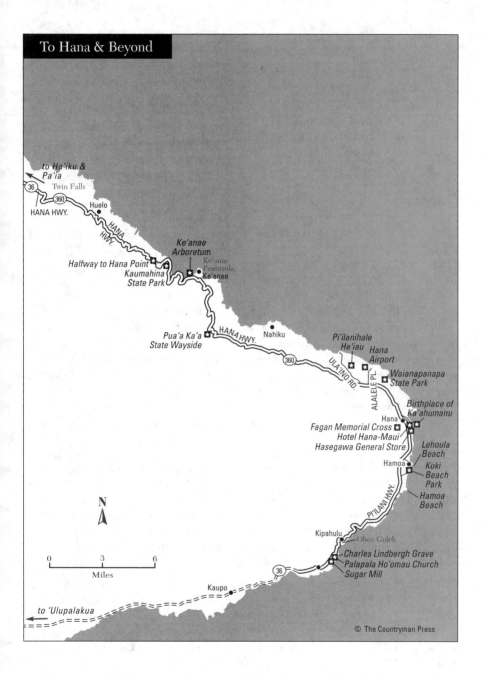

Hawai'i, upward of 50,000 to 70,000 people lived in Hana, but by the 1830s the population had plummeted to 11,000. From the 1850s to the 1930s, sugar ruled the economy and the plantations provided decent livelihoods to the locals. After World War II, though, when the local labor-intensive plantations were no longer profitable, the economy tanked.

Paul Fagan then converted his Hana Sugar Company lands and other newly acquired acreage into two businesses he hoped would provide a continuing livelihood for the native population. Ranching was the first enterprise. While Herefords have thrived in the area since and have become a Hana trademark, the *paniolo* trade could support only a small portion of the community. So the Hotel Hana-Maui became his other, bolder enterprise. In 1946, there were few hotels in Waikiki, much less in such a remote location as East Maui. Fagan envisioned a small, deluxe hideaway for adventurous travelers. It was a radical concept at the time. Since no one in Hana had enough experience with the outside world to consider the impossibility of the dream, they made it succeed. The first guests paid $5 a night for an opportunity to escape the modern world and relax in first-class comfort. It's now riding high again, easily on my list of top five places to stay in Hawai'i.

> **BUILDING BLOCKS FOR A PERFECT DAY DRIVING TO HANA**
> Stop in Pa'ia
> Drive down into Maliko Bay
> Drive down into Huelo
> Take a little hike or two
> Stop by a waterfall or three
> Drive down into the Ke'anae Peninsula
> Stop for fruit smoothies
> Check out the Black Sand Beach (1 hour) and coastal trail (4 hours) at Waianapanapa State Park

You won't find a stoplight in "Heavenly Hana," or a golf course or fast-food restaurant. What you will find is a place where you don't need a wristwatch; where ripe fruit falls from trees faster than you can eat it; where the aloha spirit is alive and well for those who stick around after the last tour van departs. Saying it's untouched by time sounds trite, but it really is true. Is it that time for you?

GETTING AROUND

By car: Don't be intimidated by descriptions of this road as "challenging" to the point of not taking the drive. It's perfectly pleasant, paved, and downright beautiful as long as you aren't rushed. In fact, only the second half of the road is really curvy and requires your utmost attention. Yes, there are dozens of hairpin turns, 50 one-lane bridges, and places where you must pull over to allow the oncoming traffic to pass. But that's part of the adventure. You'll especially want to let locals pass you, since they tend to drive faster.

Just beyond Ha'iku, the Hana Highway changes from Hwy. 36 to Hwy. 360 and the Mile Markers (MM) revert to 0. If you make it all the way out to the Pools of Oheo and Kipahulu, where Hwy. 360 becomes the Pi'ilani Highway (Hwy. 36), consider continuing along the back side of Haleakala to civilization—if the road has reopened from an earthquake-damaged bridge. (In that case, the road leads you to the "Upcountry & Haleakala" chapter.)

All Mile Marker (MM) distances are approximate.

✳ To See & Do

Exploring clockwise from the north shore around to Hana and beyond.

If you're doing Hana as a day trip (which is regrettable but perhaps understandable), leave early in the morning. I think it's best to save Pa'ia (see "Upcountry &

Haleakala") for another day, but you could always explore it on your way back from Hana (if you have time)—unless, that is, you head around the back side like I do (when the road is open and when I'm feeling defiant vis-à-vis my car rental contract, which prohibits it). Although there are little fruit smoothie stands along the way and a few places to get a soda, get food and water in Pa'ia. As for gas, it's about 50¢ per gallon higher in Hana than Pa'ia; no place in between sells it.

You can purchase a narrated audio tour of the Hana Highway, but I find these distracting. I end up spending so much energy trying to match where I am to the audio that I don't concentrate on where I am. It's your call.

On the Way to Hana

Pa'ia, *makai*, Hwy. 36. See "Upcountry & Haleakala."

✦ **Ho'okipa Beach Park**, *makai*, Hwy. 36. The windsurfing capital of Maui. See *Beaches*, "Upcountry & Haleakala."

Maliko Bay, *makai*, MM 10, Hwy. 36. This lush valley used to support a little village down by the ocean until it was destroyed by a tidal wave in the 1940s. Drive down into the gulch and head right toward the bay.

Ha'iku, *mauka*, MM 16, Hwy. 36. See "Upcountry & Haleakala." Beyond Ha'iku, the curves begin and the Hana Highway morphs from Hwy. 36 to 360.

Twin Falls, *mauka*, MM 2, Hwy. 360. The trailhead for this short hike lies just before Ho'olawa Stream. Follow the right side of the stream to reach the first falls, then continue along the right to reach the second falls.

Huelo, *makai*, MM 5. Note the colorful collection of mailboxes on the *makai* side of the road. The little hidden township of Huelo, a great place

BUILDING BLOCKS FOR A PERFECT DAY IN HANA

Doing nothing is a very good option (all day)

Pop into Hasegawa General Store (20 minutes here, 20 minutes there)

Enjoy Roselani ice cream at the harbor (30 minutes)

Drive beyond Hana to Oheo Gulch (stopping at Arabella Ark's gallery) (3 to 4 hours)

And then drive beyond Oheo Gulch as far as your heart's desire takes you (or until you can go no farther because of a washed out bridge) (timeless)

Check out the Black Sand Beach (1 hour) and coastal trail (4 hours) at Waianapanapa State Park

Go horseback riding (90 minutes)

Check out Hamoa Beach (2 hours)

Have a drink at the Hotel Hana Maui's Paniolo Bar (1 to 3 hours)

to get away from it all, spreads out below the road. Thanks to its plethora of B&Bs and vacation homes, you can experience sleepy and isolated Huelo (a tad rainy for first-time and long stays) without assuming a huge mortgage. Many Huelo residents live "off the grid," meaning that they have their own power generators. Note the New England–style **Kaulanapueo Church**, built in 1853, which still holds services about once monthly.

Koʻolau Forest Reserve, *mauka*. *Koʻolau* means "windward," and that means this area receives a lot of rainfall—about 70 inches annually. Vegetation—fruit trees, bursting with ripe pickings, and lauhala trees—is thicker than pea soup.

Waikamoi Ridge Trail, *mauka*, MM 9. The trailhead for this 1-mile round-trip hike begins near the picnic tables overlooking the Hana Highway. It passes plenty of bamboo, mahogany, and tree ferns. Restrooms.

Puahokamoa Falls, MM 11. When it's been raining, this 30-foot waterfall spills into a nice but icy swimming hole. It's a fine place for picnicking if you ant to be among hordes of day trippers, but there aren't any restrooms.

Kaumahina State Wayside Park, MM 12. Kaumahina, which means "rising moon," has flush toilets, a picnic area, and water. Head across the street to an overlook that affords a spectacular vantage point for the Keʻanae Peninsula, the Pacific, and taro fields.

⚑ **Honomanu Bay County Beach Park**, *makai*, MM 14. This deep, erosion-carved valley has a rocky, black-sand beach at its head. Because of riptides, it's not great for swimming, but you'll probably see some surfers tackling the waves. Take the rutted road slowly. Once on the beach, turn around and check out the steep sea cliffs from whence the road has been carved. No facilities.

Keʻanae Arboretum, *mauka*, MM 17. This free botanical garden displays many different varieties of taro and

SMOOTHIE CENTRAL

other plants used for medicinal purposes. Follow little Pi'ina'au Stream (in which you can swim) as it passes through to a quiet forest (about a mile walk).

Ke'anae Peninsula, *makai*, MM 17. This longtime settlement is home to one of the few remaining coastal Hawaiian communities. They still fish with traditional methods and grow taro.

Waikane Falls, MM 22. Widely considered the best falls on the road.

Nahiku, *makai*, MM 25. This old village is now home to about 80 folks, mostly Native Hawaiians, but in ancient times it boasted hundreds. In the early 1900s, a rubber plant supported the local community. The road dead-ends at the ocean.

Hana Airport, *makai*, MM 30. This tiny airstrip conjures up images of the *Little Prince* and Amelia Earhart.

Ka'eleku Caverns, *makai*, MM 31. Head 1 mile down 'Ula'ino Rd. to explore a vast system of caves. See *Outdoor Activities*.

Pi'ilanihale He'iau (808-248-8912), *makai*, MM 31 at the Kahanu Botanical Gardens. Open weekdays 10–2. Turn left onto 'Ula'ino Rd. and continue 1.5 miles beyond where the pavement ends. The state's largest *he'iau* was built in the 16th century for King Pi'ilani, the same king who built a footpath around the island. This sacred place is not a conventional tourist site, so please act with the utmost respect and reverence. Admission $10; self-guided pamphlet for the *he'iau*.

✦ **Waianapanapa State Park**, *makai*, MM 32. Spread out along a rugged volcanic shoreline, Waianapanapa, which means "glistening water," is a 120-acre park about 4 miles from Hana. It's a deservedly popular place for hiking, snorkeling (with flippers), sunbathing, and picnicking. The **Black Sand Beach** is lovely to look at, but swimming is generally a tad unsafe.

HONOR-SYSTEM FLOWERS

Ancient Hawaiians told mythic tales about the park's freshwater caves. It's said that Chief Ka'akea, who suspected his wife of adultery, found his Popoalaea hiding in one of these caves and murdered her. A few times a year, the waters around the caves

turn red with the blood of Popoalaea. (Scientists claim the color comes from tiny red shrimp that show up occasionally.) Ancient Hawaiians also walked the coastal trail that leads to Hana. It's a moderately easy hike today.

Hana

In recent years, Hana has been home to Kris Kristofferson, George Harrison, Carol Burnett, and Jim Nabors. Oprah Winfrey, who purchased a tract of ocean-front property near the Haneo'o Loop Road, was bitten by the Hana bug in 2004. Of the 2,500 or so souls who inhabit the place, the majority are indigenous Hawaiians. In fact, Hana easily has the greatest concentration of Hawaiians in Hawai'i. Hang around overnight and you will hear Hawaiian spoken.

Hana Cultural Center (808-248-8622; hookele.com), 4974 Uakea Rd., MM 35. Open 10–4 daily, except holidays. This little museum (*Hale Waiwai 'O Hana*, which means "house of the treasures of Hana") tells the story of Hana through the use of Hawaiian artifacts, daily items, and historical objects from the sugar mill, for instance. They also sell quilts and other crafts. Check out the adjacent replica *kauhale* (a thatched house with gardens).

Fagan's Cross, trailhead across from the Hotel Hana-Maui. This white stone memorial to Paul Fagan was erected in 1960 by Fagan's wife to mark his passing. The steep, 3-mile round-trip trail cuts through open grazing land, so keep your eyes peeled for patches of dung. Because of the higher elevation, you'll enjoy expansive coastal and ranchland views, particularly around sunset.

Hana Bay. If you hang around long enough, which is to say, half a lifetime, locals just might be willing to strike up a conversation. The calm bay, with a gray sand beach made of coral and ash, is fine for swimming. Just to the right of the circular bay and harbor, a trail leads to a cave where Queen Ka'ahumanu was born.

HANA

Wananalua Church. This European-style church was built in the 1830s using volcanic rocks from a nearby *he'iau*. There is absolutely no way that would be allowed to happen today!

✦ **Red Sand Beach** (aka **Kaihalulu Beach**). See *Beaches*.

See also **Hotel Hana-Maui** (under *Lodging*) and Hasegawa General Store (under *Special Shops*).

Beyond Hana

This is the best stretch of the Hana Highway, and most people don't leave enough time to explore it.

FAGAN'S CROSS

✦ **Lehoula Beach**, Haneo'o Loop Rd. off Hwy. 360, a couple of miles beyond Hana. See *Beaches*.

✦ **Hamoa Beach**, Haneo'o Loop Rd. off Hwy. 360, a couple of miles beyond Hana. See *Beaches*.

Kipahulu Ranger Station (808-248-7375), *makai*, Hwy. 360. Open 9–5 daily. Ten miles beyond Hana, this lush region is considered part of Haleakala National Park. Inquire about walks and talks led by rangers. Parking fee: $10, good for one week, unless you've already paid to go to the top of the volcano. Restrooms, but no water.

❂ **Oheo Gulch & Pools of Oheo**, Hwy. 360; park at the ranger station. Popularly but incorrectly referred to as the "Seven Sacred Pools," these pools are not sacred, nor do they number seven. In fact, there are upward of 30 of them. Although the old moniker still sticks, in late 1996 they were formally and officially renamed the Pools of Oheo. The pools, lined with volcanic basalt worn soft from years of water erosion, tumble down the gulch as Oheo Stream rushes through.

The lower pools are always more crowded than the upper ones, and all the pools are far less crowded in the morning before vanloads of day-trippers arrive. (That's another benefit of staying overnight in Hana.) Be forewarned: As fun as the pools look,

OHEO GULCH

OLD PI'ILANI HIGHWAY

each year a number of visitors die from being swept into the ocean during flash floods. Their bodies are never recovered from these shark-infested waters.

To reach the quieter pools and two waterfalls, take the **Pipiwai Trail** from the trailhead near the ranger station and walk upstream for 0.5 mile to **Makahiku Falls**. Head another 1.5 miles uphill (it's steep) through bamboo stands and across two little bridges to **Waimoku Falls**. You'll be rewarded.

Palapala Hoʻomau Congregational Church, *makai*, Hwy. 360. Just past St. Paul's Church, you'll see a tall chimney belonging to a decrepit sugar mill. And just past that, you'll see a little road leading to the church where **Charles Lindbergh's** grave is located. Lindbergh and his wife built a house in the area; he left New York City in 1974 knowing he was dying and knowing his wife wanted him to be buried here.

Old Piʻilani Highway, through to ʻUlupalakua Ranch and Kula. At press time, an earthquake had taken out a one-lane bridge that linked the Hana side of this road through to Kaupo. There was no firm date for its completion. Just in case, though, here's the scoop: This rutted road, unpaved for 4 miles through **Kaupo**, is technically off-limits to rental cars, but many folks (including me) do it anyway. Locals would prefer we didn't—it really threatens their simple ways of life—but the desertlike conditions on the back side of Haleakala are haunting and desolate, and I couldn't miss it for the world. (I'm sure some of you will end up thinking it's boring; sorry.) Except for an early stretch that consists of some blind, one-lane curves, most of the road is fine. Since it can get washed out in a few places, it's always best to ask locals at the Hana gas station or Public Works Department (808-248-8254; open 6:30 AM–3 PM) about its condition before setting out. Most of the road provides simply spectacular views of the Pacific. The Kaupo General Store (it's a big name for such a small place), about 5 miles past the Lindbergh grave, may or may not have supplies.

BEYOND OHEO GULCH

✱ Spas

Spa Hotel Hana-Maui (808-270-5290, ext. 5290 or 1-800-324-4262; hotelhanamaui.com/spa.shtml), Hana. Open 9 AM–8 PM daily. I love this low-key but entirely first-rate place. Of all the spas and treatments I enjoyed during a recent two-and-a-half-month trip across the entire state, this remained my favorite. I suspect it was

MAUI RAISES THE ISLAND

It's said that the demigod Maui—whose father held the heavens and whose mother guarded the path to the netherworld—was the smallest and weakest of his family. Still, what he lacked in physical strength he made up for with cunning intelligence. Because his brothers were better fishermen than he, Maui would distract them and pull his line against theirs to steal their fish. Soon, his brothers became annoyed and refused to go fishing with him.

When Maui's mother became aware of this, she said to Maui, her favorite son, "Go to your father, my child. There you will receive *Manai ikalani*, the hook fastened to the heavens."

When Maui returned with the hook, he enticed his brothers to invite him fishing once again by promising an abundant trip. The brothers reluctantly agreed. They paddled far into the ocean. After many hours of uneventful fishing, they turned to Maui and ridiculed him with insults, asking, "Where are those fish that you promised, brother?"

Maui rose up and stretched his neck out far. He appeared to be the largest among them. While concentrating deeply and chanting to bring the Great Fish, he threw his magical hook into the ocean. At first there was nothing; then the sea began to roar. A huge wave swept up, looming over the canoe. All were shaken except Maui, who commanded his brothers to paddle harder than they'd ever paddled before and to not look back. The brothers paddled for two straight days, while Maui held the magical line and hook taut. Suddenly, from the depths of the sea arose the tips of great mountains. As Maui tugged on the line, more of the peaks rose from the water.

When one of Maui's brothers couldn't resist the temptation to look back, Maui's line grew slack, snapped, and disappeared into the sea. The magical hook was lost forever in the depths. Maui intended to raise a great continent, but because of his brother's curiosity he pulled up only an island.

the gentle healing nature of my masseuse, combined with the soothing character of the sanctuary and the spirit of Place. It's an unparalleled trifecta.

✳ Outdoor Activities

FISHING

Shore fishing off **Hana Beach State Park** is pretty good.

HANA HIGHWAY

HIKING

Hana-Waianapanapa Coastal Trail, Waianapanapa State Park, off the Hana Hwy. This relatively flat and easy 6-mile-long trail should take about four hours. But be sure to go early in the morning or later in the day since there's no relief from the sun along the way. You'll see sea cliffs and sea caves, lots of lava and lauhala trees, up-close-and-personal ocean views, and even an ancient *he'iau*. Bring mosquito repellent—the critters are always biting.

See also **Waikamoi Ridge Trail** and **Pipiwai Trail** under *To See & Do*.

HORSEBACK RIDING

Hotel Hana-Maui (808-248-8211; hotelhanamaui.com), Hana. Your choice will probably depend on your skill level. Beginners generally take a one-hour ride that hugs the rugged coastline, strewn with black lava and loud with pounding surf. Intermediate riders head up into the mountainous ranchlands. The local guides are quite knowledgeable and the groups are small, with no more than six people. $60 per person; children ages 7–12 must be accompanied by an adult; $120 for a coast and mountain ride.

Maui Stables (808-248-7799). Contact them for rides beyond Oheo and above the pools overlooking Pipiwai Falls.

SPELUNKING

Maui Cave Adventures (808-248-7308; mauicave.com), Ka'eleku Caverns, off the Hana Hwy. Open 10:30–3:30 Mon.–Sat. and some Sun. Amateur spelunkers take note: This extensive system of ancient lava tubes dates back some 30,000 years and is full of narrow passageways, massive chambers, stalagmites, and stalactites. Three different self-guided trips are geared toward three types of different ent explorers ($12 adults, five and under free).

SPA HOTEL HANA-MAUI

✳ Beaches

In order of preference.

🏄 **Hamoa Beach**, Haneo'o Loop Rd. off Hwy. 360, a couple of miles beyond Hana. James Michener, the renowned author of the epic historical novel *Hawaii*, called Hamoa Beach "the most perfect beach in the world." He wasn't kidding. This salt-and-pepper half-moon beach, although maintained by the Hotel Hana-Maui, is open to all. The surf can be rough in winter, but summertime swimming and snorkeling are fine (especially on the left side). Bodysurfing is prime, and parking is limited. *Facilities:* a real bathroom, showers, picnic tables.

HAMOA BEACH

✦ **Red Sand Beach** (aka **Kaihalulu Beach**), just south of Hana Bay, below Kauiki, a 400-foot volcanic cone made of red cinders. As the sea eroded the cone and pummeled the rocks into red sand, a beach was born. To reach the beach, head toward the parking lot for the Hotel Hana-Maui's Sea Ranch Cottages. Turn left, pass the old cemetery, and follow the path that leads down the cliff. Don't miss it. No facilities.

✦ **Lehoula Beach** (aka Koki Beach), Haneoʻo Loop Rd. off Hwy. 360, a couple of miles beyond Hana. A lovely spot reputed to be where the goddess Pele ended her mortal existence and assumed divine longevity. Just offshore you can see ʻAlau Island, the one that the demigod Maui supposedly fished from the sea. No facilities.

✳ Lodging

Hana will reward intrepid travelers who make the time to savor her quiet riches with one of the most romantic places to stay in Hawaiʻi, prime camping cabins, and many wonderful vacation rentals. If you can, take a few days to do it right.

ON THE WAY TO HANA
Huelo Point Lookout (808-573-0914 or 1-800-871-8645; mauivacationcottages.com), off the Hana Hwy., Huelo. Thirty minutes from Paʻia and almost 30 miles from Hana, Sharon and Jeff Stone's romantic retreat is off the beaten path and well suited to those with an adventurous spirit. Down a little dirt road with few neighbors, this small compound consists of Rainbow Cottage (the finest and most lavish, awash in windows and boasting a dramatic bedroom cupola), Star Cottage (a charming little place that has an open staircase leading to a lovely sleeping loft and sitting area), Haleakala Cottage (a small studio with a private outdoor shower), and a house (with a pentagonal glass living room facing eastward and a wraparound deck). Huelo Point appeals to visitors of two extremes: those who never want to leave the property and those who are gone from sunrise to sunset. Despite the frequent rain, I never want to leave Shangri-la partly because of the free-form swimming pool and adjacent hot tub. *Rates*: $$–$$$$; discounts for weekly rentals. *Facilities and amenities*: one house and three cottages, pool, no A/C, no credit cards.

Cliff's Edge at Huelo Point (808-268-4530 or 1-866-262-6284; cliffsedge.com), off the Hana Hwy., Huelo. Ahhhhhh. I always breathe a little deeper when pulling up to the edge of this cliff—unlike most other cliffs I find myself on the edge of! The views alone, especially from the Bali and Seaside cottages, are worth the price of admission, so to speak. Seaside features a full kitchen, a sundeck with private hot tub, a gas grill, and an outdoor shower. Bali has an open floor plan, teak furnishings, a marble shower, and a private Jacuzzi. Both suites in the main residence have a large kitchenette (although a continental breakfast is included) and private lanai. It's easy enough to come for two weeks and never leave the privacy of your lanai. And with expansive North Shore views, why would you want to? *Rates*: $$–$$$; three-night minimum; shorter stays may be accommodated if slots available; due to precipitous cliff on the property, children under 13 are not allowed. *Facilities and amenities*: two cottages and two suites, saltwater pool, hot tub, satellite TV/DVD, wireless (free).

HANA

Resorts & Condos

⚓ **Hotel Hana-Maui** (808-248-8211 or 1-800-324-4262; hotelhanamaui .com), Hana Hwy. Once upon a time, there was perfection. Now there is the Hotel Hana-Maui, my favorite place to stay on Maui, and quite high on my list of top 10 places to stay in Hawai'i. This famed hideaway, returned to its former high level of service and infrastructure, is a great destination for romantics and solitude seekers. The 66-acre complex delicately blends organic vitality with handcrafted nobility. The single-story

HOTEL HANA-MAUI

cottages (and a few traditional guest rooms) are outfitted with first-class amenities, Hawaiian art, and oversized bamboo and rattan furnishings. Sea Ranch Cottages are the most luxe, most with a hot tub on the large deck. No rooms have a TV, and they're all capable of sustaining permanent exile, which is exactly how I feel after settling in here for a few days. I never want to leave . . . unless it's to trundle up to the tranquil spa (see *Spa*) or touch civilization (such as it is) at the **Paniolo Bar** (see *Entertainment*). I suspect the hotel's country-style luxury and artistic achievements will linger lovingly in your mind long after departure. *Rates*: $$$$; children free in parent's room. *Facilities and amenities*: 66 rooms and suites, two pools (including an infinity pool), shuttle to beach, two restaurants (see **Ka'uiki Restaurant** under *Dining Out*), three-hole practice golf course, two tennis courts, almost open-air fitness center, yoga classes, wet room at spa, bicycles, water sport equipment, stocked mini bar, food basket on arrival, concierge, seasonal children's programs, parking, wireless. All facilities mentioned above are included in price of room.

Hana Kai Maui Resort (808-248-8426 or 1-800-346-2772; hanakai maui.com), 1533 Uakea Rd. The Hana Kai Maui exaggerates in calling itself a resort, but these are the only condos in somnolent Hana, and they're right on top of the surging sea, so I'll have to forgive them. Most apartments here have better views than those at Hotel Hana-Maui, but the comparisons stop there. The studio and one-bedroom condos have spacious private lanais facing the Pacific pageantry, but inside, the scene is more modest and furnishings basic—although they did renovate in 2006 with more modern furnishings. One of the two low-rise buildings is so close to the surf that it sounds as if you're riding the waves to shore. Fortunately, this front building contains the larger and nicer units. *Rates*: $$–$$$; children under six free in parent's room. *Facilities and amenities*: 17 condos, Popolano Beach (black sands for walking, not swimming), no A/C, no TV, no phones.

Bed & Breakfasts

🐷 **Maui B&B at Baby Pigs Crossing** (808-248-8890; mauibandb.com), Hana Hwy., between MM 46 and 45. The last house "on the grid" of electricity way out here provides a framework for getting under Hana's skin that few places can match. It's easy to imagine yourself a resident here. At least, I always do. The guest suite, with a private entrance but linked to the main house via a covered walkway, is a very comfortable place to settle in for a while. The setting, high above the ocean with expansive views, is stunning. Part of an old-style Hawaiian home, the rental unit has a large bedroom/dining area with kitchenette and extensive continental breakfast fixings, a separate living area, and a private patio with gas grill (bring mosquito repellent). I particularly like the glassed-in, gardenlike shower setting. Host Arabella Ark is a delight and quite knowledgeable about the area. She also offers à la carte dinners (complete with wine, a protein, vegetables, and ice cream!), since this place can feel remote. To that end, there is no cell phone or wireless out here, but there is a pay phone in the studio. *Rates*: $$ nightly (weekly rates available), full breakfast included, two-night minimum. *Facili-*

ties and amenities: one unit, cable TV with DVD collection, no A/C.

Heavenly Hana Inn (808-248-8442; heavenlyhanainn.com), Hana Hwy. Attention to detail is the modus operandi at Sheryl and Bob Filippi's place, which is barely outside the center of town. This Japanese-style *ryokan* (inn) comes complete with a shared tearoom, meditation room, and meditative gardens. Each of the traditionally furnished guest rooms has its own sitting room with a futon couch, private entrance, hardwood floors, and *wabi sabi* aesthetic. It's a perfectly peaceful place to repose, inducing calm and quietude. Although there is an additional charge for breakfast, it's worth it, and the theme changes daily (from Hawaiian to Chinese to Japanese, for instance.) *Rates*: $$–$$$; no children under 15; two-night minimum. *Facilities and amenities*: three suites, full breakfast available (fee), no A/C, no phones.

VACATION RENTALS

Hana Hale Inn (808-248-7641; hanahaleinn.com), Uakea Rd. In the center of town, more or less, this hidden complex with four units is

MAUI B&B AT BABY PIGS CROSSING

situated around a lava tube, an ancient *he'iau*, a restored fishpond, and lush landscaping. It's also near a beach. The two-story tree house isn't exactly a tree house, but it does have distant ocean views. The pondside bungalow, filled with Balinese bamboo and teakwood, is great for longer stays because of its full kitchen. The modest garden suite is simply a good value. But the best accommodation is the Royal Lodge, a post-and-beam work of art with an open floor plan and magnificent spiral staircase. *Rates*: $$–$$$; continental breakfast buffet; two-night minimum; four nights at Christmastime. *Facilities and amenities*: wireless, full kitchens, Jacuzzis, no A/C.

Bamboo Inn (808-248-7718; bamboo inn.com), Uakea Rd. Adjacent to Hana Hale Inn—and thus situated around the same lava tube, ancient *he'iau*, and restored fishpond—the lushly landscaped Bamboo Inn is also near a beach. Three oceanfront suites were remodeled in 2007: Honu and Iwa have queen beds; the latter also has an outdoor shower. The two-story Nai'a sleeps up to seven people. All are decorated with Indonesian and Tahitian accents, coconut wood floors, woven bamboo siding, and Balinese bamboo and teak furnishings. *Rates*: $$; continental breakfast buffet. *Facilities and amenities*: private Jacuzzis, wireless, BBQ.

❧ **Hana Oceanfront Cottages** (808-248-7558; hanaoceanfrontcottages .com), Hana Hwy. Less than 2 miles beyond the center of Hana, and across the street from a gorgeous crescent called Hamoa Beach, these two units are poised on a corner lot with unobstructed ocean views. Hosts Sandi and Dan Simoni offer a tropical

and tasteful plantation-style unit with about 1,000 square feet of living area as well as a romantic cottage. This latter gem is the kind of place you could hole up in for seven rainy days and not go stir crazy. Thankfully, the Simonis cut no corners when planning it. It's decorated in old-Hawai'i style and features a bamboo sleigh bed, a small but top-notch kitchen, and fluffy bathroom towels. *Rates*: $$$; three-night minimum. *Facilities and amenities*: one cottage, one vacation rental, across the street from the fabulous Hamoa Beach, no A/C, phones, wireless.

Hamoa Bay House and Bungalow (808-248-7884; hamoabay.com), Hana Hwy. Just on the other side of Hana, these Balinese-inspired units are the ultimate in romantic retreats. I could easily stay for a week and forget about the world. Nestled amid ferns, bamboo, papaya trees, heliconias, and banana trees, they're a mere 10-minute walk from Hamoa Beach. The 600-square-foot bungalow sleeps two and features lots of batik and bamboo furniture, as well as a screened-in porch with a sunken tub and an outdoor lava rock shower. It has a real tree house feel to it. The kitchen is small but complete. The 1,300-square-foot, pavilion-style house sleeps four and is also furnished with attention to detail and flair. I particularly like its outdoor shower and screened-in sleeping porch. (There are two "real" bedrooms, though.) Host Robin Gaffney lives off property but is very attentive to guests' needs. *Rates*: $$–$$$; no children under 14; three-night minimum. *Facilities and amenities*: two units, full kitchens, use of water sport equipment, no A/C.

Ekena (808-248-7047; ekenamaui .com), off Hana Hwy. Very quiet and very private, Ekena is a two-story pole house that's been elegantly furnished. High above the Hana Highway, the house sits on 8 acres of cleared land with 360-degree views of forest and ocean. It's a conversation stopper every time. You'll drink in the views outside from a wraparound lanai or inside thanks to plenty of glass doors and plush couches. Stock up on groceries and whip up a nice dinner from the gourmet kitchen. The upstairs unit, Seabreeze, measures 2,600 square feet; Jasmine, on the ground floor, is half that size. Host Robin Gaffney lives off property but is very attentive to guests' needs. *Rates*: $$$–$$$$ for up to four people (big bucks for the whole house, which accommodates eight); no children under 14; three-night minimum. *Facilities and amenities*: Only one of two units rented at a time, water sport equipment (free), full kitchen, no A/C.

Camping & Cabins

Waianapanapa State Park Cabins (808-984-8109; hawaiistateparks.org/ camping/maui), Hana Hwy. In one of Hawai'i's prettiest parks, these cabins are almost as good a bargain as a frequent-flier ticket to the islands. The cabins are relatively modern (for the state park system), though extremely rustic. Mosquitos, in particular, love this place. The bedrooms have two double bunk beds; two more people can sleep in the living room. The kitchens have an electric range, a refrigerator, and a reasonable supply of utensils. Towels and linens are provided. Book months in advance, although you can sometimes get in on short notice. Twelve cabins; $ for four to six; five-night maximum. The park accepts personal checks if they are sent in 30 days prior to your visit, otherwise payment must be made by money order or cashier's check.

Oheo Gulch Campground (808-248-7375; nps.gov/hale), beyond the Kipahulu visitors center. These 100 tent sites are available on a first-come, first-served basis. No permit is necessary; no water is available; no fires; chemical toilets; three-night maximum. Don't forget to bring the tent, since it rains a great deal here. Vehicle fee $10.

✳ Where to Eat

To say that dining options in Hana are "limited" is a bit like saying Ronald Reagan was "kinda conservative." (Read: major understatement.) You won't go hungry, but you'll probably eat at every single place below if you stay more than 24 hours. Furthermore, you and the so-called grocery store will become quite intimate. Don't forget to consult listings in Pa'ia (see "Upcountry & Haleakala") if you're heading to Hana.

ON THE WAY TO HANA

Nahiku Coffee Shop, Smoked Fish Stand, and Ti Gallery, between MM 28 and 29, Hana Hwy. Coffee shop open 9–5:30 daily; fish stand open 10–5 daily (except Thurs.). Carved out of a swatch of jungle, this ingenious place comes as a something of an oasis. The makeshift café serves baked goods and smoothies, as well as smoked fish kebabs and *kalua* pork sandwiches.

HANA

Ka'uiki Restaurant Hotel Hana-Maui (808-248-8211; hotelhanamaui .com), Hana Hwy. Open for all three meals daily. With each meal served the dining room is getting up to par with the rest of the resort. While the menu changes daily to reflect the freshest ingredients available (98 percent of the produce comes from Maui, and 80 percent of it is organic), a few generalizations can be made. Cuisine is neoclassical regional Hawaiian, overseen by a New England Culinary Institute graduate, John Cox, who has trained at other Passport-owned properties. Portions from the daily tasting menu are smaller than normal, almost tapas sized. This ostensibly encourages broadening your palate to enjoy a variety of locally caught seafood and locally raised beef. Think along the lines of sautéed-potato-crusted opakapaka with Japanese mushroom ragout and sherry bacon jus. All in all, it's a lovely experience. Reservations highly recommended. A Hawaiian buffet with Hawaiian entertainment is held on Friday evenings at 7; $50 adults, $35 children. Otherwise, breakfast $$, lunch $$–$$$, dinner entrées $$–$$$$.

Hana Ranch Restaurant (808-248-8255; hotelhanamaui.com), Hana Hwy. Open for lunch daily, dinner Wed. and Fri. This pleasant and more-than-serviceable restaurant,

owned by the hotel, has indoor and outdoor seating. On my last visit, I enjoyed a simple but satisfying lunchtime burger. (Time your meal to avoid the tour-bus crush.) The take-out window dispenses an average of 3,000 meals daily—local dishes like teriyaki plate lunches and mahimahi sandwiches. Reservations required for dinner on Fridays. Window average $ per person; lunch $$, dinner entrées $$–$$$.

Tu Tu's Snack Shop (808-248-8224), on the harbor. Open Mon.–Sat. The only reason this rudimentary fast-food window is even mentioned in a guidebook is because Hana's eating options are so limited. Local plate lunches like loco moco (a burger, egg, and rice with gravy) are de rigueur. If that doesn't catch your fancy, humankind can live on Roselani ice cream alone. I've done it. (See *Roselani*.) Dishes $.

Hasegawa General Store (808-248-8231), Hana Hwy. Open 7–7 Mon.–Sat. Normally, frozen sandwiches wouldn't make it into a guidebook, but again, options are limited here! The original Hasegawa burned in 1990, but the latest incarnation, in a former theater, looks much the same, with a world of merchandise piled haphazardly in the aisles.

BEYOND HANA
You can gather sustenance from the **Seven Pools Smoothie Stand** and from **Lualima**, an environmental coffee farm beyond the Pools of Oheo.

✳ Entertainment
Ⓨ **Paniolo Bar** (808-248-8211), Hotel Hana-Maui. Open nightly. Come in the early evening (nightly except Wed. and Fri.) when musicians play and sing, and stick around for some

If That Is a Breadfruit

✪ ROSELANI

Savored for its velvety smooth texture (thanks to its 12 to 16 percent butter-fat content) and revered because it's the only ice cream made on Maui, Roselani ice cream (roselani.com) is definitely a local favorite. Ben & Jerry, step aside.

David "Buddy" Nobriga, patriarch of the Nobriga family, taught his five children not only how to make this fabulous ice cream but also to have strong values. In the words of his father, "Family comes first, business and community service follow closely." Clearly his children have learned these lessons well, because in 2000 Roselani was named Family Business of the Year and Outstanding Small Business Philanthropist of the Year. Putting their money where your taste buds are, Roselani introduced a wildly successful new flavor in 2007, Aloha Cherry Truffle, part of whose proceeds benefit the Maui Memorial Medical Center Foundation to help promote breast cancer awareness and education. Even without the altruism attached, the flavor is worth every calorie!

Buddy's only daughter, Catherine Nobriga Kim, runs the business today, and she's a self-diagnosed perfectionist. She often goes around buying Roselani ice cream from local grocery stores to test the quality. (She even has a special cooler in her car for these expeditions.) When she's not test-ing existing product, she's cre-ating new recipes like cranberry sorbet, which she makes every Thanksgiving.

Roselani ice cream is stocked by most Maui markets, but you can also find it in these scooping parlors: **Hula Cook-ies and Ice Cream**, Ma'alaea; **The Market**, at Maui Tropical Plantation, Waikapu; **Peggy Sue's**, Kihei; **Tu Tu's** (see *Where to Eat*), Hana. I must confess: I don't know whether it's all in my mind or not, but Roselani's tastes better in Hana than anywhere else on the island.

relaxing talk-story. If only someone
could bottle this laid-back vibe. . . .
You can also eat *pupus* at the bar.

✳ Selective Shopping

Visitors don't go to Hana to shop;
nonetheless, there's one fine gallery
and a historic general store.

SPECIAL SHOPS

✪ **Hasegawa General Store** (808-
248-8231; hanamaui.com), Hana Hwy.
Open daily. You can't go to Hana and
not go to Hasegawa. It's impossible.
Established in 1910, the quirky general store represents the heart of town,
its aisles overflowing with every conceivable thing you might ever need
out here. Fishing gear, perhaps?
Movies or sandals? Organic coffee?
Books about Hana? The other store in
town, **Hana Ranch Store** (808-248-
8261), Mill St., isn't nearly as interesting, but you'll probably end up there,
too, because there's nowhere else to
wander when you're in the mood to
wander.

Hana Coast Gallery (808-248-8636
or 1-800-637-0188; hanacoast.com),
Hotel Hana-Maui. Open 9–5 daily.

HASEGAWA GENERAL STORE

One of the most tasteful resort galleries on Maui, this one features
exceptionally sophisticated finds.
Look for koa furniture, *tapa* cloth,
fiber collages, feather art, sculpture,
jewelry, and finely turned bowls made
by local artists.

Arabella Ark Gallery (808-248-
4890; arkceramics.net), at Baby Pigs
Crossing, about 8 miles beyond Hana,
between MM 46 and 45. Open 11–4
daily. Arabella's raku-fired porcelain
temples are more moving than anything I've seen in a long while. No
one can describe her work better than
she: "A temple is, perhaps, the physical manifestation of the soul's longing
to touch the infinite, meet the divine.
These clay temples and fortresses,
forged in the flames of a firing, represent spiritual journeys of those quests
of the soul that transcend time, place,
nationality, race." Other work includes
whimsical but weighty teapots and
haunting, bisque-fired, paper-clay wall
tablets. Arabella fearlessly goes to
uncharted territory. Don't miss it.

See also **Nahiku Coffee Shop**,
Smoked Fish Stand, and **Ti Gallery**
under *Where to Eat*.

SMOOTHIE STAND

Lanaʻi 3

LANA'I

I like to think of visits to Lana'i as taking a vacation from my vacation. By conventional definitions, there's very little to do here. And therein lies its appeal.

Until recently, Lana'i was a destination only for trailblazers and hunters. The small island, known in the 1900s primarily for its pineapples and exotic game, had been shunned by visitors and settlers alike since Polynesians settled Hawai'i.

Old Hawaiian legends identify Lana'i as cursed, a place of evil spirits. The original trailblazer was Kaulula'au, exiled here by his father, a Maui king, for mischievous behavior. He tricked the demons into drowning themselves and made the island potentially inhabitable, but few people took the opportunity. Even would-be conquerors were repelled. When a chief from the Big Island invaded in 1778 to expand his domain, the army quickly exhausted the scarce food supply and began eating wild roots. After the diet agitated their systems, they renamed the island Lana'i Kamokuhi ("land of the loose bowels"). It's not been a history tailored to tourism.

In 1917, the Baldwin family from Maui purchased the island to grow sugar-cane. But it wasn't successful; there wasn't enough water on Lana'i. And a mere five years later, James Dole, founder of Hawai'i's pineapple industry, bought most of the island for $1.1 million and established the plantation that totally dominated the economy. The first pineapples were shipped in 1926. Until recently Lana'i, exclusively devoted to pineapples, was the world's largest pro-ducer of pineapples. Dole also constructed the little Hotel Lana'i and Lana'i City, the island's only town (where all services are located), to house Filipino plantation workers.

Castle & Cooke, a primary shareholder in the Dole Corporation, kept the focus on pineapples until the mid-1980s, when rising worker wages precluded profitability. That's when David Murdock, the chairman of Castle & Cooke, decided that tourism would be the island's savior and purchased the 140-square-mile island for $675 million. The last pineapples, save for a 100-acre patch that supplies the island's needs, were picked and shipped in 1992. Retrained in the service sector, most of the island's 3,200 residents now work for the Lana'i Com-pany, the nonagricultural subsidiary of Castle & Cooke.

The island's first cautious step into tourism back in 1990 and 1991 was modest in many respects, but not in aspiration. Almost overnight, Lana'i was trans-

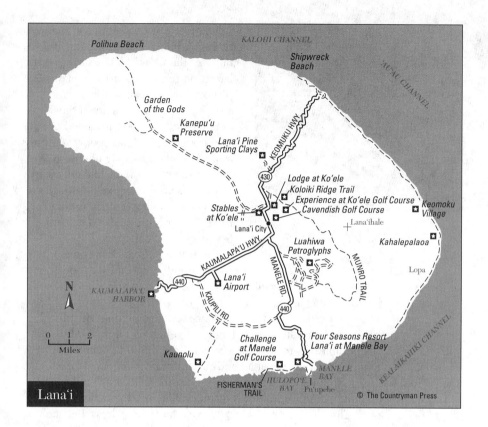

Lanaʻi

formed. The two resort hotels permitted for now—or for the foreseeable future—are absolutely stunning in elegance. The Lodge at Koʻele and the Manele Bay Hotel, both Four Seasons properties, are trailblazers for the Hawaiian tourist industry of the 21st century: They embody modern world-class luxury combined with traditional Hawaiian charm. One is a grand manse on the edge of the forest; the other is a Mediterranean-style waterfront resort. About the time that Lanaʻi traded pineapples for tourists, it also adopted the moniker Hawaiʻi's Private Island. It's not surprising, then, that gazillionaire Bill Gates chose to get married on Lanaʻi in 1993. Gates booked all the rooms at the Lodge at Koʻele and Manele Bay Hotel (and the little Hotel Lanaʻi), rented all the island's rental cars, and chartered all the nearby boats and planes that otherwise could have brought prying cameras to the island during the special event. After staying at the Lodge or Manele Bay, you will understand why someone who could get married any-where in the world chose these two hotels.

You can still hunt on Lanaʻi, you can still stay at the simple Hotel Lanaʻi, and you can still rent a four-wheel-drive vehicle and explore a whopping 30 miles of paved terrain that includes rolling green pastures, parched patches that resemble Greek islands, mist-shrouded mountain forests, and a rocky desert landscape straight out of *The Flintstones*. You can now play golf on world-class courses,

CLASSIC LANA'I LANDSCAPE

ride horseback, snorkel in a marine preserve, hike remote trails (all 100 miles of them), watch the sun set brilliantly on red rocks, or shoot clay pigeons. Or you can simply while away your days and nights in the unparalleled luxury of Manele Bay or The Lodge. Some guests only venture away from their lodging of choice to dine at the other one, while others are just too dazzled to get very far beyond The Lodge's hilltop golf course and the beach at Manele Bay. The choice is yours; don't feel guilty.

However, most visitors come on a day trip, while others come for a few nights to celebrate a special occasion at one of the two resorts. Well-to-do *kama'aina* come for a retreat, while others come because they revel in staying at the world's most posh places.

Though the changes on the island are, in some ways, momentous, it still retains its pristine charm. Residents are friendly, of generous spirit, and hospitable, waving from their cars to strolling visitors. Committed to maintaining its Hawaiian character, Lana'i remains quiet and rural, its unconventional beauty the perfect recipe for solitude seekers. There are no stoplights and barely any cars, much less a supermarket or a shopping center. Slip into the native way of life to find a new rhythm. The virgin isle may have a fancy new dress, but she's staying as pure and simple as *poi*.

GUIDANCE

Destination Lana'i (aka **Lana'i Visitor Center**) (808-565-7600 or 1-800-947-4774; visitlanai.net), 431 Seventh St., Suite A, Lana'i City. Open 9–4 weekdays. This very knowledgeable information bureau is a great go-to resource. They also have useful calendar listings: Check out the Pineapple Festival in early July; the Aloha Festival (alohafestivals.com), a state-wide event in late September or early October; and the Christmas Festival on the first Saturday of December.

Maui Visitor's Bureau (808-244-3530; visitmaui.com), 1727 Wili Pa Loop, Wailuku, Maui. Open 8–4:30 weekdays. The MVB also represents Lana'i and Moloka'i, providing maps, vacation planners, and brochures.

MORE WEB SITES

islandoflanai.com (Castle & Cook Resorts)

gohawaii.com/lanai (Hawai'i Visitor's & Convention Bureau)

state.hi.us/dlnr (Hawai'i's Department of Lands and Natural Resources)

NEWSPAPERS

Pick up a copy of the very local, weekly *Lana'i Times* for a neighborly view of what's important.

Call the **National Weather Service** (808-565-6033) to learn about wind and wave conditions.

MEDICAL EMERGENCY

Lana'i Community Hospital (808-565-6411), 628 Seventh St., Lana'i City. Open 24/7.

GETTING THERE

By air from the mainland: There are no direct mainland flights into Lana'i; you must fly through Honolulu. The Lana'i airport is 4 miles from town; from there, it takes a mere 10 minutes to get into Lana'i City, 25 minutes to Manele Bay. If you're not staying at one of the resorts, call a taxi. When the opportunity arises, I like flying in on Tuesday, the one day when bread is flown in. (You can tell that folks are new to Lana'i if they run out of bread; longtime residents always have some frozen.)

Interisland by air: It's a short hop from Honolulu. **Island Air** (808-565-6744 or 1-800-652-6541; islandair.com) operates eight daily propeller flights (30 minutes) between Honolulu and Lana'i. Tickets cost $53–90. If you're flying from a neighbor island, you have to fly through Honolulu. **Go! Express Airlines** (1-888-435-9462; iflygo.com) also flies to Lana'i from Honolulu and Maui twice daily for $49–79 one way.

Interisland by boat: **Expeditions** (808-661-3756 or 1-800-695-2624; go-lanai.com) operates a passenger ferry between Manele Harbor and Lahaina (Maui), and Manele Harbor and Ma'alaea (Maui). Consider taking Dramamine when the seas are rough; it's a small boat, and you'll feel every wave. Five or six boats ply the waters daily; the trip takes 45–60 minutes. Round-trip tickets are $50 adults, $40 ages 2–11. As a wintertime bonus, you might see whales from the boat. If you're not staying at one of the resorts, call a taxi to take you into town.

NOTHING IS VERY FAR AWAY.

GETTING AROUND

Lana'i, devoid of a single traffic light, is only 13 miles wide and 18 miles long, but it can be terribly easy to get lost on all of the unmarked dirt roads. Ask locals for directions when it seems necessary, and get a decent island map from the resorts.

Guests of the Hotel Lanaʻi, Manele Bay Hotel, and the Lodge at Koʻele have access to the hourly shuttles that run among the properties (and by extension, the famed Hulopoʻe Beach and Lanaʻi City). There are no island buses.

Lanaʻi City, more a village than anything remotely approaching a city, is picturesque, if not exactly pretty. The town's centerpiece is Dole Square, ringed with towering Cook and Norfolk Island pine trees, and surrounded by a residential neighborhood of former pineapple workers from the Philippines. The Hotel Lanaʻi is on the main street, which is great for a stroll. The Lodge at Koʻele, where it can be foggy and cool, is on the outskirts of town within easy walking distance; Manele Bay Hotel and Hulopoʻe Beach, which are perennially sunny, are a shuttle ride away on the coast.

Hwy. 440 is also known as the Kaumalapau Highway or Manele Road.

As a gauge of distance, it's 40 miles round-trip down to Shipwreck Beach and back.

By four-wheel drive or car: Since there are only 30 miles of paved road, and all the fun happens along a honeycomb of dirt roads, splurging on a four-wheel drive isn't really a splurge—it's a necessity. While there is no need to rent a car upon arrival, it would be a shame to come to Lanaʻi and not rent something for at least one day of exploring. There are a limited number of Jeeps, so reserve a vehicle a few weeks in advance, particularly during the holiday periods. Before setting out, fill up on gas, snacks, and water.

Dollar Rent-a-Car (aka **Lanaʻi City Service**) (808-565-7227 or 1-800-533-7808), at the **Lanaʻi Plantation Store**, rents cars ($60 for a compact) and four-wheel Jeeps ($139). Since there are only about 35 vehicles in the fleet, reserve early.

Adventure Lanaʻi Ecocenter (808-565-7373; adventurelanai.com), which rents Jeep Wranglers for $139–159 daily, will arrange pickup and drop-off at resorts, the ferry, or the airport. Rentals include roof racks (to carry surfboards, kayaks, and the like), an ice chest, towels, snorkeling gear, and an island map. Adventure Lanaʻi also rents quad ATVs, mountain bikes, and kayaks.

By shuttle: A complimentary resort shuttle takes guests of the Manele Bay Hotel, the Lodge at Koʻele, and Hotel Lanaʻi between town and Manele Bay throughout the day.

By taxi: **Rabaca's Limousine Service** (808-565-6670). If you're heading to The Lodge at Koʻele and you are a party of four or more, this service is cheaper ($95 for one to six people) than the one provided by the resort ($35 per person). But if you are a party of four or less heading to the Manele Bay Hotel, you're better off going on the resort shuttle at $25 per person.

TOP FIVE "MUSTS" FOR FIRST-TIME VISITORS
Snorkel at Hulopoʻe Beach
Visit Garden of the Gods
Enjoy afternoon tea in front of the fire at The Lodge at Koʻele
Hike or drive the Munro Trail
Venture out to Shipwreck Beach
Bonus Idea: Go home rested

ISLANDWIDE TOURS

By land: **Rabaca's Limousine Service** (808-565-6670). The Rabaca clan will take you wherever you want to go by car, including off road to the Garden of the Gods, Shipwreck Beach, or wherever. Private tours are $95 per hour with a three-hour minimum. If you're pressed for time, three hours will give you a good overview of the island.

TOP FIVE IDEAS FOR REPEAT VISITORS
Stay at Hotel Lana'i
Try your aim at sporting clays
Hunt for petroglyphs
Watch mist collect on Cook Island pine trees
Camp at Hulopo'e Beach

✳ To See & Do

Exploring out from Lana'i City.

Central

Lana'i City. It's a hefty moniker for such a small village. Built in the mid-1920s to house laborers from the pineapple plantation, this tiny town is basically just a grid of streets surrounding Dole Park. Almost every single visitor's service is on, or within a block of, the green park. By the time you read this, Lana'i City may have a new jail on Dole Park, but you can expect them to preserve the fascinating old one and perhaps turn it into the visitor's services outpost. Stroll around the side roads of Lana'i City to soak in the colorful, single-story plantation houses marked by tin roofs and tidy front yards.

Note the island's towering, signature Cook Island pine trees lining the main drag, Lana'i Avenue. Then note the giant Norfolk Island specimen in front of The Lodge at Ko'ele. Even longtime locals can't tell me the differences between the two varieties; try to see the distinguishing characteristics for yourself.

Situated at an elevation of 1,600 feet, Lana'i City is subject to cool evenings and mornings, occasionally overcast and damp conditions, and creeping fog banks. It comes as a welcome change to *kama'aina* from neighboring islands and to sophisticated travelers who appreciate variety on an otherwise conventionally tropical holiday.

Check out the Ka Lokahi O Ka Malamalama church, built in 1938 to serve Lana'i's growing population. It sits right next to The Lodge at Ko'ele.

Munro Trail. More commonly used as a four-wheel-drive route as opposed to a hiking trail, this rutted dirt path (not well marked at all) runs along a ridge as it winds its way to the top of Lana'ihale ("house of Lana'i"; 3,370 feet). Depending on who's measuring and from where, the trail is between 8.8 and 11 miles in length. If the mountain sports clear weather in the morning, head out spontaneously—if rentals are available at the last minute. You'll be rewarded with sweeping views of Hauloa Gulch (2,000 feet) and panoramas encompassing all the major neighbor islands except Kaua'i. It's the only spot in Hawai'i that takes in so much. By the afternoon, clouds often roll in and there's little point in going. In an effort to reforest the area and slow the soil erosion, the route was planted with Cook Island pine trees in the late 1910s by New Zealander George

Munroe. He was also aware that Cook Island pine needles siphon off upward of 40 gallons of water per hour from the fog that settles in, providing a more hospitable habitat for other growth. By all means, stay away when it's been raining, for the route turns slippery and slick. It basically becomes a big muddy mess. Even in a four-wheel drive, you'll be sliding sideways on a high and narrow "road" without shoulders. (Trust me; I know from whence I speak.) For hiking details, see *Hiking*.

To reach the trail, take Hwy. 440 south from Lana'i City for about 5 miles, turn left (*mauka*) up an unmarked red-dirt road, and keep heading upward.

Luahiwa Petroglyphs. This baker's dozen of boulders, strewn about a 3-acre site, is marked by stick-figure etchings of humans and animals. Dating back to two different periods (the 1500s and the late 1700s), these petroglyphs are among the very best in Hawai'i. No exaggeration. Perhaps fittingly, they're hard to find. Take Hwy. 440 south for 2 miles from Lana'i City and turn left onto an unmarked dirt road near a stand of pine trees. After about a mile, turn left near the water tank, then veer right and head to the end of the unmarked trail. That sounds about right.

Northeast

⚑ **Shipwreck Beach** (aka **Kaiolohia Bay**), 10 miles from Lana'i City. Half the fun of Shipwreck is getting there: The expansive views of Moloka'i, Maui, and the Pacific are dramatic. Great for beachcombing and walking, this 8-mile beach is so named because of the *Liberty Ship* grounded offshore. No one knows exactly how it got there, but this stretch of waterway has historically been treacherous to navigate. To reach it, head to the end of Keomoku Highway and turn left along a rutted and sandy route, where you'll eventually pass a ramshackle "Federation Camp," built by Filipino plantation workers in the 1950s. A few still inhabit the structures.

Keomoku. This ghost town, far off the beaten path, is really just a collection of abandoned homes, overgrown gravestones, and overrun rock walls. Built in the late 19th century to serve as the headquarters for a local sugar company, and subsequently used for ranching when the sugar industry died, this once booming community finally went bust in 1954. It also claims Lana'i's oldest church, dating to 1903 and partly restored. To reach it, continue 5 miles beyond Shipwreck Beach on an unpaved road to the right.

Northwest

Kanepu'u Preserve. Owned by The Nature Conservancy, this 590-acre tract is the last remaining stand of dryland forest in Hawai'i. It contains upward of 50 native and endangered plant species, including gardenia and sandalwood trees. One of the few Lana'i places with a well-marked trailhead, Kanepu'u has a short (15-minute) but illuminating self-guided loop trail. To reach Kanepu'u, take Polihua Road 6 miles beyond the stables in Lana'i City. When you meet the cattle guard, you've entered the preserve. See also *Hiking*.

✪ **Garden of the Gods** (aka **Keahikawelo**). Not a garden of omniscient beings, unless you believe stones have divine energy, this so-called garden is what passes for Lana'i's most visited attraction. It's really quite dramatic, especially in early morning or late afternoon when the play of light grows more intense and long shadows are cast from the gods. Barren as the South Dakota Badlands and as windswept as the moon, these rocks are an eerie sight. Erosion has taken its toll on them. As for the color palette, Benjamin Moore paint chips have nothing on them. Hues cover the spectrum from red to orange to yellow, from brown to gray to ocher and back again. The rock cairns, by the way, were built by visitors and have no more meaning than they do elsewhere. To reach the Garden of the Gods, just keep going beyond Kanepu'u Preserve.

ℱ **Polihua (Beach)**. Lovely to look at but not delightful for swimming, Polihua is usually deserted. That makes the long, wide, white-sand beach even more alluring than it would be otherwise. Except for the wind. In winter, it's a great place for humpback whale sightings. To reach it, continue a few miles beyond Garden of the Gods, to the very end of the slow dirt road.

Southwest

Palawai Basin. Although it measures a whopping 15,000 acres, you'd probably never really notice that the flat area south and east of Lana'i City was a collapsed volcanic caldera. But it is. The volcano forms the basis of the island. Notice the 100-acre pineapple field here, near the airport, which supplies all the island's mighty pineapple requirements.

Kaunolu. The island's most important historical archaeological site is a former fishing village—but not just any fishing village. Marked by stone foundations and he'iau ruins, Kaunolu dates to the late 1700s when it served as Kamehameha the Great's summer getaway. Kahekili's Leap, a 60-foot precipice with only 12 feet of water below it, was named in honor of the revered Maui chief. Warriors would try to impress King Kamehameha the Great by making this leap of faith. Look for Kaunolu only if you need excuse for exploration; the road is bumpy, and it's hot and dry here. To reach it, take Hwy. 440 south and after the airport turn left, continue 2 miles, then turn right and head 3 miles to the end of the road.

Kaumalapa'u Harbor. Built in the 1920s by the Dole Corporation to ship pineapples worldwide, this harbor is not scenic in the least. These days the only action it gets is on Thursday, when the supply barge comes in from Honolulu. If you're on the island long enough, you may notice that milk usually runs out by Wednesday. That's just one reason why the arrival of the supply ship is an event—not like the Macy's Thanksgiving Day Parade in New York City or anything, but a Lana'i-style event nonetheless. When the barge calls into port, cranes swing into action and pluck freight off the barge as locals begin guessing who's purchased a new car, for instance. To reach the harbor, continue 4 miles beyond the airport until you reach the end of the road.

TOURING THE GARDEN OF THE GODS

Manele Bay. The ferry from Maui calls here, and the island's best beach is next door. Other than that, all you'll see are 1,000-foot lava cliffs and the offshore Pu'upehe (aka Sweetheart Rock). It's said that a husband kept his beautiful wife sequestered in a sea cave here because he was afraid other men would take a liking to her. But one day the sea surged into the cave and swept her away. The dismayed husband recovered his wife's drowned body and buried her on this rock before jumping off it to his own death. Take Manele Road (Hwy. 440) south to the bottom of the hill, the end of the road.

SPECIAL PROGRAMS

𝒮 **Kids for All Seasons** (808-565-2398; lanai-resorts.com), Manele Bay Hotel. This program, for children ages 5–12, is all about the spirit of adventure and an appreciation of island culture. Small-group activities include themed arts and crafts, exploration of Hulopo'e Bay tide pools, lizard hunting, and having a ball all day long (i.e. playing various games with balls). Morning and afternoon sessions (including lunch); complimentary.

✳ Spas

Four Seasons Resort Lana'i at Manele Bay (808-565-2088; fourseasons.com/manelebay/spa). Open 8:30–7 daily. This spa is lovely to behold, complete with lots of wood, granite, and marble. You'll get all the sensory pampering and upscale services you've come to expect from this resort. Usual suspects include an aromatherapy massage, a signature banana coconut scrub, cooling ti-leaf wrap, seaweed body masks, rain forest showers, steam rooms, and saunas. The ocean views, coupled with a healthy menu of classes, may just make this your favorite spot in the resort.

Four Seasons Resort Lana'i, The Lodge at Ko'ele (808-565-7300; four seasons.com/koele/spa). At press time, The Lodge was getting a new Wellness Center and Spa; inquire about details. Although the treatment menu is limited (*lomi lomi* massages, hot stone massages, and "the big stretch"), they're so fine that they suffice except for the most hard-core spagoers. Along those same lines, the fitness center is small but sufficient, but I particularly like the heated swimming pool on a chilly afternoon.

✳ Outdoor Activities

BICYCLING/RENTALS

Mountain bikes are available to guests of both resorts to ply the rugged, red-dirt roads that lead over to heiaus and through the woods to secluded beaches.

Adventure Lana'i Ecocenter (808-565-7373; adventurelanai.com); pickup and drop-off from your lodging; $59 per day rental includes backpacks and a picnic lunch. These folks offer a few different half-day tours; call for prices. You can trek through upcountry Lana'i on a novice downhill bike trip, travel along the beach road to Kaiolohia Bay, explore a shipwreck just past Po'iwa Gulch, and hike to petroglyphs. Call 24 hours in advance.

GOLF

The Experience at Ko'ele (808-565-4653; golfonlanai.com/koele), adjacent to The Lodge at Ko'ele. Truly an "experience," this Greg Norman– and Ted Robinson–designed course is rife with wild turkeys and lush with pine trees and water, water everywhere. Waterfalls and streams will have you bubbling with fury or satisfaction in no time, depending on your play. Greens fees cost $210 for resort guests (for unlimited same-day play), $225 for non–resort guests ($50 to play Manele later in the day), $50 to replay nine holes (an option for resort guests only). Collared shirts and spikeless shoes are required. Reservations can be made by phone 30 days prior to tee time.

The Challenge at Manele (808-565-2222; golfonlanai.com/manele), adjacent to the Manele Bay Hotel. Truly a "challenge," this Jack Nicklaus–designed links course offers serious Pacific views and an 18-hole putting course. Along the way, you'll have to contend with endemic archaeological sites, lava fields, and kiawe trees. The signature 17th hole, where software gazillionaire Bill Gates was married, is a popular place for lesser mortals to tie the knot as well. Fees same as The Experience, above.

Cavendish Municipal Golf Course (no phone), adjacent to The Lodge at Ko'ele. This par-36, nine-hole course is a throwback to the 1920s, when it was built by the Dole Corporation for its plantation workers. There is no club rental or tee time sign-up—nor any clubhouse, for that matter. Free, but a small donation is appreciated.

HIKING

✪ **Munro Trail**. Pick up the trailhead at the Lana'i Cemetery (the only place where the poorly marked trail is actually marked), off Hwy. 440. Budget a difficult eight hours for this uneven terrain, which has an elevation gain of about 1,400 feet. If you're pressed for stamina or time, you can cut the hike to 8 versus 11 miles if you hike the first 4, enjoy great views of Lana'i City, and then head back from whence you came. For more details, see *To See & Do*.

Ko'ele Nature Hike. Tours depart at 11 AM from The Lodge at Ko'ele. The 5-mile trip takes about three hours and costs $15 per person.

Koloiki Ridge Trail, trailhead behind The Lodge at Ko'ele (ask the concierge for details). Sometimes called the "Ko'ele Nature Hike," this 5-mile loop trail is nice and easy. It may not be well marked, but it runs through sturdy stands of ginger and pines and affords expansive views of Maunalei Valley, Maui, and Moloka'i. Depart early in the morning for the most reliable weather and clearest views.

MUNRO TRAIL

The Nature Conservancy (808-537-4508; nature.org) leads monthly hikes within the rarefied Kanepu'u Preserve. Make the effort if the timing is right; reservations required.

Fisherman's Trail. Take an hour to follow the shoreline and cliffs around the Manele Bay Hotel and skirting the golf course. The Manele Bay hotel leads a 90-minute fitness hike on Tuesday and Friday mornings at 9 AM ($15).

HORSEBACK RIDING

Four Seasons Resort's Stables at Ko'ele (808-565-4424 information or 808-565-4555 reservations; fourseasons.com/koele). The stables across from The Lodge at Ko'ele offer both western- and English-style riding for every ability level. You can take tame *"paniolo* nose-to-tail" guided trail rides through soaring pine forests and along sweeping alpine valleys, where you'll see Maui and Moloka'i from the plateau. (Trips depart in the morning and cost $95 per person.) More experienced riders will appreciate private rides ($160 per person for 90 minutes of riding). Not to be overlooked, little cowpokes can take pony rides— 10 minutes for $10. Shuttle service from the airport available for a fee.

SCUBA DIVING

Cathedrals I and II, off Hulopo'e Beach. This site is said—by experts who know more about diving than I do—to offer the best diving in Hawai'i. It proffers the opportunity for a positively religious experience. Cathedrals, aptly named because the chambers and caverns resemble a sanctuary when the morning light floods in, also feature pinnacles rising 60 feet from the seabed. Head out in the morning when fewer boats will disturb the solitude of your sanctuary.

See Trilogy under *Water Sports*.

SNORKELING

○ **Hulopo'e Beach**, fronting the Manele Bay Hotel. Of all the major Hawaiian islands, Lana'i has the clearest waters. Add lava outcroppings, coral clusters, and tide pools, and poof: You have arguably the best snorkeling in Hawai'i. Yes, on Lana'i, all the conditions converge at Hulopo'e. Tide pools are found on the eastern side of the bay; snorkeling is best on either end of the beach. Resort guests receive complimentary snorkeling equipment.

SPORTING CLAYS & ARCHERY

Lana'i Pine Sporting Clays & Archery Range (808-559-4600; fourseasons .com/koele), off Keomuku Hwy. If you've never hoisted a shotgun and taken aim at a clay discus (aka clay pigeon), this may be your single best chance. This well-laid-out course has 14 camouflaged stations rigged to release clay targets that mimic various patterns of bird flight. Safety precautions, and gun recoil, are thoroughly discussed. By the way, women tend to have better hand–eye coordination than men, so you may want to create your own "battle of the sexes" here. Cost: $85 for 25 targets and an extensive tutorial; $90 for 50 pigeons and a short lesson, $150 for 100. Free shuttle from The Lodge.

Resort and Hotel Lana'i guests can play (free) at the Manele Bay Hotel and The Lodge at Ko'ele (808-565-2072). Public courts in Lana'i City are also free and lit for night play; call 808-565-6979 to reserve.

WATER SPORTS

Trilogy (aka **Lanai Ocean Sports**) (808-661-4743 or 1-888-628-4800; sailtrilogy .com). Lana'i's coves and bays are well protected and pollution-free, which makes scuba diving, snorkeling, and sea kayaking great experiences for all levels. In business since the early 1970s, these outfitters provide a variety of guided water activities—including catamaran and inflatable boating trips and snorkeling and adventure rafting. As a bonus, you'll get a nice dose of history to accompany your trip. Departing from Manele Harbor, you can take a snorkeling and sailing trip along the sea cliffs of Kahekili Ho'e. Lunch, snacks, and gear are included for $202 for adults, half price for children. A sunset sail will set you back $106 for adults, half price for children. Or take a scuba dive from Hulopo'e Beach. They're offered to beginning divers for $102 per person; certified divers (ages 12 and above) can shave $10 off that price. More experienced divers have a two-tank option for $213. Reservations required; book online for a savings of 10 percent. Nondiving partners can also go along for the ride for $106.

Adventure Lana'i Ecocenter (808-565-7373; adventurelanai.com). These folks rent everything you could ever possibly need for water fun: boogie boards ($10), scuba gear ($49), and kayaks with snorkeling gear ($49). And they'll even pick you up at your hotel, drive you to Manele Harbor, and give you a quick lesson on how to use your equipment. They also offer myriad excursions, including daytime and nighttime diving adventures with certified guides, four-hour surfing safaris with instruction on positioning and techniques, and small-group kayaking and snorkeling adventures led by informative guides. On any given day, they'll recommend locations based on weather and conditions. Most three- to four-hour tours cost $149 for adults; children are half price. (Call about possible age restrictions.)

TRILOGY CATAMARANS

MAMMAL SEARCH

Trilogy (808-874-5649 or 1-888-628-4800; sailtrilogy.com). Departs weekdays from Manele Harbor at 10; 90 minutes. Trilogy offers onboard naturalists who will teach you about humpback whales as you travel to their breeding habitat to observe them up close. As you make your way along the ragged coastline and protected sea caves, you'll also see large schools of spinner dolphins. $80 adults, $40 children.

✳ Beaches

𝄐 **Hulopoʻe Beach**, adjacent to Manele Harbor and Manele Bay Hotel. For decades, until 1990 when the Manele Bay Hotel was built, the cognoscenti traveled to this isolated shore from Maui, bearing picnics along with their yearnings to flee the tourist crowds. The beach still has its allure, but it's now the home of Lanaʻi's top-notch Manele Bay Hotel.

Backed by a grassy area for picnics and barbecues and providing plenty of shade, this beach is the stuff of dreams. I'll go out on a sandbar (as opposed to a limb) and say that it's one of my three favorites in Hawaiʻi. It's a Hawaiian treasure, a fine stretch on a calm cove. Rarely approaching anyone's definition of crowded, Hulopoʻe is perfect for swimming and snorkeling. Since the hotel is a five-minute walk away, and its requisite beach shack dispensary is hidden in the trees, the beach remains delightfully void of any overbearing hotel presence. Tide pools form at the eastern end of the beach, begging for exploration; look for sea stars, sea cucumbers, little shrimp, and limpets. Colorful fish congregate at both ends of the crescent-shaped bay, begging for appreciation. Pods of spinner dolphins frolic within the bay, while whales breach offshore (Dec.–Apr.). What more could a reasonable person hope for? Okay, how about this: Fortunately, Hulopoʻe is the only beach on Lanaʻi that can be reached by a paved road. It's also protected as a Marine Life Conservation District.

See also **Shipwreck** and **Polihua** Beaches under *To See & Do*.

✳ Lodging

There aren't many places to stay here, but all the varieties of lodging are at least covered—from two absolutely outstanding resorts to simple but utterly luxurious camping.

THE LODGE AT KOʻELE

A note about the two luxury properties opened in 1990 and 1991 (which also changed ownership in 2006): Perhaps not as distinctive as the extraordinary Lodge at Koʻele, the Manele Bay Hotel has a more playful spirit and a chic countenance. Castle & Cooke, original owners of both places, wanted to offer two entirely different experiences, and they succeeded admirably. Each lodging has its own following, especially since they are now under the umbrella of Four Seasons. The young and fashionable are often drawn to Manele Bay, while more experienced travelers generally prefer The Lodge. Wherever you stay, you will have full and easy access to the other hotel, a free 20-minute shuttle ride away. And if, for some reason, you decide the sister property is better suited to you once you arrive, you may change hotels if there is availability.

RESORTS

✪ **Four Seasons Resort Lana'i, The Lodge at Ko'ele** (808-565-7300 or 1-800-321-4666; fourseasons.com/koele), Keomoku Hwy. An extensive and pitch perfect $50 million renovation by the Four Seasons in 2006 really put the luster back in this grand dame. An Upcountry-elegant and world-class small hotel, The Lodge (as it's affectionately called) is breathlessly beautiful, an exquisite creation unlike any other in Hawai'i. It regularly wins a steady stream of "best this" and "best that" awards. The low-rise Lodge, a classically proportioned Victorian plantation manor, is at once evocative of both the English countryside and the rural calm of Lana'i—especially since it sits at an elevation of 1,700 feet. Everything about The Lodge is executed in an elegantly low-key manner. The Great Hall, where I spend a great deal of time, makes even the most sumptuous hotel lobbies look drab. The beamed ceiling soars to 35 feet; stenciled eucalyptus floors are covered with colorful Thai carpets. The tallest fireplaces in Hawai'i frame the ends of the hall, rising above an amazing collection of European and Asian furniture grouped in cozy conversation areas. Reflecting the layered cultures brought to the islands by settlers from around the world, the décor is both elating and relaxing. Beyond the Great Hall are smaller parlors, each distinctively different. Behind The Lodge, set on 21 acres, are a manicured garden, stone-lined reflecting pond, fitness center and pool, an Orchid House, and walking paths. As you'd expect, dining is excellent (see *Where to Eat*). As for the guest rooms, the Ko'ele and garden rooms are similar in size and furnishings. Both offer painted headboards and carved pineapple-post beds, large LCD flat-screen TVs, Roman shades, and an ample lanai; some have stone fireplaces. Views tend to be expansive. Second-floor rooms with porches offer greater privacy than first-floor rooms with lanais. All in all, The Lodge is a resort that jolts you into a new awareness of life's possibilities. If you've grown jaded by the word *unique*, as I have, The Lodge will teach you its meaning anew. *Rates*: Rooms $$$$; children free in parent's room; inquire about many packages. *Facilities and amenities*: 102 rooms, heated pool, two restaurants (the **Dining Room** and the **Terrace**), world-class golf, three tennis courts, afternoon tea in the Great Hall, cocktails and appetizers in the bar, game room, wellness center and spa, horseback riding, sporting clays, bike rentals, concierge, wireless (fee), live music in bar, children's programs (free), airport transfer fee ($35 round-trip per person).

✪ **Four Seasons Resort Lana'i at Manele Bay** (808-565-7700 or 1-800-321-4666; fourseasons.com/manele bay), Manele Rd. Another $50 million dollar renovation (see The Lodge), another extraordinary success story. This lobby takes my breath away every time I enter. It's laid out to command a stunning perspective on the Pacific as you enter the hotel. European and Asian furnishings speak of worldly grandeur, although Hawaiian murals and tropical flowers remind you of where you are. Located

MANELE BAY HOTEL'S LOBBY

a five-minute stroll from Hulopoʻe Beach, Manele Bay Hotel offers accommodations in nine low-rise Mediterranean villas connected to each other by flowing lagoons and five lush theme gardens. Views from the rooms and suites differ, but all the quarters are spacious (700 square feet is the norm) and cosmopolitan. They feature carved four-poster beds, vibrant fabrics, a substantial lanai, and 40-inch LCD TVs. The marble baths come with a double vanity, a lounging tub, and a separate shower. The garden rooms, which overlook the lovely courtyards or the pool, may offer the best value. For a close, direct Pacific view, you have to move up to an oceanfront room. Manele Bay, the sibling to The Lodge at Koʻele that has the great beach, is a grand addition to Hawaiian hotels. Once you settle into the sand, into your room, or into one of the plush armchairs in the lobby, you may find yourself disinclined to leave the grounds of this island paradise. *Rates*: Rooms $$$$;

children free in parent's room. *Facilities and amenities*: 236 rooms, large pool, fabulous beach, three restaurants (including **Ihilani**, **Hulopoʻe Court**, and **Ocean Grill**), a bar with fabulous views, world-class golf, three tennis courts, fitness center and spa, teen center, horseback riding, sporting clays, snorkeling gear (free), concierge, wireless (fee), children's programs (free), business center, airport transfer fee ($35 round-trip per person).

BED & BREAKFASTS AND INNS

✿ **Hotel Lanaʻi** (808-565-7211; hotel lanai.com), 828 Lanaʻi Ave. Until the two resorts opened in 1990 and 1991, this small lodge was virtually the only place on the island open after dark. The Hotel remains, as it has been for decades, the favorite gathering spot of Lanaʻi residents for eating, drinking, and socializing. Originally built by the Dole Corporation in 1923 for its guests visiting on company business, the putty-colored, wood-framed building was also a boardinghouse for pineapple plantation supervisors. Each guest room is smallish but dif-

MANELE BAY HOTEL & HULOPOʻE BEACH

ferent, but you can count on them being fresh and tidy and having a private bath. (The hotel underwent a complete renovation in 2005.) Hawaiian quilts, ceiling fans, and a good dose of ahola upon check-in are par for the course at this sweet place. Ask for one of the four rooms with shared lanais for a good view of the Norfolk pines surrounding the lodge. Otherwise, they have in common hardwood floors, pedestal sinks, whitewashed pine furnishings, and patchwork quilts. Since this was formerly a plantation house, the walls are none too thick. The adjacent freestanding cottage, with a separate sitting room, is ideal for families or honeymooners. This is the only accommodation with a TV. *Rates*: $$; children (under eight) free in parent's room; two-night minimum. *Facilities and amenities*: 10 rooms and one cottage, **Lana'i City Grill** restaurant, access to services and facilities at two resorts (including beach transportation), continental breakfast, no A/C.

Dreams Come True (808-565-6961 or 1-800-566-6961; dreamscometrue lanai.com), 1168 Lana'i Ave. Dating to 1925 and renovated in 2000, this family-style plantation house has four guest rooms, is decorated with Asian antiques, and has a private bath. In addition to a nice garden, Michael and Susan Hunter's property has fruit trees that provide breakfast goods. *Rates*: $. *Facilities and amenities*: four rooms, full breakfast, in-house massage, complimentary activity-booking service, Internet access available, use of refrigerator and microwave, BBQ, no A/C, no phones.

CAMPING
Hulopo'e Beach (808-565-3975; 808-565-2970 reservations), Hulopo'e

Beach Park. Surrounded by kiawe trees and far enough from the resort to make it feel private, this is one of the few places in Hawai'i where I really like to camp. *Rates*: $20 for a permit, $5 per person per night; three-day maximum; pay for permits on arrival. *Facilities*: restrooms, showers, barbecue, and picnic area. By the way, camping on the beach is reserved for residents.

✳ Where to Eat
Although the dining choices on Lana'i are limited in many ways, you'll find everything from sophisticated four-star dining to unpretentious and unassuming plate-lunch places. Because the island is so small, practically all the eateries on Lana'i are reviewed here, which isn't normally the case.

DINING OUT
Dining Room (808-565-4580; four seasons.com/koele), Lodge at Ko'ele. Open for dinner nightly. Reminiscent of the Ahwahnee Hotel in Yosemite, the Four Seasons' dining room here is understated in an elegant way;

HOTEL LANA'I

rustically upscale with fine, fine service and a fine, fine wine list. New American dishes tend to be a bit heartier here than at Manele Bay because of how the cooler Upcountry climate affects guests' appetites. Although the menu changes seasonally, you might find mac-crusted Lana'i axis venison, Colorado lamb, or roasted duck. On my last visit, I was rather partial to scallops and poached Keahole lobster. Reservations required; children's menu. Entrées $$$$.

Ihilani (808-565-7700; fourseasons.com/manelebay), Manele Bay. Open for dinner Tues.–Sat. The main formal dining room at this Four Seasons specializes in Mediterranean- and island-influenced dishes like onaga alla puttanesca, risotto, and spinach gnocchi. As for the setting, think chandeliers, crystal, and silver. It's formal, it's romantic, it's got a too-fabulous wine list, and it's aptly named: *Ihilani* means "heavenly splendor"! Reservations required; children's menu. Entrées $$$$.

Terrace (808-565-4580; fourseasons.com/koele), Lodge at Ko'ele. Open for all three meals daily. Set between the Great Hall and the English gardens, this dignified restaurant is the casual alternative to the main dining room. I use *casual* loosely; it's lovely but low-key. Breakfast is a relaxing treat here. Try the brioche French toast; macadamia nut blintzes with mango and mascarpone; or poached eggs on blue crabcakes. The latter is fabulous. At lunchtime, the Terrace ups the ante on contemporary American comfort food with pan-seared tuna on baby spinach or a Lana'i venison pastrami melt sandwich. At suppertime, grilled pork chops with apple-onion potato pie share the stage

with pan-roasted, free-range chicken and forest mushrooms. Reservations recommended for dinner; children's menu. Breakfast $$, lunch $$, dinner entrées $$$.

Hulopo'e Court (808-565-7700; four seasons.com/manelebay), Manele Bay. Open for breakfast, lunch, and dinner daily. This "islandy" restaurant, with Lana'i murals, high ceilings, and Asian décor, is a more casual alternative to Manele Bay's signature restaurant. Dinner mains range from seared opakapaka and a Hawaiian trio of seafood to kiawe-grilled lamb, chops, steaks, and mahimahi. All dishes are prepared with locally available ingredients. Reservations recommended at dinner; children's menu. Breakfast à la carte $$, breakfast buffet $$$, lunch $$, dinner entrées $$$.

Lana'i City Grill (808-565-7211; hotellanai.com), Hotel Lana'i. Open for dinner nightly. There's only one real choice between luxe and laid-back, and this is it. Miss it and you miss an integral part of Lana'i. It's more or less a countrified lodge, with a cozy fireplace, Windsor chairs, wood paneling, and small but convivial bar. (You can't go wrong with a Lana'i tai.) It's a busy place, a place where everybody eventually knows your name. Luckily, it's also very good. Bev Gannon (of Maui's Hali'imaile General Store fame) serves as the "culinary advisor." Try the spit-roasted meats, a house specialty; oyster shooters; Maryland crab cakes; Joe's meat loaf; pork chops; and the pecan-crusted catch of the day. Reservations recommended. Entrées $$$$.

EATING OUT

The Experience at Ko'ele Clubhouse (808-565-4605; fourseasons.com/koele), at the golf course. Open for lunch daily. I really enjoy this casual place that dishes up light American dishes with great ocean views. With luck you'll get a table on the lanai. On my last visit, the citrus-glazed mahimahi catch-of-the-day grabbed my taste buds, as did the oversized smoked turkey club sandwich. If you're into sweet things, the ice cream sandwich will satisfy that proverbial sweet tooth. Children's menu. Lunch $–$$.

The Challenge at Manele Clubhouse (808-565-2232; fourseasons .com/manelebay), at the golf course. Open for lunch daily. You don't have to golf here to want to eat here. You might simply come for great outdoor views of Kaho'olawe and Maui's Mount Haleakala. Some say this clubhouse has Lana'i's best outdoor tables. Then again, they also offer lots of enticing appetizers, fancy sandwiches, and first rate island influenced dishes. Children's menu. Lunch $$.

Ocean Grille (808-565-7700; four seasons.com/manelebay), Manele Bay. Open for lunch daily, dinner Thurs.–Mon. This Four Seasons poolside grill dishes up creative wok concoctions, a bevy of large and small plates perfect for noshing, and mains from free-range chicken to local seafood with Pacific Rim influences. Children's menu. Lunch dishes $$, dinner entrées $$$$.

Pele's Other Garden (808-565-9628), Houston St., on Dole Park. Open for lunch weekdays. By day this informal New York–style deli prepares box lunches to go, pizzas, soups, organic salads, burritos, and thick pastrami sandwiches. By night, it's transformed into a "real" restaurant, an Italian-style eatery with tablecloths and fancier pasta dishes. The owners,

Barbara and Mark, have a nice back patio, too. Lunch $, dinner $$.

Blue Ginger Café (808-565-6363), Seventh St., on Dole Park. Open for all three meals daily. Don't let the plastic tablecloths deter you from this friendly place. Locals hang out on the front porch here (at four tables), enjoying breakfast omelets and killer French toast, lunchtime Spam on rice or fried saimin, pigs in a blanket, and mahimahi sandwiches. You should consider doing the same. Breakfast and lunch $, dinner entrées $$.

Café 565 (808-565-6622), Eighth and Ilima Sts., off Dole Park. Open for lunch and dinner weekdays, lunch Sat. In the interest of full disclosure, this café offers hot and cold subs and pizzas. Dishes $–$$.

Coffee Works (808-565-6962), Ilima St., a block off Dole Park. Open 6–3 Mon.–Sat. This former plantation house dishes up sweet and flavorful Roselani and Lapperts ice cream, both Hawaiian made. Beware (or be happy): Their milkshakes have about five scoops of ice cream in them! A low-key gathering place for locals in

PELE'S OTHER GARDEN

the morning; I enjoy an afternoon espresso here on the deck. They also have pizzas and bagels. Dishes under $10.

✪ **Afternoon Tea** (808-565-7300), Lodge at Koʻele. Served 3–5 daily. Much anticipated by in-house and other visitors, the complimentary afternoon tea (with scones, jam, and clotted cream) in front of a warming fire at The Lodge is a wonderfully comforting tradition.

GENERAL STORES

Pine Isle Market (808-565-6488), Eighth St., on Dole Park. Open Mon.–Sat. This market supplies most islanders' needs, from fishing supplies to food and household goods.

BAMBOO STANDS

Richard's Shopping Center (808-565-3000), Eighth St., on Dole Park. Open Mon.–Sat. The other market in town was founded in 1946 by Richard Tamashiro. This general store stocks breads from Central Bakery, liquor, a bevy of T-shirts, and groceries.

International Food & Clothing Center (808-565-6433), Ilima St., barely off Dole Park. Open daily except Sat. This old-fashioned place has more food (although the international descriptor is suspect) than clothing.

Lanaʻi Plantation Store (808-565-7227), Lanaʻi Ave., barely off Dole Park. Open daily. Car rentals, groceries, and gas.

✳ Entertainment

It's the simple things in life that you'll remember. Watch the moon and stars from your resort or hotel.

Lanaʻi City Grille (808-565-7211; hotellanai.com), Lanaʻi Ave. One of the best ways to enjoy the undeveloped island is to hang out here, listen to conversations, and ask occasional questions. Linger by the fireplace in the dining room during the cool evenings or sip a Lanaʻi tai at the low-key bar. Come for "Friday Under the Stars," with food and live music on the lanai. Last call at 8:30 PM.

Lanaʻi Playhouse (808-565-7500), Seventh St., Lanaʻi City. Shows Fri.–Tues. It was a big deal when this theater opened with Dolby surround sound.

The Great Hall, at The Lodge at Koʻele. Sit in front of one of two baronial fireplaces and really read the paper. Don't just skim the headlines. Or play cards with friends. Or sink into a plush red leather chair with a glass of port and marvel at how hard it is to get up. Or listen to someone play the piano.

ROMANTIC PLACES FOR COCKTAILS

☿ **Your own** (albeit temporary) private lanai. You're paying enough for the room, so stay in and pour yourself a drink at the Manele Bay Hotel or The Lodge at Ko'ele.

Hale Ahe'ahe, at the Manele Bay Hotel. The upscale, open-air lounge at the "House of Gentle Breezes" has easy-listening evening entertainment.

✳ Selective Shopping

All these tiny shops surround, or are barely off, Dole Park. Shops are generally closed after 5 PM and all day Sunday.

Gifts With Aloha (808-565-6589; giftswithaloha.com), Seventh St., on Dole Park. Kim and Phoenix Dupree have assembled a nice collection of books, clothes, local arts (like hand-blown glass and Japanese-style pottery), and products made on Maui. Don't miss it.

Dis 'N' Dat (808-565-9170; suzieo .com), Eighth St., on Dole Park. True to their pidgin store name, Barry and Suzie Osman sell a little of this and that, including a monstrous collection of jewelry and ornaments—all quite cool and interesting, and there's tons of it! I bet it'll be difficult to leave the shop empty-handed. Don't miss it.

Lana'i Art Center (808-565-7503; lanaiart.org), Seventh St., on Dole Park. Director Greg Cohen oversees a rich island resource whose motto includes the notion that "art is the unfettered expression of the human spirit: the place where the spirit soars and explores all possibilities . . . We

need art to refresh and nourish us; to coat daily life with a gilding of light and color; to open our hearts to nature, to the loveliness of this island." As Greg suggests, stop in to witness "the possibilities of artistic creation by people who would not ordinarily have those opportunities." If you can tear yourself away from the resorts, check out the two- to three-hour art classes in silk screening, raku, or fish printing.

Mike Carroll Gallery (808-565-7122; mikecarrollgallery.com), 443 Seventh St., barely off Dole Park. Mike and his wife, Kathy, operate this working studio, whose air is thick with linseed oil. If you can't afford an original, look into a limited-edition print on canvas, a mini monthly desk calendar, or note cards.

The Local Gentry (808-565-9130), Seventh St., one storefront off Dole Park. Head here for lovely, island-style casual and evening resort garb. This sweet shop carries aloha shirts, hemp and linen shirts, beach shoes, and beach bags. Who knew you'd find such things here?

Saturday Marketplace, on Dole Park. From 7 to 11 AM each Saturday (although most vendors finish at 10),

DIS 'N' DAT

the park comes alive with a small-scale produce market, plate-lunch purveyors (Japanese and Filipino style), Nellie's vegetable or banana lumpia, low-key and locally made arts and crafts, and jams and jellies made by B&B host Dolores Fabrao. It doesn't get more homespun than this. I like to show up at 6 AM when they're setting up.

Moloka'i 4

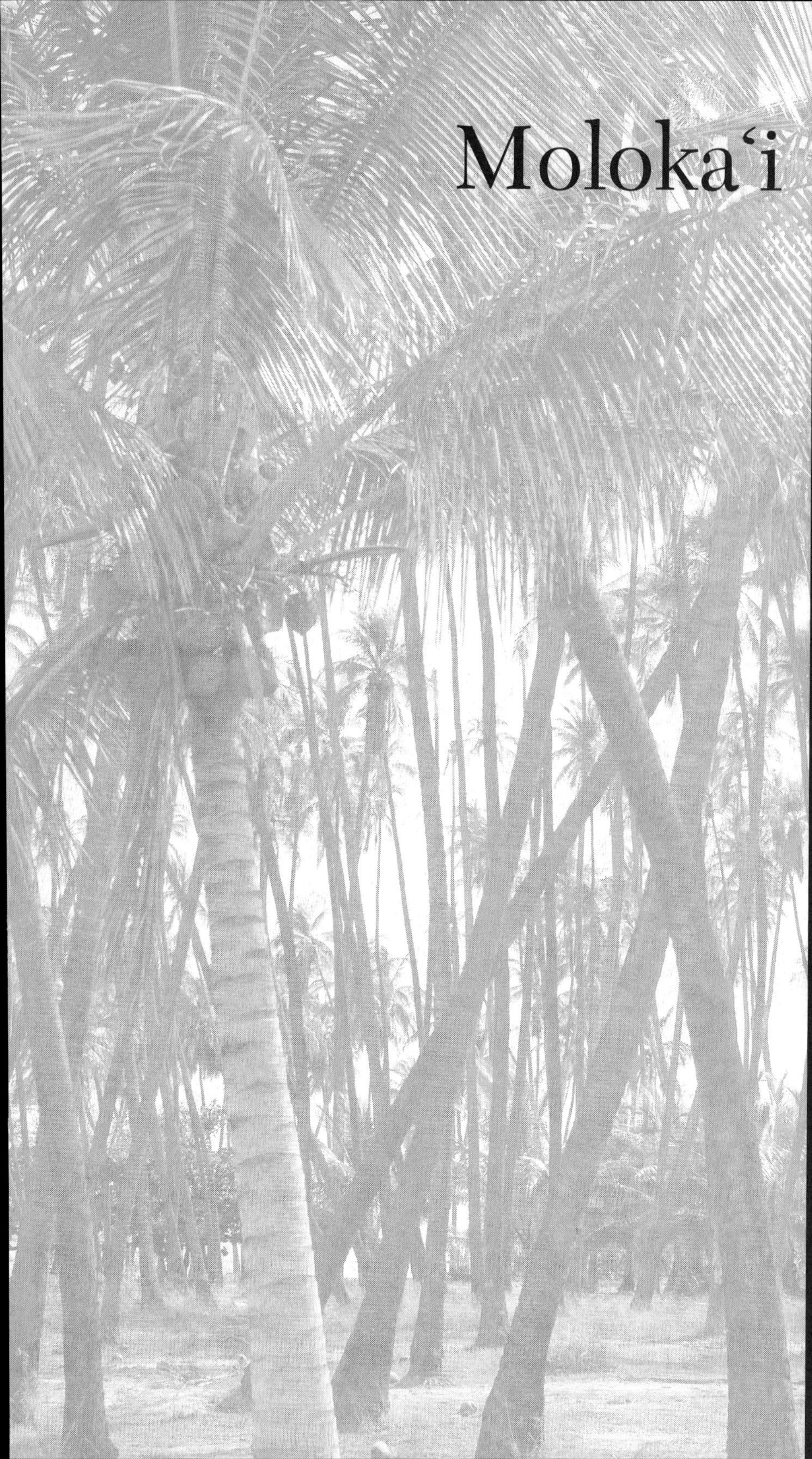

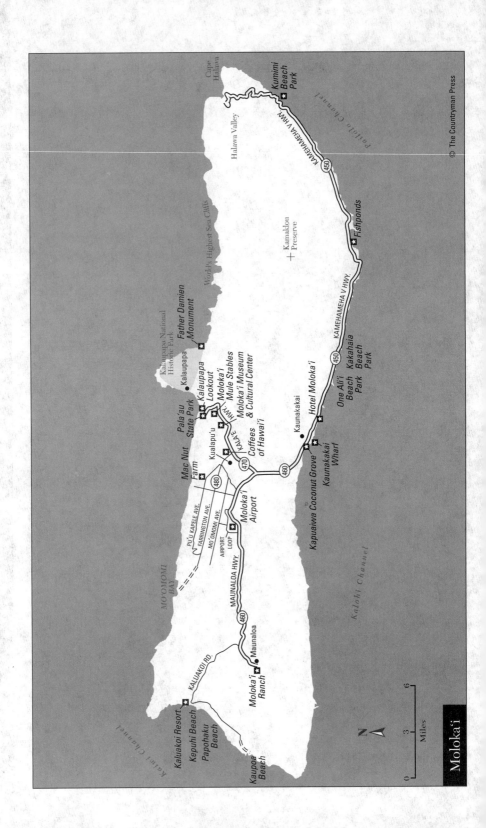

Moloka'i

© The Countryman Press

MOLOKA‘I

Moloka‘i once played with big-time progress by installing a traffic light at its busiest intersection. When it broke, no one bothered to fix it, and no one has missed it since. Progress has been stepped up lately, though; the island got its first movie theater in 1997.

Sleepy and contented, Moloka‘i earns its nicknames: the Friendly Isle and the Most Hawaiian Island. Earlier last century, it was called the Lonely Isle, a place of banishment for leprosy victims, a land of howling winds and scant population.

Going back into the mists of early Polynesian civilization, Moloka‘i was revered and feared for the spiritual strengths of its *kahunas* (priests). Lanikaula, a great prophet, lived here as a hermit. Hula was born here. In the 17th century, the poisonwood gods created an aura of sorcery on the island. Father Damien, the heroic Belgian priest who tended the exiled lepers at Kalaupapa, had a different faith but a similar intensity of devotion. The old epithet *Moloka‘i pule oo* still caries meaning: The island remains "a place of powerful prayers," where ancient legends survive and abandoned shrines and temples refuse to crumble completely.

Chances are you'll either fall in love with Moloka‘i or you'll never return. You'll wonder why the heck you ended up here or you'll accept Moloka‘i on her terms and sink into her spirit—her spirit that thrives on family, culture, and community. If you can find peace of mind anywhere, you'll find it here—where no one honks their horns or hurries or utters pretenses. Honolulu is only 25 miles away, but you might as well be in another country and century on Moloka‘i. Decide to take charming Moloka‘i on its terms or don't bother.

Even though only about 70,000 visitors step foot on Moloka‘i annually (that's less than 200 people per day), islanders are generally ambivalent about even *that* many outsiders. Resistance to conventional (or any) tourism efforts runs high. Change creeps at a glacial pace, barely perceptible. Because of that, Moloka‘i is still basically undeveloped; no buildings are higher than a coconut tree. Preservation of traditional culture is revered. Perhaps not surprisingly, a higher percentage of Native Hawaiians (more than 50 percent) live on Moloka‘i than on any of the other islands except Ni‘ihau.

Many of Moloka‘i's 7,400 residents fish and hunt just enough to get by. You may see them casting nets into the water, fishing, and collecting seaweed. You will definitely see them gathering with friends and family on Sunday—and come to think of it, on most days at sunset or at lunch, at the beach park or at the gas station.

Other than a scenic and stirring day trip to Kalaupapa, the island doesn't offer a great deal of organized activity for visitors—which is not to say there's nothing to do. There is just enough to explore on your own—from deserted beaches to sacred ruins. The East End offers a panoramic view of scenic Halawa Valley not to be missed, and the same can be said for the world's highest sea cliffs. But mostly Molokaʻi is a place for soft-adventuring. There's horseback riding and fishing, a bit of kayaking and a bit of golf. It's the place to hike undisturbed in spectacular Nature Conservancy property. It harbors Hawaiʻi's highest waterfall.

Molokaʻi is a spot to slow down (and therefore see more), step out of mainstream tourism, and absorb the spirit of an island that refuses to forget the Polynesian past. Historically, Captain Cook never set foot on Molokaʻi, but Protestant missionaries arrived in 1832. The landscape changed in 1848 when King Kamehameha V decreed that individuals could own land. By the 1870s, he had purchased much of the island from Rudolph Meyer (of the sugar mill fame). About 30 years after the king's death in 1873, *haole* Charles Cook acquired the land and converted it into a cattle ranch, which, over the intervening years, produced pineapples, sugar, and honey. Today it survives as Molokaʻi Ranch.

In late 2007, a big uproar broke out over Laʻau Point, a place of cultural significance for Molokaʻi residents and a place also owned by the ranch. The island was swimming in homegrown lawn signs pleading to SAVE LAʻAU POINT. The ranch wanted to build 200 luxury homes on 500 acres and use the proceeds to resurrect the long dormant Kaluakoi Resort and to keep day-to-day operations of the ranch running. Locals didn't want another sacred place torn up for the sake of the almighty dollar. Locals blocked the plan, and in March 2008 the ranch announced layoffs of 120 employees and the closing of the Lodge, Beach Village, Kaluakoi Golf Course, Mauna Loa gas station, Mauna Loa cinema, and its cattle raising operations. Furthermore, the ranch announced plans to cut off access entirely to its 60,000 acres.

Because Molokaʻi Ranch owns so much of the island's mass, and because it's hard to believe that they're really closing up shop for good, I was hesitant to remove all listings from this edition entirely. But at press time, it looked like a done deal. Still, I suggest asking around if the Ranch has been opened back up to tourism.

If you want to be respectful and seem like you know a thing or two about local customs, when you approach someone, it wouldn't hurt to say *Hui*—calling out to ask permission, to acknowledge that the locals are caretakers to the place.

GUIDANCE

Molokaʻi Visitor's Association (808-553-3876 or 1-800-800-6367; molokai -hawaii.com), 2 Kamoi St., Ste. #200, Kaunakakai. Open 8–4:30 weekdays. Part of the mission of the MVA is to educate visitors about culturally significant spots like fishponds and heʻiau; stop in and ask an earful of questions. Although it seems like time stands still on Molokaʻi, many tourist-related things here are more susceptible to change than on neighbor islands. The MVA will have current details.

Maui Visitor's Bureau (808-244-3530; visitmaui.com), 1727 Wili Pa Loop, Wailuku, Maui. Open 8–4:30 weekdays. The MVB also represents Lana'i and Moloka'i, providing maps, vacation planners, and brochures.

MORE WEB SITES

visitmolokai.com (events, facts, maps, and activities)

molokaievents.com (locations and calendar)

state.hi.us/dlnr (Hawai'i's Department of Lands and Natural Resources)

gohawaii.com (Hawai'i Visitor's & Convention Bureau)

honoluluadvertiser.com (daily newspaper)

starbulletin.com (daily newspaper)

NEWSPAPERS & RADIO

The charmingly local **Moloka'i Dispatch** (808-552-2781; themolokaidispatch .com) is published once a week on Wednesdays; pick it up at the grocery store or the Moloka'i Visitor's Association. If you need further evidence that the Moloka'i community is like one big extended family, the newspaper's answering machine gives the editor's home phone number.

WEATHER

Call the **National Weather Service** (808-552-2477).

MEDICAL EMERGENCY

Call **911**. The emergency room at **Moloka'i General Hospital** (808-553-5331, Puali St., Kaunakakai) is open 24/7.

GETTING THERE

By air from the mainland: There are no direct mainland flights into Moloka'i; you must fly through Honolulu.

Interisland by air: **Island Air** (1-800-323-3345; islandair.com) operates flights from Honolulu (about seven daily) and Maui (a couple daily). Because they fly relatively low, these flights almost resemble sightseeing excursions. **Pacific Wings** (1-888-575-4546; pacificwings.com) also operates several flights daily from Honolulu.

Interisland by boat: **Moloka'i Princess** (808-667-6165, 667-2585, or

FATHER DAMIEN

1-800-275-6969; mauiprincess.com) offers two ferry trips daily from Maui's Lahaina harbor to Moloka'i's Kaunakakai and back again. The 8-mile trip across the channel takes about 90 minutes. Tickets $43 adults, $22 kids (one-way).

GETTING AROUND

By car: By all means, try to get a copy of Budget Rent-a-Car's *Driving & Discovering Maui & Moloka'i* by Richard Sullivan. It's eminently useful, with descriptive color photos, road details, quick-and-easy charts, and tips on vantage points for taking the best shots.

Moloka'i is 38 miles long and 7–10 miles wide; it takes about two and a half hours to drive one-way from end to end. The airport is in the center of the island, near nothing but about 25 minutes from the West End's Moloka'i Ranch and 10 minutes to Central Moloka'i's Kaunakakai. Upon landing, you'll be forgiven for thinking your pilot has accidentally glided into rural Kansas during tornado season. You'll get used to the West End winds, and you'll soon discover that the rest of the island isn't so flat and empty.

Because there are a relatively limited number of rental cars, be sure to reserve one in advance—especially on weekends! Shuttles are available into town, but without a rental car, you'll be stranded. Gas stations are located only in Kaunakakai (which also doubles as gossip and news central) and Maunaloa. Rent cars from the national **Budget** (808-567-6877), or support the local economy more fully by renting with **Island Kine** (808-553-5242 or 1-866-527-7368; molokai -car-rental.com) or **Moloka'i Outdoors** (808-553-4477 or 1-877-553-4477; molokai-outdoors.com). First-time visitors can forgo a four-wheel drive, only necessary for serious off-road exploring.

Because of sea cliffs and dense forests, the north shore isn't particularly accessible, but don't miss the Kalaupapa Lookout. From Kaunakakai, Hwy. 460 leads to Hwy. 470 to the lookout. Along the way in little Kualapu'u, Hwy. 480 (aka Farrington Avenue) veers eastward and leads to the unpaved road for the dunes at Mo'omomi Preserve.

DESERTED WEST END BEACHES AWAIT.

Take Hwy. 460 through barren but beautiful landscape to the West End and Maunaloa. Turn onto Kaluakoi Road for the mostly deserted resort and Papohaku Beach.

The East End is as lush as the West End is dry. From Kaunakakai, take Hwy. 460 east (which becomes Hwy. 450) to its end at the dramatic Halawa Beach. This impressive road hugs the shoreline and is, in many stretches, only as wide as one car.

By boat: **Moloka'i Charters** (808-567-9400; molokaisailing.com), Kaunakakai Wharf, Kaunakakai. Moloka'i Charters offers sailing on the handsome 53-foot yacht *Hoku Kai* (*Sea Star*). Choose among half-day sails and whale-watches, full-day sails and snorkeling, and sunset sails. $300 per hour.

By land: **The Nature Conservancy** (808-553-5236; nature.org). Serious naturalists may want to schedule a Moloka'i holiday to coincide with one of the Conservancy's monthly forays into their rarefied properties. Kamaklou Preserve offers high-elevation hikers a glimpse of Moloka'i's interior rain forest, where you'll see rare native plants and insects. The rugged coastal dunes at Mo'omomi Preserve, where endangered green sea turtles nest, has been etched by trade winds. Call for reservations; space is limited.

Moloka'i Off-Road Tours (808-553-3369; molokai.com/offroad). These folks offer six-hour island tours for $98 per person with a two-person minimum. If you're time-crunched, this is a good option.

For tours of **Kalaupapa National Historic Park**, see *To See & Do*.

✴ Special Events

For a complete list of island-wide events, consult molokaievents.com or molokai-hawaii.com.

Late January: **Ka Moloka'i Makahiki** (808-553-3876 or 808-553-3673; molokai-hawaii.com), held at the Mitchell Pauole Center, Kaunakakai. Makahiki is the designated postharvest period when wars ended and peacetime commenced. In ancient times, this period lasted four months; this modern traditional celebration (which includes hula, music, chanting, and traditional Hawaiian games) lasts a day. It draws a crowd locally—more than a third of the island by some accounts.

Late March: **Prince Kuhio Celebrations**, statewide. Celebrate the birth of Jonah Kuhio Kalanianaole, a congressional delegate from 1903 to 1921.

May 1: **Lei Day**, statewide. The phrase "May Day is Lei Day" was coined by Grace Tower Warren in 1928 when Lei Day was conceived.

Mid- May: **Moloka'i Ka Hula Piko** (808-553-3876 or 1-800-800-6367; molokai-hawaii.com), Papohaku Beach Park, Kaluakoi. Take this rare opportunity to celebrate "real" hula on the island of its inception with performances and adjunct crafts, storytelling, musicians, and food stalls. The daylong event attracts some 3,000 enthusiasts with old- and new-style hula *halaus*.

Early June: **King Kamehameha Celebration** (808-586-0333; hawaii.gov/dags/king_kamehameha_commission). Hawai'i's longest-running festival is celebrated statewide to honor King Kamehameha, unifier of the Hawaiian Kingdom.

July: **Hoolaulea O Kea Kai-A Moloka'i Sea Fest** (808-553-3876 or 1-800-800-6367). A daylong celebration of the sea.

Mid- to late August: **Admissions Day**, statewide. On the third Friday in August, all islands celebrate the day Hawai'i became the 50th state.

September: **Aloha Festivals**, statewide (808-589-1771; alohafestivals.com). This event includes a floral parade down Ala Malama Street, Kaunakakai.

TOP SEVEN "MUSTS" FOR FIRST-TIME VISITORS

Visit the haunting Kalaupapa National Historic Park via mule train

Buy warm Moloka'i Sweet Bread from Kanemitsu Bakery at 10 PM

Enjoy Friday-night cocktails and entertainment at Hula Shores

Drive to the end of the road at the Halawa Valley

Take the perfect sunset photograph through a silhouetted Kapuaiwa
Coconut Grove

Post-a-Nut from the Kaunakakai Post Office

Watch sunset at Papohaku Beach, where it's practically devoid of footsteps

September–October: **Moloka'i Hoe**. At 41 miles long, this is the world's longest outrigger canoe race; it crossses the Kaiwi Channel from Moloka'i to Duke Kahanamoku Beach in Waikiki. Women race in September, men in October.

Early December: **Festival of Lights**, statewide. Moloka'i celebrates with a parade in Kaunakakai down Ala Malama Street, which begins when the sun goes down.

✳ The Three Regions

Moloka'i has one "real" town, and that's friendly **Kaunakakai**: the population and market center on the historic south coast, with Ala Malama its dusty and parched two-block shopping street. It's worth spending a little time hanging around here and watching Moloka'i's world revolve. Aging wooden storefronts and pickup trucks give the town a Wild West sort of feeling.

Head north from here through plumeria trees, alongside a coffee plantation, and up through a cooler and wetter forest to a vantage point overlooking Kalaupapa, formed by a flat "spreading" of lava. (The rugged "back side" of Moloka'i is basi-

MAIN STREET, KAUNAKAKAI

cally inaccessible wilderness, and its famed sea cliffs are viewed only from the air and by experienced kayakers.)

The island was formed by two volcanoes: the 1,381-foot Maunaloa in the West End (dominated by dry ranchland and rolling pastures) and the 4,970-foot Kamaklou in the East End (shadowed by misty and lush rain forests). A single two-lane road runs the length of the island.

The **West End** is home to Moloka'i's only tourist development: Kaluakoi Resort has 18 holes of golf and some condos, but other that than, it's mostly closed. The resort and the nearby reinvented plantation town of **Maunaloa** are secluded in a relatively unpopulated region, almost a half hour's drive from other points of interest. It's mostly home to cattle ranges, high grassy bluffs, and many dirt roads that are off-limits to visitors. Beaches along the shore are big and beautiful (especially the powder white sand at Papohaku), though they're usually unsafe for swimming. It's not uncommon to have the beach all to yourself here. The West End might seem inhospitable, but it's strangely alluring.

The jungly **East End**—full of yawning valleys and lava cliffs—is subject to brief but intense rainstorms from January to March. Heading east on this 20-mile route, the twisting, turning landscape morphs from sandy shores to rocky coastline. Along the way you'll pass fishponds, ancient *heiaus*, churches, a few condos to rent, and little tentlike A-frame structures that shelter cocks for fighting. Venture to the East End on a weekday unless you want to experience Moloka'i-style traffic: Parts of the too-narrow road are used as a sidewalk for pedestrians, and parked cars pull off onto nonexistent shoulders, which make for fun and challenging driving. When they say, "Slow down, you're on Moloka'i," they aren't kidding.

✳ To See & Do

Central Moloka'i & Kaunakakai

AROUND KAUNAKAKAI
✪ **Post-a-Nut** (808-567-6144), Hoolehua Post Office, Hwy. 480. Open 7:30–4:30 (closed 11:30–12:45) weekdays. In old movies, messages in bottles wash ashore from deserted islands, bearing tales and pleas from strange lands. Well, Moloka'i has its own variation on that theme. Your associates, nieces, and neighborhood postman will get a hoot out of delivering or receiving a coconut postcard from you in the Pacific. The Moloka'i postmaster keeps a ready supply of (free) worthy specimens on the front porch, and you can simply address it to your wackiest, nuttiest pals. Write a short and sweet "wish-you-were-here" sentiment on it, buy a priority stamp for its voyage, and off it goes.

Purdy's Macadamia Nut Farm (808-567-6601; molokai-aloha.com/macnuts), Hwy. 470 on the way to the Kalaupapa Lookout and just behind the high school, Kualapu'u. Open 9:30–3:30 weekdays, 10–2 Sat. This small family-operated mac nut farm has been amusing and educating visitors with 5- to 10-minute tours of their all-natural operation since the 1920s. There may be only 50 trees on 1.5 acres, but Tuddie Purdy knows how to work a patch (and work a crowd); he

TOP SEVEN IDEAS FOR REPEAT VISITORS
Take a once-monthly hike into the Kamaklou Preserve with The Nature
   Conservancy
Learn to fly a kite from Big Wind Kite Factory
Rent a four-wheel drive and head to Mo'omomi Dunes
Learn more than you need to know about macadamia nuts from Purdy
Kayak around the sea cliffs in the summer (for experienced paddlers only)
Hang out at Paddler's Inn
Time your visit with the annual Hula Piko Festival in May

epitomizes the island's friendly moniker. You'll learn about how nuts grow and trees bear fruit, how they're harvested, and what a tough nut they are to crack. Buy some fresh-roasted nuts or some delicious mac nut honey. Free.

Kaunakakai Wharf. Come here for local color (I'm talking sunsets and people) as well as fishing and water sports. Wintertime whale-watching is pretty good from here, the export node for local watermelon and honey.

Heading North

Coffees of Hawai'i (808-567-9490; coffeesofhawaii.com), Hwy. 480 near Hwy. 470, Kualapu'u. Morning Espresso tour at 10 AM weekdays, 9 AM Sat.; coffee bar and store open 7–5 weekdays, 8–4 Sat., 8–2 Sun. This former Del Monte pineapple plantation has been replanted with coffee trees over its 600 acres. Take a free self-guided tour or a narrated wagon ride ($35 adults, $10 children); linger over a strong cup o' joe; or browse in the modest gift shop before moving on.

Moloka'i Museum and Cultural Center (808-567-6436; hawaiimuseums .org), Hwy. 470, 2 miles south of the Kalaupapa Lookout, Kala'e. Open 10–2 Mon.–Sat. Ensconced within the 1878 Meyer Sugar Mill, Hawai'i's only remaining reconstructed mill has a cane crusher, evaporating pans, a steam engine, and every other piece of machinery needed to convert cane to sugar. It's a veritable time capsule, complete with historic photos. Many special events are held here; keep your eyes peeled. The good little gift shop may just have something with your name on it. $2.50 adults, $1 ages 5–18.

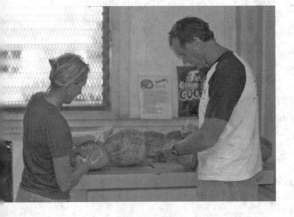

POST-A-NUT

Pala'au State Park and **Kalaupapa Lookout**. Take Hwy. 460 to Hwy. 470 to its end. Situated at about 1,000 feet, this park offers two short trails through a cool and dense 230-acre ironwood and pine forest. One trail leads to the magnificent Kalaupapa Lookout, the only place "up top" to glimpse the magnificent sea cliffs and remote peninsula (officially known as Makanalua Peninsula) where disfigured leper patients were forced to settle in the 1840s. Informational plaques are helpful here. You may have to wait a while for the clouds to part, but if you have time, it's worth the wait. The other trail leads to Phallic Rock (aka Kauleonanahoa to Hawaiians), where childless women went in hopes of boosting their fertility. Every island seems to have one of

A CHANGE OF PACE

these potent puppies, but devotees won't want to miss this particular pilgrimage. You can camp here (see *Lodging*), but it can be chilly and rainy.

✪ **Kalaupapa National Historic Park** (808-567-6802; nps.gov/kala), Makanalua Peninsula. Tours Mon.–Sat. This forlorn, inhospitable, heart-wrenching, and infamous peninsula was the final home for upward of 11,000 leprosy suffers (see the sidebar *Father Damien & Moloka'i's Leper Colony*) from the mid-1800s onward. And if you have time to do only one thing on Moloka'i, this should be it. But it does require a commitment of time (and some money). Tours are required (of the settlement), but there are myriad ways to reach the settlement (see next page). What will you see and hear on the trip? To guard the privacy of residents you can't wander freely, but you will visit a moving little museum, medical barracks, a graveyard, Father Damien's St. Philomena church, a craft store, and a memorial to Father Damien, whose final resting place is now his native Belgium. Until the 1930s his entire body was interred here, but since he was put under consideration for sainthood in Belgium, his remains were moved to that country. His right hand was returned to Kalaupapa in 1995.

The official name of the disease, by the way, is Hansen's disease, named for the Norwegian doctor who discovered a cure. Although peninsula residents still call the disease leprosy, it's not appropriate to refer to them as lepers. Today there are still about 40 residents, and although they no longer have to live here, many have known no other life and will not leave. It's their home. No children under age 16 permitted.

By van: **Father Damien Tours** (808-567-6171), Kalaupapa. This is the only outfit allowed to operate tours of the historic park, but luckily it's a great one and it's usually led by a community member. Make reservations a week in advance. One four-hour tour (Mon.–Sat.) departs at 10 AM. Adults $40; no children under 16 permitted.

By mule and van: **Moloka'i Mule Ride** (808-567-6088 or 1-800-567-7550; mule ride.com), MM 5, Hwy. 470. The mule train departs at 8 AM daily except Sun.; you'll be back up at the top by about 3:30 PM. For a personal recounting of this highly recommended trip, see the sidebar *Leading a Mule Train*. There are a few other random notes to keep in mind: wear long pants; bring rain gear; the ride can be tough on some people's backs and thighs; maximum weight is 225 pounds; and lunch is a bit skimpy, so you may wish to bring something to supplement it.

$165 for those over age 16, including the van tour (above) and a bag lunch. Make reservations a couple of weeks in advance or risk being disappointed.

By foot and van: **Hiking**. You can hike down and take the Father Damien Tour (see *By van*), but you must have a permit, obtainable from the Moloka'i Mule Ride barn. Get there by 7:30 so that you have a head start on the mule train that follows. You must reach the bottom by the time the mules and riders do, because you'll all be on the same tour van. It'll take one hour to hike down, two to hike back up.

By boat, van, foot, and air: **The *Moloka'i Princess*** (808-667-6165 or 1-800-275-6969; mauiprincess.com) from Maui packages a ferry ride that includes transportation to and from the Kalaupapa trailhead, where you'll hike down the steep 3-mile trail (and back up, which takes two hours or so), a requisite van tour, and a picnic lunch. The ferry departs for Moloka'i at 7:15 AM and returns at 4:15 PM. $264 over age 16. You can also hike down and fly out for $295 with Paragon Airlines (808-244-3356; paragon-air.com).

Heading West

✪ **Kapuaiwa Coconut Grove**, *makai*, 2 miles west of Kaunakakai. These 10 waterfront acres were planted oh-so-symmetrically with 1,000 coconut trees in 1863 to honor King Kamehameha V. Heed the warning signs and watch for falling coconuts. At sunset, this photographic backdrop makes for a great silhouetted shot. Across the street (*mauka*), the missionary-happy **Church Row** is similarly symmetrical. It's lined with seven different denomination churches that date to the late 19th century.

West End

Maunaloa. This quiet little red-dirt town was a plantation town until the mid-1920s, when pineapples began losing their economic luster. Since then, the old town has been leveled and a new one built, complete with tract houses, sidewalks, bona fide driveways, a town green, a movie theater, and a general store. Until 2008 it was a plantation-style town that revolved around the 54,000 Moloka'i Ranch. Then the Ranch decided to call it a day, and the perennial issue on Moloka'i was raised once again: development versus preserving the old way of life. Maunaloa is also a fun place on Thanksgiving, when some 3,000 folks show up for a rodeo and cookout.

CHURCH ROW

Kaluakoi. Moloka'i isn't exactly a resort mecca; locals don't embrace the development plans, nor has a critical mass of tourists ever materialized. But this failed resort still has three condo complexes, golfing, and a really fine beach.

Mo'omomi Preserve. From Hwy. 460, turn onto Hwy. 470, then left

KAPUAIWA COCONUT GROVE

onto Hwy. 480 and follow it 3 miles to the end. The dunes here are accessible only via a beautiful four-wheel-drive track, and the 900-acre preserve is accessible only through monthly guided hikes led by The Nature Conservancy (see *Islandwide Tours*). Try to visit this rare place. The preserve contains some stunning finds: ancient burial sites, endangered plants, green sea turtle nesting sites, and prehistoric bones of birds (some flightless) that lived nowhere else on our planet.

East End & the Road to Halawa Valley

This route easily makes my list of top 10 drives in Hawai'i.

Kamaklou Preserve (aka **Moloka'i Forest**). Partially cut by the Pepe'opae Trail, this 270-acre rain forest paradise is hard to penetrate. But if you do, you'll be rewarded with bogs that are a few million years old, tiny 'ohi'a trees, over 200 plant species found here and nowhere else, and lots of slow-growing lichen. This 3-mile trail takes about 90 minutes to hike with The Nature Conservancy (see *Islandwide Tours*). If you venture into its depths unassisted, you'll need a four-wheel-drive vehicle, a permit (808-553-5236), and very good directions—better than I can give you, because I didn't have time to explore it.

Ali'i Fishpond, MM 1.5 (*makai*), Hwy. 450. Ancient aquaculture, in the form of fishponds, was practically born in Hawai'i in the 1400s. At one time, almost 60 of these natural fish tanks lined Moloka'i's south shore. Today most are barely visible, but a few are still in use by locals, who trap and grow fish and collect seaweed. This particular one is undergoing serious restoration. Here's how it generally works: Rock walls made of coral or lava were laid just offshore and formed, along with a curving shoreline and a submerged gate, an enclosure over which high tide would wash. Fish would wash over the walls with the tides but remain when the tide went out. There they would swim and fatten up, to eventually be harvested by net. Ingenious.

St. Joseph's Church, MM 10–11 (*makai*), Hwy. 450. One of five churches built by Father Damien (this one in 1876), this little white wooden church is marked by a statue of the saintly man that's perpetually draped in leis. He also built the nearby **Our Lady of Sorrows Church**, MM 14–15, Hwy. 450, marked by a wooden cross, across from a fishpond.

Smith Bronte Landing, MM 11–12 (*makai*), Hwy. 450. Although the

EASTEND FISHPONDS

MAKANALUA PENINSULA'S HAUNTING ISOLATION

FATHER DAMIEN & MOLOKA'I'S LEPER COLONY

When Captain Cook arrived in Hawai'i in 1778, the population of healthy Hawaiians was estimated at 250,000 to 300,000. By 1896—because of extremely infectious diseases like the plague, smallpox, cholera, influenza, and whooping cough introduced by foreigners—the population had plummeted to about 31,000. Leprosy, introduced as Ma'i Pake (the Chinese sickness) in the early 1800s, was among the diseases.

Leprosy became an "official" concern of the Hawaiian Kingdom in 1865, when King Kamehameha authorized his government to acquire land specifically for the purpose of isolating its victims. Because it was such a highly visible and disturbing disease, victims were treated like criminals. If you were infected, it became illegal not to turn yourself in.

On January 6, 1866, the first "shipment" of leprosy sufferers was sent to Makanalua Peninsula on Moloka'i's north shore. *Sent* is perhaps too gentle a word, though. Because the land is surrounded on three sides by rough seas and the ship could not dock, patients were literally thrown overboard and left to swim ashore, holding on to what few belongings they could. Many did not make it. Because the peninsula is surrounded on the fourth side by steep 2,000-foot cliffs, the government assessed it an appropriate place to detain the victims and confine the disease. There was no way to escape.

By October 1866, 101 men and 41 women were stranded on the peninsula, boiling hot by day, fending for themselves without shelter or food. (Small amounts of food were sent from Honolulu; eventually, in 1887, the current-day mule and hiking trail was carved out of the mountainside to supply the community.) The community degenerated into lawlessness. Stories of the settlement trickled back to Honolulu, describing a desolate community filled with drunkenness and debauchery, where the strong took advantage of the weak. These tragic accounts caused family members to hide loved ones afflicted with the contagious disease, which in turn caused it to spread more. Some healthy family members, not wanting their beloved to live and die on the peninsula alone, chose to accompany them—knowing that they themselves would never return.

In 1873, four Catholic priests (led by Bishop Louis D. Maigret) decided that the settlement desperately needed a full-time pastor to oversee things and minister to the sick and dying. They set up three-month rotations; Father Damien de Veuster went first and arrived on May 10. Two days after his arrival, the Belgian priest wrote the bishop: "I am willing to dedicate my life to the leprosy victims."

Even though he made a quick and certain commitment to the people in the Kalaupapa community, Father Damien did not adjust to conditions quickly or easily. The sight of hundreds of people, many with extremely advanced cases of leprosy, was frightening. Since the smell and living conditions proved challenging, Father Damien began building sleeping quarters and started smoking a pipe to counteract the stench of open and draining sores. He did not sleep indoors until all the patients had housing.

Father Damien served as a nurse and doctor to the ailing, a parent to orphans, and a confidant and spiritual leader to the community. In a letter dated 1873, it's said that Father Damien preached "We lepers" rather than "We brethren," identifying himself with his flock long before he contracted the disease. More than 11,000 lepers arrived at the colony between 1866 and 1874.

Charles Warren Stoddard, who visited the settlement in 1868 and 1884, described Father Damien in *The Lepers of Moloka'i*: "His cassock was worn and faded; his hair tumbled like a schoolboy's, his hands stained and hardened by toil; but the flow

of health was in his face, the buoyancy of youth in his manner; while his ringing laugh, his ready sympathy, and his inspiring magnetism told of one who in any sphere might do a noble work, and who in that which he has chosen is doing the noblest of all works." Father Damien was diagnosed with leprosy three months later. In all, he worked tirelessly with these patients for 11 years, until his death in 1889 at the age of 49.

Leprosy (more sensitively called Hansen's disease) is now known to be caused by a bacillus, *Mycobacterium leprae*, and is one of the least communicable of all infectious diseases. In fact, only 5 percent of the world's population is even susceptible to it. Even though drugs became available in the 1940s to cure the disease, many people infected by the disease chose to remain on the peninsula because it was the only home they'd known.

In December 1980, President Carter established Kalaupapa National Historic Park, ensuring that the site will be preserved for the future education of visitors and that remaining patients will be guaranteed privacy and the right to live there as long as they wish.

FATHER DAMIEN'S GRAVE

landing has rather disappeared, you'll still want to know about this spot. Ernest Smith and Emory Bronte may not enjoy the cult aviation status of Charles Lindbergh, but they are in the record books. On July 14, 1927, they set out from Oakland, California, bound for Honolulu in a single-engine plane. They didn't reach Honolulu for lack of fuel, but they did make Moloka'i—25 hours and 2,500 miles later, they crashed relatively unscathed into a kiawe grove. And with that inauspicious landing, they could claim the "first trans Pacific flight" from the mainland to Hawai'i.

Ili'ili'opa'e Heiau, MM 15–16 (*mauka*), Hwy. 450. Moloka'i's largest and most revered temple (which is also the second-largest in Hawai'i) was once used for human sacrifices. It's a powerful place, having drawn *kahunas* from every shore, as well as Lono, the god of fertility. It's unclear whether it dates to A.D. 650, whether it was built in the 1100s or 1200s, whether it was built by the mythic and legendary Menehune, or by thousands of men in one night. What is known is that it consisted of four terraces and an imposing 22-foot altar and was longer than a modern-day football field. The *he'iau* is sometimes reached via a hidden 0.5-mile trail on private property, but the caretaker family has let it get overgrown and it's tough to find. In searching, you may inadvertently step on the very sacred *he'iau,* so it's best not to look in the first place. If you hike in yourself, park on the *mauka* side of the road, walk for about 10 minutes, stay on the trail, and look for the *he'iau* on the other side of a dry streambed.

Pu'u O Hoku Ranch (puuohoku.com), MM 20, Hwy. 450. Most of the rolling pastures you're passing, with great panoramic views over to Lana'i, belong to this private ranch (see *Lodging*), developed in the 1930s by Paul Fagan of Hana, Maui, fame.

✪ **Halawa Valley**, at the end of Hwy. 450. Linger at the lookout 2 miles from the valley. Moloka'i's north shore is cut by five magnificently deep valleys, but only one is even slightly accessible: Halawa. Harboring Moloka'i's earliest inhabited settlement, believed to date to A.D. 650, this paradise is the most sacred spot on the island. Despite the area being devastated by a tidal wave in 1946, a few locals still live here (growing taro and fruit), but they're not particularly enamored of outsiders. Heed the NO TRESPASSING signs, stick to exploring the beach, and watch your belongings. A 3-mile trail leads to the 250-foot Mo'aula Falls, but again, don't even think about entering the valley without a local guide. Contact **Moloka'i Fish & Dive** (808-553-5926; molokaifishanddive.com) about current tours. Their subcontracted trips depart once daily from the pavilion at Halawa Valley at 9:15, with 24 hours notice, and cost $75 per person. Or contact Pilipo Solotaio directly at 808-553-9803; keep your fingers crossed that you can reach him.

✳ Outdoor Activities

Outfitters on Moloka'i offer a little bit of everything—from kayaking to horseback riding. Instead of ordering this section by activity (as I usually do) and cross-referencing, I've listed the outfitters in order of my preference and by what activities they offer.

Moloka'i Outdoors (808-553-4477 or 1-877-553-4477; molokai-outdoors.com), at the ferry terminal, Kaunakakai. This former full-service outfitter is mostly a shuttle service now, serving all your transportation needs, but they still do a few other things. In addition to surfboard

HEADING TO THE EAST END

rentals, the friendly staff offers guided ocean kayaking trips (of fishponds and reefs), as well as full- and half-day trips of Moloka'i's cultural and natural highlights from $70 per person (if you're short on time).

Moloka'i Action Adventures (808-558-8184 or 808-553-3876; molokai-hawaii .com). These hands-on excursions are geared toward adventurous visitors who want to swim through towering waterfalls, hike brisk mountain trails, and sail alongside the world's highest sea cliffs. Call for prices and trip details.

Moloka'i Fish & Dive (808-553-5926; molokaifishanddive.com), Kaunakakai. Proprietor and photographer Jim Broker and his knowledgeable staff customize adventures of a lifetime—from diving on Hawai'i's barrier reef to night dives for those certified. They're also set up for kayaking, whale-watches, snorkeling, and horseback-riding trips.

As for easy **fishing**, cast a line off Kaunakakai Wharf, where other sailing, scuba, and snorkeling trips, as well as outfitters, are also based. Rent gear at Moloka'i Outdoors or go fly-fishing with **Moloka'i Action Adventures**.

Ironwoods Hills Golf Course (808-567-6000), Hwy. 470, Kualapu'u. Both visitors and residents like this old course, built for employees of the Del Monte pineapple plantation. Surrounded by hills and ironwood trees (hence the name), this course has great open views and fairways. Fees are shockingly inexpensive—something like $25 for 18 holes.

Kaluakoi Golf Course (808-552-0255), Maunaloa, in the West End. Tired of paying through the nose and waiting for eons to find a tee time to your liking? You won't find that here. Designed by Ted Robinson, this challenging course reopened recently after a complete refurbishment. Greens fees are $85 (for 18 holes, including a cart).

Pu'u O Hoku Ranch (808-558-8109; puuohoku.com), in the East End. Located on 14,000 remote acres, Moloka'i's largest working cattle ranch offers lush pastures and tropical forests laced with riding trails and sweeping Pacific vistas.

HALAWA

These excellent guided horseback trips also head down to the beach, where you can take a dip in the secluded waters. Half-day trips $120; one- and two-hour trail rides $55 and $75, respectively.

✳ Beaches

Central Moloka'i & Kaunakakai

🏖 **One Ali'i Beach Park**, east of Kaunakakai, MM 3–4, off Kamehameha V Highway. Generally, southern beaches aren't great for swimming, but at least their waters are usually calm. Full of locals on weekends, One Ali'i is the best beach on Moloka'i's south shore. Pronounced *O-nay*, the long and narrow beach offers safe swimming and shady picnic areas. *Facilities*: Restrooms, showers.

West End

Western beaches are marked by big bad winter waves.

🏖 ❂ **Papohaku Beach**, at the end of Kaluakoi Rd., 2 miles beyond Kaluakoi Resort. Second only to Kaua'i's Polihale Beach in length, the 3-mile Papohaku cuts a wide swath that's rarely marked by more than a few footprints. It's interesting to note that when Waikiki Beach needed sand to shore up its appeal to mainlanders, as if to confer status on the quality of its sand it dug up these grains and shipped them over to Waikiki. Swimming is safe in summer; beachcombing and sunset strolling are great year-round; camping sites are shaded by kiawe trees and palms and softened by grass; winds are calmer in the morning. *Facilities*: Restrooms, showers, picnic area, barbecue, parking.

🏖 **Pohakuloa Beach**, 1.5 miles beyond Papohaku Beach. Per usual, there are no lifeguards here or on any Moloka'i beaches; it's popular on weekends. *Facilities*: Parking.

🏖 **Kepuhi Beach**, fronting the Kaluakoi Resort. It's not good for swimming, but this beach does have some nice grassy dunes. *Facilities*: None.

🏖 **Kawakiu Beach**, a 45-minute walk (or a short four-wheel-drive ride) from Kaluakoi Road beyond the Ke Nani Kai Resort condos just north of the Kaluakoi Golf Course. If you yearn for incredible seclusion, this crescent-shaped beach has it. *Facilities*: None.

East End

🏖 **Halawa Beach Park**, at the end of Hwy. 450. There are few more perfectly or dramatically located beaches—much less black-sand beaches—than this lagoon sheltered on three sides by mountains. Locals surf in winter, but the rest of us should stay away because of dangerous currents (especially near the waterfall). Stick close to the shore in summer. *Facilities*: Restrooms, picnic pavilion, grills.

PAPOHAKU BEACH

Sandy Beach, MM 20 on Hwy. 450. Right on the road and protected by natural reefs, this popular but small patch is great for families and those needing a quick dip. *Facilities*: None.

Kumimi Beach Park (aka **Murphy Beach Park**), Hwy. 450. Open during daylight hours. Fronted by a reef that creates calm swimming and good snorkeling conditions, this white-sand beach is lined with ironwood trees that provide much-appreciated shade. *Facilities*: Picnic and barbecue areas.

✳ Lodging

Moloka'i doesn't offer an overabundance of beds to rent. And those that are available reflect the very laid-back nature of the island. The good news is that most lodging options have kitchens, so you can save money on dining if you want. From alternative (pricey) eco-camping to small B&Bs, adequate condos, and a smattering of vacation rentals, you'll find something suitable. If you're looking for full-scale resorts, à la Maui's Ka'anapali or the Big Island's Kohala Coast, you'll be better off staying there than here. Nothing here comes close.

Moloka'i is long but relatively small, so you can base yourself anywhere and get around easily. If you anticipate heading back and forth between the West and East End, you might do well by settling in between.

CAMPING

The best area is **Papohaku Beach Park** (808-553-3204 for permits), West End; restrooms, showers, and water, as well as barbecue and picnic areas. There's a three-night minimum unless it's not crowded; $3 nightly per adult, 50¢ per child. **Pala'au State Park** (808-567-6923 for permits), end of Hwy. 470, offers camping among the ironwood trees, but it can be chilly up here; $5 per night.

Central Moloka'i & Kaunakakai

Hotel Moloka'i (808-553-5347 or 1-800-535-0085; marcresorts.com), Kamehameha V Hwy., Kaunakakai. Change, but not too much, has come to Hotel Moloka'i. My hat goes off to the new manager hired in late 2007—and an infusion of $1 million; it goes a long way toward creating more comfortable rooms. Mattresses, covered with throw pillows, are firm; TVs are large; and bathrooms are spic-n-span. Nostalgia still rears its head and reigns, though, at the Polynesian-style Hotel Moloka'i. If you can't get into that spirit, you're better off staying elsewhere. Full of local character and local characters, these renovated A-frames are basic, and many of the rooms are small and dark, but they do have great views of Lana'i and a swing on each of the small lanais. It's your call. At the very least, come for drinks at sunset, when the entire island seems to show up for a party (and some stay overnight). *Rates*: $–$$; children free in parent's room. *Facilities and amenities*: 45 rooms and suites, small pool, restaurant, activity desk, mini-fridge, kitchenettes in some rooms, cable TV, and Internet.

Ka Hale Mala B&B (808-553-9009; molokai-bnb.com), 7 Kamakana Pl., Kaunakakai. Located 4 miles east of Kaunakakai, this contemporary B&B offers a spacious one-bedroom, 900-square-foot apartment with plenty of privacy, beamed ceilings, a lanai, and a fully equipped kitchen. Head up to owners Cheryl and Jack Corbiell's second-floor lanai with a view for a breakfast of taro pancakes and banana fritters. They're happy to orient guests to Moloka'i's best sights and activities. *Rates*: $. *Facilities and amenities*: one room, no A/C, no phone, no credit cards.

Molokai Vacation Rentals (808-553-8334 or 1-800-367-2984; molokai-vacation-rental.net), Kamehameha V Hwy., Kaunakakai. The friendly and professional staff at MVR will help you weed through their large inventory of condos. Three-night minimum required; $–$$.

Friendly Isle Realty (808-553-3666 or 1-800-600-4158; molokairealty .com), 75 Ala Malama Street, Kaunakakai. These folks have a good selection of cottages and condos for rent. $–$$.

West End
Paniolo Hale (808-553-8334 or 1-800-367-2984; molokai-vacation-rentals.net), adjacent to the Kaluakoi Resort, Kaluakoi. Booked through Moloka'i Vacation Rentals, these condos are individually owned, so their quality varies. Increase your chances of getting the best unit available by chatting up the reservation agents at MVR. The best value on the island, these roomy but simply furnished condos overlook a great white-sand beach (best for walking rather than swimming) and sit adjacent to a verdant swath of the Kaluakoi Golf Course. Some units have a private hot tub (available for an extra charge); some two-story units have great ocean views; all have large screened lanais, full kitchens, and access to barbecue grills. *Rates*: $–$$ studio, one-bedrooms $$ (most sleep one to four); two-bedrooms $$–$$$ (sleeps four to six); three-night minimum. *Facilities*

HOTEL MOLOKA'I

and amenities: 77 units, pool, adjacent golfing, beach, cleaning fee $75–125 depending on condo size.

East End

Pu'u O Hoku Ranch's Grove Cottage (808-558-8109; puuohoku.com), MM 25, Kamehameha V Hwy. About an hour's drive from Kaunakakai and situated on a 14,000-acre ranch, this nicely landscaped and secluded two-bedroom house has two baths, modest country-style furnishings, a fully equipped kitchen, and a covered lanai. Sitting on high with panoramic views of pasture ranchlands, organic gardens, and ocean, the sunny living room makes a perfect retreat after a day of horseback riding, hiking, and exploring. Swimming is available at the neighboring ranch lodge. Larger parties may wish to inquire about the four-bedroom house. *Rates*: $$; two-night minimum. *Facilities and amenities*: pool, TV and VCR available on request.

✳ Where to Eat

Kaunakakai has Moloka'i's only real concentration of eateries. (In fact, as you'll find out, the West End and East End have only one or two!) Unless otherwise noted, all places can be characterized as homey and unpretentious mom-and-pop places. On any other island, half of these listed below wouldn't make it into a guidebook. (Most people tend to cook for themselves in condos.) Locally caught fish is always a good bet, as is Filipino food. It's safest to assume that credit cards are not accepted anywhere in town.

Central Moloka'i & Kaunakakai

EATING OUT

Hula Shores (808-553-5347; hotel molokai.com), at the Hotel Moloka'i, Kamehameha V Hwy., Kaunakakai. Open for all three meals daily. This deeply atmospheric place boasts an oceanfront setting adjacent to a twinkling, torchlit swimming pool. You'll probably end up hanging out more than once. Once it gets under your skin, there's no turning back. Just remember, except for the popcorn shrimp, it's more about the setting than the food—although they did get

TO THE EAST END

a new chef in late 2007. At lunchtime, stick to the decent salads, steaks, and catch of the day; at night, theme dinners with prime rib and baby back ribs prevail. I've been known to hang out at the bar, noshing on appetizers and watching Sunday football—along with other wayfaring souls. A real camaraderie can form with locals at this place if you let it. Reservations recommended for dinner; children's menu. Breakfast $–$$, lunch $–$$, dinner mains $$–$$$.

Moloka'i Pizza Café (808-553-3288), Kahua Center, Old Wharf Rd., Kaunakakai. Open about 11–10 daily. This all-around favorite joint is popular with families for pasta, sandwiches, fish dinners, and veggie pizzas. Children's menu and diversions. Dishes $–$$, pizza $$–$$$.

Kualapu'u Cookhouse (808-567-9655), Farrington Ave./Hwy. 480, Kualapu'u. Open 7–2 Mon., 7 AM–8 PM Tues.–Sat. One block off Hwy. 470, this modest little plantation house offers big portions of take-out food. My last visit was less satisfying than ever (probably because of an ownership change), but if you're in the neighborhood, try the mahimahi sandwiches, chicken katsu plate lunches, loco moco breakfast plates (eggs on a bun over rice smothered in gravy), or stuffed shrimp. Breakfast and lunch $, dinner mains $$.

Paddler's Inn Restaurant and Bar (808-553-5256; paddlersinnhawaii.com), corner of Kamehameha V Hwy. 450 and Mohala St., Kaunakakai. Open for all three meals. If you want to hang out with locals (what else is new on Moloka'i), this is a friendly and hopping place to do it. Big plates and big burgers and steaks rule the menu. The parking lot is

SOUTH SHORE

jammed when there's live entertainment at night. Breakfast $, lunch $–$$, dinner mains $$$–$$$.

GROCERIES

Outpost Natural Foods (808-553-3377), 70 Makaena Pl., just off Ala Malama St., Kaunakakai. Open 9–5ish weekdays, 10–5 Sun. For organic

OUTPOST NATURAL FOODS

fruits and vegetables, bulk grains, vitamins, fruit juices, and the like, Outpost is a godsend. They also have a great little window in the back of the store, out of which they sell tofu lasagna, veggie meat loaf, and good burritos. Dishes $.

Stock up on groceries when you arrive from Kaunakakai's two competitors: **Friendly Market Center** (808-553-5595) and **Misaki's Groceries** (808-553-5505), both on Ala Malama St., both open 8:30–8:30 Mon.–Sat. Misaki's, though, won't leave you stranded on Sunday, when they're also open 9–noon.

Kualapu'u Market (808-567-6243), adjacent to the Kualapu'u Cookhouse,

Kualapu'u. Open 8:30–6 Mon.–Sat. A little grocery store.

COFFEE, ICE CREAM & SNACKS

Kamoi Snack-N-Go (808-553-3742), Kamoi Professional Center, Kaunakakai. Open 10–9 Mon.–Sat., noon–9 Sun. This convenience store is famous for Dave's Ice Cream, which uses local ingredients and is available in flavors like lychee sherbet and ube (made with sweet potatoes). Perhaps they should rename it Kamoi Sweet-N-Go, since Dave's is mouth-wateringly sublime.

✪ **Kanemitsu's Bakery** (808-553-5855), 79 Ala Malama St., Kaunakakai. Open from 5:30 AM for

---

THE 'UKELELE & INNOCENT MERRIMENT

How and when did the 'ukelele become so integral to the mainlander's idea of Hawai'i? The most reputable theory involves Joao Fernandes, who was one among 419 Portuguese immigrants from the *Ravenscrag* to land in Hawai'i on August 23, 1879. When Fernandes borrowed his friend's *braguinha* and began playing Portuguese folk songs on the beach, a growing audience of curious Hawaiians was so impressed at the speed with which he played that they dubbed the instrument *'ukelele*, or "jumping flea."

'Ukelele caught on quickly because it was easy to learn and portable. King David Kalakaua mastered the happy instrument, as did many others in the royal family, including Queen Emma, Queen Lili'uokalani, Prince Lele'iohoku, and Princess Likelike.

Much of Hawai'i's glamour from the 1920s and 1930s can be attributed to the Waikiki Beachboys (Chick, Melvin, Pu'a, Splash, Squeeze, and Freckles), who strummed their 'ukes on the beach with Bing Crosby, surrounded by graceful women, swaying palm trees, and magnificent sunsets spread across an open sky.

Today the tones and chords of the 'ukelele conjure and epitomize Hawai'i's laid-back way of life. Upon setting foot on Hawai'i's shores, you're encouraged, as Brudda Bru of 'Ukeleke Heaven says, to "sit back and take your rubbah slippahs off, put on some 'ukulele music, and *ho'omanawanui* [take it easy]."

breakfast and lunch daily. In business since 1935, this place is so renowned that you should go early or not bother. Hundreds of loaves of their famed sweet bread, perhaps infused with onions and cheese, fly out of here by 7 AM. Look for the little sign that says HOT BREAD and get it when it's piping hot from the ovens (at 10 PM); ask them to put some butter or cinnamon on it. In a nod to modern times, Kanemitsu also offers lavosh: flatbread topped with taro, Parmesan cheese, or Maui onions. Treats $.

Stanley's Coffee Shop (808-553-9966), across from Triangle Park, 125 Puali St., Kaunakakai. Open 7–4 weekdays, 7–2 Sat. Most everyone drops into simple Stanley's once for inexpensive breakfasts, lunchtime sandwiches, strong espresso, or an Internet connection. Dishes $.

Coffees of Hawai'i (808-567-9490; coffeesofhawaii.net), Hwy. 480 near Hwy. 470, Kualapu'u. Open 8–4ish daily. For espresso brewed with local beans grown on a 500-acre estate, this little semi-outdoor espresso bar offers just the right kick. (See also *To See & Do.*)

West End
Maunaloa General Store (808-552-2346), Maunaloa. Open 8–6 Mon.–Sat. When your caloric cravings can be satisfied with off-the-shelf groceries and prepackaged picnic foods, this convenience store fits the bill. Good thing, because it's the only game in town.

East End
Mana'e Goods n' Grinds (808-558-8498), MM 16, Kamehameha V Hwy. Store open 8–5 daily, counter open 6:30–3. A limited convenience store and a real neighborhood joint (for-

merly known as The Neighborhood Store), the only food source in the East End has home-style offerings like fried doughnuts, breakfast omelets, good veggie burgers, mahimahi lunches, and Maui-made Roselani's ice cream. Enjoy them at shaded picnic tables before moving on. Dishes $; no credit cards.

✳ Entertainment
After the sun sets, Moloka'i gets quiet. Now that I mention it, though, Moloka'i is quiet before the sun sets. Most so-called entertainment takes place at hotel bars and over dinner, when locals "talk story." Check the local papers and bulletin boards for really local happenings in the community. If you go with a sincere heart, you'll be welcomed.

○ Hula Shores (808-553-5347; hotel molokai.com), Kamehameha V Hwy., Kaunakakai. Open daily. If you want to know something about the heart of Moloka'i, stay overnight on a Friday. The first time I came to this beloved place, when I showed up in wrinkled khakis and a tucked-in T-shirt, I immediately went home to change into shorts, a baggy T-shirt, and old sandals. Na Kapuna, Hawaiian "aunties," and local musicians entertain appreciative audiences on Friday night (4–6 PM) with 'ukelele, guitar, hula, and storytelling. It's one of the most decidedly authentic things you can do in the entire state. Local bands also play throughout the week from 6 to 9:30.

Paddler's Inn (808-553-5256; pad dlersinnhawaii.com), corner of Kamehameha V Hwy. 450 and Mohala St., Kaunakakai. Paddler's offers one-stop shopping: Enjoy Monday night football, karaoke, comedy, and Hawaiian

SADDLING UP FOR THE RETURN MULE RIDE

LEADING A MULE TRAIN

It's pouring rain and it's chilly and it's really muddy, but we're going. And we're sizing each other up—we humans and those mules. Actually, the mules couldn't care less whether it's raining or how macho we are. Some riders are prepared with ponchos; others use makeshift garbage bags; one goes without, eager for the chance.

Mules, we quickly come to learn, have distinct personalities. And the owners of Moloka'i Mule are quick to assess our personalities and play matchmaker with their beasts. None of us wants to be told what they're seeing: Is our stubbornness or passiveness or fear written so clearly on our faces and in our body language?

I'm the last to settle into the saddle of my steed, and I quickly realize that I've been assigned the lead mule. How do I know? Because he knows. With great composure but intense determination, he quietly bulldozes his way past his compatriots to the front of the corral. Great . . . I've never led a mule train before; I've never even ridden a four-legged creature before. But it's an honor to trust one's life to the most trustworthy beast in the barn. After I give in to the trepidation—after all, these mules walk up and down this path day in and day out—the corral is opened, and off we trundle.

Down, down, down the 1,600-foot drop we go, toward the historic leper colony of Kalaupapa. At times the 3-mile trek seems nearly vertical. But that's just because I'm perched 5 feet higher off the ground than usual and because my best friend, my mule, cuts corners. (I'll never cut corners again; I promise.) He comes precariously close to each of the 26 switchbacks on the trail. He pauses at each turn, as if to carefully consider the best footing—shall we wedge the front hoof between rock and root or shall we let it slide ever-so-slightly before it lodges on that limb down there? He decides with what appears to be experienced haste. The trail is often no wider than his hoof. We pass a couple of hikers who are slip-sliding their way down. They actually look envious.

If there are two kinds of people in this world, passengers and drivers—as Volkswagen would have us believe—I'm a driver. And yet I'm quick to surrender the reins on this wet and woolly day. It takes a little while for me to become a passenger (until the third switchback or so), but it's clear that my mule operates just fine without my intervention. Gradually my mule and I become one. We zig and zag together. My calves dangle alongside his rounded belly. Keeping my waist and hips loose, I let my shoulders sway back and forth with each sure step he places. I stop pretending (for whom?—the riders behind me so they'll gain confidence?) to hold the reins loosely and let them rest on the pommel. My mind's mantra becomes *let go and settle into it*, a perfect metaphor for almost anything. I stop looking down and start looking around, drinking in the glorious scenery that was perhaps less glorious to the leprosy patients who "resettled" here. About the time I finish replaying their distressing story in my mind, we've reached the bottom of the trail, the rain has lifted, and it's time to dismount and depart for the tour. My mule heads straight for a bale of hay at the end of the rainbow. He's earned it— along with my respect. I look forward to ascending with him.

KALAUPAPA PENINSULA

BIG WIND KITE FACTORY

closed on Sunday, join what passes for the Moloka'i masses on Saturday (the only day Ala Malama Street experiences its version of traffic) to stock up on groceries, wine, and other necessary sundries. From the little-of-everything **Moloka'i Drugs** (808-553-5790) to the old-fashioned **Imamura Store** (808-553-5615), wander down Ala Malama Street to see what you see. Despite its dearth of destination shops, I dare you to visit just once.

Moloka'i Fine Arts Gallery (808-553-8520; molokaifinearts.com), 2 Kamoi St., Kaunakakai. Open daily except Sun. This good gallery has a commendable selection of arts and crafts (koa bowls, ceramics, wood carvings) made by islanders and island residents. Need a gift or commemorative souvenir? This is your best bet.

Moloka'i Fish & Dive (808-553-5926; molokaifishanddive.com), Ala Malama St., Kaunakakai. Open daily. Besides too many T-shirts, this shop has a great selection of books about Moloka'i, as well as anything you might want to buy or rent for almost every conceivable outdoor activity.

Moloka'i Wine & Spirits (808-553-5009), Ala Malama St., Kaunakakai. Open 9 AM–8 PM Mon.–Thurs., 9–9 Fri. and Sat. This fine shop, with a great selection in terms of price and vintages, would hold its own in any major tourist town in Hawai'i.

West End
The side-by-side **Plantation Gallery** (808-552-2364; molokai.com/gallery) and **Big Wind Kite Factory** (808-552-2364; molokai.com/kites) in Maunaloa are owned by the same folks and keep the same hours (8:30–5 Mon.–Sat., 10–2 Sun.). The former

music; call for nightly schedule.

Maunaloa Cinemas (808-552-2707), Maunaloa. Open for matinees and evening shows. Hard to believe, but quiet, little Maunaloa has a multiplex with first-run movies.

✳ Selective Shopping

Central Moloka'i & Kaunakakai
Let's face it—you didn't come to Moloka'i to shop. That said, whatever you need is bound to be found in Kaunakakai. Since most shops are

offers CDs featuring local musicians, local books, *lauhala* baskets, bathing suits, clothes, glassware, jewelry, and carvings—in short, everything you might consider buying on vacation. The Kite Factory sells custom- and Moloka'i-made flying contraptions, many of which are works of art bursting with great graphics. I'm partial to the hula and fish designs. Factory tours are offered daily, but be sure to ask for a free lesson (windy weather permitting) while you wrangle your free-spirited kite. Some kites, by the way, are imported from Bali and elsewhere in Indonesia.

A Touch of Moloka'i (808-552-0133), within the closed Kaluakoi Hotel, Kaluakoi Resort. This really fine gift shop stocks a great selection of aloha shirts, vacation wear, non-flower leis, and wooden bowls—and it's all made on Moloka'i.

The Big Island 5

THE BIG ISLAND IN BRIEF

The island of Hawai'i, usually referred to as the Big Island for clarity by everyone except locals, is a place of primal power, elemental *mana* (spirit). *Diversity* is its middle name, and *-est* is its calling card.

Let's start with the *-est* claims to fame. It boasts the clearest skies on the planet, the two tallest mountain peaks in the world as measured from the sea bottom, the best collection of world-class resorts (on the Kohala Coast), the most active volcano (erupting since 1983), the southernmost point in the United States (Ka Lae), the most powerful telescopes in the world (Keck), the calmest waters in the state because of prevailing winds and the position of Mauna Kea (13,796 feet) and Mauna Loa (13,677 feet), and the most feared goddess of them all (Pele), who lives in Kilauea.

The Big Island is also the youngest sibling in the archipelago (a mere 800,000 years young), the least explored, and quite obviously the biggest, even though only 10 percent of the state's population lives here. (You could put two of each of the other islands within these 4,000 square miles and still have room left over.) It's also still growing: In about 100,000 years, Lo'ihi, an underwater island near Hawai'i Volcanoes National Park, will peek above the ocean's surface as more and more lava spews from Kilauea and piles up. It has over 250 miles of coastline but the fewest swimming beaches.

It's a place where a great king was born (North Kohala) and died (Kailua-Kona); a place where royalty played and worshiped and plotted the unification of the islands; a place thick with royal fishponds, royal *heiaus* (temples), royal footpaths, and ancient petroglyphs.

Variety and dichotomy are the spice of Big Island life. She is stark with black lava and white coral, black-sand beaches and snowcapped mountaintops. Moonscapes and desert landscapes blanket her dry side, while rain forests and jungles cut a swath across her wet side. She has five volcanoes, one green-sand beach, and 11 climatic zones. In the same day you may need pants and shorts, sunscreen, and an umbrella. She is spectacularly fiery, tempting you down a hiking path to her glory, and she is lazy-making, lulling you into submission. Like a mischievous genie, the Big Island plays hide-and-seek with travelers, enticing you away from her soul.

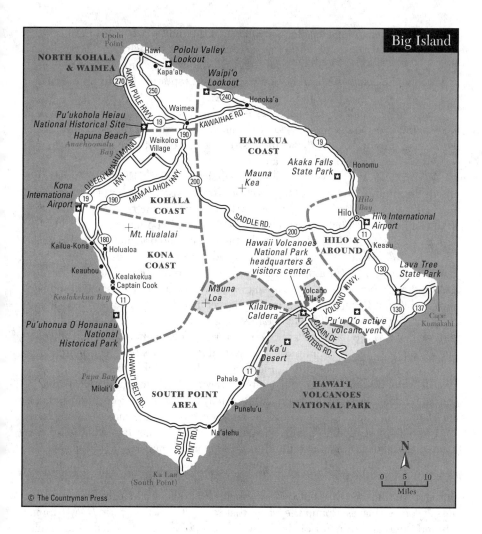

The main tourist centers on the Kohala Coast and the Kona Coast (and Kailua-Kona in particular) are a separate reality, a vacation playland that diverts most visitors from the natural and cultural richness of other regions. To experience the Big Island's bounty, you have to explore farther afield, and you must probe with patience. When you do, you'll learn precious secrets about the enduring spirit of old Hawai'i.

The volcanoes that formed all the islands are still active here. Before Mount St. Helens and Mount Redoubt erupted, the Mauna Loa and Kilauea peaks on the southern side of the Big Island were the only known live volcanoes in the United States. Unlike explosive cone volcanoes, their eruptions are not violent. They boil over slowly, sending lava snaking toward the sea at a dilatory pace. You can watch the eruptions in safety, if you are in the right place at the right time. The lucky will witness one of the most stunning sights of their lives. Typically, however, the Big Island doesn't make it easy. Mauna Loa erupts just once every few years. Kilauea is much more active, frequently spewing lava from its crater in Hawai'i Volcanoes National Park. If the lava is flowing, don't miss it.

The northern half of the island has its own natural wonders, not nearly as well known and even less accessible. On the rainy eastern side of the North Kohala Peninsula, erosion has cut through massive volcanic cliffs to create spectacular valleys such as Waipi'o and Waimanu.

Waipi'o (just over the vertical cliff on a 7-mile trail on the Hamakua Coast) and the rest of the Kohala Coast, along with the Kona Coast, are rich in Hawaiian history. Polynesians settled the Big Island first, and for the next 1,400 years, until the 19th century, it was politically and culturally the most important of the islands. It was also the home of King Kamehameha the Great, who first united all of Hawai'i under his rule. Historic sights from his era and earlier dot the western shore. A few have become tourist attractions, but some are rarely visited. The Mo'okini Heiau, the temple where Kamehameha was taken for birth rites, is one of the most significant Polynesian ruins in Hawai'i, yet it is virtually unknown to visitors.

Many Big Island small towns retain strong roots in the past. Bastions of the old ways, they have more authentic character and local personality than any of the dozen or so resort communities. Only Kailua-Kona has been commercially modernized beyond recognition of its former self. Incredibly, that is where the vast majority of tourists spend their time. They are likely to make a day trip to Hawai'i Volcanoes National Park, and they may zip through a few other spots on an island tour, but mostly they huddle together in one of the most prosaic places on Hawai'i's most sublime island. The goddess Pele, from her home in the Kilauea Crater, must roar with laughter at the contemporary tourism.

So, then, what should you do, where should you stay, how should you divide up your time? My ideal Hawaiian vacation, when I have time for only one island, is spent splitting the days between a Kohala Coast resort and a couple of smaller, less expensive places around the island that reflect her native spirit. (Day-tripping around the island from a Kohala Coast resort is possible, but, frankly, too much time is eaten up en route to wherever you're headed.)

The Kohala Coast, where the Big Island's only long, wide, sandy beaches are located, is lined with superlative and expensive resorts. Resort development on this shore, Hawai'i's premier upscale destination, has been the most sensitive and impressive in the state. If you can afford one of these resorts, by all means do it. Do beware, though, of being lulled into missing the rest of the Big Island.

Take a day trip from here into North Kohala and Kailua-Kona. Then spend a night in Waimea (a well-to-do town of cowboys, cows, and prime dining) or somewhere along the Hamakua Coast (where agriculture reigns). Or spend a night in a smaller South Kona town like Holualoa and explore that region without having to backtrack too much. Then spend a couple of nights in Hilo (a delightfully welcoming town) or Volcano Village (rife with bed & breakfasts on the edge of the national park).

The Big Island's soul is coquettish and her secrets are elusive, but they are definitely worth seeking out.

GUIDANCE

Big Island Visitor's Bureau (808-961-5797, 808-886-1655, or 1-800-648-2441; bigisland.org) has offices in Hilo and Waikoloa (near the Kohala Coast); see those sections for details.

MORE WEB SITES

eyeofhawaii.com (islandwide information)

gohawaii.com (Hawai'i Visitor's & Convention Bureau)

state.hi.us/dlnr (Hawai'i's Department of Lands and Natural Resources)

nps.gov/havo (Hawai'i Volcanoes National Park)

honoluluadvertiser.com (daily newspaper)

starbulletin.com (daily newspaper)

stayhawaii.com (Hawai'i B&B Association)

instanthawaii.com (islandwide information)

NEWSPAPERS

For local news, pick up *West Hawai'i Today* (808-329-9311 or 1-800-355-3911; westhawaiitoday.com) for coverage in and around Kailua-Kona.

The free and ubiquitous publications *101 Things to Do on the Big Island*, *This Week*, and the *Beach and Activity Guide* are full of helpful information.

WEATHER

Call the **National Weather Service** (808-935-8555 in Hilo; 808-961-5582 elsewhere on the Big Island) when it matters. If you're boating, call 808-935-9883.

MEDICAL EMERGENCY

Call 911. For hospitals, contact **Kona Community Hospital** (808-322-9311, Kealakekua); **Hilo Medical Center** (808-974-4700, Waianuenue Ave., Hilo); **North Hawai'i Community Hospital** (808-885-4444, Waimea).

GETTING THERE

By air from the mainland: The Big Island has two airports: **Kailua-Kona** (on the leeward side of the island) and **Hilo** (on the windward or eastern side); most visitors fly into the drier Kailua-Kona. **American** (1-800-433-7300; aa.com) and **United** (1-800-241-6522; united.com) offer a fair number of direct flights from San Francisco and Los Angeles to the Big Island. But the majority of flights still go through Honolulu.

At first glance the Big Island almost discourages you from landing. If you fly into Hilo, the largest town, it's likely to be raining. As the plane descends into Kailua-Kona, you see acres of desolate black lava fields that make the moon seem welcoming. At first it resembles parking lots of torn-up asphalt. However, as with any great desert, what originally seems monotonous and bleak turns out to be intriguingly diverse upon closer inspection. Don't expect to be captivated upon arrival, but I predict the lava wilderness of the Kohala Coast will grow on you.

Interisland air: **Hawaiian Airlines** (808-838-1555 or 1-800-367-5320; hawaiian air.com) and **Go! Airlines** (1-888-435-9462; iflygo.com) provide frequent interisland jet service to neighbor islands. When you book through a major carrier they will hook you up with a through flight to the Big Island.

GETTING AROUND

By car: Islanders talk about how big the Big Island is, but chances are, if you're a mainlander, it will seem quite manageable. The belt road around the Big Island is approximately 230 miles and would take about six hours to drive non-stop—a foolish thing to do, but I want to give you some perspective. Driving from Kailua-Kona to Hilo along the northern route takes about two to two and a half hours, while driving the southern route from Kona to Hilo takes about three and a half hours.

Although you can take a taxi or shuttle (**SpeediShuttle**; 1-800-242-5777; speedi shuttle.com) from the Kona airport to Kailua-Kona (where it's conceivable to stay without a car) or from the Hilo airport to downtown Hilo, I strongly recommend renting a car. The island contains 21 of 23 of the world's climatic zones, and you'll need a car to explore them. You'll only be able to give the island the attention it deserves by touring in a car. All major rental companies are represented at both airports.

A ROAD BY ANY OTHER NAME

Hwy. 19 = aka Queen Ka'ahumanu Highway (between Kailua-Kona and Kawaihae)

Hwy. 190 = aka Mamalahoa Highway (between Kailua-Kona and Waimea)

Hwy. 270 = aka Akoni Pule Highway (between Kawaihae and Hawi)

Hwy. 250 = aka Kohala Mountain Road (between Hawi and Waimea)

Hwy. 200 = aka Saddle Road (between Waikoloa and Hilo across Mauna Kea)

Hwy. 11 = aka the Hawai'i Belt Road (the road that circles the island)

Just so you know, there is also a free bus that runs around the island: **Hele-On** **Bus** (808-961-8744; co.hawaii.hi.us/mass_transit/heleonbus.html).

By most measures, the Kona Coast (specifically Kailua-Kona) and the Kohala Coast are the only truly developed tourist destinations. Hilo has toyed with tourism, but special places to stay are limited. The tiny village of Volcano, because of the nearby Hawai'i Volcanoes National Park, is increasingly popular with the B&B crowd. North Kohala, the Hamakua Coast, and the quiet South Point Area are generally off the beaten path, but each offers unusual accommodations.

For the most part, this chapter is organized as if you'll be exploring clockwise from the Kona airport.

By RV: Touring the Big Island by RV might be right up your lava flow. If so, call **Island RV** (808-334-0464 or 1-800-406-4555; islandrv.com). For about $2,200 weekly you'll get a fully outfitted, 22-foot cruiser that sleeps four and includes all campground registrations and permits. (Hawai'i laws state that you can't just pull over on the side of the road to sleep; you must stay in designated campgrounds.) Rental rates include 300 miles, but since it's about 235 miles around the island without detouring, you'll have to keep an eye on the odometer. Island RV will pick you up at the Kona airport on arrival and provide one room at the Royal Kona Resort on your last night. There is an additional charge if you're not picking up and dropping off between 9 AM and 5 PM.

ISLANDWIDE TOURS

❧ *By various modes:* **Hawai'i Forest & Trail** (808-331-8505 or 1-800-464-1993; hawaii-forest.com), 74-5035-B Queen Kamehameha Hwy., Kailua-Kona. With experienced naturalists by your side, every corner of the Big Island is open to exploration. Based on your interests and abilities, Rob and Cindy Pacheco's expert team creates adventure trips (for groups of 10 and under) to the Big Island's spectacular natural wonders. You can ride by van to Mauna Kea's summit, take an evening tour of the constellations, and return to earth to explore the volcano at Hualalai. If you're staying south of Kona, meet at headquarters; otherwise, shuttle service is available. Mauna Kea trip: $169 per person (dinner and gear included).

HAPU'U FERN

Since the Big Island also has more native bird species than any other Hawaiian island, this outfitter also offers a full-day **Rainforest Birding Adventure**. Adults and children $171; children should be able to hike on uneven terrain for extended periods. Binoculars, walking sticks, snacks, lunch, rain gear, and cold-weather gear provided.

❧ *By audio tour:* **Big Island Audio Tour** (808-896-4275; bigislandaudio

SAMPLE DRIVING DISTANCES

Kailua-Kona to Waimea: 40 miles, about 50 minutes

Waimea to Hilo: 54 miles, about 75 minutes

Hilo to Hawai'i Volcanoes National Park: 28 miles, about 45 minutes

Hawai'i Volcanoes National Park to Kailua-Kona: 110 miles, about 3 hours

tour.com). Perhaps the best investment (besides this book) that you can make to enhance your appreciation of the Big Island is to purchase this $20 CD. It entertains and educates listeners with anecdotal information and interesting tidbits on over 30 sites around the island. Order one before you fly to Hawai'i.

❦ *By air:* **Mokulele Airlines** (808-326-7070 or 1-866-260-7070; mokuleleair lines.com) departs from the Kailua-Kona airport. I highly recommend a circle island tour in one of these fixed-wing aircrafts ($349). Although the aircrafts provide a stable ride, folks prone to motion sickness may still want to take a Dramamine prior to departure.

Blue Hawaiian Helicopters (808-886-1768 or 1-800-786-2583; bluehawaiian .com). Tours depart from Hilo and Waikoloa. Take an aerial tour of a lifetime above active lava flows on their 50-minute Circle of Fire tour departing from Hilo. Or dip along the Kohala Coast for breathtaking views of ancient geological formations and lush rain forests; this two-hour tour departs from Waikoloa. Routes and times may be dictated by prevailing conditions. Prices start at $217 per person; reservations are recommended; online deals available.

By bike: Although it may seem daunting to Sunday riders, it's quite possible to circle the island in a week, but you'll have to do some advance planning. Contact **PATH** (808-936-4653; pathhawaii .org), which has a great biking guide map, or visit the **Hilo Bike Hub** (808-961-4452; hilobikehub.com), 318 East Kawili St., for information on rides around the Big Island. On the Kona side, **Kona Cycling** (808-327-0087; cyclekona.com) offers four- and six-hour tours for all levels along diverse ecosystems.

ENDANGERED SEA TURTLE

❦ *By foot:* **Hawaiian Walkways** (808-775-0372 or 1-800-457-7759; hawaiianwalkways.com). Winner of the First Annual Tour Operator of the Year Award (as conferred by the Hawai'i Ecotourism Association), Dr. Hugh Montgomery offers exceptional custom and scheduled hikes around the island that are suited to various abilities. You'll get far, far, far more out of hiking with Hugh than you will alone. Half-day prescheduled trips: $95 adults, $75 children; full-day trips: $150 adults, $95 children. Call ahead for availability.

Underwater: **Nautilus Dive Center** (808-935-6939; nautilusdivehilo.com), 382 Kamehameha Ave., Hilo. The Big Island—sometimes—offers a rare opportunity for experienced divers to dive where molten lava streams into the ocean. At press time, ever-changing conditions mandated a halt to these dives, but it's always worth checking.

Big Island Snuba (808-326-7446; snubabigisland.com), Kailua-Kona. For kids and adults with an appetite for adventure and a healthy respect for learning-before-doing, snuba might be the ticket. Compared to its scuba counterpart, equipment is pared down and lightweight. Snuba uses a simple harness and regulator for breathing, and users always remain tethered to a hose attached to a tank on a raft. Packages include a more-than-adequate 15-minute lesson on how to safely descend 25 feet, the perfect depth for beginners to view aquatic life up close while still enjoying the comfort of a nearby instructor. Take a 90-minute beach dive from King Kamehameha Kona Beach Hotel or a longer boat dive from various locations along the Kona Coast (depending upon weather conditions). Instructor-led Snuba Doo packages offer flotation vests and regulators for children ages 4–7. Instructor certification programs are also available. Dives $49–165 per person; Snuba Doo $69–110.

Golf: **Stand-by Golf** (1-888-645-2665; stand-bygolf.com). While frequent fliers know about standby flights, golfing enthusiasts should know about Stand-by Golf. Unsold tee times at some of the best courses on the island are available at the last minute for lower prices ($70–150) than if you'd booked ahead. Tee times are available for many courses on Kaua'i, Maui, and O'ahu, too. For same-day reservations, call between 7 AM and 1:30 PM; for next-day tee times, call 6–10 PM.

TOP 10 "MUSTS" FOR FIRST-TIME VISITORS
Marvel at creation at Hawai'i Volcanoes National Park
Descend into Waipi'o Valley
Hike to Akaka Falls
Hang in Hilo and absorb local culture
Ascend Mauna Kea for serious stargazing
Drink Kona coffee in a Holualoa café
Snorkel at Kealakekua Bay, skirting sea caves
Spend lazy days at Hapuna Beach or Mauna Kea Beach
Linger at the Pololu Valley Lookout
Visit black sand and sea turtles at Punalu'u Beach Park

TOP 10 IDEAS FOR REPEAT VISITORS

Explore HVNP much more thoroughly

Tour Pu'uhonua O Honaunau National Historical Park

Don't move from your perch at a five-star North Kohala resort

Test your patience and skills at Hapuna and Mauna Kea Golf Courses

Look for petroglyphs at the Pu'ako Archaeological Petroglyph District

Go whale-watching with Captain Dan McSweeney

Stand on the very southern tip of South Point

Understand the importance of Pu'ukohola Heiau National Historic Site

Take a night dive to watch manta rays

Plan your trip to witness the Merrie Monarch Festival

✳ Special Events

For a complete list of islandwide events, consult calendar.gohawaii.com.

Mid-March: **Kona Brewers Festival** (808-331-3033; konabrewersfestival .com), King Kamehameha Kona Beach Hotel, Kailua-Kona. Come for the beer tasting and stay for the cause—raising hundreds of thousands of dollars for environmental and cultural organizations.

Late March: **Prince Kuhio Celebrations**, statewide. On March 26, Hawai'i celebrates the birth of Jonah Kuhio Kalanianaole, who served as a congressional delegate from 1903 to 1921.

LAVA FLOW AS SEEN FROM A HELICOPTER

Easter: **Merrie Monarch Hula Festival** (808-935-9168; merriemonarch festival.org), Hilo. This weeklong cultural event begins the day after Easter Sunday, and the hula competition takes place the following weekend. (The solo Miss Aloha Hula is on Thursday, *kahiko* is Friday night, and *halau* is on Saturday night.) Reserve your tickets months in advance.

May 1: **Lei Day**, statewide. The phrase "May Day is Lei Day" was coined by Grace Tower Warren in 1928 when Lei Day was conceived.

June: **King Kamehameha Celebration** (808-586-0333; hawaii.gov/dags/ king_kamehameha_commission), statewide. Hawai'i's longest-running festival honors King Kamehameha, unifier of the Hawaiian Kingdom.

Late June: **Great Waikoloa Food, Wine & Music Festival** (808-886-1234; hiltonwaikoloavillage.com), Hilton Waikoloa Village. At this festival, part of the Hilton's Dolphin Days celebration, chefs from around the world gather to flaunt their latest tastes.

July 4: **Parker Ranch Horse Races & Rodeo** (808-885-7311; parker ranch.com/events), Waimea. Let this group of *paniolos* (cowboys) show you the ropes—with horse racing, pony rides, food, and lots of other action.

Turtle Independence Day (808-881-7911; maunalani.com), Mauna Lani Bay Hotel & Bungalows, Kohala Coast. On July 4th, visitors can watch as turtles bred in captive are ceremoniously returned to the ocean.

Late July: **Crater Rim Run & Marathon** (808-967-8222; volcano artcenter.org), Hawai'i Volcanoes National Park. One of the toughest but most beautifully sited marathons also holds a noncompetitive, 5-mile run-walk.

August: **Hawaiian International Billfish Tournament** (808-329-6155; konabillfish.com), Kailua-Kona. Anglers from around world descend on Hawai'i.

Mid-August: **Hawaiian Cultural Festival** (808-882-7218; nps.gov/puhe), Kawaihae. This weekend celebration at Pu'ukohola Heiau National Historic Site includes canoe rides and arts and crafts workshops. Because of the 2007 earthquake, which caused damage to the *heiau*, the traditional opening ceremony and the morning sunrise service in Hawaiian will probably not be held.

Mid- to late August: **Admissions Day**, statewide. On the third Friday in August, all islands celebrate the day Hawai'i became the 50th state.

Late August: **Slack-Key Guitar Festival** (808-226-2697; slackkey festival.com), Kailua-Kona. Some of Hawai'i's most accomplished folk musicians gather to play the slack key guitar, steel guitar, and 'ukulele.

TOP DOZEN PLACES TO STAY AROUND THE BIG ISLAND

Best Romantic Hideaways
Waianuhea (Hamakua Coast)
Volcano Places (Nohea) (Hawai'i Volcanoes National Park)
The Inn at Kulaniapia (Hilo & Around)
The Cliff House (Hamakua Coast)

Best Intimate & Affordable Lodgings
Hale Ohia Cottages (Hawai'i Volcanoes National Park)
Dolphin Bay Hotel (Hilo & Around)
Waimea Gardens Cottage (North Kohala & Waimea)

Best B&Bs
Waianuhea (Hamakua Coast)
Waipi'o Wayside Bed & Breakfast Inn (Hamakua Coast)
Shipman House Bed & Breakfast (Hilo & Around)

Best Unusual Places
The Hobbit House (The South Point Area)
Wood Valley Temple Retreat & Guest House (The South Point Area)
(See also *Top 10 Places to Stay on the Kona Coast*, p. 376, and *Top Places to Stay on the Kohala Coast*, p. 401.)

TOP PLACES TO EAT BEYOND THE KONA & KOHALA COASTS

Pricey
Merriman's (North Kohala & Waimea)

Moderate
Café Pesto (North Kohala & Waimea)
Bamboo (North Kohala & Waimea)
Hilo Bay Café (Hilo & Around)
Seaside Restaurant and Aquafarm (Hilo & Around)

Cheap Eats
Simply Natural (Hamakua Coast)
(See also *Top 10 (Plus One) Places to Eat in Kona & Kohala*, p. 382.)

Late August–early September: **Big Island Festival** (808-326-7820; bigislandfestival.com). One of the Big Island's largest festivals offers food, wine, spa events, and golf.

First weekend in September: **Queen Lili'uokalani Long Distance Canoe Races** (808-324-1541 or 808-334-9481; kaiopua.org), between Kailua-Kona Pier and Honaunau. Thousands of spectators gather for the world's largest long-distance canoe race.

September: **Aloha Festivals** (808-589-1771; alohafestivals.com), statewide. Big Island festivities include parades, hula, beauty contests, and a festival at Parker Ranch.

Poke Contest (808-880-3028; pokecontest.com), Hapuna Beach Prince Hotel and Mauna Kea Beach Resort. Part of the festival is dedicated to finding the best *poke* (pieces of raw fish mixed with local ingredients) recipes.

Mid-September: **Kupuna Hula Festival** (808-322-1812; alohafestivals.com), Keauhou Sheraton, Kailua-Kona. Hawaiian elders gather for a hula competition while lessons are offered in the hotel lobby; arts and crafts demonstrations are also offered.

Mid-October: **Ironman Triathlon World Championship** (808-329-0063; ironmanlive.com), Kailua-Kona. Spectators watch for free as competitors swim 2.4 miles from the Kailua-Kona Pier, bike 112 miles up the Kona Coast to Hawi and back, and then run 26.2 miles.

Mid-November: **Kona Coffee Cultural Festival** (808-326-7820; konacoffeefest.com). This 10-day event includes coffee-picking contests, living-history farm tours, art exhibits, and a parade.

BANANA LEAVES

THE KONA COAST

Kailua-Kona used to be a peaceful fishing and agricultural village. Mark Twain and Robert Louis Stevenson marveled at its rustic charm around the turn of the 20th century. There are still vestiges of the past, such as Hawai'i's oldest missionary church and a replica of Kamehameha the Great's last home. Almost 200 years ago, the king dedicated his residence to Lono, the god of good harvests and prosperity, who would likely have misgivings about today's forms of bounty. Since 1970, the population has quadrupled and concrete consumption has zoomed astronomically.

Residential housing, condos, and hotels now line Ali'i Drive for about 10 miles. From Kamehameha's home in the north to the Keauhou condo and shopping developments in the south, the coastal boulevard bulges with monuments to a new kind of prosperity. The northern sector of Ali'i Drive is the center of the action, which in Kailua is largely confined to shops and eating at good-time restaurants.

Other than convenience, perhaps the best reason to stay in Kailua-Kona is ready access to deep-sea fishing. The construction of Kailua-Kona Pier in 1915 near Kamehameha's home virtually eliminated the town beach. But today the pier is the center of the famous marlin fishing industry and the International Billfishing Tournament each August. Charters go out daily and return in the late afternoon to weigh giant catches on huge scales. Kailua-Kona is also home to the increasingly popular Ironman Triathlon in October.

You may have heard *kona* used to describe leeward-side weather; basically *kona* redefines the words *sunny* and *dry*.

At the 70-mile stretch south of Kailua-Kona, tourist development abruptly halts and the rural calm of Kailua's past reemerges. Highway 11 parallels the rocky coast, about 1,000 feet above the Pacific, down to the southern tip of the United States (see "The South Point Area"). The farther south you go, the more macadamia nut trees you'll see. The Big Island, by the way, produces 90 percent of the state's nuts. The road is heavily traveled by visitors going to Kealakekua Bay, a popular marine sanctuary for snorkeling and kayaking, and where Captain Cook was killed; Pu'uhonua O Honaunau National Historical Park, an ancient religious sanctuary; or all the way to Hawai'i Volcanoes National Park (see that chapter).

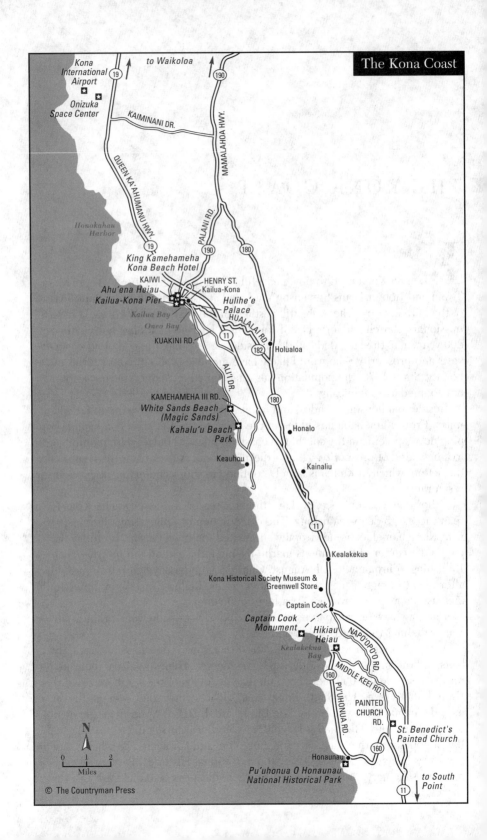

The Kona Coast

Kona International Airport

Onizuka Space Center

to Waikoloa

KAIMINANI DR.

QUEEN KA'AHUMANU HWY.

MAMALAHOA HWY.

PALANI RD.

Honokohau Harbor

King Kamehameha Kona Beach Hotel

KAIWI

Ahu'ena Heiau

Kailua-Kona Pier

Kailua Bay

Oneo Bay

HENRY ST.
Kailua-Kona

Hulihe'e Palace

HUALALAI RD.

KUAKINI RD.

Holualoa

ALI'I DR.

KAMEHAMEHA III RD.

White Sands Beach (Magic Sands)

Kahalu'u Beach Park

Honalo

Keauhou

Kainaliu

Kealakekua

Kona Historical Society Museum & Greenwell Store

Captain Cook

Captain Cook Monument

Hikiau Heiau

Kealakekua Bay

NAPO'OPO'O RD.

MIDDLE KEEI RD.

PU'UHONUA RD.

PAINTED CHURCH RD.

St. Benedict's Painted Church

Honaunau

Pu'uhonua O Honaunau National Historical Park

to South Point

N

0 1 2
Miles

© The Countryman Press

Located on the fertile slopes rising up to Mauna Loa, the village of Holualoa was once agricultural but is now an artists' community with galleries occupying the church and former post office. It's still the heart of Kona coffee district; the old coffee mill is now an artist's workshop and studio. Lots of cafés serve 100 percent Kona coffee.

GUIDANCE

Kona Historical Society (808-938-8825; konahistorical.org) offers excellent **walking tours of downtown** with colorful commentary. Tours are booked by reservation only; $15 adults; $7 ages 5–12.

GETTING AROUND

By car: For planning purposes, it takes about two hours nonstop to drive from Kailua-Kona south to the turnoff for South Point. If you're trying to get to a boat tour on time, keep in mind that traffic around Kailua-Kona creeps during morning and afternoon rush hours. Holualoa is about a 15-minute drive from Kailua-Kona; take Hwy. 19 to Hualalai Road and head uphill along the winding tropical road. The free **Keauhou Trolley** (808-930-4900, ask for the concierge) stops at major resorts, Kahalu'u Beach Park, and shopping areas. It only runs every 90 minutes or so, but if someone in your party has taken the car and you want to go into town, you can't beat it.

✳ To See & Do

✪ *In Kailua-Kona*

The main part of Ali'i Drive, shaded by regal banyan trees, is a mere half mile long. It's most convenient to park at the King Kamehameha Kona Beach Hotel (75-5660 Palani Rd.), although it's not free. Many tourist-oriented and specialty shops—bursting at the seams with *lilikoi'i* jam, Kona coffee, and macadamia

---

BUILDING BLOCKS TO SEVEN PERFECT DAYS IN PARADISE

These regional planners will get you started on how best to dip into the island. Use them as building blocks to create perfect days. But a word of caution: If you try to do everything mentioned, you might not feel like you're on a vacation. Use them merely as a guide.

Building Blocks for the Perfect Day on Kona Coast

Stroll historic Kailua-Kona in early morning before it gets too hot and over-run with tourists (90 minutes)

Pop in and out of cafés and galleries in Holualoa (2 hours)

Kayak around and swim in Kealakekua Bay (3 hours)

Explore Pu'uhonua O Honaunau National Historical Park (three hours)

Take a snorkeling and catamaran trip with Hula Kai or Fair Wind (4 to 5 hours)

nuts—are housed in somewhat atmospheric, open-air shopping malls here, like the boardwalk-style Kona Inn Shopping Village.

King Kamehameha's Kamakahonu (808-329-2911; konabeachhotel.com/ history.cfm), 75-5660 Palani Rd., adjacent to the King Kamehameha Kona Beach Hotel. After conquering and unifying the islands by 1810, the king lived at this royal compound from 1813 to 1819 (when he died). At that point, his bones were secreted away somewhere in the North Kona area, safely tucked away in a cliffside cave so no one could steal his *mana*. When the king died, his son Liho-liho assumed the throne and promptly upended the apple cart. He decreed that gods needn't be revered above all else, and he broke tradition by dining with his mother, Ke'opuolani, and the king's principal wife, Ka'ahumanu. The **Ahu'ena Heiau** (an impressive replica, especially considering that you're seeing only about one-third of its actual size) is fascinating. The king lived on these grounds during peacetime, and he dedicated the temple to Lono, the god of harvest and rain. *Kahunas* gathered at Ahu'ena to give the king advice, but there is no confirmation that human sacrifices were actually made. The hotel has an informative pamphlet for free self-guided tours, or you can call and reserve a place on a guided tour (donations; 808-327-0123). Perhaps you'll get lucky, like I did, with a docent whose father restored the *heiau*.

Kailua-Kona Pier (808-329-4997), downtown, Ali'i Dr. Dating to 1918, this pier is a hub of activity. You'll find sunset sailing boats docked here, fishing charters, outrigger canoeists, and the like. The Ironman Triathlon also begins here with a 2.4-mile swim, and locals fish with rods and nets from the seawall.

🏵 **Hulihe'e Palace** (808-329-1877; daughtersofhawaii.org), 75-5718 Ali'i Dr. Open 9–4 daily. This two-story, New England–style church constructed of coral, lava, 'ohi'a, and *koa* wood in 1838 originally served as the vacation home for the

HULIHE'E PALACE

island's governor, who royally enjoyed entertaining royalty here. In the 1880s, King David Kalakaua also used it as a summer home; it's only one of two royal palaces in the United States. (The other is in Honolulu.) After the palace fell into disrepair, the Daughters of Hawai'i restored it in the mid-1920s and opened it to the public. (At press time it was under renovation again, scheduled for a late 2008 reopening.) Guided tours are quite informative; you'll probably not forget the massive four-poster bed or the stunningly intricate inlaid table. Hula shows are held on the palace grounds at 4 PM on the third and fourth Sunday of each month, except June (when it's on King Kamehameha Day) and December (when it's on Christmas). $6 adults, $1 children.

Moku'aikaua Church (808-329-0655), 75-5713 Ali'i Dr. Across the street from the palace, this New England–style church is the island's oldest Christian church. It began life as a thatched hut in 1820 but was replaced by this black stone and white coral edifice in 1836. The lava stones, by the way, were taken from a *heiau* that was supposedly no longer in use.

Beyond Downtown

Lekeleke Burial Grounds and Kuamo'o Battlefield, at the southern end of Ali'i Dr. This sacred spot, about a 10-minute drive from downtown, is the burial site of about 300 soldiers. When Liholiho became king and changed the laws, Chief Kekuaokalani challenged him here and much blood was shed.

✎ **Ellison S. Onizuka Space Center** (808-329-3441; hawaiimuseums.org/mc/ ishawaii_astronaut.htm), at the Kona airport, 1 Keahole St. Open 8:30–4:30 daily. About 7 miles north of Kailua-Kona, this center is dedicated to the Big Island– born astronaut who perished in 1986 in the space shuttle *Challenger* tragedy. Interactive exhibits include what it feels like to be weightless in space and in a shuttle launch; it's great fun for kids. $3 adults, $1 ages 12 and under.

Natural Energy Laboratory of Hawai'i Authority (NELHA) (808-329-7341; nelha.org) near MM 94, 73-4460 Queen Ka'ahumanu Hwy. Open 8–4 week-days. If you're an NPR Science Friday type or a *New York Times* Science Tues-day type, NELHA will fascinate you. A combination of sun and science create conditions here for novel aquaculture techniques and ground-breaking oceanic conservation. Self-guided tours free; reservations ($8 for adults, $5 for students and seniors) required for public presentations Mon.–Thurs., third Saturday of the month, from 10 AM.

NELHA

Honokohau Harbor, off Hwy. 19 about 5 miles north of Kailua-Kona. Many boating and snorkeling trips depart from here. You'll find whale-watching and fishing charters here, too.

✪ **Coffee** and **Holualoa**, Hwy. 180. This funky little village is the heart of Kona coffee country, a region that stretches for about 20 miles, where trees thrive at an elevation of 1,000 to 1,400 feet. Before setting out for deep exploration in search of the ever-elusive perfect brew, pick up the *Coffee Country Driving Tour* brochure from the Big Island Visitor's Bureau in Waikoloa (see *Guidance* under "The Kohala Coast"). The Big Island is the only place in the United States where coffee is commercially grown. It was first planted on Oʻahu in 1825 and migrated in 1828 to the Big Island, where it thrives in rich volcanic soil. When coffee began its gourmet ascent in the 1980s, Kona coffee beans rose with the market's tide. The commodity is priced like barrels of crude oil these days: sky high. Thanks to the lobbying efforts of Governor Linda Lingle, the White House began serving exclusively Kona coffee in 2003. For more information, see *Coffee . . . Did You Know?* (p. 371).

Holualoa has cultivated more than coffee trees, though. It has a nice blend of galleries, cafés, little shops, many B&Bs, and even an old-fashioned gas station and an old general store. You should also come to Holualoa for the shade and moderate temperatures.

South of Kailua-Kona (from North to South)

Kainaliu, around MM 113, Hwy. 11. This blink-and-you'll-miss-it village is worth a momentary diversion for its authentic Aloha Theater and some marvelous old Japanese-owned stores (like Kimura's, dating to the 1920s).

Kona Historical Society Museum (808-323-3222; konahistorical.org), between MM 111 and 112, Hwy. 11, Kealakekua. Open 10–2 weekdays. Also known as the **Greenwell Store**, this mid-19th-century homestead consisted of a post office, cattle ranch, houses, and a general store; the latter is all that remains. It houses artifacts and photographs that help illuminate what daily life was like on a ranch back in the 1850s. You can also glean some information about the world of Kona coffee. $7 adults, $3 children.

By late 2008 a fancy new visitors center should be completed. Also, keep your ears open about their new Kona Heritage Ranch, which will depict a day in the life of a Big Island rancher circa 1890.

The organization offers excellent **tours of the circa-1900 coffee farm** that depicts life for a Japanese farm family, complete with costumed docents playing the parts. It's quite illustrative. Open 10–2 Mon.–Fri.; $20 adults, $7.50 ages 5–12.

Hikiau Heiau, end of Napoʻopoʻo Rd., off Hwy. 11. When Captain Cook landed on the Big Island in 1778, he was honored as a god at this *heiau,* where only the stone platform remains.

✪ **Kealakekua Bay**, end of Napoʻopoʻo Rd., Captain Cook. This protected marine park is home to sea caves, pods of dolphins, healthy coral reefs, abundant colorful fish that live within them, and snorkelers who want to be part of their ecosystems for a few hours. (See *Outdoor Activities.*) Before Captain Cook arrived here in November 1778, it was considered the center of Hawaiian life. It's safe to say that by landing here, he changed the course of Hawaiʻi's history. When Cook returned the second time, he was killed here.

COFFEE . . . DID YOU KNOW?

- Kona coffee is the only coffee grown in the United States for commercial use.
- Kona coffee is grown only on the western slopes of the great volcanic mountains Mauna Loa and Hualalai, between 800- and 2,000-foot elevations.
- The coffee tree takes two years to produce "first fruit," but four years to reach full maturity and produce a commercial crop.
- In one year, one coffee tree will produce only enough fruit to make 1 pound of roasted coffee.
- The coffee tree is a member of the gardenia family.
- More than a billion pounds of coffee are consumed every year in the U.S.

Terms Describing Green Coffee Beans (Prior to Roasting)

- *Color:* From blue-green to yellow-green and brown dependent on geographic origin, species, age, method of processing, maturity, and conditions of storage and transport
- *Black jack:* Coffee that has turned black after the full process during transportation or during processing
- *Clean:* A well-graded coffee free of defects
- *Parchment:* Dried coffee still in the outer skin prior to hulling
- *Quakers:* Often referred to as stinkers or floaters, these are unripe or blighted beans—coffee picked when the coffee cherry is still green
- *Screen:* The general term for size gradings based on the mesh or screen size through which the beans may be retained while grading
- *Sound:* Good marketable coffee
- *Bold:* A large to very large, well-formed, and even coffee bean

Terms Describing Brewed Coffee

- *Acid:* Sharp and pleasing characteristic particularly strong with certain origins—as opposed to one with a caustic, overfermented, sour, or bitter flavor
- *Body:* Strong, full, pleasant characteristic as opposed one tasting thin
- *Coarse:* A raspy and harsh flavor; one lacking finesse
- *Erpsig:* Potato flavor
- *Earthy:* Groundlike, wet-earth flavor that comes after storage with damaged coffees
- *Fiery:* Bitter charcoal taste generally due to overroasting
- *Grassy:* Greenish grassy or greenish flavor, particularly strong with early-crop Arabics that have been picked prematurely
- *Muddy:* Dull, indistinct, and thickish flavor, perhaps due to grounds being agitated
- *Rank:* Dirty, unpleasant flavor due to contamination or overfermentation
- *Fine:* Coffee with distinct quality characteristics such as acid, body, etc.

—Compliments of Hawai'i Coffee Company (see *To See & Do,* "Greater Honolulu," in the O'ahu section)

Cook and his sailors were welcomed with open arms when they first sailed into the bay. It was harvest season, and he was considered by many to be the personification of the god Lono. Cook sailed out of the bay four months later, but he was forced to return because of bad weather. His second coming was not greeted as kindly. Upon learning that one of his longboats had been stolen, Cook and his men went to retrieve it, and he wound up getting shot on Valentine's Day 1779.

Captain Cook Monument, alongside Kealakekua Bay. This obelisk marks the spot where Cook was killed. But because of his observations to the outside world, changes had already been put in motion. It wouldn't be long before missionaries and whalers, drunken sailors and disease would irrevocably alter this paradise. Most visitors see the monument from a snorkeling tour or land with their rental kayak. But you can also hike here. The trailhead for this three-hour (2.5-mile) intermediate hike is near the three royal palm trees on Napoʻopoʻo Rd. near the intersection with Hwy. 11. Per usual, bring plenty of water.

St. Benedict's Painted Church (808-328-2227), off Hwy. 160. Belgian priests worked hard at converting Hawaiians. This quirky and somewhat Gothic church is filled with hand-painted scenes from the Bible. Because Hawaiians were illiterate, the Belgian priest-painter figured the pictures would help explain the stories and teachings. This vantage point affords great views of Kealakekua Bay.

✪ **Puʻuhonua O Honaunau National Historical Park** (808-328-2288; nps.gov/puho), on Hwy. 160, off Hwy. 11, Honaunau. Visitors center open 8–5 daily; park open 7 AM–8 PM daily. About 3.5 miles off Hwy. 11 and about 20 miles south of Kailua-Kona, this 16th-century sacred place of refuge was beautifully restored and converted into a national historical park in 1961. You'll want to take a very good self-guided tour, looking for thatched *hales*, fishponds, burial sites, and other areas that illuminate the earliest ways of life in Hawaiʻi. It's called a "place of refuge" for very specific reasons. If you broke any of the strict laws of the times (pertaining to sex or land ownership, for instance), there was only one way to achieve absolution. If you could get here—through, around, or over the 10-foot-high, 17-foot-thick, and 1,000-foot-long wall surrounding the place—before the "authorities" got to you, you'd be safe. Don't miss the royal *heiau* on the premises, Hale-o-Keawe. $5 per vehicle or $3 per person.

CAPTAIN COOK MONUMENT

BICYCLING

Hawaiian Pedals (808-329-2294; Kona Inn Shopping Village, Aliʻi Dr.) and **HP Bike Works** (808-326-2453; hpbikeworks.com), both in Kailua-Kona. These shops carry a wide range of cycling clothes and accessories if you forgot to pack your gear, and they'll recommend cycling routes based on your preferences and abilities. Mountain bikes and hybrids rent by the half day ($15), full day ($20), or week ($70); add another $5 daily for a rack. More advanced cyclists will want to stop by **HP Bike Works** at 74-5583 Luhia St., where a larger rental selection of bikes is available. Rent a rack and head to Volcano Village or ask about many nearby road excursions that are traversed for the Ironman Triathlon.

DIVING

Since I've never been diving, contact the experts: **Jack's Diving Locker** (1-800-345-4807; jacksdivinglocker.com) or **Bottom Time** (808-331-1858; bottomtime hawaii.com), both in Kona, for the lowdown on the deep down. Highly consider night diving with the graceful **manta rays** with either outfitter. According to friends, it's otherwordly, and it's changed the lives of everyone I know who's done it.

FISHING

Honokohau Marine Charters (808-329-5735 or 1-888-566-2487; charterdesk .com), Honokohau Harbor, north of Kailua-Kona. Trips daily. You don't have to travel far to catch big game: blue marlin, mahimahi, swordfish, and yellowfin tuna are common just 3 miles offshore. If you want to keep your catch, discuss your options when making reservations. This company books over 50 vessels—choose your boat based upon availability, what type of fish you're looking for, and your group size. Parties of up to six can charter the 35-foot *Cabo Howbaddoy-ouwantit*; when you tire of fishing, you can soak up the sun on its beautiful bridge. An eight-hour excursion costs $700 ($500 for four hours). Regular charters run $500–900 for a full day, $300–600 for a half day.

GOLF

⛳ **Swing Zone** (808-329-6909), 74-5562 Makala Blvd., Kailua-Kona. Open 10–9 daily. Though this par-3 practice course may be only six holes, it's not child's play. To brush up your skills, play an unlimited number of rounds for a one-time fee of $14; club rentals cost $11. There's also a driving range (60 balls for 6 bucks) and a newly refurbished 18-hole putting course ($7) shaped like the Big Island. Batting cages keep kids occupied while you're loosening your hips and perfecting your swing.

PUʻUHONA O HONAUNAU

THE BIG ISLAND

HIKING

See **Captain Cook Monument** under *To See & Do.*

HORSEBACK RIDING (& SNORKELING)

King's Trail Rides (808-323-2388; konacowboy.com), near MM 111, Hwy. 11, Kealakekua. Trips daily. This outfit leads small groups of six and fewer people down hills dense with vegetation that lead to sweeping views of Kealakekua Bay. Bring a bathing suit (they'll supply a snorkel and mask), because riders can also swim and explore along the bay's protected marine preserve. The four-hour trip includes a two-hour ride and picnic lunch at Captain Cook Monument; children over seven welcome. $135 weekdays, $150 weekends.

KAYAKING & CANOEING

Aloha Kayak (808-322-2868; alohakayak.com), MM 114, Hwy. 11, 8 miles south of Kailua-Kona. Trips Mon.–Sat. If you're interested in mixing natural history and culture lessons with kayaking, take their four-hour cave and snorkeling expedition ($79 adults, $40 ages 12 and under) that explores hidden coastal recesses. It's a personal favorite. Perhaps surprisingly, the most relaxing tour is a six-hour open-water paddle to Captain Cook Monument ($159 adults, ages 12 and under half price). Gear, snacks, and beverages are included on all trips. Aloha Kayak also rents boats for $35 single, $60 double; reserve at least 24 hours in advance.

HULA KAI

SNORKELING & BOAT TRIPS

✪ **Snorkel Bob's** (808-329-0770; snorkelbob.com), 75-5831 Kahakai Rd. (at Huggo's), Kailua-Kona. Open daily. For rental gear galore, nobody beats Bob's. Don't skimp on equipment—top-of-the-line gear costs $11 daily ($44 weekly) for a mask, snorkel, and fins. Bob's will point you to the Big Island's best snorkeling spots based on your abilities. Start out about 4 miles south of the store in Kahalu'u; head 30 miles south to Kealakekua Bay for pristine waters accessible by boat or kayak near Captain Cook Monument; or continue farther to City of Refuge (Pu'uhonua O Honaunau National Historical Park).

✪ **Hula Kai** (808-322-2788 or 1-800-677-9461; fair-wind.com), office at 78-7130 Kaleiopapa St., Kailua-Kona; boats depart from Keauhou Bay; inquire about parking nearby. Since

SEA QUEST EXCURSIONS

this high-tech hydrofoil is able to bring passengers farther than any other boat plying these waters, you'll reach two snorkeling sites (including Pali Kaholo) the likes of which you've probably never seen. The crew is top-notch, the healthy food is delicious, and the snorkeling is brilliant. When the boat is stopped, patio-style umbrellas are brought out to shelter you from the sun while dining and dipping into the water. Expect a whopping three hours of snorkeling time. Bring sunscreen, towels, a swimsuit, and a light jacket. $149 per person; the five-hour trip departs at 9:30 AM.

Fair Wind Cruises (808-322-2788 or 1-800-677-9461; fair-wind.com), office at 78-7130 Kaleiopapa St., Kailua-Kona; boats depart from Keauhou Bay; inquire about parking nearby. Trips daily. Perfect for practically everyone, this 60-foot catamaran carries 100 passengers and heads to the Kealakekua Bay marine sanctuary at Captain Cook Monument, where calm waters draw spinner dolphins. Snorkelers can peer below the water's surface while sun soakers can float above it. There's even a water slide on board (and toilets); all gear is included. The four-and-a-half-hour morning trip has longer periods of bright sunshine; it includes continental breakfast and barbecue lunch. The slightly shorter after-noon cruise (departing at 2 PM) includes snacks. $109–119 adults, $69–75 ages 12 and under.

Captain Zodiac (808-329-3199; captainzodiac.com), 5 miles south of the Kona airport at Honokohau Harbor. Trips daily. How is this snorkeling trip to Keala-kekua different from the others? It uses those rigid-hull, inflatable boats used by Navy SEALs and carries only 18 passengers (including crew). Since the ride can be bumpy and the boat fast moving, pregnant women, small children, and deli-cate adults should seek a more tranquil tour like Fair Wind. This four-hour expe-dition includes snorkeling and cruising alongside the canopy of sea caves and lava tubes in Kealakekua Bay—home to spinner dolphins and their offspring. $90 adults, $75 ages 4–12; snacks and beverages included.

Sea Quest (808-329-7238; seaquesthawaii.com), Keauhou Bay Pier; inquire about parking. Trips daily. Because groups are limited to six or 12 people, this is an intimate trip in small inflatable boats that hug the coastline. These boats allow passengers to check out sea caves and lava tubes tucked into protective coves where most other boats can't go. Snorkelers explore pristine coral reefs at the Place of Refuge (Honaunau), where green sea turtles congregate, and then con-tinue on to Kealakekua and the Captain Cook Monument for more snorkeling. Unlike the big boats that must anchor, these small, hard-bottomed rafts slowly drift along the bay. The four-hour morning trip costs $89 adults ($72 ages 5–12); the three-hour afternoon trip (which doesn't include a stop at Honaunau) is $15–20 less; gear, drinks, and snacks included.

SUBMARINE

Atlantis Submarine (1-800-548-6262; atlantisadventures.com), 5656 Kuakini Hwy. (below Cassandra's Restaurant), Kailua-Kona. Daily departures 10–1. Explore the waters off Kailua-Kona Pier in a state-of-the-art, 48-passenger sub. From a dry bench seat, you can observe an extensive coral reef teeming with tropical fish, white tip reef sharks, moray eels, and manta rays. Although the vessel is 100 feet below sea level, cabin pressure is the same as it is on the surface. Check in 30 minutes before departure at the pier, where you'll take a short boat ride to the vessel and descend by ladder to the cabin below. The hour-long trip includes 35 minutes underwater and 25 minutes back and forth from the pier. Claustrophobic visitors need not apply. $80 adults, $42 ages 12 and under.

SURFING

Ocean Eco Tours (808-324-7873; oceanecotours.com), Kailua-Kona. Daily trips. Big Island surfing is best left to the already initiated. Swells are big on the north and leeward shores in the wintertime; the opposite shores get summertime waves. If you have your heart set on learning, call these guys and they'll teach you in two and a half hours ($95 per person, including gear).

If you're heading out on your own, go to **Pacific Vibrations** (808-329-4140; across from the Kailua-Kona Pier) for board rentals, which cost $15 for short boards, $20 for long boards.

WHALE-WATCHING

☙ ✪ **Captain Dan McSweeney** (808-322-0028; ilovewhales.com), 5 miles south of the Kona airport at Honokohau Harbor. Twice-daily trips mid-Dec.–April; thrice weekly July–mid-Dec. A humpback whale expert since the late 1970s, marine mammal researcher Dan McSweeney captains *Lady Ann* and heads into humpback breeding ground where you'll likely hear them singing and observe newborn calves and mating behavior. The popular morning cruise tends to be calmer and cooler and affords better lighting for photos. Book as early as possible; reservations are required. During the summer months, Captain Dan also knows where to find the pilot, sperm, and other whales that summer here. If Captain Dan doesn't find the whales (highly unlikely), he'll take you out again. Three-hour cruises; boarding begins at 7 AM and 11 AM. $80 adults, $70 ages 11 and under.

TOP 10 PLACES TO STAY ON THE KONA COAST

Best Intimate & Affordable Lodgings
Kona Tiki Hotel
Horizon Guest House

Best Resorts & Condos for Families
Outrigger Kanaloa at Kona
Sheraton Keauhou Bay Resort & Spa

Best B&Bs
Holualoa Inn

Best Values
Kona Magic Sands
Outrigger Keauhou Beach Resort

Best Unusual Places
Silver Oaks Guest Ranch
Dragonfly Ranch
Manago Hotel

✳ Beaches

In order of preference.

🏄 **Kahaluʻu Beach Park**, Aliʻi Dr., between Kailua-Kona and Keauhou. Really, really popular with locals and visitors, especially on the weekends, Kahaluʻu is great for swimming and snorkeling because of a good offshore reef. Families like the shallow waters and spotting endangered sea turtles, but watch out for a strong riptide during winter high tides. *Facilities:* restrooms, showers, limited parking (even though it receives upward of 1,000 people a day), lifeguard, water activity rentals.

🏄 **White Sands Beach** (aka **Magic Sands Beach** and **Disappearing Sands Beach**), Aliʻi Dr., about 4.5 miles south of Kailua-Kona between Kailua-Kona and Keauhou. So nicknamed because winter and high tides wash the grains away, this is a small patch of white sand. Its calm waters are perfect for learning how to boogie board and snorkel. *Facilities:* restrooms, showers, limited parking, lifeguard, volleyball.

✳ Lodging

About half the island's beds are located in condos and hotels along a 5-mile, lava-strewn, oceanfront strip in and around Kailua-Kona. Most are relatively modestly priced (but showing some age) and convenient to activities. When planning a trip, remember that high season generally runs mid-Dec.–mid-April. Also, Kailua-Kona is packed for the Ironman Triathlon in mid-Oct. The little village of Holualoa, upslope, is markedly different.

RESORTS & HOTELS

Kailua-Kona

Kona Tiki Hotel (808-329-1425; konatiki.com), 75-5968 Aliʻi Dr. About a mile south of town and thus well removed from the bustle, this friendly three-story is a great value. Perhaps one of the best in the state. Along with oceanside lanais and a complimentary breakfast served poolside (which is also oceanside), the traditional hotel has guest rooms with pleasant décor. Book early or tempt disappointment; don't bother getting your hopes up for the winter season. *Rates:* $; three-night minimum (seven-night minimum Oct. and Dec.). *Facilities and amenities:* 15 rooms and suites, pool, no TVs or phones in room, no credit cards.

King Kamehameha Kona Beach Hotel (808-329-2911 or 1-800-367-6060; konabeachhotel.com), 75-5660 Palani Rd. Known locally as the King Kam, this hotel is situated on the same grounds where the former king lived. (In the lobby you'll find a display of artifacts from his life including an *ahuʻula*, a feather cape, and a *mahiʻole*, a feather helmet.) Because of that, and because it's next to the pier, the place sees a lot of foot traffic. One person's "central location" is another person's "Penn Station." Although the guest rooms won't win any awards for aesthetics, they're clean and simple and great for families. Try to get a room on the top two floors, and ask about packages. *Rates:* $$–$$$; children free in parent's room. *Facilities and amenities:* 460 rooms and suites, pool, small beach, water sport rentals, activity desk, parking (fee).

Uncle Billy's Kona Bay Hotel (808-961-5818 or 1-800-367-5102; uncle billy.com), 75-5739 Ali'i Dr. Across the street from the ocean, with a prime downtown location, these two- and four-story buildings are something of an institution with visitors from neighbor islands. Public space has serious Polynesian overtones. As for the guest rooms, they were renovated in 2006, but the décor remains simple and the modest amenities keep the prices down. All of the rooms have a mini fridge. If you're a light sleeper, sleep elsewhere. *Rates:* $–$$; children free in parent's room; Internet specials available. *Facilities and amenities:* 144 rooms and suites, shallow pool.

South Kailua-Kona

⚓ **Sheraton Keauhou Bay Resort & Spa** (808-930-4900 or 1-866-837-4256; sheratonkeauhou.com), 78-128 Ehukai St., Keauhou. New to the scene in 2004 (when it reopened after a $70 million renovation and after re-branding as a Sheraton), this resort is about 15 minutes south of Kailua-Kona proper. Because it's perched on a rocky lava shoreline, it pays special attention to its water features—a two-tiered pool system linked by little rivers, a lava tube water slide, and a separate children's pool with a sandy bottom. There's no beach, but there *are* unobstructed views of Keauhou Bay, which don't get much better in this neck of the woods. As for the guest rooms, they're large and comfortably elegant with a natural color palette and plush bedding. Staff is friendly. Don't miss having a drink in the lounge at sunset. *Rates:* $$$–$$$$; children free in parent's room. *Facili-*

ties and amenities: 521 rooms and suites, pools, beach, two restaurants (including **Kai**, see *Dining Out*), three tennis courts (free), Ho'ola Spa, concierge, children's programs, parking (fee).

Outrigger Keauhou Beach Resort (808-322-3441 or 1-800-688-7444; outrigger.com), 78-6740 Ali'i Dr., Keauhou. There's a fair amount to recommend in this value-oriented hotel. Sea turtles lounge on the shoreline of the 10-acre, seven-story property, much of which hangs out over a lagoon; it's adjacent to the great Kahalu'u Beach (for snorkeling); golf is within a mile; the grounds are lush and include a reconstructed 19th-century summer cottage of King Kalakaua (the resort sits on royal land); and the resort underwent a soft renovation in 2007. As for the rooms, they're on the small side; space aside, spring for the ocean-view quarters. *Rates:* $$–$$$$; children free in parent's room. *Facilities and amenities:* 309 rooms and suites, pool, nice oceanside bar, forgettable restaurant, six tennis courts, fitness room, concierge, spa, children's programs, water sport rentals, Internet in room, parking (fee).

Manago Hotel (808-323-2642; man agohotel.com), Hwy. 11, Captain Cook. They don't make 'em like this anymore. This family-owned and family-operated institution hasn't changed much since it was built in 1917. Walk through the front door, and you'll feel like you're in a time warp. (Even if you don't stay here, stop in and have a gander.) Although all rooms are Spartan (to say the least), splurge for one with a private bath and hope for one on the top floor because of (distant) ocean views.

Rooms surround a quaint Japanese courtyard garden with a koi pond. The very friendly Manago family will be pleased to make your acquaintance. The hotel is about 12 miles south of downtown Kailua-Kona. *Rates:* $ with private bath. *Facilities and amenities:* 64 rooms (42 with private bath), restaurant, bar, no phones or TVs (or anything much hanging on the walls).

CONDOS & APARTMENTS

Kailua-Kona

Kona By The Sea (808-327-2300 or 1-877-997-6667; resortquesthawaii .com), 75-6106 Ali'i Dr. This Resort-Quest property, last renovated in 2004, is a good find for families and friends, as long as you don't mind driving to the beach. The one- and two-bedroom condos are spacious; all have ocean views. Reserve one close to the ocean, and you'll hear waves crashing throughout the night. There's no better place to be at sunset than on your lanai. *Rates:* $$$–$$$$; Internet specials available (especially during low season); two-night minimum. *Facilities and amenities:* 71 units, oceanfront pool, concierge, spa, tennis courts, Internet (fee), free parking.

🌸 Kona Magic Sands (808-329-3333 or 1-800-244-4752; konahawaii.com), 77-6452 Ali'i Dr. If you want to swim from this condo complex, you'd better stay in the summer; the beach disappears because of tides in winter. A great value (especially given that it is oceanfront, wedged between two beaches), the studios here are all individually owned but generally are oceanfront, large, and airy. They all have great westward-facing lanais, too. *Rates:* $–$$. *Facilities and ameni-*

ties: 15 units in the rental pool, restaurant, pool, Internet in some units (fee), free parking.

Royal Sea Cliff Resort (808-329-8021 or 1-800-688-7444; outrigger .com), 75-6040 Ali'i Dr. The Royal Sea Cliff looks like a sleek Dallas apartment complex lost in the Pacific—the design fits handsomely on a lava-rock shoreline that fronts the property. Fountains, waterfalls, and fishponds tumble toward the sea, through a tiered courtyard between the two wings of the condominium. The building is large and sprawling, but the architecture conceals its size, and lanais offer a sense of privacy. The priority for lodging here should be an oceanview unit close to the Pacific, preferably one of the corner units with a big concrete sundeck in addition to the tiled lanai. Condos are furnished in a minimalist style; kitchens are fully equipped; there's daily maid service. *Rates:* $$–$$$; children free in parent's room. *Facilities and amenities:* 62 apartments, two pools, tennis court (free), activity desk.

South of Kailua-Kona

🌸 🐚 Outrigger Kanaloa at Kona (808-322-9625 or 1-800-688-7444; outrigger.com), 78-261 Manukai St., Keauhou. These handsome, brown, low-rise wooden buildings—the most exclusive accommodations in the Kailua-Kona area—are nestled between the rocky shores of Keauhou Bay and the green fairways of the Kona Country Club. Although there is shoreline access for snorkeling, there is no beach. Two of three free-form swimming pools, though, take center stage on the property. Another pool is seaside. Kanaloa condos have one or two bedrooms, although some two-bedroom units are actually lofts that can sleep eight people. Most are furnished in similarly smart fashion. All units have *koa* kitchen cabinets; some oceanfront units have whirlpool tubs. If you don't need a gleaming white beach outside your door, your dollar goes a long way here. *Rates:* one-bedrooms $$$$, two-bedrooms $$$–$$$$; children free in parent's room. *Facilities and amenities:* 166 units, three pools, oceanside bar, decent Bar & Grill restaurant, two tennis courts (free), concierge, golf, dial up Internet (fee), free parking.

BED & BREAKFASTS AND COTTAGES
Kailua-Kona
Silver Oaks Guest Ranch (808-325-2000 or 1-877-325-2300; silveroaks ranch.com), 73-4570 Mamalahoa, Kailua-Kona. This family-friendly place is one of the most welcoming places to stay on the island. Your resoundingly knowledgeable hosts, Amy and Rick Decker, offer a 10-acre working ranch complete with goats, horses, and chickens. Although it's 5 miles north of downtown and sits at a pleasant elevation of 1,300 feet, it's a world away. Guest rooms are lovely, starter breakfast items are supplied for your first night, and all the little amenities you can think of are provided. *Rates:* $–$$; five-night minimum. *Facilities and amenities:* three cottages and two rooms (one with a kitchen), pool, hot tub, beach gear, TV, phone, no A/C, no smoking, full kitchens, WiFi (free), washer-dryer.

Nancy's Hideaway (808-325-3132 or 1-866-325-3132; nancyshideaway .com), 75-1530 U'anani Pl., Kailua-Kona. A few miles above Kailua-Kona in Upcountry, Nahele Cottage is a one-bedroom guest house with ocean-views and a kitchenette. Nohea Studio

is separate from the main house, with a private entrance and the same expansive views. Both are light and airy with functional furnishings and not a lot of fuss. *Rates:* $; three-night minimum; not suitable for children under 13. *Facilities and amenities:* two units, TV, phone, no A/C, smoking on lanai only, continental breakfast, WiFi (free).

South of Kailua-Kona
❀ **Holualoa Inn** (808-324-1121 or 1-800-392-1812; holualoainn.com), 76-5932 Mamalahoa Hwy., Holualoa. In the cool hills above bustling Kailua-Kona, this contemporary open-air retreat sits nestled among grazing cattle and Kona coffee fields. It's a different world up here, an enchanting balance of the artistic and agrarian. Westerly ocean views from the rooftop gazebo and swimming pool are expansive. Cool, gentle breezes drifting through the house are magical, the sensibilities relaxed. Converted to a B&B in 1988 after a stint as the vacation home of a Hawaiian art collector and newspaperman, the inn is now owned by Sandy Hazen, an area coffee farmer. She offers a stylish alternative to resort and condo living. Rough cedar walls and eucalyptus floors are a treat. More than 7,000 square feet of casually comfortable space rambles under high, open-beam ceilings. A ground-floor common area holds guest refrigerators, a microwave, loaner coolers, and beach mats, as well as the inn's only TV. *Rates:* $$$; children over 13 welcome; two-night minimum. *Facilities and amenities:* six suites, large pool, Jacuzzi, full breakfast by a bona fide chef, no A/C, no phones.

Hale Hualalai (808-326-2909; hale -hualalai.com), 74-4968 Mamalahoa

Hwy., Holualoa. One of the best aspects of staying here is host Lonn Armour's breakfasts. A professional chef for 25 years, Lonn serves up fancy breakfasts alongside his own 100 percent Kona coffee. As for the contemporary rooms, each suite has an expansive ocean view, a private (westward facing) lanai, and a private entrance for utmost privacy. The 675-square-foot spaces are outfitted with beamed ceilings and lots of wood. *Rates:* $$; two-night minimum. *Facilities and amenities:* two rooms, TV, phone, no A/C, no smoking, full breakfast, WiFi (free), Jacuzzi.

Dragonfly Ranch (808-328-2159 or 1-800-487-2159; dragonflyranch.com), 84-5146 Keala O Keawe Rd., Honaunau. Easily characterized as an eco-treehouse straight out of a Swiss Family Robinson movie, this is one of the most unique indoor and outdoor retreats in the state. Only communal, almost-rustic types need apply; it's an easygoing, bohemian atmosphere. The host, Barbara Moore, offers *lomi lomi* massages as a gift to guests, and you may join her and other guests in the preparation of communal dinners. Every configuration of accommodation is here: studio, room, cottage, and suite. Check out the Web site for colorful photos that do it justice. Dragonfly is about 20 miles south of Kailua-Kona. *Rates:* $–$$; five-night minimum requested. *Facilities and amenities:* six units (three-night minimum), phone, no A/C, no smoking, full and organic (excellent) breakfasts, kitchenette in cottage, WiFi (free), communal suppers available upon request.

Horizon Guest House (808-328-2540 or 1-888-328-8301; horizonguesthouse.com), Honaunau. Want to really get away from it all? This gated place sits on 50 acres at 1,100-foot elevation, is within a 10-minute drive of a small beach, boasts panoramic ocean views from every room, and has a beautiful (clothing optional) infinity pool and hot tub. Originally built as a B&B, it has four guest rooms staggered for privacy and outfitted with Hawaiian antiques, king beds, and hand-stitched quilts. For quiet nights, when you don't want to trek into town for dinner, there's a well-stocked barbecue area and a media room for movies, music, or reading (preferably not all at once). And to fully take advantage of its airy and cool surroundings, the house completely opens to the outdoors. *Rates:* $$$; two-night minimum. *Facilities and amenities:* nice buffet breakfast, media room, Internet access, pool, beach gear, no smoking, no A/C, no phones in rooms (but house phone available).

Aloha Guest House (808-328-8955 or 1-800-897-3188; alohaguesthouse.com), Honaunau. Located 45 minutes south of the Kona airport at 1,500-foot elevation, this tropical property is best accessed with a four-wheel-drive vehicle. (The road can be intimidating.) All of the five units have private bath and ocean views, but some have 180-degree ocean views, and one has a Jacuzzi. Outdoor communal space includes many lanais and a hot tub; indoor shared space includes a kitchen and a living area with TV, DVD, Internet access, and a video library. The charming German host offers the option of breakfast delivered to your room or served in the main dining area. The cottage (with phone and TV) is perfect for those wanting more privacy and your own kitchen; it requires a five-night minimum stay. *Rates:* $–$$$. *Facilities and amenities:* five rooms, full breakfast, beach gear, Internet, phone, TV, no smoking.

Tara Cottage (1-800-262-9912; bestbnb.com), Honaunau. Even if you lived in the Kealakekua Bay area, you'd probably want to vacation at this first-class cottage. (At the very least, you'd put your relatives up here.) It's a romantic, honeymoon kind of place where details matter. A large lanai overlooks exquisitely landscaped grounds and the bay below, a tropical outdoor shower feels very private, and a complete kitchen is tucked into an alcove. Unless you need something from the owner, you'll be on your own here—which is precisely why you chose Tara Cottage, right? Enjoy morning coffee from beans grown on the farm. *Rates:* $$; three-night minimum. *Facilities and amenities:* phone, no A/C, no smoking.

CAMPING

For information about camping near **Pu'uhonua O Honaunau National**

HUGGO'S

TOP 10 (PLUS ONE) PLACES TO EAT IN KONA & KOHALA

Pricey

Hualalai Grille (The Kohala Coast)

Roy's Waikoloa Bar & Grille (The Kohala Coast)

Canoe House (The Kohala Coast)

Brown's Beach House (The Kohala Coast)

Norio's Sushi Bar & Restaurant (The Kohala Coast)

Kenichi Pacific (The Kona Coast)

Moderate

Jackie Rey's Ohana Grill (The Kona Coast)

O's Bistro (The Kona Coast)

Cheap Eats

Island Lava Java (The Kona Coast)

The Coffee Shack (The Kona Coast)

Java on the Rocks (The Kona Coast)

Historical Park or at **Ho'okena Beach County Park**, contact the Department of Parks and Recreation (808-961-8311; hawaii-county.com). The two parks are approximately 10–15 miles apart.

✴ Where to Eat

Plenty of restaurants line Ali'i Drive and have full-on ocean views, but there aren't a lot that'll knock your culinary senses silly. That said, there are a few gems, and none will disappoint. There's no shortage of places to get a caffeine buzz on.

DINING OUT

Kailua-Kona

🍴 ✎ **O's Bistro** (808-327-1153), Crossroads Shopping Center, 75-1027 Henry St. Open 10–9 daily. Noodles rule at O's Bistro—oodles and oodles of them, in fact! O's global menu ranges from saimin with Peking duck and pad Thai to udon, orzo, and vermicelli. It's a whole lotta fun here, and the setting is quite pleasant. Noodles $$–$$$, main dishes $$$–$$$$.

Ⓨ **Huggo's** (808-329-1493; huggos .com), 75-5828 Kahakai Rd. Open for lunch and dinner daily. In business since 1969, Huggo's is many things to many people. At sunset the thatched-roof **Huggo's on the Rocks** is *the* place for torch-lit tropical drinks, appetizers, and light meals of burgers, sashimi, or salads. In the morning, ♪ **Java on the Rocks** (open 6–11 AM daily) takes over and is *the* great spot for coffee and breakfast. There's truth in advertising here: This water's-edge location is truly "on the rocks," complete with crashing waves. The "regular" Huggo's still has great water views, but dishes are more serious: seafood (including local lobster, Kona *poke*, and blackened ahi sashimi) is its raison d'être. Portions are quite hefty. It's also the kind of place where the most popular dessert is Hualalai Pie, an ice cream sundae by any other name. Reservations recommended; children's menu. Breakfast $, lunch $$, dinner entrées $$–$$$$.

Ⓨ ♪ **Kona Inn Restaurant** (808-329-4455), Kona Inn Shopping Village, 75-5744 Ali'i Dr. Open for lunch and dinner daily. Sunsets are pure perfection from this breezy (but touristy) waterfront location, outfitted with luxurious *koa* woods, Oriental carpets, and comfy chairs. Come for drinks and appetizers and you might just stay for dependable local fish dishes; mahimahi, ahi, and daily specials are the way to go—even though the menu is more far-reaching. You'll also find

steaks, sandwiches, and Caesar salads. Their **Café Grill** has lighter and less expensive specials worth checking out—with the same views. Children's menu. Lunch $–$$, dinner entrées $$–$$$$.

Keauhou

Kenichi Pacific (808-322-6400), Keauhou Shopping Center, 78-6381 Ali'i Dr. Open for dinner daily. Tucked away in a shopping center, Kenichi Pacific is worth seeking out. Very worth seeking out. When you feel like rubbing shoulders with locals who are living it up with great sushi and signature rolls in upscale surroundings, come here. If for some strange reason you don't want sushi, their macadamia crusted lamb is highly recommended. Then again, you could nosh on a wide range of appetizers and call it a day, too. Save room for the decidedly decadent warm molten chocolate cake. If you're heading north, they also have a location at the **Shops at Mauna Lani** (see "The Kohala Coast"). Dinner entrées $$$–$$$$.

♪ **Kai** (808-930-4900, sheraton keauhou.com), Sheraton Keauhou Bay Resort & Spa, 78-128 Ehukai St. Open for breakfast and dinner daily. The best thing about this restaurant is its big picture windows that are open to the ocean's edge. You can often watch manta rays feeding here at night. On my last visit, the Pacific Rim and Hawaiian fusion cuisine was okay, and it matched the service. For sure, try the seared ahi appetizer. The family-friendly breakfast buffets are a good bet, as is the all-you-can-eat seafood buffet (Sat.) and crab night (Wed.). Breakfast $–$$, dinner entrées and buffets $$$–$$$$.

South of Kailua-Kona

Ke'ei Café (808-322-9992), near MM 113, Hwy. 11, Kealakekua. Open for lunch weekdays, dinner Tues.–Sat. This lovely bistro is attractive with hardwood floors, local artwork, and coastal views. And it doesn't ignore its mission of providing creative food at moderate prices. The eclectic menu of Asian-, Latin-, and Mediterranean-inspired cuisine utilizes fresh ingredients for its chowder, curries, tofu fajitas, and salads. You can almost taste the earth. Traditional bread pudding made by the Pilgrims doesn't hold a candle to this, suffused with bananas and pineapple. The café is about 15 minutes south of Kailua-Kona. Be prepared to wait—both to be seated *and* once you're seated. Lunch $–$$, dinner entrées $$–$$$.

Kailua-Kona

EATING OUT

✑ **Jackie Rey's Ohana Grill** (808-327-0209; jackiereys.com), 75-5995 Kuakini Hwy. Open 11–5 weekdays and dinner nightly. Slightly out of the way and up the hill from downtown Kailua-Kona, this neighborhood grill (and sports bar and family-friendly eatery) is particularly known for its

lunches. Think fancy sandwiches, burgers, *poke,* and excellent fries. At happy hour, think drinks and *pupus*. Dinners are more extensive; think wasabi-crusted ahi (with organic greens), short ribs, and seafood. On Friday and Saturday evenings they have live music. They offer a lot of bang for the buck. Children's menu. Lunch $–$$, dinner entrées $$.

🍲 **Island Lava Java** (808-327-2161), 75-5799 Ali'i Dr. Open 6 AM–10 PM daily. Not only does this fashionable little place have unobstructed ocean views across the street, but it now serves lunch and dinner. Yahoo! From the day it changed hands in 2000, it was famous for its cinnamon rolls and "pull-aparts" (muffins, scones, breads, and croissants, all baked on-site). Now they serve sandwiches and burgers for lunch and get more ambitious at dinnertime with butternut squash lasagna, blackened fish salad, and fish tacos (all three of which are recommended). There are a few tables inside and outside, and counter service only inside. Breakfast and lunch $–$$, dinner entrées $–$$$.

🍲 ✑ **Big Island Grill** (808-326-1153), 75-5702 Ku'akini Hwy. Open for breakfast, lunch, and dinner Mon.–Sat. Not known outside local circles (but certainly well known within them!), this grill's slogan is "Well worth the wait." (It's true—on both accounts—you will wait, and it is worth it.) Folks are dazzled by and appreciative of large portions of good mainland dishes that have been influenced by island ingredients and concepts. (Try the roast pork plate or the coconut shrimp salad.) You won't break the bank eating here, either. Breakfast and lunch $–$$, dinner entrées $–$$$.

✐ **Fujimamas** (808-327-2125, fuji mamas.com), 75-5719 Ali'i Dr. Open for lunch and dinner daily (except no lunch on Sun.). New in 2006, this place dishes up meals "'ohana-style" (family-style) in a variety of dining areas, each with its own Asian motif. Choose from sushi rolls at the bar or something more formal in a private tatami room. Everything seems to taste better, including stir-fry dishes, when it's served on the bamboo-encircled patio. Dishes $–$$; children's bento meals available.

Pancho & Lefty's (808-326-2171), 75-5719 Ali'i Dr. Open 8 AM–9 PM daily. Sometimes you're just in the mood for a good (strong) margarita and nachos, even if you're in the middle of the Pacific on a once-in-a-lifetime trip. Look for it across the street from the Kona Marketplace, where you'll also find its competitor, **Tacos El Unico** (808-326-4033), whose margaritas aren't as strong but whose food is just as good and cheaper. Dishes $–$$.

♈ **Mixx Bistro** (808-329-7334), 75-5626 Kuakini Hwy., King Kamehameha Mall. Open noon 'til late weekdays, 4:30–late weekends. Perfect for a light lunch, afternoon drinks, or a late night bite, Mixx mixes it up with an extensive selection of wines by the glass and beer. Along with appropriate cheese platters to complement the wines, they also have a healthy selection of appetizers (*pupus*) and live nightly entertainment. Light dishes $–$$.

Kona Natural Foods (808-329-2296), Crossroads Center, 75-1027 Henry St. Open daily. When your body craves an infusion of organic greens and a healthy sandwich instead of a typical plate lunch, this shop will set you on a corrective path. They also have vitamins and such.

Keauhou
Peaberry & Galette (808-322-6020), 78-6831 Ali'i Dr., Keauhou Shopping Center. Open daily. Next to the cinema, this little crêperie sports a charming retro-modern look and serves savory and sweet crêpes, sandwiches, salads, and rich homemade desserts. And espresso, of course. Dishes $–$$.

South of Kailua-Kona
♜ ✐ **The Coffee Shack** (808-328-9555; coffeeshack.com), near MM 108, Hwy. 11, Captain Cook. Open 7:30–3 daily. Pull over here right now; you needn't wait for a coffee attack. Between a breezy lanai overlooking tropical gardens and stunning bay views, this casual haunt makes a great pit stop for eggs Benedict, gargantuan sandwiches made with homemade breads (and salmon or roast beef), and pizzas. Dishes $, pizza $–$$.

♜ **Manago Hotel** (808-323-2642), near MM 110, Hwy. 11, Captain Cook. Open for all three meals Tues.–Sun. About 20 minutes south of Kailua-Kona, this renowned but run-down hotel is incredibly popular with locals. And if you want to feel like an insider, you'll stop by. In return you'll get long-lasting memories: hearty servings of pork chops (purported to be among the island's best), T-bone steaks, and fried *ono* (or other island fish like *opelu* or *akule*) served with a friendly attitude at long Formica tables. Where else? Breakfast $, lunch and dinner $–$$.

Teshimas (808-322-9140), 79-7251 Mamalahoa Hwy., Honalo. Open for all three meals daily. About 9 miles south of Kaiula-Kona, this authentic Japanese restaurant is very local and very friendly. Folks make a beeline for sashimi, Teshima's miso soup, sukiyaki, bento boxes, and shrimp tempura at very reasonable prices. Don't pass it up. Dishes $–$$; no credit cards.

✪ COFFEE

Starbucks has infiltrated Kailua-Kona, but you have lots of other local options that celebrate the famed Kona bean, especially up in Holualoa. Most cafés serve light meals, so they are interspersed above. For a primer on Kona coffee, see *Coffee . . . Did You Know?* (p. 371).

Holualoa Kona Coffee Company (808-322-9937; konalea.com), 77-6261 Mamalahoa Hwy., MM 2, Holualoa. Open 8–3 weekdays. Before or after you indulge in a savory brew, take a free tour (8–3 weekdays) of this organic coffee bean farm.

Holuakoa Café & Restaurant (808-322-2233), 76-5900 Mamalahoa Hwy., Holualoa. Café open 6:30–3 weekdays, 8–3 weekends; restaurant open for lunch and dinner Tues.– Sat. and brunch on weekends. Using rarefied Kona Blue Sky beans from the 400-acre Twigg-Smith coffee estate, this café brews one strong espresso. Although I didn't get a chance to eat there, the new restaurant specializes in local and organic food. Lunch and brunch $–$$, dinner entrees $$$.

Kona Blue Sky Coffee Company (808-322-1700; konablueskycoffee .com), 76-973A Hualalai Rd., Holualoa. Open 9–4 Mon.–Sat. You can tour the farm where these beans are grown, harvested, dried, roasted, and ground—all by hand or with natural methods. It goes a long way in explaining the price.

Island Lava Java (808-327-2161), Ali'i Sunset Market Plaza, Ali'i Dr., Kailua-Kona. Open 6 AM–10 PM. When it's time for a local jolt.

✳ Entertainment

The Big Island isn't exactly big-time quiet, but it almost is. The scene mostly consists of low-key live music and homegrown hula in hotel bars and lobbies that face a setting sun. The **Kona Inn** is particularly popular. Not so shabby, but maybe not what you had in mind? Only two towns might fit another bill, and Kailua-Kona is one. Consult with *West Hawai'i Today* for up-to-the-minute information.

𝒴 **Kona Brewing Company & Brewpub** (808-334-2739; konabrewingco.com), 75-5629 Ku'akini Hwy., Kailua-Kona. Open 11–10 Sun.–Thurs., 11–11 Fri.–Sat. This enjoyable place, atmospheric with a *koa* bar and driftwood benches, features locally flavored brews like *lilikoi'i* wheat ale. Pair a pint with an organic pizza for a nice match. When in Rome. . . . You can also take a quick tour of the facilities before embibing and nibbling on pizzas and salads.

𝒴 **Huggo's** (808-329-1493), 75-5828 Kahakai St., Kailua-Kona. Open 11:30 AM–2 AM. For shoreline sunset cocktails.

MOVIES

The Makalapua Stadium Cinema (808-327-0444, 74-5469 Kamakaeha) and Keauhou 7 Cinemas (808-324-0172, 78-6831 Ali'i Dr., in the Keauhou Shopping Center) make for a perfect escape from an already escapist holiday. Both are in Kailua-Kona.

✳ Selective Shopping

In general, Ali'i Drive in Kailua-Kona is chock-full of souvenirs and bursting with T-shirts galore. Head up to the village of Holualoa for great art galleries and independent coffee shops.

ART GALLERIES

Holualoa Gallery (808-322-8484; lovein.com), 76-5921 Mamalahoa Hwy., Holualoa. Open 10–5 Tues.– Sat. With inspired ceramics, jewelry, calabashes, glass, and sculpture, as well as block prints and other island-style works, this gallery is diverse and dazzling. Look for the lovely raku (Japanese pottery).

Studio 7 (808-324-1335), 76-5920 Mamalahoa Hwy., Holualoa. Open 11–5 Tues.–Sat. Ready your senses to be serenaded. This tranquil space occupies the heart of the gallery scene in town. Although both owners are artists, they also offer ceramics, wood objects, and sculptures by other creative types.

Kailua Village Artists Gallery (808-329-6653; kailuavillageartists.com), Kona Beach Hotel, 75-5660 Palani Rd., Kailua-Kona. Open 9:30–5:30 daily. This co-op features artists working in a variety of media; have a look around.

BOOKSTORES

Borders. See Crossroads Shopping Center under *Shopping Areas*.

CLOTHES

Kimura Lauhala Shop (808-324-0053), 77-996 Mamalahoa Hwy. at Hualalai Rd., Holualoa. Open Mon.–Sat. This teensy place offers every conceivable item that could be woven with pandanus fronds.

Kona Farmer's Market, off Queen Ka'ahumanu Hwy., Kailua-Kona. Open 8–2:30 Sat.–Sun. Follow the locals' lead for produce and flowers to this unlikely industrial location.

Ali'i Gardens Marketplace, 75-6129 Ali'i Dr., Kailua-Kona. Open 9–5 Wed.–Sun. Upwards of 50 vendors sell fresh juices, local coffee, and crafts on this 5-acre plot.

✳ Shopping Areas

Crossroads Shopping Center, 75-1000 Henry St. (Kuakini Hwy.), Kailua-Kona. Head here when you need a Borders bookstore and Safeway supermarket.

Coconut Grove Market Place (808-329-5300), Ali'i Dr., Kailua-Kona. Open daily 9 AM–10 PM. Surrounding sandy volleyball courts, this warren of buildings has restaurants, a gallery, and a coffee shop or two.

Makalapua Center, Makalapua Ave., Kailua-Kona. Just north of town off Hwy. 19, this center is anchored by Macy's and KMart.

✳ Special Shops

The Grass Shack (808-323-2877), at the corner of Konawaena and Mamalahoa Hwy., Kealakekua. Open Mon–Sat. Since the 1970s, this little grass shack has been offering pricey Ni'ihau shell leis, objects made with rare and unusual woods, or 'ukuleles.

Kimura Store (808-322-3771), Mamalahoa Hwy., Kainaliu. Open Mon.–Sat. 9–5:30. Family owned for generations, this is the kind of general store you find only in Hawai'i.

THE KOHALA COAST

The Kohala Coast is a historic region, and its resort developments deserve considerable credit for restoring and preserving sights on their property. They make it possible to surround yourself with the ultimate in refined luxury and leisure recreation while still experiencing much of the true temper of the Big Island. There are abundant ancient *heiaus*, royal fishponds, and well-preserved petroglyphs scattered throughout the region. An ocean of folded black lava is interrupted only by emerald fairways, pink bougainvillea, tufts of billowy golden grasses, and white coral rocks arranged as graffiti.

Hawaiian royalty played here, so it seems only fitting that we do, too.

There are four distinct, entirely separate coastal resort areas, including Ka'upulehu, which is officially in the North Kona district but has more in common with Waikoloa, Mauna Lani, and Mauna Kea than with Kailua-Kona (which is in the South Kona district). These spots share some of the most predictable weather in Hawai'i—it's almost always sunny, dry, and moderate in temperature. While these areas are not far from one another or the coastal highway, the configuration of the shore and lava fields makes them secluded hideaways, each barely visible to another or to passing motorists. In fact, you may find yourself saying incredulously, "We're staying *where*?" when all you see is miles of moonscape lava. If you can't afford to stay here, make lunch, dinner, or golf reservations and allow for some time to wander the public areas. The resorts are attractions in and of themselves. Each is an oasis, really, in what some might describe as a barren wasteland, a load of lava lobbed over the volcano's edge by the angry god-

BUILDING BLOCKS FOR A PERFECT DAY ON THE KOHALA COAST

Explore petroglyphs and fishponds (90 minutes)

Swim and sun at Hapuna or Mauna Kea Beaches (3 hours)

Lunch on the beach at a resort (2 hours)

Play a round of world class-golf (4 hours)

Drive across Saddle Road and back (4 hours)

Friday night *lu'au* at Kona Village (4 hours)

Dinner on the beach at a resort (3 hours)

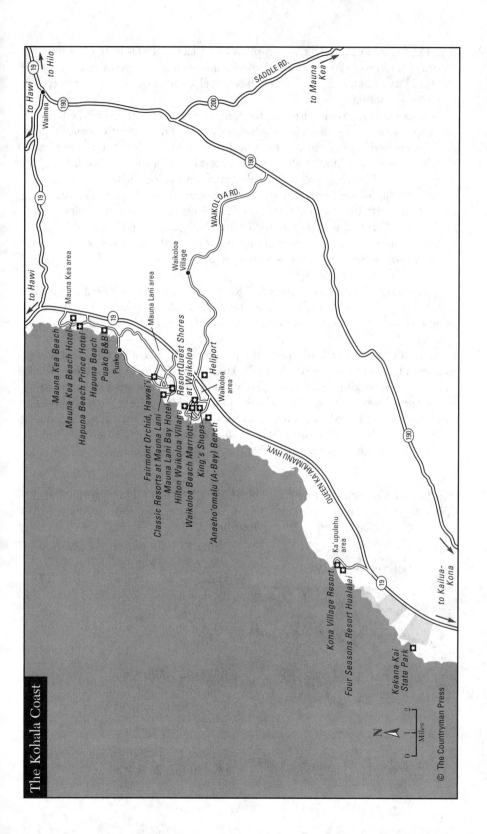

The Kohala Coast

to Hawi
to Hilo
19
190
Waimea
SADDLE RD.
to Mauna Kea
200
190
WAIKOLOA RD.
to Hawi
19
Mauna Kea area
Waikoloa Village
Mauna Lani area
Mauna Kea Beach
Mauna Kea Beach Hotel
Hapuna Beach Prince Hotel
Hapuna Beach
Puako B&B
Puako
ResortQuest Shores at Waikoloa
Heliport
Waikoloa area
Fairmont Orchid, Hawai'i
Classic Resorts at Mauna Lani
Mauna Lani Bay Hotel
Hilton Waikoloa Village
Waikoloa Beach Marriott
King's Shops
'Anaeho'omalu (A-Bay) Beach
190
QUEEN KAAHUMANU HWY.
Ka'upulehu area
Kona Village Resort
Four Seasons Resort Hualalai
19
to Kailua-Kona
Kekana Kai State Park

N

0   1   2
Miles

© The Countryman Press

dess Pele. (Mount Hualalai's last eruption took place in 1800–1801.) For the record, I could spend weeks on end amid this seemingly "barren wasteland" and still find beauty and drama on a daily basis. It challenges expectations and conventional definitions.

Mauna Lani and Mauna Kea are the most impressively refined of the four areas and have a few similarities. Both enjoy a pair of dramatically beautiful golf courses, created at enormous cost out of the lava bedrock, and two of the most enticing beaches in Hawai'i. Neither is overdeveloped in any way. Each has a couple of grand hotels, along with a select number of elegant condominiums.

Ka'upulehu houses two distinctly upscale hotels. When it opened in 1996, the Four Seasons Resort Hualalai raised the bar for elegance and service along the coast. Kona Village is a different breed, specializing in a single brand of Polynesian escapism rather than worldly abundance. One of the most venerable resorts in Hawai'i, it's a delightful treat when you're in the mood to make believe you're marooned in the South Seas.

The Waikoloa, with golf courses and King's Shops, constitutes South Kohala's headquarters. While Mauna Lani and Mauna Kea cater to small and moderate-sized meetings, Waikoloa attracts major conventions in addition to independent travelers.

Last, but most importantly, resist the temptation to take a piece of lava home as a souvenir. Madame Pele doesn't take kindly to it and seeks retribution. You'll hear stories about folks who ignore the warning and fall prey to an unusual string of bad luck. The stories usually end with a Priority Mail package to a U.S. post office on the Big Island with a note that says, "Would you please leave this rock on the side of the road? Thanks." The Waikoloa Beach Marriott Resort & Spa ceremonially repatriates lava rocks that they receive in the mail.

GUIDANCE

Big Island Visitor's Bureau (808-886-1655 or 1-800-648-2441; bigisland.org), 250 Waikoloa Beach Dr., Waikoloa. Open 8–4:30 weekdays. Pick up their informative *Coffee Country Driving Tour* brochure.

THE FAIRMONT ORCHID, HAWAI'I

Kona-Kohala Resort Association (808-886-4915 or 1-800-318-3637; kkra.org), 69-275 Waikoloa Beach Dr., Waikoloa. These folks don't encourage drop-ins, but they will answer questions if you happen by. Contact them in advance of your visit.

GETTING AROUND

By car: It's about 33 miles from Kailua-Kona north to Kawaihae, where Hwy. 19 splits and heads to Waimea and Hwy. 270 heads to North Kohala, both of which are discussed in "North Kohala & Waimea."

❋ To See & Do

✧ ✪ **Petroglyphs**. The Big Island has more ancient rock tableaus than any other Hawaiian island, and you'll find rousing clusters at a few distinct places on the Kohala Coast. The **Pu'ako Archeological Petroglyph District** (Holoholokai Beach Park, within the Mauna Lani area) encompasses a whopping 230 acres and contains the largest depository of petroglyphs in the state. There's an easy 1.5-mile trail that begs for exploration.

LOCAL-STYLE GRAFFITI

You'll need a reservation to tour the **Kaupulehu Petroglyphs** (808-325-5555) at Kona Village Resort; there's no other way to get beyond the guard shack. If you make the effort, though, you'll be rewarded with some 3,000 lava rocks on which you'll see stick figures canoe paddling, walking, dancing, and all basically telling the stories of animals, gods, and families. Tours are usually held on Tues. and Sat. mornings.

An informative and free walking tour highlighting petroglyphs along the **King's Trail** (aka Mamalahoa Trail) is offered Thur.–Sun. at 10:30. Meet at the Food Court at the King's Shops (808-886-8811, Waikoloa Beach Dr., Waikoloa Beach Marriott Resort & Spa). Even if you don't take the tour, you can still walk this ancient footpath through the lava fields.

TOUR LIKE AN ANCIENT MARINER AT THE FAIRMONT ORCHID

Fishponds. Ancient Hawaiians were ingenious at catching and raising fish in closed and open ponds. Closed ponds were basically inland ponds, without direct ocean access. Open ponds involved the building of sea-walls and gates to trap the fish. At high tide they'd come over the wall, where they'd remain and fatten up as the tide went out and left them behind. The Waikoloa Beach Marriott Resort & Spa has done a great job protecting and preserving both kinds at the **Kahapapa** and **Ku'uali'i Fish**

✪ MAUNA KEA & SADDLE ROAD

This is one lofty perch. No matter the time of day, the Big Island's center is full of possibility. Make time to explore at night, when the velvety dark skies yield near-perfect conditions for pondering the inexplicable questions—about what life, if any, resides in deep space. Make time to explore by day, when silence is deafening and you dream of a dozen words that describe the sound of wind.

Before getting too dreamy, first things first: Your rental car contract may forbid you to drive across Saddle Road, Hwy. 200, which links Hilo to Waimea (almost). This is usually because the rental agencies don't want to come get you should you break down. It has nothing to do with the quality of the road. Nonetheless, for current **road conditions** to the summit, call 808-935-6268. For current **weather conditions**, call 808-961-5582.

Second things second: 24 hours prior to summiting, drink plenty of water, try to limit your caffeine and alcohol intake, and try to limit (or stop)

smoking. The visitors center sits at a lofty 9,300 feet, while the summit tops off at 13,796 feet. The air is pretty thin between the visitor's center and the summit, where there's 40 percent less oxygen than at sea level. Pregnant women, children under age 16, and anyone with heart or serious

health problems should not go farther than the visitors center. Scuba divers should wait at least 24 hours from their last dive. Wear lots of sunscreen and be aware of altitude sickness and dizziness. If you're heading up on your own, bring all the warm clothing you brought to Hawai'i—the summit averages 30 degrees Fahrenheit, and it's windy. Don't overexert yourself at the summit, and don't be macho.

Third things third: You have a few choices about how far to go and how to get there. You can simply drive across **Saddle Road** and admire Mauna Kea from the emptiness of the road. Since little vegetation survives (much less thrives) along this seemingly desolate road, you'll find yourself looking for the world in a patch of lichen.

You don't need a four-wheel drive to take the unmarked Summit Road (at about MM 28) 6 miles up to the **Onizuka International Astronomy Visitor Center** (808-961-2180; ifa.hawaii.edu/info/vis), named for Hawai'i's astronaut who died in the *Challenger* explosion. The center is open 9 AM–10 PM daily, but perhaps the best time to visit is during the (free) nightly stargazing sessions held 6–10 PM. These include a film, lecture, Q & A period, and a chance to peer through a telescope.

Beyond the visitors center you'll need four-wheel drive. The visitors center leads (free) caravan-style summit trips if you have your own four-wheel drive. The three-hour trips begin at 1 PM on Sat. and Sun. and include a tour of an observatory and a guided walk at the summit. Along the way, the topography morphs into a moonlike landscape. It's no wonder the Apollo astronauts trained here.

The visitors center is about one hour from Hilo or Waimea and 90 minutes from Kailua-Kona. If you're continuing to the summit, another 45 minutes farther, take time to get acclimatized. Breathe deeply (you probably won't be able *not* to!) to get enough oxygen.

Thirteen observatories, operated by NASA and countries from around the world, crown the summit. Since this rarefied atmosphere is almost completely free from clouds, dust, and light pollution,

and since it sits so close to the equator, almost 90 percent of the stars in the universe are visible from here. It gives a whole new meaning and dimension to the notion of stargazing. On weekdays 8–4:30, you can visit a model of the world's largest telescope, the **Keck Telescope** (808-885-7887; keckobser vatory.org), operated by the University of California and the California Institute of Technology. You also get an astonishing impression of Mauna Kea's neighbor, Mauna Loa, and Maui's Mount Haleakala. It's an impression that will remain indelibly imprinted on your psyche for years to come. If you have a four-wheel drive to reach the summit, you can visit the **Subaru Telescope** (808-934-5056; subarutelescope.org) for a 30-minute tour. Book tours a week in advance; they are held weekdays at 10:30, 11:30, and 1:30.

Mauna Kea Summit Adventures (808-322-2366 or 1-888-322-2366; maunakea.com) also leads a seven- to eight-hour tour of the summit that includes pickup in Kailua-Kona, a very good picnic-style dinner, and warm parkas. Most importantly, though, it includes a sophisticated layperson's discussion about the unique geography, geology, and Hawaiian mythology related to Mauna Kea. Trips $197 per person.

Hawai'i Forest & Trail (808-331-8505 or 1-800-464-1993; hawaii-forest

Ponds (808-886-6789) adjacent to its resort. Over at the Mauna Lani Bay Hotel & Bungalows, the **Kalahuipua'a Fish Ponds** (808-885-6622) are similarly preserved and quite historic. The hotel also offers tours at 10:30 AM on Tues., Thurs., and Sat.

The latter have the added benefit of being adjacent to the **Eva Parker Woods cottage** (808-885-6622), a tiny 1930s beach house originally built by Frank and Eva Woods, descendants of John Palmer Parker (founder of the Parker Ranch). The cabin was later acquired by Francis I'i Brown, who used it to wine and dine wealthy friends and visit his mistress, Winona Love, a beautiful and acclaimed hula dancer. The house contains samples of *tapa* cloth, household items, and dis-

.com). On my last trip to the summit, I went with these folks (who offer a similar trip to MKSA), and I couldn't have been happier. I highly recommend them. Trips $169 per person (dinner and gear included).

Don't feel left out if you don't reach the summit. Instead, stop in at the **Keck Observatory Control Center** (808-885-7887; 65-1120 Mamalahoa Hwy., Waimea), where you can watch a highly informative film about the goings-on at the observatory and check out some telescopes. Open 8:30–4 weekdays.

Although you can't see it from Summit Road, the glacial **Lake Waiau** sits at 13,000 feet. It's only half a mile off Saddle Road and quite worth stopping; ask for directions from the visitors center.

Bird-watchers flock to the **Hakalau Forest**, on Saddle Road just east of Summit Road, a national wildlife refuge that's open only on weekends. Although you must secure a permit and access code to get through the gate, it's worth it if you're searching for rare and endangered species like the *nukupu'u*, the *akiapola'au*, and the *alala*. Stop in Hilo (32 Kino'ole St., Suite 101) for permits.

The only places to sleep up here are the **Mauna Kea State Park Cabins**

(808-974-6200; hawaii.gov/dlnr), off Saddle Rd., about 30 miles from Hilo. Situated at 6,500 feet, these four cabins have flush toilets but no running water for cooking purposes. Cabins sleep six, and bedding is provided. *Rates:* $35 per cabin nightly.

plays on fishing and Hawaiian canoes. It's open during the Mauna Lani Bay Hotel & Bungalows historic tour, offered most Tuesdays, Thursdays, and Saturdays at 9 AM.

Hotel art. Pop into the sedate **Mauna Kea Beach Hotel** (808-882-7222, Mauna Kea area) to drink in the striking collection of original art from the Far East, Hawai'i, and the South Pacific. And then head to the decidedly bustling **Hilton Waikoloa Village** (808-886-1234, Waikoloa area) to tour their hallways— three distinct walks feature highly illuminating reproductions from Asia and Southeast Asia, Oceania, and an "East-Meets-West" collection. If you missed the Eastern version of Art History 101, it's not too late to learn a thing or two (or seventeen). Ask the front desk or concierge for information and perhaps a self-guided walking tour map.

Waikoloa Village, *mauka*, off Hwy. 19. Not to be confused with the resort area, this little village has contemporary housing for islanders, a supermarket, and other practical shops.

✳ Spas

Four Seasons Resort Hualalai (808-325-8000; fourseasons.com/hualalai). Perhaps without equal, this spa consistently ranks at the top of "World's Best Spas" lists. As are all fine spas in the state, it is decidedly Hawaiian in its approach, ethos, and offerings. I've never received a treatment here that wasn't worth every penny. It's easy to linger at the oh-so-exclusive and private spa and sports club all afternoon.

Kohala Spa (808-886-1234; kohalaspa.com) at the Hilton Waikoloa Village This 25,000-square-foot facility offers everything from astrology readings and Pilates classes to cardio rooms and kids' programs. Oh, and of course, plenty of treatments.

Mauna Lani Spa (808-885-6622; maunalani.com) at the Mauna Lani Bay Hotel & Bungalows. From detox lava treatments and specialized Aquatic Body Therapy to massages and specialized baths, this first-rate facility rises above most others in the state. Try their open-air lava sauna, where you can lather yourself in wet clay, bake in the sun, rinse, and remoisturize with their signature oils.

✳ Outdoor Activities

BICYCLING

Mauna Kea Mountain Bikes (808-883-0130 or 1-888-682-8687; bikehawaii .com), Waikoloa Village. Rentals cost $35 daily, $135 weekly. Take them anywhere—especially along Mana Road—which offers cross-country-style rides with gradual climbing.

NENE

Nene—standing 2 feet tall with long necks, muted yellow-buff cheeks, and black heads—are on the brink of extinction. The only reason that Hawai'i's state birds, believed to have evolved from a Canada goose injured during migration, have lasted this long is because they're a model of evolutionary prowess. Over time their webbed feet morphed into clawlike ones and their wing structure changed to adapt to shorter flights. In the late 1700s, about 25,000 nene inhabited the islands. When a restoration project began in 1951, the number of recorded nene was 50. The bird has made an impressive comeback, but there are still only about 500 wild creatures, primarily surviving because of strictly enforced protection laws and captive breeding. Look for them here at Mauna Kea State Park and at Haleakala National Park on Maui. Breeding season is Nov.–June.

✤ **Dolphin Quest** (808-886-2875; dolphinquest.org), at the Hilton Waikoloa Village, Waikoloa area. This one-of-a-kind offering allows visitors a rare interaction with the gentle but wild creatures in calm and shallow waters. With the Encounter Program (30 minutes), kids ages 10 and older don a snorkel and mask to play with the friendly mammals. The Kid's Quest includes hands-on educational activities and 30 minutes interacting with dolphins. $150–350 per person; reservations accepted up to two months in advance.

GOLF

Serious golfers could spend a week playing different courses, all renowned, on leeward Big Island.

○ **Hapuna Golf Course** (808-880-3000; hapunabeachhotel.com), Hapuna Beach Prince Hotel, Mauna Kea area. Environmentally friendly—par excellence (no pun intended)—this Arnold Palmer–designed, links-style course kicks up its heels with some seriously challenging elevation gains. It's easily one of the best courses in Hawai'i. Greens fees cost $165 ($125 for resort guests) and drop to $145 ($105 for resort guests) at 1 PM. Make reservations up to 30 days in advance.

○ **Mauna Kea Golf Course** (808-882-5400; maunakeabeachhotel.com), Mauna Ken Beach Hotel, Mauna Kea area. Could a course be more beautiful? Robert Trent Jones Jr. designed a winner, but like other courses on the leeward side, trade winds challenge even the fiercest players. The course was set to reopen in late 2008 after sustaining earthquake damages in 2007.

Mauna Lani Francis I'i Courses (808-885-6655; maunalani.com), Mauna Ken Beach Hotel, Mauna Lani Dr. Laid out on lava fields, the **North Course** is dressed with a fair amount of native flora, but the oceanfront **South Course** is much more open—and dramatic! Since there's lava, lava everywhere, count on losing a few balls—they bounce on lava in all manner of directions, rarely to be seen again. North and South Course greens fees are $210 ($145 for resort guests) and drop to $100 after 3 PM. Make reservations three weeks in advance.

Waikoloa King's Course (808-886-7888; waikoloabeachresort.com), Waikoloa Beach Marriott Resort, adjacent to the Outrigger and Hilton, Waikoloa area. This links-style course has its share of trade winds. Greens fees are $195 ($130 for resort guests) and drop to $95 after 1 PM.

Waikoloa Beach Course (808-886-6060; waikoloabeachresort.com), Waikoloa Beach Marriott Resort, adjacent to King's Course, Waikoloa area. As designer Robert Trent Jones Jr. himself said about his course, it's certainly tough to make par here. Greens fees are $195 ($130 for resort guests) and drop to $95 after 1 PM. Make reservations up to a year in advance. Golfers will be pleased that the **Waikoloa Beach Grill** (808-886-6131; open for lunch and dinner daily) is now a bona fide destination worthy of your eclectic palate. Try any of the local fish dishes, but whatever you do, save room for David Brown's delectable desserts.

Waikoloa Village Golf Course (808-883-9621; waikoloa.org), Waikoloa Village. About 6 miles off the main highway, this oft-overlooked course surprises out-of-towners who play here. It's a challenging Robert Trent Jones Jr. course, rife with pesky traps and lovely fairways. Greens fees run $80 and drop to $40 after 4 PM. Make reservations up to a week ahead.

Hualalai Golf Course. It's simply outstanding, but you have to be a Four Seasons Resort Hualalai guest to play here. For fanatics, the Nicklaus-designed course is worth every single penny.

HIKING
See **petroglyphs** under *To See & Do*.

✳ Beaches
In order of preference.

Although at last count the Big Island had 80 beaches, it doesn't have an overabundance of great *swimming* strands. In general, the ones it does have, though, are doozies or at least quite unusual. Around the island, you'll have a choice between white or golden sand, black or green, and salt-and-pepper. Here on the Kohala Coast, which boasts the Big Island's top three swimming beaches, they're perfect golden crescents.

𝆑 ✪ **Hapuna Beach**, at the Hapuna Beach Prince Hotel, Mauna Kea area. A whopping half mile long and quite wide, this golden crescent is one of the best in the entire state for swimming and snorkeling—in summer! In winter, the gradual slope of the bay gives way to waves that can pester the shoreline. Lava outcroppings cap the north and south edges; the northern boundary has a little cove with tide pools. A casual resort restaurant feeds all comers. Given this beach's preeminent stature, it's always surprising that it isn't more overrun. *Facilities:* restrooms, showers, parking, camping cabins (see *Lodging*).

𝆑 ✪ **Mauna Kea Beach** (aka **Kaunaoa Beach**), at the Mauna Kea area. Nothing, not even an upscale resort located on its edge, can take away from the splendor of this near-perfect beach. The white crescent is generally calm for

HAPUNA BEACH

swimming year-round and attracts manta rays in the evening (thanks to hotel floodlights that draw the gentle creatures) and sea turtles by day. It's bookended by lava-rock promontories, which attract colorful fish. *Facilities:* restrooms, showers, sometimes limited parking.

MAUNA KEA BEACH

🏄 **ʻAnaehoʻomalu Beach** (aka **A-Bay**), at the Waikoloa Beach Marriott Resort & Spa. The best Waikoloa area beach (and one of the Big Island's top three) offers great swimming, snorkeling, lots of water activity rentals, and lots of palm trees. It rarely gets more picture perfect. A-Bay has the added bonus of being surrounded by ancient fishponds and petroglyphs (see *To See & Do*). At the southern end, snorkelers can watch endangered sea turtles. *Facilities:* restrooms, showers, picnicking, parking. **Ocean Sports** (808-885-5555; hawaiioceansports.com) has a gear rental hut on the beach.

🏄 **Kekana Kai State Park**, about 2 miles north of the Kailua-Kona airport. Open 8–8 daily. Head *makai* down a rough road (four-wheel drive needed on my last trip) for 5 miles until you reach a series of bays and coves with perfectly calm waters for swimming—unless it's winter, when the surfers come out and we mere mortals should stay dry watching from the sidelines. *Facilities:* restrooms, barbecue area, no drinking water.

🏄 **Holoholokai Beach Park**, at the Fairmont Orchid, Hawaiʻi, Mauna Lani area. It's smallish, but its calm water makes for good swimming, and its rocky areas make for good snorkeling. When you're done sunning, wander around the nearby Puʻako Archeological Petroglyph District (see petroglyphs under *To See & Do*). *Facilities:* restrooms, parking, barbecue, picnicking.

✳ Lodging

These appear in geographic order, from south to north, instead of my normal preferential order.

The Kohala Coast boasts an exceptional collection of resorts. Truly. Perfect for honeymooners, stressed-out professionals, well-off families, or once-in-a-lifetime savers, you can't go wrong here. Although the lodgings all have some degree of high-end amenities, services, and facilities, they're all quite differentiated from one another.

KEKANA KAI STATE PARK

Yes, the famed Kohala Coast properties pack a heck of a wallop. Whenever I stay here, my biggest problem is always forcing myself off the property to explore.

✿ RESORTS

✿ ❦ **Four Seasons Resort Hualalai** (808-325-8000 or 1-800-819-5053; fourseasons.com/hualalai), Kaʻupulehu area. Quite simply, this is a highly vaunted, treasured oasis—a magical place designed in 1996 to enhance its surroundings rather than compete with them. After you're warmly welcomed by name, personalized service continues at the reception desk, where you drink in panoramic views of dormant Mauna Kea. The lobby is suffused with mahogany rafters (airy but down to earth), rattan furnishings, and a slate floor. From there, lushly landscaped walkways lead to detached, two-story bungalow crescents (Sea Shell, Palm Grove, Beach Tree, and King's Pond), each with its own swimming pond or pool. By night, gardens are particularly roman-

FOUR SEASONS RESORT HUALALAI

tic, lit by hundreds of torches. King's Pond boasts an enclosed saltwater swimming lagoon, great for snorkeling since it's stocked with manta rays and colorful fish. Those who live for the beach will no longer be disappointed at Hualalai. Although only a thin ribbon of sand fronts the lava-rock shore, Four Seasons guests now have access to the lovely beach at Kona Village, just a five-minute shuffle from heaven. (Still, I rarely can pry myself away from the infinity pool and attendant service.) Even the nonmotivated, though, will want to experience the exceptional open-air, state-of-the-art health club and spa. It's been ranked the *world's best* spa. As for the guest rooms (each with an ocean view), intimacy and quiet luxury pervade. Hardwood, slate, and stone appointments are softened by luxurious linens; exceptional amenities abound. Bungalows are now even better than ever, some expanding to include a sitting area. To enhance the spirit and feed your mind, the Kaupulehu Cultural Center teaches Hawaiian values, heritage, and practices. If I had only one month to live and unlimited funds, it'd be here. *Rates:* $$$$; one child

FOUR SEASONS RESORT HUALALAI

free in parent's room. *Facilities and amenities:* 243 rooms and suites, five pools, four restaurants (including **Pahu i'a** and **Beach Tree Bar & Grill**; see *Dining Out* and *Eating Out*), eight tennis courts (fee), fitness center, spa, water sport rentals, concierge, shops, children's programs, parking (fee for valet).

🐚 **Kona Village Resort** (808-325-5555 or 1-800-367-5290; konavillage .com), 1 Kahuwai Bay Dr., Ka'upulehu area. A romantic's dream of South Seas tranquility, Kona Village is one of Hawai'i's most exotic places to stay. If you aren't able to forget your worries here, you're probably doomed to a life of stress. Take a cue from Steve Jobs, who retreated here with his family when deciding whether or not to retake the reins of Apple way back when. It's almost a requirement to switch off the outside world when you check in. What's so special? Just ask another computer magnate, Michael Dell, whose investment firm purchased Kona Village in early 2007. (He's also the owner of next door neighbor Four Seasons Hualalai.) The 82-acre village consists of Polynesian-style bungalows (*hales*) dispersed along a secluded beach and around an ancient Hawaiian fishpond. Sandy paths connect them. I always half expect Gilligan and his comrades to wash ashore at some point. When the resort opened in 1965, the remote region was accessible only by a small airstrip nearby. Although you drive in today, Kona Village still prides itself on not having TVs, radios, phones, clocks, or A/C (although that may change, along with furnishings). But I also measure luxury by other quotients: How is the service, and how quickly can I relax? Kona Village brings you down to earth and pampers your soul rather than your whims. The staff-to-guest ratio may be similar to that at other luxury properties, but service aspirations are different. Not only will you be referred to by name after a day or so, but when you put a coconut in front of your *hale*, it's the Kona Village version of a DO NOT DISTURB sign. While the most expensive bungalows are oceanfront, I think the idyllic tropical lagoon locations are just as nicely sited. If you can afford it, I recommend starting or ending a holiday here. *Rates:* $$$$, with and without meals, use of all facilities, and beach gear. *Facilities and amenities:* 125 cottages, two pools, swimming beach with offshore dock, two restaurants, three tennis courts, fitness room, concierge, **lu'au** (fee; see *Lovely Lu'au*), children's programs (free), parking (free).

TOP PLACES TO STAY ON THE KOHALA COAST

Best Romantic Hideaways
Four Seasons Resort Hualalai
Kona Village Resort

Most Worldly Resorts
Four Seasons Resort Hualalai
The Fairmont Orchid, Hawai'i
Hapuna Beach Prince Hotel

Best Resorts & Condos for Families
Four Seasons Resort Hualalai
Kona Village Resort
The Fairmont Orchid, Hawai'i
Mauna Lani Bay Hotel & Bungalows
Hilton Waikoloa Village

Best Resort Values
Waikoloa Beach Marriott Resort & Spa

KONA VILLAGE RESORT

✐ ❦ **Waikoloa Beach Marriott Resort & Spa** (808-886-6789 or 1-800-922-5533; waikoloabeachmarriott.com), 69-275 Waikoloa Beach Dr., Waikoloa area. If you haven't been to this Marriott recently, you're in for a big surprise. After a serious infusion of time and resources, the Waikoloa is better than ever. It always provided a great value. Now it provides flat screen TVs, an infinity pool (for adults only), glass railings on the lanais, and comfy (signature) bedding. This resort still doesn't try to compete with the lavishness of its neighbors, but it's still a very attractive alternative if your pockets aren't quite as deep. With a noble bearing and an appreciation of Hawaiiana that the monarch would admire, the hotel sits on land that King Kamehameha the Great claimed, making the half-mile beach *kapu* (forbidden) to commoners in his day. To preserve the royal fishponds, the hotel was situated back a fair distance from the ocean. Exclusive Cabana Club rooms (renovated after the earthquake in 2006) sit on the lagoon's edge, but most other guest rooms are located in two six-story wings farther from the beach. (Families are best matched to deluxe rooms.) Best of all, perhaps, it's located on the fabulous Anaeho'omalu Bay (A-Bay), where you can swim or snorkel along the half-mile white-sand beach or go windsurfing or catamaran cruising. *Rates:* $$$–$$$$; children free in parent's room. *Facilities and amenities:* 556 rooms and suites, two pools, beach, two restaurants (including **Hawai'i Calls**), lounge with entertainment, fitness center, Mandara Spa, water sport rentals, concierge, activity desk, children's programs, Hawaiian cultural programs, resort fee (includes self parking, daily mai tais, and WiFi Internet).

✐ ❦ **Hilton Waikoloa Village** (808-886-1234 or 1-800-445-8667; hilton waikoloavillage.com), 425 Waikoloa Beach Dr., Waikoloa area. I really appreciate this place; it knows what it is and executes it with aplomb. This Hilton is as much amusement park as hotel; it's a vast, sprawling playground with beds. Distances are so vast that a monorail shuttles guests from one end to the other. A magnificent art collection lines miles of covered walkways. Christopher Hemmeter conceived the resort as the ultimate fantasy experience, and he succeeded in some respects and failed in others. The center of attention is a 4-acre saltwater lagoon designed for swimming, sunbathing, and snorkeling. The main swimming pool, almost an acre itself, features waterfalls, a 175-foot-long water slide, and three Jacuzzis. Eight hundred chaise lounges line the decks. Even the Pacific is there somewhere, on ⅔ mile of rocky shoreline, if you get an urge for the real thing. Most guests admire it from a distance and splash the day away in their imaginative water wonderland. The Hilton has the only **Dolphin Quest** program in Hawai'i, where guests can swim with dolphins supervised by marine science specialists. Reservations three months in advance is recommended. As for the guest rooms, they're all similar except for view and bed size, and they all enjoy a lanai, as well as upscale furnishings and luxury conveniences. They all received a complete renovation in 2006. *Rates:* $$$–$$$$; children free in parent's room. *Facilities and amenities:* 1,240 rooms and suites, three pools, nine restaurants (including **Donatoni's**, **Imari**, and **Kamuela Provisions**), golf putting course, eight tennis courts (fee), fitness center, **Kohala Spa**, water sport rentals, concierge, activity desk, shops, children's programs, parking (fee).

🔱 🐚 **Mauna Lani Bay Hotel & Bungalows** (808-885-6622 or 1-800-367-2323; maunalani.com), 68-1400 Mauna Lani Dr., Mauna Lani area. The tone is established immediately: You're greeted beneath the porte cochere with a fragrant lei and led past teeming koi ponds into the lobby, where chilled fruit juice is served on a silver platter while you register. Few other Hawaiian hotels blend resort excellence with enchantment so well. When you consider the historic park next door, you've got the cultural element as well. Tennis and golf are superlative; in fact, the Francis H. I'i Brown North and South Courses

KICKIN' BACK IN STYLE

could be the most beautiful 36 holes in Hawai'i. The resort is also well situated for sun tanning on the beach; the main strands spread radiantly and broadly across groves of palms hung with hammocks. Swimming is utterly satisfying in a protected cove. As for the guest rooms, about 90 percent have some sort of ocean view. Regular rooms have handsome furnishings,

HILTON WAIKOLOA VILLAGE

large private lanais, and two dressing areas. The bungalow suites are basically 4,000-square-foot mansions, complete with a dedicated butler and maid who seek to satisfy every whim. No matter where you roost, you'll never want to leave. *Rates:* $$$$; children free in parent's room. *Facilities and amenities:* 343 rooms and suites, pools, beach, four restaurants (including the **Canoe House**), superb North and South Golf Courses, superb tennis courts (fee), superb Sports and Fitness Club (about five minutes away), spa, water sport rentals, concierge, activity desk, children's programs, parking (free).

✿ ✎ **The Fairmont Orchid, Hawai'i** (808-885-2000 or 1-800-251-7544; fairmont.com/orchid), 1 N. Kaniku Dr., Mauna Lani area. With each visit, I am always newly impressed with the Orchid. They are always improving and raising the standard here. As they say and mean: *E Komo Mai* (Welcome). This 32-acre resort is stunning, the facilities and services exceptional, and the staff knowledgeable. Beginning life as a Ritz-Carlton (which set the luxury

THE FAIRMONT ORCHID, HAWAI'I

tone) and then a Sheraton (which restored Hawaiiana in the décor and staff of traditional beach boys), The Fairmont is now firmly its own being. The hotel design on the whole may be more formal than you expect, but the mood is relaxed and sunny. The aura extends into the rooms, which are plush without being pompous. They feature vintage prints, large tile lanais (on the first floor), expansive views of the ocean, and artfully landscaped grounds. Views from even the least expensive garden rooms are wonderfully lush. The large marble baths feel decadent. The waterfall at The Fairmont is an aesthetic delight, flowing and splashing its way over lava rocks toward the 10,000-square-foot heated pool—one of the island's best. The first-rate Spa Without Walls offers private seaside *and* waterfall massage huts. The white sandy lagoon is a popular spot, beyond which the beach stretches toward the horizon in an inviting natural state, beckoning guests to walk and hide away. Endangered sea turtles favor this stretch of beach. Stop one evening (or every night) in the smartly renovated Luana Lounge for cocktails. It's an inviting place—made more so with a hula dancer at sunset and local artwork. Don't miss stargazing on Friday nights, and don't forget to do nothing here, too, before or after dining at one of their many great restaurants. *Rates:* $$$–$$$$; children free in parent's room. *Facilities and amenities:* 540 rooms and suites, pool, beach, five restaurants (including **Nori's Sushi Bar & Restaurant**, **The Grill**, and **Brown's Beach House**), golf course, nine tennis courts (fee), fitness center, spa, water sport rentals, concierge, shops, children's programs, parking (fee).

⚜ Hapuna Beach Prince Hotel
(808-880-1111 or 1-866-774-6236;
hapunabeachhotel.com), 62-100 Kaunaoa Dr., Mauna Kea area. First im-
pressions matter. On seeing the
palm-tree-lined driveway and massive
pillars at the entryway, you know the
Hapuna Beach Prince is a deliciously
different and refreshing contemporary place. Opened in 1995, the
Prince appeals to a hip, 40-something
crowd (and certainly those younger
who have the cash). The low-rise
structures are nestled into the bluffs
and blend harmoniously with the
environment. Slate walkways lead
through the terraced courtyard down
to the sweeping beach and large pool.
The hotel sits at one end of the absolutely fabulous Hapuna Beach—
easily one of the state's best. The
wide, white sands epitomize lounging
perfection, but the surf can get a little
rough for swimming. Golf is *the* fea-
tured recreation, and the links-style
course, designed by Arnold Palmer
and Ed Seay, challenges players with
unforgiving fairways. In the guest
rooms, the tone is one of tasteful
understatement. Each of the spacious
beauties (at 631 square feet, the
largest on the Kohala Coast) enjoys
an ocean view, although the magnificence of the view grows with the rate.
It tops out at the Hapuna Suite, the
most luxurious in Hawai'i. The 8,000-
square-foot hideaway has four master
bedrooms, a luxury kitchen, 24-hour
butler service, and a seductive private
swimming pool. You don't have to
book a suite, though, to be treated
like royalty at this oasis of the spirit.
Rates: $$$$; children free in parent's
room. *Facilities and amenities:* 350
rooms and suites, pool, beach, six
restaurants (including **Coast Grille**

and **Hakone**), golf course, 11 tennis
courts (fee), spacious fitness center,
spa, water sport rentals, concierge,
activity desk, shops, children's programs, valet parking (free).

⚜ Mauna Kea Beach Hotel (808-
882-7222 or 1-866-774-6236; mauna
keabeachhotel.com), 62-100 Mauna
Kea Beach Dr., Mauna Kea area.
Due to 2007 earthquake damage, the
hotel was undergoing an extensive
renovation through 2008. Specifics
were unavailable at press time. I can
tell you what *used to be* true, though.
Laurance S. Rockefeller chose beach
locations for his select RockResorts
with extraordinary vision. In 1960,
the 1,839-acre Mauna Kea Beach
Hotel was the culmination of his
genius—and one of the boldest and
most far-sighted decisions in the his-

HAPUNA BEACH PRINCE HOTEL

MAUNA KEA BEACH HOTEL

tory of modern tourism. He carved an imaginative, architecturally significant, art-filled hotel out of an inaccessible and forbidding patch of black lava on one of the grandest natural beaches in Hawai'i. Although time has marched on since the Mauna Kea's original inspiration, its recreational facilities remain superior, boasting Palmer and Trent Jones golf courses, a tennis park, and a pearly, expansive beach that's ideal for any surfside pastime. Additional activities abound, including manta ray diving excursions and tours of the hotel's art collection. Although the terraced rooms were small by today's norms (but that may change), and the furnishings were simple (that may change), the focus is really on the outdoors (that won't change). When booking, it's worth noting that "oceanview" rooms are better than "beachfront." *Rates:* $$$$; children free in parent's room. *Facilities and amenities:* 310 rooms and suites, pool, beach, restaurants (including **Batik**), golf courses, 13 tennis courts, fitness center, spa, water sport rentals, concierge, activity desk, children's programs, parking.

CONDOS
☙ Classic Resorts at Mauna Lani
(1-800-642-6284 reservations or 1-877-827-3994 information; mauna lanipoint-px.rtrk.com), 68-1050 Mauna Lani Point Dr., Mauna Lani area. These condominiums make most other Hawai'i condos look like housing projects. If there were Academy Awards for condos, Mauna Lani would win for best special effects; the panorama outside includes lava rock, pounding surf, and the fabled 15th hole of the Francis H. I'i Brown South Golf Course. The one-, two-, and three-bedroom units in the rental program are contemporary, plush, and spacious. The large master bathrooms boast a large soaking tub and two marble vanities, while the spacious living room opens onto an enormous lanai. Housekeeping services look after you daily, and the kitchens are very nicely equipped. Guests may use all the exceptional recreational facilities within the Mauna Lani area at discounted rates: If the stunning golf courses don't call to you, take a short shuttle ride to play tennis at the Mauna Lani Sports & Fitness Center. Or head to the Point's private beach club, secluded from the masses. *Rates:* $$$–$$$$; children free in parent's room. *Facilities and amenities:* 116 condos, pool, golf course, parking (free).

ResortQuest Shores at Waikoloa (808-886-5001 or 1-877-997-6667; resortquesthawaii.com), 69-1035 Keana Pl., Waikoloa area. Sited between the Waikoloa Beach Marriott and the Hilton, the Shores is closer to the Waikoloa Beach Golf Course than either of them, which conveniently surrounds the grounds. The 11 contemporary but classic Mediterranean-style buildings rise three stories above a series of lagoons that flow gently by the pool, Jacuzzi, and barbecue grills. Most buildings are oriented toward the Pacific-setting sun, but none get a good water view. Although there are plenty of restaurants and beaches at nearby resorts, you'll find neither at the Shores. The condominiums do allow you, though, to enjoy recreational abundance and area history in spacious privacy. Apartments are large and well appointed; the fully equipped kitchens, bathrooms, and huge lanais gleam with tile. Bathtubs are oversized and, in some units, separate from the shower. Daily maid service is a treat. *Rates:* $$$–$$$$; children free in parent's room; Internet deals available. *Facilities and amenities:* 120 rooms and suites, pool, two tennis courts (free), fitness center, concierge, children's programs, parking (free).

BED & BREAKFASTS

Puako Bed & Breakfast (808-882-1331 or 1-800-910-1331; big island-bedbreakfast.com), 25 Puako Beach Dr., Puako. One host at this bed & breakfast is a Hawaiian *kumu hula* (*hula* instructor) who entertains at many resorts and embodies the *aloha* spirit. Local culture, important here, surrounds you. You'll enjoy the generous breakfast served in the common kitchen–dining area. The largest unit has a living room with a king futon, a lanai, a queen bed, en suite bath, and cathedral ceilings. The other private-bath guest room is also quiet and comfortable, with a king bed and nice bath; it opens onto a private garden area. The B&B is *mauka* (on the mountain side) but has easy beach access. Oh, and by the way, sunny Puako only receives 7 inches of rain annually. *Rates:* $$; two-night minimum. *Facilities and amenities:* four rooms (some with private bath), A/C, TV, breakfast, no smoking.

VACATION RENTALS

Vintage Beach Cottage (808-896-0732; 2papayas.com), Puako. While not oceanfront, this cottage—one of the island's most comfortable and nicely furnished—is only a one-minute walk from a beach access point. Although Puako was a dust bowl for years, these days it's a mecca for Silicon Valley transplants. The proud property owners live in a separate residence, privately tucked behind the cottage, and they anticipate your every need. From a welcome breakfast basket to high-end kitchen appliances, they've done a

NEAR PUAKO

POTLUCK: STORIES THAT TASTE LIKE HAWAI'I

Potluck—a collection of short stories by Catherine Bridges Tarleton—speaks to our longings for and about Hawai'i. In them, Catherine has tasted Hawai'i's flavor and ways of life and writes with humor and insight about her experiences as a mainlander who immigrated to the islands. From "Everything I Need to Know about Life I Learned from Potluck" to "The Bard of Hamakua," from the real to the imaginary, Catherine's stories wax with modern-day sensibilities. Her glossary alone is worth the price of admission!

From "Pulakaumaka (Obsession)":

I try to call Hawai'i but Hawai'i never calls back . . .

I try to call Hawai'i from the car phone when I am stuck in traffic. Screaming at the lights and idiots. Screaming at the cold defrost that makes the window fog worse and the stupid sticking lighter and the smartass D.J. with too many opinions and the rattlesnake voice . . .

Sometimes I get recordings, which is not too bad, and I listen to the steel guitars six thousand miles away. I listen to the Brothers Caz who never get old and are always headed back home, in the islands, back home, in the islands. It eases the need a little. It makes my left ear warm . . .

Sometimes an operator says *aloha* and *mahalo* for calling the 800 number for some hotel chain to ask about room rates and job openings and just to hear the sound of Hawai'i's voice. As soon as I hang up I replay the tape

---

great job. The place has a very tropical feel, just like a beach house should. Built in the 1940s and immaculately preserved, it's now outfitted with a king-sized bed, very comfy living room, indoor and outdoor showers, a washer-dryer, and a carport; the lanai off the bedroom has a sliver of an ocean view. You'll undoubtedly end up swinging in a hammock or barbecuing on one of several lanais. *Rates:* $$; five-night minimum, cleaning fee, security deposit. *Facilities and amenities:* kitchen, TV, VCR, phone, A/C, no smoking.

CAMPING & CABINS

Hapuna Beach Shelters (808-974-6200; hawaii.gov/dlnr/dsp), Mauna Kea area. These small A-frame shelters are set back from the famed Hapuna Beach, with easy access to the parking lot. Bring a sleeping pad for the wooden bed frames. Hot showers, toilets, drinking water, and cooking facilities are located in an adjacent communal building. Since there's no tent camping allowed here, this is the only way to stay on the beach. *Rates:* $; reservations recommended at least a month in advance; checks only.

in my brain over and over until every word is burned in solid state, then I dial again to hear *aloha* and *mahalo* and *aloha* and *mahalo* for calling. Until I believe it . . .

If I can get through the busy busy busy busy signal, I will beg Hawai'i to take me away. From everything gray and everything boring and everything freezing and sodden and awful. Then I will tell Hawai'i that I want, I deserve, and I need to be there, need to be. And that I will quit smoking if, lose twenty pounds if, stop all the crying if if if if the place will take me in. I will do whatever Hawai'i wants, and I will be whatever Hawai'i wants me to be. In Hawai'i, I can . . .

In Hawai'i, I can lie in the sand and vibrate with the rhythm of surf and earthquakes . . .

In Hawai'i, I can walk on rocks, walk on water, walk on clouds to the top of Mauna Kea . . .

In Hawai'i, I will eat mangos three meals a day. I will build a house in a mango tree and bathe in mango puree. I will live with the mango tribe and run with the mango herd and howl at the mango moon with a mouthful of mango dripping down my chin like blood from the mango vampire's desperate hunger . . ."

✳ Where to Eat

From south to north.

Each of these staggeringly luscious resorts has one fine-dining room (serving high-end cuisine from a sophisticated staff) and another one that's a notch down in atmosphere and cost (barely—for those times when you don't want to dress up a smidgeon for dinner). Asking my preference would be akin to choosing a favorite child—it depends on the day of the week, right? So, unlike my usual method of ordering reviews by preference, these listings appear as you'd find them when driving from south to north. Reservations are recommended at all establishments.

DINING OUT

🌺 🐟 **Pahu i'a** (808-325-8000; fourseasons.com/hualalai), Four Seasons Resort Hualalai, Ka'upulehu area. Open for breakfast and dinner daily. While the Four Seasons' ultra-elegant dining room features an aquarium (or *pahu i'a*), its focal point is the vast cobalt-blue ocean within arm's reach. Try to secure a table on the terrace; there may be no finer oceanfront tables in the entire state. And that's no exaggeration! The oh-so-sophisticated restaurant, in fact, feels like a floating island since you must cross a natural anchialine (brackish) pond via an 'ohi'a wood bridge to reach it. As for the nuanced dinner menu, it emphasizes Hawaiian fish, Pacific Rim preparations, and Asian dishes. Be adventurous in the morning by ordering a full Japanese breakfast, highlighting broiled salmon and miso soup. The buffet is the best among a coastline of superb buffets. Or throw caution to the wind and dive into the lavish buffet (almost without peer in the state). Children's menu. Breakfast buffet $$$$, dinner entrées $$$$.

✿ ♈ **Hualalai Grille** (808-325-8525; hualalairesort.com), Ka'upulehu area. Open for dinner daily. This new temple to Hawai'i regional cuisine, by chef Alan Wong (famous by way of the Kohala Coast's Canoe House and of Alan Wong's and the Pineapple Room in O'ahu), catapulted into the hearts of food lovers as soon as the doors opened in 2004. The stylish interior highlights *koa*, marble, and local artwork—a perfect palette for Wong's culinary artistry. Wong's soups are justifiable renowned; try the sublime chilled yellow and red tomato soup. Lunchtime burgers are a cut above the competition, while dinner dishes may feature ginger-encrusted onaga or royal moi steamed to perfection. Children's menu. Entrées $$$–$$$$.

✿ ♣ **Norio's Japanese Restaurant and Sushi Bar** (808-887-7387, fairmont.com/orchid), The Fairmont Orchid, Hawai'i, N. Kaniku Dr. Open nightly for dinner. Leave it to the Fairmont to have the best Japanese restaurant on this side of the island. When they do something, they do it right. Master sushi chef Norio hails

from Tokyo, and his menu showcases traditional Japanese delicacies as well as melt-in-your-mouth sushi and sashimi. I've rarely had better. Don't miss the Japanese abalone, Maine lobster, prawns, and Atlantic flounder, much of which is farmed down the road. Diners can watch the artistry from the beautiful sushi bar or the main dining room. Or savor it from a private dining room while contemplating the serenity of a Japanese garden and koi pond. Children's menu. Entrees $$$–$$$$.

✿ **The Grill** (808-885-2000; fairmont.com/orchid), The Fairmont Orchid, Hawai'i, Mauna Lani area. Open for dinner Tues.–Sat. Except on the hushed terrace, The Grill is awash in rich *koa* woods, which lend a comfortably clubby, handsome, and formal atmosphere. (A grand piano at the entryway also helps.) As for the distinctly Hawaiian menu, it offers well-executed lamb and veal specialties as well as fish and seafood that will leave you worshiping Neptune. The brilliant dessert menu features a chocolate soufflé that'll rock your world. And lastly, a truly exceptional wine list is made more so with the expert assistance of a savvy sommelier. Children's menu. Entrées $$$$.

✿ **Donatoni's** (808-886-1234; hilton waikoloavillage.com), Hilton Waikoloa Village, Waikoloa area. Open for dinner nightly. One of half a dozen resort restaurants, this romantic villa-style eatery stands head and shoulders above the crowd, even if you include every single Italian restaurant in the state in the "crowd." From start to finish, from exquisite service to impeccable presentation, the entire northern Italian experience couldn't be more refined. Dishes are sublime;

even seemingly simple pasta dishes excel. Top off the evening with classic tiramisu. Children's menu. Entrées $$$–$$$$.

✐ **Imari** (808-886-1234; hiltonwaikoloa village.com), Hilton Waikoloa Village, Waikoloa area. Open for dinner nightly. Even though I didn't get a chance to eat here for this edition, Imari's sushi, tempura, shabu shabu, and teppanyaki get consistently high grades from my foodie friends and contacts. Expect a hushed and tranquil tone. Reservations recommended, elegant resort attire required; children's menu. Entrées $$$–$$$$.

✐ ☪ **Roy's Waikoloa Bar & Grille** (808-886-4321; roysrestaurant.com), Waikoloa Beach Dr., King's Shops, Waikoloa area. Open for dinner daily. Although my intellect questions whether executive chef Roy Yamaguchi can possibly maintain his high standards with so many different locations (the same question can be raised about other noted chefs), my taste buds have a quick retort: Roy can and does. Although each of Roy's (exposed) kitchens is run by a different chef, each dishes up incredibly consistent, creative cuisine like hibachi-style salmon. And if you feel like forgoing fish for once, Roy's baby back ribs are a signature dish. The classy bistro overlooks a big lake and gets buzzy and sceney at night. Children's menu. Entrées $$$$. BYOB ($20 corkage fee).

✐ **Canoe House** (808-885-6622; maunalani.com), Mauna Lani Bay Hotel, Mauna Lani area. Open for dinner nightly. This famed restaurant was placed squarely on the culinary map in 1989 by chef Alan Wong, one of the forefathers of Hawai'i regional cuisine. And although Wong departed

in 1995, the pioneering tradition lives on—although it's not quite as exalted and vaunted as it once was. It's tough following the embodiment of perfection. Make it a point to arrive at the open-air, torch-lit restaurant and terrace for sunset cocktails and appetizers like nori-wrapped tempura ahi (not to be missed!). Then let sautéed *ono* served on wasabi smashed potatoes melt in your mouth. Although there are always five different seafood preparations from which to choose, the baby back ribs and rack of lamb are good alternatives to ocean delicacies. Trust the wine steward with pairings and get ready for romantic dining to the nth degree. Reservations recommended; children's menu. Entrées $$$–$$$$.

🍴 ✐ **Hawai'i Calls** (808-886-6789; marriott.com), Waikoloa Beach Marriott Resort & Spa, Waikoloa area. Open for breakfast, lunch, and dinner daily. Nostalgia may reign in the atmosphere department, but cuisine from the kitchen is pure contemporary Hawaiian. From grounds glowing with tiki torches and glistening ponds to a lovely open-air setting, this tasteful restaurant is quite satisfying. Hawai'i Calls may not have the upper-crust panache of other Kohala resorts, but it more than makes up for it in value. An expansive 'ohana spirit infuses everything. The Friday and Saturday night prime rib and seafood buffet is a bargain at $45. Children's menu. Breakfast buffet $$–$$$, dinner entrées $$$–$$$$.

✐ ☪ **Kamuela Provisions** (808-886-1234; hiltonwaikoloavillage.com), Hilton Waikoloa Village, Waikoloa area. Open for dinner nightly. The torch-lit terrace here is one of my favorite places on this coast for an

KAMUELA PROVISIONS

but the fine Japanese cuisine will do, nothing but Hakone will do. Since Prince Hotels have historically catered to a Japanese clientele, you can trust the grace inherent in Hakone's service and execution. What it lacks in water views it makes up with exquisitely plated dishes. The sushi and sukiyaki are excellent. Reservations required; children's menu. Japanese buffet $$$–$$$$, dinner entrées $$$–$$$$.

See also Sansei Seafood under *Selective Shopping.*

almost elegant but exceedingly comfortable meal. Sweeping views on the point are beyond compare. Try the macadamia pesto-encrusted pork chop or the guava chicken. The popular wine bar offers an impressive selection of wines by the glass. When they're perfectly paired with appetizers, you could spend the evening here and leave quite satisfied. Children's menu. Entrées $$$–$$$$.

✆ **Coast Grille** (808-880-1111; hapunabeachhotel.com), Hapuna Beach Prince Hotel, Mauna Kea area. Open for dinner nightly. If the unusual circular dining room (which affords spacious ocean views) indicates any such level of innovation from the kitchen, you're in luck. From seafood and steaks to mouthwatering oysters, the menu doesn't disappoint. Banquettes and wicker furnishings also lend a high relaxation quotient. Reservations required; children's menu. Entrées $$$–$$$$.

✆ **Hakone** (808-880-1111; hapuna beachhotel.com), Hapuna Beach Prince Hotel, Mauna Kea area. Open for dinner Fri. and Sat. When nothing

EATING OUT

✪ ⛾ ✆ ♟ **Brown's Beach House** (808-885-2000; fairmont.com), The Fairmont Orchid, Hawai'i, Mauna Lani area. Open for lunch and dinner nightly. I'm always tempted to eat every meal of every day here because of the setting. No joke. Torch lit and casually elegant in its simplicity, this beachside eatery (complete with an open kitchen) offers Hawaiian regional dishes with a Japanese flair. We're all lucky that the food is as superb as it is, because with a setting like this, I (for one) would be tempted to eat their sand just to sit here. On my last

BROWN'S BEACH HOUSE

trip to the Big Island I had seared ahi every day for lunch, to do an unrivaled taste test, and I can say that Brown's rules! Lastly, there's nothing like white tablecloths on the beach. The adjacent **Brown's Deli** offers pastries in the morning and pizzas and salads in the afternoon. Entertainment nightly. Children's menu. Lunch $$–$$$, dinner entrées $$$–$$$$.

🍸 **Beach Tree Bar & Grill** (808-325-8000; fourseasons.com/hualalai), Four Seasons Resort Hualalai, Ka'upulehu area. Open for lunch daily and dinner Sun.–Fri. For the perfect intersection of price, cuisine, and venue, the Beach Tree is almost unmatched. The beachside and poolside service is divinely casual, and the offerings are as diverse as ahi sashimi, sandwiches, vegetarian dishes, grilled fish, and wildly diverse salads. There's often evening entertainment. Children's menu. Lunch $$–$$$, dinner entrées $$$–$$$$.

🍸 **Merriman's Market Café** (808-885-6822; merrimanshawaii.com), Waikoloa Beach Rd., King's Shops, Waikoloa area. Open for lunch and dinner weekdays. What a great concept: Take chef Peter Merriman's expertise (see Merriman's in "North Kohala & Waimea"), apply it to Mediterranean dishes, and offer it in a laid-back market and gourmet deli setting with indoor and outdoor seating. It's a refreshing change of pace. It's also a nice place for solo diners, who can eat outside, have a glass of wine, and people-watch. Reservations recommended for dinner; children's menu. Lunch $$$, dinner entrées $$$–$$$$. BYOB ($20 corkage fee).

✪ LOVELY *LU'AU*

Polynesia Revues are held at the Hilton Waikoloa Village, Waikoloa Beach Marriott Resort & Spa, and Mauna Kea Beach Hotel on the Kohala Coast and at the King Kamehameha Kona Beach Hotel in Kailua-Kona, but none holds a tiki torch in atmosphere to the *lu'au* at **Kona Village Resort** (808-325-5555; Ka'upulehu area; $98 adults with an open bar; $67 ages 6–12; $40 ages 3–5).

By now you probably know what goes into a good (and bad) *lu'au*: a steamed pig that cooked all day in an earthen *'imu;* entertainment in the form of hula, chanting, and fire dancing; and buffets featuring local food. It's just not always this well done. The Kona Village revue is exceedingly laudable, the food is bountiful and tasty (*laulau, lomi lomi* salmon, ahi *poke,* coconut pudding), the open-air dining room a treat, and, most importantly, the *aloha* spirit genuine. The remote setting is rarefied, too: Tiki torches light sandy paths while the tranquil lagoons and bay shimmer under the full moon.

The Kona Village *lu'au* is held on Wednesday and Friday evenings. The property opens at 4:45 PM (when you should come if you're not staying here; see *Lodging*), the *'imu* ceremony, dinner, and show runs from 5:15 until 8:45 PM. You'll really feel transported to another time and place.

☀ Entertainment

On the Kohala Coast, fine dining is generally considered the evening's entertainment.

○ **Twilight at Kalahuipua'a** (808-885-6622), Mauna Lani Bay Hotel, Mauna Lani area. Once monthly, on the Sat. closest to the full moon, folks start gathering at about 5:30 PM. Celebrating Hawai'i's cultural traditions, residents and visitors assemble with blankets and picnics (or plate dinners) to talk story and appreciate local music and dance. Don't miss it.

Y **Clipper Lounge** (808-886-6789), Waikoloa Beach Marriott Resort & Spa, Waikoloa area. Open 11–11 daily.

Y **Atrium Bar** (808-885-6622), Mauna Lani Bay Hotel, Mauna Lani area. Open 5:30–7:30 Mon.–Sat. Cozy and stylish, this upscale space offers Hawaiian music and a nice selection of wines, unless you're more of a mind for a Stoli and stogie.

Y **Reef Lounge** (808-880-1111), Hapuna Beach Prince Hotel, Mauna Kea area. Open 5:30–10:30 nightly. A nice, open-air place for cocktails and Hawaiian music.

See also **Beach Tree Bar & Grill** and **Kamuela Provisions** under *Where to Eat*.

☀ Selective Shopping

King's Shops (808-886-8811; waikoloabeachresort.com), Waikoloa Beach Dr., Waikoloa area. This pricey, pleasant outdoor mall has upscale gift shops, a few upmarket retailers along the lines of Louis Vuitton, a bathing suit shop, galleries, a juice bar, a Starbucks, and several restaurants.

Queen's Marketplace (808-886-8811; waikoloabeachresort.com),

MERRIMAN'S MARKET CAFÉ

across from the King's Shops, was only partially occupied at press time. Eateries include **Sansei Seafood** (808-886-6286; dkrestaurants.com; open nightly), which specializes in Japanese-based Pacific Rim cuisine and is outstanding wherever it goes. Promised eateries include outlets specializing in noodles and Thai and Chinese cuisine. Starbucks was opened from the get-go.

Shops at Mauna Lani. This high-end retail and restaurant complex includes chains like Ruth's Chris Steakhouse and Tommy Bahama as well as locally known Kenichi Pacific. Look for galleries and jewelry shops, too.

NORTH KOHALA & WAIMEA

North Kohala is a relatively small peninsula on a Big Island map, but a devoted explorer could spend weeks probing its layers of diversity. The Parker Ranch sprawls around the rural and rolling pastures of the peninsula, from the ocean to the slopes of Mauna Kea, which dominates the southern perspective. The largest family-owned ranch in the United States, the Parker spread has a colorful history dating back to the days of Kamehameha the Great.

The spirit of the king himself is present throughout the Kohala region. His birthplace is marked near the 1,500-year-old Mo'okini **Heiau** in the far north, and just down the coast is the Pu'ukohola **Heiau** National Historic Site, where he started his conquest and unification of the islands.

Speaking of kings, sugar was once also king in Kohala; in its heyday, there were seven plantations. The former sugar towns of Hawi and Kapa'au, although only a few blocks long and lined with old wooden buildings, are well worth poking around. While the northwestern territory is arid, the northern shore can be surprisingly hot and humid up here.

The region's principal town, a fast-growing place with well-off residents and a decidedly *paniolo* atmosphere, sits at a 2,500-foot elevation and cannot decide on its name. The post office calls it Kamuela, which is Hawaiian for "Samuel," in honor of Samuel Parker, grandson of the founder of the Parker Ranch. But most residents refer to it as Waimea, its original appellation and the one I use. Whatever you call the burg, it's a fine base for developing an appreciation of the Big Island's magnificence, which extends even to the food offered at Merriman's—arguably the best on the island. And if you don't make it up to the observatory on

BUILDING BLOCKS FOR A PERFECT DAY IN NORTH KOHALA & WAIMEA

Visit Lapakahi State Historical Park (90 minutes)

Wander the shops and eateries in Hawi (90 minutes)

Drive to the Pololu Valley Lookout (90 minutes)

Drive the Kohala Mountain Road (90 minutes)

Understand *paniolo* life and horse-back ride at Parker Ranch (3 hours)

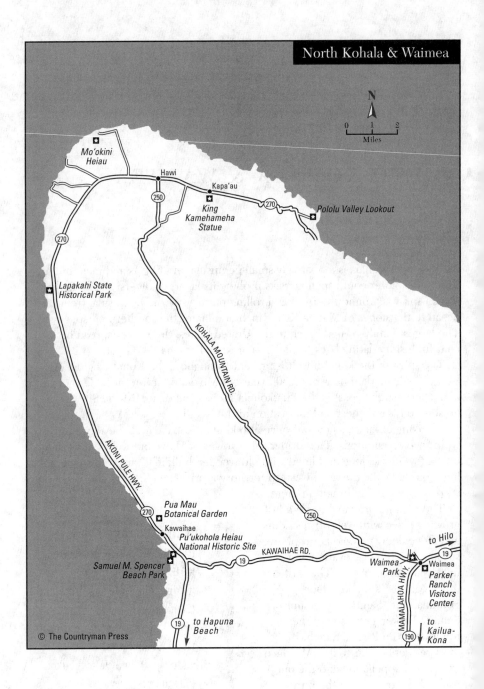

Mauna Kea (see *Mauna Kea & Saddle Road* in "The Kohala Coast"), you can always stop in at the Keck Observatory Control Center in Waimea.

GETTING AROUND

By car: Allot a nice leisurely day to explore this region; from Kailua-Kona or the Kohala Coast resorts, take Hwy. 19 north to Hwy. 270 and follow it to its end.

Backtrack for a short while through Kapaʻau and Hawi, and then take Hwy. 250 south to Waimea.

✳ To See & Do

Exploring clockwise around the North Kohala Coast.

✪ **Puʻukohola Heiau National Historic Site** (808-882-7218; nps.gov/puhe), 62-3601 Kawaihae Rd., off Hwy. 270, about 1 mile south of Kawaihae. Open 7:30–4 daily. It was prophesied that if King Kamehameha I would build this coastal *heiau*, he'd conquer and unify the Hawaiian Islands. He did (in 1790–1791), and he did (in 1810). It was also suggested by the prophets that he needed to sacrifice his adversary at this huge stone platform for the same reason. Thus, he invited his cousin to the temple's dedication, killed him, and proceeded with his campaign to control the islands. Ironically, this *heiau* overlooks another, Mailekini, built earlier in the 1200s to honor peace between the Big Island and Maui.

Kawaihae Harbor, off Hwy. 270. Used by King Kamehameha I when he sailed off to take control of the neighbor islands, and used by Captain George Vancouver in 1793 to bring Mexican longhorn cattle to the Big Island, this harbor—these days—is busy on weekends with paddlers and commercial traffic. (It's the largest on this side of the island.) In winter you can see whales offshore from here.

Pua Mau Botanical Garden (808-882-0888; puamau.com), *mauka*, Ala Kahua Dr. (Kohala Estates), near MM 6 off Hwy. 270, Kawaihae. Open 9–4 daily. Take a self-guided tour of this 45-acre garden, which features over 200 varieties of hibiscus, bronze sculptures, and plumeria trees. $15 adults, $5 ages 6–16, free ages 5 and under.

🏄 **Lapakahi State Historical Park** (808-974-6200 or 808-882-6207), *makai*, Hwy. 270. Open 8–4 daily. Although it'll be hot and parched (with no relief in the form of shade), you should take one of the short, mile-long trails to this mid-14th-century fishing village, *Koaiʻe*, the island's best preserved. You'll see only stone walls and ruins, but there are good interpretive displays on shelters, fishing, legends, and such. Sections of the park are sacred, so walk with respect. Go early in the morning or late in the afternoon to beat the heat, and do yourself another favor by wearing sturdy shoes. Self-guided tour available.

Moʻokini Heiau, off Hwy. 270 (turn *makai* where you see the sign for ʻUpolu Airport), North Kohala. Dedicated to the god of war, Ku, this National Historic Landmark dates back to A.D. 480 and is the state's oldest and largest. It's highly sacred. Said

PUʻUKOHOLA HEIAU

to have been built by 18,000 workers who passed stones one by one along a 14-mile trail from the Pololu Valley to here, the three-tiered temple was also used for human sacrifices by Tahitian priests a few hundred years later. Additionally, the future King Kamehameha I was born in 1750 about 1,000 yards from here. Although the *heiau* is located about 1.5 miles down an unpaved road that requires a four-wheel drive, you are only permitted to visit on the third Saturday of each month by helping the Moʻokini Preservation Foundation (808-373-8000) with their work.

✪ **Hawi** and **Kapaʻau**, Hwy. 270. These two former sugar plantation towns are chock-full of western-style buildings that have been restored and resurrected with galleries, shops, and cafés.

King Kamehameha Statue, Hwy. 270, Kapaʻau. This 8.5-foot-high statue, which towers over its onlookers with outstretched arms, came to this location in a roundabout way. An American sculptor cast it in Europe in 1880, but it was lost when the transport ship carrying it sank off the coast of the Falkland Islands. A replacement was soon recast and took its place of honor in front of Aliʻioni Hale in Honolulu (see the Oʻahu section). As the story goes, the original was found in a junkyard and shipped here, near the king's birthplace. On King Kamehameha Day (June 11), enormous leis are draped from the statue.

✪ **Pololu Valley Lookout**, end of Hwy. 270, Kapaʻau. The road abruptly ends where lush cliffs and steep jagged mountains fall into a swirling ocean. It's thought that in the fifth century, lava rocks from this valley were used to build the Moʻokini Heiau, 14 miles away. If you look with attention, you can see waterfalls that originate from the same source that fed the Kohala Ditch, the ditch that irrigated sugarcane and allowed the industry to flourish.

✪ **Kohala Mountain Road Lookout**, Hwy. 250. It always seems superfluous to designate Hawaiʻi roads as scenic—because they all are! Still, some roads are more scenic than others. This is one of those. When heading to Waimea (or even back down the Kohala Coast, for that matter), take this alternate route; it's about 22 miles from Hawi to Waimea, where it joins up with Hwy. 19. On a clear day, you can see Kawaihae Harbor and the Kohala Coast resorts from here, although the road is often shrouded in mist. The curvy road offers sweeping vistas, rolling hills, loads of ironwood trees, casuarina pine trees, and cattle, which replaced cane as the industry of choice.

NORTH KOHALA

Waimea (aka Kamuela)

✪ **Waimea** (aka **Kamuela**) is rainbow country, an old cowboy town with horseback riding, but also one where new housing developments are threatening to impact the very charming reasons why the newcomers wanted to settle here in the first place.

Parker Ranch Visitor's Center & Museum (808-885-7655; parkerranch .com), Hwy. 19 and Hwy. 190, Waimea. Visitors center open 9–5 Mon.–Sat.; historic homes open 10–5 Mon.–Sat. In 1809, New Englander John Parker went AWOL from his ship and soon found himself cleaning the fishponds and tending the cattle of King Kamehameha; he conveniently married the king's granddaughter and ended up with a couple of acres of his own. The ranch was formally established in 1847, and today it consists of 150,000 acres (one of the largest in the United States) and over 30,000 head of cattle; about a dozen *paniolo* (cowboys) work the ranch, which, though privately owned, is overseen by a trust.

Visitors have a few options for learning more about this vital part of the Big Island's history. The **museum** holds artifacts and photographs pertaining to six generations of Parkers that illuminate the family and life on the ranch. Two historic homes are located about 2 miles south of town. **Mana Hale**, a rustic New England saltbox-style house made from *koa*, was built in 1874 and served as the original family residence. It's almost hard to appreciate so much *koa*, which was used for the bed's headboard, the walls, ceilings, and floors. **Pu'uopelu** was built later by other Parker descendants and houses an impressive collection of works by European masters like Pissarro, Degas, and Renoir along with priceless objets d'art from Japan and China. $8 for museum, $9 per house. The ranch hosts rodeos on July 4 and Labor Day.

'Imiola Congregational Church (808-885-4987), Church Row, off Hwy. 19, Waimea. The congregation was founded in 1832, but this church dates to 1857. It's particularly noteworthy for its beautiful *koa* interior and the *koa* calabashes that are suspended from the ceiling.

See also **Keck Observatory Control Center** under *Mauna Kea & Saddle Road* in "The Kohala Coast."

✳ Outdoor Activities

ATV RANCH RIDES

ATV Adventure at Kahua Ranch (808-882-7954), Waimea. Located on the western slopes of the Kohala Mountains, above Highway 250, this ranch spreads outward to encompass 8,500 stunning acres. See the ranch like a Hawaiian *paniolo*: cruising on an ATV. Trips: two hours for $95 per person, $40 ages under 16, including riding instruction. While you're at it, inquire about their evening ranch programs (808-987-2108).

THE NORTH KOHALA COAST

HIKING

Pololu Valley, at the end of Hwy. 270, Kapaʻau. A steep, 3-mile switchback trail leads down into the valley, where you'll find wild boars, horses, and fallow *taro* fields. The valley trail eventually leads to Waipiʻo Valley, but it's appropriate only for a few readers since it's hard-core.

HORSEBACK RIDING & MULE RIDES

Kohala Naʻalaea (808-889-0022; naalapastables.com), MM 11, Hwy. 250, Waimea. Rides offered daily. Twelve thousand acres of wide-open pastures and mountain ranges offer plenty of drama to entice high-spirited riders ($68 for 90-minute rides; $89 for two hours). Along with introducing spectacular Big Island vistas, experienced *paniolos* will show you the ropes of this working ranch. Families, in particular, enjoy ranch tours in old-fashioned wagons pulled by Percheron geldings ($37 adults, $18 children).

This outfit also offers nicely paced and informative trail rides deep within **Waipiʻo Valley** (808-775-0419), where riders explore towering waterfalls, *taro* fields along the valley floor, and lush rain forests. Rides are offered Mon.–Sat.; the morning and afternoon tours last two and a half hours ($89 per person); children must be over 8 years old, and adults must weigh less than 230 pounds.

LAUHALA WEAVING

Parker Ranch (808-885-7655; parkerranch.com), Waimea. The magnificent 150,000-acre Parker Ranch is the largest single-owner ranch in the United States and emblematic of traditional *paniolo* (cowboy) spirit. Two-hour rides are scheduled at 8:15 AM and 12:15 PM ($79 per person); the 90-minute afternoon ride starts at 4 PM ($79 per person); children ages seven and older are welcome; private rides are also available.

❊ Lodging

Temperatures can be deliciously cool at night in cowboy country.

BED & BREAKFASTS

🐚 **Waimea Gardens Cottage** (808-885-8550; waimeagardens.com), off Mamalahoa Hwy., Waimea. This romantic English-style cottage hideaway in the hills is one of Hawai'i's best. Barbara and Charlie Campbell built their contemporary home on the site of an old plantation house, preserving sections of the rustic washroom as the anteroom of a country cottage for B&B guests. In the Kohala cottage, you step down onto eucalyptus floors in the main room. A full kitchen, with pots dangling from the ceiling, occupies one corner; opposite it sits a queen-sized bed. Remodeled in 1998, the bathroom features lots of custom woodwork and opens onto a private enclosed garden. The Waimea Cottage shares the same comfortable country décor and amenities as its sister. But it also has a fireplace and French doors that open onto a brick terrace and lovely garden. The most recent addition, the Garden Studio, is attached to the main residence but has a separate entrance and an enclosed garden. Encircled by flowers, the cottages pull off a perfect blend of bucolic charm and functional grace. It's a short drive to the beach or into the center of Waimea, but you may not want to wander too far. *Rates:* $$; three-night minimum on two rooms. *Facilities and amenities:* three rooms, continental breakfast, TV, phone, no A/C, no smoking, no credit cards.

🐚 **Aaah, the Views!** (808-885-3455 or 1-866-885-3455; aaahtheviews .com), 66-1773 Alaneo St., Waimea. True to its name, this streamside upcountry home operated with care by Derek and Erika Stuart, offers to-die-for views from each of the four units. Only 15 minutes from Hapuna Beach, the property boasts a little of everything for every budget: a studio apartment, rooms that share a bath, and a nice deck and sauna. It offers a great value. *Rates:* $. *Facilities and amenities:* four rooms, continental breakfast, TV, WiFi Internet, no smoking rooms, no credit cards.

Jacaranda Inn (808-885-8813 or 1-800-262-9912; jacarandainn.com), 65-1444 Kawaihae Rd., Waimea. The Jacaranda is a good bet for affordable privacy and luxury. Managers won't dote and hover here. Built in 1897, the upcountry spread was purchased in the early 1960s by Laurance Rockefeller, who used it as a personal retreat and a companion property for his luxurious Mauna Kea Beach Hotel. Today the 11-acre estate consists of luxe hideaways, all set far back from the road behind a fence and hedge. All eight guest rooms are connected by covered walkways and surround the original building, which houses a "great room," breakfast room, library and billiards room, and

OLD MAMALAHOA HIGHWAY, WAIMEA

a lounge and little-used formal dining room. Most of the sumptuously furnished guest rooms are, in fact, 450- to 650-square-foot suites with separate sitting rooms and spacious, luxury baths. Bedding makes you feel like you're sleeping on air, and keeping the windows open on a cool Waimea evening only enhances the effect. Furnishings and details vary from Victorian elegance to Indonesian motif to upscale hunting lodge. *Rates:* $$ for rooms, $$$$ for cottage. *Facilities and amenities:* eight rooms, full breakfast available, two rooms with TV, no A/C, no phone.

Hale Hoʻonanea (808-882-1653 or 1-877-882-1653; houseofrelaxation .com), Ala Kahua Dr., Waimea. Proprietors Bruce and Melanie Biddle offer a tranquil retreat on 3 acres in the Kohala estate. There aren't many options besides big resorts in this neighborhood, but this is a good one. Savor spectacular panoramic ocean views from your private lanai or venture out to explore the rich history of the Kohala Coast. Hapuna Beach is only five minutes away; shopping and dining are nearby in Waimea. If you want to save some money for activities, this perch will preserve your options. All units are detached from one another to ensure a bit more privacy than you might expect at a small place. *Rates:* $-$$; two-night minimum. *Facilities and amenities:* three suites, TV, no phone, no A/C, no smoking, continental breakfast, kitchenette, private lanai, Internet access.

MOTEL

Kamuela Inn (808-885-4243 or 1-800-555-8968; hawaii-bnb.com/ kamuela.html), 65-1300 Kawai Hae Rd., Waimea. These former motel rooms and suites (some with a kitchen) vary from unit to unit, but they're pleasant and tasteful. Splurge for the larger suites and settle in for a while as you explore. Since they're set back from the main drag, they're fairly quiet. *Modesty* is the buzz word here. *Rates:* $-$$. *Facilities and amenities:* 30 rooms and suites, TVs, continental breakfast, phones in some rooms.

COTTAGES & VACATION RENTALS

Tina's Country Cottage (1-800-262-9912; bestbnb.com), Waimea. Fifteen minutes from Hapuna Beach and 1 mile from Waimea center, this cottage is privy to the best of both worlds. Located on the drier and sunnier side of Waimea, it's an immaculate two-bedroom, two-bath cottage with a loyal following; book early. It features a bright and fully equipped eat-in kitchen (great for gathering) and a homey and comfortable living room. Surrounded by spacious lawns and flowering trees, Tina's is also popular with families. The front lanai overlooks the old rodeo grounds, so if you're really lucky, you can watch some cowboys practicing in the corral. Remember, you're at a 2,500-foot elevation here, so evenings tend to be cooler. *Rates:* $$; four-night minimum. *Facilities and amenities:* no A/C, no smoking, phone.

Makai Hale (808-880-1012 or 1-800-262-9912; bestbnb.com), Kawaihae. Favored because of its location, location, location, this property books early, so plan ahead. The two guest rooms (one with an ocean view) are located in a separate guest wing from the sweet owners (who tend to keep to themselves unless they're needed), who never book the rooms to two separate parties. Guests have access to a microwave and kitchenette stocked with goodies, but they also get a poolside breakfast each morning. *Rates:* $$; three-night minimum. *Facilities and amenities:* two rooms, continental breakfast, pool, hot tub, TV, phone.

CAMPING

The island's best camping is at **Spencer Beach Park** near Kawaihae. Contact the Department of Parks and Recreation (808-961-8311; hawaii-county.com) in Hilo to obtain a mandatory camping permit. Facilities include showers, running water, and barbecue pits.

✳ Where to Eat

Waimea's cowboy country is home to arguably the island's best restaurant, a number of other worthy and sophisticated ones, and some darn good coffee shops. You won't come close to starving when you're tooling around North Kohala.

DINING OUT

✐ **Merriman's** (808-885-6822; merrimanshawaii.com), Opelu Plaza, Waimea. Open for lunch weekdays, dinner nightly. Few restaurants in the state serve more consistently stellar cuisine. Chef Peter Merriman was one of the first to cast off old traditions and pioneer the new Hawai'i regional cuisine. Wok-charred ahi that literally melts in your mouth was a staple on his menu before some chefs learned that tuna wasn't born frozen or plucked from a can. For Merriman's premier version of the dish, come at dinnertime. Strongly consider the catch of the day in a choice of preparations, vegetarian specialties, and wonderfully seasoned, free-range

beef, lamb, and chicken. Lunch selections are simpler—sandwiches, soups, and salads. Don't miss his organic Lokelani tomatoes that, if he ever removed them from the menu, would likely instigate World War III. Reservations recommended for dinner; children's menu. Lunch $–$$, dinner entrées $$$–$$$$.

✐ **Daniel Thiebaut** (808-887-2200; danielthiebaut.com), 65-1259 Kawaihae Rd., Waimea. Open for dinner nightly. Ensconced in a historic general store that dates to 1900, Daniel Thiebaut's Mediterranean-French-Pacific-Asian fusion cuisine elates sophisticated palates. From Hunanstyle rack of lamb to lobster bisque flavored with brandy to seared catch-of-the-day paired with a European-style sauce, he does it with flair—and by seriously highlighting local ingredients. Even vegetarians get the royal treatment with macadamia-crusted tofu and crispy avocado spring rolls with smoked tomato coulis. High ceilings, historic items that one might have found in the general store, and perfectly scaled dining rooms add up to one big impression. Before making a recommended reservation, inquire whether Chef Daniel is in that night. Follow through only if he is. Children's menu. Entrées $$$–$$$$.

✐ ☙ ♈ **Bamboo** (808-889-5555; bamboorestaurant.info), Hwy. 270, Hawi. Open for lunch and dinner Tues.–Sun. Islandy to the max, this deservedly popular "Island saloon" makes for colorful off-the-beaten-path destination dining. A comfortable and spacious eatery with unfinished floors, local artwork, and rattan furnishings, Bamboo offers creative Asian-style seafood preparations and fried noodles worth the drive if you're staying south of here. Both the fish and produce are as fresh as it gets; sometimes the chef cooks up his own catch of the day. Burgers and stir-fries at lunchtime are a great value. And then there's the Sunday brunch—popular for its signature eggs Benedict. Bamboo's exceptionally tasty *lilikoi'i* margaritas seem to go down nicely any time of the day. Check out the live music on Friday and Saturday evenings. Children's menu. Sunday brunch $–$$, lunch $$–$$$, dinner entrées $$–$$$$.

🌶 ✍ **Café Pesto** (808-882-1071; cafepesto.com), Kawaihae Shopping Center, Akoni Pule Hwy., Kawaihae Harbor. Open for lunch and dinner daily. This ever-popular café (with a branch in Hilo) dishes out gourmet pizzas topped with local lobster and large portions of inventive pasta dishes, risotto, and calzones. The organic greens alone inspire patrons to drive from miles away. Children's menu. Lunch $$, dinner entrées $$–$$$.

EATING OUT

🌶 **Sushi Rock** (808-889-5900), 55-3435 Akoni Pule Hwy., Hawi. Open for lunch and dinner Thurs.–Tues. This groovy little chef-owned place, perfectly presided over by Anita, dishes out the freshest *and* most creative sushi combos on the Big Island. Their new wave rolls defy the rules and dance in your mouth. Kamikaze this and samurai that . . . put yourself in their hands and let them tickle your fancy. Try the fresh wasabi root, a rarity. Dishes $–$$$.

✍ **Kawaihae Harbor Grill & Seafood Bar** (808-882-1368; kawaihae-restaurants.com), Hwy. 270, Kawaihae Harbor. Open for lunch and dinner daily. For reasons that

HAWI TOWN'S MAIN DRAG

don't cut the mustard (for me), this place is always packed even though it's across from an industrial area. The food, served in a historic 1850s building with lots of old Hawaiiana paraphernalia on the walls, is okay and portions sizeable. Decent choices include Hawaiian-style steamed fish, locally grown Maine lobster, Thai seafood curry, and Asian baby back ribs. Check out the daily blackboard specials and *pupus* in the upstairs **Seafood Bar**. Children's menu. Lunch $–$$, dinner entrées $$$–$$$$.

🌶 ✍ **Tako Taco** (808-887-1717), 64-1066 Mamalahoa Hwy., Waimea. Open 11–8:30 daily. It doesn't get simpler than this: fish burritos (or veggie choices topped with tomatillo pineapple salsa), good margaritas, and Mexican wedding cakes to complete the trifecta. It's a mellow place, all about the purity of ingredients—from the beans and rice to the fish and guacamole. Dishes $–$$.

🌶 ✍ **Kohala Rainbow Café** (808-889-0099), Hwy. 270, Kapa'au. Open 11–5 weekdays. It's hard to beat these healthy wraps (their specialty), piled high with locally grown and often organic veggies. You'll also find soups, salads, and burgers. Children's menu. Dishes $.

COFFEE, ICE CREAM & MORE

Kohala Coffee Mill (808-889-5577), Hwy. 270, Hawi. Open daily. Who needs a community center when there's this happenin' little place with great caffeinated beverages and cooling chai alongside light snacks like burgers, bagels, and ice cream—and not just any old ice cream, but the famed **Tropical Dreams Ice Cream**. In my humble opinion, the world doesn't need another flavor of ice cream besides Tropical Dreams Tahitian Vanilla. For wireless and shave ice, head to the backyard **Upstairs at the Mill** (808-889-5015).

Nanbu Courtyard (808-889-5546), Nanbu Hotel, Hwy. 270, Kapa'au. Open 6:30–2 weekdays, 7–2 Sat. Hang out in the courtyard behind the hotel with an espresso and hot sandwich.

✳ Entertainment

Kahilu Theatre (808-885-6868; kahi luthreatre.org), Hwys. 19 and 190, Waimea. The only real venue of its ilk on the island, the Kahilu hosts good performances: drama, hula, musicals and musical groups, symphonies, and the like. If something's being staged here, it's probably worth seeing.

See also **Bamboo** under *Dining Out*.

✳ Selective Shopping

Enough interesting one-of-a-kind shops and galleries line Kapa'au and Hawi—like **Elements** (808-889-0760, Kapa'au) for jewelry and **Bamboo** (808-889-1441, Kapa'au) for handmade wood items and *aloha* wear—to make poking around fun.

ART GALLERIES

Ackerman Galleries (808-889-5971; ackermangalleries.com), Hwy. 270, Kapa'au. Gallery open noon–5 Mon.–Sat.; gift shop open daily. With a fine-art gallery and gift shop a few blocks away from each other (on opposite sides of the street), they've got the market for your money covered. The gallery highlights Gary Ackerman's paintings, along with furniture and sculpture.

Harbor Gallery (808-882-1510; har borgallery.biz), Kawaihae Shopping Center., Hwy. 270, Kapa'au. Open daily. This two-story gallery highlights paintings and drawings, along with a huge variety of work in various media.

BOOKSTORES

Kohala Book Shop (808-889-6400), Hwy. 270, Kapa'au. Open 11–5 Mon.–Sat. Housed within the perfectly restored historic Nanbu Hotel, the state's largest used book store has exceptional Hawaiiana and Oceania collections and staggeringly rare first editions. Don't be surprised to linger longer than you'd expect.

CLOTHES

As Hawi Turns (808-889-5023), Hwy. 270, Hawi. Open daily. No, they don't specialize in beautiful turned

KOHALA BOOK SHOP

HAWI TOWN IS LINED WITH GALLERIES.

koa bowls. But they do sport bright island wear, good vintage clothes, and stylish designs—items you don't generally need but are fun on holiday shopping sprees.

FARMER'S MARKETS

Waimea is **lei-making country**, and two competing markets offer fresh flowers and produce: the **Waimea Farmer's Market** and the **Parker School Farmer's Market**. Both are held Sat. about 7 to noon.

SHOPPING AREAS

Parker Ranch Shopping Center, Hwy. 19, Waimea. Corralling more than 30 shops and the Parker Ranch Visitor's Center, this center has a natural and conventional grocery store along with a Starbucks (for when you gotta have it).

Parker Square, Hwy. 19, Waimea. Smaller boutiques like the Gallery of Great Things (below) make their home here. It's worth wandering around.

SPECIAL SHOPS

Gallery of Great Things (808-885-7706), Parker Square, Hwy. 19, Waimea. Open daily. With a name like that, they'd better deliver—and they do if you're into gifts from Polynesia and Indonesia; some local artists and art are represented, too, including lovely and typically pricey Niʻihau shell necklaces.

Nakahara Grocery Store & Nakahara General Store (808-889-6449), Hawi. Open daily. These stores are so classically Hawaiian that you have to drop in, even if you don't need any hard goods or foodstuffs.

HAMAKUA COAST

T his lush and rural landscape, once undulating with fields of sugarcane, now grows diverse agricultural crops—from macadamia nuts and specialty vegetables for four-star restaurants to papayas and pot (*pakalolo*). Along the way the panoramas include as many open and rolling fields as dense pockets of vegetation, ravines, and sea cliffs. As you head out of Waimea, arid ranching country gives way to the tropical luxuriance of the Waipi'o Valley, one of the state's most remote, mystical, and mysterious places. There aren't many places to stay or eat along the way, but the quaint and sleepy Honoka'a makes a pleasant stop. Don't miss Akaka Falls, which offers a big scenic bang for a relatively little expenditure of energy.

GUIDANCE
Economic Development Board (808-935-2180; hiedb.org), 117 Keawe St., Hilo. Look for their *Hamakua Heritage Coast* driving booklet that covers this glorious stretch between Waimea and Hilo.

GETTING AROUND
By car: The Waipi'o Valley, the star attraction of the north shore, is about 45 minutes from Hilo or 30 minutes from Waimea.

✳ To See & Do
Exploring clockwise, from west to east.

Old Mamalahoa Highway, *mauka*, off Hwy. 19. A few miles east of Waimea, this old road runs parallel to Hwy. 19 and is more intimately connected with the rolling hills and ranchland that surrounds it.

✪ **Waipi'o Valley**, *makai*, Hwy. 240. This sacred valley, a veritable Garden of Eden, is easily one of the five or six most remote places in the entire

> **BUILDING BLOCKS FOR A PERFECT DAY ON THE HAMAKUA COAST**
> Tour Waipi'o Valley (2 hours)
> Detour along Heritage Drive and Scenic Drive (1 hour)
> Visit one of two botanical gardens (2 hours)
> Hike to Akaka Falls (1 hour)

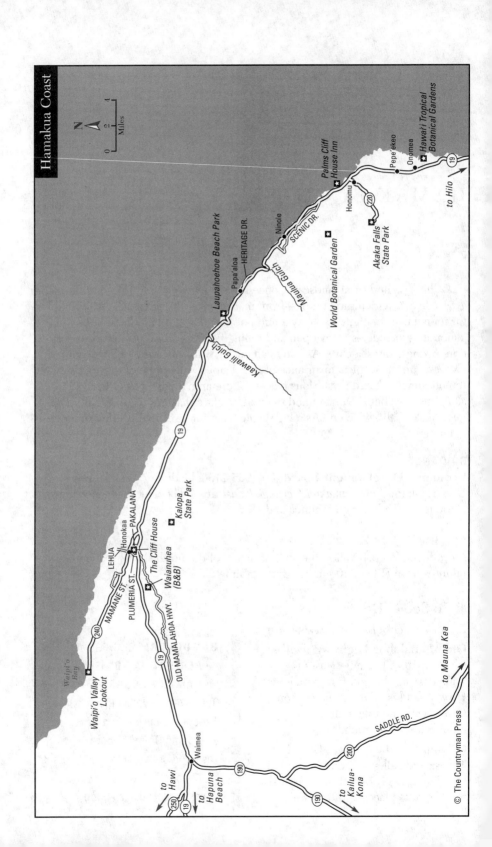

Hamakua Coast

© The Countryman Press

archipelago. It's certainly off the grid, and the 50 or so people who live here like it that way. The pastoral valley has no services and only a handful of houses; wild horses roam free. Unless you walk down (see *Down, Down, Down into Waipi'o Valley*, p. 432) or take a tour, it's impossible to get a sense of it. Even if you don't have time to walk or tour, though, at least drive to the lookout and marvel at the valley's inaccessibility. It's about 1 mile wide and 6 miles long.

It's said that between A.D. 1200 and 1600, between 4,000 and 20,000 people lived here. Once the highly favored haunt of ancient Hawaiian royalty (many of whom are buried here), this is where the future King Kamehameha was whisked off to mature in safety—and to gain the requisite training that would make him a great warrior. When Caucasian explorers "discovered" it in 1823, only about 1,500 Hawaiians lived here, farming taro and harvesting bananas, guava, and other fruit from the abundant landscape. In 1946, a tidal wave rushed in and wiped out the place.

If you do hike down into Waipi'o (which means "curving water"), you'll encounter an ethereal world along with a 1,200-foot waterfall, plenty of streambeds, and a **black-sand beach** from which surfing is fun for experienced riders only. (It is absolutely not a beach for swimming.) It's best to cool off in the stream and pond that feed into the ocean. Switchback trails are barely perceptible on the opposite valley wall, where the cliffs reach about 2,000 feet.

Waipi'o Valley Shuttle (808-775-7121), Hwy. 240. Operates 9–3 Mon.–Sat. The valley, steeped in oodles of legends and myths, is accessible via this two-hour four-wheel-drive tour. The tour does not include a stop at the black-sand beach, though; there are local taboos against it. $50 adults, $25 ages 3–11. Purchase tickets at the Waipi'o Valley Art Works (808-775-0958), Hwy. 240.

Waipi'o Valley Wagon Tour (808-775-9518; waipiovalleywagontours .com), Hwy. 240. Operates 9:30–3:30 Mon.–Sat. The 90-minute, fully narrated tour departs from the WOH Ranch on Hwy. 240. $55 adults, $25 ages 4–12.

✪ **Honoka'a**, *makai*, Hwy. 19 and Hwy. 240. One of Honoka'a's claims to fame is that the island's first macadamia nuts were planted here. It then bustled with life from the sugar plantations. Now this funky and sleepy little town feels very "real." Its western-style storefronts and boardwalks hold a few mellow cafés and mom-and-pop antiques stores.

Kalopa State Park (808-974-6200), *mauka*, 3 miles off Hwy. 19, Honoka'a. Open 7 AM–8 PM daily. This

HAMAKUA COAST WATERFALL

100-acre forest of eucalyptus, 'ohi'a, and koa trees makes a nice picnic stop; there's an easy 0.75-mile trail here, perfect for stretching your legs.

Laupahoehoe Beach Park (808-961-8311), *makai*, off Hwy. 19. This little peninsula, shaped like a lava leaf and hence the name Laupahoehoe, has a sad story. The 1946 tidal wave rolled in and swept 21 schoolchildren and their three teachers out to sea. It's not a place for swimming, but the light is particularly lovely in the late afternoon.

✪ Take **Heritage Drive**, *makai*, just south of Papa'aloa, Hwy. 19, and the 3-mile **Scenic Drive**, *mauka*, between Ninole and Hakalau, off Hwy. 19, to get even closer to the lush nature of this area.

❧ **World Botanical Garden** (808-963-5427; wbgi.com), *mauka*, near MM 16 off Hwy 19, Umauma. Open 9–5:30 daily. Purported to be the largest of its ilk in the state, this former sugarcane plantation, which occupies 275 acres, has over 5,000 species of plants cultivated within a 10-acre area. The ever-evolving place has a kid's maze (made of 5-foot jasmine plants that cover an acre) and interesting medicinal plants. You can also see the trilevel **Umauma Falls** from here; an easy 0.25-mile walk through the rain forest leads to a great viewing area. $13 adults, $6 ages 13–17, $3 ages 5–12.

Honomu, *mauka*, 2 miles off Hwy. 19. This teensy town, with tin-roofed houses, a café, an old plantation store, and a gallery or two, makes a nice interlude on the way to or from Akaka Falls.

✪ **Akaka Falls State Park**, *mauka*, 3.5 miles off Hwy. 19, just past Honomu. About 10 miles from Hilo, this park actually has two falls: Akaka (measuring 442 feet) and Kahuna (about 400 feet). A paved, 1-mile path (steep in a few places but hardly impossible) leads through thick stands of ginger and yellow- and green-striped bamboo; a few banyan trees are thrown in for good measure.

Four-Mile Scenic Drive, *makai*, between Pepe'ekeo and Onomea, off Hwy. 19. Take this little detour (also known as Old Mamalahoa Hwy.) that runs more or less parallel to Hwy. 19 to enjoy better views of Onomea Bay and the quaint town of Pepe'ekeo.

Hawai'i Tropical Botanical Gardens (808-964-5233; htbg.com), 27-717 Old Mamalahoa Hwy., Papa'ikou. Open 9–5 daily (last tickets sold at 4 PM). Off the Four-Mile Scenic Drive and about 8 miles north of Hilo, this 17-acre preserve is lined with walkways and lush with banyan and banana trees, orchid and bromeliad collections, streams and waterfalls. In fact, there are almost 2,000 different kinds of plants, flowers, and trees.

BIRDS OF A FEATHER

The place graciously dispenses umbrellas upon entry; what does that tell you?
$15 adults, $5 ages 6–16, free ages 5 and younger.

✳ Outdoor Activities

GOLF
🏌 **Hamakua Country Club** (808-775-7244; gvhawaii.com), Honoka'a. These
nine holes are a bargain at $20 per person for the entire day. But what's really
great is the layout: The course is perched on a steep hill, with great ocean views
and a wacky design where fairways cross each other. Visitors have access on
weekdays; tee times aren't necessary.

HIKING
Hawaiian Walkways (808-775-0372 or 1-800-457-7759; hawaiianwalkways
.com), Honoka'a. When you're ready for some challenging small-group hiking
with well-trained and informed guides, this outfitter fits the bill. Slow down and
see more on their half-day, 3.5-mile expedition above the Hi'ilawe falls. This
unforgettable trail, laced with natural springs and hand-built irrigation canals,
was constructed for the sugar plantations in the late 1800s. Over the rivers and
through the woods, you'll cross log bridges and use ropes and walking sticks to
steady yourself. $95 adults.

Waipi'o Valley. See *To See & Do*.

HORSEBACK RIDING
See **Kohala Na'alaea** in "North Kohala & Waimea" under *Outdoor Activities*.

✳ Lodging

BED & BREAKFASTS AND INNS
🏠 ✐ **Waianuhea** (808-775-1118 or
1-888-775-2577; waianuhea.com),
45-3503 Kahana Dr., Honoka'a.
Waiahuhea is off Hwy. 19, near MM
43 between Waimea and Hilo. I must
say: This place may not have a rival in
the whole state. No expense has been
spared to create a one-of-a-kind destination. On those occasions when
you're seeking stylish accommodation
as destination, look into Waianuhea. I
could come for a week's retreat and
depart a new person. It's remote and
it's luxurious; it's peaceful and it's off
the grid. (You'll be stunned by that
fact at dusk, when all the house lights
are aglow!) At first blush, it's hard to
conceive of a place so special *in* a
place so special. On closer inspection,
yes, it excels in all aspects. Every contemporary, stylish, soothing, and
sophisticated detail—from fine toiletries to flat-panel TVs—has been
attended to with your care and comfort in mind. From cozy and sweet to
spacious and suite, the five accommodations speak to pampering and privacy. The private hot tub and
made-to-order breakfast are two of
many, many pluses. Since dining
options are limited, the inn stocks
high-end microwave foods (for a tiny
fee). *Rates: $$$; children under eight
free in parent's room. Facilities and
amenities:* five rooms, full breakfast,
evening wine hour with fancy hors
d'oeuvres.

DOWN, DOWN, DOWN INTO WAIPI'O VALLEY

"What time would you like me to come up and get you?" she offered toward the end of the call. Not wanting to inconvenience the friend of a friend, I begged off. "Don't worry about it; I'll walk down." She was audibly dumbfounded and bemused. "No one has *ever* offered to walk down before." Travel writers have a sense of pride about these things, so I was pleased to be the first real adventurer she'd dealt with. Little did I know, I would soon be eating my words and uttering my own audible sounds of disbelief (among other things). "But I *will* take directions since I don't know where you are."

Her informational tips went something like this: "Walk downhill for about a mile. At the bottom, head to the left until you reach a green house where the road dips a bit. Head upstream to the third *taro* patch. Behind the shack you'll hear the river. If the river isn't too high, ford it." (Uh, sorry, hold on a sec: How do I know if the river is too high? "Throw a rock in, and if you can't see or hear it hit the bottom, it's too high. In that case, wait on the far side and someone will drive over to pick you up." Okay.) She finishes: "Otherwise, cross the stream and follow the road until you see the compound with the tree houses. That's me."

I jot everything down. Sounds straightforward enough. But as I head downhill, questions arise at each juncture. The first is simple: Good God, why didn't she insist on picking me up? She lives here; she knows better. This downhill walk was no walk in the park. The muscles in my thighs were burning and my toes were turning black and blue, I was just sure of it. My toes couldn't be more jammed into the tips of my boots if my life depended on it. This was no average hill; this was a hill with a grade of what felt like 45 percent. The *Oxford English Dictionary* needs a new word for this kind of hill—besides *inhumane*. Of course, I knew that visitors weren't allowed to drive down because of the steep grade and that only four-wheel-drive vehicles could manage it. But who *knew*?

At the bottom of the hill, more doubts set in. Is this *really* the bottom, or is it just leveling off a bit? Am I supposed to head left *here*? I do. When I come to the green house, a man is fixing a car that looks like it's never run. He lifts his

HIDDEN DEEP WITHIN THE WAIPI'O VALLEY

head only after I inter-
rupt with a gentle
"excuse me" three
times. I haven't seen
anyone else the whole
time. I'm sure he doesn't
see many people. He
doesn't care. When I
ask him if this is the way
to "C.'s" house (not her
real initial), his expression straddles the fence
between bemusement
and confusion. He

WAIPI'O VALLEY

shrugs, and without uttering a word simply points over to the left, on the
other side of the river. When C. said "head upstream to the *taro* patch," I
didn't realize she meant that the road *was* the stream—that I was supposed
to walk upstream in the stream. Blood is just starting to flow more normally to
my toes; now my feet are going to be soggy for the rest of the trip. But up the
stream I go.

I thought I knew what a *taro* patch looked like, but down here, I'm not
sure of anything anymore. These look more like fields than patches. But the
valley is clearly a different world, with its own set of measures and definitions. There is hope, though. I can recognize a shack when I see one. But
hold on: That looks more like a house than a shack. Is that what she meant?
My life has been one of fairly exacting language until this moment, but it
needs to start loosening up out of necessity. This ordeal (er, trek) has been
going on two hours, and I don't want to take one more waterlogged step. It's
decided: This is a patch and that's a shack.

I have a big belly laugh when I first catch sight of the stream, but no one
can hear me: The river is rushing so furiously that it drowns out every other
sound in the valley. I don't need to conduct C.'s oh-so-technical experiment
of throwing a rock in to see if it's too high to ford. But I do anyway. I wait. For
whom? For what?

Twenty minutes or so pass. Who knows how long, really. Time stands still
or, at the very least, is warped in Waipi'o Valley. A red pickup stops on the
other side just long enough to let a dog jump out the window. It starts paddling furiously, and eagerly, to get to my side. The truck follows slowly. "Are
you Kim?" "Yeah; I guess you're here to pick me up?" He's surprised I've
made it this far. He apologizes: C. kept him from setting out an hour earlier.
Suki, the wonder dog, hops back in, too tired to make the return crossing.
And we set out for their tree house. Who *are* these people? But that's another story.

When you head into the Waipi'o Valley, get a ride.

WAIANUHEA

Waipi'o Wayside Bed & Breakfast Inn (808-775-0275 or 1-800-833-8849; waipiowayside.com), near Honoka'a. When you're ready for a real bed & breakfast experience, the five units at Jackie Horne's nicely furnished, plantation-style house have something for everyone. Perched on a beautiful lawn, with white picket fence in front and views of the water, it serves as a prime base for exploring Waipi'o Valley and visiting the funky little town of Honoka'a, about 8 miles away. Surprise, surprise: The most popular room is the largest room with ocean views. Another upstairs room has sloped ceilings, great for those who like a cozy, attic feel. The other three first-floor rooms are pleasant and bright, filled with antique furniture; they have somewhat of a gingham-country feel. For breakfast, the host goes the distance trying to supply all-organic ingredients and work around dietary restrictions. *Rates:* $$; two- to three-night minimum. *Facilities and amenities:* five rooms, full breakfast, DVD library, in-room dataport, TV, no smoking.

The Cliff House (808-775-0005 or 1-800-492-4746; cliffhousehawaii.com). This two-bedroom getaway, with a full kitchen and lovely (islandy) furnishings, has views visitors only dream about. It truly is on the edge of a cliff, with an expansive lanai that takes in the panoramic sweep of the coast.

Secluded on 40 acres of pastureland, it's a great spot for four friends. It's equidistant from Hilo and Waimea, an hour from each. *Rates:* $$; two-night minimum. *Facilities and amenities:* TV, Internet access.

CABINS

Kalopa Cabins (808-974-6200; hawaii.gov/dlnr/dsp), about 6 miles south of Honoka'a. These two simple cabins sleep 8–16 people; bedding is supplied. A communal dining and cooking area has a stove and rudimentary utensils. *Rates:* $ nightly for eight people.

Camping is permitted at **Waipi'o Valley** and **Kalopa State Park** (see *To See & Do*).

✱ Where to Eat

Although pickings are slim, you'll not come up empty-handed in little Honoka'a. Plan to stop here and pack a picnic, or wait until you reach Hilo or Waimea (depending on which direction you're going).

🍲 Simply Natural (808-775-0119), Mamane St., Honoka'a. Open 8–4 daily. This low-key deli makes delicious banana-*taro* pancakes, open-faced turkey sandwiches, and other healthy meals using ultrafresh vegetables and ingredients. On first glance, you might pass by this small joint, but really, try the superb locally smoked chicken and tempeh. Dishes $.

Tex Drive-In (808-775-0598), Hwy. 19, Honoka'a. Open 6:30 AM–8 PM daily. Join the locals for the Big Island's best *malasadas*, basically a fried dough dessert that's the equivalent of a holeless doughnut, either plain or stuffed with something sweet like papaya jam. Have 'em as a meal or have one after a plate lunch, chicken katsu, saimin, or a

TEX DRIVE-IN

wrap. This institution is as much an attraction as a fast-food restaurant; you can also watch the *malasadas* being made. Dishes $.

Café Il Mondo (808-775-7711), 45-3626-A Mamane St., Honoka'a. Open for lunch and dinner Mon.–Sat. The combination of local art, a dramatic *koa* bar, and stone-oven pizzas make for one surprisingly satisfying interlude. Even though the pesto and vegetable pizzas remain the most popular offerings, the café also makes very respectable soups and sandwiches. Children's menu. Dishes $–$$; no credit cards.

What's Shakin' (808-964-3080), 27-999 Old Mamalahoa Hwy., Pepe'ekeo. Open 9:30–5 daily. The fruit smoothies are the freshest possible since the fruit comes from owner Patsy and Tim's farm, but if you're in need of protein, try the chicken and fish wraps or anything with homemade salsa. Dishes $–$$.

✴ Entertainment

Honoka'a People's Theater (808-775-0000), Mamane St., Honoka'a. Built in 1930 as a movie theater by the same folks who built the Aloha Theater in Kainaliu (on the Kona Coast), this restored palace screens movies and hosts an October music festival.

✴ Selective Shopping

Waipi'o Valley Artworks (808-775-0958; waipiovalleyartworks.com), 48-5416 Kukuihale Rd., Kukuihale. Open daily. At the end of Hwy. 240 near Waipi'o Overlook, this boutique–gallery–craft store displays an assortment of wooden objects made by islanders—from large tables to small gifts like bowls.

Kama'aina Woods (808-775-7722; hulihands.com), Lehua St., Honoka'a. Open 9–5 weekdays. Rich *koa* wood is transformed into bowls, plates, boxes, and more here, where you can watch 'em create great stuff in the workshop.

Honoka'a Trading Company (808-775-0808), Mamane St., Honoka'a. Open daily. This shop will grab your interest for antiques, Hawaiiana from the '30s and '40s, kimonos, and all sorts of items made with *koa*.

HONOMU TOWN

HILO & AROUND

For many visitors, quiet Hilo is a desirable destination only in early April when the Merrie Monarch Festival exhibits the best in Hawaiian hula. For many visitors, the main problem with Hilo is the rain. As residents say, people don't tan in Hilo; they rust. Skies are often overcast; clouds bust open with heavy-duty rain or they weep with mist; the air is heavy with humidity. The upside? There's a bonanza of rainbows, and it's very lush.

Despite the presence of the University of Hawai'i, the former sugar plantation town isn't exactly exciting, either. When a freighter inadvertently dumped 900 tons of molasses into the bay in 1984, wags claimed the slow-moving solution brought the pace to a total standstill. For some reason, Hilo once thought it could be another big destination like Honolulu and built lots of high-rise hotels on the bay. But the masses never materialized, so now Hilo is a good budget destination. (There are an increasing number of fine and pricey B&Bs, too.)

For many visitors, Hilo simply serves as a gateway to Hawai'i Volcanoes National Park, about 45 minutes south.

But I love friendly Hilo. It's decidedly real. If you aren't in a race to notch your belt with tourist attractions, Hilo offers many moments you'll find nowhere else. Compared with the suburban malls of Kailua-Kona, commerce in Hilo is exotically old-fashioned. Catch the state's most stirring farmer's market; drop into mom-and-pop shops owned by long-time Japanese immigrants; or wake early any morning except Sunday for the Suisan Fish Auction, when the large, multiethnic fishing fleet sells its catch downtown. Or visit Hilo's nurseries, which grow 22,000 varieties of

BUILDING BLOCKS FOR A PERFECT DAY IN AND AROUND HILO

Pay a morning visit to Rainbow Falls, Pe'epe'e Falls, and Boiling Pots (90 minutes)

Take a walking tour of downtown Hilo (2 hours)

Plan to visit the farmer's market (30 minutes)

Pop into the Pacific Tsunami Museum (1 hour)

Cruise Banyan Drive (15 minutes)

Visit the outpost: the Puna District & Pahoa (3 hours)

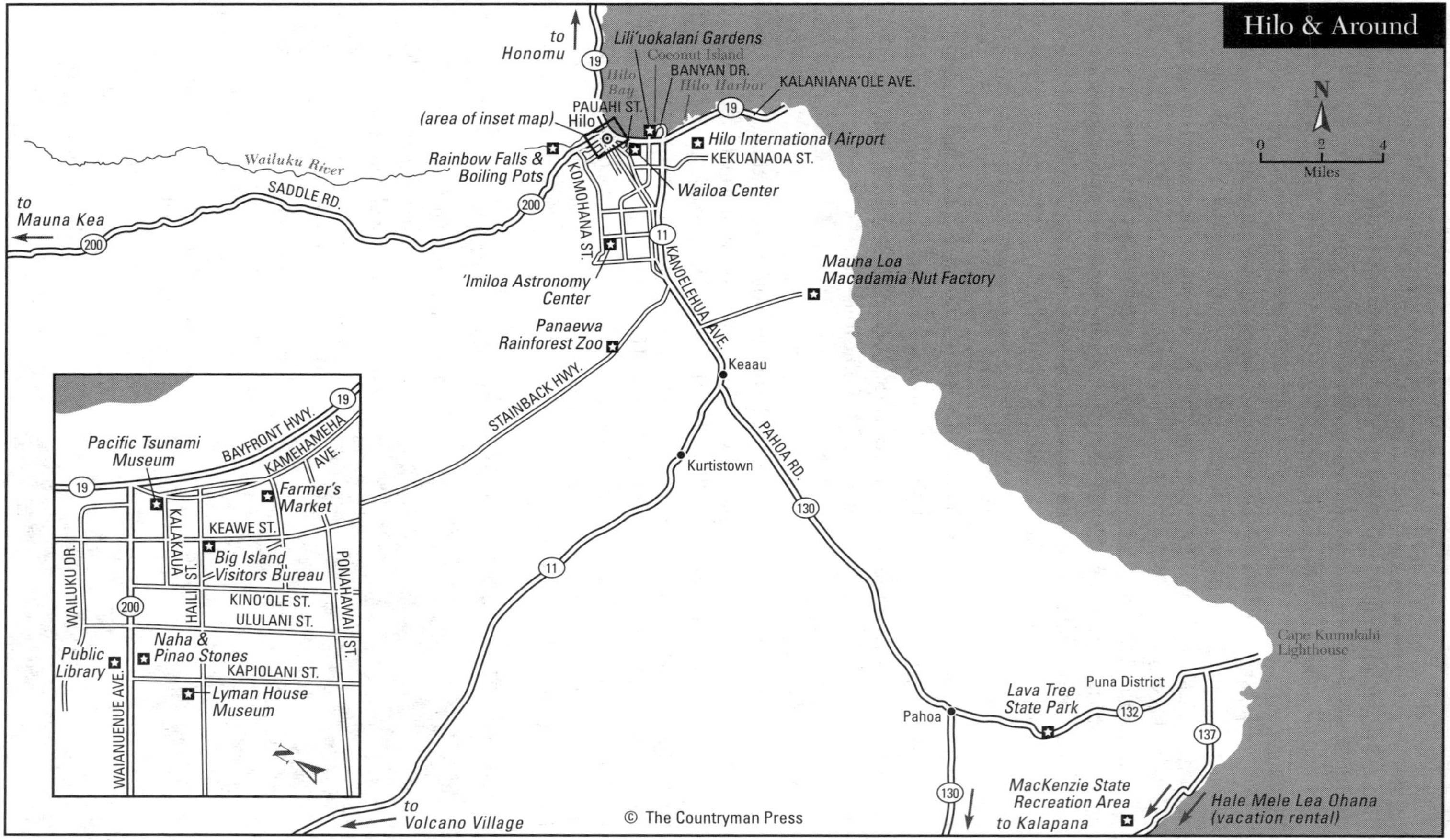

Hilo & Around

0 2 4
Miles
N

to Mauna Kea
Wailuku River
SADDLE RD.
to Honomu
Rainbow Falls & Boiling Pots
(area of inset map)
Liliʻuokalani Gardens
Coconut Island
Hilo Harbor
BANYAN DR.
Hilo Bay
PAUAHI ST.
Hilo
KOMOHANA ST.
ʻImiloa Astronomy Center
Panaewa Rainforest Zoo
KEKUANAOA ST.
Wailoa Center
Hilo International Airport
KALANIANAʻOLE AVE.
Mauna Loa Macadamia Nut Factory
KANOELEHUA AVE.
Keaau
Kurtistown
STAINBACK HWY.
PAHOA RD.
Pahoa
Puna District
Lava Tree State Park
Cape Kumukahi Lighthouse
Hale Mele Lea Ohana (vacation rental)
MacKenzie State Recreation Area
to Kalapana
to Volcano Village

© The Countryman Press

Pacific Tsunami Museum
KAMEHAMEHA AVE.
BAYFRONT HWY.
Farmer's Market
KEAWE ST.
Big Island Visitors Bureau
KINOʻOLE ST.
ULULANI ST.
PONAHAWAI ST.
KALAKAUA ST.
HAILI ST.
Naha & Pinao Stones
KAPIOLANI ST.
Lyman House Museum
WAIANUENUE AVE.
Public Library
WAILUKU DR.
N

orchids, thanks to the rain, earning the city its title of Orchid Capital of America.

Downtown is charmingly quaint, full of tin-roofed houses and Victorian manses; many buildings are on the National Register of Historic Places. Although some are ramshackle, many more house restaurants, shops, and cafés. To my taste, the island's best cup of espresso is found in Hilo (at Bears' Café; see *Where to Eat*).

Full of Japanese, Chinese, and Filipino former sugarcane workers and their descendants, the state's second-largest city sits proudly on Hilo Bay. Because of its location, though, it was twice devastated by tsunamis; don't miss the museum that tells the story.

Southeast of Hilo, the Puna District is the Big Island's most off-the-beaten-path region. Reward yourself with half a day exploring its tide pools, pristine coastline, remote villages surrounded by lava flows, natural thermal pools, the eastern rift of Kilauea, and large swaths of tropical rain forest.

GUIDANCE

Big Island Visitor's Bureau (808-961-5797 or 1-800-648-2441; bigisland.org), 250 Keawe St., Hilo. Open 8–4:30 weekdays.

Downtown Improvement Association (808-935-8850; downtownhilo.com), 329 Kamehameha Ave., Hilo. Open 8:30–4:30 Mon.–Sat.

GETTING AROUND

By car: Hilo is about 45 minutes north of Hawai'i Volcanoes National Park, while the **Puna District** is easily explored via a loop route on your way to the national park (or as a day trip from Hilo). The 25-mile route takes two to three hours, depending on how much you stop. From Hilo, take Hwy. 11 south to Pahoa, then Hwy. 132 to Hwy. 137 to the lighthouse. Head south along the shoreline on Hwy. 137, a narrow, slow, and winding road. In short, a great road. Follow it to the end and then backtrack a short distance to pick up Hwy. 130 back up to Pahoa and beyond to Hwy. 11.

AMELIA EARHART'S TREE, BANYAN DRIVE

AMELIA EARHART
JAN. 6, 1935

✻ To See & Do

✪ The Downtown Improvement Association publishes a great, self-guided historic **walking tour** brochure of downtown. Since walking is the best way to get around, it provides a convenient way to organize your wanderings. Although Kamehameha Avenue is the main thoroughfare, Keawe Street is particularly representative of Hilo. Many of its 1920s and '30s plantation-style buildings have been revitalized and rehabbed, and they stand side by side with others that haven't.

Morning temperatures are more conducive to exploring; it gets pretty darn humid in the afternoon. Brief showers and bona fide rainstorms happen frequently, so if you have an umbrella, don't leave it in your suitcase.

Around Downtown Hilo

✪ **Banyan Drive**, near the Naniloa Resort. Stretched out along the waterfront, this canopy of 50 or so trees with thick dangling root systems was planted from 1933 to 1972 by visiting dignitaries like Franklin D. Roosevelt, Babe Ruth, Cecil B. DeMille, Amelia Earhart, and Richard Nixon (whose tree fell in a storm; another was planted by Pat Nixon on a subsequent visit).

LILI'UOKALANI GARDENS

Coconut Island, near the Naniloa Resort across from Banyan Dr. Reached via a little footbridge, this 1-acre island is a pleasant picnic place. Local fishermen work the waters, kids play in tide pools, and the rest of us simply enjoy the expansive views of Hilo Bay. On a clear day there are unobstructed and towering views of Mauna Kea from here.

✪ **Lili'uokalani Gardens** (808-961-8311), Banyan Dr. at Lihiwai St. Open sunrise–11 PM. This 30-acre formal Japanese garden, developed in the early 1900s to honor Japanese sugar workers (but named in honor of the queen), is filled with pagodas, arched bridges, koi ponds, stone lanterns, and wooden gates. It's particularly popular with local families on Sunday. Free.

✪ **Hilo Farmers Market** (808-933-1000; hilofarmersmarket.com), Kamehameha Ave. at Mamo St. The best market in Hawai'i, this colorful collection of open-air stalls offers everything from flowers (like orchids and anthuriums) to local products (like freshly roasted coffee beans, baked goods, and mac nuts). The latter are less expensive and much better quality than you'd get in Long's Drugstore—which is where you should go if you can't make it here. The market hums on Wed. and Sat. (6 AM– 4 PM), but it's open daily, a shadow of itself. Go as early as possible on its two big days.

✎ ✪ **Pacific Tsunami Museum** (808-935-0926; tsunami.org), 130 Kamehameha Ave. Open 9–4

Mon.–Sat. This captivating and informative museum has interactive displays on the "walls of water" that rolled over Hilo in 1946 and 1960, devastating the town and killing dozens of residents. Among other things, you can learn about the difference between a tidal wave and tsunami, learn how earthquakes trigger the waves, and see what Hilo looked like before the tsunami struck. Many of the friendly staff members lived through the most recent tragedy, so they bring quite a poignant perspective. There's also a good kid's area. $7 adults, $2 ages 6–17.

Mokupapa Discovery Center (808-933-8193; hawaiireef.noaa.gov), 308 Kamehameha Ave. Open 9–4 Tues.–Sat.

Naha & Pinao stones, 300 Waianuenue Ave., across from the Hilo Public Library. The future King Kamehameha I is said to have moved the 5,000-pound Naha stone when he was 14 years old. Before he did, it was prophesied that whoever moved the oblong boulder would unify and rule the archipelago. The Pinao stone once stood as a sentinel to an ancient *heiau* near the Wailuku River.

✍ **Lyman House Museum** (808-935-5021; lymanmuseum.org), 276 Haili St. Open 9:30–4:30 Mon.–Sat.; call for house tour times. The Big Island's oldest wooden structure dates to 1839, is topped with Hilo's first corrugated tin roof, and was built by New Englanders David and Sarah Lyman, Hilo's first missionaries. During their stay here, they met with all the important folks who came through Hilo, from Mark Twain and Robert Louis Stevenson to Hawaiian royalty. The house contains items related to their daily life, along with objects from the monarchy. The adjacent Earth Heritage Gallery is devoted to area ecology, while the Island Heritage Gallery is devoted to Hawai'i's cultural history, from the arrival of the Hawaiians to the impact of the island's five ethnic immigrant groups. $10 adults, $3 ages 6–17.

Near Downtown

Rainbow Falls, off Wainuenue Ave., just past Kaumana Dr. Come early in the morning for the best views and chances to catch a rainbow glistening over the falls—hence its name.

LYMAN HOUSE MUSEUM

Pe'epe'e Falls and **Boiling Pots**, Waianuenue Ave., about 3 miles north of downtown. Four streams feed and cascade into these falls and get trapped in a jumble of rocks below, a veritable roiling cauldron.

'Imiloa Astronomy Center of Hawai'i (808-969-9700; imiloa hawaii.org), 600 'Imiloa Pl. Open 9–4 Tues.–Sun. Since it opened in late 2005, 'Imiloa, which translates as "exploring new knowledge," has become one of the hottest tickets in the state; don't miss it. Consider budgeting two to four hours here with or without children. Part of the Uni-

RAINBOW FALLS

versity of Hawai'i Hilo campus, this 40,000 square-foot gallery houses over 300 exhibits that relate Mauna Kea and the exploration of astronomy to Hawaiian culture. Billed as a voyage through time and space, the interactive exhibits and planetarium shows educate, inspire, and elucidate mysteries held dear to all of humanity. Primarily funded by NASA, the architecturally arresting center sits on 9 acres of UH's Science and Technology Park. $17.50 adults, $9.50 ages 4–12.

Wailoa Center (808-933-0416), Wailoa State Park, off Kamehameha Ave. Open 8:30–4:30 weekdays (from noon on Wed.). This center has changing local art exhibits. Free.

Nani Mau Gardens (808-959-3500; nanimau.com), 421 Makalika St., about 3 miles south of downtown off Hwy. 11. Open 9:30–4:30 daily. Nani Mau, which means "forever beautiful," is an apt name for this 20-acre botanical museum, which features over 200 kinds of thematically arranged flowering plants, fruit trees, orchids, ginger, and other exotic flora. $10 adults ($16 with tram tour, four person minimum), $5 ages 4–10 ($11 with tram tour).

Mauna Loa Macadamia Nut Factory (808-966-8618; maunaloa.com), Macadamia Rd., about 10 miles south of downtown off Hwy. 11. Open 8:30–5:30 daily. Follow rows of mac trees leading to the factory, where you can learn about the growing and processing of these addictive nuts. Watch a little film, take a self-guided tour, and do some firsthand taste-testing. Free.

 Panaewa Rainforest Zoo (808-959-9233; hilozoo.com), Panaewa Rainforest Reserve, Stainback Hwy., off Hwy. 11 near MM 4 south of downtown. Open 9–4 daily. The only outdoor rain forest zoo in the United States is a relatively quiet place. Its 12 acres are home to endangered nene, monkeys, peacocks, parrots, a white Bengal tiger, and about 50 other species. Free.

PAHOA TOWN

○ *Puna District*

Pahoa, Hwy. 130 at Hwy. 132. With Wild West–style raised boardwalks and false-front wooden buildings, the heart of the region feels like a modern-day outpost. In addition to low-key galleries, shops, and restaurants, the town offers **Pahoa Natural Groceries** (808-965-8322, Pahoa Village Rd.), a small market with all the right fixings for assembling a picnic when you're in this neck of the woods. Open daily.

Lava Tree State Park (808-974-6200), Hwy. 132, 2 miles from Pahoa. Open sunrise–sunset. The 1790 eruption of Kilauea turned a lively 'ohi'a forest into something that resembles a bunch of single-story smokestacks. It's definitely worth a look. Free.

Cape Kumukahi Lighthouse, 1.5 miles east of intersection of Hwys. 132 and 137, Kapoho. Some say thanks to Madame Pele, this lighthouse was spared in a most unusual way during a devastating 1960 eruption. Lava flowed around the lighthouse on both sides, but not through it.

Ahalanui Park (aka **Pu'ala'a**), 2.5 miles south from intersection Hwy. 132 and Hwy. 137. This 3-acre park has a large, thermally heated swimming pond. Facilities include restrooms, showers, and picnicking.

MacKenzie State Recreation Area, Hwy. 137. In addition to containing a considerable chunk of the King's Trail (a royal transportation route), this ironwood-forested park has a dramatic rocky shore. It makes a nice location for picnicking.

Star of the Sea Painted Church, Hwy. 137. When the 1990s eruption started oozing lava, townspeople rallied to move this church from Kalapana to safer ground. It's noteworthy for interior biblical paintings done by a Belgian missionary.

Kalapana, at the end of Hwy. 137. A 1990s volcanic eruption destroyed most of the town, and it's still quite eerie. There's definitely an end-of-the-road quality to it.

HILO BAY

✳ Outdoor Activities

GOLF

Hilo Municipal Golf Course (808-959-7711; gvhawaii.com), 340 Haihai St., Hilo. Popular with locals on weekends, this relaxed course gets a lot of rain—which makes for green, green fairways and green greens. But it can also make for some slow play. Greens fees $29 weekdays, $34 weekends; carts $16.

Naniloa Golf Course (808-935-3000; gvhawaii.com), 120 Banyan Dr., Hilo. This nine-hole course is more challenging than it looks; you'll have fun here. Greens fees run $45 for the 18-hole course, $30 for the nine-hole; carts cost $9; rental clubs available.

Beaches

In order of preference.

✂ **Leleiwi Beach Park**, Kalaniana'ole Ave., about 4 miles east of downtown Hilo. The best and most picturesque beach on this side of the island, Leleiwi claims spring-fed tide pools that are great for families. The presence of sea turtles makes for rich snorkeling.

✂ **Richardson Ocean Beach Park** is adjacent to Leleiwi, has a lifeguard, and—since it's a marine reserve—has great snorkeling. *Facilities*: restrooms, showers, picnicking, lifeguards.

✂ **Onekahakaha Beach Park**, Kalaniana'ole Ave., about 3 miles east of downtown Hilo. This white-sand beach is popular with families because of a protective breakwater and shallow depths. *Facilities*: restrooms, showers, and lifeguards.

Lodging

Unless you book very far in advance, it's impossible to get a room during the Merrie Monarch Festival (see *Hula as We Know It* and *Entertainment*). Also, unless otherwise noted, all lodging is located in Hilo. Hilo is often used as a base for exploring Hawai'i Volcanoes National Park, even though it's 45 minutes south of town. When deciding whether or not to stay in Hilo or Volcano Village, note that Hilo B&Bs are generally more sophisticated and Hilo has more restaurants. Hilo also has many large, outdated hotels on Banyan Drive that fill with tour groups, but I barely review one.

HOTELS

❀ **Dolphin Bay Hotel** (808-935-1466 or 1-877-935-1466; dolphinbay hotel.com), 333 Iliahi St. This motel is the city's most amiable hostelry. The small and personable cinderblock motel is situated in a quiet residential neighborhood four blocks from downtown and three blocks from Hilo Bay. Manager John Alexander is one of the most attentive and helpful hosts in Hawai'i and provides immaculate lodgings and lush tropical surroundings. The moderate-sized standard studios are the most basic; larger superior studios come with a queen-sized bed and nicer bathroom; one-bedroom suites have lanais and can accommodate four. Each has a full kitchen and ceiling or table fans. I prefer second-floor rooms, which feel more spacious thanks to a peaked ceiling. Most visitors use Dolphin Bay as a base for exploring Hawai'i Volcanoes National Park, and John's firsthand knowledge about the park flows as freely as hot lava. When you're here, the staff treats you like a family member. *Rates*: $–$$. *Facilities and amenities*: 18 rooms and suites, full kitchens, continental breakfast, TV, no A/C, no phones.

Uncle Billy's Hilo Bay Hotel (808-961-5818 or 1-800-367-5102; uncle billy.com), 87 Banyan Dr. It's noisy, it's old, and the lobby borders on Polynesian tacky. Then why stay here? Because it's inexpensive, it's oceanfront, an informal Hawaiian spirit prevails, and it offers great packages that include a rental car and a three-night

HULA AS WE KNOW IT

Let's get right to the heart of hula. In the beginning, hula was, it's believed, a religious expression in which only men participated. I say "it's believed" because the Hawaiian language was originally an oral one, and early history was passed down in poetic chants rather than written words. Even hula's place of origin is indefinite—many believe it was "born" on Moloka'i; others believe the fire goddess Pele's youngest sister, Hi'iaka, was the first to perform hula (as we understand hula) on the Big Island. The point is, traditional hula has nothing to do with coconut bras and cellophane skirts. And since the mid-1970s—the beginning of the renaissance of Hawaiian language, culture, and art—traditional hula has become newly, widely, and wonderfully popular.

Hula kahiko is the Hawaiian phrase for traditional hula, the form accompanied by only the human voice and percussion instruments traditionally made from gourds, coconut stumps, and smooth stones. Costumes, too, are made (whenever possible) from native plants and natural fibers. If you see dancers wearing carnation leis and long velvet dresses, they are not doing *hula kahiko*!

The missionaries, who arrived in the 1820s, saw hula as pagan ritual and did everything in their power to outlaw it. They succeeded only in driving it underground . . . but not for long. A few decades later the Merrie Monarch, King David Kalakaua, led its revival—that's when *hula 'auana* (modern hula) was born. Often accompanied by beautiful singing and musicians playing guitar, 'ukulele, and standing bass, *'auana* (which means "wandering") is the form with which most visitors are familiar. Appearing to float across the stage, women dancers wear long *holoka* (gowns, really), and men wear crisply pressed slacks and shirts.

Now, back to those coconut bras and cellophane skirts. They did, indeed, have their day, one now known as the Sweet Leilani era, when visi-

minimum stay. If you're dining out, exploring the national park, and using the room only to sleep, save some money by staying here, where rooms consist of little more than a bed, television, and phone. Ultra laid-back and the oldest among the Banyan Drive hotels, Uncle Billy's is a popular haunt among neighbor islanders. *Rates:* $;

children free in parent's room. *Facilities and amenities:* 143 rooms, pool, continental breakfast buffet.

BED & BREAKFASTS AND INNS

🌺 **Shipman House Bed & Breakfast** (808-934-8002 or 1-800-627-8447; shipmanhouse.com), 131 Kaiulani St. This magnificent house

tors began arriving on large ships and groups of island women would greet the visitors with hula and lei. Sweet Leilani comes from the many *hapa haole* songs—similar to Tin Pan Alley tunes—played to accompany these hula.

This brings us to the heart of today's matter—the difference between "hotel" hula and "real" hula. There is nothing wrong with the hula you will see at your hotel. It's beautiful and filled with *aloha*. It's just the same as the hula being taught in island *halau* (schools), which might be compared to ballet companies. The commitment to a *halau* is huge; the training and practice are difficult and time consuming. Serious students are passionate, and for many, hula is their lives. There isn't, frankly, much opportunity for visitors to experience this kind of hula.

✪ If you want to see "real" hula, consider attending the **Merrie Monarch Hula Festival.** The competitions could be described as the "Olympics of Hula." Quite simply, it's astounding. Ask anyone about his or her first time at the Merrie Monarch, and they will undoubtedly speak first about the fragrance. Imagine entering a 5,000-seat, open-air arena filled with the intoxicating fragrance of *maile, pikake, pakalana*, and plumeria, among others. They take the form of lei and other adornments, as well as arena décor. Although your hotel television set will offer an infinitely better vantage point for the competition, you'll miss the experience. But it's not easy attending Merrie Monarch. The weeklong Hilo festival begins on Easter Sunday with craft fairs (some say the island's best) and free entertainment; a general air of festivity continues throughout the week; the three-night hula competition begins on Thursday. Tickets are more difficult to come by than hotel rooms and rental cars (which are almost impossible to secure). Hundreds of dancers, their families, and their friends descend on Hilo each year and have "standing" reservations. Consult the festival Web site (merriemonarchfestival.org) for details. Good luck. And in whatever way you can on your trip, enjoy the hula.

—Bonnie Friedman

has remained in the same family since it was built in 1899. Today it's owned by the original Shipman owner's great-granddaughter, who opened it as a B&B in 1997. Barbara Ann and her husband, Gary, have done a fine job renovating the mammoth house and retaining much of the original furnishings. The craftsmanship and details are stunning: a porte cochere entryway, wraparound porch, curved windows with hand-rolled glass. Common space includes a grand hallway, double parlor, dining room, and library featuring Jack London's letter of introduction to the Shipmans, dated from his monthlong April 1907 visit. Hawai'i's last queen, Liliuokalani, was

SHIPMAN HOUSE

Mary Shipman's friend, and the queen came to the house often. She played the Steinway and had her favorite chair at the massive, round dining room table. (It takes very little effort to imagine Hawaiian royalty in this setting.) Barbara enjoys regaling guests with family stories and has a keen desire to keep the house "just so." Breakfast—a highlight in a house brimming with highlights—utilizes a bounty of local ingredients and preparations. The Shipmans were avid horticulturists, and the 5 acres overflow with fruits and flora. Ask when the local hula class practices on the premises and try to stay at that time. *Rates:* $$; children not encouraged because of a steep backyard gulch. *Facilities and amenities:* five rooms, extraordinary breakfast, no phone, no TV.

🦩 **Bay House Bed and Breakfast** (808-961-6311 or 1-888-235-8195; bayhousehawaii.com), 42 Pukihae St. Hilo has undergone a recent renaissance in regard to lodging, and this newer home is partly responsible for the upturn. The Big Island's best oceanfront B&B has qualified and considerate hosts (who live in a separate section of the house) and is within walking distance of downtown. Of the three tastefully decorated, light, and airy rooms (all with private bath), I prefer the one on the end because of its extra windows and king bed. Although rooms tend to be smallish, they do have lanais with direct bay views—as does the communal hot tub. *Rates:* $$. *Facilities and amenities:* three rooms, hot tub, generous continental breakfast, no A/C, no smoking, no phones in room (but house phone available).

The Palms Cliff House Inn (808-963-6076 or 1-866-963-6076; palms cliffhouse.com), Hwy. 19. Near Akaka Falls and about 15 miles north of Hilo, this boutique hostelry on 3½ acres overlooks Pohakumana Bay and offers more services and amenities than most traditional B&Bs. Your hosts, Michele and John Gamble, will do everything to see that your stay is a pleasant one. The sumptuous décor in each room is fit for a Victorian king or queen. To do them justice, it's best to check room photos online. You'll also enjoy the morning paper and a full breakfast on the back veranda (to the sound of crashing surf 150 feet below), which boasts the same views as from your private lanai. *Rates:* $$$–$$$$; children under 13 not allowed. *Facilities and amenities:* eight suites, TV, phone, A/C in some rooms, gas fireplaces in some rooms, Jacuzzi, concierge, no smoking, full breakfast, dial up Internet, sketchy cell phone reception.

The Inn at Kulaniapia (808-935-6789 or 1-866-935-6789; waterfall .net). Located in the middle of a 2000-acre mac nut farm, this 22-acre property feels like another world, but it's only 15 minutes from downtown

Hilo. Hosts Len and Jane Sutton have created a welcoming, country retreat (in three buildings) from which you can swim in the Kulaniapia waterfall pond, barbecue, and explore bamboo gardens. Or do nothing. Accommodations are luxurious, spacious, comfortable, and all quite different from one another. Harmony House features five rooms with rosewood furniture and Chinese antiques; the three-story Pagoda House sleeps six; and The Residence has five suites with private balconies and marble bathrooms. *Rates:* $$. *Facilities and amenities:* 11 units, spa with body treatments, hot tub, TV, phone, no A/C, no smoking, full breakfast, kitchen and laundry facilities in guest house, Internet access.

The Falls at Reed's Island (808-935-7920 or 808-635-3649; reeds island.com), 82 Halaulani St. This secluded retreat is lusciously situated near cascading waterfalls and rivers. The location is truly magical and perfect for a couple or a group of friends. *Rates:* $$$; two-night minimum; $145 cleaning fee; $35 per additional person. *Facilities and amenities:* three rooms, TV, phone, no A/C, no smoking, full kitchen, gas grill, hot and cold soaking tubs, laptop with free WiFi.

Waterfalls Inn Bed & Breakfast (808-969-3407 or 1-888-808-4456; waterfallsinn.com), 240 Kaiulani St. In an exclusive neighborhood and within walking distance of downtown Hilo and the bay, this historic plantation-style home sits on the banks of the Wailuku River—so you'll be falling asleep to the sound of water. Built in 1916, the home has been expertly restored, right down to the 'ohi'a floors and bathroom fix-

tures. Guest rooms are island simple, and hosts George and Barbara Leonard enjoy providing great service and breakfasts (best enjoyed on the grand veranda). *Rates:* $$; two-night minimum. *Facilities and amenities:* four rooms (with whirlpool or soaking tubs), TV, no phone, no A/C, no smoking, continental breakfast, WiFi (free).

Hale Kai Hawaii Bed & Breakfast (808-935-6330; halekaihawaii .com), 111 Honoli'i Pl. Overlooking a popular surfing beach, Hale Kai boasts fabulous ocean views from each of the guest rooms and their lanais. Hosts Maria and Ricardo have really spiffed up the place, and Maria whips up some of the best breakfasts on the island—think coconut macadamia pancakes, basil and feta frittatas, apricot scones. *Rates:* $$; two-night minimum; no children under 13. *Facilities and amenities:* three rooms and one suite, full breakfast, oceanfront pool, hot tub, private lanais, cable TV, no phone, no A/C, no smoking, kitchenette in suite, WiFi (free).

THE PALMS CLIFF HOUSE INN

Emerald View Bed & Breakfast
(808-961-5736 or 1-800-262-9912;
emeraldview.com) 272 Kalulani St.
Located on the Wailuku River within
walking distance of downtown, this
two-room B&B has very friendly and
accommodating hosts (one of whom is
Japanese and speaks fluently) who live
in the house. Totally remodeled in
2004, the largest unit has a king bed
with views (and sounds) of the rushing river; the other room has two full-
sized beds. Both units have a private
en suite bath finished with granite
and river rock. Breakfast is delivered
to your room so that you can enjoy it
on your private riverside lanai. But
there's also a common living area for
guests. *Rates: $$*; not appropriate for
children. *Facilities and amenities:* two
rooms, full breakfast, hot tub, Inter-
net, TV, no smoking, no phone.

Puna District
🦐 **Hale Mele Lea Ohana** (415-640-
0443 or 808-965-7141), Waioleka Dr.,
Kehena. With a Pacific view from
your private lanai, this clean and quiet
apartment makes a great tropical
retreat. With island-style wicker and
rattan furnishings, a handy outdoor
shower, well-placed reading lights,
and comfy chairs, the cute unit boasts
sliding doors that let in coastal trade
winds and lots of sunshine. It also has
a king-sized bed, a large dressing
area, and a spacious living-dining area
that is decorated in cool, fresh colors.
The new and fully equipped kitchen
is stocked with everything you need to
prepare a snack or full meal (except
produce and protein). To ensure your
privacy, the apartment is only rented
when the upstairs owner's quarters
are unoccupied. The unit is a 45-
minute drive from Hawai'i Volcanoes
National Park, a 45-minute drive from

Hilo, and only a 10-minute stroll away
from Kehena, a clothing-optional
black-sand beach. *Rates: $. Facilities
and amenities:* Kitchen, phone, water
sport equipment, no smoking, no A/C.

✳ Where to Eat
Hilo has a fair number of eateries,
mostly geared toward locals, the
mainstay of the economy. With a cou-
ple of notable exceptions, the atmos-
phere won't induce you to linger over
your meal longer than necessary. But
you will encounter friendly service at
these primarily family-operated places.
All eateries are located in Hilo unless
otherwise noted.

DINING OUT
🦐 ⅄ **Hilo Bay Café** (808-935-4939),
Prince Kuhio Plaza, 315 Maka'ala St.
Open for lunch and dinner Mon.–
Sat., dinner Sun. If I didn't have to
eat in a different restaurant every day,
I'd eat all my meals here. Really. And
for these prices! The kitchen opened
in late 2003 to great reviews, and no
wonder. I say: eat early and eat often.
Enhanced by orchid sprays and light
jazz, the atmosphere is almost stylish
but definitely easygoing (ignore its
strip mall location). The creative dish-
es range from a well-executed chicken
potpie to blackened ahi. Caesar salads
are very good. Martinis and a nice
wine list round off the evening.
Reservations recommended; chil-
dren's menu. Lunch $–$$, dinner
entrées $$–$$$.

⅄ **Seaside Restaurant and Aquafarm** (808-935-8825), 1790 Kalanianaole Ave. Open for dinner Tues.–
Sat. When a place has its own aquafarm, you can bet it serves fresh fish.
About 2 miles east of downtown, and
an "only in Hilo" kind of place, this

eatery, owned and operated by the Nakagawa family, was washed away by the 1946 tidal wave (and subsequently rebuilt). These days it's surrounded by about 30 acres of fishponds—the kind that Hawaiians have been traditionally fishing for hundreds of years—that contain catfish, carp, mullet, trout, and the rare *aholehole*. Seaside is purported to be the only place in Hawai'i that serves *aholehole*; order it a day in advance. (Even then, though, it's sometimes not available.) In fact, if you want *any* fish to be pond-fresh, you must call in your order. Fish is either fried or steamed. Since the dining room is set with plastic chairs and simple tables, arrive early to snag an outdoor table overlooking the pond for sunset. Reservations recommended; children's menu. Entrées $$$.

♣ ♂ **Café Pesto** (808-969-6640; cafepesto.com), S. Hata Bldg., 308 Kamehameha Ave. Open for lunch and dinner daily. With high ceilings, tasteful décor, and well-spaced tables, this congenial café is a welcome oasis. The menu is similar to its sister in Kawaihae Harbor (see "North Kohala & Waimea"), predominantly serving Italian dishes of risotto, pasta, kiawe-infused brick-oven pizza, and calzones with Asian overtones. Children's menu. Lunch $$, dinner entrées $$–$$$. BYOB ($8 corkage fee).

Harrington's (808-961-4966), 135 Kalaniana'ole. Open for lunch weekdays, dinner nightly. Because it owns the loveliest perch in Hilo (overlooking a koi pond near the waterfront) and has a hoppin' happy hour, Harrington's gets a conservative nod. The Slavic steak (slathered in butter and garlic) and catch-of-the-day are dinnertime specialties of this steak and seafood house; at lunchtime it's burgers. Lunch $–$$, dinner entrées $$$.

Pescatore (808-969-9090), 235 Keawe St. Open for lunch and dinner daily, breakfast on weekends. Authentic southern Italian cuisine at a fancy but not off-putting trattoria is a nice change of pace for Hilo. It stands in marked contrast to the many ethnic hole-in-the-walls. Venture beyond pasta to catch-of-the-day and ahi carpaccio. Lunches are lighter and revolve around panini sandwiches and chicken parm, while breakfast concentrates on omelets and crêpes. Children's pasta dishes. Breakfast $, lunch $–$$, dinner entrées $$–$$$.

CAFÉ PESTO

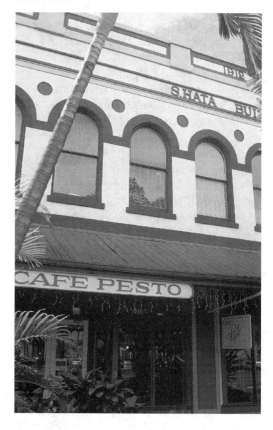

Ocean Sushi Deli (808-961-6625), 250 Keawe St. Open for lunch and dinner Mon.–Sat. It's way more about the food than the atmosphere at this hole-in-the-wall: Try to overlook the Formica tables and concentrate on the inexpensive ocean-fresh sushi and excellent seafood. You'll find conventional choices as well as many that push the envelope, like oyster nigiri. Dishes $–$$$$.

Royal Siam Thai Restaurant (808-961-6100), 70 Mamo St. Open for lunch Mon.–Sat., dinner nightly (closed midafternoon). *Authentic* gets bandied about a bit too easily these days, but it applies at Royal Siam. Although the décor is simple, the curries, noodles, and stir-fries rule the roost. Dishes $$.

Miyo's (808-935-2273), Waiakea Villas, 400 Hualani St. Open for lunch and dinner Mon.–Sat. (closed midafternoon). I can tell all I need to know about a Japanese restaurant by its miso and tempura (in this case ahi tempura): Miyo's is the real deal. News flash: I'm not the only one who thinks so. From teriyaki to sukiyaki, from sesame chicken to hordes of vegetarian dishes, you'll feel like you're dining farther across the Pacific than you are—until you catch glimpses of Mauna Kea through open shoji screens. Lunch $–$$, dinner entrées $–$$.

Ken's House of Pancakes (808-935-8711), 1730 Kamehameha Ave. Open 24/7. The parking lot is always jammed at this local favorite—famous for the original loco moco. Sure Ken's is known for namesake pancakes, but there are upwards of 200 other items on the menu. (No, I didn't count, but I did a quick scan.) Come as much for

local ambience as for French toast made with Portuguese sweet bread. Tuesdays feature all-you-can-eat tacos (3–8 PM), Wednesdays highlight prime rib, Thursdays are Hawaiian plates, Fridays are oxtail soup, and Sunday rolls out the red carpet with all-you-can-eat spaghetti (3–8 PM). You gotta love it. Breakfast $, lunch and dinner $–$$.

Kuhio Grill (808-959-2336; marriottwaikiki.com), Prince Kuhio Plaza, 2552 Kalakaua Ave. Open daily. A typical Hilo place, in that it has no atmosphere to speak of, this place is famous for 1-pound *laulau* (*taro* from Waipi'o Valley and pork), along with plate lunches, saimin, chicken yakitori, and fried rice. Classic all around. Children's menu. Breakfast $–$$, lunch $–$$$, dinner entrées $$$.

Big Island Pizza (808-934-8000; bigislandpizza.com), 760 Kilauea Ave. Open 11–9 daily. If you're not heading down to Volcano, where choices are more limited than they are in Hilo (and you're likely to be ordering pizza), this place will satisfy those cravings we all get for pizza. Pies are over-the-top gourmet; crusts are chewy *and* crispy. Dishes $–$$$.

COFFEE & SNACKS

Bears' Café (808-935-0708), 106 Keawe St. Open daily. The epitome of a local café, this groovy place has indoor and sidewalk tables where you can hang with a cup o' joe, pastries, morning eggs, or a sandwich.

Abundant Life Natural Foods (808-935-7411), 292 Kamehameha Ave. Open daily. Head here for organic produce, smoothies, and sandwiches, all sold alongside earthy-crunchy shampoos, lotions, and potions.

> **LOOSEN UP**
>
> Slack key guitar, called *ki ho'alu* in Hawaiian, is a finger-picking style that can be used on any guitar. Its origins date back to the early 19th century when Mexican cowboys started strumming with a thumb to get a strong, steady bass. Although these Mexican *paniolos* introduced the guitar and the picking, Hawaiians quickly developed their own style. *Ki ho'alu* literally means "loosen the key" because the guitar strings are slacked to produce one-of-a-kind tunings. Hawaiian music rose in popularity in the 1970s principally because of the slack key stylizing of Gabby Pahinui, Leonard Kwan, Ray Kane, and the more modern Keola and Kapono Beamer brothers.

✳ Entertainment

Merrie Monarch Hula Festival (808-935-9168; merriemonarchfestival.org), Edith Kanakaole Tennis Stadium, Hilo. The largest festival of its kind—a lusciously astounding and profoundly moving spectacle—always begins on Easter Sunday. For a description of the festival, see *Hula as We Know It*. Tickets (if you're lucky enough to get them) $10–25.

Uncle Billy's Hilo Bay Hotel (808-961-5818), 87 Banyan Dr., Hilo. If you're heading here for dinner, they have free hula shows on Friday and Sunday nights.

Hawai'i Volcanoes Resort (808-969-3333), 93 Banyan Dr., Hilo. Head to the hotel's Crown Room to hear Hawaiian musicians from neighbor islands. This dependable Big Island venue is on most circuits.

MOVIES

When it rains, you have options; for islandwide show times, call 808-961-3456.

Palace Theater (808-934-7010), 38 Haili St., Hilo. This neoclassical 1925 theater has been lovingly restored and now shows art movies and film festivals and hosts special events.

Kress Discount Cinemas (808-935-6777), 174 Kamehameha Ave., Hilo. Second-run movies for $1.

Prince Kuhio Stadium Cinema (808-959-4595), 111 E. Puainako St., Prince Kuhio Plaza, Hilo. First-run flicks.

KRESS DISCOUNT CINEMAS

✳ Selective Shopping

You'll generally find that goods are less expensive here because the shops cater so locally. Unless otherwise noted, all shops are in Hilo.

Basically Books (808-961-0144; basicallybooks.com), 160 Kamehameha Ave. Open daily. Just as easily renamed "Basically Maps," this terrific place has a huge selection of hiking, USGS, and topo maps, among others. They are also heavy into environmental titles, natural history, geology, Hawaiiana, and the Pacific Rim.

Dan DeLuz Woods (808-968-6607; deluzwoods.com), near MM 12, Hwy. 11, Mountain View. Open 9–5 daily. When you've had your fill of *koa* (could that happen?), you'll appreciate master woodworker and bowl turner extraordinaire Dan DeLuz. His versatility with monkeypod, mango, sandalwood, milo, Hawaiian ash, and other native woods is impressive, to say the least.

Sig Zane Designs (808-935-7077; sigzane.com), 122 Kamehameha Ave. Open Mon.–Sat. Sig's designs, classic and ever-evolving, have a cult following. The patterns, bold colors, and motifs used in his truly original clothing and household accessories celebrate Hawaiian culture. As you might expect, the shop is as aesthetically pleasing as the fabric designs. Sig Zane, who opened his first store in 1985, is about as close to Hawaiian culture as anyone in the retail business. He's a great hula dancer (a *kuma hula*), and his wife is even more accomplished in the field.

Hana Hou (808-935-4555), 164 Kamehameha Ave. Open daily. Head here for *lauhala* weavings, new and "vintage" *aloha* shirts, feather leis, and other gifts.

Big Island Candies (808-935-8890; bigislandcandies.com), 585 Hinano St. Open 8:30–5 daily. This factory makes hand-dipped chocolate cookies and other treats. The free samples alone could set you back a few pounds.

SHOPPING AREAS

Prince Kuhio Shopping Plaza, off Hwy. 11, heading toward Volcano. With two movie theaters, one Christian bookstore, Safeway, Sears, Macy's, and a Hilo Hattie store (great for Hawaiian apparel), you'll probably end up here at some point. For coffee and macadamia nuts, Long's Drugstore has the best prices.

Waiakea Center, off Hwy. 11, heading toward Volcano. Across the street from Prince Kuhio, with a Borders bookstore and a food court.

HAWAI'I VOLCANOES NATIONAL PARK

Every Big Island visitor needs to experience the drama and power of Hawai'i Volcanoes National Park. There are very few places on earth where you can feel Mother Nature so acutely; you can literally see her growing, smell her sulfurous belching, touch her elemental heat. Creation happens here. Even if you only have a few hours, drive along Crater Rim Road and stop at the Thurston Lava Tube, Devastation Trail, and the Halema'uma'u Overlook. If you have a few days to explore (which is ideal), serious and Sunday hikers will find enough trails to keep them occupied for several days. The park has it all: steaming, gaping crevasses; moonlike surfaces; lava tubes; cinder cones; steam vents; rain forest retreats; ohelo berries favored by Pele, and *hapu'u* ferns.

Mystical Volcano Village has Japanese roots but also attracts off-the-grid types, artists, and New Agers who want to be left alone to do their thing. They're invisibly tucked back in residential areas camouflaged by tree ferns and a constant gentle mist. Other than that, the village consists of a few restaurants, a convenience store, and lots of charming B&Bs. Situated at 4,000 feet, it's chilly here at night, so remember to pack a sweater.

GUIDANCE

Hawai'i Volcanoes National Park (808-985-6000; nps.gov/havo), Hwy. 11, Volcano Village. Park open 24/7; **Kilauea Visitor's Center** open 7:45–5 daily. An invaluable resource, the visitors center has mountains of information on ranger-led walks, current eruptions (hvo.wr.usgs.gov), native flora and fauna, and, of course, local geology. You might even refer to yourself as an amateur volcanologist upon departure. Park rangers are *the* source for hiking information; the park also publishes an invaluable and inexpensive drive guide. Don't miss the film on recent eruptions, which is shown hourly and is particularly illuminating. Folks with respiratory or heart problems and pregnant women should take particular caution and avoid some areas. Backcountry permits are required to park in the camp overnight. Entrance fee $10 per vehicle, valid for seven days.

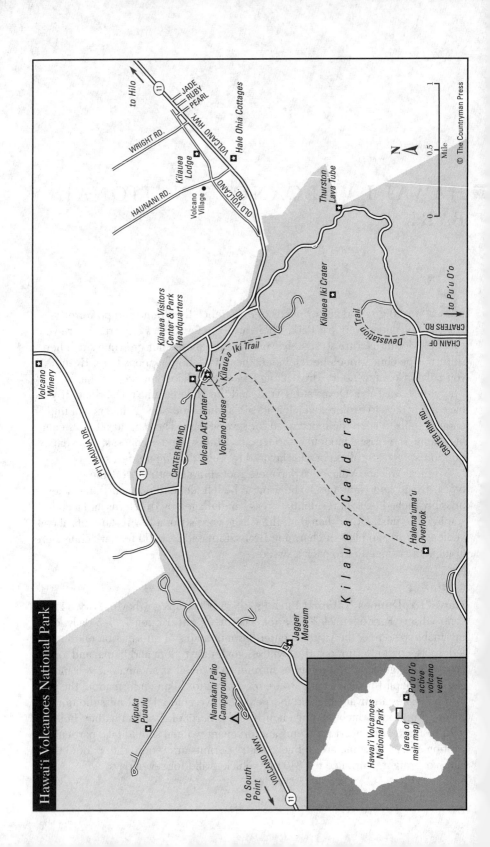

Hawai'i Volcanoes National Park

to Hilo

11

JADE
RUBY
PEARL

VOLCANO HWY.

Hale Ohia Cottages

WRIGHT RD.

Kilauea Lodge

HAUNANI RD.

OLD VOLCANO RD.

Volcano Village

Thurston
Lava Tube

N

0.5   1
Mile
0

© The Countryman Press

Kilauea Iki Crater

to Pu'u O'o

Devastation Trail

CHAIN OF CRATERS RD.

Kilauea Visitors
Center & Park
Headquarters

Kilauea Iki Trail

Volcano Winery

Volcano Art Center

Volcano House

CRATER RIM RD.

11

PI'I MAUNA DR.

CRATER RIM RD.

Kilauea Caldera

Halema'uma'u
Overlook

Jagger
Museum

Kipuka Puaulu

Namakani Paio
Campground

VOLCANO HWY.

to South
Point

11

Pu'u O'o active
volcano vent

Hawai'i Volcanoes
National Park

(area of
main map)

BUILDING BLOCKS FOR A PERFECT DAY AT HAWAI'I VOLCANOES NATIONAL PARK

Get oriented at the visitors center (1 hour)

Circle the Crater Rim Drive, stopping to hike and photograph along the way (3 hours)

Drive Chain of Craters to the end, stopping along the way to explore (3 hours)

Pop into the Volcano Art Center (30 minutes)

Cruise into tiny Volcano Village and drive its back roads in the fog (1 hour)

BUILDING BLOCKS FOR ANOTHER PERFECT DAY ON THE BIG ISLAND

Take a helicopter tour of the island (2 hours)

Tour the summit of Mauna Kea with Hawai'i Forest & Trail (8 hours)

Design a customized hike with Hawaiian Walkways (half or full day)

Do absolutely nothing at your classy Kohala Coast Resort (all day & night)

GETTING AROUND

By car: The national park is about 30 miles (45 minutes) from Hilo and 110 miles (two and a half to three hours) from Kailua-Kona. The park is quite easy to navigate; the visitors center has a good, free map. The village, laid out in a grid pattern, is just a few miles from the national park.

✴ To See & Do

✎ ✪ **Hawai'i Volcanoes National Park**. Life rarely gets more elemental. In so many ways, there's nothing like it in the United States. In fact, it's the only volcanic rain forest park in the country. As is the case in most U.S. national parks, most visitors simply drive along the paved roads and rarely get out of the car.

But to fully feel its power, you really need to feel the heat and smell the sulfur here. It measures about 350 or so square miles and has upward of 150 miles of hiking trails. The park is without state peers as far as natural attractions are concerned; over 2 million people visit annually. Established as a national park in 1916, the area has received tourists since the mid-1800s.

HAWAI'I VOLCANOES NATIONAL PARK

✪ **Eruptions**. They're on every visitor's mind. When Kilauea spews molten lava, primarily from the **Pu'u O'o vent**, it's not the fiery and fast stuff that folks run *from*—they actually run *to* it to bear witness, to photograph it, to stand in awe of something that's truly awesome. Since January 3, 1983, Kilauea has crawled over and consumed more than 15,000 acres and added another 500-plus. (She's constantly taking and giving.) Her eruptions have covered beaches, villages, roads, a visitors center (in 1989), churches, and about 200 homes. People have died walking *on* hardened (and hollow) lava, but no one has died by being in Kilauea's direct path. No one knows when she will cease gurgling, but she'd been quiet for the previous 25 years, and volcanologists don't have much experience with eruptions that last more than a few months. By way of comparison, Mauna Loa last erupted in 1984, but prior to that she'd been dormant for nine years. She hasn't spoken since.

Lava. There are two principal types of lava: *pahoehoe* (pronounced *pa*-HOY-*hoy*), which looks like curled rope and is the result of a fast flow, and *a'a* (pronounced AH-*ah*), which looks like torn-up asphalt and results from a slow flow.

Night viewing. It's dramatic, but you must be prepared. Essential ingredients include a flashlight, lots of water, closed-toe shoes with good traction, a sweater or jacket, a good sense of balance, an intrepid nature, and a healthy dose of wonder. Since Mother Nature isn't predictable, you must call the visitors center (808-985-6000), consult the exceptional Web site (hvo.wr.usgs.gov), or read the bulletin board at the visitors center (a decidedly low-tech but effective approach) to find out if the lava flow is visible, where it's located, how far a walk it requires, and how to reach it. I last glimpsed its mystery off Hwy. 130 at the end of the road past Pahoa (see *Puna District* in "Hilo & Around"). Try to get there an hour or so before sunset and be prepared to walk back over uneven lava in the utter darkness (with only the aid of a flashlight). A high plume of smoke will signal that you're getting hotter, and closer. As the lava crawls to the sea, it seems compelled to do so, like some kind of creature going home. When the lava finally hits the ocean, it's so hot that it remains on fire for quite a long while.

Touring. The best way to see the park, besides driving its length and hiking to your ability, is to splurge on a **helicopter or plane ride** over it. (See *Islandwide Tours* under "Big Island in Brief.")

Kilauea Visitor's Center, inside the park entrance, Crater Rim Dr. This should be everyone's first stop. See *Guidance*.

✪ **Volcano Art Center** (808-967-7565 or 1-866-967-7565; volcanoart-center.org), next to the visitors center, Crater Rim Dr. Open 9–5 daily. There's nothing like a good volcano—mixed with a dose of Pele's powerful mythology—to inspire artists and craftspeople. The cultural nexus of the village's artistic expression lies within these walls, where it's all about the power of the volcano. It's a crowd pleaser, that's for sure. In addition to educational exhibits, look for expressions in paint, jewelry, block prints, *koa*, watercolors, and more. The center carries the largest selection of artists (upward of 300) on the island.

Volcano House (808-967-7321; volcanohousehotel.com), across from the visitors center, Crater Rim Dr. This aging 1941 hotel caters to tour groups, but it has magnificent picture-window views from its dining room and lobby of Kilauea and Halema'uma'u Craters.

✪ Crater Rim Drive. This 11-mile loop drive takes in spectacularly expansive vistas and circles **sulfur banks** (which smell like rotten eggs), **steam vents** (which really lend the impression that the earth is breathing), and huge deserts of lava.

Kilauea Caldera. This active crater measures about 2.5 miles long, 2 miles wide, and 400 feet deep, but you can hike within and around it.

Kilauea Iki Trail. The trailhead starts at the visitors center. This 4-mile, two-hour trek starts in a lush fern forest but descends onto the floor of Kilauea Iki, which erupted for a month or so in 1959.

✦ ✪ Thomas Jagger Museum (808-985-6000), Crater Rim Dr., about 3 miles west of the visitors center. Open 8:30–5 daily. Stop here to collect some Madame Pele lore, watch fiery films on eruptions, and check out the seismographic instruments that detect earthquakes, early indicators of forthcoming volcanic activity. Free.

✪ Halema'uma'u Overlook, a 10-minute walk from the Jagger museum. Peer into the 1,000-foot-deep steaming fire pit and across its half-mile width and imagine Pele living here. And don't forget to pull your jaw up off the ground as you stand in awe. The 3.5-mile (one-way) **Halema'uma'u Trail** departs from the visitors center and descends into and crosses the pit. This is a great hike, but bring plenty of water and sunscreen.

✪ Devastation Trail. Kilauea Iki's 1959 eruption ripped through this former 'ohi'a forest and took no prisoners; the barren trees are mere empty shells, bleached and barkless bones. It's haunting. Don't miss taking the 30-minute walk along a 1-mile paved route (round-trip).

✪ Thurston Lava Tube, Crater Rim Dr. After so much unrelenting sun on the crater rim, this shady, cool, and moist spot comes as a relief. The tube, with a 10-foot-high clearance so you can easily walk through it (without a flashlight), was formed when its top and outer layers cooled as lava continued running like a stream through its center. The fern forest

END OF THE CHAIN OF CRATERS ROAD

VOG

VOG

When characteristically brilliant blue skies are replaced by uncharacteristically hazy gray skies, it's a little unsettling—especially when it lingers for days. This is supposed to be paradise, after all. But what is it? It's not fog or smog—it's vog. That's right, vog. This volcanic smog is an atmospheric effect caused by sulfuric gases escaping from Big Island's volcanic vents. In short, it's air pollution that can have hazardous effects on people already suffering from respiratory ailments like asthma and emphysema. When the trade winds ebb during fall and winter, vog can envelop the Big Island (especially) like a soft blanket, but it's also felt on Maui and O'ahu. If you are easily affected by air quality, are pregnant, or have heart or respiratory trouble, you're well advised not to visit Hawai'i Volcanoes National Park, and you should think about staying indoors on bad days. It wouldn't be enough to keep you home, though. On the upside, vog heightens the drama of sunsets along the Kona and Kohala Coasts.

surrounding it is thick with singing birds. Head half a mile farther into the tube if you have a flashlight.

○ **Chain of Craters Road.** This dramatic, 22-mile road descends from the crater's rim at 4,000 feet and dead-ends at sea level, passing old roads covered by lava flows. It takes at least two hours to drive up and back, and much longer if you stop along the way! (There are no services along the way.)

Pu'u Loa Petroglyphs, between MM 15 and 16, Hwy. 11. An easy 30-minute, 2-mile boardwalk loop trail will reward you with carvings and pictograms of people and animals. It's a sacred spot, used by ancient Hawaiians for burying the umbilical cords of their babies.

✎ **Kipuka Puaulu**, south on Hwy. 11 from the park and right on Mauna Loa Rd. This self-guided, 1-mile walk leads to a forest oasis not consumed by lava streams. Also known as "Bird Park," the 100-acre sanctuary provides a rich habitat for native birds and uncommon flora. A trailhead display identifies what you should be looking for. Go early in the morning or toward dusk for best sightings.

NENE CROSSING

✳ **Outdoor Activities**

BIRDING

Within and around the national park. Get out your binoculars and start searching: Gentle 'ohi'a forests provide a protective canopy for feath-

ered creatures. Additionally, endangered nene often nest at the aptly named
Kipuka Nene Campground (on Hilina Pali Rd.). Pheasants occasionally gravitate
to the golf course as well.

DIVING

Nautilus Dive Center (808-935-6939; nautilusdivehilo.com), 382 Kamehameha
Ave, Hilo. Very experienced divers can descend near where live lava flows into
the sea. Due to the dangerous and unpredictable conditions, dives are often suspended. But for the more adventurous among our ranks, it's worth checking.

GOLF

Volcano Golf & Country Club (808-967-7331; gvhawaii.com), near MM 30,
Hwy. 11, Volcano Village. Sitting pretty above 4,000 feet, this unusual par-72
course is dotted with sweet 'ohi'a trees. Greens fees are $68 and drop to $54
after noon; reservations recommended.

HIKING

Hawaiian Walkways (808-775-0372 or 1-800-457-7759; hawaiianwalkways
.com); meet at Kilauea Visitor's Center. This outfitter offers full-day ecotours of
Kilauea Volcano that suit hard-core *and* weekend hikers. Lunch, snacks, and rain
gear are provided. $150 adults, $95 ages 12 and under; advance reservations
required.

Arnott's Lodge (808-969-7097; arnottslodge.com), 98 Apapane Rd., Hilo, offers
guided night walks of the volcano. The hostel-style lodge attracts a younger
adventurous crowd; the night/dusk hike takes about four hours and costs $85.

✳ Lodging

Vacation rentals and B&Bs are the
order of the day in quirky Volcano
Village, so delightfully close to the
national park. But if you long for
some regularity in your rooms, it's
best to stay in Hilo. Unless otherwise noted, all lodging is in Volcano
Village.

Hawaii Volcano Vacations (1-800-
709-0907; hawaiivolcanovacations
.com) represents a good variety of
freestanding cottages and private
houses in the village that I can't
review here because of space limita-
tions. But you can trust them to help
on these "one-off" places.

BED & BREAKFASTS & INNS

☄ 🐾 ✪ **Hale Ohia Cottages** (808-
967-7986 or 1-800-455-3803; hale
ohia.com), 11-3968 Hale Ohia Rd.,
across from Volcano Village. I love
this place. These charming cottages,
and a historic main house built in

HALE OHIA COTTAGES

1931, are magically hidden from the road and surrounded by acres of botanical-style Japanese gardens. The shingled main house, topped with red turrets, contains a simple but elegant two-room suite with a lanai and separate entrance. The most deluxe cottage, 'Ihilani, boasts a fireplace, leaded-glass windows, a private garden with a fountain, and an updated bathroom. It was completely redone in late 2007. The two-story Hale Ohia is enormous, but I particularly like the one-bedroom Hale Lehua, built to be a private study. It's very cozy and romantic with a fireplace, stained glass, a covered lanai, and a wisp of a kitchenette. The 'Iiwi and Camellia Suites are the least expensive because they're on the ground floor, with less natural light, but they're still fine choices, and they have private entrances. All come with continental breakfast fixings. Ask about owner Michael Tuttle's two **vacation rentals**; they're great deals! *Rates:* $–$$; two-night minimum for some of the cottages. *Facilities and amenities:* four cottages, four suites, two vacation rentals, continental breakfast (on-site), no smoking, WiFi (free).

🐚 ✒ **Kilauea Lodge** (808-967-7366; kilauealodge.com), Old Volcano Rd.

PAHOEHOE LAVA

Fifty years after its 1938 opening as a YMCA camp, this historic lodge was reborn as a handsome upcountry inn. Owners Lorna and Albert Jeyte converted the former dormitory into cozy accommodations and the lodge into the area's finest dining room. Three of the four second-floor rooms in **Hale Maluna** have Hawaiian décor and handcrafted quilts; the fourth is Japanese in style. All have functioning fireplaces (perfect to dull the chill from cool Volcanoes nights) and bathrooms brightened by skylights. And each has some distinct characteristics—either stained glass, *koa* furniture, or a private entrance. **Hale Aloha** was built in 1991 and has larger rooms and a common great room. **The Cottage** (originally the caretaker's place) has a gas fireplace, a private porch, and a full sitting area with a sofa bed. A couple of blocks from the lodge, **Tutu's Place** is a cheery, 1929 free-standing cottage that's been completely updated. Great for families, the **Pi'i Mauna House**, located 4.5 miles from the main lodge, sits on the sixth fairway of the Volcano Golf Course. The house can accommodate up to six guests and includes a hot tub, a gas fireplace, a spacious lanai, and lots of peace and quiet. *Rates:* $$. *Facilities and amenities:* 12 rooms and two cottages off property, restaurant (see *Where to Eat*), full breakfast, hot tub, no phones, WiFi in some areas.

COTTAGES & VACATION RENTALS

🐚 ✒ **Volcano Places** (808-967-7990 or 1-877-967-7990; volcanoplaces .com). Kathryn Grout has built and renovated four great places to stay. The one-bedroom "jewel box" called **Nohea** offers handcrafted beauty unequaled in Volcano. The private treasure boasts a state-of-the-art entertainment system, a vertical spa on one wall of a two-headed shower, a whirlpool spa, and beautiful furnishings. It's magical. The **Bungalow** is a family-friendly, three-bedroom, one-bathroom historic home. The covered front porch is a great place to enjoy a morning brew while watching native birds fly among tall 'ohi'a trees. The house features a large, comfy living room warmed by a gas stove, high ceilings, hardwood floors, and a fully equipped old-fashioned kitchen (very generously stocked with nonperishable food items). **Kate's Volcano Cottage**, a knotty-pine studio, has a built-in entertainment center and a full but small kitchen, with everything downsized to match the proportions of a small cottage. It also has a lovely view of the rain forest from across the large covered lanai. Lastly, **Kahi Malu** is set among tree ferns, hydrangeas, and camellias and offers two bedrooms and equally private surroundings. *Rates: $–$$; two-night minimum; seventh night free. Facilities and amenities:* continental breakfast provisions, warming pads on the mattresses, TV, DVDs, CDs, phone, no smoking.

🐚 **Volcano Teapot** (808-967-7112; volcanoteapot.com), 19-4041 Kilauea St. Set on 2.5 acres, this 1912 fairy-tale cottage was completely restored by Bill and Antoinette Bullough (a cabinetmaker and O'ahu native, respectively). The whitewashed interior provides an uncluttered backdrop for country décor and comfortable, refurbished antiques. To maintain the feel of a 1900s-era plantation house, the Bulloughs chose traditional green, red, and white for the front porch. Inside, it's sunny by day and warm in the evening, thanks to a gas fireplace in the living room. The master bedroom is dominated by a quilt-covered,

A BIRD'S EYE VIEW OF KILAUEA CRATER

pencil-post bed, while the second guest room has a set of twins. The bathroom is small but cute and complete, as is the kitchen. If you want to inject some calm and order into your getaway, you won't find a tempest in this teapot. *Rates: $$;* two-night minimum. *Facilities and amenities:* one cottage, continental breakfast, full kitchen.

CABINS
Hawai'i Volcanoes National Park Cabins (808-967-7321; volcanohouse hotel.com/cabins.htm), off Crater Rim Rd. within the national park. When you consider the spaciousness surrounding you outdoors, these rustic cabins can feel claustrophobic. But then again, it's not every day you get to sleep within a volcano. Such are life's trade-offs. A few details: It's a 3-mile hike to the cabins. Each has a fireplace grill, but you must bring your own firewood. Since cabins have only one blanket and a thin mattress per bed, and they're perched at a 4,000-foot elevation, you might want to bring a sleeping bag and pad. The cabins have electricity but no electrical outlets. The communal building has two toilets and one hot shower. *Rates: $;* register at Volcano House (within the national park), where you pick up bedding and keys. *Facilities:*

10 cabins, shared bathhouse, outdoor barbecue, no smoking.

❋ Where to Eat

There may be limited options, but the variety fits the bill.

EATING OUT

Kiawe Kitchen (808-967-7711), 19-4005 Haunani Rd. Open daily. Even if this *weren't* Volcano Village, where options are limited, I'd still recommend these wood-fired gourmet pizzas with thin crusts. For lighter fare at lunchtime, I like their salads and soups. Since the availability of ingredients is more subject to market vagaries in the village than most other places on the Big Island, nightly specials are the key to their successful kitchen. Rack of lamb is always a good fallback position. Dishes $$–$$$.

Kilauea Lodge (808-967-7366; kilauealodge.com), Old Volcano Rd. Open nightly. This Jackson Hole–style lodge looks lost in the tropics, a rugged domain dominated by an enormous fireplace made entirely of stones from around the world (including ones from the Acropolis and the Dead Sea) and covered from floor to ceiling with international coins and memorabilia. At this nippy and damp altitude, its frequently lit fire is homey. Meat lovers unite; fish eaters make do. The woodsy lodge with *koa* tables features lamb Provençal, ever-popular duck à l'orange, and hasenpfeffer (braised rabbit), owing to Chef Albert's German roots. The service isn't the fastest in the West, but hopefully you won't have anywhere to go. Reservations recommended; children's menu. Entrées $$$–$$$$.

Thai Thai Restaurant (808-967-7969), 19-4084 Old Volcano Rd. Open for dinner nightly. Pleasant and friendly, Thai Thai offers dependable standbys like pad Thai, along with chicken satay, myriad tasty stir-fries, lots of dishes with coconut milk, and mahimahi that's spiced up with your choice of five different curries. Like the other places in town, this is a good place for solo diners. Children's menu. Entrées $$–$$$.

Lava Rock Café (808-967-8526), Hwy. 11. Open 7:30 AM–9 PM Tues.–Sat., Sun.–Mon. until 4 PM. This cheery little place, albeit one under a plastic ceiling, whips up good omelets and pancakes as well as chicken teriyaki and burgers. They also pack "seismic sandwiches" to take on your park hikes. Dishes $–$$.

Volcano Golf & Country Club (808-967-7331), Hwy. 11, about 2 miles west of the park entrance. Open for breakfast and lunch daily. This local hangout featuring local dishes is a rare bird. Watch fog and mist roll in over volcanic greens and fairways, perhaps with a rare nene crossing your path. Pair it with burgers, teriyaki chicken, saimin, or a fish sandwich, and you've entered the realm of the real. Dishes $.

❋ Selective Shopping

Kilauea Kreations (808-967-8090; kilaueakreations.com), Old Volcano Rd. Open 9:30–5:30 daily. There are a lot of rainy days in Volcanoes; no wonder a quilting co-op came to fruition.

Akatsuka Orchid Gardens (808-967-8234 or 1-888-967-6669; akatsuka orchid.com), near MM 22, Hwy. 11. Open 8–5 daily. This region is flower central for the Big Island, and possibly the state. Wander around this greenhouse garden nursery, choose

VOLCANO VILLAGE

center also has a great selection of anthuriums and other inexpensive cut flowers that they'll carefully ship to the mainland for you. You can even call in an order.

Volcano Winery (808-967-7479; volcanowinery.com), 35 Pi'i Mauna Dr., MM 30 off Hwy. 11 south of the park. Open 10–5:30 daily. Just for fun, try some wine flavored with *lilikoi'i*, guava, or lehua blossom. Conveniently, the tasting room doubles as a gift shop.

Fuku-Bonsai (808-982-9880; fuku bonsai.com), 17-856 Ola'a Rd., halfway between Hilo and Volcano Village, in Kurtistown. Open 8–4 Mon.–Sat. Get a primer on pruning and caring for these tiny but expressive plants and then have one shipped home.

See also **Volcano Art Center** under *To See & Do*.

your orchids among hundreds in this impressive collection, and have them shipped home. Think twice, though, if you live in the desert. Remember, orchids like cool moisture.

Volcano Store (808-967-7210), Haunani Rd. and Old Volcano Rd. Open 5 AM–7 PM daily. The single gas pump outside and creaky floors inside are quaint, but this veritable community

THE SOUTH POINT AREA

Windswept, barren, haunting, and borderline surreal, the **Ka'u District** resembles little else in America. If you're doing a circle tour of the Big Island, you can't miss it. But neither *should* you miss it. It's a land of extremes, with dense rain forests, undulating grasses, and spacious deserts with scorched earth where lava flows tumble from the top of Mauna Loa into the ocean. In fact, the Ka'u Desert has been subject to repeated flows. The district is big, too, as big as the entire island of O'ahu. Although it's barely populated now, Ka'u was once the most populous place on the Big Island. (What a difference a millennium makes!) It's a land of macadamia nut farms, old sugar towns like Pahala and Na'alehu, little churches, friendly residents, and ancient fishing villages that date to A.D. 700, when Polynesians paddled across the Pacific (probably from Tahiti) and set foot here. It's where you'll find the difficult-to-access green-sand beach and the southernmost point in the United States. Without a doubt, there is an inescapable end-of-the-world feel here.

GETTING AROUND

By car: For planning purposes, it's about an hour between Hawai'i Volcanoes National Park and the turnoff for Ka Lae (South Point). It's another two hours or so from the turnoff to Kailua-Kona. The Punalu'u Bake Shop (see *Where to Eat*) acts as an unofficial regional visitors center.

✳ To See & Do

Exploring clockwise from Volcanoes around to Kailua-Kona.

Wood Valley Temple Retreat & Guest House (808-928-8539; nechung .org), off Hwy. 11, Pahala. This divinely serene and tranquil Tibetan Buddhist

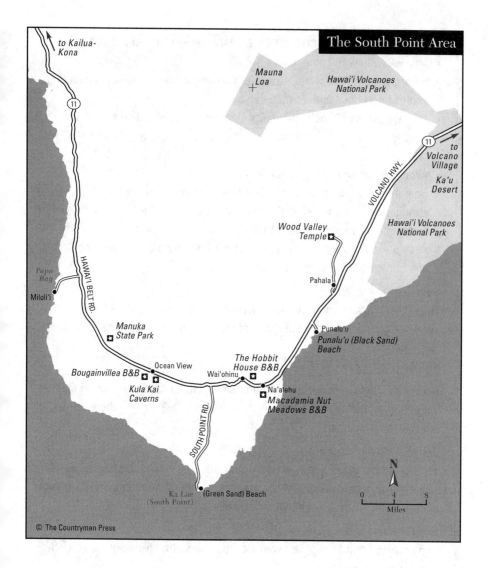

to Kailua-Kona

Mauna Loa

Hawai'i Volcanoes National Park

11

to Volcano Village

Ka'u Desert

VOLCANO HWY.

Wood Valley Temple

Hawai'i Volcanoes National Park

HAWAI'I BELT RD.

Papa Bay

Miloli'i

Pahala

Manuka State Park

Punalu'u

Punalu'u (Black Sand) Beach

Ocean View

The Hobbit House B&B

Bougainvillea B&B

Wai'ohinu

Kula Kai Caverns

Na'alehu

Macadamia Nut Meadows B&B

SOUTH POINT RD.

Ka Lae (South Point)

(Green Sand) Beach

N

0   4   8
Miles

© The Countryman Press

retreat center conveys a sense of timelessness and purpose. Established in 1973 and dedicated by His Holiness the Dalai Lama in 1980, the 25-acre plot of paradise offers guests the chance to meditate and contemplate Buddhist teachings. Come for a full-blown retreat or just a few quiet days of solitude. The guest house is tucked into a fragrant eucalyptus forest; rooms are furnished with Asian Pacific décor; a full kitchen is available. Day visitors $5; singles, doubles, dorms $.

✪ **Punalu'u Beach Park** (808-961-8311), *makai*, off Hwy. 11, 27 miles from Hawai'i Volcanoes National Park. Before a 1947 tidal wave destroyed an active sugar port that was here, this place bustled. Today it offers an easily accessible

BEACH SAFETY TIPS (COURTESY OF THE AMERICAN RED CROSS)

- Always swim with companions.
- Before entering the water, check for warning signs or red flags indicating that hazardous conditions may exist.
- Ask lifeguards or beach attendants about current ocean and surf conditions.
- Always check the water depth; never dive into unknown water or shallow, breaking surf.
- Avoid swimming in shorebreak areas.
- Be careful during periods of high surf and riptide. If you're caught in a strong current, don't panic. Wait until it subsides, and then swim parallel to shore and across the current to safety.
- Keep a watchful eye on the ocean; study it and note rocks, breakers, reefs, and currents. If in doubt, stay out!

Sunburn

Tropical sun is extremely strong, and even on hazy, overcast days overexposure can occur. Use high sunscreen protection and wear long sleeves, pants, and a hat.

Coral

Coral can cause multiple cuts and abrasions, which require thorough cleaning and possible medical attention. Avoid swimming in areas where coral may cause problems.

Jellyfish & Man-of-Wars

Tentacles from these nearly transparent creatures may cause reactions ranging from a mild sting to shock, nausea, or respiratory difficulty. If contact occurs, seek medical attention immediately.

Sea Urchins

Sea urchins are covered with sharp, brittle spines that frequently break off when they penetrate hands or feet. Be careful not to step on them. However, if you come in contact with one, soak the area in hot water and seek medical attention.

Beware of the Terrible "Too"s

Too tired. Too cold. Too far from shore. Too much sun. Too much hard play.

BEACH CONDITIONS

These conditions may exist at any time. Check with beach and pool attendants about present conditions. Always exercise caution while in or near the ocean.

black-sand beach—not good for swimming, but good for picnicking, camping, and watching endangered turtles nesting. Before leaving, wander up to the fishponds, just inland.

Mark Twain's Monkeypod Tree, near MM 64, Hwy. 11, Wai'ohinu. Twain, who absolutely loved the region, planted this tree in 1866, but a storm took it down in the 1950s. Still, new life sprang from the roots; another fine specimen rises today.

PUNALU'U BEACH PARK

✪ **Ka Lae** (aka **South Point**), near MM 70; drive 12 miles *makai* down bumpy South Point Rd. past horses and cows and acres upon acres of windswept land to the boat ramp. Park, and then walk another 2.5 miles (about one hour) over lava and pastures toward an inactive cinder cone (Pu'u o Mahana) and Green Sand Beach. If you have a four-wheel drive, you can drive most of this 2.5-mile stretch—which is tough even with a four-wheel drive—but you'll still have to clamber down the steep cliff over lava rocks to the beach. It's relatively easier (but still very tricky) to get down to the southern end. Use caution and wear shoes with good traction. Or just peer down onto it from above.

There isn't a sign that says YOU ARE HERE AT THE SOUTHERNMOST POINT OF THE UNITED STATES, but you'll feel the remoteness of it. Polynesians must have, too. They landed here in A.D. 750 (some historians peg it at A.D. 300). If you look hard, you can still see holes in the rocks where ancient Tahitian fishermen tied up their canoes in around A.D. 750. King Kamehameha I also fished here, while King Kamehameha II surfed. Ah, royal free time.

🏄 **Green Sand Beach** (aka **Papakolea Beach**). See *Beaches*.

Ocean View, Hwy. 11. This mountainside "estate development" stretches for a whopping 11,000 acres up the side of a lava flow.

Kula Kai Caverns (808-929-7539; kulakaicaverns.com), between MM 78 and 79, off Hwy. 11, Ocean View. Although it's easy to forget because the visible topography is so mesmerizing, there is a wildly extensive system of lava tubes and caves beneath your every step in this neck of the woods. No matter your level of experience or (dis)comfort, there's a hike with your name on it—from an easy 30-minute walk to a two-hour adventure to a half-day extravaganza. Wear sturdy

TOP BEACHES ON THE BIG ISLAND
For Swimming & Sunbathing
Hapuna Beach (The Kohala Coast)
Mauna Kea Beach (The Kohala Coast)
For Snorkeling & Water Sports
'Anaeho'omalu Beach (The Kohala Coast)
For Families
Kahalu'u Beach Park (The Kona Coast)
Leleiwi Beach Park (Hilo & Around)
For Drama
Green Sand Beach (The South Point Area)

shoes; they'll supply helmets, lights, knee pads, and such. Hey, you're on the Big Island, have fun. All tours are by reservation only. $15–95 adults, $10–65 ages 8–12; children must be at least 12 for the half-day tour.

Manuka State Park (808-974-6200), near MM 81, Hwy. 11. Open 7–7 daily. A nice place to have a picnic, this park is basically an arboretum of upland forest that's slowly but surely gaining a toehold on the lava flow. A rough-and-ready, 2-mile loop trail leads past kukui and hau trees.

Miloli'i, *makai*, off Hwy. 11. If you have time, take the long road down to this old-fashioned fishing village, wedged between lava flows and the ocean, where they still use canoes and nets to fish.

✳ Beaches

Because of tides and other natural environmental conditions that cannot be denied, beaches come and go all the time. A little bit of sand gets moved from here and deposited there; it's barely noticeable to the casual onlooker. Not so on the Big Island. Lava flows can create and destroy beaches practically overnight. During an active 1989 flow, a beautiful half-mile beach at Kamoamoa was formed, but then it was completely covered by a 1992 flow.

🏖 **Green Sand Beach** (aka **Papakolea Beach**), off South Point Rd. from Hwy. 11. It's much too rough to swim here, and the winds blow hard, but if you make it this far, you'll be rewarded with the rare sight of olivine sand that formed during an 1886 eruption when Mauna Loa dumped hot lava into a cold ocean. You'll also find a fair number of sunbathers in the buff. For directions, see Ka Lae under *To See & Do*. *Facilities*: none; there's no shade or fresh water, either.

✳ Lodging

There are a limited number of good places to stay along this undeveloped part of the Big Island.

🏠 **Macadamia Nut Meadows B&B** (808-929-8097 or 1-888-929-8118; macadamiameadows.com), Na'alehu. Host Charlene Cowan rolls out quite a welcome mat—especially to families since Charlene has children of her own. Rooms are nothing fancy, but they come with a healthy dose of Hawaiian hospitality. Since the B&B is surrounded by a macadamia nut orchard, the hosts offer complimentary tours of the 8-acre working farm. The Green Sand and Black Sand Beaches are quite near, and the B&B is equidistant (about 45 minutes) from

Volcano National Park and Pu'uhonua O Honaunau National Historical Park. *Rates:* $–$$; $10–15 per additional person depending on age; two-night minimum. *Facilities and amenities:* five rooms, cable TV, mini-fridge, no phone, no A/C, no smoking, full breakfast, WiFi (free), large pool, tennis court.

✿ **Bougainvillea B&B** (808-929-7089 or 1-800-688-1763; bougain villeabedandbreakfast.com), three blocks off Hwy. 11, Ocean View. Carved from a subdivision of lava plots that don't remotely resemble mainland subdivisions, Don and Martie's oasis is perched on the edge of the world, halfway between Kona and Hilo. Perfect for *really* exploring the most unexplored region of the Big Island, this B&B offers full breakfasts on the lanai or in the airy dining room, a hot tub and pool, and guest rooms with private entrances. Martie's slogan is true: "Easy to find, hard to leave." It's a really friendly and communal place with superior stargazing. *Rates:* $. *Facilities and amenities:* four rooms, pool, hot tub, exercise equipment, satellite TV, horseshoes, small kitchen area.

✐ **The Hobbit House** (808-929-9755; hi-hobbit.com), Wai'ohinu. Perfect for independent self-starters, this is one of the more unusual places to stay I've ever seen. The whimsical hilltop house, built plank by plank by the energetic and hospitable Bill and Darlene Whaling, resembles a hobbit's house with its undulating roofline, art deco window frames, and tree-trunk porch supports. You'll enter the four-room apartment through a low, curved door. It has whitewashed walls and wooden ceilings and is furnished in a refreshingly Spartan fashion. Window crossbeams are carved from curved tree limbs and accented with Darlene's stained glass. Although Darlene offers a substantial breakfast each morning, the unit has a large, fully equipped modern kitchen that operates on solar and wind power. *Rates:* $$; three-night minimum. *Facilities and amenities:* one apartment, breakfast, no A/C, no smoking, no credit cards, house phone available.

See also **Wood Valley Temple Retreat & Guest House** and **Punalu'u Beach Park** (camping) under *To See & Do*.

✳ Where to Eat

Shaka Restaurant (808-929-7404), Hwy. 11, Na'alehu. Open 10–8:30 daily. It won't win any awards (except perhaps for large portions), but it'll seem like an oasis between Volcano Village and Kailua-Kona if you're hankering to sit down for a meal. Stick to burgers and burritos or fresh catch-of-the-day and count yourself lucky. Children's menu. Lunch $$, dinner entrees $$–$$$.

Punalu'u Bake Shop (808-929-7343), Hwy. 11, Na'alehu. Open 9–5 daily. About 45 minutes from Hawai'i Volcanoes National Park. Pick up some poha berry (gooseberry) jam when you're here.

Kaua'i 6

KAUA'I IN BRIEF

I know this much is true: Few islands in the world rival Kaua'i in natural grandeur.

The oldest of the Hawaiian archipelago, it erupted from the sea 5 million years ago. Its highest point (5,148 feet) is an extinct volcano in the center of the island. The top of this mountain, Mount Wai'ale'ale ("overflowing water"), is also one of the wettest spots on earth and siphons from omnipresent clouds about 500 inches of rain a year. The island's age and the rainfall produce dazzling effects: eroded peaks that spiral with geometric decisiveness; cascading currents of water that fall freely; jungle valleys so unexplored that some natives believe they are home to a mysterious race of people; the gorge that Mark Twain call the "Grand Canyon of the Pacific"; breathtaking bays and beaches buffeted by a relentless sea for so long that they shimmer with perfected defiance.

Kaua'i challenges us to live fully, with each and every sense. To smell sweet ginger wafting through the forest. To touch a rainbow. To contemplate the passage of time. To listen as endangered songbirds test their voices to see if humanity can still hear. To taste rain. To continually see with wondering eyes as each curve brings yet another eye-popping beach, emerald valley, or jagged cliff.

Kaua'i's dramatic scenery dazzles Hollywood. John Wayne, Dorothy Lamour, Charlton Heston, Rita Hayworth, Mitzi Gaynor, and Elvis Presley all made films on Kaua'i's beaches. Secluded tropical valleys served as backdrop locations for *Jurassic Park*, *Raiders of the Lost Ark*, and *King Kong* starring Jessica Lange. The most famous set is on the North Shore, where a pair of rugged peaks took on the enduring identity of Bali Hai with the shooting of *South Pacific*. Bali Hai may be the single most perfectly positioned pinnacle in the world.

You may have been to Kaua'i via your local cineplex, but that's no substitute for actual experience. The nobility of the island is exhilarating, even if the resort areas are a bit commonplace. Just bring good hiking shoes and enough money for a rental car. The more you explore, the more enduring the memory will be. Although she doesn't give up her goods as easily as other islands, Kaua'i is for the active visitor. (Guided tours abound, because two-thirds of the island is inaccessible wilderness.) And Kaua'i is also a place for healing; a place for lazy days and watching sunsets. Misty and mystical, laid-back Kaua'i is not overrun by

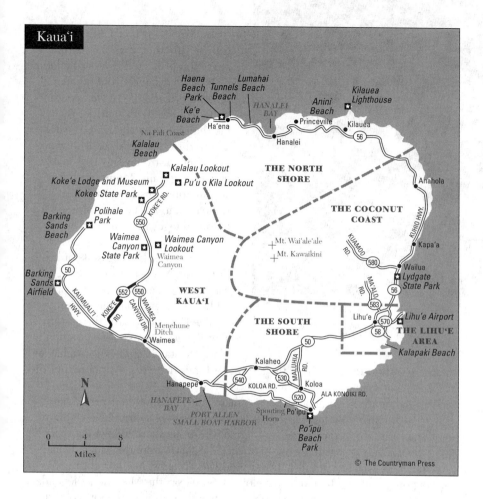

Kaua'i

tourism, yet it has a strong tourism infrastructure. Everything you could possibly want is here, except a healthy dose of nightlife.

And let's not overlook the folks who live here. Kaua'i's nickname may be the Garden Isle, but her *mana* has had a decided influence on the residents. They're arguably (I use the word loosely, considering the context) the friendliest in the state.

Development on Kaua'i has done little to enhance or destroy its natural majesty, though developers are working hard to leave their marks. Kaua'i has avoided the blotching of the coastal horizon by high-rises, but the resort areas that line the popular shores on either side of the Lihu'e area tend to be architecturally undistinguished, with buildings often mismatched and certainly mundane against the dramatic natural backdrop. Almost everyone flies into Lihu'e, an ordinary commercial center.

The South Shore boasts the most popular resort area, Po'ipu, whose lively and developed beach is choice and where the chance for sunshine is very good. But Po'ipu is a moderate drive from the island's natural sights.

HANALEI BAY & BALI HAI

In West Kaua'i, you'll find Waimea Canyon, another stunning natural attraction protected from exploitation by both its distance from popular resort areas and the rugged contours of the colorful terrain. More accessible than the Na Pali Coast, it can be admired from several roadside viewing points or from many reasonably easy hiking trails. Limited cabin accommodations are available at Koke'e State Park or in restored plantation cottages in Waimea. The dry west coast has one of the grandest beaches, Polihale, accessible only by dirt roads. Many of its lush fields of waving sugarcane are being supplanted by coffee and macadamia nuts.

The Coconut Coast (the eastern shore), with a dense concentration of places to stay in sprawling Wailua and Kapa'a, is a short distance from the airport. It tends to be dry over here, but the beaches are not the best for swimming.

Kaua'i abounds in gorgeous beaches, many unspoiled, often deserted, and dangerous for swimming in winter. The finest collection is on the North Shore, where rain is more frequent and where one wondrous shore follows another along the sparsely populated main highway. The sands around Kilauea, Hanalei, Lumahai, and Ke'e are fit for fantasies. And Kaua'i's most magnificent regions are too powerful to be tamed by developers. Some say the Menehune, legendary dwarfs credited with creating archaeological wonders, inhabit the savagely wild valleys of the Na Pali Coast. At least they haven't opened a hotel yet! The only route through Na Pali is a 22-mile round-trip trail, extremely treacherous at points though just moderately tricky for the first 2 miles starting at Ke'e Beach.

Often called the "separate kingdom" because she resisted King Kamehameha's advances for so long, Kaua'i still retains an independent spirit. Interestingly, sights and attractions on Kaua'i are indicated with an image of the king replete with royal feather cape and helmet. It makes touring easy.

Oh, and about that red dirt: It doesn't come off. Bring socks, pants, and shorts that you won't mind relegating to your next Kaua'i trip. That's also one reason for removing your shoes before entering someone's home (or your rental condo).

GUIDANCE

Kaua'i Visitor's Bureau (808-245-3971 or 1-800-262-1400; kauaivisitors bureau.com), 4334 Rice St., Suite 101, Lihu'e. Open 8–4:30 weekdays. Look for their free Island of Kaua'i Travel Planner and pocket map.

County Parks & Recreation Department (808-241-4463), for general beach information.

A PERFECT DAY FOR A HELICOPTER TOUR

8:00	Eat a big omelet at Olympic Café
10:30	Head to the skies on a helicopter tour
12:00	Try oxtail stew at Tip Top Café
1:00	Learn about the island and shop for gifts at the Kaua'i Museum
3:00	Snorkel at Lydgate State Park
5:00	Take a sunset stroll on the Lydgate Beach Park Coastal Trail
6:30	Enjoy live music and scrumptious veggies at Blossoming Lotus
9:00	Groove the night away at The Point (Sheraton)

MORE WEB SITES

poipu-beach.org (Po'ipu Resort)

state.hi.us/dlnr (Hawai'i's Department of Lands and Natural Resources)

honoluluadvertiser.com (daily newspaper)

starbulletin.com (daily newspaper)

gohawaii.com (Hawai'i Visitor's & Convention Bureau)

kauaiworld.com (local daily newspaper)]

kauai-hawaii.com (Kaua'i Visitor's Bureau)

alternative-hawaii.com (good tourism information)

bnbkauai.com (Bed & Breakfast Kaua'i)

NEWSPAPERS & RADIO

The *Garden Island* newspaper (kauaiworld.com) is widely available.

For some classic Hawaiian tunes, tune your radio to 570 AM KQNG. The island's only commercial-free station (KKCR, at 90.9 and 91.9 FM) features local-issue talk shows as well as jazz, reggae, blues, and rock.

WEATHER

Check current weather conditions before heading out on a hike (808-245-6001) or for an expensive boat trip (808-245-3564 for marine conditions). In summer ocean swells quiet down on the North Shore; in winter they're dangerously large on the North Shore. The rainy period, most acutely felt on the North Shore, falls (no pun intended) Nov.–Mar.

MEDICAL EMERGENCY

Wilcox Memorial Hospital (808-245-1100), Lihu'e; open 24/7.

Kaua'i Veterans Memorial Hospital (808-338-9431), Waimea; open 24/7.

GETTING THERE

By air from the mainland: First things first: Try to sit on the left side of the air-craft on the approach; the views are luscious. Many carriers fly daily direct from the West Coast, including American, United, Alaska, Hawaiian, US Airways, and Aloha. **Pleasant Holidays** (1-800-742-9244; pleasantholidays.com) puts together good packages from the mainland.

Interisland air: **Hawaiian Airlines** (808-838-1555) has direct service from Kaua'i to Maui or O'ahu. **Go! Airlines** (1-888-435-9462) has direct service between Lihu'e and O'ahu (which means you'll eat up time at the airport if you plan to head to another island). Kaua'i, by the way, lies almost 100 miles north of O'ahu.

By sea: Unless you have a friend with a yacht or you take a cruise through the islands, the only other way to arrive to Kaua'i is the **Hawaii Superferry** (1-877-443-3779) . . . well, maybe. At press time, the Superferry (after an uproar by local protesters) suspended ferry service between Lihu'e and O'ahu. But plans are still in the works. Call them directly to see if the car ferry is currently shuttling passengers and for current rates.

GETTING AROUND

By car: Kaua'i is not encircled by one road. Fifteen miles of coastline, with cliffs too steep for a road, are completely cut off. This calls to true explorers, those not satisfied with today's all-too-easy drive-by culture. But it also means that unless you divide your lodging between the North and South Shores, you are probably going to be backtracking.

Traffic crawls between Lihu'e and Kapa'a during the rush hours (6:30–8:30 and 3:30–5:30). Try to time your trip accordingly.

Heading north from Lihu'e, take Hwy. 51 (aka Kapule Highway) up through Kapa'a and the Coconut Coast (the eastern shore) along Hwy. 56 (aka Kuhio Highway) to the North Shore. In Hanalei, Hwy. 56 morphs into little Hwy. 560 until it dead-ends in Ha'ena at Ke'e Beach.

Heading south from Lihu'e, take Hwy. 51 (aka Kapule Highway) to Hwy. 58 (aka Nawiliwili Road) to Hwy. 50 (aka Kaumuali'i Highway) toward Po'ipu, Waimea, and Polihale Beach. To reach Po'ipu, take Hwy. 50 to Hwy. 520 (aka Maluhia Road).

By bus: **Kaua'i Bus** (808-241-6410) operates Mon.–Sat. 6:30 AM–7 PM. This inexpensive system isn't really practical for sightseeing because it doesn't stop at the big resort areas, but you might still find it valuable for something. It cruises between Hanalei on the North Shore and Kekaha on the South Shore. The visitor's bureau often has schedules.

By taxi: Contact **Kaua'i Taxi Company** (808-246-9554) if you find the need.

DRIVING TIMES & DISTANCES

Lihu'e to Po'ipu = 14 miles, about 30 minutes

Lihu'e to Waimea = 25 miles, about 60 minutes

Lihu'e to Koke'e State Park = 36 miles, about 90 minutes

Lihu'e to Wailua/Kapa'a = 10 miles, about 15 minutes

Lihu'e to Hanalei/Princeville = 30 miles, 50–60 minutes

By land: **Kaua'i Backroad** (aka **Aloha Kaua'i Tours**) (808-245-6400 or 1-800-452-1113; alohakauaitours.com). These half-day, narrated jaunts (in an air-conditioned SUV or van) cruise through the 22,000-acre Grove Farm Plantation, where you'll see rugged coastline, the south cliffs, Kilohana Crater, and a cool 2,200-foot sugar mill tunnel. You'll also learn a bunch of interesting historical tidbits. For instance, the tunnel was built so that cane didn't have to be hauled all the way around the mountain. And AOL's Steve Case, whose grandfather was an accountant for the Wilcox's and Grove Farm, now owns these sugar fields. (He happens to be the second-largest landowner on Kaua'i.) You never know what you're going to pick up by riding around with a local tour guide for four hours. Aloha Kaua'i also offers other outings. Depending on your interests, consider snorkeling the South or North Shore or taking a 3-mile hike into Wai'ale'ale Crater with these folks. Tours $70 adults, $50 ages 5–12.

Hawai'i Movie Tours (808-822-1192 or 1-800-628-8432; hawaiimovietour.com). Kaua'i's awesome grandeur, impossible to re-create on a movie set, has provided the backdrop for dozens of films and TV shows, including *Fantasy Island*, *Gilligan's Island*, *South Pacific*, *King Kong*, *Six Days & Seven Nights*, *Blue Hawai'i*, *Jurassic Park*, and *Raiders of the Lost Ark*. This tour takes folks to many famed movie locations in the relative luxury of air-conditioned mini buses and four-wheel-drive vans. Since they're all equipped with digital video and surround sound, you can watch the scene in the van and compare it to what's outside the window. Depending on your prism, it could be a bit cheesy, but movie buffs will easily get seduced. Regardless, one of the best aspects of the tour is the stunning scenery that you couldn't see without a permit. Tours $111 adults, $92 children.

By foot: **Sierra Club** (808-246-8748; hi.sierraclub.org), Lihu'e. This club offers a great resource page for hikers on its Web site, as well as many organized outings. Do take advantage.

Kaua'i Nature Tours (808-742-8305 or 1-888-233-8365; kauainaturetours.com). If you are interested in learning about Kaua'i's geological and botanical history, take a daylong walking tour with this small group of scientists. Tours head through Waimea Canyon and along the Na Pali Coast, and they include lunch, bottled water, and other snacks to keep your energy up. Here's a word of warning, though: Some of these hikes can be challenging, but they're all well worth your while. Children (inquire about special rates) must like to hike and be at least six years of age. Tours $100–130 per person.

✪ *By air:* Most of Kaua'i is inaccessible. For unparalleled views of the

ALOHA KAUA'I TOURS

best of the best—Mount Wai'ale'ale, Hanalei Valley, Waimea Canyon, and the Kalalau Valley—take to the skies. It's well worth your money. Most helicopter tours originate from the heliport at the Lihu'e Airport. Among the companies that fly, you'll find **Jack Harter Helicopters** (808-245-3774 or 1-888-245-2001; helicopters-kauai.com) and **Island Helicopters** (808-245-8588 or 1-800-829-5999; islandhelicopter.com).

Will Squyres Helicopter Tours (808-245-8881 or 1-888-245-4354; helicopters -hawaii.com). If you want a thrilling view that will knock your socks off, tour the island of Kaua'i in an ASTAR 350 helicopter. This 60-minute narrated tour takes you over, around, and through Waimea Canyon, Wailua Falls, and the legendary Na Pali Coast. If the idea of flying in a chopper doesn't sit well in the pit of your stomach, don't worry; Will's company started in 1984 and has a perfect safety record. (Don't forget the Dramamine.) The local lore and colorful commentary can't compete with the Technicolor greenery, but they sure complement it. The grand tour costs $229–275 per person. Kids need to weigh at least 40 pounds.

Underwater: **Dive Kaua'i** (808-822-0452; divekauai.com; Kapa'a), **Sea Sport Divers** (808-742-9303; kauaiscubadiving.com; Po'ipu), and **Bubbles Below Scuba Charters** (808-332-7333; bubblesbelowkauai.com; Ele'ele) offer myriad rentals for shore dives or boat trips. Because Kaua'i is the oldest major island, the coral reefs have had more time to develop and therefore offer great diving possibilities. Dives are particularly weather dependent here. Most offshore dives take place off the South Shore (at the Sheraton Caverns), but diving is also good on the North Shore in summer (at the Oceanarium). The eastern Coconut Coast has a popular offshore wreck that also makes a good destination. As for shore dives, talk to the shop pros about South Shore spots like Koloa Landing and Tortugas and North Shore spots such as Tunnels Beach, Ke'e Beach, and Cannons Beach (just beyond Ha'ena Beach Park).

✳ Special Events

For a complete list of islandwide events, consult calendar.gohawaii.com.

February: **Waimea Town Celebration** (808-245-3971), Waimea. Canoe races, a rodeo, and a marathon are held to celebrate the town where Captain Cook first landed. This two-day event draws some 10,000 people.

Late March: **Prince Kuhio Celebrations** (808-826-9272), Lihu'e. Hawai'i celebrates the birth of Jonah Kuhio Kalanianaole, a congressional delegate from 1903 to 1921. Although this day is celebrated on all the islands, Kaua'i—the birthplace of this venerable leader—puts on the best show.

TOP 10 "MUSTS" FOR FIRST-TIME VISITORS

Peer into Waimea Canyon

Take a Na Pali Coast boat trip

Swim at Po'ipu Beach Park

Enjoy sunset drinks at Bali Hai

Drive the North Shore

Take a helicopter ride

Visit the Kaua'i Museum

Hike 2 miles of the Kalalau Trail

Explore Limahuli Garden

Watch the sunset at Polihale

May 1: **Lei Day** (808-245-6931), state wide. Contests are held for the most beautiful lei at the Kaua'i Museum, a queen is crowned, and modern and traditional hula competitions are held. The phrase "May Day is Lei Day" was coined by Grace Tower Warren in 1928 when Lei Day was conceived.

May through August: **Outrigger Canoe Season** (808-261-6615; y2kanu.com), statewide. Canoe races are held most weekends across the state.

Early June: **King Kamehameha Celebration** (808-245-3971; state.hi.us/dags/kkcc). Hawai'i's longest-running festival is celebrated statewide to honor King Kamehameha, unifier of the Hawaiian Kingdom.

July: **Koloa Plantation Days** (808-822-0734; koloaplantationdays.com). This nine-day festival celebrates the rich sugar industry history of Koloa.

Mid- to late August: **Admissions Day**, statewide. On the third Friday in August, all islands celebrate the day Hawai'i became the 50th state.

TOP 10 IDEAS FOR REPEAT VISITORS

Hike at Koke'e State Park

Kayak the Hanalei River

Snorkel at Ke'e Beach

Gallery hop on Hanapepe Art Nights

Paddle into the Hule'ia National Wildlife Refuge

Indulge your senses at ANARA Spa

Tour Na Aina Kai Botanical Gardens

Hike 2 more miles of the Kalalau Trail

Dine at hole-in-the-walls in Lihu'e

Learn to surf in Hanalei Bay

September: **Aloha Festivals** (808-589-1771; alohafestivals.com), statewide.

Early December: **Festival of Lights** (808-828-0014), Lihu'e. Crowds gather at the historic county building on Rice Street to witness this lighting ceremony at 6 PM on the first Friday of the month; a parade follows.

THE LIHU'E AREA

Everyone flies into Lihu'e, and *almost* everyone leaves fairly quickly. But those in the know return to the island's commercial center for good local restaurants. While Lihu'e hosts the local seat of government and Nawiliwili Harbor, it's of interest to visitors because of Kalapaki Beach, the Hule'ia National Wildlife Refuge, the Menehune Fishpond, and the informative Kaua'i Museum.

Lihu'e was built by the sugar industry, and vestiges of the past are still evident in the rusting hulk of the Lihu'e Sugar Mill, in the undulating area sugarcane fields, and in the ancestors of Japanese and Filipino immigrant workers.

GETTING AROUND
By car: Rice Street is the main thoroughfare.

✳ To See & Do
Exploring in no particular order.

✪ **Kaua'i Museum** (808-245-6931; kauaimuseum.org), 4428 Rice St., Lihu'e. Open 9–4 weekdays, 10–4 Sat. This downtown museum, dedicated to telling the story of Kaua'i and preserving the art and artifacts of Hawai'i, consists of several galleries with changing exhibits. Basically it covers all the bases: geological, mythological, and cultural. Of course it touches on the all-important sugar industry, monarchy, and Captain Cook's arrival in 1778. You can even watch an aerial film of the island, which is great if you can't afford a helicopter ride. Back on solid ground, check out Ni'ihau shell necklaces and human-hair leis, missionary quilts and carved koa containers, *poi* pounders and photographs,

KAUA'I MUSEUM

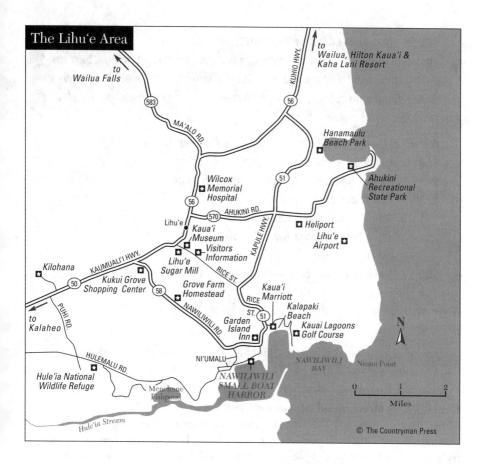

The Lihu'e Area

to Wailua Falls

to Wailua, Hilton Kaua'i & Kaha Lani Resort

KUHIO HWY.

583
56

MA'ALO RD.

Hanamaulu Beach Park

51

Wilcox Memorial Hospital

Ahukini Recreational State Park

56

AHUKINI RD.

570

KAPULE HWY.

Heliport

Lihu'e

Kaua'i Museum

Lihu'e Airport

Visitors Information

Kilohana

KAUMUALI'I HWY.

Lihu'e Sugar Mill

RICE ST.

50

58

Kukui Grove Shopping Center

Grove Farm Homestead

Kaua'i Marriott

RICE

PUHI RD.

NAWILIWILI RD.

ST.

51

Kalapaki Beach

to Kalaheo

Garden Island Inn

Kauai Lagoons Golf Course

N

HULEMALU RD.

NI'UMALU

NAWILIWILI BAY

Ninini Point

Hule'ia National Wildlife Refuge

Menehune Fishpond

NAWILIWILI SMALL BOAT HARBOR

0   1   2

Miles

Hule'ia Stream

© The Countryman Press

full-length capes and feather helmets. One building is dedicated to Kaua'i and Ni'ihau. Don't miss the excellent gift shop. $7 adults, $5 seniors, $1 ages 6–12. Free on the first Sat. of every month.

Menehune Fishpond, Ni'umalu Rd.; take Rice St. to Nawiliwili Rd. to Ni'umalu Rd. Built by a race of industrious miniature people said to have lived here before the Polynesians arrived, this intricate fishpond has walls that are 4 feet thick and 5 feet high. Mullet are raised within its walls. The mysterious and playful

MENEHUNE FISHPOND

SEVEN-DAY PERFECT-DAY PLANNER

These regional, hour-by-hour planners will get you started on how best to dip into the island. But a word of caution: If you try to do everything mentioned in the time alloted, you might not feel like you're on a vacation. Use them merely as a guide.

A Perfect Day in the Lihu'e Area & on the Coconut Coast

8:00	Eat banana pancakes at Ono Family Restaurant
9:30	Kayak the Hule'ia National Wildlife Refuge
12:30	Check out Wailua Falls
1:15	Slurp saimin at Hamura's Saimin
2:30	Sip a latte at Small Town Coffee
3:30	Swim at Lydgate State Park
5:30	Unwind with cocktails at Coconuts Island Style Grill
7:00	Eat super fresh fish at Hukilau Lanai

stonemasons, who liked to work at night and indulged in taro and shrimp, were said to number about 75 in the late 1700s, but no one knows for sure.

⚘ Kalapaki Beach. See *Beaches*.

Grove Farm Homestead Museum (808-245-3202), 4050 Nawiliwili Rd. Tours Mon., Wed., Thurs. at 10 and 1. This two-hour walking tour of one of the oldest plantations on Kaua'i will give you a good historical overview of the sugar industry, immigrant workers, and plantation life. The 80-acre homestead was purchased in 1864 by George Wilcox, the son of a missionary who spun sugar into gold, and it stayed in the family until 1973. By beginning to use irrigation ditches and more modern steam plows, Wilcox revolutionized the sugar industry. $10 donation. Reservations required.

Lihu'e Sugar Mill, corner of Hwy. 50 and Hwy. 51. Kaua'i's first sugar mill was built in 1836 and remained an economic force until the early 1990s.

Nawiliwili Harbor, Wa'apa Rd. Passenger cruise ships, container ships, and the U.S. Navy all call at Kaua'i's principal port.

♂ ☉ Hule'ia National Wildlife Refuge. Accessible only by kayak, this refuge offers great endangered-bird-watching; look for blue herons and Hawaiian gallinules (the legendary latter is a nonmigratory and rather secretive bird that stands 13 inches and is graced with a red forehead). So utterly picturesque that *Raiders of the Lost Ark* was filmed here, the refuge feeds into Nawiliwili Harbor via the shallow Hule'ia Stream. Take a meandering paddle alongside the jungle-like shores lined with mangroves; you'll feel richly rewarded.

Wailua Falls. From Kuhio Highway head north; turn left on Ma'alo Road. Drive 4 miles until the road ends. Does this 100-foot waterfall look familiar? The producers of *Fantasy Island* found this gusher breathtaking enough to showcase it in the opening credits of the show. And even though much of the water has been rerouted for irrigation, it is still quite a sight.

Kipu Falls. See *Zip Line Adventures*, "The South Shore."

✴ Outdoor Activities

BIRD-WATCHING
See **Huleʻia National Wildlife Refuge** under *To See & Do*.

FISHING
Charters in search of tuna and mahimahi are available out of **Nawiliwili Harbor**.

Deep Sea Fishing Kauaʻi (808-634-8589; deepseafishingkauai.com) and **Kai Bear Sportfishing Carters** (808-652-4556; kaibear.com) take people out on four-, six- and eight-hour charters. Prices run $149–319 per person, all the way into the thousands for private charters. Both companies offer rates for spectators (though it can be a choppy ride).

FITNESS CENTER
Kauaʻi Athletic Club (808-245-5381), 4370 Kukui Grove St., Lihuʻe. This full-service club offers day passes for $12.50.

DO YOU BELIEVE?
You may know something about fairies, leprechauns, and hobbits, but what do you know about the Menehune? These hairy, dwarflike creatures, said to be about 2 feet high (although some can be as small as 6 inches), have been known to erect large monuments in a single night by passing stones down a long line. Legend has it that a prince and princess commissioned the Menehune to build the famous **Alekoko** ("rippling blood") **Fishpond**, better known as the **Menehune Fishpond**. Though the two royals were forbidden to watch the Menehune work, curiosity got the better of them. When night fell and they peeked at the toiling spirits, the pair was subsequently transformed into the two stone pillars visible on the ridge above the pond.

Scholars hypothesize that the Menehune could have been a different race that inhabited the islands before the Polynesians arrived, or perhaps an inferior social class.

Even to this day, one can invoke the hardworking Menehune's presence. It's often done at wedding feasts or at large parties, in a prayer that the work can be done in a single night while all humans are fast asleep. But to make this work, you have to clap your hands and *really* believe. (I've been clapping so much while writing this book that my palms are sore.)

THE SWEET SMELL OF SUGAR SUCCESS?

With over 40 varieties of wild sugarcane (*ko*) from which to choose, ancient Hawaiian families and tribes found plenty to do with the sweet sticks that grew on the islands. They used the plants for everything from medicine and baby food to aphrodisiacs and toothbrushes.

In 1835 King Kamehameha III granted permission to Ladd & Co. to convert over 1,000 acres of land into a sugar plantation, the first such lease of its kind granted to outsiders. William Hooper, who was only 26 years old at the time, was sent to establish the plantation in Koloa with the help of 25 *kanakas* (Native Hawaiians). Thanks to lush soil and plenty of rain, wild sugarcane was already prevalent in Koloa, so Hooper knew it would be a good area for cultivating this increasingly valuable commodity. Clearing land was backbreaking work for the *kanakas*, who had to move from their coastal villages. Among other things, it involved dragging plows, drilling soil with *'o'o* (digging sticks), and crushing cane.

In a mere four years the plantation had grown to employ 100 *kanakas*, who were paid with coupons that could only be redeemed at the company store. Women sugar boilers were paid 6¢ a day, which was less than half the wage of the men. Not willing to act as virtual slaves for sugar plantation owners, many Hawaiians became frustrated and disgruntled and started to ignore their duties. Dissatisfied with the work of the *kanakas*, Ladd & Co.

GOLF
Kaua'i Lagoons Golf Course (808-245-5061 or 1-800-634-6400; kauailagoons golf.com), Kalapaki Beach, Lihu'e. This newly renovated, Jack Nicklaus–designed Kaua'i Kiele Championship Course weaves along sheer cliffs and across 40 acres of freshwater lagoons. Greens fees for Kiele cost $175 and drop to $125 after noon. You can make reservations up to a month ahead of time.

KAYAKING
True Blue Island Adventures (808-245-9662; kauaifun.com), Nawiliwili Harbor. Whether you're a beginner or an expert, paddling up the Hule'ia River with the wind at your back is a tranquil way to spend half a day. These folks lead morning kayaking tours (daily except Sun.) up through Hule'ia National Wildlife Refuge to Papakolea Falls, where you'll swim, eat lunch, and relax. Actual paddling time is about two and a half hours one-way before a 20-minute hike to the waterfall; then the outfitter will drive you back. $89 adults, $69 ages seven and older.

TENNIS
The Tennis Club at the Kaua'i Lagoons (808-241-6000), on the grounds of the Kaua'i Marriott, Lihu'e. This place boasts a fancy tennis stadium and four courts for those who aren't ready to take center stage. Court time $20 an hour.

began employing Chinese immigrants. It soon became standard at plantations to house different races of people separately.

Ladd & Co. went bankrupt soon thereafter, but sugar production on the site continued until 2000. When you're in Koloa, look for a ruined chimney with a commemorative plaque just north of town. It's all that remains of the original sugar mill.

SUGAR MILL

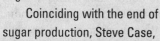

Coinciding with the end of sugar production, Steve Case, of AOL fame, started buying up Grove Farm's sugar land (and their debt). Is it because his grandfather was Grove Farm's moneyman that he needed to buy this ailing Kaua'i land? Whatever the case, he now owns a bunch of acreage in Lihu'e, on the southwest side, and the land leading up to the sacred Maha'ulepu Beach.

Kaua'i County Parks and Recreation Department. The islandwide recreation department maintains two lighted courts in Lihu'e County Park located on Hardy St., Lihu'e.

TUBING

Kaua'i Backcountry Adventures (808-245-2506; kauaibackcountry.com), Lihu'e. With exclusive access to the irrigation network of Lihu'e's once booming sugar industry, this crew will deposit you in an inner tube and slide you through Kaua'i's interior. Tours last three hours, head out four times daily, and run $100 a person. Children over five are welcome as long as they meet height and weight requirements (kids must be over 43 inches; adults can't weigh more than 300 pounds).

✳ Beaches

✯ **Kalapaki Beach**. Park just beyond the front entrance of the Kaua'i Marriott off Rice St. This quarter-mile crescent fronts the lavish Marriott and offers good swimming thanks to a sheltering jetty. Stunning views of the folded Haupu Ridge range are slightly marred (for me) by the commercial harbor activity. Still, it's the best beach in the area. Small waves make for "okay" windsurfing; rental equipment is available on the beach. *Facilities*: lifeguard, showers, parking, restrooms.

✻ Lodging

The main (and only) reason for staying in Lihu'e is that it's centrally located between the natural sights on the North and South Shores.

RESORTS

🐚 **Kaua'i Marriott Resort & Beach Club** (808-245-5050 or 1-800-220-2925; marriott.com), 3610 Rice St. Just a mile from the airport (and thus within the flight path of air traffic), this waterfront resort is great for families and those dividing their time between the North and South Shores. Equal parts time-share and full-service resort, the Marriott began life as a lavish, fantastical Westin in the late 1980s. But in 1992, Hurricane Iniki practically wiped it off the face of Kaua'i. Although you still have to descend an elevator to the lobby (which feels disconcerting), there are water features everywhere, including a 5-acre pool complete with whirlpools and waterfalls. If you don't feel like lounging around the magnificent pool, the good Kalapaki Beach is within a sandal shuffle. As for the nicely appointed guest rooms, they have beach or garden views. *Rates:* $$$–$$$$; children free in parent's room. *Facilities and amenities:* 356

KAUA'I MARRIOTT RESORT & BEACH CLUB

rooms and suites (plus 208 time-share units), the largest pool on Kaua'i, located on good Kalapaki Beach, five restaurants, access to Jack Nicklaus–designed golf course, access to seven tennis courts (fee), excellent fitness center and day spa, water sport rentals, concierge, shops, children's programs, parking (fee).

Hilton Kaua'i Beach Hotel Resort (808-245-1955 or 1-888-805-3843; hilton.com), 4331 Kaua'i Beach Dr. This Hilton is situated just 3 miles north of Lihu'e (equidistant from Lihu'e and Wailua) and perfect for those who can't decide between the North and South Shores. From the plantation-style lobby to guest-room lanais (with mountain, ocean, or garden views), this beachfront resort always comes as a pleasant surprise to me. The guest rooms are fairly spacious, set in U-shaped low-rises that surround a sculpted pool with a (novel) sandy bottom, waterfalls, and an impressionistic fern grotto. Be sure to catch the complimentary afternoon mai tais, torch lighting, and Hawaiian music. *Rates:* $$–$$$$; children free in parent's room. *Facilities and amenities:* 350 rooms and suites, three pools, restaurant, adjacent to Wailua's public golf course, four tennis courts (free), WiFi, resort fee (includes parking, Sunset Cocktail Party, torch-lighting ceremony and Polynesian dance show, local phone calls, and airport shuttle service).

MOTEL

🐚 **Garden Island Inn** (808-245-7227 or 1-800-648-0154; gardenislandinn .com), 3445 Wilcox Rd. This ultra-friendly, colorful low-rise motel is the perfect antidote to high-priced resort rooms. Top-of-the-line quarters (orchid rooms and suites) are spacious and have lanais with ocean views across the main street. (Road noises should die down just about the time you'll want to go to sleep.) The best values are second-floor rooms, but all units are breezy, with original art on the walls. They also rent a couple of reasonably priced two-bedroom condos next door. *Rates*: rooms $–$$, two-bedrooms $$; children free in parent's room. *Facilities and amenities*: 21 units with kitchenettes (condos have full kitchens), water sport equipment (free), across the street from Kalapaki Beach, A/C.

CONDOS

Kaha Lani Resort (808-822-9331 or 1-800-367-5004; castleresorts.com), 4460 Nehe Rd. This slightly remote oceanfront condo complex on the northern edge of Lydgate Beach Park rents one- to three-bedroom units perfect for families. I like the top-floor units because of their vaulted ceilings. *Rates*: $$$–$$$$; children free in parent's rooms. *Facilities and amenities*: 74 units, pool, tennis courts (free), putting green, full kitchens, daily maid service, and free local phone calls.

✴ Where to Eat

Dining here isn't generally about gourmet food or romantic settings. Having said that, there are many good options to suit various moods. A few homey neighborhood places bear experimentation, as does the island's best saimin joint. Unless otherwise noted, all eateries are located in Lihu'e.

DINING OUT

Gaylord's (808-245-9593; gaylords kauai.com), Kilohana Plantation, 3-2087 Kaumuali'i Hwy. Open for all three meals daily, Sun. brunch. Housed in a former plantation manager's estate and landlocked with distant views of Mount Wai'ale'ale, the experience here is a tad on the formal side in terms of atmosphere (a candlelit flagstone patio), service, and cuisine (classic and Continental with a hint of Hawaiian influence). Lovely lunches revolve around salads, sandwiches, and lighter fare, while dinner tends toward rack of lamb, venison, and specialty ribs. Gaylord's also puts on a popular Sunday brunch. Reservations recommended; children's menu. Breakfast buffet and lunch $$, dinner entrées $$$–$$$$, Sunday brunch $$$.

Café Portofino (808-245-2121; cafe portofino.com), adjacent to the Kaua'i Marriott, 3501 Rice St. Open for dinner daily. Locals and tourists alike are attracted by candlelit Italian dinners, a harpist strumming in tune with the waves, and the open-air setting above Kalapaki Beach. I always go for the

A PERFECT DAY FOR RELAXING	
9:00	Chow down on all-you-can-eat brunch at Gaylord's
11:30	Schedule a massage at ANARA spa
1:30	Bliss out in the Po'ipu Beach sun for the afternoon
4:30	Unwind with sunset cocktails at Brennecke's
7:00	Treat yourself to divine seafood at Tidepools

vegetable pasta dishes because they're sure to be fresh, unlike at a lot of other high-end spots. Reservations recommended; children's menu. Entrées $$$–$$$$.

✂ ♈ **Duke's Canoe Club** (808-246-9599; dukeskauai.com), adjacent to the Kaua'i Marriott Resort & Beach Club on Kalapaki Beach, 3610 Rice St. Open for lunch and dinner daily. Paying homage to surfer Duke Kahanamoku with thematic décor, Duke's is the funnest choice around. They've concocted a winning formula with myriad choices like mahi burgers, stir-fry cashew chicken, and an extensive salad bar. Personally, I always zero in on the daily-catch specials. The two-tiered, informal eatery features an indoor pond and waterfall, and a happenin' bar downstairs. Come on by for late-afternoon Taco Tuesday, featuring $2.50 fish tacos and $3.25 draft beers. Reservations recommended; children's menu. Lunch $$, dinner entrées $$–$$$.

♈ **JJ's Broiler** (808-246-4422; jjs broiler.com), Anchor Cove, 3146 Rice St. Open 11–11 daily. Overlooking Kalapaki Bay with great views, the open-air JJ's is a lively and popular hangout for *pupus* (along the lines of potato skins and calamari), drinks, and burgers. I much prefer the downstairs bar to the upstairs Pacific Rim. JJ's, by the way, is known for their Slavonic tenderloin. Reservations recommended; children's menu. Lunch $$, dinner entrées $$$.

EATING OUT

🦐 **Hamura's Saimin** (808-245-3271), 2956 Kress St. Open for lunch and dinner daily. This diner-style eatery, complete with a U-shaped counter and swivel seats, dishes up the best bowls of steaming saimin on Kaua'i. Period. (Their wontons and udon are also terrific.) This unadorned local landmark, said to serve 1,000 portions of saimin daily, features an entertaining open kitchen, but you may still prefer take-out. For those not interested in noodles, chicken satay and teriyaki provide good fallback options. Dishes $–$$; no credit cards.

✂ 🦐 **Tip Top Café** (808-245-2333), 3173 Akahi St. Open for all meals

A FRESH PERSPECTIVE ON KAUA'I'S LUSHNESS

Tues.–Sun. Locals swear by this cafeteria filled with big gray booths. And for good reason. This is the place to try out local favorites like oxtail stew, saimin, or plate lunches at some of the lowest prices around. At night this spot becomes Sushi Katsu, serving up decently priced Japanese food, but lacking the local talk story that makes Tip Top so appealing. Dishes $–$$.

Barbecue Inn (808-245-2921), 2982 Kress St. (off Rice St.). Open for all three meals (closed midafternoon Mon.–Sat.). A fixture in the local community since the early 1940s, this joint has great specialty organic salads, makes its own breads and pies, and features Japanese-American dinner combos and plate lunches (with shrimp tempura, ribs, or Cajun seafood, for instance). I always gravitate toward the specials. Children's menu. Breakfast $, lunch $–$$, dinner entrées $$–$$$.

❧ **Kako's** (808-246-0404), 2980 Ewalu St. Open 10:30–1:30 Mon.–Sat. Formerly of the North Shore, this beloved phenom dispenses handmade broth and noodles (with barbecue chicken or teriyaki chicken strips) to appreciative patrons. They have incredibly cheap burgers, too. Dishes $; no credit cards.

✳ Entertainment

❦ **Barefoot Bar at Duke's Canoe Club** (see *Dining Out*) has contemporary Hawaiian music on Aloha Friday evenings, when tropical drinks are served up at good prices. Open for drinks until midnight.

✳ Selective Shopping

BOOKSTORE

Borders (808-246-0862; borders.com), Kukui Grove shopping center, Nawiliwili Rd. It's conveniently located, just west of downtown, on your way to Po'ipu. Open daily.

FARMER'S MARKET

Sunshine Market (808-241-6390), Vidinha Stadium, stadium parking lot, Ho'olako Hwy. Held Fri. at 3.

SHOPPING CENTER

Kukui Grove (808-245-7784), Kaumuali'i Hwy. Open daily. The island's big mall has big-box retailers like Kmart and Sears, along with a grocery store.

SPECIAL SHOPS

Kaua'i Museum Gift Shop (808-245-6931; kauaimuseum.org), 4428 Rice St. Open Mon.–Sat. This shop offers interesting prints, local arts and crafts, and great *lauhala* weavings.

Kaua'i Products Store (808-246-6753), Kukui Grove shopping center, Kaumuali'i Hwy. Open daily. Stop here for long-lasting seed leis, koa boxes, and other gift items. As for the quilts, they've been designed by locals but are made overseas.

Kilohana Plantation (808-245-5608; kilohanakauai.com), Kaumuali'i Hwy. Open daily. One mile west of downtown and home to Gaylord's (see *Dining Out*), this Tudor-style manse, which sits prettily on a former sugar plantation, houses a few galleries, a craft shop, and a clothing store.

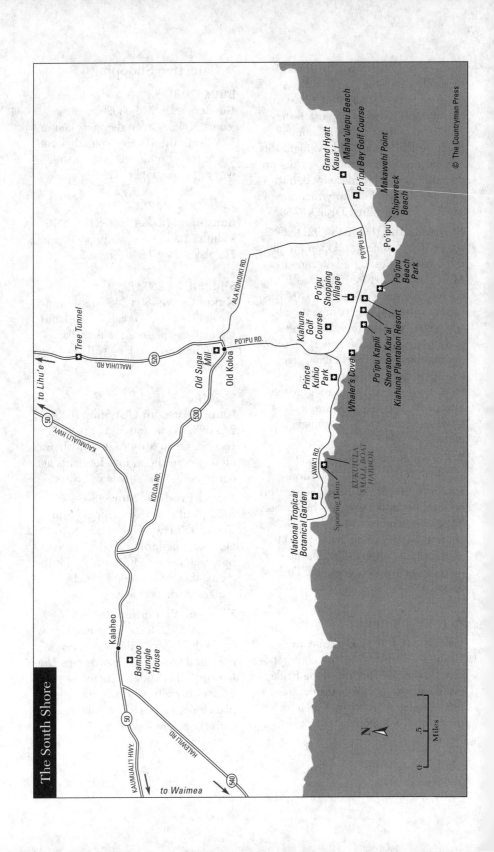

The South Shore

© The Countryman Press

to Lihu'e →

to Waimea →

KAUMUALI'I HWY.
KAUMUALI'I HWY.
HALEWILI RD.

KOLOA RD.

MALUHIA RD.

ALA KONOIKI RD.

PO'IPU RD.
PO'IPU RD.
PO'IPU RD.

LAWA'I RD.

Kalaheo

Bamboo Jungle House

National Tropical Botanical Garden

Old Sugar Mill

Old Koloa

Tree Tunnel

Kiahuna Golf Course

Po'ipu Shopping Village

Prince Kuhio Park

Whaler's Cove

Po'ipu Kapili
Sheraton Kaua'i
Kiahuna Plantation Resort

KUKUI'ULA SMALL BOAT HARBOR

Spouting Horn

Grand Hyatt Kaua'i

Po'ipu Bay Golf Course

Maha'ulepu Beach

Makawehi Point

Shipwreck Beach

Po'ipu

Po'ipu Beach Park

N

0   .5   1
Miles

THE SOUTH SHORE

The South Shore is the most dependably sunny and dry place on Kaua'i. Great golden beaches, clear azure skies, and lots of golf and tennis draw flocks of faithful visitors, making **Po'ipu** the most popular resort on the island. And in your spare time, between stints swimming at Po'ipu Beach, walking at Maha'ulepu Beach, horseback riding along the coastline, and mountain biking through sugarcane fields, put the botanical garden high on your list of things to see and do. When you tire (which you will), pamper yourself at Kaua'i's best spa, ANARA.

Developers have long known the virtues of this sunny resort area and have recently moved in like nobody's business. And in Hawai'i, that's saying something! At press time, eight new resort and condo complexes were kicking up mounds of red dirt, causing some local shops to close. The area is undergoing a transformation the likes of which Kaua'i has never seen. Even while the bulldozers rage on, the sunshine will always remind you why you're willing to pay the big bucks to stay here.

The former sugar mill town, **Old Koloa**, offers a bit of low-key shopping; **Kalaheo** and **Lawa'i** are delightfully residential, full of the descendants of Portuguese immigrants who originally came to fish and work on the plantations.

GUIDANCE
Po'ipu Beach Resort Association (808-742-7444 or 1-888-744-0888; poipu -beach.org), at the Sheraton Kaua'i Resort, Po'ipu Beach, Koloa. Open 9–5 weekdays. You can request their free maps and guides to this region and make online reservations through their Web site.

GETTING AROUND
By car: From Lihu'e, take Hwy. 50 past the Hoary Head Mountains to the Koloa Gap at Hwy. 520. Mount Wai'ale'ale is on your right, and Hoary Head is on your left. Take Hwy. 520 through the Tree Tunnel toward Po'ipu. Pass through tiny Koloa, then turn onto Po'ipu Rd., which will eventually veer left for most condos, Po'ipu Beach, the Hyatt, and eventually Maha'ulepu Beach. Or you can veer right onto Lawa'i Rd. to reach Spouting Horn.

THIRTEEN-MILE TREE TUNNEL LINES THE ROAD TO PO'IPU.

✳ To See & Do

Exploring from North to South

Tree Tunnel, Hwy. 520 (aka Maluhia Rd.). For many locals, this dramatic entryway to the Po'ipu area signifies that they're home. Originally planted in the early 20th century to serve as a windbreak for acres and acres of sugarcane fields (and nearly decimated by Hurricane Iniki in 1992), the far-reaching eucalyptus branches now cover the roadway and embrace drivers.

✪ **Old Koloa and the Old Sugar Mill**, Koloa. This plantation-style town, more or less the intersection of two main streets, is charming. Complete with a general store and lots of little shops ensconced in wooded storefronts, Old Koloa presents as a not-so-Wild-West town. But in actuality, Kaua'i's first sugar mill opened here in 1835, and little sugar shacks sprung up to serve the industry. In addition to a little **Sugar History Museum**, plaques on buildings around town tell the fascinating story of sugar, plantation life, and the all-important ethnic workers. Vestiges of sugar also remain—you can still see the old mill's smokestack, and a plot of sugarcane varieties has been cultivated for educational purposes. At press time, developers were bulldozing monkeypod trees to create the new **Shops at Koloa**. Hopefully this new shopping center won't alter the old charm of this little town.

Exploring Westward along Lawa'i Road

Prince Kuhio Park, Lawa'i Rd., behind the Po'ipu Lawa'i Condominiums. This little way station commemorates Prince Kuhio Kalanianaole, a great politician, the "man who might have become king" had the monarchy survived. His birthday, March 26, is celebrated throughout Hawai'i.

A PERFECT DAY ON THE SOUTH SHORE

8:00	Eat Loco Moco at Joe's on the Green
9:30	Explore the National Tropical Botanical McBryde Gardens
12:00	Marvel at the Spouting Horn phenomenon
12:30	Order a plate lunch at Koloa Fish Market
1:00	Chill out at Mahuʻalepu Beach
3:00	Head over to Poʻipu Beach for shave ice
4:30	Explore art galleries and surf shops of Old Koloa Town
5:30	Watch the sunset from The Point (Sheraton)
7:00	Indulge in seafood at the Plantation Gardens restaurant
9:00	Grab a nightcap at the Stevenson Library (Grand Hyatt)

Kukuiula Small Boat Harbor, Lawaʻi Rd., Poʻipu. Monk seals and sea turtles are popular visitors along the southwestern coast. If you spot reclusive monk seals snoozing on the beach (I frequently see them here), please don't disturb them. Chances are they're digesting a big meal, or they're tired and need to rest from swimming out a storm. To learn more about endangered Kauaʻi monk seals, contact the **Kauaʻi Monk Seal Watch Program** (kauaimonkseal.com).

Spouting Horn, Lawaʻi Rd., Poʻipu. This lava tube geyser, the Old Faithful of Hawaiʻi, shoots up plumes of seawater that reach 10 feet into the air on a quiet day (and up to 60 feet during winter storms). Spouting Horn also offers something for your ears as well as eyes: You can't photograph it, but listen for the groaning and moaning coming from an adjacent airhole. It's tempting to walk out onto the rocks to get a closer look, but don't; stay on the paved path. The rocks are slippery, and people have died here.

✪ **National Tropical Botanical Garden** (808-742-2623; ntbg.org), 4425 Lawaʻi Rd., Poʻipu. Allerton (tours only) at 9, 10, 1, and 2 Mon.–Sat.; McBryde (self-guided tours) 9:30–4 daily; last tram leaves at 2:30; both tours leave from the visitors center on Lawaʻi Rd. The Allerton Garden, a 100-acre gem designed by landscape designers and art connoisseurs Robert and John Allerton, purports to have the largest collection of rare and endangered plants in the world. There's also a good collection of fruit and spice trees. Monkeypod, bamboo, kukui nut, and palms are all well represented. The formal

SPOUTING HORN

McBryde Garden, sited on Queen Emma's late-19th-century vacation getaway, is replete with fountains, statues, terraced taro patches, lily ponds, and water features. The 250-acre research center is dedicated to preserving the biodiversity of Hawai'i's flora and fauna. *Allerton: $40 adults, $20 ages 10–12, no children under 10 allowed; McBryde: $20 adults, $10 ages 6–14.*

Exploring Eastward along Po'ipu Road

❡ **Po'ipu Beach Park** (which includes **Brennecke's Beach**). See *Beaches.*

❡ **Shipwreck Beach** (aka **Keoneloa Beach**), at the Grand Hyatt Kaua'i Resort & Spa. This relatively uncrowded and quiet beach, about 2 miles long, has poor swimming but good windsurfing at the eastern end. It's named after an offshore wreck.

Makawehi Point, east of Shipwreck Beach; trailhead just east of the Grand Hyatt Kaua'i Resort & Spa. It's only a 10-minute walk past coves, forests, and World War II bunkers to the point, where you can drink in stunning views of the Pacific Ocean from the ridge of a 50-foot sand dune. You can also see Maha'ulepu Beach and the Haupu Ridge from here.

❡ **Maha'ulepu Beach**. See *Beaches.*

✴ Spas

✪ **ANARA Spa** (808-742-1234; kauai.hyatt.com), Grand Hyatt Kaua'i Resort & Spa, Koloa. One of the best in Hawai'i and without equal on Kaua'i, ANARA offers everything from fitness equipment to fresh clean cuisine to logo wear. But their real claim to fame, of course, lies in treatments. Soothe yourself with a traditional Hawaiian lomi lomi massage done by a sensitive practitioner or a cooling ti-leaf wrap for sunburns. Afterward, simply enjoy the open-air, lava-rock showers in an incredibly verdant garden. The name ANARA, by the way, stands for "A New Age Restorative Approach."

✴ Outdoor Activities

ATV TOURS

Kaua'i ATV Tours (808-742-2734; kauaiatv.com), Kalaheo. Though ATVs are responsible for tearing up precious land (especially local beaches), this exhilarating tour still enchants visitors. These outfitters take adventurers looking to get down and dirty (read: muddy) into Kaua'i's otherwise inaccessible interior. Four-hour tours (that depart four times a day) speed through waterfalls, cruise past famous movie sites, and head deep into the jungle. Not for pregnant women or people under 16. Tours $135–155, including lunch.

BICYCLING

Outfitters Kaua'i (808-742-9667; outfitterskauai.com), Po'ipu Plaza, 2827A Po'ipu Rd. Open 8–5 daily. The flat Po'ipu area is good for biking, especially through the cane fields to Maha'ulepu Point, as long as you don't mind a little red dirt in your face and stuck to your skin. Road and mountain bikes are available ($25–45 adults, daily) from these centrally located outfitters. You can bike from their front door along the coast from Spouting Horn to Maha'ulepu.

Kiahuna Plantation Golf Course (808-742-9595; kiahunagolf.com), 2454 Kiahuna Plantation Dr., Koloa. Set amid archaeological sites, this par-70 course is one of Robert Trent Jones Jr.'s best designs. Popular among locals and visitors, it features rolling hills, lava tubes, tough greens, tougher trade winds, a *heiau*, and plenty of water hazards. Greens fees run $95 and drop to $70 after 3 PM. Reservations can be made up to 30 days in advance.

Kukui'o lono Golf Course (808-332-9151), 854 Pu'u Rd., Kalaheo. This wooded, playful nine-hole, par-36 course shouldn't give golfers many problems, unless you're distracted by ab-fab coastal views. Greens fees are $8 per day, cart rental is $7, and club rental is $7. Be there by 3 PM if you plan on renting clubs. There are no reserved tee times; it's first come, first served.

Po'ipu Bay Golf Course (808-742-8711; kauai.hyatt.com), 2250 Ainako St., Koloa. Nestled along Po'ipu Bay, this par-72, links-style course offers an in-cart navigational system that gives the exact distance from the hole and pin placement. The PGA Grand Slam tournie has been held here for years. Greens fees are $125–200 and drop to $75 after noon. You can make reservations up to 30 days in advance.

HIKING

See **Makawehi Point** under *To See & Do*.

HORSEBACK RIDING

CJM Country Stables (808-742-6096; cjmstables.com), 1731 Kela'ukia St., 2 miles beyond the Grand Hyatt Kaua'i Resort & Spa, Koloa. If your idea of a romantic vacation includes horseback riding on a beach, these stables have a trotting steed with your name on it. Head off along coastline trails with a small group and an experienced guide. Of the various two- and three-hour trips, one departs early in the morning so riders can enjoy the sun glimmering off the water. Another heads over Hidden Valley and along Ha'upu Ridge to Maha'ulepu Beach. Some rides include swimming and picnicking; trips cost $98–125. CJM also offers a free monthly rodeo series that features *paniolo* (cowboy) events.

SURFING

✍ **Margo Oberg's Surfing School** (808-332-6100; surfonkauai.com), in front of the Sheraton on Po'ipu Beach, Po'ipu. This family-owned and family-operated concession of professional surfers will have you feeling like a pro (almost) after a couple of hours. There's no need for a wet suit since the water is warm and the waves gentle (enough) for beginners. Sign up for a two-hour private ($125) or group ($65) lesson.

See also **Nukumoi Surf Shop** under *Water Sports*.

TENNIS

Kiahuna Tennis Club (808-742-9533), Po'ipu Rd., Po'ipu. These 10 hard courts rent for $10 per person for one and a half hours, but if the courts aren't busy, you can keep playing as long as you want. At $45 per couple, the weekly pass is a bargain.

Kaua'i County Parks and Recreation Department. The islandwide recreation department maintains two lighted courts at Kalawai Park on Pu'uwai Road in Kalaheo. There are also lighted courts in Koloa at Anne Knudsen "Koloa" Park.

WATER SPORTS

Snorkel Bob's (808-742-2206; snorkelbob.com), 3236 Po'ipu Rd., Po'ipu. Open 8–5 daily. Po'ipu Beach is great for bodysurfing, boogie boarding, and snorkeling, and Bob has all the equipment you'll need. Snorkels rent for $5–8, boogie boards for $26.

Nukumoi Surf Shop (808-742-8019; nukumoi.com), Brennecke's Beach, off Honowili Rd. from Po'ipu Rd. Fulfilling your every desire for playing at the beach, these folks rent surfboards ($20–30 daily), boogie boards ($5), snorkel gear ($5), and beach chairs ($5). Their hip shop also sells clothing and accessories.

ZIP LINE ADVENTURES

Outfitters Kaua'i (808-742-9667 or 1-888-742-9887; outfitterskauai.com) 2827A Po'ipu Rd., Po'ipu. If you want to visit Kipu Falls (in Lihu'e), this is the best (and most exciting) way to do it. This reputable tour company will take you on a kayak through the jungle, on a 2-mile hike, and then strap you into a harness to zip over the treetops of Kaua'i. Afterwards, you can swim at the locally favored watering hole without getting too much stink eye from territorial locals. Tours last almost eight hours and run $175 for adults and $135 for kids 14 and under.

PO'IPU BEACH

✳ Beaches

In order of preference.

In general, South Shore beaches offer good wintertime swimming and gentle summertime body- and board surfing.

✦ ✪ **Po'ipu Beach Park**. This stunningly beautiful crescent of white-golden sand is the stuff of sunning, walking, and swimming dreams. It actually consists of five crescents separated by sandbars. Come hell or high water, don't miss sunset here. To the left of the Sheraton Kaua'i Resort, reached via Honowili Rd. off Po'ipu Rd., you'll find a large beach park

MAHA'ULEPU BEACH

(and **Brennecke's Beach**) with a broad lawn littered with coconut palm trees, a playground, and a picnic and barbecue area. It's quite popular on weekends. To the right of the Sheraton, reached via Ho'onani Rd. from Lawa'i Rd., the beach is well suited to swimming, snorkeling, and surfing. Windsurfing, boogie boarding, bodysurfing, and shore fishing are also popular. *Facilities:* parking, restrooms, showers, lifeguard.

✦ **Maha'ulepu Beach**. Take Po'ipu Rd. 3 miles past the Grand Hyatt Kaua'i Resort & Spa along a rutted red-dirt, cane-hauling road until you reach a T. Turn

---

TOP 10 PLACES TO STAY ON KAUA'I

Best Romantic Hideaway
Hanalei Bay Resort (The North Shore)

Best Intimate & Historic Lodging
Waimea Plantation Cottages (West Kaua'i)

Most Worldly Resorts
Grand Hyatt Kaua'i Resort & Spa (The South Shore)
Princeville Resort Kaua'i (The North Shore)

Best Condos
Po'ipu Kapili (The South Shore)
Hanalei Colony Resort (The North Shore)

Best B&Bs
Rosewood Bed & Breakfast (The Coconut Coast)
Hale Puka Ana (West Kaua'i)

Best Family Resorts
Kaua'i Marriott Resort & Beach Club (The Lihu'e Area)
Grand Hyatt Kaua'i Resort & Spa (The South Shore)

right, go through the gate, and follow it for another 1.5 miles to the end. Okay, now for the good part: This is arguably the most beautiful beach in Kaua'i, perhaps even in the state. I know, I know, we all have our favorites. But Maha'ulepu is worlds away from civilization, 2 miles long, and great for walking, hanging out, and simply drinking in the natural splendor. It's surrounded by sugarcane fields, sand dunes, and casuarina trees and sits at the base of the dramatic Haupu Ridge. What more could you want? Facilities? Sorry, there aren't any. Oh, and it's best not to swim here.

✳ Lodging

Except for the major new development at press time, Po'ipu was never really a planned resort. That's its advantage (in terms of the diversity of accommodations) and its liability (for aesthetic coherence and consistency of style). Other than a four-story limit on building height, common all over Kaua'i, there is no pattern to Po'ipu development. A large luxury hotel may share a beach with a less-impressive, smaller hotel and a condominium designed in a plantation style.

Lodging recommendations here reflect the diversity of the area, ranging from luxe resorts and value-conscious condos to fine B&Bs and vacation rentals. Most are stretched out along several miles of Po'ipu and Lawa'i Roads, which head in separate directions along the coast. For my purposes, and unless otherwise noted, addresses in Koloa and Po'ipu are practically indistinguishable.

GRAND HYATT KAUA'I RESORT & SPA

RESORTS

♂ **Grand Hyatt Kaua'i Resort & Spa** (808-742-1234 or 1-800-742-2353; kauai.hyatt.com), 1571 Po'ipu Rd., Koloa. Easily one of the finest resort hotels in the state, this Hyatt opened in 1990 and boasts languorous pools (for swimming and snorkeling), an exceptional spa, and authentic Hawaiian flavor. With delightful low-rise architecture reminiscent of the islands in the 1920s and 1930s, the hotel does a wonderful job re-creating the classic charm of long ago, right down to the postcard-perfect vista of the Pacific framed like a painting from the open-air lobby. The 50-acre ocean-front resort, replete with serious tropical gardens, also revels in its aquatic features. In fact, this Hyatt's water playground is perhaps the most successful and smartest in Hawai'i. The Hyatt's Hawaiian feel also extends to the guest rooms, which are some of the most distinctive in Hawai'i and certainly boast the customary luxuries. The vast majority have an ocean view, though it's usually fairly distant, and the lanai lookout perch is on the small side. *Rates*: rooms $$$$; children free in parent's room. *Facilities and amenities*: 602 rooms and suites, two giant pools, saltwater lagoon, decent natural beach for sunning but not swimming, six restaurants (see **Dondero's** and **Tidepools** under *Dining Out*), adjacent Robert Trent Jones Jr.–designed

PO'IPU KAPILI

golf course, four tennis courts (fee), excellent fitness center, really excellent ANARA Spa (see *Spas*), bike rentals, concierge, **Stevenson's Library** for drinks, shops, great children's program under the auspices of "Camp Hyatt," resort fee (includes parking), WiFi (fee).

⚓ **Sheraton Kaua'i Resort** (808-742-1661 or 1-800-782-9488; sheraton kauai.com), 2440 Ho'onani Rd., Koloa. After years of wrangling with insurance companies following Hurricane Iniki in 1992, the 20-acre Sheraton injected $40 million into restorations and reopened in late 1997. It might as well be brand new. The original Sheraton was almost as old as Po'ipu. In fact, the two had grown up together as resorts since the 1960s when both were small and virtually unknown. While Po'ipu might show a little middle-age spread, the Sheraton looks spry if low-key. Its most compelling feature hasn't changed: a prime location on the famed Po'ipu Beach. There are three types of rooms, all diverse in style and views—none of which are from a building taller than a mature coconut tree. Choose direct Pacific views from an oceanfront wing; views of the white sandy beach from a beachfront wing; or tropical garden views (with koi-filled ponds, ginger, and anthurium) from a garden wing. The strength of these latter rooms lies in the pricing, solidly appealing to those who don't mind a short shuffle to the sands. They're a tad smaller than their counterparts, but at night, when the gardens are illuminated, there's a certain visual appeal that's lacking in the oceanfront rooms. At dusk, I retire to the oceanfront Point, where cocktails are the perfect way to welcome the

sunset with open arms. *Rates*: $$$$; children free in parent's room. *Facilities and amenities*: 394 rooms, two pools, great beach, four restaurants, three tennis courts, fitness room, water sport rentals, concierge, library with Internet, shops, children's programs, resort fee.

CONDOS & APARTMENTS

Po'ipu Kapili (808-742-6449 or 1-800-443-7714; poipukapili.com), 2221 Kapili Rd., Po'ipu. This small, elegant cluster of oceanside condos is a favorite of mine. If you're looking for style, the convenience of condo living, and proximity to the ocean, classy Kapili has it. Built in 1981, the one- and two-bedroom low-rise units are spacious, each with a lanai that provides either a frontal ocean view or an angled one. Deluxe and regular ocean views differ only in that the former offer Pacific views from inside and outside. Superior rooms are coveted corner units. Rooms are individually decorated; you can expect modern kitchens, tropical upholstery, and rattan furnishings. It's too rocky to swim in front of Kapili, but you can take a drink to the seawall and watch the sun set. Or you can walk three minutes down the road to the island's best swimming and most lovely sandy shore (Po'ipu Beach). *Rates*: $$$– $$$$; children free in parent's room;

10-night minimum during Christmas vacation. *Facilities and amenities:* 60 one- and two-bedroom units, pool, lighted tennis courts (free), activity desk, book and DVD rentals.

Whaler's Cove (808-742-7571 or 1-800-225-2683; whalers-cove.com), 2640 Pu'uholo Rd., Koloa. This upscale and stylish condo appeals to the discriminating and sits smack on the ocean (albeit on a rocky lava perch from which you cannot swim). Unless you've been to Hawai'i before, you may not be familiar with koa, a cherished and rare hardwood native to the islands. That will change after staying here: These intimate enclaves are each filled with $10,000 worth of koa. By the end of your stay, koa will likely have entered your dreams. It's the kind of touch that separates a good getaway from a truly memorable one. All units enjoy good ocean views, prime enough to be called oceanfront in many places. But the term here is reserved for apartments with the peak perspective, so near the water that you can hit it with an ice cube tossed from your lanai. No two condos are exactly alike, but most are certainly bright, airy, and spacious. Most are single-level suites that share access to an ocean-view terrace. Count on plush furnishings and upgraded kitchens. *Rates:* $$$$. *Facilities and amenities:* 39 one- and two-bedroom units, renovated free-form pool perched over the splashing surf, activity desk, no A/C, resort fee (includes WiFi).

Kiahuna Plantation Resort (Outrigger: 808-742-6411 or 1-800-688-7444; outrigger.com; Castle Resorts: 808-742-2200 or 1-800-367-5004; castle resorts.com), 2253 Po'ipu Rd., Koloa. This large beachfront condo complex boasts hotel-like services and was one of Kaua'i's original resort condos; it's still among its finest. Accommodations are less opulent than at some places, and most aren't in shouting distance of the ocean, but the grounds front the fine sands of Po'ipu Beach with activities close by. (A pool, golf course, and 10 free tennis courts are across the street.) The 35-acre estate was once part of Hawai'i's first sugarcane plantation, and the main house survives as an atmospheric check-in area and restaurant (see **Plantation Gardens** under *Dining Out*). The condos sprawl in 42 plantation-style buildings; only a few have ocean views. *Rates:* one-bedrooms $$$–$$$$, two-bedrooms $$$$. *Facilities and amenities:* 333 units; great beach; access to pool, tennis, and golf (across the street); restaurant; water sport rentals; use of Sheraton's children's programs (fee); concierge; WiFi (fee).

❧ **Waikomo Stream Villas** (808-742-2000 or 1-800-742-1412; grantham -resorts.com), 2721 Po'ipu Rd., Po'ipu. If you can bear being away from the ocean, these condos are the best deal on the island. Spacious one- and two-bedroom condos with lofts are hidden within junglelike landscaping. Don't forget to bring earplugs, though, because otherwise you'll hear bullfrogs chattering in the stream throughout the night. *Rates:* $–$$; five-night minimum. *Facilities and amenities:* 60 condos, pool, no A/C, tennis courts, kitchen, WiFi (free).

Kaua'i Banyan Inn (1-888-786-3855; kauaibanyan.com), 3528 B Mana Hema Place, Lawa'i. Up in the hills of Lawa'i, these low-key studios make me feel like I scored my own island *hale*. Nice touches like tiled kitchens, king-sized beds, hardwood floors, earplugs, and breakfast fixings (plus local information from the chatty owner, Lorna) make this a good choice for visitors who want to experience rural island life. *Rates:* $$; three-night minimum; $45 cleaning fee; no children under 10. *Facilities and amenities:* five suites and a cottage, no A/C, hot tub, free beach equipment, kitchenette.

Suite Paradise Po'ipu Kai (808-742-6464 or 1-800-367-8020; suite-para dise.com), 1941 Po'ipu Rd., Po'ipu. This huge condo complex stretches 70 acres from Po'ipu Road to the beach. Of all the rental companies in the South Shore, Suite Paradise offers the best deals for studios to five-bedroom condos. *Rates:* $–$$$$; two-night minimum; cleaning fee. *Facilities and amenities:* 306 condos in their rental pool, seven pools, no A/C, kitchen, WiFi (free).

Hale Kua Guest Cottages (808-332-8570 or 1-800-440-4356; halekua .com), 4896 E. Kua Rd., Lawa'i. Bird-watchers who want proximity to Po'ipu will love these simply decorated vacation rentals. Between one-bedroom condos or a three-bedroom cottage, you won't be disappointed. It'll end up being a nice home base thanks to a dense canopy of trees (including a Bodhi and a killer star-fruit crop), resident cats, dogs, birds, and the friendly Cowerns. *Rates:* $$. *Facilities and amenities*: four condos and a three-bedroom cottage, no A/C, kitchen, washer and dryer, beach gear, DVD lending library.

BED & BREAKFASTS AND INNS
🌺 **Po'ipu Plantation** (808-742-6757 or 1-800-634-0263; poipubeach.com), 1792 Pe'e Rd., Koloa. More like a small hotel than a B&B; most accommodations here resemble condos rather than homey rooms. The choicest quarters are the nine spacious and bright apartments that occupy a trio of

low-rise wooden buildings at the back of the property, which sits in a residential neighborhood just across from the Pacific. These well-maintained units include a full kitchen with good-quality appliances; most of the lanais have an ocean view. I tend to prefer the second-floor units with cathedral ceilings. The four traditional B&B rooms (two of which are suites) occupy the main plantation house. Guests staying here have access to the entire house—perfect for a larger family or friends traveling together—as well as a large breakfast that might include eggs *and* French toast. *Rates:* rooms $, condos $$; three-night minimum. *Facilities and amenities:* 13 rooms and condos, breakfast included with rooms (not apartments), A/C, phone, TV, WiFi (free).

🌺 **Bamboo Jungle House** (808-332-5515 or 1-888-332-5115; kauai-bed andbreakfast.com), 3829 Waha Rd., Kalaheo. Thanks to private lanais and entrances, these theme rooms—waterfall, jungle, and safari—each create a feeling of being in your own private sanctuary. Two of the three guest rooms in this plantation-era house have ocean views from the lanai, but all guests will appreciate the hot tub; lush gardens; clean, tropically decorated rooms; common space; and 10-foot solar-powered waterfall. The waterfall suite—the most romantic—also has a kitchenette. *Rates:* $$; three- to five-night minimum; cleaning fee $35–45. *Facilities and amenities:* three rooms, lap pool, full breakfast, no A/C, no phones.

Poi'pu Beach Club (808-962-0100 or 1-800-262-9912; poipubeachclub .com), Po'ipu. If you're looking for a waterfront place with a hammock strung between palm trees and a more traditional-style bed & breakfast, this is it. Unusual for Hawai'i, the owners, who live next door, will come over in the morning to prepare breakfast. The property faces a small bay where charters come and go, and it's a one-minute walk from a small sliver of beach. So if you want to swim, you'll have to watch out for boats. Now back to the guest rooms, one of which is waterfront, the other of which faces the road: Although they're smallish, there is a communal living and break-fast room. I don't really recommend the unit in the owner's house. *Rates:* $$; two-night minimum. *Facilities and amenities:* three rooms, TV, phone, breakfast.

Marjorie's Kauai Inn (808-332-8838 or 1-800-717-8838; marjorieskauaiinn .com) 3307-D Hailima Rd., Lawa'i. Nestled high above the National Botanical Tropical Gardens with great views, this tropical and hidden haven utterly enchants guests, some of whom never want to leave. The B&B offers smallish rooms with all the styl-ish décor you'd expect from world traveling owners, along with a saltwa-ter lap pool and breakfasts that fea-ture farmer's market produce. I bet you'll be lolling on the hammock long after checkout time. *Rates: $$. Facili-ties and amenities:* three rooms, TV, phone, continental breakfast, kitch-enette, free beach gear, bikes, kayaks, BBQ, pool, hot tub, massages (by prior arrangement), WiFi.

MOTELS

✂ 🐾 **Kalaheo Inn** (1-888-332-6023; kalaheoinn.com), 4444 Papalina Rd., Kalaheo. If you're interested in value, this single-story hostelry will float your boat. Studios and one-, two-, and three-bedroom suites, all equipped with kitchenettes; perfect for budget-

conscious families. New California owners upped the prices a bit, but the place is about as low-key as you can get on the South Shore. *Rates:* $–$$. *Facilities and amenities:* 15 rooms, water sport equipment (free), no A/C, no phones, WiFi access in office (free).

VACATION RENTALS

Hale Nu'u (808-742-2333 or 1-866-425-3688; halenuu.com), Po'ipu. This three-story residence is a bargain (especially for two couples traveling together) relative to so many condos on the water. While it's not oceanfront, it's a mere 10-minute walk to a great beach. The retired owners, who live on the second floor but travel frequently, rent the first and third floors. Both units have private entrances. I prefer the upper-level unit, measuring a whopping 1,800 square feet with 10-foot ceilings, two large bedrooms, a Jacuzzi tub, spacious living and dining areas, and a high-end European-style kitchen. You'll probably spend a great deal of time drinking in 180-degree ocean views from the very large lanai. As for the ground-floor unit, it has a huge kitchen, queen bed, living room (with sleeper sofa), lanai with barbe-cue, and 10-foot ceilings. *Rates:* $–$$$; five-night minimum (some flexibility). *Facilities and amenities:* two units, TV, phone, barbecue, full kitchen.

Po'ipu Beach Vacation Rentals (808-742-2850; gloriasvacationrentals .com). For a fabulous selection of condominiums, cottages, and luxe oceanfront houses, you can't go wrong with their offerings.

The Parrish Collection Kauai (808-742-2000 or 1-800-325-5701; parrish kauai.com), 3176 Po'ipu Rd., Suite 1, Koloa. These folks represent over 150 area condos and houses, with properties in all price ranges. Tell them what amenities and facilities you need, and they'll find a well-suited place. Their **Waikomo Stream Villas** (see above) condos offer high-end furnishing for miniscule prices. If you want to fall asleep to waves crashing but don't want to mortgage your home, check out **Nihi Kai Villas**. Or maybe you are searching for the perfect five-bedroom oceanfront abode that could be showcased in *Architectural Digest*. Well, these are the people to call. They generally book the most nicely decorated units in the rental pools at **Kiahuna Plantation**, **Po'ipu Kai**, **Whaler's Cove**, and **Po'ipu Crater**.

✳ Where to Eat

In general, the food isn't going to be cheap in Po'ipu and Koloa, but it will be quite good. Foodies will salivate at Roy's and the Beach House. If money is more of an object, head to Old Koloa town and Kalaheo.

DINING OUT

Y **Beach House** (808-742-1424; the-beach-house.com), 5022 Lawa'i Rd., Po'ipu. Open for dinner nightly. For extraordinary Hawai'i regional cuisine that never disappoints, smooth service, and the South Shore's absolute best oceanfront setting, look no further. While the Beach House might not have to flex its culinary muscle given its privileged perch, it certainly does! With sliding glass doors flung open to sea breezes, this utterly romantic restaurant never misses a beat with fire-roasted ahi and paella. (The menu does change daily, though.) Make reservations for an hour before sunset and don't forget to bring the sunglasses. Reservations

highly recommended; children's menu. Entrées $$$–$$$$.

Y **Roy's Po'ipu Bar & Grill** (808-742-5000; roysrestaurant.com), Po'ipu Shopping Village, 2360 Kiahuna Plantation Dr., Po'ipu. Open for dinner nightly. Opened in 1994, Roy's is still delivering the trademark goods. Customers thrive on eclectic, Euro-Asian-Pacific specialties served with aplomb. You're likely to see upward of 25 nightly specials. Because of the enticing variety, I often order a bunch of apps and skip the main courses. As is true for all Roy's, the wine list is exemplary, the kitchen open, the chocolate soufflé sublime, the decibel level high, and the scene "sceney." Reservations recommended; children's menu. Entrées $$$–$$$$.

Tidepools (808-742-1234; kauai-hyatt.com), Grand Hyatt Kaua'i Resort & Spa, 1571 Po'ipu Rd., Koloa. Open for dinner nightly. Romance seekers look no further. You'll do right by your partner to dig deep into your wallet and indulge at this open-air, candlelit, Bali hut perched on an expansive koi pond. Seafood is the way to go here, with ambitious takes on opah, opakapaka, ahi, and swordfish (my favorite is the vanilla hollandaise opah), though there are plenty of vegetarian and meat options

BEACH HOUSE RESTAURANT

to satisfy. Reservations required; children's menu. Entrées $$$–$$$$.

✂ ♀ **Plantation Gardens** (808-742-2121), Kiahuna Plantation Resort, 2253 Po'ipu Rd., Koloa. Open for dinner nightly (from 5 PM for *pupus*, pizza, and cocktails). Ensconced in a former plantation house, this fine choice is perhaps the most atmospheric and historic dining option on Kaua'i. The lush garden and large lanai is lit with tiki torches, while the interior is awash in rich woods and a South Seas décor. As for the food, you can have it both ways: The seafood and nightly (fresh, fresh, fresh) fish specials are all about contemporary island cooking. But you could also delve into more traditional dishes like lamb, pork tenderloin, and roasted chicken. Reservations recommended; children's menu. Entrées $$$.

Casa di Amici (808-742-1555), 2301 Nalo Rd., Po'ipu. Open for dinner nightly. When Randall Yates opened this plantation-style eatery, a cheer went up with local foodies. Soon, though, unorganized reservations practices (where you had to wait a while for a table), slow service, an overly ambitious menu, and too-creative cuisine turned locals away. And it turned Casa di Amici into a popular venue for tourists with money. Because of the wait, I always end up ordering an appetizer when I'm really hungry (even though the main dishes are substantial). I find traditional Italian meals superior to the fusion style pasta creations. Piano music on Saturday evenings. Reservations recommended. Entrées $$$–$$$$.

Dondero's (808-742-1234; kauai-hyatt.com), Grand Hyatt Kaua'i Resort & Spa, 1571 Po'ipu Rd., Koloa. Open for dinner Tues.–Sat. On my last visit to this Italian restaurant, nothing seemed to be firing on all cylinders: I was disappointed by service (servers were way too pushy), atmosphere (lighting was way too bright for the prices), and the pasta dishes (food was way too rich to finish). If a new executive chef finds his

---

TOP 10 PLACES TO EAT (PLUS ONE MORE) ON KAUA'I

Pricey
Roy's Po'ipu Bar & Grill (The South Shore)
Beach House (The South Shore)
La Cascata (The North Shore)

Moderate
Hanapepe Café & Espresso Bar (West Kaua'i)
Caffe Coco (The Coconut Coast)
Lighthouse Bistro (The North Shore)

Cheap Eats
Hamura's Saimin (The Lihu'e Area)
Duane's Ono-Char Burger (The Coconut Coast)
Papaya's Natural Foods (The Coconut Coast)
Kilauea Fish Market (The North Shore)
Kilauea Bakery & Pau Hana Pizza (The North Shore)

or her way here, you may want to check out the lush garden and ocean seating (as well as indoor seating enhanced by marble floors and lovely tile work). Reservations highly recommended; children's menu. Entrées $$$–$$$$.

EATING OUT

✒ ☿ **Keoki's Paradise** (808-742-7534; hulapie.com), Po'ipu Shopping Village, 2360 Kiahuna Plantation Dr., Po'ipu. Open 11 AM–midnight daily. Perhaps it's the open-air Polynesian atmosphere, complete with a verdant human-made lagoon, waterfall, and thatched bar, that attracts content customers. Or perhaps it's the far-ranging menu that has something for everyone—from ahi sandwiches and Thai shrimp sticks to steaks and ribs. Or perhaps it's the family-friendly prices, good tropical drinks, and absurdly popular hula pie (with Oreo cookies, chocolate sauce, mac nut ice cream, and whipped cream). Local tip: Eat in the bar, where prices are lower and the food is just as good. Children's menu. Lunch $$, dinner entrées $$$–$$$$.

Casablanca (808-742-2929), at the Kiahuna Swim and Tennis Club, 2290 Po'ipu Rd., Koloa. Open for lunch and dinner daily. Locals and tourists-in-the-know flock here for open-air Mediterranean dining that's nicely set between a pool and tennis court. Lunchtime dishes revolve around reasonably priced sandwiches, salads, and smoothies. I like to come for tapas and cocktails during happy hour. Dinner delights patrons with a signature *zarzuela* or North African rack of lamb. Reservations recommended; children's menu. Lunch $$, dinner entrées $$–$$$.

✒ ☿ **Brennecke's Beach Broiler** (808-742-7588; brenneckes.com), 2100 Ho'one Rd., Po'ipu. Open 11–10 daily. Although the décor isn't much to look at inside and there are certainly better places to eat, the popular and fun Brennecke's has managed to draw in beachgoers since opening in the late 1980s. It might have something to do with sitting directly across from Po'ipu Beach Park. (Try to get a second-floor table to best appreciate it.) As for the food, you can get kiawe-grilled fish and steaks, Alaskan king crab, big salads from a salad bar, and burgers. Portions are large. There's a take-out deli on the first floor. Children's menu. Lunch $$, dinner entrées $$–$$$$.

Joe's on the Green (808-742-9696), 2545 Kiahuna Pl., Koloa. Open for all three meals daily. This is my favorite place for breakfast in Po'ipu. Locals and tourists head here for reasonably priced egg and griddle fare served in a festive and sporty environment on the Kiahuna golf course, complete with glimpses of the Pacific. Lunch offers sandwiches and salads, while dinner focuses on meat dishes. Children's menu. Breakfast and lunch $$, dinner entrées $$–$$$.

✒ **Brick Oven Pizza** (808-332-8561), 2-2555 Kaumuali'i Hwy., Kalaheo. Open 11–10 Tues.–Sun. Since the late 1970s, this brick-oven pizzeria has delivered Kaua'i's best pizza. Easily, hands down. It's garlicky, and you have a choice of regular or wheat crust. Dishes $–$$$$.

🦐 **Koloa Fish Market** (808-742-6199), 5482 Koloa Rd., Koloa. Open daily. You will not find cheaper (or better) plate lunches or *poke* on the island. This literal hole-in-the-wall serves up heaping plates of meat or

KOLOA TOWN

fish, macaroni salad, rice, and seaweed salad. Since there are only two chairs on a small lanai, plan to take your food to go. Dishes $–$$.

See also **Kalaheo Coffee Co. & Café** under *Coffee & More*.

COFFEE & MORE

Kalaheo Coffee Co. & Café (808-332-5858; kalaheo.com), 2-2436 Kaumuali'i Hwy., Kalaheo. Open (more or less) 6 AM–2 PM, and for dinner Wed.–Sat. As might be expected, this independent coffeehouse brews a good variety of serious coffee. And it's served up with a good alternative vibe. They also make mean breakfast burritos and omelets, as well as lunchtime turkey burgers. Dinners satisfy family palates with everything from burgers to nachos to seafood. Breakfast and Lunch $–$$, dinner entrées $$–$$$.

✳ Entertainment

Keoki's Paradise (see *Eating Out*) often has live music on weekends.

Ⴘ **The Point at the Sheraton**

Kaua'i Resort (see *Lodging*) draws folks from all over the island for live music, DJs, and even a happening disco night.

ROMANTIC PLACES FOR COCKTAILS

Ⴘ **Beach House** (see *Dining Out*) is the South Shore's premier spot for sunset drinks and apps.

Ⴘ **Grand Hyatt Resort** (see *Lodging*) is a close runner-up, though, with live Hawaiian music at dusk.

✳ Selective Shopping

FARMER'S MARKETS

Sunshine Markets (808-241-6390) are held at two South Shore locations: the Koloa Ball Park (Mon. at noon), and the Kalaheo Neighborhood Center (Tues. at 3).

SHOPPING AREAS

Koloa, Koloa Road, consists of one long block of low-key, wooden storefronts with raised wooden boardwalks. Don't overlook a few shops tucked behind the main drag.

Shops at Koloa. At press time, plans were in the works for this new shopping area.

Po'ipu Shopping Village (808-742-2831), Po'ipu Rd., Po'ipu. Open daily. There are a few restaurants and couple of dozen shops here, including boutiques with casual resort wear, a shop specializing in exotic black pearls, and Sand People gift shop.

SPECIAL SHOP

Mederios Farms (808-332-8211), 4365 Papalina Rd., Kalaheo. Open Mon.–Sat. Condo dwellers will be keen on Mederios's farm-raised meats and chicken.

WEST KAUA'I

This remote section of Kaua'i has a terribly alluring and desolate beach at **Polihale State Park**, literally at the end of the road. It's one of my favorite places on Kaua'i. But the biggest draws are the dramatic **Waimea Canyon** and **Koke'e State Park**, which offer fabulous hiking and easily accessible view-points. Along the way you won't want to miss a detour into sweet **Hanapepe**, which boasts a restaurant whose reputation supersedes the town's.

There are only a few reasons to base yourself here: You plan on spending the majority of your holiday exploring Koke'e and Waimea Canyon; you really like to live on the edge; or you love historic accommodations.

GETTING AROUND
By car: Hwy. 50 (aka Kaumuali'i Highway) runs from Lihu'e through Waimea to the end of the road at Polihale State Park. To reach Koke'e State Park and Waimea Canyon, you have two choices in and beyond Waimea. Hwy. 550 (Waimea Canyon Drive) is narrower but also more scenic than the second choice. Hwy. 552 (Koke'e Road) in Kekaha is steeper and wider. Although I usually drive up one and down the other, it's no matter; they both converge into Koke'e Road after a few miles. Waimea and Koke'e State Park are 20 miles and a world away from each other.

✳ To See & Do
Exploring from east to west.
Kukui'o lono Park (808-332-9151), *makai*, off Papalina Rd. from Hwy. 50. Open 6–6 daily. Just beyond Kalaheo village, this park has panoramic views and lovely Japanese gardens. It makes a great place for a picnic. Free.

Kaua'i Coffee Company (808-335-3237), *makai*, off Hwy. 540 (aka Halewili Road) from Hwy. 50. Open 9–5 daily. Over 3,400 acres of sugarcane have been converted into the crop of the future: coffee. At this little visitors center (really just an excuse for a retail shop) you can still see a restored sugar-camp house, as well as old grinders and roasters. Free.

Hanapepe Scenic Overlook, Hwy. 50, *mauka*. (If you take the side road to Kaua'i Coffee Company, above, you will miss this scenic overlook unless you

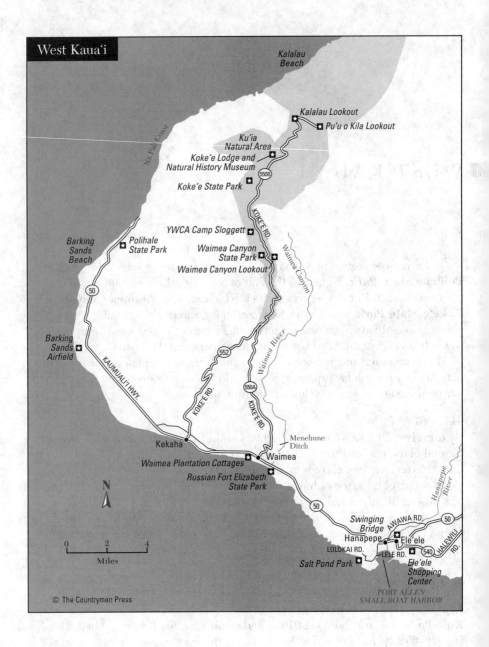

West Kaua'i

Kalalau
Beach

Kalalau Lookout
Pu'u o Kila Lookout

Ku'ia
Natural Area
Koke'e Lodge and
Natural History Museum
550B
Koke'e State Park

YWCA Camp Sloggett

Barking
Sands
Beach
Polihale
State Park
Waimea Canyon
State Park
Waimea Canyon Lookout

Waimea Canyon

KOKE'E RD.

50

552

Barking
Sands
Airfield
KAUMUALI'I HWY
KOKE'E RD.
550A
KOKE'E RD.

Waimea River

Menehune
Ditch
Kekaha
Waimea
Waimea Plantation Cottages
Russian Fort Elizabeth
State Park

N

0   2   4
Miles

50

Swinging
Bridge
Hanapepe
AWAWA RD.
50
Ele'ele
LOLOKAI RD.
LELE RD.
540
HALEWILI RD.
Salt Pond Park
Ele'ele
Shopping
Center

Hanapepe River

PORT ALLEN
SMALL BOAT HARBOR

© The Countryman Press

backtrack.) This roadside spot, overlooking a gaping canyon draped in a rich orange-and-red palette, marks the spot where the last battle on Kaua'i, led by King Kaumuali'i's son Humehume, took place in 1824.

✪ **Hanapepe**, Hanapepe Rd., *mauka* off Hwy. 50. Often referred to as a dusty ghost town, tiny Hanapepe developed as a plantation village populated by Chinese rice farmers. Today you'll find a few galleries, a great restaurant, a happening Friday Night Art event, and a fun swinging footbridge that crosses the

A PERFECT DAY ON WEST KAUAI

7:30	Enjoy breakfast and coffee on your lanai; pack a take-out lunch
9:00	Beat the masses to spectacular views at Koke'e's Kalalau Valley
10:00	Hike the Alaka'i Swamp Trail
1:00	Enjoy a picnic lunch overlooking Waimea Canyon
2:30	Grab a shave ice at Jo-Jo's clubhouse
4:00	Watch the sunset at Polihale State Park
7:00	Dine at Wrangler's Steakhouse
9:00	Down a microbrewed beer at Waimea Brewing Company

Hanapepe River in the middle of town. Don't leave town without walking across it.

Port Allen, Waialo Road, *makai*, off Hwy. 50. The main west coast shipping port is also the departure point for snorkeling, diving, and Na Pali Coast boat trips.

𝄆 **Salt Pond Beach** (*makai*). See *Beaches*.

Russian Fort Elizabeth, *makai*, Hwy. 50. Stop here for good views of the Waimea River and the island of Ni'ihau. Just before the Waimea River Bridge, this visually uninteresting and overgrown site nonetheless has an interesting history. Anton Scheffer, a Russian posing as a doctor, befriended King Kamehameha I and provided him with health care. In gratitude, the king gave him this land, upon which Scheffer built a fort in 1816. When Scheffer raised a Russian flag, the king seized the fort and expelled him. Then Scheffer befriended the king of Kaua'i and plotted with him to oust King Kamehameha I. When the real Russian military sailed into Kaua'i and exposed Scheffer for a fake, he was finally ousted.

HANAPEPE SWINGING FOOTBRIDGE

Menehune Ditch (aka Kiki a Ola), *mauka*, a couple of miles up Menehune Road off Hwy. 50 just after the Waimea River Bridge. Only a 2-foot-high section of this old aqueduct is visible because of the highway, but it still carries water to taro patches. Predating the documented arrival of the first Polynesians, its very existence gives credence to the existence of the Menehune and their previously unknown building methods.

Waimea, *mauka*, Hwy. 50. Once the capital of Kaua'i and commanding an important place in Kaua'i's history, Waimea is a sleepy place today. Captain Cook landed here in 1778; a little monument stands in tribute to him on the *mauka* side of the road. The first missionaries on Kaua'i also set up shop here in 1820. And Kaua'i's last king, Kaumuali'i, ceded control of this island to Hawai'i's unifying King Kamehameha here. Pick up a self-guided walking tour at the **Waimea Visitor's and Technology Center** (808-338-1332), 9565 Kaumuali'i Highway. They also lead guided tours on Mon. at 9:30 AM; reservations required.

✪ **Waimea Canyon**, *mauka*. The Grand Canyon of the Pacific (according to Mark Twain) measures 3,600 feet deep by 10 miles long by 2 miles wide. Subject to the effects of wind and water erosion over eons of time, the red-dirt canyon is awash in a million shades of green, red, orange, and brown. It's a constantly changing parade of hues; the quality of light changes throughout the day. Having said that, afternoon light is usually better for photography. From the **Waimea Canyon Lookout** (MM 10) you'll see desertlike conditions, cliffs (where seemingly precarious yet sure-footed goats scramble), the thin ribbon of the Waimea River running through it, and breathtaking peaks. Many vantage points offer great glimpses and edgy cliffside views, including that at **Pu'u Hinahina**, between MM 13 and 14. There are a few ways to access the canyon: You can peer into it, fly over it, or hike around it.

✪ **Koke'e State Park**, *mauka*, Hwy. 550. At over 4,500 acres, this wilderness park is thick with rain forests and swamps, and it offers 45 miles of dramatic hiking trails of varying length and difficulty. You'll encounter native 'ohi'a and iliau as well as imported redwood and eucalyptus. (See *Hiking* under *Outdoor Activities*.) At 4,000 feet in altitude and often shrouded in clouds, it also offers relief from heat and hordes of tourists. It gets cool here after sunset, so you'll want to bring layers. Outdoorsy types could easily spend three days in seventh heaven hiking here. Once filled with koa that was used for making surfboards (among other things), Koke'e was also home to rare birds whose feathers were plucked to make capes and helmets for royalty. It's another world from the one left behind in Waimea.

KOKE'E STATE PARK

Two miles beyond Koke'e Lodge, the **Kalalau Lookout** is often shrouded in the afternoon, but be patient. The wind blows clouds in and out. And when it clears, look out—to inspiring views of waterfalls, folded mountains, and a thick tree canopy. Five million years of wind and water erosion have

NI'IHAU

Separated from Kaua'i by the 17-mile Kaulakahi Channel, Ni'ihau is a dry desert island primarily used for sheep and cattle ranching. It's been privately owned since 1864, when Elizabeth Sinclair, a widow with five children, decided to buy it for $10,000 from King Kamehameha. Instead of purchasing a parcel of O'ahu that now includes Waikiki (which was originally offered to her), Sinclair negotiated for Ni'ihau, lush and green after an especially rainy winter. When Ms. Sinclair realized that Ni'ihau was not much use agriculturally, she began to acquire real estate on Kaua'i, and her descendants (the Robinson family) have continued to do so ever since.

From the get-go, the Robinsons imposed a strict lifestyle on the island's residents; this included attending church. After Hawai'i became annexed by the United States, the Robinsons became convinced that it was their responsibility to preserve traditional Hawaiian culture. It is the only island where Hawaiian is the official language.

To this day the relationship between the native islanders and the Robinsons is a bit confusing. Some observers liken it to a kind of serfdom with overlords, but islanders are able to leave the island whenever they choose. The Robinsons could make much more money selling the land to developers, but they keep it because they feel they have a responsibility to the residents. Most of the confusion arises because the islanders live in poverty. Because there is no communal electricity, most residents use generators and have now started using solar power. Until very recently, the only way to communicate with the mainland was homing pigeons, but they were recently replaced by two-way radios. Most of the island's 160 residents live in Pu'uwai ("heart")—raising livestock, making charcoal, gathering honey, and producing delicate (and very expensive) shell leis.

Outsiders usually need a personal invitation from the owners to visit, but you can also visit on a tour, which was not allowed until 1987. Contact **Ni'ihau Safaris** (808-335-3500 or 1-877-441-3500). **Ni'ihau Helicopter** (808-335-3500; niihau.us) gives three- to four-hour tours for $365 per person (lunch included). The latter touches down far from Pu'uwai, so don't expect to see many residents.

created jagged, notched mountain ridges. The lookout is the highlight of the drive. If you're even remotely alive, the landscape will literally take that breath away. Head 1 mile farther for the **Pu'u o Kila Lookout**, from where the road was at one time planned to continue on to the North Shore. Any commonsense person would think not.

Koke'e Natural History Museum (808-335-9975; kokee.org), almost at the end of the road, next to the Lodge at Koke'e. Open 10–4 daily. This little spot, a good place to pick up trail information and maps, has some local memorabilia and displays on area weather, wood, flora, fauna, and Hawaiian tools. They also have a great selection of local books. Suggested donation $1.

Kekaha, Hwy. 50 at Hwy. 552. The air in this red-dirt plantation town is thick with molasses and sugar. During harvest season, Apr.–Oct., you'll see big tractor-trailers full to overflowing under the weight of cut sugar stalks. The Robinson family still owns one-third of Kaua'i, and their sugar mill, although nonunionized, pays decent wages.

Barking Sands Pacific Missile Range Airfield, *makai*, Hwy. 50. Part of an early warning system designed after the attack on Pearl Harbor, this remote testing facility has access to over 40,000 square miles of open ocean and airspace that is otherwise unoccupied.

✿ **Polihale State Park** and **Barking Sands Beach**, *makai. See Beaches.*

✳ Outdoor Activities

BICYCLING

Outfitters Kaua'i (based in Po'ipu; see "The South Shore") offers daily guided bike tours that begin at the top of Waimea Canyon. One starts as the sun peeks over the rim of the canyon; one is timed with sunset. The 12-mile trips are 100 percent downhill, include a couple of short hikes, and last about four hours. $98 adults, $78 children 12–14; no kids under 12 allowed.

BIRD-WATCHING

Terran Tours (808-335-3313 or 808-335-0398). Koke'e State Park is a key location for spotting endangered and native birds like the apapane, iwi, honeycreeper, anianiau, and plenty of moa. Real birders, wildlife enthusiasts, and natural history buffs will want to book a great trip with naturalist David Kuhn, an experienced guide who leads custom and private tours. He devises trips from half a day to three days, depending on your skills and interests; rates vary as well.

MOA (AKA JUNGLE CHICKENS)

BOAT EXCURSIONS

Holoholo Charters (808-335-0815; holoholocharters.com), Port Allen, Ele'ele. This charter company offers whale-watching, sightseeing, and snorkeling trips on catamarans or an aluminum custom-designed monohull. Heading out to the Na Pali Coast and along the coast of the forbidden island of Ni'ihau, trips last five hours. Afternoon trips generally have better light for picture taking. Snorkeling tours $120 adults, $80 children over six;

sunset tours $80 adults, $60 children five and over; all tours include meals and drinks.

✪ **Captain Andy's** (808-335-6833 or 1-800-535-0830; napali.com), Port Allen, Ele'ele. Sail the *Spirit of Kaua'i*, a 55-foot catamaran, or the *Discover*, a 24-foot rigid hull, for a more adventurous trip in an inflatable boat. The latter gets closer to sea caves along the rugged shoreline. Andy's four-hour Na Pali Coast tour ($105) includes a buffet dinner and open bar, while the five-hour snorkeling trip ($139) includes all meals.

SPIRIT OF KAUA'I CATAMARAN TOURS.

Captain Zodiac (808-329-3199; captainzodiac.com), Port Allen, Ele'ele. This four-hour trip, aboard a hard rubber (motorized) raft that holds 15 passengers, allows sightseers a more intimate experience than they'd get on a catamaran. This is especially exciting when dolphins are swimming alongside the vessel. But be warned: These rides are bumpy. (Still, I prefer them.) Snorkeling is included, as is sea cave exploring and a beach landing (if water conditions permit). $90 adults, $75 ages 5–12. Participants must be in good physical condition, without back problems; the trip is not recommended for pregnant women.

HIKING

Consult the folks at **Koke'e Natural History Museum** under *To See & Do* for current weather and trail conditions before setting out. Also before heading out, make sure you have plenty of water, sunscreen, and food.

Nature Walk, Koke'e State Park. From the Lodge, a 20-minute (0.25-mile) trail leads along a path that identifies native plants.

Halemanu-Koke'e Trail, Koke'e State Park, trailhead near MM 15. This easy 2.5-mile round-trip hike heads through koa and 'ohi'a forests alive with singing birds.

A PERFECT DAY FOR SAILING THE NA PALI COAST	
6:30	Order coffee and banana bread at Kalaheo Coffee Company
7:00	Hop on a catamaran to cruise the Na Pali Coast
12:00	Eat a veggie burger at Hanapepe Café & Espresso Bar
1:30	Explore Hanapepe's art galleries
3:00	Cool off in the ocean with monk seals at Salt Pond Beach
5:00	Snag a seat at the Beach House for sunset cocktails and *pupus*
7:00	Chow down on big pizza pies at the Brick Oven Pizza

Alaka'i Swamp Trail, Koke'e State Park, trailhead just off Mohihi Rd. This serious 7-mile trail heads through a rainy swamp that's home to rare species of plants and birds. Because of seriously muddy conditions, important sections of the trail run along a boardwalk. Consider yourself really lucky if the clouds part; you might even see Hanalei.

Awa'awapuhi Trail, Koke'e State Park, trailhead near MM 17. This six-hour (6.5-mile) round-trip trail is tough, but hikers are rewarded with unparalleled views of ravines and steep ridges. It's not recommended for those who fear heights. Hike early for the best light.

Iliau Nature Walk, Waimea Canyon, trailhead just before MM 9. This short trail gives it up with great views after a mere 10 minutes.

Kukui Trail, Waimea Canyon, trailhead near MM 9. Of the three trails that go into the canyon, this one takes about three to four hours (5 miles round-trip) and is relatively well maintained. Remember: What goes down, must come up. The trail descends about 2,000 feet into the canyon.

Pu'u o Kila Lookout Trail, Waimea Canyon. Just beyond the Kalalau Lookout, this one-hour (2-mile) trail runs along the ridge and offers incredible views.

TENNIS

Kaua'i County Parks and Recreation Department (808-241-4463). The islandwide recreation department maintains four courts (two of which are lighted) at the Waimea High School (Ha'ina Road, Waimea) and two lighted courts at Kekaha Park on Elepaio Road in Kekaha.

✳ Beaches

In order of preference.

✦ ✪ **Polihale State Park and Barking Sands Beach**, at the end of Hwy. 50. If you're drawn to wide-open spaces, Polihale delivers! To reach the longest beach in Kaua'i, you'll have to drive 30 minutes along a rutted and bumpy road through sugarcane fields. (If it's been raining, forget about it.) But you'll be rewarded with a 15-mile-long beach that's 300 yards wide, sits at the very base of the soaring Na Pali Coast, and is remarkably devoid of human beings. On weekends, locals cruise in dune buggies and shore-fish. In winter, big surf and rip currents keep everyone well away from the shoreline. Striking and quiet, this is my favorite place to picnic at sunset. It's hard to beat. You'll also have a good view of Ni'ihau from here. As for Barking Sands Beach, this 3-mile-long

KOKE'E STATE PARK

dune gets its name from the noise that's made when your footsteps crunch the sand. Be particularly careful about parking in deep sand and leaving valuables in the car. *Facilities:* camping, restrooms, picnicking, showers.

✄ ᚠ **Salt Pond Beach**, barely beyond Hanapepe, off Lele Rd. and Lokokai Rd. from Hwy. 50. This is the only park in Hawai'i where salt is harvested as it has been since the late 18th century. Seawater evaporates here in the sun and is left atop impermeable clay pits. Used as seasoning and alternative health therapies, this reddish sea salt is available in shops around the island. As for beach activities, the white crescent is perfectly protected by a reef. As such it's great for swimming (for all ages), fishing, windsurfing, and snorkeling. There are also tide pools to explore. *Facilities:* camping, parking, restrooms, lifeguard, showers, picnicking.

✳ Lodging

If you're going to do a lot of hiking in Koke'e State Park or Waimea Canyon, hang out at the desolate Polihale Beach for a few days, or if you're partial to historic accommodations, West Kaua'i is for you.

COTTAGES

✄ **Waimea Plantation Cottages**
(808-338-1625 or 1-800-992-4632; waimea-plantation.com), 9400 Kaumuali'i Hwy., Waimea. Set on 27 acres of the old Waimea Sugar Mill plantation (established in 1884), these cottages are a loving tribute to a bygone way of life. A century after the plantation's founding, heirs of the initial owner embarked on a major historical restoration of the property. They refurbished a group of homes built originally for plantation workers and bosses and added some new bungalows, constructed in the same simple mode by following the 1919 blueprints. After a decade of careful work, this result is one of the most unusual and special places to stay in Hawai'i. The accommodations vary considerably in size and price but never in quality of furnishings. The majority are inland from the shoreline (but certainly within eyesight of the ocean)

in villagelike clusters oriented to gardens and a vast coconut grove. Period furnishings of mahogany, koa, rattan, and wicker grace all the cottages, though they also come well equipped with conveniences like phone, TV, stereo, simple kitchen appliances, and weekly maid service. Tin-roofed lanais beckon for lounging; hardwood floors are nicely maintained; simple white curtains billow in the breeze; and old-fashioned wooden Venetian blinds are

WAIMEA PLANTATION COTTAGES

evocative. Although the atmosphere is nostalgic, you can be sure the original occupants never enjoyed these upgraded amenities. *Rates*: $$–$$$$; *children free in parent's room*. *Facilities and amenities*: 54 one-, two-, and three-bedroom cottages, pool, beach (not for swimming), restaurant (see **Waimea Brewing Company** under *Dining Out*), no A/C, shop, spa.

BED & BREAKFASTS AND INNS

Hale Puka Ana B&B (808-652-6852; westkauaisunset.com), 8240 Elepaio, Kekaha. If you want to spend your days trekking around Koke'e but appreciate high thread-count sheets at night, this is *the* place for you. Decorated with spare yet high-end flair, it's easy to settle in to this small B&B. Since the property is in remote Kekaha, owners Partick and Jules built an outdoor BBQ area and kitchen—though you'll have to do most of your shopping back on the South Shore. *Rates*: $$; three-night minimum stay. *Facilities and amenities*: three suites, outdoor shower, access to a great beach, outdoor kitchen and grill, A/C, continental breakfast, WiFi, TV, free beach gear.

Waimea Inn (808-338-0031; innwaimea.com), 4469 Halepule Rd., Waimea. Owned by the same folks as the Waimea Plantation Cottages, this little inn (in a restored church) and vacation rental units are a welcome addition to the neighborhood. Though rooms may not inspire sonnet writing, they are mellow resting places after a day of hiking. Spring for the Banana Suite so you can relax in the Jacuzzi tub. *Rates*: $–$$; two-night minimum stay. *Facilities and amenities:* four rooms and suites, three two-bedroom cottages, shared living room, WiFi.

CAMPING & CABINS

Koke'e Lodge (808-335-6061), Hwy. 550, Koke'e State Park. These rustic, rudimentary mountain cabins are as close as you can stay (indoors) to Kaua'i's awe-inspiring natural wilderness. At the 4,000-foot elevation, on top of Na Pali valleys and Waimea Canyon, you're likely to need the woodstoves that provide the only source of heat (firewood available). Cabins come with a kitchen, basic utensils, hot showers, and bedding. *Rates*: $ per night; five-night maximum. *Facilities and amenities*: 12 cabins (some with kitchenette), restaurant at the Lodge, no phones, no credit cards. Note: There has been a lot of talk about bulldozing these

---

DON'T THEY EVER SLEEP?

Those dang roosters are on Pacific Standard Time, I'll tell ya, even though they arrived in Kaua'i with the Polynesian settlers. No need for an alarm clock, and if you are a light sleeper bring some earplugs, because come 4 AM these Kaua'i residents start partying.

You can blame Hurricane 'Iniki for that. When those winds came raging through the island, tearing apart these roosters' cages, these guys let out a whoop and chacha-ed their way from Haena to Kekaha. You'll spot roosters up in Koke'e and down in Lydgate Park, strutting across the street in Lihu'e, and unfortunately hanging out under your hotel window.

cottages to make room for a lodge, but there was no firm information at press time.

Polihale State Park (808-274-3444), Hwy. 50. This end-of-the-universe beachfront camping (with some shade provided by thorn-bearing kiawe trees) is as remote as it gets. I love it here because of the beach, but it does draw an "interesting" mix of locals, hippies, and mainlanders who revel in its seclusion from authorities and civilization. *Rates*: $5 per site per night; five-consecutive-night maximum. *Facilities*: restrooms, showers, drinking water, picnic tables, barbecue area.

HOSTEL

YWCA Camp Sloggett (808-245-5959; campingkauai.com), Kokeʻe State Park, Hwy. 550. In addition to tent camping in an open field on the property, this YWCA has dorm-style bunk beds. You can also rent the caretaker's cottage or the Sloggett Lodge. *Rates*: $25 per person for hostel and family cabins in Sloggett Lodge; $85–120 for the caretaker's cottage; $7 for tent camping. *Facilities and amenities*: 66 beds, one cottage, one lodge.

✳ Where to Eat

Although the number of dining options dwindles as you head westward, those listed here are good.

DINING OUT

🍲 ✐ ᵧ **Waimea Brewing Company** (808-338-9733; waimeabrewing.com), Waimea Plantation Cottages, 9400 Kaumualiʻi Hwy., Waimea. Open 11–9 daily. This deservedly popular eatery has friendly service and delivers large portions of consistently good food at reasonable prices. I couldn't ask for anything more. I'm partial to the ale-battered fish-and-chips, chicken quesadillas, and barbecue ribs, but you can also be more serious with, perhaps, seared ahi covered in furikake (seaweed). The authentic plantation house is airy (and open air) and pleasant, with rattan and hardwood floors, but the tiki-lit deck is also quite nice. Choices, choices! Children's menu. Dishes $–$$$.

🍲 ᵧ **Hanapepe Café & Espresso Bar** (808-335-5011), 3830 Hanapepe Rd., Hanapepe. Open for lunch weekdays, dinner Fri. A real favorite because of the fun and funky atmosphere, as well as their commitment to creative cuisine, this café with a trademark U-shaped counter is lively and lovable. It's one of the friendliest eateries on Kauaʻi. Although the café creates a new dinner menu every week, it always showcases local seafood and cheesey vegetarian options with Italian influences. Save room for outrageous desserts. Dinner reservations recommended; children's menu. Lunch $–$$, dinner entrées $$$.

✐ **Wrangler's Steakhouse** (808-338-1218), Kaumualiʻi Hwy., Waimea. Open for lunch and dinner weekdays, dinner only Sat. This family-friendly former general store has all the atmospheric *paniolo* trappings you might expect: saddles, log booths, a stagecoach, and denim seats. (Or you can bypass that and eat on the back deck.) Big steaks sizzle at dinnertime, but lunch is more fun if you order a three-tier lunch pail filled with teriyaki, shrimp tempura, and rice. Children's menu. Lunch $$, dinner entrées $$–$$$$.

LAPPERT'S ICE CREAM

EATING OUT

Toi's Thai Kitchen (808-335-3111), Ele'ele Shopping Center, Kaumuali'i Hwy., Ele'ele. Open for lunch and dinner Mon.–Sat. (closed midafternoon). This casual place has loyal patrons who come for pad Thai, veggie curries, and lemongrass- or coconut-infused tofu, meat, and seafood dishes. Many of the herbs used are grown by the owners. Dishes $–$$.

Shrimp Station (808-338-1242), *makai*, 9652 Kaumuali'i Hwy., Waimea. Open for lunch daily. If you are craving shrimp, this roadside truck stop (literally) is the perfect spot for a breezy snack. The little guys are cooked almost every way imaginable. Dishes $$.

ICE CREAM & SHAVE ICE

Lappert's Ice Cream (808-335-6121), 3555 Kaumuali'i Hwy., Hanapepe. Open daily. First made in 1983 by a retired Hanapepe resident who wanted to keep busy, this rich ice cream is now sold islandwide. Try it with liliko'i, papaya, or lichee. Look

for outlets at the Coconut Marketplace in Kapa'a (The Coconut Coast) and on Koloa Road in Koloa (The South Shore).

Jo-Jo's Clubhouse 9734 Kaumuali'i Hwy., Waimea. Open 10:30–5:30 daily. Locals and tourists alike wait in line for this sticky sweet shave ice. And with 60 flavors of this popular Hawaiian treat, you'll know why. My favorite is the liliko'i with *azuki* beans.

JUST SO YOU KNOW

Koke'e Lodge (808-335-6061), at the end of Hwy. 550 in Koke'e State Park, is a rustic lodge perched at 3,600 feet that serves basic and hearty breakfasts and simple lunches. (I'd rather picnic.)

✳ Entertainment

Waimea Brewing Company (see *Dining Out*), which really does make

HANAPEPE SHOPPING

its own beer, often has live music at their pleasant bar. There's Hawaiian music on Thursday.

Hanapepe Café & Espresso Bar (see *Dining Out*), also has live music on Friday evenings.

✪ **Hanapepe Art Night**, Friday evenings 6–9. Okay, so it's not high art. But this is the best cultural event on the island. Wander Hanapepe's old streets while you sip wine, eat cheese and chocolate, listen to street musicians, and explore galleries that stay open late along Hanapepe Road. Paired with dinner at **Hanapepe Café** (see *Dining Out*), this is a wonderful way to spend a Friday evening.

✳ Selective Shopping

BOOKSTORES
Koke'e Natural History Museum (808-335-9975), at the end of Hwy. 550 within Koke'e State Park. Open daily. Among the top 10 bookstores in the state for all things relating to Hawai'i and Kaua'i, this book and gift shop is a great source for hiking maps.

Talk Story Books (808-335-6469), 3567 Hanapepe Rd., Hanapepe. Open on weekdays and Friday evenings, this bookshop/café sells new and used titles.

FARMER'S MARKETS
Sunshine Market (808-241-6390), Kekaha Neighborhood Center, Kekaha (Sat. at 9), and at Hanapepe Park (Thur. at 3).

SHOPPING AREAS
Hanapepe, off Hwy. 50, is basically a few blocks long and lined with little wooden storefronts. Still, you'll find a few excellent places that are definitely worth a stop.

Kekaha's little town center (on Hwy. 50), with a few local shops, is the last stop before heading up to Koke'e.

SPECIAL SHOPS
Koa Wood Gallery (808-335-5483), 3848 Hanapepe Rd., Hanapepe. Open 9–7 daily, Fri. until 9. (If the door is locked, head around the back, where you'll find Al working.) I can't keep my hands off Al's buttery-smooth koa creations in this fabulous gallery. From high-end tables and chairs to less expensive end tables, shipping these beautifully crafted pieces to the mainland is more affordable than you might think.

Kaua'i Fine Arts (808-335-3778), 3905 Hanapepe Rd., Hanapepe. Open weekdays 9:30–4:30, Fri. until 9. This is the best gift shop in the area.

Collectibles and Fine Junque (808-338-9855), Kaumuali'i Hwy., Waimea. Open Mon.–Sat. As the name implies and geography infers, you'll find Hawaiian collectibles and aloha shirts here.

Taro Ko Chips Factory (808-335-5586), 3940 Hanapepe Rd., Hanapepe. Open 8–5 weekdays. These handmade chips, laced with trademark purple taro "threads," are brought to you by the same farmers who grew the crops.

Red Dirt Shirt (808-335-5670; dirtshirt.com), 4350 Waialo Rd., 'Ele'ele. Open daily. The ubiquitous red dirt shirts are made here.

THE COCONUT COAST

The Coconut Coast, on the eastern shore of Kaua'i, is a fabled area rife with legends and myths, especially the area alongside the navigable **Wailua River**. The coastal Hwy. 56 (aka Prince Kuhio Highway), which runs along the entire shore, is riddled with a disproportionate number of coconut palm trees—hence its moniker. It's also lined with dozens of condos, hotels, and strip malls.

The center of the neighborhood, for visitors at least, is the Wailua River (with great kayaking) and **Lydgate State Park** (with the area's best swimming). A couple of good hikes and an intense mountain bike trail also originate here. Shopping is concentrated in the Coconut Plantation, but little strip malls on Hwy. 56 also harbor one-of-a-kind shops. The Wailua Golf Course is one of the top municipal values in a state known for its costly courses.

Kapa'a is a funky little town of wooden storefronts that looks like an old plantation town. But in actuality, most of it has been rebuilt since 1992 when Hurricane Iniki pounded everything to smithereens. You'll find the outstanding Blossoming Lotus or Hukilau Lanai here, as well as a surprisingly wide range of eateries, most of which are big on healthy options.

GETTING AROUND

By car: Hwy. 56 (aka Kuhio Highway) runs all along the eastern shore. Hwy. 580 (aka King's Highway, because it leads to an area rich with royal history) spurs *mauka* off Hwy. 56 in Wailua. Hwy. 581 (aka Olohena Road) spurs *mauka* off Hwy. 56 in Kapa'a. Traffic, by the way, grinds to a crawl during the morning and afternoon rush hours; try to come through here between 9:30 and 3:30, or after dark.

✳ To See & Do

Exploring from South to North along Hwy. 56
✿ ⨍ **Lydgate State Park**. See *Beaches*.

East to West on Hwy. 580
Wailua River State Park, *mauka*. The wettest place on Kaua'i, Mount Wai'ale'ale, feeds the 20-mile Wailua River, which is navigable by kayak and runs parallel to much of Hwy. 580. The region is said to have been founded by Puna, a Tahitian

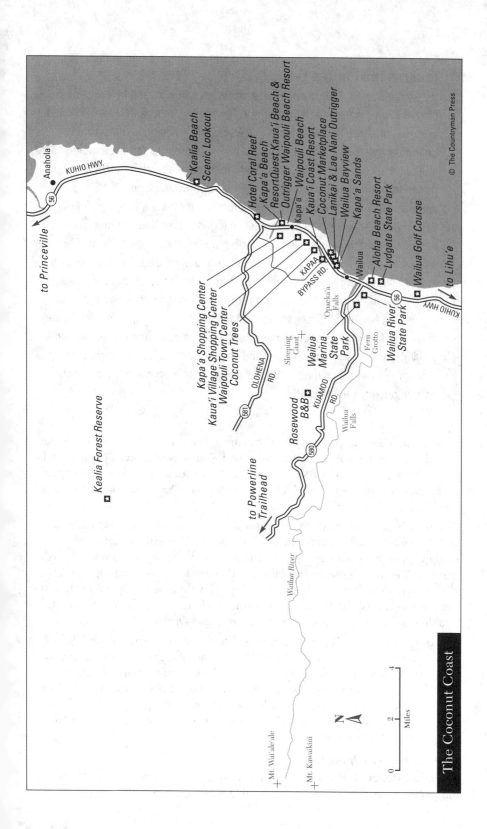

The Coconut Coast

LOOKING INIKI IN THE EYE

On September 11, 1992, Kaua'i residents were jolted awake by the shrill cry of civil sirens. After snapping on their TVs, they quickly learned a hurricane hovering offshore had escalated to a F5 rating and made a sharp turn in their direction. With only a few hours' notice, residents gathered their loved ones and barricaded themselves inside their homes to wait. Hurricane Iniki ripped through their communities with average wind speeds of 145 mph. A whopping 227 mph wind rating was recorded on Makaha Ridge in Koke'e State Park. The eye of the storm passed directly over Kaua'i, and right when people thought the worst was over, another devastating gust struck. Miraculously only six people died that day, but the total repair bill was estimated at $1.6 billion. With homes demolished, forests flattened, and resorts ragged, the people of Kaua'i banded together to rebuild. Nature, too, has a way of repairing devastation. Things on the island are certainly back to normal, and in most places you'd never even know they were once destroyed. However, you will pass by an occasional gutted building, its renovation postponed by insurance claims disputes. If you get a chance to watch a video of Iniki's horrific power, don't miss it.

priest from whom all of Kaua'i's royalty came. The state park encompasses this sacred land and contains the remains of no less than seven ancient *heiaus* and royal birthing stones. All of Kaua'i's nobility was born against these stones; the umbilical cords of the future chiefs were wrapped in kapa and placed inside a crack in these boulders.

Poli'ahu Heiau, off Hwy. 580, which was built by Kaua'i's last king (Kaumuali'i), and **'Opaeka'a Falls**, a dramatic 40-foot cascade (the name means "rolling shrimp"), are just up the street from the state park. Once upon a time, the falls were so filled with these crustaceans that they could be seen roaring over the cliff from quite a distance. Across the street, way down in the Wailua Valley, you can see the huts of the **Kamokila Hawaiian Village**, a decent re-creation that doubled as an African village in Dustin Hoffman's *Outbreak*.

Sleeping Giant, *mauka*; turn onto Hale'ilio Road from Hwy. 56. Look for a horizontal profile of the mythical creature that ate the villagers' *taro* and fish, promptly fell asleep, and never woke up. Better yet, hike the well-marked trail to the top of the slumbering fella. The 1.75-mile trail has a 1,000-foot ascent, so it's not for grannies in sneakers, but it should take midlevel hikers about an hour one-way. Toward the end of the trail there's a left turn, so to speak, that yields stunning views of the east coast.

Continuing North on Hwy. 56

ϔ **Wailua Beach**. If you simply can't wait to get in the water, it's okay here as long as the waves are small. Novice surfing is also okay here.

⚓ **Kapaʻa Beach Park**, near Hwy. 581. Locals predominate at this beach park, which is geared to barbecuing and picnicking.

⚓ **Kealia Beach**, at the Kapaʻa Stream Bridge. More suited to suntanning than to swimming, this is nonetheless a scenic area.

✳ Spas

Angeline's Muʻolaulani (808-822-3235; auntyangelines.com), Anahola. For 20 years Angeline has been treating sore muscles her way—with four hands. Though not actually a day spa, you'll be more than relaxed after her signature salt scrub, steam, and four-handed *lomi lomi* massage.

✳ Outdoor Activities

BICYCLING

Powerline Trail, trailhead at the end of Hwy. 580 at the Keahua Forest Arboretum. This challenging 12-mile mountain bike and hiking trail ends in Princeville and offers great views of Mount Waiʻaleʻale. The first half of the trail is far more interesting than the second half, so instead of arranging transportation pickup in Princeville or riding back, just bike or hike the first half and turn around. Among other things, it's often very muddy; you'll want to bring plenty of water and food and talk with the local bike outfitters.

GOLF

Wailua Golf Course (808-241-6666), 3-5350 Kuhio Hwy., Lihuʻe. Rated one of the top 10 municipal golf courses in the United States, this 18-hole, par-72 course is open to the public daily. It attracts a dedicated crowd, so it can get busy. Greens fees run $32 weekdays and $44 weekends. You can make reservations seven days ahead of time.

HIKING

Kuilau Ridge and Moalepe Trails, from the Keahua Forest Arboretum on Hwy. 580; trailhead on the right where Hwy. 580 and 581 cross the riverbed at the arboretum. These two trails, 4 miles round-trip each, offer great bang for the buck. Take 45 minutes and hike the first 1.25 miles for ridgetop views of Mount Waiʻaleʻale, primal valleys, and the coast. Or better yet, keep going for another mile beyond that (along a narrow but well-marked trail) for even more stunning views. Along the way, you'll pass through lots of dense foliage and thimbleberries.

Also see **Sleeping Giant** under *To See & Do*, as well as *Bicycling*, above.

HAWAIʻI'S ONLY NAVIGABLE RIVER, THE WAILUA

LEIS

The custom of wearing flower garlands was first recorded by a member of Captain Cook's crew in 1779. Since then visitors have been as enchanted by wearing leis (pronounced *lays*) as they have been by the ritual of receiving one. May 1, or Lei Day, is a glorious, all-island day of celebration when everyone is adorned with colorful and exquisitely crafted leis.

Marie McDonald, prizewinning lei artist and author of *Ka Lei*, a history of lei making, provides insight into the act of giving a lei. "Many people have difficulty saying 'I love you.' In Hawai'i, we get around the words by giving a lei," she explains. "Giving a lei lets someone know you love, respect, and honor them. Even though a floral lei lasts a short time, the thought behind it lingers."

Although vintage episodes of *The Love Boat* suggest that everyone in Hawai'i receives a lei upon arrival, this is not the case. Still, if you have your heart set on "getting leid" on arrival, there is hope. **Kama'aina Leis, Flowers & Greeters** (808-836-3246 or 1-800-367-5183) charges $16 on O'ahu and $20 on neighbor islands; give them three days' notice. **Greeters of Hawai'i** (1-800-366-8559; greetersofhawaii.com) charges $25–50 per person (or $15 for a *keiki*, or a candy lei) and requires 48-hour advance notice.

Leis on each island feature local native plants. **Big Island** leis are made of lehua blossoms from 'ohi'a lehua trees, which grow around volcanoes. The flowers (mostly red, but also white, yellow, and orange) are sacred to the volcano goddess Pele. **Kaua'i**'s long-lasting leis are made with purplish berries from mokihana, which smell like anise and are strung like beads. On **Kaho'olawe** the stems and flowers of hinahina, a silver-gray plant found on local beaches, are braided into lovely leis. On **Lana'i** light orange, threadlike strands of the kaunaoa (a parasitic vine) are twisted together to make leis. **Maui**'s pink lokelani or "rose of heaven" makes for a sweet-scented and very delicate lei. On **Moloka'i** the leaves, white flowers, and nuts of the silver-green kekui, or candlenut, tree are braided together. On secretive **Ni'ihau** white puka shells found along the shoreline are pierced and strung on cords and sold for lots of money. On **O'ahu** the yellow-orange 'ilima lei, sometimes called a royal lei, is velvety, paper-thin, and very delicate.

KAYAKING

Wailua River Kayak Adventures (808-822-5795; kauaiwailuakayak .com), Kuhio Hwy., Kapa'a. If you feel like renting your own kayak, packing your own picnic, and setting out up the Wailua River (with map in hand), these conveniently located folks rent kayaks ($25–50 a day).

Kaua'i County Parks and Recreation Department. The islandwide recreation department maintains two lighted courts at Kapa'a New Park on Olohena Road in Kapa'a; two lighted courts at Wailua Homesteads Park on Kamalu Road in Wailua; and two lighted courts at Wailua Houselots Park on Nounou Road in Wailua.

WATER SPORTS

Snorkel Bob's (808-823-9433; snorkelbob.com), 4-734 Kuhio Hwy., Kapa'a. Open 8–5 daily. This one-stop shop has something for every aquatic adventurer. Their enthusiastic and knowledgeable staff can outfit folks with gear for all levels. Snorkeling gear costs $5–8 daily, boards $22–32.

✳ Beaches

In general, swimming on the Coconut Coast isn't great because of rip currents, waves, often windy conditions, and jellyfish. But that doesn't mean there aren't plenty of places to suntan and enjoy sweeping Pacific views. There is one place, though, that stands out along the shore.

✦ **Lydgate State Park**, *makai*, off Leho Rd. from Hwy. 56, 5 miles north of Lihu'e, at the mouth of the Wailua River. A wall has created a natural pool to protect the area from pounding surf, making it one of the few places on the eastern shore to safely swim and snorkel. It's popular and blessed with ironwood trees, a coconut grove, lava pools, and ancient *heiaus*. Before Captain Cook arrived, this was a place of refuge for Hawaiians who'd broken *kapu* (or committed crimes). If they reached this place before their punishers did, they'd avoid punishment—which frequently meant being spared their lives. *Facilities*: restrooms, lifeguards (most of the time), playground, parking, nice picnicking, showers, camping, barbecue area.

✳ Lodging

The Coconut Coast, not a particularly trendy area, remains a value-conscious choice. It's also popular among those splitting their time between the North and South Shores—those who don't want to drive the entire length of the island after adventuring all day. Many of my lodging suggestions are on the bay, where the sands are good for sunning and strolling but not necessarily for swimming. You'll also find some good B&Bs and vacation rentals inland, surrounded by great mountain views and friendly residents.

RESORTS & HOTELS

ResortQuest Kaua'i Beach at Makaiwa (808-822-3455 or 1-866-774-2924; resortquesthawaii.com), 650 Aleka Loop, Kapa'a. Formerly a Courtyard by Marriott, this beachfront property underwent a huge renovation in 2006. Smallish rooms, decorated in Indonesian teak, speak to a plush and contemporary Hawaiian aesthetic. Set amid a historic coconut grove, it's quite convenient to shopping and dining. Ask about their Tahitian-style lu'au, which is one of the best shows on the island for the lowest price. *Rates*: $$$–$$$$; children free in parent's room. *Facilities and amenities*: 311 rooms, pool, beach (unsafe swimming), two restaurants, lounge with nightly entertainment, tennis courts, health club, spa, concierge, parking (fee), resort fee (includes discounts on spa treatments and WiFi).

♫ **Aloha Beach Resort** (808-823-6000 or 1-888-823-5111; abrkauai .com), 3-5920 Kuhio Hwy., Kapaʻa. This might be the best resort deal on the island, hands down. When you consider the old-school Hawaiian aloha, rooms renovated in 2006, and its location on the Coconut Coast's best beach—it's hard to beat. It's a great choice for budget-conscious couples *and* families. *Rates*: $$; children free in parent's room. *Facilities and amenities:* 216 rooms and suites, two pools, two restaurants, tennis courts, close to a great beach, lounge, fitness room, concierge, children's programs, parking (free).

♨ **Hotel Coral Reef** (808-822-4481 or 1-800-843-4659; hotelcoralreef .com), 1516 Kuhio Hwy., Kapaʻa. This old-fashioned budget haven has appealed to bargain hunters since the 1960s. Friendly and small, the hotel has a great location; you simply can't get any closer to a white-sand beach than this. New owners have big dreams of turning this into a "resort" and have renovated the rooms, but you can still get pretty good deals. I'd splurge for the oceanfront rooms; the two-room units have a separate living room with a pullout sofa for families. *Rates*: $–$$; children free in parent's room. *Facilities and amenities:* 24 rooms, beach (safe swimming), pool, activity desk, A/C, some rooms with kitchenettes, parking (free).

CONDOS & APARTMENTS

♫ **Outrigger Waipouli Beach Resort & Spa** (808-822-6000 or 1-866-508-9565; outriggerwaipouli beachcondo.com), 4-820 Kuhio Hwy., Kapaʻa. If you want the perks of a resort *and* your own kitchen, look no further. Spacious one- and two-bedroom condos, though individually owned, generally cater to folks who want subzero refrigeration, Jacuzzi tubs, and Tommy Bahama décor. *Rates:* $$$–$$$$; children free in parent's room; two-night minimum stay. *Facilities and amenities:* 118 condos, two pools (and water slides), full kitchen, fitness room, concierge, **Aveda Spa & Salon**, A/C, water sports rentals, WiFi (free), parking (free).

Kauaʻi Coast Resort at the Beachboy (808-822-3441 or 1-877-977-4355; shellhospitality.com), 520 Aleka Loop, Kapaʻa. This oceanfront timeshare is doing something right. Maybe it is the red, green, and gold accents, or the carpeting, or perhaps the hardwood furnishings. Most likely the rooms are filled because of its close proximity to the ocean and sweet deals on tours (if you're willing to suffer through a time-share presentation). Regardless, it's a good deal. *Rates:* $$–$$$ (shop online for discounts). *Facilities and amenities:* 108 studios; one-, two-, and three-bedroom condos; excellent restaurant (see **Hukilau Lanai** in *Dining Out*); pool; lounge with nightly entertainment, A/C, condos have kitchens, high-speed Internet (fee).

Lae Nani Outrigger (808-822-4938 or 1-800-688-7444; outrigger.com), 410 Papaloa Rd., Kapaʻa. It's nothing fancy, but this beachfront condo complex with safe swimming offers one- and two-bedroom units with separate

HUNTING WILD PIGS

In March 2006, steady rainfall kept us from hiking many of Kaua'i's trails. But for one brief period the downpour stopped, and we resolved to hike the Kuilau Ridge Trail, famed for its spectacular views. It was an easy ride up to the trailhead, and we kept wondering why we saw so many pickups with dogs in them. Arriving at the trailhead, we parked and began the beautiful steady upward climb. We met no one. Our trail resembled a creek more than a trail due to the heavy storm system visiting the island. Looking out over the heavily forested misty valley below, I recalled scenes from *Jurassic Park* and half-expected to see a T. Rex chasing down its prey. As we drew close to the top of the mountain, we rounded a corner and there, standing right in the middle of the trail, stood a heavyset man, machete in one hand and pit bull sitting by his side. My heart took a leap. I recalled that just the day before, on another trail, we'd seen a poster saying that a hiker had been missing for two months. Could this man standing in the trail with a machete be a killer? I whispered to my husband, "Should we turn around?" He said, "No, we've climbed this far, I'm going to the top!" But I could see that he, too, was nervous. So we continued to walk straight toward him. He continued to stare at us, machete in hand, and pit bull by his side. As we passed him, my husband greeted him in a light, cheery fashion, "Good morning! How's it going?" The man grunted.

We made it to the top and marveled at the breathtaking view. This trail is definitely worth the hike. But we had to return by the same trail. (The Moalepe Trail intersects with the Kuilau Ridge Trail, but it takes you down another watershed and ends at 'Olohena Road, far from where we parked our car.) As we turned around and started back down, I reviewed with my husband how we would do hand-to-hand combat with a machete-wielding man with a pit bull. I worried about the dog; my husband fretted about the machete. When we came to the spot where we had encountered the man, he was gone. The return trip was uneventful.

On our way down the road, we stopped at a roadside stand to buy coconut milk—something every visitor to the island should try. The vendor sticks a straw right into the coconut and you sip right out of it! I told the Hawaiian about our encounter. He laughed, and said, "Oh, you just met a real Hawaiian wild pig hunter! The native way to hunt wild pigs is to hamstring them with a machete while the dog distracts them. Then they kill them. Usually they lose a dog or two in the process!"

—Ann Rutherford

living rooms, large lanais, and full kitchens. That's about all you need around here. Oh, it's also adjacent to the Coconut Marketplace. Rosewood and Castle also rent units here—often for much cheaper than Outrigger, but without the resort frills. *Rates: $$– $$$$. Facilities and amenities:* 59 rooms, pool, beach (sandy and swimmable), full kitchens, tennis courts (free), concierge, parking (free).

Kapa'a Sands (808-822-4901 or 1-800-222-4901; kapaasands.com), 380 Papaloa Rd., Kapa'a. Few Kaua'i lodging places reviewed in this guide enjoy a higher year-round occupancy rate than this beachfront condo. It's a small, unassuming property on a side street off busy Kuhio Highway, near Wailua Beach and almost camouflaged from sight by palms, pines, and lush foliage. Five buildings sit directly on the Pacific; the others are only a bit farther back. The two-level, two-bedroom units, which sleep five, should also be seriously considered by couples. I like that the upstairs master bedroom has its own ocean-facing lanai. As for the ground-floor studios, some feel a tad cramped, but otherwise the individually decorated condos are ideal. In order to increase the sense of spaciousness, ask for one with a Murphy bed in the living room rather than one with two twins. The beach here is a bit scruffy, but you can walk along it to better sands. Once you discover Kapa'a Sands, one of those semiprecious gems underrated by conventional wisdom, you'll probably join the parade of returning guests. *Rates: $–$$;* cleaning fee; three-night minimum stay. *Facilities and amenities:* 21 units, pool, kitchen, beach, no A/C.

Lanikai (808-822-7700 or 1-800-367-5004; castleresorts.com), 390 Papaloa Rd., Kapa'a. The most exclusive condos in the area overlook an oceanfront pool and scenic Wailua Bay. Other condos on both sides share the shore, but at Lanikai you will feel as if you are on a private estate, aloof from the nearby crowds. The apartments are spacious (at 1,450 square feet) and contemporary, featuring every convenience you might want, except air-conditioning in most cases. The condos differ mainly in the location of the master bedrooms. Half are on the Pacific side; the others are on the street side. Request the ocean-oriented version, which also has a larger lanai running the length of the apartment, with entrances from both the living room and bedroom. The beach in front is scrawny, but if you don't mind mixing with the masses temporarily, you can easily walk to better sands nearby. And when you return to your select enclave later, you can refresh yourself at the wet bar and toast the Lanikai's swanky detachment. *Rates: $$$–$$$$;* children free in parent's room. *Facilities and amenities:* about half of the 18 two-bedroom units are rented; pool, no A/C, kitchen, daily maid service.

🌀 **Wailua Bayview** (1-425-391-0207 or 1-800-882-9007; wailuabay.com), 320 Papaloa Rd., Kapa'a. Situated just above Wailua Beach on a slight rise, these small seaside condos sit closer to the ocean than any others in the neighborhood. And their lanais have a great vantage point, looking down on the expansive beach. For the money, these units are perhaps the best on Kaua'i. For the optimum view, get an apartment on the second or third floor of the low-rise wooden building. Units are individually decorated, but you can probably count on tropical décor replete with rattan. *Rates: $$;*

maximum four people per unit; four-night minimum stay. *Facilities and amenities:* 45 one-bedroom units, pool, beach (safe for swimming, depending on tidal conditions), A/C and WiFi in most units.

BED & BREAKFASTS

☙ Rosewood Bed & Breakfast

(808-822-5216; rosewoodkauai.com), 872 Kamalu Rd., Kapaʻa. From the moment you spot the white picket fence surrounding the tidy front yard, you know that Rosewood is a cut above other B&Bs in Hawaiʻi. Rosemary and Norbert Smith began renting rooms in the late 1980s and never looked back. But you, you'll look across the street to a mesmerizing panoramic mountain range and valley. There are as many rental options here as there are colors in a rainbow. Colleen's Dream cottage, tucked away behind the main house, features a wicker king-sized bed and a screened porch (with kitchenette). It's delightfully private, right down to the outside shower. The upscale Victorian guest house is plum pickings, complete with a modern kitchen, hardwood floors, tidy layout, master bedroom, and an upstairs loft (great for kids). You could easily settle in for a week. The B&B suite in the main house offers splendid mountain vistas and the chance to have breakfast with your generous hosts. Three tiny but efficient bunk-style rooms (with shared bath) are perfect for backpackers and adventures. If you've splurged at an expensive resort and are ready to do some hiking, stay here! (Not to be outshone, these rooms also enjoy an outdoor shower.) The latest acquisition is a beauty: an adjacent free-standing house called Shannon's Serenity, with upscale but comfort-able furnishings and a spacious layout that accommodates socializing and privacy for a family or two couples traveling together. I could easily settle in for a couple of weeks. *Rates:* $–$$; children free in parent's room; three-night minimum. *Facilities and amenities:* three cottages, bunkhouse with three shared bathrooms, B&B suite, breakfast on the first and last morning, no A/C, free Internet, phones, no credit cards.

Kauaʻi Country Inn (808-821-0207; kauaicountryinn.com), 6440 Olohena Rd., Wailua. Attention Beatles fans: You won't want to miss this place. Owners Mike and Martina have created quite a Beatles museum (that houses one of the band's original Mini Coopers). The attention to detail that energetic Mike spends on his affection for the Fab Four seeps into the rooms as well. No, you won't find Beatles memorabilia taped to the bathroom walls. Instead you'll find Hawaiian-motif rooms with colorful murals, marble baths, private BBQs and lanais, hardwood floors, comfy beds, and sweeping mountain views. *Rates:* $–$$; four-night minimum; no children under 12. *Facilities and amenities:* five one- to two-bedroom

ROSEWOOD BED & BREAKFAST

suites and one three-bedroom cottage, hot tub, no A/C, free beach gear, full kitchen or kitchenette, WiFi (free).

🦐 🐚 **Inn Paradise** (808-822-2542; innparadisekauai.com), 6381 Makana Rd., Kapa'a. Located on 3 somewhat residential acres, complete with a stream and seasonal waterfalls, this place is ideal for a six-person group, especially since the outside lanai is connected to all three units. Although the décor and furnishings are modest rattan and wicker, it's all immaculately maintained by the friendly owners who live next door. (Guests are entirely welcome to use the hot tub at their house.) As for sleeping quarters, all units have king beds, one unit has two bedrooms, and one has a Murphy bed for additional guests. Each unit also has a kitchen, whether it's merely a kitchenette or full-sized. And for a refreshing change with smaller accommodations, children are welcome. *Rates:* $; three-night minimum. *Facilities and amenities:* three units, TV, welcome basket, hot tub.

VACATION RENTALS

Rosewood Kaua'i Vacation Rentals (808-822-5216; rosewoodkauai.com). Proprietor, all-around island booster, and perfectionist businesswoman Rosemary Smith runs a great rental agency. I trust her selection of properties implicitly, and her Web site is easy to navigate. What more could you want? I'm particularly head over heels about their River Rim Villa property, a stunning house magnificently situated overlooking the Wailua River. Measuring almost 5,000 square feet, the three-bedroom and three-bath house is a bargain. It's outfitted with upscale appointments, luxe

linens, a gourmet kitchen, and a baby grand piano. As an added bonus, a gazebo and hot tub overlook the river. Why bother waiting another minute to reserve?

🦐 **Rainbow's End** (808-823-0086; rainbowsendkauai.com), 6470 Kipapa Rd., Kapa'a. Don't need surf and sand? Want a great central location that also provides value? Look no further. Located just 3 miles inland from Kapa'a, this rural and perfectly renovated Victorian cottage is a personal favorite. While "rural" in Hawai'i may mean only an acre, at least this cottage is surrounded by vegetation and feels very private. Although smallish (guests are advised to travel light), the cottage more than makes up for it in detail and amenities. The owners, who are available next door but will respect your privacy, have lovingly restored this little Fabergé jewel—right down to lovely hinges, a period telephone, a claw-foot Jacuzzi tub, and a two-person outdoor shower. High-quality toiletries and linens are luxurious; the queen bed linens change with the seasons. (Upcountry winters may require a blanket.) If it gets too quiet for you in the evenings, a TV and VCR are nicely tucked into custom casework in the bedroom. In the morning, filtered sun streams through stained-glass windows into the galley kitchen as you enjoy a continental breakfast culled from the stocked refrigerator. *Rates:* $–$$. *Facilities and amenities:* one cottage, continental breakfast, TV, phone.

🦐 **Opaeka'a Falls Hale** (1-888-822-9956; opaekaafallskauai.ws), 120 Lihau St., Kapa'a. True to its name, this residential property sits on a cliff overlooking the Wailua River just inland from Kapa'a. Based simply on central location and price, it's a great find. Both units (one up and one down) have private entrances and a full kitchen; they share the beautifully landscaped grounds, which include a pool, hot tub, and barbecue area. The upper unit, with a king-sized bed, has an elevated lanai for better river viewing. *Rates*: $–$$; three-night minimum; $50 cleaning fee. *Facilities and amenities*: TV, phone, welcome basket, pool, no credit cards.

✴ Where to Eat

Foodies flock to Blossoming Lotus, but there are a surprising number of other fine choices that are both palate pleasing and healthful. Also check out the Tahitian lu'au at the ResortQuest Kaua'i Beach at Makaiwa (see *Lodging*). Kapa'a, by the way, happens to be fast-food central.

DINING OUT

☙ ✪ **Hukilau Lanai** (808-822-0600), Kaua'i Coast Resort at Beach Boy, 520 Aleka Loop, Wailua. Open for dinner nightly. Locals head to this seafood spot when they're ready for a fine night out. Torch-lit patio dining on super-fresh fish (prepared with sweet sauces) gives me enough reason to return over and over again. Throw in live music in the lounge, great cocktails (including 20 wines for under $20), reasonable prices, friendly staff, and killer desserts, and you've got a must-visit for Coconut Coast diners. Entrées $$$.

☙ ✪ **Blossoming Lotus** (808-822-7678; blossominglotus.com), 4504 Kukui St., Kapa'a. Open for dinner nightly and Sunday brunch. Even if a meal without meat, fish, or dairy seems odd, give this vegan restaurant a try. It's the foodie spot du jour.

Ensconced in a spacious yet small dining room, you'll not be disappointed by their creative takes on Indian, Greek, Mexican, and American food (my favorite is the enchilada casserole). Though dinners are spectacular (especially paired with organic beer and wine, live music, and a friendly staff), I'm partial to their inexpensive brunch offerings. The corn bread is out of this world (which may be why it's called "cosmic"), and the spelt cinnamon-raisin French toast will have you wondering, "What *was* all the fuss about eggs anyway?" Sunday brunch $, dinner entrées $$.

☙ **Caffe Coco** (808-822-7990), 4-369 Kuhio Hwy., Kapa'a. Open for dinner Tues.–Sun. This little roadside café, set back from the highway, is utterly appealing in a delightfully funky way. Surrounded by tropical trees that bear fruit used in many recipes, you'll dine on surprisingly creative dishes in an outdoor, tiki-lit gravel courtyard. Expect large portions of healthful *and* gourmet cuisine—from salads and fish to vegetarian dishes, and lots of mosquitoes. Dinner entrées $$–$$$. BYOB.

DOVES ROOSTING IN A BANYON TREE

ISLAND FLORA

African Tulip Tree

At over 50 feet tall with scarlet-red flower buds that form a ball-shaped cluster, this fun tree is prime for play: The banana-shaped flower buds are filled with water and form a natural water pistol when squeezed. And when the ripe pods split open, they're good for boat races.

ANTHURIUM

Anthuriums

At first glance these heart-shaped bracts look plastic; their feel and texture is rubbery and shiny. But since they last a long time and come in many shades of red, pink, green, white, and pastel, they're highly valued in cut-flower displays.

Banyan Tree

Soaring some 60 feet, with canopies stretching nearly across a city block, these romantic trees look surreal. Sharing the same genus as the common fig tree, banyan branches send shoots toward the ground that eventually take root. These, in essence, become additional trunks and create a labyrinth of limbs supporting the main trunk.

Bird-of-Paradise

Originally from South Africa, this tropical herb flower belongs in the banana family. The flowers (several on each stalk) resemble a long-beaked bird with orange and blue plumes jutting from the crown of its head.

Breadfruit Tree

Hawai'i has the world's largest collection of 'ulu, which was harvested for canoes, surfboards, and drums. It's so important, in fact, that an entire institute is dedicated to breadfruit (breadfruit.org). And yes, the 2- to 5-pound fruit (before it's fully ripened) tastes like fresh bread.

Bromeliad

Although there are over 2,700 bromeliad species, the pineapple is by far the best known. All bromeliads sport spiral leaf arrangements called rosettes; with few exceptions, a flower stalk rises from the rosette's core.

Coffee

Hawai'i is the only U.S. state that produces commercial coffee. Thriving at elevations of 800 to 2,000 feet, a coffee tree needs two years to produce its first fruit, but four years to produce its first crop. You'll find plantations on the Big Island (Kona side), Kaua'i, Moloka'i, and Maui. The plant's flower, by the way, is a small, fragrant white blossom. And the "cherries" (or berries) produced by the flowers turn red when they ripen.

Ginger

This gorgeous, juicy-red flower shaped like a beehive is almost essential in tropical bouquets and grows natively in Hawai'i. The root is used in culinary dishes, while the flower can be used as shampoo.

Hibiscus

With over 200 species and large, ostentatious flowers that range in color from lily white to shocking magenta, hibiscus are very much associated with Hawai'i. And why not? The state flower is the endemic yellow hibiscus, and hibiscus shapes are plastered on fabrics all around the island.

Jacaranda

This impressive tree comes alive in spring. After the evocative, bell-shaped, bright purple flowers burst open, they fall quickly and cover the ground in a soft carpet.

Macadamia

Originally from Australia, these trees are cultivated for their large sweet nuts, which grow in clusters and are a delicacy all over the world.

Monkeypod Tree

One of the largest trees in Hawai'i, monkeypods can grow more than 80 feet tall and 100 feet across.

Orchid

With intoxicating aromas and dazzling colors, orchids are alluring. For dazzling displays, check out Big Island farms near Hilo or the gardens at Kiahuna Plantation on Kaua'i.

Pandanus (Hala)

Hala is easy to recognize: An exposed nest of roots helps support the tree, and its strange fruit looks like a sectioned pineapple. Hawaiians still weave pandanus leaves (*lauhala*) into useful items like hats and bowls.

Plumeria

This tropical flowering tree (sometimes called frangipani) comes in a plethora of colors and sizes and is prized for its flowers and use in ornamental landscaping.

Protea

Belonging to an ancient family of flowering plants, the ancestors of proteas can be traced back 300 million years. Strangely alluring, their flower heads have a thistlelike quality. One of the most impressive, the king protea (*Protea cynaroides*), looks like an artichoke.

Silversword

Almost lost to extinction in the 1920s because of vandalism and grazing, this distinctive plant is a great conservation success story. Still, it's found only on the Big Island and the Haleakala Crater on Maui. Please, give its roots a wide berth by treading lightly around it. Otherwise, you risk killing it. When the plant eventually flowers, it produces a stalk up to 6 feet high that's decorated with hundreds of sunflower like heads.

Taro

Ancient Hawaiians felt *taro* was so integral to their daily survival that the word for "family" (*'ohana*) is derived from the word *'oha*, which describes the shoot that grows from the *taro* plant. *Taro* root is still used to make food today. *Taro* chips are delightful and addictive; *poi*, a *taro* root mash, is so sacred to Hawaiians that fighting is not permitted when a bowl of *poi* is offered.

Ⓨ **Coconuts Island Style Grill** (808-823-8777) 4-919 Kuhio Hwy., Kapa'a. Open 4–10 Mon.–Sat. Popular with the *pupu*-and-tropical-drinks crowd, Coconuts also features a worthy, eclectic main menu. Try the spicy lobster bisque, tempura ono with ginger wasabi, or even the polenta. A tropical atmosphere prevails thanks to a liberal use of coconuts and bamboo. Reservations recommended; children's menu. Entrées $$$.

EATING OUT

Ⓢ **Mermaids Café** (808-821-2026), 1384 Kuhio Hwy., Kapa'a. Open 11–8:45 daily. Healthy foods with fresh flavors predominate in Mermaid's wraps and chicken satay. Since this teensy sidewalk café has limited seating (which is subject to road noise and exhaust), consider taking your food out. Dishes $.

Ⓢ **Papaya's Natural Foods** (808-823-0190), Kaua'i Village Shopping Center, 4-831 Kuhio Hwy., Kapa'a. Open Mon.–Sat. Filled with earthy-crunchy, granola-munching hippies, this whole-food store has great salads, sandwiches, and the like. After stocking up on natural groceries, take your lunch or dinner to one of the few outside tables. Dishes $–$$.

Ⓢ **Duane's Ono-Char Burger** (808-822-9181), 4-4350 Kuhio Hwy., Anahola. Open 11–6 daily. This roadside burger stand serves *ono* (delicious) char burgers, if they do say so themselves. And they can, because they really do. I bet you've never had a burger like Duane's. The avocado burger is a personal favorite, but vegetarians won't feel slighted—Duane's also makes a nonbeef patty. Dishes $.

Monico's Taqueria (808-822-4300), Kinipopo Shopping Village, 4-356D Kuhio Hwy., Kapa'a. Open for lunch and dinner Wed.–Mon. This family-owned Mexican restaurant serves up some of the best tacos on the island. I always call ahead and take my food to the beach. Dishes $–$$.

Ono Family Restaurant (808-822-1710), 4-1292 Kuhio Hwy., Kapa'a. Open 7:30–1:30 daily. Breakfast at this local hole-in-the-wall is as the name *ono* brags—delicious. Don't waste your time looking at the menu: order the griddle fare. Fast. I still dream about their homemade coconut syrup, served piping hot. Dishes $.

Olympic Café (808-822-5825), 4-1354 Kuhio Hwy., Kapa'a. Open daily 7 AM–9 PM. On the second floor in the center of Old Kapa'a Town, this open-air restaurant is deservedly popular with locals, who sit on stools and watch the action on the street below. There's plenty of fresh breakfast fare for meat lovers and vegans, and for lunch—gigantic salads, sandwiches, Mexican-themed *pupus*, and plate lunches (I love the ahi salad). A healthy cocktail menu makes this a happening spot all hours of the day. Breakfast $–$$, lunch and dinner $$–$$$.

Pono Market (808-822-4581), 4-1300 Kuhio Hwy., Kapa'a. Open 7–7 most days (until 8 PM Fri. and 4 PM Sun.). Inexpensive and delicious plate lunch specials with daily specials bring out the Hawaiian in us all. This little market in the center of town is a dependable choice for beach picnics or take-home dinners for the family. You can also buy *leis* here. Dishes $.

Small Town Coffee (808-821-1604; smalltowncoffee.com), 4-1495 Kuhio Hwy., Kapaʻa. Open daily 5:30 AM– 9 PM, until 4 PM on Sun. Though it doesn't offer much in the way of food, this is the best coffeehouse on the island, brewing up award-winning lattes. People drive from all over the island to hang on the lanai, listen to live music, or surf the Web.

Kintaro Restaurant (808-822-3341), 4-370 Kuhio Hwy., Wailua. Open Mon.–Sat. for dinner. Okay, I don't love this massive sushi and *teppan* table restaurant, but it seems everyone else on the island does. Big sushi rolls (that rely heavily on eel and salmon) and loud cocktail libations have locals and tourists lining up. Reservations recommended for *teppan* tables. Entrées $$–$$$.

JUST SO YOU KNOW

Bull Shed (808-822-3791; bullshed restaurant.com), Kuhio Hwy., Kapaʻa. Rather like Sizzler chain restaurant, the Bull Shed is popular because of its waterfront views and reasonably priced steaks.

✻ Entertainment

Coconut Marketplace Movie Theater (808-822-3641), Kuhio Hwy., Kapaʻa. Two screens for first-run flicks.

Coconuts Island Style Grill (see *Dining Out*) serves cocktails and *pupus.*

Hukilau Lanai (see *Dining Out*) has live music and delicious cocktails.

See the ResortQuest Kauaʻi Beach at *Makaiwa* (*Lodging*) for their **Tahitian luʻau.**

✻ Selective Shopping

FARMER'S MARKETS

Sunshine Market (808-241-6390), at Kapaʻa New Town Park, Kahau Rd., Kapaʻa. Wed. at 3 PM.

Kauaʻi Products Fair (808-246-0988; kauaiproductsfair.com), Kuhio Hwy., Kapaʻa. Open Thur.–Sun., but there are lots more vendors on the weekend. You'll find more than food here; crafts, arts, and collectibles are all represented.

SHOPPING AREAS

Coconut Marketplace (808-822-3641), Kuhio Hwy., Kapaʻa. With almost 75 shops (and a few not-particularly-recommended restaurants) in one open-air-style pavilion, this marketplace could keep shoppers busy for a while. Look for coveted Niʻihau shell leis at Kauaʻi Gold (808-822-9361). Open daily.

Kapaʻa, strung out along Kuhio Hwy., is lined with a few tasteful strip malls and many independent shops.

SPECIAL SHOPS

Hula Girl (808-822-1950), 4-1340 Kuhio Hwy., Kapaʻa. Open daily. For aloha shirts, as well as fanciful and fun gifts, Hula Girl has it (and so could you).

Tin Can Mailman Fine Books and Curiosities (808-822-3009), 4-356 Kuhio Hwy., Kapaʻa. Open Mon.–Sat. On a rainy day you can get lost in this antique-map and used-bookstore. Not only will you find an excellent selection of titles for beach reading, but also a healthy array of tapa cloth and Hawaiiana books.

Kela's Glass Gallery (808-822-4527; glass-art.com), Hee Fat Marketplace,

4-1354 Kuhio Hwy., Kapaʻa. Open daily. For stunning handmade glass that's either functional or frivolous, this is the island's best bet.

South China Sea Trading Company (808-823-8655; sochinasea.com), Hee Fat Marketplace, 4-1354 Kuhio Hwy., Kapaʻa. Open Mon.–Sat. Since I never manage to get to the South China Sea myself, I relish taking the voyage vicariously through this selection of imports. The smell of wood particularly heightens my senses. From affordable to not, these accessories always lure me into parting with some money unexpectedly.

Bambulei (808-823-8641; bambulei .com), 4369 Kuhio Hwy., Wailua. Open daily. This fine boutique has an impressive selection of *muʻumuʻus* (some of which sell for upward of $2,000), 1930s and 1940s collectibles, antiques, and accessories, all in a 1930s-style plantation house.

Kauaʻi Fruit & Flower Company (808-245-1814; kauaifruit.com), 3-4684 Kuhio Hwy., Kapaʻa. Open 9–5 weekdays, Sat. 9–1, closed Sun. Stop here to arrange shipment of native fruits and flowers to anywhere in the world. Or stop in for a fruit smoothie made from a bounty of locally grown fruits.

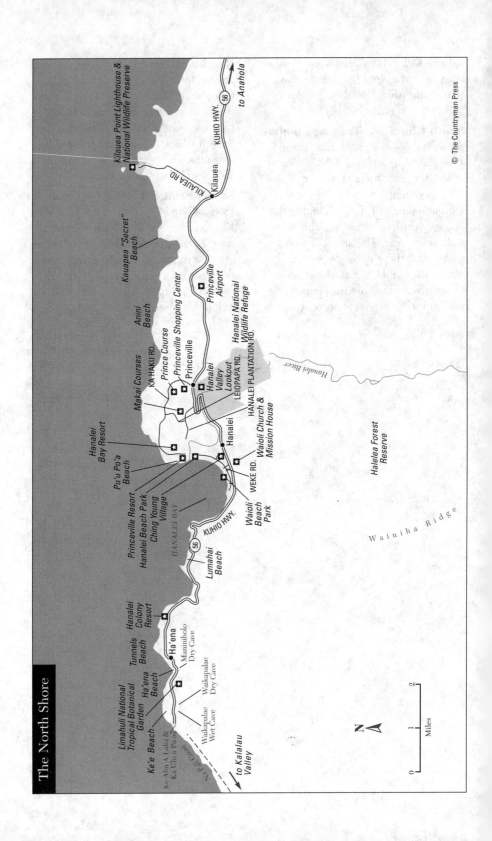

The North Shore

Ke Aim A Laka & Ka Ulu a Paoa
Na Pali Coast
Ke'e Beach
Limahuli National Tropical Botanical Garden
Ha'ena Beach
Tunnels Beach
Waikapalae Wet Cave
Waikapalae Dry Cave
Maniniholo Dry Cave
Ha'ena
Hanalei Colony Resort
Lumahai Beach
KUHIO HWY.
56
HANALEI BAY
Ching Young Village
Hanalei Beach Park
Princeville Resort
Pu'u Po'a Beach
Hanalei Bay Resort
Makai Courses
Prince Course
KA HAKU RD.
Princeville Shopping Center
Princeville
Waioli Beach Park
Waioli Church & Mission House
WEKE RD.
Hanalei
HANALEI PLANTATION RD.
LEI'OPAPA RD.
Hanalei Valley Lookout
Hanalei National Wildlife Refuge
Princeville Airport
Anini Beach
Kauapea "Secret" Beach
Kilauea Point Lighthouse & National Wildlife Preserve
KILAUEA RD.
Kilauea
KUHIO HWY.
56
to Anahola

Hanalei River

Halelea Forest Reserve

Waini ha Ridge

to Kalalau Valley

N

Miles
0   1   2

© The Countryman Press

THE NORTH SHORE

Y ou've heard the tourist-brochure hype before, the hype about "experiencing the Hawai'i of your dreams." Well, it's true about the North Shore of Kaua'i, and most specifically about Hanalei. Sandy crescent bays are backed by fluted and folded mountains. Stunningly verdant gorges are as gorgeously chiseled as Meryl Streep's cheekbones. If the velvety cliffs of Bali Hai can lure even the hard-hearted from their self-imposed shells, imagine what can happen to full-fledged, self-proclaimed romantics. They (we) have a field day. Most of my travel-writer colleagues agree: The North Shore is among the top two or three favorite destinations in the whole state. Many movie celebrities and musicians agree; they're secretly ensconced in digs all around here.

You have to admire **Hanalei**. On one of Hawai'i's loveliest bays, flanked by a spectacular landscape, the small town enjoys a setting that would be worth untold millions to developers. But Hanalei refuses to consider the possibility and even insists on maintaining the narrow, one-lane bridges on both sides of town that keep big tour buses away. If you want to get away from something or get back to yourself, there's a patch of sand with your name on it here.

Down the road from Hanalei, **Princeville** is sometimes called "*Haole*-wood," *haole* being the term for "Caucasian foreigner." The modern, 11,000-acre development lacks native character, but so does most of Hawai'i, from Hanalei's perspective. Located on an expansive plateau that offers outrageous views of Hanalei Bay and Bali Hai, Princeville's main claim to fame is 45 holes of golf, including two courses ranked by *Golf Digest* as being among the best in the state. The posh Princeville Resort is also known for notable views and dining.

While the weather is never predictable here, the winters can be stormy and cool, the summers often sunny. Spring and fall temperatures can fluctuate hour to hour. December and January receive the most rainfall. The old volcano and its nearby peaks and lush valleys are a glorious sight, but they wouldn't be so stunning without the frequent rain.

The **Na Pali Coast**, established as a protected area in 1984, encompasses 6,500 acres of truly, madly, deeply, wildly rugged land. If you think of Kaua'i as a pie, the Na Pali ("the cliffs") area is like one giant wedge, really, whose crust runs from Polihale State Park in the west to Ke'e Beach in the east. Koke'e State Park offers high vantage points for peering into it. It's a veritable Garden of

A PERFECT DAY ON THE NORTH SHORE

7:00	Hike the first 2 miles of the Kalalau Trail
10:30	Snorkel at Ke'e Beach State Park
12:00	Enjoy falafels at Mediterranean Gourmet
1:30	Explore the lush Limahuli Garden
4:00	Take a quick dip in Hanalei Bay
5.30	Sip mai tais at the Princeville Resort
7:00	Delight in fish and pasta at La Cascata
9:30	Head to Hanalei Gourmet for brews and live music

Eden, the single most traditionally stunning place in Hawai'i. You can't drive through it (the road ends here), but you can sail around it (with or without cocktails in hand), helicopter over it, or hike through it. Whatever you do, do not miss exploring—however you can manage. The legendary and famed **Kalalau Valley** is simply the largest valley along the Na Pali Coast.

The North Shore offers exceptional birding, lazy kayaking, high-yield hiking, a choice of superlative botanical gardens, and great swimming and snorkeling at many of the most beautiful beaches in the world.

Then there's that indescribable, end-of-the-road, end-of-the-universe quality about the place. It's so rare. It appeals to my quiet, lazy, escapist side. I figure if it's good enough for Puff the Magic Dragon to live here by the sea, I, too, could frolic in the autumn mist in a land called Hanalei—for weeks on end.

GETTING AROUND

✪ *By car:* Hwy. 56 (aka Kuhio Highway) morphs into the smaller Hwy. 560 beyond Princeville, when the road changes dramatically. From here to Ke'e Beach, the road hugs the shoreline and offers breathtaking beach views that alternate with peaceful pasturelands and majestic mountain peaks. One-lane bridges are common. If someone is already on the bridge or approaching it, pull over and wait your turn. (Local custom says if there is a line of cars waiting across the bridge and you are the fifth car to cross, that's when you should stop.)

TOURS

By land: **North Shore Cab Tours** (808-639-7829), Hanalei. These three-hour North Shore tours include plenty of history, myths, and legends. Call for pickup at area lodging places. $60 per hour, up to six passengers.

KILAUEA POINT LIGHTHOUSE

Exploring east to west

🐚 ✪ **Na Aina Kai Botanical Gardens** (808-828-0525; naainakai.org), *makai*, 4101 Wailapa Rd., before MM 21, Kilauea. Open for guided tours (only) 9:30–1:30 Tues.–Fri. More than a mere botanical garden, this one-of-a-kind creative endeavor stretches for 240 acres and offers a unique blend of flora, fauna, and visual art. (There are over 60 bronze sculptures scattered around.) Great for gardeners and nongardeners alike, it has 12 diverse gardens with hardwoods, orchards, carnivorous plants, and orchids. There's even a great children's area, a path to the ocean, fountains, a teahouse, a maze, and gazebos. Tours: one and a half hours $25; three hours $35; five hours with lunch $70; make advance reservations.

Kilauea, *makai*, Hwy. 56. This former plantation town, which has recently turned to raising prawns as a source of livelihood, has an old general store (the Kong Lung Co.) dating to 1892, lots of fresh fruit stands worth a detour, two little churches, a highly creditable but tiny cluster of shops and eateries, and a 1913 lighthouse atop a wildlife preserve. Take some time to poke around a bit.

Kilauea Point National Wildlife Refuge (808-828-0168), Kilauea Rd., *makai*, 1 mile north of Kilauea off Hwy. 56. Open 10–4 daily. This 200-acre seabird sanctuary is home to the largest concentration of rare and endangered birds on any major Hawaiian island. The rocky cliffside juts out onto a promontory, where, with a bit of luck, you'll probably spot frigates, albatross (which rarely alight on land), nene, shearwaters, and boobies. With binoculars, you might see offshore seals, dolphins, and wintertime whales. $3 adults, free ages 16 and under.

🏄 **Anini Beach County Park**. See *Beaches*.

Princeville, *makai*, off Hwy. 56. Once a sugar plantation, this sprawling estate was bought in the 1890s by Albert Wilcox, who converted the highlands for cattle ranching and the lowlands for rice farming. Today the manicured, cliffside enclave is the most exclusive on Kaua'i.

Queen's Bath. See *Hiking*.

Hanalei Valley Lookout, *mauka*, Hwy. 56. Even if you've started to bypass scenic turnouts because you've become too jaded by Hawai'i's beauty (shame on you), stop here. Arguably the single most easily accessible, watercolor-like stop on Kaua'i, this roadside parking area peers down onto a patchwork of taro fields and a wildlife refuge. Bisected by the meandering Hanalei River and flanked by spirelike mountains, the patterned, abstract fields look to be colored with 20 shades of green crayons. Until the early 1900s these fields were filled with rice farmed by Chinese immigrants.

Hanalei Bridge, Hwy. 56. Built in 1912, this creaky, decrepit, one-lane steel truss bridge is the precarious—and only—link between Princeville and Hanalei.

Hanalei National Wildlife Refuge, *mauka*, off Ohiki Rd. from Hwy. 560. This 900-acre refuge, home to endangered migrating shorebirds and waterfowl, is closed to the public, but you can drive down the dirt road that veers left from

THE ONLY ROUTE INTO HANALEI CROSSES
THIS BRIDGE.

the other side of the Hanalei Bridge. It runs alongside the fields, passes an old rice mill, and yields great open views. I'll never forget parking here for hours under the light of a full moon, watching two owls hunt.

✪ **Hanalei**, Hwy. 560. One of the first places in Hawai'i settled by Polynesians, Hanalei was transformed from a swampy area into fertile farmland because of savvy irrigation systems. This funky town, once a happenin' hippie paradise in the 1970s, is still counterculture at its core. Feel like dropping out? Drop in here. Whether you're here to rest hard or to play hard—try hiking, kayaking, and surfing—you may never want to leave. Full of shops and delightful eateries, Hanalei has a spirit all its own. Picture-postcard-perfect *Hanalei*, by the way, simply means "crescent bay." For a real slice of local life, head down to Hanalei Pier on the weekend (take Aku Road off Hwy. 560 and turn right onto Weke Road). The area is called "Black Pot" locally because, in the olden days, locals would hang out at the beach park all day, cooking up dishes to share from black pots.

 Hanalei Beach Park. See *Beaches*.

Waioli Church and Mission House Museum, *mauka*, Hwy. 560, Hanalei. Tours Mon., Wed., and Thurs., 10 and 1. Two missionary teachers from Connecticut, Abner and Lucy Wilcox, moved to this tidy house in 1837. A guided tour will give you a great idea of what life was like in this remote location. Unlike most other missionaries' homes, this two-story house utilizes local materials. The house boasts simple koa furniture, 'ohi'a floors, and a lava-rock chimney. (The Wilcoxes' son George went on to amass a fortune and name for himself in the sugar industry.) Free.

 Lumahai Beach, *makai*, between MM 4 and 5 on Hwy. 560. The beach—made famous in *South Pacific* by Mitzi Gaynor washing that man right out of her hair—is difficult to

TOP SEVEN BEACHES ON KAUA'I
For Swimming & Sunbathing
Po'ipu Beach Park (The South Shore)
Anini Beach County Park
   (The North Shore)
For Sunsets
Hanalei Beach Park
   (The North Shore)
Tunnels Beach (The North Shore)
For Families
Salt Pond Beach (West Kaua'i)
Anini Beach County Park
   (The North Shore)
For Walking
Maha'ulepu Beach
   (The South Shore)
Polihale State Park (West Kaua'i)
For All-Around Water Sports
Po'ipu Beach Park (The South Shore)
Hanalei Beach Park
   (The North Shore)

"WASH THAT MAN RIGHT OUTTA YOUR HAIR" AT LUMAHAI BEACH

reach, but there is a steep trail down. If you make the effort, limit your activity to strolling, picnicking, and suntanning rather than swimming since the currents are tricky here.

Haʻena, Hwy. 560. Less a town than a 4-mile stretch of road, Haʻena is marked by beautiful bays, gardens, vest-pocket beaches, lagoons, and good snorkeling and surfing. The current boundaries of Haʻena State Park encompass land originally owned by Elizabeth Taylor's brother Hugh. In the 1970s, more than 50 hippies started hanging out on his land, building shelters and getting rather out of hand (even in a place known for tolerance). So the state purchased the land, forced them out, and set it aside as a park.

⚑ **Tunnels Beach**. See *Beaches*.

⚑ **Haʻena Beach Park**. See *Beaches*.

Maniniholo Dry Cave, *mauka*, Hwy. 560, across from Haʻena State Park. This grotto was a place of worship in ancient times.

❂ **Limahuli Garden** (808-826-1053; ntbg.org), *mauka*, located 0.25 mile from Keʻe Beach, Haʻena. Open 9:30–4 Tues.–Sat. This ultralush National Tropical Botanical Garden, located on 17 acres of serpentine paths, has terraced steps lined with taro. While it will keep serious botanists and herbalists enthralled (it's a veritable encyclopedia of information), it's also quite appealing for laypeople. The staff is devoted to preserving the habitat of native plants once abundant in this region—plants used for medicine, clothing, shelter, and food. The stream that runs through it even supports endangered freshwater fish. Be prepared for mosquitoes and slippery paths. Self-guided tours: $15 adults; guided tours $25; both tours free ages 12 and under.

Waikapalae and **Waikanaloa Wet Caves**, *mauka*, Hwy. 560, just before MM 10; it is a short climb to one of the caves. It's suggested that Pele

TERRACES AT LIMAHULI GARDEN

A SISTER AND A CHIEF

One of the most famous stories about Pele, the Hawaiian volcano goddess, takes place near Ke'e Beach. Although there are many different versions of the story, they all involve Pele's sister, Hi'iaka, and the Kaua'ian chief, Lohi'au.

Pele, it's said, sometimes sent her spirit wandering through the islands while she was asleep. One night she came upon a group of sacred hula dancers, including Lohi'au. Instantly attracted to him, Pele morphed herself into a beautiful mortal woman and seduced him. Knowing that her actual body was awakening far away on Kilauea, Pele promised to come back for him.

At home in Kilauea Crater, Pele blessed her sister Hi'iaka with magical powers and sent her off to fetch Lohi'au. Hi'iaka passed through many trials. Often relying on her magic to defeat mo'o (giant lizards) and other creatures, Hi'iaka reached Lohi'au's home.

But Hi'iaka was too late. Lohi'au had already hanged himself with grief, having pined away for Pele. So Hi'iaka caught his free-floating soul and pushed it back into his body through a slit in his toe. After he was revived, they set off for Kilauea.

But Lohi'au was shocked when he finally saw Pele's bodily form, for she was a wizened crone. He was instead drawn to Hi'iaka's beauty, and they fell in love.

Although touched by the man's longing, Hi'iaka had fully intended to fulfill her mission and bring Lohi'au to Kilauea. But Pele was a jealous spirit, and she soon began to burn while imagining Hi'iaka in Lohi'au's arms. In a fury, the volcano goddess killed Hi'iaka's best friend (the poet Hopoe) and scorched Hi'iaka's lovely gardens.

Filled with desperation and loss, Hi'iaka and Lohi'au made love. Pele then burned the man to death but could not destroy her immortal sister. Hi'iaka descended to the underworld to free Lohi'au's soul and brought him back to Kaua'i, where he purified himself by surfing at Ke'e Beach.

It's said that the rock formations on the nearby cliffs are remnants of the giant creatures Hi'iaka killed on her magical journey, and also that Lohi'au's grave is above Waikapalae wet cave.

hollowed out these depressions. Whatever you believe, it's best not to swim in them.

⚲ **Ke'e Beach State Park**. See *Beaches*.

Ke Ahu a Laka (and **Ka Ulu a Pa'oa**), on the west side and above Ke'e Beach. The most important *hula halau* in Hawai'i took place here, at these separate sacred sites that sit at the base of a cliff in a clearing on a hillside. (The path is unmarked and overgrown but still manageable.) On the upper level, or platform, an altar to Laka, the goddess of hula, is often draped with revered leis, vines, and kapa from students and devotees making the important pilgrimage. The *mana* is quite palpable here to those who are quiet; please be respectful.

✳ Spas

Princeville Health Club & Spa (808-826-5030; princeville.com), Princeville Resort Kaua'i, Princeville. I'd happily pay $20 a day to work out here simply for the views. (But golfers at Princeville can enjoy the extensive health club facilities for free.) The spa offers most treatments imaginable.

✳ Outdoor Activities

BICYCLING

Pedal 'n Paddle (808-826-9069; pedalnpaddle.com), Ching Young Village, Hanalei. Open 9–6 daily. Cruise Kaua'i's stunning North Shore on a mountain bike or, better yet, rent a tandem for tooling around Princeville. Locks and helmets included. Rentals $12–20 daily, $50–80 weekly.

BIRD-WATCHING

See **Kilauea Point National Wildlife Refuge** and **Hanalei National Wildlife Refuge** under *To See & Do*.

BOAT EXCURSIONS

The surf is calmest in spring and summer; excursions are prone to cancellation in winter due to rough surf conditions. Outfitters will let you know what's happening on any given day. Trips have the added bonus of dolphin and sea turtle sightings.

Except for **Captain Sundown Catamaran** *Ku'uipo* (808-826-5585, captain sundown.com), Hanalei, most trips around the **Na Pali Coast** depart out of **Port Allen** (see "West Kaua'i"). When the sea is manageable (which isn't as often as you might hope in winter), this Native Hawaiian crew takes you on a five-hour catamaran tour. Though they pride themselves in being the only outfit to depart from Hanalei, you must call for a weather check at 7 AM because occasionally you'll have to depart from Lihu'e. The five-hour tours include snorkeling, lunch, and fishing lines. Costs are $120–138 adults; $99–120 children 7–12; no children under 7; no trips on Sunday. Book your trip early in your stay so that if it gets canceled, there's time to reschedule.

TARO FIELDS NEAR HANALEI

TAKE THE ONE LESS TRAVELED BY

Nothing beats hiking the Na Pali Coast for experiencing the natural splendor of Hawai'i. Part of what makes it glorious is that no road cuts through here. It is pristine wilderness, home to more than 120 rare and endangered plant species, golden monarch butterflies, and long-plumed tropical birds. If you need a visual image, think *Jurassic Park*, which was filmed here. How to enjoy it? The untouched expanse of wilderness is accessible only via an ancient footpath: the rigorous, 22-mile (round-trip) **Kalalau Trail** that leads to **Kalalau Valley**.

But what if you're not an experienced backpacker? You're still in luck. The first mile of the trail, which is uphill, actually affords the most impressive views. Still, though, you can't be a novice hiker, and it's best if you don't suffer from vertigo (a few parts of the path are no wider than a foot, with scary vertical drops). Still feel left out? At least walk to the top of the first bend in the trail, 400 feet above the ocean; the expansive views of Lumahai Beach will remain with you for a long time. I've never met anyone who was disappointed by the effort they made.

ALONG THE KALALAU TRAIL

GOLF

Makai Courses (808-826-3581; princeville.com), Princeville. Easily Kaua'i's best course, and one of the hardest in the state, these 27 holes consist of Makai Ocean, Makai Woods, and Makai Line—all of which take in the best of Princeville's natural surroundings. Greens fees run $175 but drop to $95 after 1:30 PM, and then to $50 after 3 PM. You can make reservations up to 30 days in advance.

A few more particulars before setting out for the day: bring plenty of water (even if you're hiking only 1 mile), gobs of mosquito repellent, sunscreen, an adventurous spirit, and sturdy shoes that will stand up to mud. It's always slippery and covered in loose rocks. The trail is best hiked in summer, when it's driest. It's downright tough mid-Oct.–mid-May.

It takes about four hours (round-trip) to hike the first section to **Hanakapi'ai Beach** (no permit required). Set out early; in addition to enjoying cooler temperatures, you'll avoid the crowds as the day wears on. After the first uphill mile, you'll wind down into a lush valley, hop over several streams, and descend to Hanakapi'ai Beach. *Do not be lulled into challenging the ocean here!* This lovely beach is one of the most deadly in Kaua'i. Large signs warn people about rough swimming conditions and list those who've died in swimming accidents since 1995. Because of currents and the fact that there is no reef, it can even be dangerous to wade at the shoreline. Most folks turn around here.

Head another 2 miles (one-way) inland to the striking **Hanakapi'ai Falls**: quintessential Hawai'i. Ripe guavas litter this section of the slippery trail, which is lined with groves of wild ginger and home to hundreds of exotic birds. Allow another three hours for this stretch, plus some time if you swim beneath the 120-foot waterfall. If you do take a dip, pick some wild ginger (which looks like red beehives on the top of a long, narrow stem) and wash your hair in the falls. It feels pretty exotic. Squeeze the clear, sticky, sweet-smelling liquid from each of the fist-sized flowers and then suds up.

The remainder of the trail requires a permit and leads deep into Kalalau Valley. It's the most strenuous hike in Hawai'i—even for the most experienced hikers and serious backpackers. Because of erosion, the treacherous-feeling trail can be a mere 10 inches wide in places, with dizzying 1,000-foot sheer drops into the ocean. Attempt this trail only in summer when it's dry. During winter, portions of the trail disappear, and flash floods are dangerous. For more information about camping and hiking permits, contact the **Department of Lands and Natural Resources** (808-274-3444; kauai-hawaii.com). Or request a permit by writing to 3060 Eiwa St. (Room 306), Lihu'e, HI 96766.

Prince Course (808-826-5001; princeville.com), Princeville. This Robert Trent Jones Jr. masterpiece is Kaua'i's most difficult, but the frustration and pain are lessened by fabulous ocean views. Greens fees are $200 and drop to $125 at noon, and then to $70 at 3 PM. You can make reservations up to 30 days in advance.

HIKING

⚙ **Kalalau Trail**, Na Pali Coast State Park, trailhead at Ke'e Beach. (See *Take the One Less Traveled By*.) Because the Kalalau Valley provided plentiful fresh water, natural terracing for taro planting, and natural protection from adjacent-valley invaders, this area was probably settled as early as the late 900s A.D. Ancient *heiaus* are scattered throughout the valley, as are historic home sites. During more recent times, up until the 1920s, the valley supported coffee and taro harvesting. And in the late 1970s, the state came through and swept out hippies who'd set up camp here.

Queen's Bath. Take Ka Haku Road, turn right on Punahele Road, and look for a dirt parking lot on the right where the trail begins. This hike should not be attempted in winter. But during other seasons, if the skies have been clear for a couple days and the sea is mellow, this hike will deposit you at a lava-rock ocean pool.

HORSEBACK RIDING

Princeville Ranch Stables (808-826-6777; princevilleranch.com), Hwy. 56, just east of the Princeville entrance, near MM 27, Princeville. Trips daily. This working cattle ranch provides several guided rides, as well as an opportunity to help with a cattle drive at dawn. One look at the majestic views of Bali Hai and the Hanalei Mountains from this verdant valley ranch, and you'll know you're not in Kansas anymore. The midday waterfall and picnic trip, which crosses an open prairie and lasts three or four hours (with most of it spent in the saddle), includes a short hike to an 80-foot waterfall where you can swim and have lunch. $125–135; children must be eight or older; book one week in advance.

KAYAKING

⚙ **The Hanalei River**, which meanders through the Hanalei National Wildlife Refuge, makes for a perfectly lazy paddle. Its relative stillness means it's great for folks of all ages and abilities. You'll be lulled into submission with the mountains as a backdrop and taro patches and rare birds in the foreground.

Kayak Kaua'i (808-826-9844; kayakkauai.com), Hwy. 560, Hanalei. Open daily. The only outfitter with a private dock on the river, these folks offer rental sea kayaks ($42–65 daily) and guided three-hour snorkeling and kayak tours ($60).

Pedal 'n Paddle (808-826-9069; pedalnpaddle.com), Ching Young Village, Hanalei. Open 9–6 daily. These single ($20 daily) and double ($40 daily) kayaks can be used only on the nearby Hanalei River, which is fine since it's the best place around. If you're worried about scratching your rental car when transporting the kayak, use their Styrofoam rack.

SURFING

Remember, Hanalei in wintertime is reserved for the pros.

Windsurf Kaua'i (808-828-6838), Anini Beach, Hanalei. Always wanted to try windsurfing? These folks will teach you on a stretch of beach that's protected by an ocean reef with plenty of wind to get you going. The rest—that is, staying upright—is up to you. Beginner's lessons are held weekdays at 9 and 1 ($85 per person for three hours). Rentals are $25 per hour, $75 for a half day.

Hanalei Surf Company (808-826-9000; hanaleisurf.com), Hwy. 560, Hanalei, rents boards for $20 a day.

TENNIS

Princeville Racquet Club (808-826-1230; princeville.com), Princeville Resort Kaua'i. Open 9–4:30 daily. The facility has six hard courts that rent for $12 per person and offers a women's clinic Sat. morning for $15.

✳ Beaches

In order of preference.

In general, it's too rough for wintertime swimming.

✹ **Hanalei Beach Park** (including **Waioli Beach Park**). From Hwy. 560 turn *makai* on Aku Road, then right on Weke Road. No beach in Hawai'i enjoys a better location. This magnificent half crescent is 2 miles wide and reaches 1 mile inland from the open ocean. With all this space for folks to spread out, it never feels crowded (except around the pier on weekends). For swimming, snorkeling, bodyboarding, and kayaking, the water is calmest around the pier; windsurfing is best left to those with prior experience. While there can be strong currents in the bay, swimming is generally okay year-round. Do keep an eye on things, though. *Facilities:* restrooms, showers, lifeguard.

✹ ✪ **Ke'e Beach State Park**, about 7.5 miles from Hanalei, at the end of Hwy. 560. If your jaw isn't dropping here, check your pulse. Thanks to an offshore lagoon reef, the underwater snorkeling is great, but the unspoiled view above the water is pretty spectacular, too. *Facilities:* restrooms, showers, parking.

✹ **Tunnels Beach**. At MM 8.5, turn *makai* onto a dirt road off Hwy. 560. Few places rival Tunnels for watching the sunset as an ever-changing palette of pastels sweeps across the dusky sky. And although I'm loath to use "picture-perfect" again, it really is. Quieter than its next-door neighbor, Ha'ena, this well-protected beach offers good swimming and snorkeling year-round. (It's always advisable to check surf conditions in winter before playing in the water, though.) Windsurfing is best left to those with experience. *Facilities:* none, but a stand of ironwood trees provides nice shade.

HA'ENA BEACH PARK

✦ ✹ **Anini Beach County Park**. From Hwy. 56, turn onto Kalihiwai Rd. between MM 25 and 26, and then turn left on Anini Beach Rd. The place where the puka shell necklace craze began is still good for shelling. The 3-mile, golden-white beach is protected by a 2-mile reef, so it's good for beginner snorkelers,

intimidated swimmers, and novice windsurfers. The azure lagoon couldn't be prettier; if you haven't lounged on a South Seas beach in this lifetime, consider it done. *Facilities:* restrooms, shower, barbecue, picnic, parking, camping.

Ha'ena Beach Park, MM 8 off Hwy. 560. Across from the caves, this beach offers excellent swimming and snorkeling in summer. *Facilities:* restrooms, showers, parking, camping, picnic, barbecue.

✳ Lodging

The planned community of Princeville has two resorts and an assortment of condos. But as you might expect, lodging is severely limited in Hanalei. All accommodations up here are surrounded by Kaua'i's dramatic beauty and are near the Na Pali Coast, but the closer you get to Mount Wai'ale'ale, the more likely you are to get showers.

RESORTS

Princeville Resort Kaua'i (808-826-9644 or 1-800-826-4400; princevillehotelhawaii.com), 5520 Ka Haku Rd., Princeville. Somewhere in the world there must be a resort hotel that rivals the Princeville for spectacular views, but no place in Hawai'i comes close. Sloping down a bluff above perfect Hanalei Bay, tumbling toward peaks popularly known as Bali Hai, this hotel enjoys absolutely sublime ocean and mountain vistas. The hotel's unusual physical structure ensures that water views are optimized. Built in a series of tiers, the building descends rather than ascends and thus does not overpower the setting. The only drawback is that some guests have to take a couple of elevators and a short hike to reach the beach (itself a bit gravelly—but perfect for surveying the scenery). At press time, a gigantic renovation (slated for six months, but still going 12 months later) was morphing this palace of grandeur from a Starwood property to a St. Regis. Knowing what this property was before the renovation, I have full confidence recommending it to you. Just breathing the regal air is sure to make you want to stay. If you decide to stay elsewhere (especially if you want consistently sunny winter weather), at least drop by for a sunset cocktail. As Hawaiian musicians strum and the sun sinks majestically into the Pacific, casting a warm red glow on Bali Hai, the magical moment is bound to bring you back for more. *Rates:* $$$$; children free in parent's room. *Facilities and amenities*: 242 rooms and suites, oceanside pool, beach (good swimming), three restaurants (including **La Cascata**, see *Dining Out*), two golf courses, tennis courts (fee), health club and spa, water sport rentals, concierge, shops, children's programs, parking (fee).

Hanalei Bay Resort (808-826-6522 or 1-800-827-4427; hanaleibayresort.com), 5380 Hono'iki Rd., Princeville. A 22-acre resort that shares the same stunning location as its upscale neighbor, the Princeville, this excellent resort is simply less expensive, less pretentious, and a bit farther from the ocean. In my mind, though, it's perhaps easier to savor the sublime and breathtaking grandeur here. Guest rooms are spread across a bluff above Hanalei Bay in a variety of low-rise buildings. Shuttles (which can take a while to arrive) haul guests around the expansive grounds and even to the beach below. (It's a steep walk.) Many guests, though, don't wander farther than the attractive pool, a free-form lagoonlike place fed by two waterfalls. The studios with kitchenettes and spacious one-bedroom quarters are, in general, handsomely furnished, ideal for longer stays and families (as well as couples). All rooms have lanais, but the ocean-view quarters provide a particularly good perspective of the sea. This is also a time-share resort. *Rates*: $$–$$$$; children free in parent's room. *Facilities and amenities*: 236 rooms and one-bedroom suites, two pools, beach (good swimming), two restaurants (see **Bali Hai**, *Dining Out*), kitchens or kitchenettes, eight free tennis courts, water sport rentals, concierge, parking (free).

CONDOS
Hanalei Colony Resort (808-826-6235 or 1-800-628-3004; hcr.com), 5-7130 Kuhio Hwy., Hanalei.

HANALEI BAY RESORT

HANALEI COLONY RESORT

This beachfront condo complex, about five minutes west of Hanalei village, offers the only accommodations in this scenic neighborhood other than a few vacation rental homes. It sits alone on a striking beach, one that is too rocky for swimming but splendid for romantic strolls. The 13 low-rise buildings, some arrayed along the shore, contain four apartments each. Décor is seaside simple—what you would want in a basic hideaway cabin along any coast. Both bedrooms open onto the living room with louvered doors, giving the unit more of a studio feel than a traditional two-bedroom feel. Bathrooms and kitchens are smallish but completely fine. For my money the oceanfront condos are worth the added expense, especially the ones called premium oceanfront. These are virtually the only accommodations directly on the sea on Kaua'i's North Coast. And these are a bargain for Hawai'i. A swimming pool, barbecue gazebo, and guest laundry are grouped at the rear of the grounds. *Rates*: $$$–$$$$; children free in parent's room; five-night minimum;

seventh night free. *Facilities and amenities*: 48 condos, pool, beach (great for sunning and strolling but not for swimming), the **Mediterranean Gourmet** restaurant (see *Eating Out*) concierge, activity desk, children's programs during summer, parking (fee), no A/C, no phones, no TVs.

BED & BREAKFASTS AND INNS

Hale Ho'o Maha (808-826-7083 or 1-800-851-0291; aloha.net/~hoomaha), 7083 Alamihi Rd., Hanalei. The energetic hosts of this B&B attract an international crowd. As such, guests often end up swapping travel tales in the hot tub, over breakfast, or in the shared BBQ area. The Asian and Polynesian décor, the endless supply of books, and the general feeling of being holed up in a remote house on stilts (close to Hanalei, but just far enough away) make this a terrific option. *Rates*: $$; no children under seven. *Facilities and amenities:* four suites, close to beach, expanded continental breakfast, no A/C, hot tub, access to Internet.

🌺 **Hanalei Inn** (808-826-9333; hanaleiinn.com), 5-5468 Kuhio Hwy., Hanalei. Even though these clean rooms have kitchenettes, A/C, and a reasonable amount of space for the price, this motel still reminds me of a hostel. With darkish rooms, a shared outside space with a soda machine and a hammock, and a few cats, the Hanalei Inn is one of the cheaper spots on the North Shore. And it's the only inn in Hanalei. They also rent a room and a couple apartments a block from Hanalei Bay for a bit more money. *Rates*: $$. *Facilities and amenities:* five studios, two one-bedroom apartments, walk to beach, A/C.

CONDOS

Pu'a Po'a (808-245-8841 or 1-800-367-5025; kauaivacationrentals.com), 5454 Ka Haku Rd., Princeville. Ahhhh! This is the ultimate luxe condo complex in Princeville. Located next to the Princeville Resort, perched on a cliff, and overlooking Bali Hai, these units are best suited to people who don't want to leave the condo. *Ever.* Windows stretch from floor to ceiling (except for the bedrooms); the private lanais are as big as most hotel rooms; and owners generally have stellar decorating taste. *Rates:* $$$; three- to five-night minimum; cleaning fee. *Facilities and amenities:* 56 two-bedroom condos, pool, close to beach, kitchen, some units have free WiFi.

🏄 **Pali Ke Kua** (808-245-8841 or 1-800-367-5025; kauaivacationrentals .com), 5300 Ka Haku Rd., Princeville. This is an excellent condo option for families or two couples. These one- and two-bedroom units are spacious, situated on the cliffs overlooking Bali Hai, and still have an old Hawai'i feel about them. Book early; these popular condos sell out fast. *Rates:* $$–$$$; three- to five-night minimum; cleaning fee. *Facilities and amenities:* 96 condos, pool, trail to beach, kitchen, some units have free WiFi.

🐚 🏄 **Sealodge** (808-826-6585 or 1-800-222-5541; oceanfrontrealty .com), 3700 Kamehameha Rd., Princeville. These one- and two-bedroom condos are a steal for the location. Set atop the Princeville cliffs, most units might not give expansive ocean views (and can be dark), but walk a few feet and you'll feel as regal as the folks who forked over the big bucks to stay at the Princeville. *Rates:* $–$$; three-night minimum; cleaning fee. *Facilities and* *amenities:* 86 condos, pool, kitchen, hiking trail to beach.

COTTAGES

Aloha Sunrise & Sunset Inn (808-828-1100 or 1-888-828-1008; kauai sunrise.com), 4899-A Waiakalua Rd., Kilauea. If you care where you stay, stay here. Seriously. This 10-acre farm, complete with an organic vegetable garden, offers two cottages furnished in a relaxed vintage-1940s Hawaiian style. Although the two-story cottage is attached to the owner's residence, it still feels private. *Rates:* $$, cleaning fee; not appropriate for children. *Facilities and amenities:* no A/C, no credit cards.

Secret Beach Hideaway (808-828-2862 or 1-800-820-2862; secretbeach hawaii.com), 2884 Kauapea Rd., Kilauea. Set on 11 gated acres near the Kilauea Lighthouse, these three jewel-like cottages are as magical as the setting high atop an oceanfront plateau. Trails zigzag from the cottages through maturing botanical gardens down to Secret Beach. Each of the 500-square-foot cottages is beautifully appointed with top-of-the-line amenities: everything from Gaggenau appliances and 500-thread-count sheets to teak lanai furniture and marble bathrooms. Every inch of the contents was custom-made on Kaua'i by highly skilled craftspeople. Hale Lani has wonderfully soothing Japanese overtones; Hale Nanea has great views of Bali Hai; and Hale Ke Aloha, the most secluded, is best positioned for taking in sunsets. *Rates:* $$$$; $200–300 cleaning fee. *Facilities and amenities:* private paths to beach, no A/C.

VACATION RENTALS

Hanalei North Shore Properties (808-448-3336; hanaleinorthshore properties.com), Princeville. This out-fit represents some of the best condo and vacation rental listings on the North Shore. Listing over 60 properties, these agents generally guarantee stocked kitchens, a TV, and washers and dryers; some units have A/C and WiFi. Straight shooters, HNSP has been up to this for over 30 years. No credit cards; cleaning fees.

Pure Kaua'i (808-828-0380 or 1-866-457-7873; purekauai.com), Kilauea. Favored by celebs and people who want some serious pampering, this vacation rental/go-to company does it all. From finding you that perfect oceanfront villa to arranging a gourmet breakfast, private drivers, and spa services, this company delivers. Of course, it comes with a hefty price tag.

CAMPING

Kalalau Valley. In order to hike and camp here, you must obtain a permit from the **Department of Lands and Natural Resources** (808-274-3444; kauai-hawaii.com), 3060 Eiwa St., Lihu'e. *Rates:* $10 per person.

YMCA Camp Naue (808-246-9090 or 808-826-6419), 4 miles past Hanalei, between MM 7 and 8, *makai.* For $10 a person, guests are allowed to tent camp near the ocean and use the BBQ pavilions and bathrooms. They also rent out beds in the bunkhouse on a first-come, first-served basis.

✳ Where to Eat

Tiny Hanalei has the all-around best cluster of restaurants on Kaua'i, while the Princeville eateries reviewed here have Kaua'i's absolute best sunset views. Plenty of smoothie stands will also draw you in.

La Cascata (808-826-9644; prince ville.com), Princeville Resort Kauaʻi, 5520 Ka Haku Rd., Princeville. Open for dinner nightly. The most elegant dining on Kauaʻi, La Cascata boasts drop-dead views of Hanalei Bay and Bali Hai. It'd be foolish not to arrive an hour before sunset. The artfully presented Sicilian menu features classic beef dishes, rack of lamb, and pasta dishes with Pacific touches. Reservations recommended. Entrées $$$$.

🦐 🍴 **Lighthouse Bistro** (808-828-0480; lighthousebistro.com), Kilauea Rd. (off Hwy. 56), Kilauea. Open for lunch Mon.–Sat. (closed mid-afternoon) and dinner daily. Set in a plantation-style building with high ceilings, bamboo chairs, and local art-work, the bistro is a very pleasant place to enjoy fine Continental, Pacific Rim, and Italian cuisine. (I hate to sound like a broken record, but the fresh catch of the day is always a very good bet.) Lunches can be particularly creative and upscale or as simple as sandwiches and wraps. And, by the way, despite the name, there are no

SMOOTHIES IN HANALEI

lighthouse views here. Reservations recommended; children's menu. Lunch $–$$, dinner entrées $$–$$$$.

Postcards Café (808-826-1191), Kuhio Hwy., Hanalei. Open for dinner nightly. Postcards, another plantation-style cottage where *healthful* is not a bad word, emphasizes local ingredients in big, creative ways. The menu—inspired by Asian, Indian, and Mediterranean foods, as well as Hawaiʻi regional cuisine—ranges from fresh fish, pasta, and vegetarian dishes to Thai curries and a daily special. It's hard to go wrong here. Eat indoors or out. Reservations recommended. Entrées $$–$$$.

Bali Hai (808-826-6522), Hanalei Bay Resort, 5380 Honoʻiki Rd., Princeville. Open for breakfast and dinner daily. Because the stunning perch overlooks Bali Hai and is rivaled only by the same westward views at La Cascata, I really only think about this open-air restaurant for sunset dinners. Might as well play to their strengths. Pacific Rim–style fish specials are the most popular dishes, but the comfortable and spacious dining room has lots of lobster and steak dishes as well. For breakfast, try the *poi* pancakes or fried *taro*. Reservations recommended; children's menu. Breakfast about $–$$, dinner entrées $$–$$$$.

Bar Acuda (808-826-7081; restaurant baracuda.com), 5-5161 Kuhio Hwy., Hanalei. Open for dinner Tues.–Sun. Foodies rejoice. If you are willing to part with a hefty hunk of cash while *not* staring at Bali Hai over dinner and drinks, this San Francisco–inspired restaurant is a wonderful choice. Serving up tapas (small shared plates) and a few seasonal meat, seafood, and vegetarian dinner-sized

BALI HAI RESTAURANT

🦐 🐟 **Kilauea Fish Market** (808-828-6244), 4270 Kilauea Lighthouse Rd., Kilauea. Open 11 AM–8 PM Mon.–Sat. I'm always sorry I didn't find this little fish shack sooner. Locals come out in droves for gigantic ahi or veggie wraps, farm-fresh meat, salads, plate lunches, and locally caught seafood at low, low prices. There's no ambience here—just seriously *ono kine grindz*. Dishes: $–$$.

Hanalei Dolphin Restaurant (808-826-6113; hanaleidolphin.com), 5-5016 Kuhio Hwy., Hanalei. Open for lunch and dinner daily. Because it claims the only waterfront dining in Hanalei (on the Hanalei River), this nautical-themed seafood spot gets to charge tourist prices for okay food. I'm partial to their salads (free with entrées) and *pupus*. Since no reservations are accepted, get here early, or better yet, pick up some fish from their fish market and grill it up yourself. Dishes $$$–$$$$.

🦐 ▼ **Mediterranean Gourmet** (808-826-9875), Hanalei Colony Resort, 5-7132 Kuhio Hwy., Ha'ena. Open for lunch and dinner Mon.–Sat. After a number of incantations, Charo's restaurant just might have found a winning combination: oceanfront Mediterranean dining, live music, and a great wine list. I love coming here after a hike to gorge on fresh fruit smoothies, salads, and hummus. Other darn good choices include steak or rack of lamb dinners. It doesn't get much better than watching the sun explode over the Pacific while you sip wine and groove to live music. Lunch and dinner entrées $$–$$$.

Red Hot Mamas (808-826-7266), 5-6607 Kuhio Hwy., Ha'ena. Open 11–5. The only fast food option in Ha'ena serves up organic burritos,

entrées, Bar Acuda specializes in sustainable cuisine prepared in creative ways. Think steak rubbed with coffee and cocoa, Humboldt Fog cheese plates, and *bacalao*. Reservations highly recommended. Entrées $$$–$$$$.

EATING OUT

▼ **Hanalei Gourmet** (808-826-2524), 5-5161 Kuhio Hwy., Hanalei. Open 8 AM–10:30 PM daily. From picnics-to-go to *pupus*, soups, salads, stir-fries, and roasted eggplant sandwiches, this little place has all the bases covered for a casual stop. The deck in front is prime, but you can also get food to take out. Previously incarnated as a schoolhouse, the lively eatery still has old-fashioned blackboards and wooden floors. The popular bar is often tuned to a TV sporting event or live music. Children's menu. Dishes $–$$$$.

tacos, and Mexican fare using hormone-free chicken, grass-fed beef, and organic vegetables. Dishes under $.

🌺 ✐ ⚘ **Kalypso** (808-826-9700), 5-5156 Kuhio Hwy., Hanalei. Open for lunch and dinner daily. This most hip hangout has a prime outdoor deck and kitschy, fantasy tropical indoor décor. The roadside joint is absolutely packed at lunchtime for soups and salads, even more packed during happy hour (when cheap beer and tacos rule). Dinner is a bit more eclectic—from burgers to burritos and fish to fettuccine. Children's menu. Lunch $–$$, dinner entrées $$–$$$.

🌺 **Kilauea Bakery & Pau Hana Pizza** (808-828-2020), Kong Lung Center, Kilauea Rd. (off Hwy. 56), Kilauea. Open 6:30 AM–9 PM daily. Legendary pizzas (with wheat and white crusts as well as cheese choices that run the gamut from goat to Gorgonzola to feta), sourdough bread (made with *poi* or guava), and fruit-infused pastries rule here. It's a bright and fashionable little place, with some outdoor picnic tables. I seem to make repeated trips here at all hours of the day. Dishes $–$$.

✐ **Bubba Burgers** (808-826-7839; bubbaburgers.com), *makua*, Kuhio Hwy., Hanalei. Open 10:30–8 daily. Burger central on the North Shore, Bubba's is without equal (don't tell Duane—see *Eating Out* in "The Coconut Coast"). With a little sassy attitude on the side, Bubba's also makes popular Budweiser chili and tempeh burgers to enjoy at little thatched picnic tables. Dishes less than $.

JUST SO YOU KNOW
Banana Joe's Tropical Fruit Stand (808-828-1092), 5-2719 Kuhio Hwy.,

Kilauea. You can't miss this bright yellow roadside stand, nor should you.

Hanalei Taro & Juice Company (808-826-1059), Hwy. 560, Hanalei. When taro is mixed with local fruits, the concoction is irresistible.

✴ Entertainment

Lu'aus. Commercial *lu'aus* are produced on Kaua'i by a few resorts (chief among them the **Princeville Resort Kaua'i** and **Grand Hyatt Kaua'i Resort & Spa**—see "The South Shore") and independent operators, but I haven't been to one I can recommend wholeheartedly. (If you're going to Maui, save the experience for the Old Lahaina Lu'au. If you're not going to Maui, simply save your money.)

⚘ **Hanalei Gourmet** (see *Eating Out*) is a friendly place with live jazz, folk, and rock music that begins after nightfall.

⚘ **Kalypso** (see *Eating Out*) is the hippest hangout in town, with a huge selection of microbrews, cocktails, and martinis.

⚘ **Sushi & Blues** (808-826-4105), Ching Young Village, Kuhio Hwy., Hanalei. Open nightly. With shiny copper tables and a shiny copper bar, this happenin' place specializes in . . . you guessed it: sushi and blues. But they also have jazz and rock and roll. Call ahead to confirm the varied lineup of live music on Wed., Thur., and Sun.

⚘ **Tahiti Nui** (808-826-6277), 5-5134 Kuhio Hwy., Hanalei. This spirited daily happy hour (4–6) is popular with visitors and locals for good reason. I head elsewhere when I get hungry, though.

ROMANTIC PLACES FOR COCKTAILS
Y ☺ **Anywhere overlooking Hanalei Bay**. No sensible person could argue for a more romantic place to watch the sunset than looking over the perfectly curved Hanalei Bay, Bali Hai, and the Na Pali Coast. How you experience it is up to you: Enjoy a bottle of wine discreetly on the beach (please drive safely afterward); head to the Happy Talk Lounge at Hanalei Bay Resort (see *Lodging*); or settle into the Living Room bar (808-826-9644) at the upscale Princeville Resort Kaua'i (see *Lodging*).

✳ Selective Shopping

FARMER'S MARKETS
Sunshine Market (808-241-6390), Kilauea Neighborhood Center, Kilauea. Thur. at 4:30.

Farmer's Market, behind the post office, Hwy. 560, Hanalei. Sat. 11:30–1:30. The goods are primarily organic at this fun market.

Hawaiian Farmers of Hanalei, Hwy. 560, Hanalei. Tues. at 2. Look for tropical flowers, tropical fruits, and organic veggies.

SHOPPING AREAS
Hanalei, Hwy. 560. Two low-key, low-slung shopping areas spar across the street from one another. Open daily. Although Ching Young Village (808-826-7222) looks a bit rough around the edges, I bet you'll linger and loiter there. None of the goods are high art, but you'll probably buy something.

SPECIAL SHOPS
Kung Long (808-828-1822), Kung Long Shopping Center, Kilauea Rd. (off Hwy. 56), Kilauea. Open daily.

My absolute favorite shop on the island (because the shopping experience is completely aesthetic), this place sells goods with an Asian feel, including home accents, women's clothes, jewelry, ceramics, and books.

Lotus Gallery (808-828-9898), Kung Long Shopping Center, Kilauea Rd. (off Hwy. 56), Kilauea. Open daily. One owner is a gem expert; the other is a jeweler. It's a glistening match.

Yellowfish Trading Company (808-826-1227), Hanalei Center, Hwy. 560, Hanalei. Open daily. Take home a little piece of vintage Hawai'i (circa 1940), treasures that look like they came off the set of *From Here to Eternity*, unique retro furniture, and accessories.

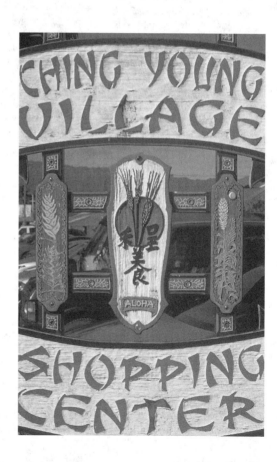

INDEX